Juvenile Delinquency
THEORY, PRACTICE, AND LAW

To Our Families

Juvenile Delinquency —————
THEORY, PRACTICE, AND LAW

Larry J. Siegel, Ph.D.
University of Nebraska, Omaha

Joseph J. Senna, M.S.W., J.D.
Northeastern University

WEST PUBLISHING COMPANY
St. Paul • New York • Los Angeles • San Francisco

Photo Credits

Part One—Stock Boston; George W. Gardner, photographer
Part Two—Stock Boston, W. B. Finch, photographer
Part Three—Magnum Photos, Bruce Davidson
Part Four—Leo de Wys, Rhoda Sidneir
Part Five—Corrections Magazine, Bill Powers
Part Six—Roy Lustig
Part Seven—Stock Boston, Betsy Cole

COPYRIGHT © 1981
By WEST PUBLISHING CO.
  50 West Kellogg Boulevard
  P.O. Box 3526
  St. Paul, Minnesota 55165

Libary of Congress Cataloging in Publication Data

Siegel, Larry J.
    Juvenile delinquency—theory, practice, and law.

    (Criminal justice series)
    Bibliography: p.
    Includes index.
    1. Juvenile delinquency—United States.
    2. Juvenile justice, Administration of—United States.
    I. Senna, Joseph J., joint author.   II. Title.
    III. Series.

HV9104.S43   364.3'6'0973   80-25533

ISBN 0-8299-0414-X

Preface

America's juvenile justice system is in the midst of reexamining its fundamental theories, operations, and institutions. Over eight decades have passed since the establishment of the first juvenile court in America, but a clear and concise view of how to prevent and control juvenile criminality has not yet been developed. On the one hand, reformers with a social welfare orientation argue that delinquency requires treatment by social agencies dispensing personalized individual justice to needy children. On the other hand, those with a law enforcement orientation suggest that efforts to treat children under the concept of *parens patriae* have neglected the victims of delinquency, and that serious offenders need to be punished rather than rehabilitated.

These different perspectives on juvenile justice and delinquency are reflected in the changes going on in this field today. First of all, the definition of *delinquency* has become unclear. It covers many different acts that children commit and many different situations in which they become involved. Second, the philosophical ideas underlying juvenile justice throughout the twentieth century have been questioned. Third, understanding the theories of delinquency and its causes is an incredibly complex task. Fourth, society in general has become critically concerned about rising rates of juvenile crime and about violent young offenders. The perplexing nature of these issues and the fact that treating and controlling juvenile offenders is one of the great challenges of modern times have made the authors believe there is a need for this text.

The purpose of the book is to comprehensively and objectively describe concepts and theories of delinquency, the juvenile justice system, and the rights and responsibilities of children under law. The book provides an in-depth analysis of delinquency and juvenile justice by examining historical data, statistical information, sociological theories, legal issues, and significant practices in juvenile justice. It is intended primarily for use by undergraduate and graduate students studying delinquency and juvenile justice and law. It can also be used as an addition to a criminology or even a social deviance course. It may even be useful to practitioners and to those who have a general interest in the subject of juvenile delinquency and justice.

The book is divided into seven major parts.

Part 1 discusses juvenile delinquency in America. It examines the definition of delinquency and ways of measuring the problem of delinquency.

Part 2 describes the theoretical framework of juvenile delinquency studies by examining the variety of theories that seek to explain the causes of delinquency. These theories include individual theories of delinquency, social structure approaches, social process concepts, theories of social control such as labeling and conflict theory, and theories of female delinquency.

Part 3 discusses the issue of environmental influences on delinquency. It covers such areas as peers and delinquency, the juvenile gang, schools and delinquency, and the relationships among family, delinquency, and child abuse.

Part 4 begins the study of the entire juvenile justice system. First, it presents an overview of the system. Then it offers significant information about the history and philosophy of juvenile justice and an analysis of the legal rights of juveniles who are processed by social control agencies.

Part 5 is devoted to how children who commit crimes and status offenses are handled by police, courts, and correctional agencies. Police work with children, early court processing, and the juvenile trial are included here.

Part 6 focuses on postadjudication procedures for juveniles. It deals with community treatment and institutionalization.

Finally, Part 7 explores the rights of minors under the law.

In sum, this book seeks to describe and analyze the phenomenon known as juvenile delinquency and the social control agencies that deal with it. It provides a comprehensive and nonbiased approach to understanding antisocial behavior by children in America. The text is intended to make teaching and learning about the concept of delinquency and juvenile justice effective and enjoyable for both teachers and students.

A number of pedagogical features are used to achieve this goal. Each chapter contains a chapter outline, a summary, and questions for discussion. Highlights or vignettes of actual juvenile justice practices are included to explain theories or programs. Unique chapters on the gang, family and delinquency, child abuse, and the rights of minors have been developed. These features should substantially help in the overall understanding of the problems of delinquency and juvenile justice.

As with any project of this kind, completion would not have been possible without the help of others. Special acknowledgment is in order for two people who helped in the construction of the text: Elizabeth Mills and Elena Natalizia.

We are indebted to the following sources for allowing us to use material: American Bar Association, Law Enforcement Assistance Administration, National Council of Crime and Delinquency, and *Boston Globe*. Special appreciation also is given to Diana White and Janie Burcart for permission to use their material.

We also wish to thank the following reviewers for their assistance in the overall development of the text: Linda Anderson, Daniel Bell, Martin Miller, Joseph Rankin, and Donald Weisenhorn.

Larry J. Siegel
Joseph J. Senna

Contents

PART I   THE NATURE OF DELINQUENCY

Chapter 1   The Concept of Delinquency   3

Introduction; The Concept of Delinquency; The Juvenile Delinquent;
Parens Patriae and Legal Responsibility; Becoming a Delinquent; Status
Offenders; The Status Offender Controversy

Chapter 2   Measures of Official Delinquency   21

Introduction; The Uniform Crime Reports; Other Forms of Official
Statistics Used as Research Tools; Analysis of Official Statistics

Chapter 3   Unofficial Sources of Juvenile Statistics   41

Introduction; Self-Report Studies; Ways of Validating Self-Reports;
Victimization Surveys; Observation and Biographical Data

PART II   THEORIES OF DELINQUENT BEHAVIOR

Chapter 4   Individualistic Theories of Delinquent Behavior   67

Introduction; Classical Theory; Individualistic Theories of Delinquency; Positivist Theory; Critique of Individualistic Theories

Chapter 5   Social Structure Theories   97

Introduction; Cultural Transmission Theory; Strain Theory; Subcultural
(Strain) Theory; Middle-Class Delinquency; Policy and Social Structure
Theory

ix

Chapter 6   Social Process Theories   **125**

Introduction; Differential Association Theory; Neutralization Theory;
Control Theory; Containment Theory; Policy Implications of Social
Process Theories

Chapter 7   Social Reaction Theories   **151**

Introduction; Labeling Theory; Conflict Theory; Policy Implications of
Social Reaction Theory

Chapter 8   Female Delinquency   **177**

Introduction; The Inherent Nature of Female Delinquency; Developmental Theories of Female Delinquency; Theories of Economic and
Social Determinism; Delinquent Girls and the Juvenile Justice System

PART III   ENVIRONMENTAL INFLUENCES ON DELINQUENCY

Chapter 9   Juvenile Gangs in America   **197**

Introduction; Definition of Gangs; History of Gangs; Gang Structure;
Causes of Gang Delinquency; Types of Gangs; Extent of the Gang
Problem

Chapter 10   Schools and Delinquency   **219**

Introduction; The School in Modern American Society; Educational
Factors and Delinquency; Delinquency in the Schools; The Role of the
School in Delinquency Prevention

**Chapter 11   The Family and Delinquency:
                    Child Abuse and Neglect**   **247**

Introduction; The Family and Delinquency; The Family's Influence on
Delinquency; Child Abuse and Neglect; Definition and Scope; Causes
of Abuse and Neglect; Philosophy and Practice of the Child Protection
System; Desposition of Abuse and Neglect Cases; Treatment and
Termination; Abuse, Neglect, and Delinquency

PART IV   JUVENILE JUSTICE ADVOCACY

Chapter 12   An Overview of the Juvenile Justice System   **271**

Introduction; The Field of Study; The Definition of Juvenile Justice; The
Development of Juvenile Justice; The System of Juvenile Justice; The
Process of Juvenile Justice; Comparison of the Criminal and Juvenile

Justice Systems; Early Efforts to Distinguish Between the Juvenile and the Adult Justice Systems; The Goals of Juvenile Justice; Current Issues in Juvenile Justice Administration

Chapter 13   The History and Philosophy of Juvenile Justice   299

Introduction; Care of Children in the Middle Ages; Child Care in the Fifteenth and Sixteenth Centuries; Early English Developments and the Chancery Court System; Children in Colonial America; Developments in Great Britain in the Nineteenth Century; Developments in America in the Nineteenth Century; The Establishment of the Illinois Juvenile Court in 1899; The Modern Juvenile Court: 1899-1967

Chapter 14   The Legal Right of Juveniles   321

Introduction; Supreme Court Decisions; The Juvenile Justice Process and Lower Court Decisions; The Organization of the Juvenile Court; Juvenile Court Jurisdiction; Criticisms of the Juvenile Court

PART V   PROCESSING THE JUVENILE OFFENDER

Chapter 15   Police Work With Juveniles   347

Introduction; The Role of the Police and Juvenile Offenders; Organization of Police Service for Juveniles; Recruitment and Training of Juvenile Police Officers; Legal Aspects of Police Work with Juveniles, Police Discretion with Juveniles; Factors Affecting Police Discretion; Police Work and Delinquency Prevention; Directions in Police Work with Children

Chapter 16   Early Court Processing   367

Introduction; The Concept of Detention; How a Child Enters Detention; Current Detention Problems; Standards for Detention Care; The Intake Process; Diversion; Illustrations of Diversion Programs; The Petition; Bail for Children; The Plea and Plea Bargaining in Juvenile Justice; Transfer Proceedings

Chapter 17   The Juvenile Trial and Disposition   391

Introduction; The Prosecutor in the Juvenile Court, Functions of the Juvenile Prosecutor; Role of the Juvenile Court Judge; Selection and Qualifications of Juvenile Court Judges; The Defense Attorney in the Juvenile Justice System; Public Defender Services for Children; Adjudication; Constitutional Rights at Adjudication; Dispositions; Trends in Juvenile Sentencing; Predisposition Report; The Child's Right to Appeal in the Juvenile Court

PART VI JUVENILE CORRECTIONS

Chapter 18 Community Treatment of the Juvenile Offender 417

Introduction; Juvenile Probation; The Organization and Administration of Juvenile Probation Services; Restitution as a Form Community Treatment; The Trend Toward Deinstitutionalization; Residential Treatment Alternatives to Incarceration; Nonresidential Community Treatment; Criticisms of the Community Treatment Approach

Chapter 19 Institutionalization 443

Introduction; History of Juvenile Institutions; Institutionalized Youth—A Profile; Juvenile Institutions; Treatment of Juveniles Within the Institution; Female Juveniles in Institutions; Institutional Rules and Discipline; Juvenile Aftercare; Violent Young Offenders

PART VII CHILDREN'S RIGHTS

Chapter 20 Rights of Minors 479

Introduction; Children's Rights Within the Family—Medical Care and Privacy; Children's Rights Outside the Family; The Rights of Special Children; A Bill of Rights for Children

APPENDIXES

Appendix A Glossary 501

Appendix B Excerpts from the U.S. Constitution 515

Appendix C Children's Rights 517

INDEX

Subject Index 521

Name Index 539

PART I

THE NATURE OF
DELINQUENCY

Chapter 1

Chapter Outline

Introduction
The Concept of Delinquency
The Juvenile Delinquent
Parens Patriae and Legal Responsibility
Becoming a Delinquent
Status Offenders
The Status Offender Controversy
Chapter Summary

Key Terms, Names, and Cases

juvenile delinquency
juvenile delinquent
status offenders
child savers
parens patriae
mens rea
due process
Judge Lindsay Arthur
National Advisory Commission on Criminal
    Justice Standards and Goals

The Concept of Delinquency

INTRODUCTION

- Four members of a local street gang chance upon a young woman walking home late at night. They force her into an abandoned building, where each in turn rapes her. Later, they threaten her with death if she reports them to the police.
- Two young boys skip school to go on a shoplifting spree. In a suburban sporting goods store, they are apprehended by a security guard when they attempt to leave the premises without paying for some tennis balls.
- A young girl is taken into police custody by two juvenile detectives. Her mother has filed a complaint charging her with running away, staying out late at night, dating an older boy, and being disobedient at home.

Each of the strikingly different activities described here is a common form of youthful misbehavior that occurs daily in our society. The first involves a gratuitously violent act by an organized street gang. The second involves a relatively minor theft by two young boys. The third involves no crime at all but rather unapproved behavior of an adolescent girl. All three activities are in the general category of juvenile delinquent behavior.

Such activities have become a familiar and disturbing feature of our daily lives. It is not uncommon for local newspapers to be filled with vivid stories of youth crime and passionate calls for harsher punishment for young offenders.

State governments have begun to review their juvenile court legislation. New York, for example, has made serious attempts to toughen the legal penalties for crimes committed by youthful offenders.[1]

Despite such measures, the average citizen may feel that little can be done to control delinquency. Arguments for the use of harsh penalties and prison terms for delinquent minors do little to allay this growing national concern. The prospect of locking thousands more young people in prison-like facilities appears inherently self-defeating. "Won't they emerge from their ordeal more seriously damaged than when they began it?" and "How can the threat of prison sentences control the behavior of youths who have engaged in anti-social behavior since they were three years old?" are questions that are not readily answerable. It is unlikely that severely punished youths will eventually learn skilled trades or finish their education. How, then, can they be expected to compete in a world where even college graduates are unemployed?[2]

In a similar vein, the American citizen may be somewhat skeptical about the exclusive use of rehabilitation and nonpunitive treatment for court adjudicated minors. To treat youths who commit serious criminal acts as misguided children in need of a helping hand seems to violate one of society's basic instincts: to punish wrongdoers and compensate victims. Moreover, rehabilitation just does not seem to work. As commentator C. Ray Jeffrey laments: "We have not found a way to rehabilitate the criminal after the offense has occurred and the rehabilitative ideal has meant sacrificing individual rights as well as reducing the effectiveness of criminal law."[3]

Extensive research efforts have weakened the argument for rehabilitating delinquents by revealing that no single treatment effort effectively restricts recidivism (repeated criminal behavior.)[4]

Considering the magnitude of the problem, it is not surprising that a great deal of attention has been devoted to studying delinquent behavior. One goal has been to identify the factors that actually cause extralegal activity. This search has two main branches: (1) the study of contributing sociocultural factors and (2) the search for a unified theory of the causes of delinquency. The first approach leads experts to study the effects of such diverse social factors as IQ levels, education, and neighborhood environment on the behavior of youth. (These factors will be discussed throughout this text.) The second approach is directed at discovering the factor (or factors) that will explain delinquent behavior in all its varied forms (see Chapters 4 through 8).

In addition to these two approaches, research projects sponsored by federal and state governments and by private foundations have attempted to evaluate the effectiveness and efficiency of the police, the courts and the correctional agencies that administer to delinquents. These efforts can also be divided into two branches: (1) the study of system operations and (2) the evaluation of treatment. Studies of system operations include the analysis of such diverse topics as the way police behave when arresting youths,[5] the way lawyers function in juvenile court,[6] the training and competence of juvenile court judges,[7] and the decisions of probation officers.[8] The evaluation of treatment has focused more directly on the results of the various rehabilitative (or punitive) measures used with children after they have been adjudicated (tried) in juvenile court. Such research investigates the effectiveness of pretrial treatment, of juvenile probation, and of institutional programs like training schools and halfway houses. (See Chapters 14 through 18.)

Government agencies, private foundations, and the university community have accumulated a great deal of information. More is known about delinquency than ever before, but a great deal of controversy about its cause and prevention still abounds. Therefore, the purpose of this text is to examine the theoretical, practical, and legal issues surrounding juvenile delinquency in order to equip the reader with a better understanding of the field.

The purpose of this first chapter is to introduce the reader to the concept of *juvenile delinquency*. To accomplish this task, we will initially make some general statements about the currency and seriousness of the delinquency problem. Then we will generate a working definition of juvenile delinquency by exploring the origin and philosophical basis for the idea of a separate legal (and social) category for youthful law violators. We will also separate the two "types" of youthful law violators—*status offenders* and *juvenile delinquents*—in order to better understand why this distinction is made.

The first chapter, then, concerns itself with the nature of the delinquency concept. Following chapters will explore the amounts and causes of delinquency, as well as the social factors related to it. They will also deal with the treatment of juvenile delinquents by the law.

THE CONCEPT OF DELINQUENCY

One of the most serious problems facing those concerned with juvenile delinquency is their confusion over what constitutes delinquent behavior. Delinquency involves both *legal* and *social* factors. Usually, a variety of antisocial behaviors brings troubled young people to the attention of the juvenile authorities: family disputes, poor school attendance, illegal activity, conflicts with neighbors and other citizens, and so on. In addition, the youths manifest a variety of social and personal problems. Reading and school adjustment problems, mental and emotional instability, alcoholism and drug dependence, physical handicaps, and low self-esteem are but a few. These legal, social, and personal problems are so intertwined that the concept of delinquency is ambiguous. In fact, most states define two distinct and sometimes independent types of youthful offenders: *juvenile delinquents* and *status offenders*. Juvenile delinquents have violated a criminal law. Status offenders either have been accused by their parents, teachers, or other authority figures of being *ungovernable, unmanageable, truant,* or *otherwise disobedient* or have engaged in behavior that is legally prohibited solely because of their minority status—for example, skipping school, staying out late, or drinking alcohol. Youths in both categories can be taken into police custody, can be given a trial or hearing before a juvenile court judge, and can be placed in custodial care.

Since these two categories may be conceptually independent of one another and comprise differing sets of problems, they will be analyzed separately.

THE JUVENILE DELINQUENT

Juvenile delinquency is currently defined as *an act committed by a minor (an individual who falls under a statutory age limit, in most states either seventeen or eighteen) that violates the penal code of the government with authority over the area in which the act occurred.*

Because of their minority status, juveniles are usually kept separate from adults and receive different consideration and treatment. For example, most large police departments employ police officers whose sole responsibility is children. Every state employs an independent juvenile court system with its own judges, probation department, and other facilities. Terminology is also different. Adults are tried in court; children are adjudicated. Adults' can be punished; children are given treatment. If treatment is mandated, children can be sent to secure detention facilities, but, under normal circumstances, they cannot be committed to adult prisons. (See Chapter 12 for a more complete analysis of these differences.)

Children also have their own unique legal status. A minor who is apprehended for a criminal act can be charged only with being a juvenile delinquent regardless of the crime that was committed. In addition, delinquency proceedings are usually confidential, trial records are kept secret, and the name, behavior, and background of delinquent offenders are not made public. Eliminating specific crime categories and maintaining secrecy are efforts to shield children from the stigma of a criminal conviction and to prevent youthful misdeeds from becoming a lifelong burden.

Our current treatment of juvenile delinquents is a by-product of the development of a national consciousness of the problems of youth. The designation *delinquent* first became popular toward the end of the nineteenth century, when the first separate juvenile courts were instituted. (Chapter 13 contains a more complete discussion of the history of juvenile justice and delinquency.) Advocates of a separate legal status for youth argued that treating minors and adults equivalently violated the humanitarian ideals of American society. Reformers, known today as *child savers*,[9] favored a philosophy of *parens patriae* (literally, the state is the father). This doctrine viewed minors who engaged in extralegal behavior as victims of improper care, custody, and treatment at home. Illegal behavior was a sign that the state should step in and take control of the youth before more serious crimes occurred. The state, through its juvenile court authorities, should act in the best interests of the child. This meant that children should not be punished for their misdeeds but instead should be given the care and custody necessary to remedy and control wayward behavior. It made no sense, therefore, to find children guilty of specific crimes such as burglary or petty larceny because that stigmatized them and labeled them as thieves or burglars. Instead, the delinquency label was substituted; it indicated that the child needed the care, custody, and treatment of the state.

PARENS PATRIAE AND LEGAL RESPONSIBILITY

The *parens patriae* philosophy is still followed in most jurisdictions, and consequently every state maintains a separate legal status for minors within its legal code. The *parens patriae* doctrine places the juvenile delinquent somewhere between criminal and civil law. Criminal laws are state statutes that prohibit activities believed to be so harmful that they injure society as well as their victims, for example, theft and rape. Criminal law violations therefore involve a conflict between the individual and the state. Civil law, on the other hand, involves activities that harm the victims but not the broader society. Libel, negligence, and violations of contracts break civil laws. Under the *parens patriae* doctrine, delinquent acts are not considered criminal violations. Delinquents are not considered criminals. They cannot be found guilty of a crime and punished like adult criminals. The legal action against them is considered a civil action.

However, the U.S. Supreme Court, recognizing the sanctions and disabilities delinquent youth may be forced to suffer at the hands of the law, has granted minors many of the same legal protections that adults enjoy. These include the right to an attorney at trial and the right to remain free from self-incrimination. Furthermore, young persons are to be found delinquent at a hearing only if the evidence shows them to be so beyond all reasonable doubt.

Thus, the delinquency concept and the juvenile justice process fall somewhere between criminal and civil actions. In many respects, the treatment of delinquent youth is similar to that given to those, like the mentally ill, who cannot care for themselves and whom the state must care for. These issues will be discussed in more detail in Chapter 13.

The development of the delinquency concept can be traced to the roots of our Anglo-Saxon legal tradition. Early English jurisprudence held that children under seven were legally incapable of committing crimes.[10] Children between the ages of seven and fourteen had somewhat more responsibility for their actions, but they were still sometimes treated differently from adults who had committed the same crime. This was especially true in the case of the death penalty, which was used comparatively rarely with young offenders.

The basis for the special treatment of youths lies in the legal concept of *mens rea*, or guilty mind. Under English law, it is not enough to engage in a forbidden or illegal act in order to be convicted of a crime. An individual must also intend to commit the act. For example, if an individual accidentally takes a book from the library, it is not a crime because the intention of committing the act (*mens rea*) is absent. Without *mens rea*, an illegal act is viewed as unintentional and accidental, a product of a mental defect. The individual cannot be held legally responsible.

Our society believes that young people are incapable of mature adult judgments and therefore their responsibility for their acts is legally limited. Children can intentionally steal cars and know full well that the act is illegal, but they may also be incapable of fully understanding the consequences of their behavior and the harm it may cause. The law, therefore, does not punish a youth as it would an adult and holds youthful misconduct as evidence of unreasoned or impaired judgment.

The many attacks on *parens patriae* center on the seriousness of some juvenile crimes and the physical and emotional maturity of many delinquents. Some experts have called for the end of "coddling" youthful criminals and administering to them as if they were legally adults—that is, making them eligible for criminal labels, prison sentences, and so on.[11]

In fact, many youths who are deemed dangerous, mature, and responsible for their acts are *not* treated as juvenile delinquents. Through a process called *waiver* or *transfer*, their cases are handled by adult courts (see Chapter 14). They can then be tried, convicted, and punished as an adult would be. Transfer proceedings are instituted when a child commits a serious crime, such as rape or murder, and if it can be shown at a hearing before a judge that the state's juvenile justice system is not equipped to handle the case.

The trend toward advocating harsher punishment is a response to the rising delinquency rate and the failure of the *parens patriae* philosophy to effectively control it.

BECOMING A DELINQUENT

Approximately 95 percent of the nation's youths have committed acts which would have brought them to the attention of juvenile authorities had they been apprehended.[12] But the process of becoming an official delinquent is very selective. Later on, we will discuss in great detail the process by which police, courts, and correctional authorities decide to label a youth a delinquent. Now, we will briefly describe some of the more important operations of this process.

Young people first come to the attention of the juvenile authorities because someone—a teacher or school official, a neighbor, a victim of crime, or even a parent—complains about them to the police or to the juvenile court. In addition, the police themselves can apprehend a youth as a result of their own observation while on patrol. If the police apprehend a child, the first important decision is: Should the child be taken into custody or simply warned never to do the act again? The decision is based on a number of different factors. How serious was the delinquent act? Was there a victim, or was it a victimless crime, such as smoking marijuana or using alcohol? Is the child a known and persistent troublemaker, or is this an isolated incident? Does the child associate with older criminal companions? Is the child defiant and brazen or apologetic, scared, and contrite? Since so many different factors enter into the decision to hold or release a child, some youths who have committed serious crimes are eventually released, while others whose acts are less serious are held for the juvenile court.

If a complaint is filed with the juvenile court authorities, a second round of decision making occurs, this time by the judge and the staff of the juvenile court. Again, important questions must be answered: Did the youth commit the act? What is the best response—community treatment, institutionalization, or a simple warning? What is the child's home situation like? A number of steps can then be taken. The child can be given a warning and released. He or she can be placed directly in an informal community treatment program, for example, an alcohol clinic, a drug abuse center, or a mental health facility. Alternatively, after a formal hearing, the youth can be found to be a juvenile delinquent and placed on probation (community supervision by the court) or given another form of community treatment such as placement in an after-school program. In very serious cases, delinquents can be removed from their homes and placed in secure institutional facilities. These are often referred to as camps, training schools, ranches, farms, homes, or reformatories. This entire process is quite formal, with hearings, lawyers, witnesses, and procedures similar to those found in the adult justice system. And even though the juvenile court procedure is closed and confidential, neighbors, local businesspeople, and teachers often become aware of a child's problems with the law.

Becoming an official delinquent therefore involves a lengthy process of decision making that begins when a complaint is registered with the police or brought directly to the attention of juvenile court authorities and ends when a youth is placed in a treatment category that suits his or her particular needs. Treatment ranges from no formal action to extended institutional care. At each step along the way important questions are posed about the youth, and the answers determine the outcome of the case. Children become official juvenile delinquents through a slowly evolving process. At each juncture, agents of the justice system decide whether an act is a single unfortunate incident of never-to-be-repeated antisocial behavior or whether it is the forerunner of a pattern of escalating and persistent criminality. Sociologist Robert Emerson has suggested that the process of becoming delinquent depends not on determining whether the child committed a delinquent act but on whether the child is incorrigible and therefore in specific need of juvenile justice services.[13]

Even when juvenile justice authorities believe they are acting in the best interests of the child, the label they bestow is likely to have serious and far-reaching consequences. In Chapters 12 through 19 we will give a great deal of attention to the consequences of becoming a delinquent; for now, it is important to note that the process has a powerful and long-term effect.

STATUS OFFENDERS

A child can become subject to state authority because of conduct that is illegal only because the child is under age. Such acts are known as status offenses. They include but are not limited to:

- Truancy from school
- Sexual misconduct
- Using profanity
- Using tobacco
- Using alcohol
- Disobeying school officials
- Curfew violation
- Idleness
- Running away
- Disobeying parents
- Having delinquent friends
- Immoral conduct

State control over a child's noncriminal behavior is considered consistent with the *parens patriae* philosophy and is used to protect the best interests of the child. Usually status offenders are put in the hands of the juvenile court when it is determined that their parents are unable or unwilling to care for or control them and their behavior will eventually hurt themselves and society.

There is a historical basis for status offense statutes. It was common practice early in the nation's history to place disobedient or runaway youth in orphan assylums and houses of refuge.[14] When the first juvenile courts were founded in Illinois, the Chicago Bar Association described part of their purpose as follows:

The whole trend and spirit of the [1899 Juvenile Court Act] is that the State, acting through the Juvenile Court, exercises that tender solicitude and care over its neglected, dependent wards that a wise and loving parent would exercise with reference to his own children under similar circumstances.[15]

Until recently, however, almost every state treated status offenders exactly like juvenile delinquents, referring to them either as *wayward minors* or *delin-quent children*. A recent trend, begun in the 1960s, has resulted in the creation of separate status offense categories, called Children, Minors, Persons, Youths, or Juveniles in Need of Supervision (CHINS, MINS, PINS, YINS, JINS) in different states. A recent survey by the National Assessment of Juvenile Cor-rections Project indicates that eighteen states still categorize status offenders with delinquents, eight states have mixed categories (judges use their discretion to label offenders either delinquent or status offender), and the remaining twenty-four and the District of Columbia have separate status offense catego-ries.[16] Another recent practice has been to separate delinquents and status offenders when they are held in a detention facility prior to trial (see Chapter 16) or if they are institutionalized as a consequence of their juvenile court hear-ings (Chapter 18).

Separate status offense categories may avoid some of the stigma associated with the delinquency label, but they have little practical effect on the child's treatment. Youths in either category can be picked up by the police and brought to a police station. They can both be petitioned to the same juvenile court, where they have a hearing before the same judge and come under the supervi-sion of the probation department, court clinic, and treatment staff. Not all states provide separate detention facilities or custodial institutions. Thus, at a hearing, status offenders may see little difference between the treatment they receive and the treatment of the delinquent offenders sitting across the room. Highlight 1–1 illustrates the case history of two "typical" female status offenders.

Highlight 1–1. Marie and Melissa.

Marie

Marie is 14 years old, white, and four months pregnant. The father of her expectant child is black. She is the only daughter of a family that lives in a wealthy suburb. Her father is a school principal and her mother is a housewife and an avid club woman. Marie is pretty and of average intelligence. She is very interested in art and started staying out of school just before her 13th birthday to go to art museums or art galleries in the city. Her father demanded that she attend school and prohibited her from enrolling in art courses in her school Her grades continued to be between B's and C's, which, while satisfactory by most standards, were not good enough for her

father. He insisted that they improve. Her mother was too busy with her clubs and volunteer work to spend time with Marie.

The pressure became so great that she ran away. When she was picked up by the police, her parents demanded that she be charged with incorrigibility. Marie was sent to a juvenile detention center where she stayed for three months. During her stay she became pregnant. She was then sent to the state training school where during the routine entrance physical, she learned she was pregnant.

The next few weeks were a confusing, tense time. Her parents wanted her to have an abortion but she refused. The training school personnel insisted that she could not remain there because of inadequate programs for pregnant girls. Because of her history of running away, it was decided not to place her in a home for unwed mothers.

Finally, foster care arrangements were made on the condition that she would give up her baby for adoption as soon as it was born. Just before her transfer to the foster home, Marie developed complications with her pregnancy and had to be hospitalized. A conflict arose, as to who was responsible for her medical bills, so, after she was released, Marie returned to the training school. Three weeks later the issue was resolved, and Marie was placed in a foster home. She is still there awaiting her baby and has not seen her parents.

Melissa

Melissa was 15 when she was first arrested. She was living with her parents and her two sisters. Her father supported the family on his $7,000 annual salary. Melissa is an attractive young woman and, until the time of her first arrest, was doing well in school. According to school officials she is intelligent, made excellent grades and had a good attitude about school.

Within a month's time Melissa was arrested twice. The first time her mother called the police requesting that they pick Melissa up because she refused to go to school, and because lately she had been "getting upset too easily and having lots of emotional scenes." When the police arrived Melissa had left the house. They found her a few minutes later walking in the rain a short distance away. She was arrested and charged with running away. Melissa explained to the police that she did not want to return home because she and her mother were not getting along and because her father beat her. She asked the police if she could go to live with an aunt. However, her mother would not give her approval because "it wouldn't look right." Melissa then spent

eight days in detention before she was returned to her parents' home. A few days later the police received a call from Melissa asking that they please come get her because she had just had an "argument" with her father and she was afraid he would hurt her. When the police arrived, they arrested Melissa at her request and again charged her with running away.

This time Melissa waited in detention for two weeks until she was placed with a foster family and ordered to attend a day school for troubled girls where she could receive counseling. Melissa was unhappy at the new school and eventually was dismissed for fighting with other girls. A few days later she was also asked to leave her foster home for "abusing the telephone" and having a "belligerent and non-conforming attitude," according to her foster parents.

Melissa was then placed at St. Ann's, a residential parochial school for "difficult" boys and girls. After a month and a half she ran away from there. While on the street she tried unsuccessfully to find a new foster home so she would not be returned to St. Ann's. Apprehended by the police, she refused to go back to St. Ann's and was placed in detention where she remained for two weeks.

She was then placed in a community residential program but was soon dismissed for leaving without permission to attend a local fair and for spending time with an unknown young man. She was returned to the detention center for four months before being committed to the state training school for girls.

Source: Excerpted from U.S. Department of Justice, Office of Juvenile Justice and Delinquency Prevention, *Little Sisters and the Law* (Washington, D.C.: Government Printing Office, 1977).

THE STATUS OFFENDER CONTROVERSY

The status offender concept has come under considerable fire. To some it remains an exercise in futility since it places the moral welfare of a minor in the hands of a justice system ill-equipped to effectively handle it. For others, it allows a frightening exercise of state power. It has been estimated that almost 30 percent of all youths coming in contact with the law have committed no crime but are unruly, truant, or runaways. (Of incarcerated youth, 35 percent are believed to be status offenders.[17]) Critics commonly take issue with the wording of status offense statutes. The vague and confusing language of these laws is considered unfair to youths. A typical example is Ohio's Unruly Child Law presented in Highlight 1–2.[18] Notice the use of such terms as *wayward or habitually disobedient, habitual truant,* and *found in a disreputable place.* Some legal scholars argue that such language, though benevolently intended, violates a child's constitutional right to be treated fairly under the law, a concept known as *due process.*[19] They argue that it is difficult to avoid illegal behavior when one cannot be exactly sure how that behavior is defined. For example, how can a child avoid being habitually disobedient when the law does not state how much disobedience constitutes habitual disobedience. Most state statutes employ vague terms; yet appellate courts have consistently upheld their legality since they are viewed as necessary for exercising prompt and flexible supervision over the child.[20]

By making the state's control over a child broad and far-reaching, the law allows intervention when there exists a reasonable belief that the conditions of the child's life are poor or damaging.[21] However, states do not place youths in custody for the merest suggestion of misbehavior or wrongdoing. No national standard exists, but many court cases have held that wayward behavior must be habitual and continuous if a child is to be placed under state control

---

Highlight 1–2. Ohio Unruly Child Statute

2151.022 Unruly child defined.
As used in sections 2151.01 to 2151.54, inclusive of the Revised Code, "Unruly child" includes any child:

(A) Who does not subject himself to the reasonable control of his parents, teachers, guardian, or custodian, by reason of being wayward or habitually disobedient;

(B) Who is an habitual truant from home or school;

(C) Who so deports himself as to injure or endanger the health or morals of himself or others;

(D) Who attempts to enter the marriage relation in any state without the consent of his parents, custodian, legal guardian, or other legal authority;

(E) Who is found in a disreputable place, visits or patronizes a place prohibited by law, or associates with vagrant, vicious, criminal, notorious, or immoral persons;

(F) Who engages in an occupation prohibited by law, or is in a situation dangerous to life or limb or injurious to the health or morals of himself or others;

(G) Who has violated a law applicable only to a child.

Source: Ohio Rev. Code Ann., Sec. 2151.022.

and that parents must show some documented proof of youthful wrongdoing if they expect court action.

The status offender category has also come under attack because it is sometimes used to mask parental neglect or abuse.[22] A child may run away from home or stay out late at night to avoid a traumatic and unpleasant home life. The physical, mental, and sexual abuse of children has become a growing national scandal, with many reported cases involving serious injury and even death (see Chapter 11). Parents may perceive the juvenile court as a convenient solution to family problems, but the parents themselves may be at fault.

In some instances, a thorough investigation by the juvenile court's social service staff will reveal family conditions accurately, and the court will place status offenders within a different legal category, that of *neglected* or *dependent children*. This procedure shifts the legal burden to the parents, and the court can order them to alter their behavior lest they themselves become subject to sanctions and punishments (see Chapter 11). Unfortunately, limited resoures often make accurate assessments of the home situation impossible. The status offender label remains intact, and the child is punished for the parents' misdeeds.

Experts are particularly concerned with the type of treatment status offenders receive when they are held in secure custody prior to trial (pretrial detention) and after sentencing. The issue is two-fold: (1) the frequency of detention and (2) the holding of status offenders and delinquents in the same facility. It is quite common to keep status offenders in custody.[23]

One study found that 25.6 percent of all youth committed to juvenile institutions in Texas during a one-year period were status offenders (55 percent of all first-offender females).[24]

Rosemary Sarri discovered that 43 porcent of all children held in upper New York State institutions were noncriminal youth. In fact, it has been estimated that 70 percent of all girls and 23 percent of all boys held in custody nationwide are status offenders.[25]

Objections have also been raised to the housing of status offenders and juvenile delinquents in the same institution (both pre- and posttrial). Some states have outlawed this custom, but many still retain it. In some instances, separate wings or sections of adult facilities are actually used for young people. The federal government has moved to eliminate this practice with the 1974 Juvenile Justice and Delinquency Prevention Act. It denies federal support to facilities that house both delinquents and status offenders.[26]

Support for the Status Offense Concept

Not all students of juvenile delinquency believe that status offense categories are harmful and should therefore be discontinued. Status offenders may have ongoing, long-term problems at home, at school, and in the neighborhood. Delinquents may have committed a single petty crime such as a minor theft or public intoxication.[27] In fact, a number of legal cases have upheld the housing of status offenders and delinquents in the same correctional facility because, in reality, they share many of the same problems.[28]

Lawrence Martin and Phyllis Snyder have raised another argument for maintaining the jurisdiction of the juvenile courts over the status offender.[29] They suggest that the failure of the courts to take control over wayward youths neglects the rights of concerned parents who are incapable of controlling their children. They suggest:

> The court would be abdicating its responsibility if it did not attempt to support these parents with its authority and thus speak for the society that will soon confer adult status on these children. Though the behavior of status offenders may not be criminal, it is unlawful. Unless we believe that truancy and waywardness are good for children, we ought to concern ourselves with all avenues of service that might change such behavior.[30]

Judge Lindsay Arthur supports this position, suggesting that the status offense should remain a legal category so that juvenile courts can "force" a youth into receiving treatment.[31] While he recognizes the stigma associated with a court appearance, Judge Arthur counters that the stigma may be less important than the need for treatment.[32]

Charles Thomas has conducted one of the few studies to address the status offender controversy through actual empirical research.[33] Employing a sample of youths referred to the juvenile court in Virginia, Thomas found that many who appeared on status offense charges had had previous experiences as delinquents. Furthermore, many status offenders later returned under delinquency petitions. He further discovered that a status offender's future conduct did not result from being stigmatized by court authorities and that the behavior that initially brought a youth to court was a poor predictor of future behavior.[34] Thomas's research indicates that status offenders and delinquents are not as different as some reformers would like to believe.

The Future of the Status Offender Concept

A number of national commissions seeking to reform the treatment of status offenders have called for the abolition of the juvenile courts' authority over status offenders. For example, the National Juvenile Justice Standards Project, which was designed to promote significant improvements in the way children are treated by the police and the courts, has called for the end of juvenile court jurisdiction over status offenders. In its standard for dealing with noncriminal youth it states:

1.1 Noncriminal Behavior
A juvenile's acts of misbehavior, ungovernability or unruliness which do not violate the criminal law should not constitute a ground for asserting juvenile court jurisdiction over the juvenile committing them.[35]

One of the more influential critiques of the status offense concept has been put forward by the National Advisory Commission on Criminal Justice Standards and Goals. In 1976, a task force of the commission proposed a national policy for the treatment of status offenders that, in essence, suggests: "The only conduct that should warrant family court intervention is conduct that is clearly self-destructive or otherwise harmful to the child."[36] To meet this standard, the commission suggested that the nation's juvenile courts confine themselves to controlling the five status offenses illustrated in Highlight 1–3.

Highlight 1-3. National Advisory Commission on Criminal Justice Standards and Goals—Categories for Status Offenses.

1. *School Truancy.* This is defined as a pattern of repeated or habitual unauthorized absence from school by any juvenile subject to compulsory education laws. The court's power to intervene in cases of truancy should be limited to situations where the child's continued absence from school clearly indicates the need for services.

2. *Repeated Disregard for or Misuse of Lawful Parental Authority.* Family court jurisdiction under this category should be narrowly restricted to circumstances where a pattern of repeated disobedient behavior on the part of the juvenile or a pattern of repeated unreasonable demands on the part of the parents creates a situation of family conflict clearly evidencing a need for services.

3. *Repeated Running Away From Home.* Running away is defined as a juvenile's unauthorized absence from home for more than 24 hours. Family court jurisdiction in this category should be the last resort for dealing with the juvenile who repeatedly runs away from home, refuses or has not benefited from voluntary services, and is incapable of self-support. Where the juvenile is capable of self-support, the family court should give serious consideration to the dispositional alternative of responsible self-sufficiency discussed below.

4. *Repeated Use of Intoxicating Beverages.* This is defined as the repeated possession and/or consumption of intoxicating beverages by a juvenile. In this category, the family court should have the power to intervene and provide services where a juvenile's serious, repeated use of alcohol clearly indicates a need for these services.

5. *Delinquent Acts Committed by a Juvenile Younger Than 10 Years of Age.* A delinquent act is defined as an act that would be a violation of Federal or State criminal law or of local ordinance if committed by an adult. Family court delinquency jurisdiction covers juveniles of age 10 and above. This category is intended to cover the situation where a juvenile younger than 10 years repeatedly commits acts that would support a delinquency petition for an older child or where the "delinquent acts" committed are of a serious nature.

Source: Excerpted from National Advisory Commission on Criminal Justice Standards and Goals, *Juvenile Justice and Delinquency Prevention* (Washington D.C.: Government Printing Office, 1977), p. 310.

Thus, the commission recognizes a middle ground. Abolishing status offenses outright would be wrong. Instead the juvenile court's jurisdiction should be limited to easily defined and especially harmful behavior. In addition, the commission suggests that the court take control over all parties involved in the child's predicament:

[Jurisdiction should extend] not only to the child but also to the parents or guardians and any public institution or agency with the legal responsibility or discretionary ability to supply services to help in dealing with these problems. In this way the family court will have a direct jurisdictional tie to any person, school system, treatment facility, or service associated with the child's behavioral problem.[37]

Some states have begun to make sweeping changes in their policy toward status offenders. Florida, for example, has eliminated the use of its status offender category, and now treats such youths as dependent children.[38] Massachusetts's new law covering children in need of supervision expressly forbids the housing of status offenders in the same facilities as delinquents.[39]

Despite these changes, it is likely that in the near future both the status offender and the juvenile delinquent category will continue to exist in the nation's juvenile court jurisdictions. Furthermore, it is also likely, considering the impact of federal legislation, that the categories will become even further separated in terms of pre- and posttrial treatment.

CHAPTER SUMMARY

Juvenile delinquents are youths who have violated provisions of their state's criminal code. Status offenders are youths who have participated in actions such as truancy, running away, or disobedience to parents that are prohibited to people their age. Some states separate these categories by law; others combine them, using a term like wayward minor to designate both delinquents and status offenders.

Juvenile delinquency has been defined by statute since 1899. Separate status offense statutes appeared in the 1960s. The concept of treating children differently from adults has its roots in the *parens patriae* philosophy, which maintains that the state should give care and custody to people who cannot care for themselves. Nineteenth-century reformers argued that this doctrine should be applied to minors because their illegal and wayward behavior was not the product of a mature mind and they often came from backgrounds that inspired their troublesome behavior. These reformers are called child-savers.

Today, status offenders and delinquents are handled in a justice system that is separate from that of adult offenders. Some states prohibit status offenders and delinquents from being held together prior to trial (detention) or after adjudication (in secure treatment facilities). Though the federal government encouraged separate detention with passage of the 1974 Juvenile Justice and Delinquency Prevention Act, many states still treat status offenders and delinquents together.

Controversy still rages over the status offense concept. The most important issue is whether the juvenile justice system should retain control over status offenders or whether a separate agency should handle them.

DISCUSSION QUESTIONS

1. Is it fair to have a separate legal category for youths? Does this unfairly penalize adults?
2. Are juveniles actually incapable of understanding the serious consequences of their actions?
3. Is it fair to institutionalize a minor simply for being truant or running away from home?
4. Should delinquency proceedings be secretive? Does the public have the right to know who juvenile criminals are?

SUGGESTED READINGS

Allinson, Richard, ed. *Status Offenders and the Juvenile Justice System.* Hackensack, N.J.: National Council on Crime and Delinquency, 1978.

Arthur Lindsay. "Status Offenders Need a Court of Last Resort." *Boston University Law Review* 57 (1977): 631–644.

Empey, LaMar. *Juvenile Justice.* Charlottesville: University of Virginia Press, 1979.

Gold, Martin. *Delinquent Behavior in an American City.* Belmont, California: Brooks/Cole, 1970.

Hahn, Paul. *Juvenile Offenders and the Law,* 2d ed. Cincinnati: Anderson Publishing, 1978.

Hickey, William. "Status Offenders and the Juvenile Court." *Crime and Justice Abstracts* 9 (1977): 91–122.

Ketcham, Orville. "Why Jurisdiction over Status Offenders Should Be Eliminated from Juvenile Courts." *Boston University Law Review* 57 (1977): 645–662.

Platt, Anthony. *The Child Savers.* Chicago: University of Chicago Press, 1969.

Sarri, Rosemary C. *Under Lock and Key: Juveniles in Jail and Detention.* Ann Arbor, Mich.: National Assessment of Juvenile Corrections, 1974.

Streib, Victor. *Juvenile Justice in America.* Port Washington, N.Y.: Kennikat, 1978.

REFERENCES

1. See Chap. 878, Laws of 1976, New York Family Court Act 71-769, 29A, *McKinney's Consolidated Laws,* 1977.

2. See, generally, Edwin Schur, *Labeling Deviant Behavior: Its Sociological Implications* (New York: Harper & Row, 1971). See also Edwin Schur, *Radical Nonintervention: Rethinking the Delinquency Problem* Englewood Cliffs, N.J.: Prentice-Hall, 1973).

3. C. Ray Jeffrey, "Theoretical Structure of Crime Control," in *Juvenile Justice Philosophy,* ed. F. Faust and P. Brantingham (St. Paul, Minn.: West Publishing, 1974), p. 15.

4. Robert Martinson, "What Works? Questions and Answers about Prison Reform," *Public Interest* 35 (1974): pp. 25–43.

5. See, for example, Irving Piliavin and Scott Briar, "Police Encounters with Juveniles," *American Journal of Sociology* 70 (1964): pp. 206–214.

6. David Duffee and Larry Siegel, "The Organization Man: Legal Counsel in the Juvenile Court," *Criminal Law Bulletin* 7 (1971): p. 544.

7. See, for example, Justine Wise Polier, "Prescriptions for Reform: Doing What We Set Out to Do," in *Juvenile Justice,* ed. LaMar Empey (Charlottesville: University of Virginia Press, 1979), pp. 213–244.

8. See, generally, Anne Mahoney, "The Effect of Labeling upon Youths in the Juvenile Justice System: A Review of the Evidence," *Law and Society Review* 8 (1974): pp. 583–615.

9. Anthony Platt, *The Child Savers: The Invention of Delinquency* (Chicago: University of Chicago Press, 1969).

10. See Philippe Aries, *Centuries of Childhood* (New York: Knopf, 1962). A detailed discussion of the history of childhood juvenile justice is contained in Chapter 12.

11. For a general discussion, see David Rothman, "The Progressive Legacy: Development of American Attitudes toward Juvenile Delinquency," in Empey, *Juvenile Justice,* pp. 34–69.

12. This fact is borne out by many self-reports of delinquency studies. See Chapter 3 for a further discussion of this topic.

13. Robert Emerson, "A Note on 'Serious' Cases," paper presented at the American Sociological Association meeting, Washington, D.C., 1970.

14. See, generally, David Rothman, *The Discovery of the Asylum* (Boston: Little, Brown, 1971).

15. Reports of the Chicago Bar Association Committee, 1899, cited in Platt, *The Child Savers*.

16. Mark Levin and Rosemary Sarri, *Juvenile Delinquency: A Comparative Analysis of Legal Codes in the United States* (Ann Arbor: University of Michigan, National Assessment of Juvenile Corrections, 1974).

17. Rosemary Sarri, "Status Offenders: Their Fate in the Juvenile Justice System," in *Status Offenders and the Juvenile Justice System,* ed. Richard Allison (Hackensack, N.J.: National Council on Crime and Delinquency, 1978), p. 66.

18. Ohio Unruly Child Statute, 2151.022.

19. For an analysis of the role of due process in juvenile justice, see Larry Siegel, Joseph Senna, and Therese Libby, "Legal Aspects of the Juvenile Justice System," *New England Law Review* 12 (1976).

20. In re L.N., 109 N.J. Super. 278, 263 A 2d., 150 (1970).

21. *Commonwealth v. Brasher,* 359 Mass. 550; 270 N.E. 2d 389 (1971).

22. See, for example, Naomi Fegelson Chase, *A Child Is Being Beaten* (New York: McGraw-Hill, 1976); and V. J. Fontana, *Somewhere a Child Is Crying* (New York: Macmillan, 1973).

23. Howard Abadinsky, "The Status Offense Dilemma: Coercion and Greatment," *Crime and Delinquency* 22 (1976): p. 458.

24. R. L. Barrett, "Delinquent Child: A Legal Term without Meaning," *Baylor Law Review* pp. 352–371.

25. Rosemary Sarri, "The Detention of Youths in Jails and Juvenile Detention Facilities," *Juvenile Justice* 26 (1973): p. 4.

26. See, generally, Sarri, "Status Offenders."

27. See, generally, Howard James, *Children in Trouble* (New York: David McKay, 1969).

28. See, for example, *In re Lovette,* M. 35, N.Y. 2d. 136, 359 N.Y.S. 2d. 41 (1974). See, generally, Sarri, "Status Offenders."

29. Lawrence Martin and Phyllis Snyder, "Jurisdiction over Status Offenses Should *Not* Be Removed from the Juvenile Court," *Crime and Delinquency* 22 (1976): pp. 44–47.

30. Ibid., p. 45.

31. Lindsay Arthur, "Status Offenders Need a Court of Last Resort," *Boston University Law Review* 57 (1977): pp. 631–644.

32. Ibid.

33. Charles Thomas, "Are Status Offenders Really So Different?" *Crime and Delinquency* 22 (1976): pp. 438–455.

34. Ibid., pp. 454–455.

35. American Bar Association Joint Commission on Juvenile Justice Standards, Section 1.1.

36. National Advisory Committee on Criminal Justice Standards and Goals, *Juvenile Justice and Delinquency Prevention* (Washington, D.C.: Government Printing Office, 1977), p. 311.

37. Ibid., p. 318.

38. See David Gilman, "How to Retain Jurisdiction of Status Offenses," *Crime and Delinquency* 22 (1976): p. 48.

39.   See Elizabeth Vorenberg, "How Massachusetts Has Shifted Care of Status Offenders to a Social Services Unit," *Criminal Justice Newsletter* 9 (1978): pp. 1–2.

══════════════════════Chapter 2═

Chapter Outline	Key Terms, Names, and Cases
Introduction	official delinquency
The Uniform Crime Reports	Uniform Crime Report (UCR)
Other Forms of Official Statistics Used as Research Tools	crime rate
	burglary
Analysis of Official Statistics	larceny
Chapter Summary	robbery
	murder
	assault
	birth cohort
	motor vehicle theft
	Marvin Wolfgang

Measures of Official Delinquency

INTRODUCTION

The present chapter will explore the amount, the nature, and the extent of official delinquent behavior. The term *official delinquent* refers to youths whose delinquent behavior has come to the attention of law enforcement agencies, including local and state police departments and juvenile courts and correctional authorities. Thus, youths with a public record are official delinquents, and their actions are considered *official delinquency*.

Youths whose criminal acts are undetected by law enforcement authorities and youths who are apprehended but released without any formal action being taken are secret, hidden, or unofficial offenders. (See Chapter 3 for a discussion of self-reported, unofficial youth crime.)

The concept of official delinquent behavior is important for a variety of reasons. For one thing, it specifically refers to minors who have been *formally* processed by the agencies of the justice system—young people who have been taken into police custody, petitioned to juvenile court, placed on probation, and even housed in secure treatment facilities. This constitutes a most important group of offenders, perhaps the most important, for criminological study. Official statistics can therefore help criminologists better understand who the serious delinquents are, their backgrounds, their personal characteristics, and, significantly, what effect official processing has on their subsequent behavior. Furthermore, although the records of official delinquents are often by law or statute confidential, military, government, and even business authorities can sometimes see juvenile files.[1] Thus, minors who are recorded as official delinquents may be subject to the pains of stigma and social rejection associated with the delinquency label. They may be prevented from gaining future employment and made to suffer other types of social ostracism. This factor also highlights the importance of official delinquency.

Researchers, theorists, and social planners use official statistics to study the causes and prevention of delinquency. Major academic studies have relied on the records of police, court, and correctional agencies.[2] Government policy is often based on the trends uncovered in official statistics.[3] Unfortunately, some critics have charged that official data leads to a spurious view of delinquency, one dominated by the biases of police, court, and correctional decision makers.[4]

* For example, critics point out that local police departments and juvenile courts are more likely to process black and lower-class white youths. Conversely, they are more likely to give children of the middle class a "break" by handling their cases informally, for example, letting them go with a warning.[5] Thus, it is not surprising that police records reflect a disproportionate involvement in delinquency by poor black and white youths.[6] Keeping this in mind, it can be argued that official delinquency is more a product of police (and court) behavior than youthful misbehavior. Attempts, therefore, to use official statistics in delinquency research or program planning will only lead to a distorted picture of the delinquency problem. Nonetheless, official statistics continue to be widely used in governmental and academic circles because, after all, they are one of the few sources that tell us a great deal about youths who have run afoul of the law and have suffered at its hands.

Official delinquency statistics have been organized and collected on the local, regional, and national level. Almost every major city police department and court agency maintains extensive records on the youth taken into custody or processed. In addition, some state governments make annual surveys of the youths who have been processed to juvenile court as well as those who occupy residential correctional facilities within the state.[7]

Perhaps the most widely used source of official crime and delinquency statistics has been the annual effort of the U.S. Justice Department's Federal Bureau of Investigation (FBI) to accumulate information gathered by the nation's police departments on the number of criminal acts reported by citizens, and the number of persons arrested each year for criminal and delinquent activity. Called the *Uniform Crime Reports (UCR)*, the FBI's effort constitutes our best known and most widely used source of national crime and delinquency statistics.[8]

Despite the extensive effort by the FBI to survey over 10,000 police agencies every year, critics have charged that the UCR is of questionable validity and that its findings must be interpreted with extreme caution.[9] And, as we shall see later in this chapter, the future of the UCR is uncertain.

In the following sections, we will review in some detail two of the most important collections of official delinquency statistics. First, the UCR will be examined in order to provide some indication of the nature and extent of official delinquent behavior in America. Then, an important study, *Delinquency in a Birth Cohort*, will be examined to illustrate how official statistics have been used to explore the factors related to delinquent behavior.[10]

THE UNIFORM CRIME REPORTS

When people say the "crime rate is skyrocketing" or "delinquency is getting out of hand," they are usually referring to information provided in the FBI's

Uniform Crime Reports (UCR). Based on the efforts of over 10,000 law enforcement agencies across the nation, the UCR provides a yearly report of the crime in the United States as measured by offenses coming to the attention of the nation's law enforcement agencies.[11] The FBI focuses on seven crimes that, because of their seriousness, frequency, and the likelihood of their being reported to police, are considered the most necessary to monitor. These crimes, known as Index Crimes, include murder and nonnegligent manslaughter, forcible rape, robbery, aggravated assault, burglary, larceny and theft, and motor vehicle theft (see Highlight 2–1). In addition, the FBI collects data on the race, sex, and age of offenders who are *arrested* for almost any other crimes except traffic violations. These data are our national crime statistics.

Highlight 2–1. Definitions of Index Crimes.

Murder and Nonnegligent Manslaughter
Murder and nonnegligent manslaughter, as defined in the Uniform Crime Reporting Program, is the willful (nonnegligent) killing of one human being by another.

The classification of this offense, as in all other Crime Index offenses, is based solely on police investigation as opposed to the determination of a court, medical examiner, coroner, jury, or other judicial body. Not included in the count for this offense classification are deaths caused by negligence, suicide, or accident; justifiable homicides, which are the killings of felons by law enforcement officers in the line of duty or by private citizens; and attempts to murder or assaults to murder, which are scored as aggravated assaults.

Forcible Rape
Forcible rape, as defined in the Program, is the carnal knowledge of a female forcibly and against her will. Assaults or attempts to commit forcible rape by force or threat of force are also included; however, statutory rape (without force) and other sex offenses are not included in this category.

Robbery
Robbery is the taking or attempting to take anything of value from the care, custody, or control of a person or persons by force or threat of force or violence and/or by putting the victim in fear.

Aggravated Assault
Aggravated assault is an unlawful attack by one person upon another for the purpose of inflicting severe or aggravated bodily injury. This type of assault is usually accompanied by the use of a weapon or by means likely to produce death or great bodily harm. Attempts are included since it is not necessary that an injury result when a gun, knife, or other weapon is used which could and probably would result in serious personal injury if the crime were successfully completed.

Burglary
The Uniform Crime Reporting Program defines burglary as the unlawful entry of a structure to commit a felony or theft. The use of force to gain entry is not required to classify an offense as burglary. Burglary in this Program is categorized into three subclassifications: forcible entry, unlawful entry where no force is used and attempted forcible entry.

Motor Vehicle Theft
In Uniform Crime Reporting, motor vehicle theft is defined as the theft or attempted theft of a motor vehicle. This definition excludes the taking of a motor vehicle for temporary use by those persons having lawful access.

Larceny-theft

Larceny-theft is the unlawful taking, carrying, leading, or riding away of property from the possession or constructive possession of another. It includes crimes such as shoplifting, pocket-picking, purse-snatching, thefts from motor vehicles, thefts of motor vehicle parts and accessories, bicycle thefts, etc., in which no use of force, violence, or fraud occurs. In the Uniform Crime Reporting Program, this crime category does not in-

clude embezzlement, "con" games, forgery, and worthless checks. Motor vehicle theft is also excluded from this category for crime reporting purposes in as much as it is a separate Crime Index offense.

Source: Federal Bureau of Investigation, *Crime in the United States, Uniform Crime Reports*, 1978 (Washington, D.C.: Government Printing Office, 1979).

The FBI cannot calculate the number of delinquent youths who commit Index Crimes since, in most instances, their identities remain unknown. However, national arrest data give some indication of the nature, extent, and trend of delinquent behavior in America. We will now examine this data and try to draw some conclusions about the extent of American delinquency.

Arrest Trends

The most recent FBI statistics indicate that 7 percent of all persons arrested were under the age of fifteen, 23 percent were under eighteen, and 40 percent were under twenty-one. In suburban areas, the arrest rate for teenagers was even greater. Twenty-eight percent of all arrests in these areas were youth eighteen and under. As Figure 2-1 indicates, offenders between the ages of thirteen and twenty-one were arrested at a rate disproportionate to their share of the total population. For example, sixteen to eighteen-year-olds made up more than 15 percent of all people arrested, but they constituted only 5 percent of the nation's population.

For reasons of comparison, arrests of males and females in the years 1969 and 1978 are illustrated in Table 2-1 (p. 26). In viewing the data in Table 2-1, we should remember that the population of youths eighteen and under actually *declined* 10 percent during this ten-year period—from 70,754,000 to 63,425,000.[12] Keeping this in mind, the changes recorded in the number of juvenile arrests takes on even greater significance. Table 2-1 shows that arrests in almost every serious crime category increased dramatically with the exception of motor vehicle theft by males. With the exception of sex offences and public order offenses such as drunkenness, vagrancy, curfew and loitering, arrests increased in minor crime categories also. The decline in these categories can be explained in part by changes in state law and practice. Many jurisdictions have removed the legal penalties from vagrancy, curfew, and other similar offenses to free crowded court dockets. Similarly, youths with drug and alcohol problems and those who have run away because of family problems are often referred directly to community-based treatment programs without official action being taken.

Figure 2–1. Distribution of Arrests by Age.

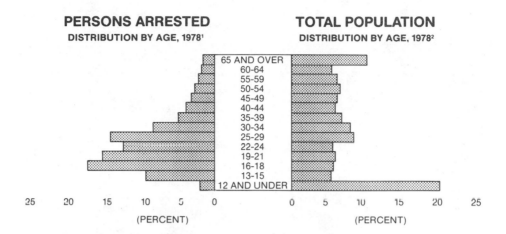

PERSONS ARRESTED
DISTRIBUTION BY AGE, 1978[1]

TOTAL POPULATION
DISTRIBUTION BY AGE, 1978[2]

(PERCENT)   (PERCENT)

[1]PERSONS ARRESTED IS BASED ON REPORTS
RECEIVED REPRESENTING POPULATION.

[2]THE TOTAL POPULATION IS 218,059,000 FOR
THE U.S., BASED ON BUREAU OF CENSUS
PROVISIONAL ESTIMATES, JULY 1, 1978

Source: Federal Bureau of Investigation, *Crime in the United States, Uniform Crime Reports,
1978* (Washington, D.C.: Government Printing Office, 1979), p. 185.

People eighteen and under seem to be getting arrested much more often today than they did a decade earlier. The *population* of this group declined by 10
percent, but the number of boys arrested for serious index crimes increased by
almost 19 percent, in ten years, and the number of girls increased a dramatic 61
percent. (We will discuss the background of female delinquency more fully in
Chapters 3 and 8.) Let us take a closer look at trends in serious violent and property arrests.

Violent Crime

In the 1960s and 1970s, a wave of violence swept through America, raising the
amount of crimes against persons to unprecedented heights. For example, the
number of robberies reported to police tripled between 1963 and 1971; the number of murders, which had actually declined between 1933 and 1963 rose from
14,760 in 1969 to over 20,000 in 1974. In general, the number of reported violent
crimes rose from 661,870 in 1969 to over 1.1 million in 1979 (the latest figures
available from the FBI at the time of this writing).

Youths certainly perpetrate violent crimes, but they are not arrested as often
as adults. As Table 2–2 (p. 26) indicates, people over eighteen arrested for the
most serious crimes of violence—murder, rape, and assault—far outnumber
people under eighteen. For the crime of robbery, however, 34 percent of all
people arrested were under eighteen.[13] Teenage robbery rarely involves skill or
professionalism. Instead, it is a brutal attack by a street tough on a weak victim.
Sometimes, robbery is used as a means for a gang boy to prove his toughness or
manhood. Consider this statement by a former teenage gang member:

Table 2-1. Total Arrest Trends by Age and Sex, 1969–1978.

[3,608 agencies; 1978 estimated population 114,764,000]

	Males						Females					
	Total			Under 18			Total			Under 18		
Offense charged	1969	1978	Percent change	1969	1978	Percent change	1969	1978	Percent change	1969	1978	Percent change
TOTAL	4,195,086	4,424,628	+ 5.5	975,556	1,074,142	+ 10.1	659,638	917,618	+ 39.1	252,296	297,099	+ 17.8
Murder and nonnegligent manslaughter	7,777	8,988	+ 15.6	845	960	+ 13.6	1,453	1,582	+ 8.9	85	97	+ 14.1
Forcible rape	11,705	15,877	+ 35.6	2,355	2,643	+ 12.2	—	141	—	—	48	—
Robbery	55,827	74,035	+ 32.6	17,833	23,773	+ 33.3	3,534	5,739	+ 62.4	1,148	1,707	+ 48.7
Aggravated assault	79,565	117,849	+ 48.1	12,718	20,082	+ 57.9	11,274	17,818	+ 58.0	1,675	3,459	+106.5
Burglary	198,496	261,321	+ 31.7	108,128	139,524	+ 29.0	9,001	17,289	+ 92.1	4,709	8,974	+ 90.6
Larceny — theft	312,139	459,261	+ 47.1	169,722	209,342	+ 23.3	115,194	224,850	+ 95.2	53,239	84,445	+ 58.6
Motor vehicle theft	97,101	78,724	– 18.9	56,705	41,202	– 27.3	5,465	7,545	+ 38.1	3,153	4,446	+ 41.0
Violent crime[1]	154,874	216,749	+ 40.0	33,751	47,458	+ 40.6	16,261	25,280	+ 55.5	2,908	5,311	+ 82.6
Property crime[2]	607,736	799,306	+ 31.5	334,555	390,068	+ 16.6	129,660	249,684	+ 92.6	61,101	97,865	+ 60.2
Crime Index total	762,610	1,016,055	+ 33.2	368,306	437,526	+ 18.8	145,921	274,964	+ 88.4	64,009	103,176	+ 61.2
Other assaults	193,664	226,830	+ 17.1	31,438	43,942	+ 39.8	26,422	37,226	+ 40.9	7,263	11,256	+ 55.0
Arson	6,280	8,881	+ 41.4	4,076	4,800	+ 17.8	606	1,264	+108.6	345	519	+ 50.4
Forgery and counterfeiting	22,895	27,621	+ 20.6	2,721	4,058	+ 49.1	7,058	13,107	+ 85.7	802	1,775	+121.3
Fraud	39,467	64,514	+ 63.5	1,850	2,669	+ 44.3	14,058	44,803	+218.7	455	1,130	+148.4
Embezzlement	3,839	3,050	– 20.6	131	434	+231.3	1,064	1,112	+ 4.5	57	145	+154.4
Stolen property; buying, receiving, possessing	29,562	55,350	+ 87.2	10,514	20,545	+ 95.4	2,801	7,222	+157.8	819	2,035	+148.5
Vandalism	81,028	122,801	+ 51.6	59,703	72,645	+ 21.7	6,417	11,401	+ 77.7	4,068	6,024	+ 48.1
Weapons; carrying, possessing, etc.	68,936	84,753	+ 22.9	12,441	14,546	+ 16.9	4,802	7,424	+ 54.6	596	921	+ 54.5
Prostitution and commercialized vice	7,816	19,588	+150.6	236	814	+244.9	27,499	40,806	+ 48.4	617	1,748	+183.3
Sex offenses (except forcible rape and prostitution)	36,044	35,154	– 2.5	7,020	6,515	– 7.2	5,932	3,497	– 41.0	2,190	687	– 68.6
Drug abuse violations	145,864	298,220	+104.5	35,182	72,412	+105.8	29,062	51,185	+ 76.1	10,075	14,756	+ 46.5
Gambling	50,010	32,928	– 34.2	1,309	1,297	– .9	4,366	3,293	– 24.6	44	68	+ 54.5
Offenses against family and children	41,521	20,638	– 50.3	531	1,109	+108.9	4,232	3,152	– 25.5	181	732	+304.4
Driving under the influence	277,972	500,299	+ 80.0	3,112	11,370	+265.4	19,296	49,170	+154.8	138	1,301	+842.8
Liquor laws	153,995	155,295	+ .8	49,182	54,268	+ 10.3	22,825	29,255	+ 28.2	10,129	16,069	+ 58.6
Drunkenness	1,178,850	626,369	– 46.9	32,652	21,399	– 34.5	88,822	51,785	– 41.7	4,680	3,666	– 21.7
Disorderly conduct	422,959	380,070	– 10.1	84,138	71,301	– 15.3	65,645	76,902	+ 17.1	16,697	15,055	– 9.8
Vagrancy	67,818	16,633	– 75.5	6,279	2,733	– 56.5	7,305	4,092	– 44.0	1,099	573	– 47.9
All other offenses (except traffic)	468,358	637,951	+ 36.2	129,137	138,131	+ 7.0	87,362	130,013	+ 48.8	39,889	39,518	– .9
Suspicion (not included in totals)	72,802	10,070	– 86.2	15,805	3,232	– 79.6	12,697	1,682	– 86.8	2,574	553	– 78.5
Curfew and loitering law violations	69,788	45,499	– 34.8	69,788	45,499	– 34.8	17,192	11,355	– 34.0	17,192	11,355	– 34.0
Runaways	65,810	46,129	– 29.9	65,810	46,129	– 29.9	70,951	64,590	– 9.0	70,951	64,590	– 9.0

[1]Violent crimes are offenses of murder, forcible rape, robbery, and aggravated assault.
[2]Property crimes are offenses of burglary, larceny — theft, and motor vehicle theft.

Source: Federal Bureau of Investigation, *Crime in the United States, Uniform Crime Reports,* 1978 (Washington, D.C.: Government Printing Office, 1979), p. 189.

Table 2-2. Total Arrests of Persons under 15, 18, 21, and 25 Years of Age, 1978.

[11,872 agencies; 1978 estimated population 207,060,000]

Offense charged	Grand total all ages	Number of persons arrested				Percent of total all ages			
		Under 15	Under 18	Under 21	Under 25	Under 15	Under 18	Under 21	Under 25
TOTAL	9,775,087	728,198	2,279,365	3,909,507	5,536,862	7.4	23.3	40.0	56.6
Murder and nonnegligent manslaughter	18,755	244	1,735	4,519	8,136	1.3	9.3	24.1	43.4
Forcible rape	28,257	1,102	4,517	9,266	15,231	3.9	16.0	32.8	53.9
Robbery	141,481	13,086	48,088	79,933	106,693	9.2	34.0	56.5	75.4
Aggravated assault	257,629	11,508	41,253	79,368	126,485	4.5	16.0	30.8	49.1
Burglary	485,782	93,652	250,649	346,122	407,760	19.3	51.6	71.3	83.9
Larceny — theft	1,084,088	194,680	454,994	636,749	778,028	18.0	42.0	58.7	71.8
Motor vehicle theft	153,270	20,146	77,534	106,970	126,451	13.1	50.6	69.8	82.5
Violent crime[1]	446,122	25,940	95,593	173,086	256,545	5.8	21.4	38.8	57.5
Property crime[2]	1,723,140	308,478	783,177	1,089,841	1,312,239	17.9	45.5	63.2	76.2
Crime Index total	2,169,262	334,418	878,770	1,262,927	1,568,784	15.4	40.5	58.2	72.3

Source: Federal Bureau of Investigation, *Crime in the United States, Uniform Crime Reports,* 1978 (Washington, D.C.: Government Printing Office, 1979), p. 196.

I wanted everybody to know that I was one of the baddest guys that walked the street, so I walked around with my zip gun exposed or my switchblade knife in my hand. Then I started hanging out with a bunch and we wanted to be *something*, because everybody else, they weren't really doing nothing, they really wasn't makin' that money. So we started mugging.[14]

Fear of armed robbery and other violent youth crimes has helped to change the patterns of American life. Suburban shopping centers have replaced downtown stores because people are afraid of the criminal element in urban areas. City parks and other public areas are no longer used at night. Reducing the rate of violent youth crime has become a top priority of public officials on the state, local, and national levels of government.

Property Offenses

As Table 2-2 indicates, people under eighteen make up a significant number of all people arrested for property crimes (45.5 percent). In fact, more than half of all people arrested for burglary and motor vehicle theft were under eighteen, and more than 40 percent of the more than 1 million people arrested for larceny were under eighteen.

Stealing is a way for minors to get desired goods and luxuries even though their earning capacity is extremely limited. For example, the FBI estimates that the average value of the property lost from a larceny-theft was $219 and from a burglary was $526.

The theft of motor vehicles and parts is especially prevalent among young offenders. The automobile has long served as an expression of adolescent freedom, and joy-riding in souped-up cars is still a favorite pastime of rebellious adolescents, fuel shortages notwithstanding. This phenomenon is reflected by the fact that in 1978, 70 percent of those arrested for motor vehicle theft were under twenty-one, and those under eighteen accounted for about 51 percent of the total arrests (77,534). These acts are common among urban teenagers. One-third of the arrests for larceny-theft in the nation's cities and suburbs involved youths under eighteen (21 percent in rural areas). In addition, larceny-theft involves many other acts common to youth, including thefts from coin machines, shoplifting, purse snatching, and theft of bicycles.

Race and Delinquency

Racial prejudice has long been linked to the conflict between minorities and agencies of the law. It has become commonplace to charge either that (1) blacks are disproportionately involved in serious criminal activity or (2) that police, court, and correctional agencies discriminate against racial minorities, causing their crime rate to appear higher than that of whites. Such claims have led to major racial confrontations, including the Miami riot of May 1980. Many people died over a conflict that started when four police officers were found innocent of charges stemming from the beating to death of a young black man.

Table 2-3 shows the arrest distribution of youth under eighteen by racial background. Though the population of whites in this age group is more than six times that of blacks (61 million to 9 million), blacks appear to get arrested at a far greater rate. In fact, Table 2–3 indicates that black youths actually outnumbered whites in the critical area of arrests for serious violent crimes (49,596 to 42,404). White youths preponderate in the arrest statistics for crimes such as vandalism, drug abuse, driving under the influence, liquor laws, drunkenness, and the catchall category, "All Other Offenses," which includes many status offenses. How can we explain these findings? That blacks have resorted to violence in response to racism and oppression has been documented by a number of social commentators, including author Charles Silberman, who discusses this issue in Highlight 2–2.

Table 2–3. Arrests of Minors by Race.

Offense charged	Arrests under 18							Percent distribution[1]						
	Total	White	Negro	Indian	Chinese	Japanese	All others	Total	White	Negro	Indian	Chinese	Japanese	All others
TOTAL	2,268,317	1,685,854	525,628	16,399	2,013	1,399	37,024	100.0	74.3	23.2	0.7	0.1	0.1	1.6
Murder and nonnegligent manslaughter	1,732	821	830	10	3	2	66	100.0	47.4	47.9	.6	.2	.1	3.8
Forcible rape	4,501	1,914	2,454	18	1	1	113	100.0	42.5	54.5	.4	—	—	2.5
Robbery	48,005	14,672	31,418	154	47	24	1,690	100.0	30.6	65.4	.3	.1	(²)	3.5
Aggravated assault	41,213	24,997	14,894	282	59	11	970	100.0	60.7	36.1	.7	.1	—	2.4
Burglary	249,453	176,327	65,715	1,455	147	233	5,576	100.0	70.7	26.3	.6	.1	.1	2.2
Larceny-theft	453,395	306,653	134,065	3,346	627	497	8,207	100.0	67.6	29.6	.7	.1	.1	1.8
Motor vehicle theft	77,014	57,485	16,313	777	104	45	2,290	100.0	74.6	21.2	1.0	.1	.1	3.0
Violent crime[3]	95,451	42,404	49,596	464	110	38	2,839	100.0	44.4	52.0	.5	.1	—	3.0
Property crime[4]	779,862	540,465	216,093	5,578	878	775	16,073	100.0	69.3	27.7	.7	.1	.1	2.1
Crime Index total	875,313	582,869	265,689	6,042	988	813	18,912	100.0	66.6	30.4	.7	.1	.1	2.2
Other assaults	82,200	52,582	27,024	532	72	33	1,957	100.0	64.0	32.9[4]	.6	.1	—	2.4
Arson	8,694	7,107	1,380	33	9	4	161	100.0	81.7	15.9	.4	.1	—	1.9
Forgery and counterfeiting	9,957	7,833	1,970	52	6	2	94	100.0	78.7	19.8	.5	.1	—	.9
Fraud	18,867	9,798	8,601	46	69	1	352	100.0	51.9	45.6	.2	.4	—	1.9
Embezzlement	909	735	160	3	2	—	9	100.0	80.9	17.6	.3	.2	—	1.0
Stolen property; buying, receiving, possessing	37,245	25,400	10,753	207	50	22	813	100.0	68.2	28.9	.6	.1	.1	2.2
Vandalism	127,538	107,847	17,177	560	83	40	1,831	100.0	84.6	13.5	.4	.1	—	1.4
Weapons; carrying, possessing, etc.	23,613	16,196	6,522	98	51	19	727	100.0	68.6	27.6	.4	.2	.1	3.1
Prostitution and commercialized vice	4,203	2,137	1,970	11	11	—	74	100.0	50.8	46.9	.3	.3	—	1.8
Sex offenses (except forcible rape and prostitution)	11,803	8,240	3,244	44	40	8	227	100.0	69.8	27.5	.4	.3	.1	1.9
Drug abuse violations	140,406	121,099	16,759	576	65	105	1,802	100.0	86.2	11.9	.4	(²)	.1	1.3
Gambling	2,137	367	1,630	2	4	6	128	100.0	17.2	76.3	.1	.2	.3	6.0
Offenses against family and children	2,866	2,162	665	14	4	1	20	100.0	75.4	23.2	.5	.1	—	.7
Driving under the influence	26,641	25,187	899	329	10	10	206	100.0	94.5	3.4	1.2	—	—	.8
Liquor laws	126,089	120,786	2,803	1,754	39	31	676	100.0	95.8	2.2	1.4	—	—	.5
Drunkenness	42,944	39,565	2,472	724	17	4	162	100.0	92.1	5.8	1.7	—	—	.4
Disorderly conduct	123,872	91,705	28,657	844	34	14	2,618	100.0	74.0	23.1	.7	—	—	2.1
Vagrancy	6,566	4,971	1,527	21	4	2	41	100.0	75.7	23.3	.3	.1	—	.6
All other offenses (except traffic)	339,512	248,419	85,696	1,679	319	167	3,232	100.0	73.2	25.2	.5	.1	—	1.0
Suspicion	6,146	4,331	1,667	108	1	3	36	100.0	70.5	27.1	1.8	—	—	.6
Curfew and loitering law violations	78,823	58,815	18,597	902	44	29	436	100.0	74.6	23.6	1.1	.1	—	.6
Runaways	171,973	147,703	19,766	1,818	91	85	2,510	100.0	85.9	11.5	1.1	.1	—	1.5

See footnotes at end of table.

Source: Federal Bureau of Investigation, *Crime in the United States, Uniform Crime Reports,* 1978 (Washington, D.C.: Government Printing Office, 1979), p. 179.

Highlight 2–2. Charles Silberman on Racial Violence

When one reflects on what has been done to black people in this country, in short, what is remarkable is not how *much*, but how *little*, black violence there has always been. Certainly, it would be hard to imagine an environment better calculated to evoke violence than the one in which black Americans have lived.

The caste system is disappearing rapidly, white Americans are learning to avoid overtly racist remarks and behavior. But the racial attitudes the caste system engendered are a good bit more durable—in the North as well as in the South. It was only a few years ago that the white housekeeper inspecting my wife's hospital room bestowed a

An alternative explanation is that black youths are arrested more often for violent crimes because the police patrol black neighborhoods more heavily and because they discriminate against blacks. Conversely, the police may be less willing to arrest black youngsters for drug, liquor, or vandalism violations, feeling that these are community problems that are of no concern to the official agencies of justice. There has been much debate over this issue. Some critics charge that police and juvenile courts do indeed discriminate in their handling of black and poor white youths, or as one commentator suggests:

In our society, lower-class children more than middle-class ones, black children more than white ones, and boys more than girls, face high probabilities . . . not only of engaging in rule-violation in the first place, but also of becoming enmeshed in official negative labeling processes.[15]

Nonetheless, some research has uncovered evidence that race is less influential than such factors as prior record, seriousness of offense, and other personal factors in determining whether a child will be arrested and subsequently processed to juvenile court.[16]

In either event, FBI data indicate that white youths are arrested over 1.6 million times a year and black youths over 0.5 million times, surely a startling and serious matter for concern.

Conclusions of the Uniform Crime Reports

Analysis of UCR data indicates that a significant number of young people are arrested every year for serious crimes. In addition, the proportion of youth arrested today is much higher than it was ten years ago (based on the fact that while the population of people eighteen and under has declined 10 percent, the number of youths arrested has increased).

Minors are arrested by the police over 2 million times a year. If the ratio of arrests to criminal acts is 5:1 (based on the overall ratio between crimes reported to police and arrests), then it is possible that youths account for over 10 million serious crimes a year. And, of course, youths are responsible for many criminal acts that are never reported to police and for so-called victimless crimes that go unrecorded such as gambling and soft-drug use. Thus, the total of youth crime in the United States has reached awesome proportions.

---

gracious compliment on the black porter who had washed the floor. "The floor looks beautiful," she told him. "You're a good boy, Jimmy." Jimmy was 48 years old.

Whites continue to patronize blacks and, in the process, deny their existence as full human beings. This white assumption of black invisibility cuts to the marrow, for it denies black peoples' existence as full human beings. In time, it makes them wonder if they really do exist—if they really are full human beings. It also makes them angry.

Source: Charles Silberman, from an address cited in *Correction Today*, September–October, 1979, p. 13.

As we shall see later in the chapter, the UCR has been criticized for being inaccurate and methodologically unsound. Its future remains in doubt, but it will most likely be taken out of the hands of the FBI and given to the newly formed Office of Justice Statistics in the United States Justice Department. In addition, the crime of arson will be added as an Index Crime in the near future.

OTHER FORMS OF OFFICIAL
STATISTICS USED AS RESEARCH TOOLS

In addition to the UCR, criminologists frequently use other official delinquency records as research tools. They examine raw police files in order to determine (1) the types of youths who get arrested for delinquent acts and (2) what happens to them after their arrest. For example, Theodore Ferdinand and Elmer Luchterhand examined police records and found that law enforcement officers are more likely to arrest black and low-income white boys than middle-class youth.[17]

In a similar study, Edward Green examined police records in Michigan and discovered that there was a disparity in black and white arrest rates because blacks were predominantly of lower-class status.[18] Use of official records has provided a conflicting picture of police-juvenile relationships.

Juvenile court records have also been used to explore the nature of the delinquency problem. Issues of significant importance to criminologists include defining the factors that influence the intake decision, adjudication, and the choice of disposition after the trial is over. Prominent among studies of this type is Robert Terry's analysis of juvenile court records in Racine, Wisconsin.[19] Terry found that while the court treated minority and lower-class white youths more severely, these groups actually had more prior offenses and engaged in more serious delinquent acts. Yona Cohn used court records differently in her study of the criteria that probation officers used in deciding to recommend probation or more severe dispositions (such as institutionalization) to juvenile court judges.[20] Cohn found that gender (girls were more often institutionalized), school activities, family, and a child's personality were all of greater importance to probation officers than crime seriousness.

Still another example of the use of official statistics in criminological research includes the use of correctional records to compare institutionalized youth with noninstitutionalized youth, or to compare the effects of different types of institutions.[21]

Problems with obtaining and processing official records hinder their usefulness. Public agencies are often reluctant to open their archives to researchers since they fear loss of client privacy. Official records also tend to be inconsistent—different agencies keep records in different ways. It is also time-consuming and tedious to go over thousands of records, take notes, and then transfer the information into a format that lends itself to data analysis. In general, records of justice agencies tend to be spotty and incomplete.

Perhaps the most well known and influential study of delinquency using official records was the pioneering attempt of Clifford R. Shaw and Henry D. McKay to determine the effect of ecological and cultural factors on delinquent careers (see Chapter 5).[22] In the spirit of the Shaw-McKay research effort, Marvin Wolfgang, Robert Figlio, and Thorsten Sellin recently conducted a study of the lives of delinquent youth, *Delinquency in a Birth Cohort*, which used official records extensively.[23] This is a landmark study, so we have analyzed its methodology and findings in detail.

Delinquency in a Birth Cohort

Wolfgang, Figlio, and Sellin used official records to follow the delinquent careers of a cohort of 9,945 boys born in Philadelphia, Pennsylvania, in 1945, until they reached eighteen years of age in 1963. The authors believed that:

Such an inquiry would permit us to note the age of onset and the progression or cessation of delinquency. It would allow us to relate these phenomena to certain personal or social characteristics of the delinquents and to make appropriate comparisons.[24]

Official police records were used to identify delinquents. About one-third of the boys (3,475) had some police contact. The remaining two-thirds (6,470) had none. Each delinquent's actions were given a seriousness weight based on the Wolfgang-Sellin Delinquency Index, which provides a weighted score for every particular delinquent act.[25] The weighting of delinquent acts allowed the researchers to differentiate, for example, between a simple assault requiring no medical attention for the victim and a serious assault in which the victim needed hospitalization.

Wolfgang et al. obtained data from school records, including subject IQ scores and measures of academic performance and conduct. Socioeconomic status was determined by locating the residence of each member of the cohort and assigning him the median family income for that area. The levels used were: $4,000 and under, poverty; $4,000-$4,500, deprivation; $4,501-$5,783, semideprivation; $5,784-$6,799, modest but adequate; above $6,799, comfort.

Findings

Of the 9,945 boys in the final sample, slightly over one-third (3,475) had at least one contact with the police during their minority.

Race was found to be the most significant predictor of eventual police contact. Of the 2,902 nonwhite subjects, 1,458 had police contact (50.24 percent). Of the 7,043 white youths, 2,017 (28.64 percent) were similarly treated.[26] Wolfgang and his associates also noted that minority youth tended to fall in the lower-class category (84.2 percent of nonwhites, and 30.8 percent of whites were from lower socioeconomic levels). However, when youths from the same socioeconomic levels were compared, nonwhites still had a higher level of police contact. After further analysis, the researchers were forced to conclude that no single variable predicted juvenile police contact better than racial background.[27]

School Achievement

Wolfgang et al. found that school-related variables were also significantly related to delinquent behavior. (See Chapter 10 for a more detailed discussion of schools and delinquency.) For one thing, the types of schools a youth attended influenced whether he would eventually be picked up by police. A greater proportion of delinquents spent the major part of their school years in public schools, and fewer delinquents than nondelinquents attended parocial schools. Furthermore, 4 percent of delinquents, compared to 1 percent of nondelinquents, attended a public disciplinary institution.[28]

Nondelinquents received more education than delinquents (11.24 years completed versus 9.96). While this relationship was consistent across racial lines, it was equally apparent that nonwhites averaged significantly less schooling than whites.

Another school-related factor, IQ also distinguished delinquents from nondelinquents. (See Chapter 4 for a more detailed analysis of the relationship between I.Q. and delinquency.) The average IQ for nondelinquents was 107.87; for delinquents, it was 100.95. Again this relationship was consistent across racial lines.

In a similar vein, school achievement levels were significantly related to delinquent activities: 12.8 percent of nondelinquents were rated "very low" on school achievement; 27.46 percent of delinquents received such negative ratings. Conversely, 19.48 percent of nondelinquents received a "very high" rating, while only 5.63 percent of delinquent youth received that rating. However, the researchers found major differences between the races in school achievement, with blacks doing considerably less well.[29]

Multiple Offenses

Fifty-four percent (1,862 youth) of the boys who committed delinquent acts committed more than one offense. The remaining 46 percent (or 1,616) were one-time offenders. Recidivists were more likely to be nonwhites in the lower socioeconomic strata who had lower IQ scores, finished fewer school years, and maintained lower school achievement levels.[30]

The 3,475 recorded delinquents in the sample were responsible for 10,124 delinquent acts. Whites were involved in 44 percent, nonwhites in 56 percent. Racial differences were also significant with respect to type of delinquent act committed. Nonwhites were apprehended for significantly more rapes, robberies, assaults, burglaries, and auto thefts. Furthermore, based on the Wolfgang-Sellin seriousness scale, the offenses of nonwhites were found to be five times as serious as those of whites.[31] However, there were no significant differences in the seriousness level between the races for one-time offenders who shared similar socioeconomic backgrounds.[32] In fact, the greatest differences in seriousness of offense were between nonwhite recidivists and nonwhite single offenders. Weapons were rarely used in the recorded delinquent acts, but boys from lower socioeconomic status families were six times more likely to use weapons than higher-class youth, and nonwhites were ten times as likely to use weapons as whites.[33]

Wolfgang and his associates concluded that:

it is clear that preventing the group of nonwhite lower SES (socio-economic status) boys from continuing delinquency after their first offense would indeed produce the maximum delinquency reduction . . . the most serious acts—those involving physical violence or assault on others—could also be drastically decreased.[34]

Age

The percentage of youth of all races and economic strata involved in delinquent behavior increased steadily from age ten to just less than sixteen. Delinquency then decreased from that point to age eighteen.[35] Both white and nonwhite youth committed greater numbers of violent crimes as they aged. The number of property offenses declined with age for nonwhites and remained unchanged for whites. However, as a general rule, the authors found that as nonwhites became older they became somewhat less delinquent, and as whites became older they became somewhat more delinquent.

Wolfgang and his associates pinpoint race as the single most important factor in disposition.[36] Nonwhites received significantly stricter sentences than whites, and this relationship holds up when socioeconomic status is controlled for. In addition, disposition was inversely related to chronic delinquency; that is, the stricter the disposition he received, the more likely the youth would engage in repeated delinquent behavior. Strict dispositions also increased the probability that further court action would be taken. Two factors therefore stand out as encouraging recidivism—the seriousness of the original offense and the severity of disposition.

Wolfgang et al. were forced to conclude that their analysis cast grave doubts on the efforts of the juvenile justice system to control or eliminate delinquent behavior:

The judicial process and the correctional system do not seem to function effectively to restrain, discourage, or cure delinquency. Not only do a greater proportion of those who receive a severe disposition violate the law, but these violations are serious and rapid.[37]

Conclusions of Wolfgang, Figlio, and Sellin

It is difficult, as the authors themselves admit, to tie this vast array of data into a convenient and easily understood explanation of delinquent activity. However, some striking conclusions can be drawn that have major implications for understanding the nature and causes of male delinquency:

1. Race is a predominant factor in predicting official contact by police and court agencies. It is the strongest factor in determining the probability of a delinquent career.
2. Socioeconomic status and educational factors including IQ, drop-out rate, and school achievement are all indirectly related to delinquent behavior through their association with race. That is, nonwhites are likely to come from low status families and experience school failure. This in turn relates to being an offender, a recidivist, and committing serious acts.
3. A small number of youth commit a large percentage of official delinquent acts. Once caught they are likely to commit even more delinquent acts and become chronic offenders. Stricter punishments provided by the juvenile justice system are likely to encourage rather than eliminate further delinquent participation.

Thus, the picture Wolfgang and his associates draw of the chronic, serious offender is a picture of an outcast from society. He is a poor member of a minority group, and he has an unstable family. He has a low IQ and poor school achievement, and he is unlikely to finish his education. Moreover, he is likely to be officially labeled by the justice system and severely punished.

Critique of Delinquency in a Birth Cohort

Delinquency in a Birth Cohort is a major contribution to the literature of crime and delinquency. Nonetheless, the study must be read somewhat critically in light of what we know about police enforcement methods. The disproportionate number of lower class and minority youth included in police records may be more a function of police patrol and arrest practices than the actual participation of minorities in delinquent activity. That is, police departments may devote more attention to minority sections of the city and may also enforce laws more thoroughly there. Moreover, it is also possible that white youths who are apprehended are more likely to be released at the point of initial police contact without official action. Despite these considerations, the differences that Wolfgang's study disclosed between delinquents and nondelinquents *within* each racial grouping are important enough to warrant intense study of the cohort data. In fact, a number of recent studies have used cohort data to indicate how such factors as IQ level and school achievement interact with delinquent behavior.[38] The cohort study remains the premier study utilizing official records in the last twenty years.

ANALYSIS OF OFFICIAL STATISTICS

A great deal of criticism has been directed at the national crime statistics and official statistics in general. Methodological problems have compelled some experts to advocate their total abandonment.[39] Two main issues most disturb the critics: (1) the neglect or refusal of many citizens to report delinquent and criminal acts to police and (2) the problems caused by variations in law enforcement practices. Each of these issues will be discussed separately below.

Reporting Practices

American citizens are believed to report less than half of all criminal and delinquent acts to police. The reasons for this phenomenon are varied. Many individuals in lower-class areas neglect to carry property insurance and therefore believe it is useless to report theft-related offenses to police since nothing can be done. In other cases, the victims may fail to notify police because they fear reprisals from friends or family members of the offenders.

A number of national surveys have attempted to uncover the factors that cause citizens to decide not to report delinquent or criminal acts to the police. In 1966, the President's Commission on Law Enforcement and the Administration of Justice sponsored one such effort.[40] Utilizing a nationally drawn sample of ten thousand citizens, the commission found the most common citizen responses to be that the police couldn't do anything about the matter, that the crime was a private not criminal affair, that the person was not sure if the real offenders would be caught, and that the police would not want to be bothered.

In a more recent study conducted by the National Crime Survey (NCS),[41] a large, nationally-drawn sample of citizens was used to determine the factors that affect the reporting or nonreporting of delinquent and criminal activity. (See Chapter 3 for a more detailed discussion of the NCS.) The NCS data revealed that the reasons given for not reporting crime varied according to the type of criminal behavior examined. For example, rape and attempted rape victims said that they did not report the crime because it was a private matter (37 percent) and because they feared reprisals (21 percent). Assaults remained unreported because people felt that they were a private matter (23 percent). People did not report crimes such as robbery, burglary, and larceny because they believed nothing could be done, victimization was not important enough, or the police would not do anything about the matter.

In an analysis of NCS data, Michael Hindelang and Michael Gottfredson found that for each category of personal, household, and business victimization, completed criminal acts were more often reported to police than attempted acts.[42] Similarly, the seriousness of delinquent or criminal activity influenced reporting. For example, if a weapon was used in the crime, it increased the likelihood that police would be notified. Additionally, as the value of monetary loss increased, so did the probability that the act would be reported to police.

Law Enforcement Practices

The way police record and report criminal and delinquent activity also affects the validity of UCR statistics. For example, in New York City for the period 1948 to 1952, burglaries rose from 2,726 to 42,491 and larcenies increased from 7,713 to 70,949. These significant increases were found to be related to the change from a precinct to a centralized reporting system for crime statistics.[43] A new central reporting system instituted in Philadelphia in 1952 resulted in a sharp rise in Index Crimes from 16,773 in 1951 to 28,560 in 1953.[44]

Problems of a similar sort were encountered by Duncan Chappell, Gilbert Geis, Stephen Schafer, and Larry Siegel in their study of urban rape rates. The initial purpose of their research was to discover the social factors that might account for the dramatic differences in the rape rates of two urban centers, Boston and Los Angeles (7.7 and 35.4 per 100,000 respectively). Careful examination of their data source—raw files submitted to the UCR—indicated that the most important factor differentiating the two cities was police discretion in reporting rapes. Los Angeles police used extreme amounts of discretion and flexibility in their crime reporting. Many alleged rapes occurring in Los Angeles in fact bore no resemblance to the UCR's definition of the deed.[45]

Serious allegations have been made that police officials deliberately alter reported crimes in order to put their departments in a more favorable light with the public. Seidman and Couzens suggest that police administrators may falsify crime reporting to improve their image.[46] For example, they may deliberately undervalue the cost of goods so that an index larceny will be relegated to a nonreportable offense category.

Beyond these immediate problems, it is also quite likely that police arrest and patrol practices vary significantly among neighborhoods within individual police jurisdictions and also among the thousands of independent city police departments. Consequently, *any* delinquency reporting system may be inherently flawed and invalid. For example, police may release some suspects, especially juveniles, at the point of initial police contact since the arresting officer believes, often justifiably, that the delinquent activity in question is a matter best dealt with by the youth's own family. And, of course, this practice may vary depending upon the recognition the family has in the community, its social standing, racial characteristics, the youth's attitude, the arresting officer's discretion, and so on. Therefore, any subsequent research effort that uses police arrest reports runs the risk of being biased and misleading.

CHAPTER SUMMARY

Official delinquents are those youths whose illegal behavior has come to the attention of police, courts, and correctional agencies. Because their misbehavior is recognized by the state authority, they maintain an official police (or juvenile court) record that can follow them for the rest of their lives.

The Federal Bureau of Investigation tabulates crimes that citizens report to the nation's police departments and then publishes this information in its annual report, *The Uniform Crime Report* (UCR). UCR arrest information shows that the problem of youth crime has increased markedly in the last ten years. Youths are committing more serious crimes such as burglary, robbery, and assault. Females are less likely to be delinquent than males, but their criminal acts are increasing at a relatively faster rate. Despite the tremendous resources that have been directed at the elimination of juvenile delinquency in the last decade, the problem of youth crime seems in no way to have abated.

Criminologists have used official records in a number of different research efforts designed to measure the extent and nature of delinquent behavior. One recent project is the cohort study of Wolfgang, Figlio, and Sellin. These researchers followed the official delinquent careers of males born in 1945 until their eighteenth birthdays in 1963. Their research indicates that about one-third of the subjects in their sample of almost 10,000 boys had police contact and that poor, minority youths were the most likely to commit delinquent acts. Wolfgang and his associates also found evidence that poor IQ and school achievement influenced the likelihood that a boy would be arrested. Wolfgang's study, which indicates that official delinquency is especially prevalent among poor minority youth, is typical of research studies that use official police and court statistics for their data base (see Chapter 5).

A number of criminologists have questioned the validity of official records. On the one hand, many people simply refuse to report crime due to fear, embarrassment, or disinterest. On the other hand, police practices may vary so widely that police records are inconsistent and misleading. It has been alleged that, at best, official records reflect racial and class biases. At worst, they have been willfully manipulated by police departments to present the police in a favorable light.

The general mistrust of official statistics has raised questions about the value of basing delinquency prevention policy and theory on them. In addition, as we shall see in the following chapter, a major effort has been undertaken to collect delinquency information that is free from the inherent biases of official data.

DISCUSSION QUESTIONS

1. Have you ever been the victim of crime or delinquency and failed to report it to the police?
2. Do you believe that the police treat certain ethnic and racial groups in a discriminatory fashion?
3. What can be done to combat the rising juvenile crime rate?
4. What factors do you think have caused the increase in official female delinquency?

SUGGESTED READINGS

Amir, Menachem. *Patterns in Forcible Rape.* Chicago: University of Chicago Press, 1971.

Bell, Daniel. "Crime as an American Way of Life." *Antioch Review* 13 (1953): 131–154.

Black, Donald. "Production of Crime Rates." *American Sociological Review* 35 (1970): 733–748.

Black, Donald, and Reiss, Albert. "Police Control of Juveniles." *American Sociological Review* 35 (1970): 63–77.

Brownmiller, Susan. *Against Our Will: Men, Women and Rape.* New York: Simon and Schuster, 1975.

Kamisar, Yale. "How to Use, Abuse—and Fight Back with Crime Statistics," *Oklahoma Law Review* 25 (1972): 239–258.

Kitsuse, John, and Cicourel, Aaron. "A Note on the Uses of Official Statistics," *Social Problems* 11 (1963): 131–139.

Nettler, Gwynn. *Explaining Crime.* 2d ed. New York: McGraw-Hill, 1978.

Department of Health, Education and Welfare, Office of Youth Development. *Juvenile Court Statistics, 1978.* Washington, D.C.: Government Printing Office, 1979.

Wolfgang, Marvin; Figlio, Robert; and Sellin, Thorsten. *Delinquency in a Birth Cohort.* Chicago: University of Chicago Press, 1972.

FOOTNOTES

1. The actual destruction of juvenile records, called "expungement," is rare. Most jurisdictions simply close or "seal" them.
2. Marvin Wolfgang, Robert Figlio, and Thorsten Sellin, *Delinquency in a Birth Cohort* (Chicago: University of Chicago Press, 1972).
3. Most commonly used statistics are the Federal Bureau of Investigation, *Crime in the United States: Uniform Crime Reports,* 1978 (Washington, D.C.: Government Printing Office, 1979). (Cited hereafter as *Uniform Crime Reports.*)

4. For a critical analysis of official data, see Ronald Beattie, "Criminal Statistics in the United States," *Journal of Criminal Law, Criminology and Police Science* 51 (1960): p. 49.

5. For an important study, see Terrence Thornberry, "Race, Socioeconomic Status and Sentencing in the Juvenile Justice System," *Journal of Criminal Law and Criminology*, 64 (1973): 90-98.

6. See, for example, Irving Piliavin and Scott Briar, "Police Encounters with Juveniles," *American Sociological Review* 70 (1964): p. 206.

7. For a composite of these statistics, see U.S. Department of Justice, *Children in Custody* (Washington, D.C.: Government Printing Office,), no. SD-JD-3F, 1975.

8. See *Uniform Crime Reports*, 1978.

9. See, for example, David Seidman and Michael Couzens, "Getting the Crime Rate Down: Political Pressure and Crime Reporting," *Law and Society Review* 8 (1974): p. 457.

10. Wolfgang, Figlio, and Sellin, *Delinquency in a Birth Cohort.*

11. *Uniform Crime Reports*, 1978. Data in this section are the most recent available at the time of this writing.

12. U.S. Department of Commerce, Bureau of the Census, *Current Population Reports: Population Estimates and Projections, Estimates of the Population of the United States by Age, Race, and Sex, 1967–1969 and 1976–1979* (Washington, D.C.: Government Printing Office, 1980).

13. For a detailed look at robbery, see John Conklin, *Robbery and the Criminal Justice System* (Philadelphia: Lippincott, 1972).

14. See Morton Hunt, *The Mugging* (New York: Segment, 1972).

15. Edwin Schur, *Radical Nonintervention: Rethinking the Delinquency Problem* (Englewood Cliffs, N.J.: Prentice-Hall, 1973), pp. 125–126.

16. Robert Terry, "The Screening of Juvenile Offenders," *Journal of Criminal Law, Criminology and Police Science* 58 (1967): pp. 173–181.

17. Theodore Ferdinand and Elmer Luchterhand, "Inner-City Youth, the Police, the Juvenile Court, and Justice," *Social Problems* 17 (1970): pp. 501–527.

18. Edward Green, "Race, Social Status, and Criminal Arrest," *American Sociological Review* 35 (1970): p. 119.

19. Terry, "The Screening of Juvenile Offenders," p. 175.

20. Yona Cohn, "Criteria for the Probation Officer's Recommendation to the Juvenile Court Judge," in *Becoming Delinquent*, ed. P. Garabedian and D. Gibbons (Chicago: Aldine Publishing, 1970), pp. 190–207.

21. Thomas Enyon and Jon Simpson, "The Boy's Perception of Himself in a State Training School for Deliquents," in Garabedian and Gibbons, in *Becoming Delinquent*, pp. 238–246.

22. Clifford Shaw and Henry McKay, *Juvenile Delinquency and Urban Areas* (Chicago: University of Chicago Press, 1942).

23. The following analysis comes from Wolfgang, Figlio, and Sellin, *Delinquency in a Birth Cohort.*

24. Ibid., p. 4.

25. See Thorsten Sellin and Marvin Wolfgang, *The Measurement of Delinquency* (New York: Wiley, 1964), p. 120.

26. Wolfgang, Figlio, and Sellin, *Delinquency in a Birth Cohort*, p. 54.

27. Ibid.

28. Ibid.

29. Ibid., p. 57.

30. Ibid., p. 64.

31. Ibid., p. 65.

32. Ibid., p. 75.

33. Ibid., p. 79.

34. Ibid., p. 82.

35. Ibid., p. 251.

36. Ibid., pp. 219–220.

37. Ibid., p. 243.

38. See Chapter 4 for an analysis of his work, especially that conducted by Michael Hindelang and Travis Hirschi.

39. For example, see Beattie, "Criminal Statistics in the United States."

40. Philip Ennis, *Criminal Victimization in the United States, Field Survey II: A Report of a National Survey*, President's Commission on *Law Enforcement and Administration of Justice* (Washington, D.C.: Government Printing Office, 1967).

41. Nicolette Parisi, Michael Gottfredson, Michael Hindelang, and Timothy Flanagan, *Sourcebook of Criminal Justice Statistics 1978* (Washington, D.C.: Government Printing Office, 1070), p. 363.

42. Michael Hindelang and Michael Gottfredson, "The Victim's Decision Not to Involve the Criminal Justice Process," in *Criminal Justice and the Victim*, ed. William F. McDonald (Beverly Hills, Calif.: Sage, 1976), pp. 57–74.

43. Paul Tappan, *Crime, Justice, and Corrections* (New York: McGraw-Hill, 1960).

44. Daniel Bell, *The End of Ideology* (New York: Free Press, 1967), p. 152.

45. Duncan Chappell, Gilbert Geis, Stephen Schafer, and Larry Siegel, "Forcible Rape: A Comparative Study of Offenses Known to the Police in Boston and Los Angeles," in *Studies in the Sociology of Sex*, ed. James Henslin (New York: Appleton-Century-Crofts, 1971), pp. 169–193.

46. Seidman and Couzens, "Getting the Crime Rate Down: Political Pressure and Crime Reporting," p. 457.

Chapter 3

Chapter Outline

Introduction
Self-report Studies
Ways of Validating Self-reports
Victimization Surveys
Observation and Biographical Data
Chapter Summary

Key Terms, Names, and Cases

self-report surveys
National Crime Survey
social class
validity
victimization
life-histories
Michael Hindelang
first-person accounts
James Short
Ivan Nye
Maynard Erickson
Martin Gold

Unofficial Sources of⸺
Juvenile Statistics

INTRODUCTION

The questionable validity of official delinquency data has been a serious problem for criminologists concerned with the causes and prevention of delinquent behavior. If criminologists base their work on inaccurate data, then all subsequent theory and policy decisions will be equally biased and misleading. Sociologists Roger Hood and Richard Sparks have commented on the problem of statistical uncertainty:

In relying on this [unofficial] data the theorist is faced with two problems. First, he must estimate to what extent those convicted differ from those who have committed identical acts but have not been caught or prosecuted. Secondly, he must try to disentangle those factors which explain criminal behavior from those which explain why a person has become officially processed as a delinquent or a criminal.[1]

The problems associated with official statistics have led many criminologists to seek alternative sources of information on delinquent behavior in order to assess the true extent of American youth crime. In addition, official delinquency statistics do not say much about the personality, attitudes, and behavior of individual delinquents. Official statistics may illustrate broad concepts, such as trends in the relative frequency of delinquent behavior, but they are an inadequate source of information about narrower theoretical issues, such as the relationship between the individual personality and delinquent behavior. Thus, alternative sources about delinquent behavior are needed to determine its true extent, develop valid theories and test them, and to make effective policy.

This chapter will review three of the more important unofficial sources of delinquency statistics: self-report studies; the National Crime Survey (NCS), a nationwide survey of the victims of crime; and first-person accounts of delinquency in which delinquents tell their own stories.

SELF-REPORT STUDIES

Criminologists have used self-report studies of delinquency frequently for over thirty years.[2] They are a valuable source of information on the delinquent activities of youths who have had formal contact with the juvenile justice system and those who have so far escaped official notice of their delinquent acts.

Self-report studies are designed to let youthful subjects personally reveal information about their violations of the law. The studies have many different formats. For example, youths arrested by police can later be interviewed about their delinquent activities. A survey that asks subjects to tell about their delinquent behavior without revealing their identities can be distributed to an entire school. Boys in the lunchroom of a youth detention center can be issued a questionnaire asking them about their delinquent acts. Youths in an after-school neighborhood center can be surveyed during a club meeting.

Self-report studies can be conducted on a one-to-one basis through an interview or a self-administered questionnaire, but more commonly, they are conducted through a mass distribution of questionnaires. The subjects can be known, but more frequently they remain anonymous. The basic assumption of self-report studies is that the anonymity of the subject and the promise of secrecy backed by the researcher's highly respected academic credentials will allow youths to describe their illegal activities honestly. According to Richard Hood and Roger Sparks, self-report studies can serve three different functions:

First, they make possible an assessment of the *number of people* in the population as a whole who commit (or have committed) various deviant acts and the frequency with which they have done so. Secondly, by abolishing the artificial dichotomy between delinquents and nondelinquents under which all of the latter are presumed "innocent," they lead to the conception of delinquency as a *variable* and thus to the development of a scale on which to measure individuals' involvement in delinquency—ranging from the completely innocent to the completely committed. Thirdly, and most important of all, they enable a comparison of those who have been officialy labelled as delinquent—who have a record—with those who have not.[3]

James Short and Ivan Nye have described self-report studies similarly:

Certain theoretical and immediately practical advantages to this type of study are apparent. In the study of juvenile delinquency, for example, the extent and nature of various types of conduct and its variability can be investigated. This, in contrast to the usual procedure of assuming that a group of institutionalized children are delinquent and comparing them with a group of noninstitutionalized who are defined as nondelinquent. Further, such investigations *can* be made in all *segments* of the population, rather than in the socioeconomically biased institutionalized or officially apprehended group.[4]

Sample Survey

Highlight 3-1 contains an example of a self-report survey. Subjects check off appropriate spaces to indicate how many times they have participated in illegal or deviant behavior. Other formats allow subjects to write in the precise number of times they engaged in each delinquent activity. Note that the sample sur-

Highlight 3–1. Self-Report Survey.

PLEASE INDICATE HOW OFTEN IN THE PAST TWELVE MONTHS YOU DID EACH ACT. (Check the best answer.)

	Never did act	One time	2–5 times	6–9 times	10–13 times	14–17 times	18+ times
1. Stole something worth less than $10	__	__	__	__	__	__	__
2. Stole something worth more than $10	__	__	__	__	__	__	__
3. Snorted or sniffed heroin	__	__	__	__	__	__	__
4. Injected heroin	__	__	__	__	__	__	__
5. Used amphetamine pills (such as uppers, crystal meth, dex)	__	__	__	__	__	__	__
6. Shot up amphetamines	__	__	__	__	__	__	__
7. Got drunk on beer	__	__	__	__	__	__	__
8. Got drunk on hard liquor	__	__	__	__	__	__	__
9. Got drunk on wine	__	__	__	__	__	__	__
10. Used marijuana (pot)	__	__	__	__	__	__	__
11. Used downers (valium, librium, darvon, thorazine, etc.)	__	__	__	__	__	__	__
12. Used psychadelics (LSD, mescaline)	__	__	__	__	__	__	__
13. Used cocaine	__	__	__	__	__	__	__
14. Been in a fist fight	__	__	__	__	__	__	__
15. Carried a weapon such as a gun or knife	__	__	__	__	__	__	__
16. Fought someone using a weapon	__	__	__	__	__	__	__
17. Stole a car	__	__	__	__	__	__	__
18. Used force to steal	__	__	__	__	__	__	__
19. (For boys) Forced a girl to have sexual relations against her will	__	__	__	__	__	__	__
20. Driven a car while drunk or high	__	__	__	__	__	__	__
21. Damaged property worth more than $10	__	__		__	__	__	__

Source: Larry Siegel, University of Nebraska, and Spencer Rathus, New Mexico State University.

vey limits the reporting period to the past twelve months, thereby focusing on relatively recent behavior.

Surveys measuring self-reported delinquency are also likely to contain items not directly related to delinquent activity—for example, items requesting information on such diverse topics as subjects' self-image; intelligence; personality; attitudes toward family, friends, and school; leisure activity; and school activities. Self-report surveys also gather personal information on subjects' family background, social status, race, and sex. Reports of delinquent acts can then be used with this other information to create a much more complete picture of delinquent offenders than official statistics can provide.

Self-Report Data

Most self-report studies indicate that the number of children who break the law is far greater than had previously been believed.[5] In fact, when truancy, alcohol consumption, petty theft, and soft drug use are included in self-report scales, almost every child tested has violated some law.

Self-report studies indicate that the most common offenses are truancy, drinking alcohol, using a false I.D., shoplifting or larceny under $5, fighting, using marijuana, and damaging the property of others.[6]

Table 3-1, which contains data from a recent study, illustrates the extent and nature of self-reported delinquency. The subjects were all students in a high school in an upper-middle-class neighborhood in the northeastern United States. Although the official delinquency rate (crime known to the police) in this area was quite low, it is evident that the teenage population engaged in serious and widespread delinquent behavior. Moreover, these statistics are not atypical of other self-report efforts.[7]

Table 3-1. Percent of Respondents Admitting to One or More Acts During Past Twelve Months.

Delinquent Act	Males %	Females %	Total %
Theft under $10	62.2	43.6	52.9
Theft over $10	28.3	12.5	20.4
Sniffed heroin	3.4	3.1	3.3
Shot up heroin	2.7	1.1	1.9
Used uppers	9.9	8.1	9.0
Shot up uppers	3.5	2.4	3.0
Drank beer	68.5	58.0	63.3
Drank liquor	52.5	50.7	51.6
Drank wine	35.3	38.3	36.8
Used marijuana	52.0	47.0	49.5
Used downers	8.0	10.3	9.2
Used LSD	11.9	9.1	10.5
Used cocaine	7.1	2.4	4.8
Engaged in fist fighting	65.7	20.3	43.0
Carried weapons	38.2	8.2	23.2
Fought with weapon	12.5	2.6	7.6
Stole car	9.4	1.9	5.7
Used force to steal	6.9	1.7	4.3
Engaged in forcible sex	6.6	—	—
Engaged in drunk driving	22.1	13.6	17.9
Destroyed property	41.8	12.1	27.0
(N)	(786)	(883)	(1669)

Source: From a study by Larry Siegel, University of Nebraska, and Spencer Rathus, New Mexico State University.

During the twelve months prior to the survey, more than half the male respondents engaged in petty theft, drank beer, used hard liquor, used marijuana, and engaged in fist fighting. In addition, a significant number drank wine, carried weapons, destroyed property, and stole something worth more than $10.

The frequency of serious criminal acts is much lower, but a number of the youths in the sample used heroin, fought with a weapon, forced girls to have sexual relations, and used uppers or downers (methedrine, amphetamines, angel dust, and so on).

The results are suprisingly similar for the girls who participated in the survey. Though the level of their participation was somewhat lower, the girls seemed to be engaging in the same types of behavior as the boys. They were quite likely to drink, steal, and use marijuana. They were less likely, however, to engage in fist fights, carry a weapon, or damage property.

When the results of recent self-report surveys are compared with various studies conducted over a twenty-year period, a uniform pattern emerges. The use of drugs and alcohol has increased markedly, especially among girls, although theft, violence, and damage-related crimes seem more stable. Although a self-reported crime wave has not occurred, neither has there been any visible reduction in teenage delinquency.

The following sections will review self-report data about the sex, peer activity, status, race, and drug use of the youths surveyed.

Social Class and Delinquency

Official delinquency data persistently find social class to be a major predictor of delinquency. Whether this is bias in the official data or a picture of reality is frequently debated.[8] Theorists who have based their efforts on official police statistics (see Chapters 4, 5, and 6) maintain that those who think delinquency is spread throughout the social classes are just wishful thinkers: "Egalitarian proclivities and sentimental humanitarianism dispose us to minimize the dispro portionate concentration of delinquency among the less prosperous, powerful, and respected."[9] For the most part, theoretical pronouncements on delinquency have assumed that serious youth crime is almost entirely a lower-class phenomenon. Even those theorists who recognize that delinquency is spread throughout the social classes note that middle-class youths are involved in delinquency to a much lesser extent and that middle-class delinquency is much less serious:

The isolated offender—as the middle class offender more often is—is not likely to evoke serious concern on the part of law enforcement officials, who recognize that delinquent behavior tends to be less stable when peer supports are weak or absent.[10]

However, the first few self-report studies, specifically those conducted by James Short and Ivan Nye, did not find a direct relationship between social class and delinquency.[11] In fact, only one major self-report research project, conducted by Martin Gold in 1966,[12] posited such a relationship; and Gold, as we shall see, later uncovered findings that caused him to rethink his conclusions.[13]

Most early self-report studies found that socioeconomic class was related to official processing by police, court, and correctional agencies but not to the actual commission of delinquent acts. For example, Short and Nye found that delinquent behavior had no relationship with class when they used self-reports as the criterion of delinquency but that it had a clear relationship when they used institutionalization.[14] In addition, factors generally associated with lower-class membership, such as broken homes, were found to be related to institutionalization but not to admissions of delinquency.[15] Ivan Nye, James Short, and Virgil Olsen studied two areas of the country and several schools. Using father's occupation as an indicator of class, they were unable to support the contention that a relationship exists between self-reported delinquency and socioeconomic class.[16]

In another study, Robert Dentler and Lawrence Monroe found no relationship between amount of admitted delinquency and class.[17] Most researchers did conclude, however, that lower-class youths were more likely to receive official notice from the justice system. Therefore, they appear to be overrepresented as official delinquents. Middle-class delinquency, on the other hand, remained hidden.

In a subsequent research effort, John Clark and Eugene Wenninger suggested that both the self-report studies and the official data could be correct.[18] They argued that self-report studies often used nonrepresentative samples. For example, Short and Nye sampled largely rural areas, and Dentler and Monroe used three Kansas communities—a middle-class suburb, a rural farm town, and a rural nonfarm community. On the other hand, the theorists who stress the role of social class in delinquency deal with large metropolitan areas, particularly inner-city regions.[19]

Clark and Wenninger thus hypothesized that class is not a good predictor of delinquency in rural and small town areas but does hold in the large cities. They tested this hypothesis by comparing youths from four different types of communities—rural farm, small lower-class urban, small upper-class urban, and large industrial urban. They found no significant difference between classes of youth within the rural area and the two small urban areas. However, they found significant differences between the admitted behavior of industrial urban youth and lower-class urban youth and the admitted behavior of upper-class urban and rural farm youth. The first two areas produced much more delinquency. The greatest difference occurred between the upper- and lower-class urban communities. Lower-class urban youth admitted to acts that were more serious—acts that are generally viewed as "real delinquency." Upper-class urban youth engaged in generally more trivial behavior.

Clark and Wenninger concluded that class per se did not predict the distribution of delinquency. Rather, community-wide norms govern what goes on among youth, and the community consists of whole towns. Within industrial cities and metropolitan areas, "status areas" constitute self-contained communities for the youths within them. Within these status areas, class has no bearing on the amount of delinquency committed. Clearly, class is a major factor dividing one status area from another. However, the youths of one class who live in an area dominated by another class will generally adhere to the norms of the majority—hence the finding that class has no bearing when all youths sampled are from a given status area.

Some self-report studies have supported Clark and Wenninger's influential study; others have contradicted it. For example, William Arnold studied a sample of 540 youths from schools within a city of 200,000. Using father's occupation as a measure of class, he found no relationship between class and delinquency as measured by assault and theft scales, and only a weak relationship using a vandalism scale.[20] This was the reverse of the direction that Clark and Wenninger predicted for a city of this size; the youths from the higher socioeconomic levels admitted more delinquency than those from the lower levels.

LaMar Empey and Maynard Erickson sampled 180 boys in high schools in small cities in Utah (including those who had no court record and those with one court appearance), probationers, and boys in the state juvenile institution.[21] Like Arnold and others, they found no significant relationship between class and delinquency, and the only differences that did exist were "because of the general activities of one whole group versus another."[22] Middle-class youths constituted 55 percent of the total sample, but they admitted 59 percent of the total violations and two-thirds of the serious violations.[23]

Ronald Akers, studying youths from a large northeastern community, also found no relationship between class and delinquency.[24] Harwin Voss took a sample of 620 youths in the Honolulu schools, classifying them by their father's occupation.[25] For the females, there was no significant difference between socioeconomic groups, but for the males there was such a differing. Males in the upper two categories were significantly more delinquent than those in the lower, with the second category—the sons of white collar workers and small businesspeople—being the most delinquent. As far as seriousness was concerned, the direction of this class distribution remained, but the differences were not statistically significant.

Although, in his first few studies, Martin Gold found an inverse relationship between class and delinquency,[26] his later work with Jay Williams showed no statistically significant differences among classes (controlling for race and sex) in terms of amount of admitted delinquency.[27] The only statistically significant relationship indicated that higher status white males were more seriously delinquent than other white males. When race was not controlled, it confounded the class variable and produced no significant relationship between class and delinquency.

In a more recent study, Richard Johnson carefully compared youths who had families at the poverty level, on welfare, or unemployed with working-class and middle-class youths in Seattle, Washington. Once again, the relationship between social class and delinquency was either weak or nonexistent.[28]

Despite this seemingly clear-cut evidence that delinquency and class are not related, a recent study by Delbert Elliott and Suzanne Ageton once again muddies the waters.[29] Using a carefully drawn national sample of 1,726 youths aged eleven to seventeen and a sophisticated self-report instrument, Elliott and Ageton found lower-class youths to be much more likely than middle-class youths to engage in serious delinquent acts such as burglary, assault, robbery, sexual assault, and vandalism. Moreover, lower-class youths were much more likely to have committed "numerous" serious personal and property crimes (more than 200) than middle-class youths. These findings forced Elliott and Ageton to conclude that self-report data give findings about class and delinquency that are actually similar to those of official data. (For example, see Chapter 2 for Wolfgang, Figlio, and Sellin's studies.) Furthermore, the authors charge that studies showing middle- and lower-class youths to be equally delinquent rely on measures that are weighted toward minor crimes and status offenses (for example, using a false I.D. or skipping school). When serious crimes like burglary and assault are compared, lower-class youth are significantly more delinquent. In sum, the issue of class and delinquency is still being debated, and further research is needed to clarify it.

Sex Differences

In recent years, differences among delinquents that can be attributed to their sex have been given close attention. In the past, studies often ignored female youths, assuming that they were not delinquent. Theorists (see Chapters 4 through 7) described sex differences in delinquency with such statements as: "The delinquent is a rogue male. His conduct . . . may be viewed as the exploitation of untrammelled masculinity." On the other hand, "the female's station in society . . . depends . . . on the kinds of relationships she establishes with members of the opposite sex" and "it is no accident that 'boys collect stamps, girls collect boys.'"[30]

Self-report studies of delinquency have made it possible to review in some detail the similarities and differences between male and female participation in delinquent behavior. Studies that have included females have found that they are less delinquent than males, but the sex ratio is not as great as the official data show it to be.

Self-report studies that include sex comparisons show that females' delinquency is much higher than expected. For example, Gary Jensen and Raymond Eve found that females' admission rates ranged from 31 percent for petty theft to 1 percent for grand larceny on a self-report questionnaire containing theft, violence, and damage-related items.[31] Michael Hindelang found an average ratio between male and female delinquency of 2.5 to 1, with a range of only 1.2 to 1 for cheating on tests to 4.8 to 1 for promiscuity.[32] Although James Short and Ivan Nye gave no overall ratio for male and female delinquency, they found that the overall sex ratio was much lower than expected.[33] For example, they found that for the unauthorized use of a motor vehicle, the male-female ratio was 4 to 3 in a sample of noninstitutionalized youth. In the same group, the petty larceny rate was 2 to 1. The sex ratios were even closer for institutionalized youth. For example, the male-female ratio for fighting was 3 to 2.5. However, not all studies concur. In a national study, Jay Williams and Martin Gold found that boys were twice as likely as girls to be "frequently delinquent" and that male delinquency was twice as serious as female.[34]

One of the barriers to understanding female delinquency has been the attitude of police and court personnel. Juvenile justice agents frequently assume that girls have been sexually deviant when they are arrested or petitioned to juvenile court. As a result, official records reflect girls' sexual behavior and downplay their criminal activities. Commenting on their finding, Short and Nye offer an explanation for this phenomenon.

The fact that a significantly higher proportion of boys in both samples (institutionalized and non-institutionalized) report engaging in heterosexual relations and the fact that girls are most often referred to court for such activities presumably refers to society's greater concern for the unsupervised activity of girls.[35]

Chapter 8 will explore some of the theoretical issues related to female delinquency and will reexamine some relevant self-report data. However, for now we can conclude that female delinquency is different from the picture of it painted by official police and court statistics and that it is far more extensive.

Race and Self-Reported Delinquency

Self-report studies have not been used extensively to measure delinquent behavior among minority youths. They have simply not taken place in areas with enough minority representation for meaningful comparisons to be made. Parents and school officials in communities with large minority populations often mistrust university-based researchers who want to measure the misdeeds of their children. However, some studies have looked specifically at the relationship between race and delinquency, testing the old notion that black youths actually have a higher delinquency rate.

Leroy Gould, for example, sampled the central area of Seattle and obtained representatives of black, white, and Oriental youths.[36] He compared each youth's official and self-reported delinquency and obtained the usual relationship between race and official delinquency. Blacks had the most official delinquency and Orientals the least. On the other hand, the relationship between race and self-reported delinquency was virtually nonexistent. Gould found a very weak association between overall admissions of specific offenses and official records. Controlling for race, however, the data indicated that for whites there was a relationship between official and self-reported delinquency. For both blacks and Orientals there was none.

Voss investigated the relationship between official and self-reported delinquency and race in Honolulu.[37] For official delinquency, he found the assumed racial distribution. Forty percent of official male delinquents were Hawaiian, although they are only 25 percent of the population. Japanese, who are 33 percent of the population, accounted for only 18 percent of the official delinquents. However, the highest delinquency rate was for the residual category, Other, which included blacks, Puerto Ricans, and Koreans. The delinquency rate for this group was 459.2 per 1,000, as opposed to the Hawaiian rate of 201.8 and the Chinese rate—the lowest—of 26.7. The self-report data (620 school youths and 183 incarcerated youths) revealed that Chinese and white youths are consideraly more delinquent than official data would suggest and that the Hawaiians are considerably less delinquent.

The results of two recent studies contradict previous findings that there is no real relationship between delinquent behavior and race. Using victimization data from the National Crime Survey (see the following section of this chapter), Michael Hindelang found blacks to be substantially over-represented in the serious crimes of robbery, rape, and assault. Moreover, Hindelang concluded that blacks are over-represented in the official statistics (that is, the Uniform Crime Reports of the FBI) because they actually commit these crimes and not because police officers and official statistics are biased.[38] Similarly, Delbert Elliott and Suzanne Ageton found, in a nationally selected sample of 1,726 youths, that black youths were quite a bit more delinquent than white and that they committed more serious crime, like assault, robbery, sexual assault, and burglary.[39] In addition, black youths were much more likely than white youths to be frequent offenders (more than 200 reported acts). Elliott and Ageton also support the finding that the Uniform Crime Report may be a more accurate measure of delinquent and criminal behavior than previously believed.

In sum, early self-report studies contradicted the findings of official delinquency sources about the relationship of race and class to delinquency. However, some recent surveys have indicated that this relationship is less clear-cut. White middle-class youths do in fact commit serious and frequent delinquent acts, but these studies suggest that lower-class and black youths are actually the most seriously delinquent. Nonetheless, it is still difficult to draw an absolute conclusion about the validity of either position. These findings must be kept in mind when we discuss the various theories concerning the cause of delinquent behavior in Chapters 4 through 8.

Gang Activity versus Lone Delinquency

Work in delinquency has generally assumed that it is a group phenomenon.[40] However, self-report data bring this assumption into question. Although some studies have found that the majority of self-report acts occur in groups,[41] the amount of delinquent group activity may be overestimated. Maynard Erickson, for example, showed that when youths commit an act in a group, their chances of apprehension and of thus becoming official delinquents are increased. This factor may distort the extent of group delinquency.[42] Erickson's work also showed that between 37 and 42 percent of the total admitted acts were committed alone. Additional support for the notion that gang activity may be overestimated is provided by Michael Hindelang.[43] In gathering opinions about group and lone delinquents from 140 sheriff's deputies, he found the following. First, the deputies were more likely to arrest youths who verbally abused them. Second, they believed that verbal abuse occurred more when suspects were in a group than when they were alone. Third, they believed that juveniles were more likely to commit crimes in a group than alone. If the opinions of these deputies are held by other law enforcement officers, there can be little doubt that a juvenile runs a greater risk of being arrested when in a group than when alone.

However, recent findings by Walter Miller (which will be discussed in greater detail in Chapter 9) suggest that the amount of group delinquency may be higher than self-report surveys indicate.[44] These contradictory findings mean that greater effort is needed in this area of research.

Drug and Alcohol Abuse

Self-report surveys can be quite informative about the prevalence of illegal drug and alcohol use by American youth. These so-called victimless crimes are quite likely to escape the notice of law enforcement authorities and therefore remain hidden from the official statistics of delinquency. Nonetheless, the use of drugs and alcohol by youths is a problem of growing national concern to parents, educators, and public officials.

To provide information on the extent of drug and alcohol abuse, the National

Institute on Drug Abuse of the U.S. Department of Health and Human Services has conducted a nationwide self-report survey using a scientifically selected sample of almost 7,000 subjects. Highlight 3–2 presents some of the results of this survey.

Highlight 3–2. Highlights of a Government Survey on Drug Abuse

The number of Americans who have used illicit drugs has increased dramatically in the past two decades, according to two studies released in June 1980 by the Department of Health and Human Services.

A *Drug Retrospective: 1962 to 1980,* prepared by HHS' National Institute on Drug Abuse, states that over the past 18 years the proportion of persons who have used marijuana has increased from 4 percent to 68 percent, and the proportion who have tried harder drugs—cocaine, heroin and hallucinogens—has increased from 3 percent to 33 percent in the high risk 18- to 25-year age group.

The National Survey on Drug Abuse, which surveys the non-medical drug use of more than 7,000 Americans 12 years of age and older, shows that between 1972 and 1979 experience with marijuana and cocaine has doubled among 12- to 17-year-olds and among those over 25 years of age. Between ages 18 and 25, the percentage of cocaine use has tripled and marijuana use has increased from 48 percent to 68 percent. The survey was conducted by the Social Research Group at George Washington University and the Response Analysis Corporation in Princeton for the National Institute on Drug Abuse.

Experience with inhalants and hallucinogens has also shown a marked increase since the early 1970s, says the survey.

Only the illicit use of stimulants, sedatives and tranquilizers reported by 12- to 17-year-olds and those over age 25 has remained relatively constant over the last decade. However, these drugs showed large increases by 18- to 25-year-olds until 1977, finally leveling off in 1979. Experience with heroin has also been constant during the

1970s with about 3 percent or less, depending on age, reporting they have tried it.

"These two reports show that the deep concerns of the American people in general, and parents in particular, about the rapid rise in illicit drug use over the past few years are well founded," said HHS Secretary Patricia Roberts Harris.

Dr. Julius B. Richmond, assistant secretary for health and surgeon general, said: "Although widespread drug abuse began in the 1960s, it was during the 1970s that the American people paid the resulting costs—financially and physically as well as psychologically. We must now try to work together as a nation to ensure that the effects of drug use in the past decade—including impaired health, productivity, school performance, motivation and driving ability—are not repeated in the next."

The institute cautions that both the survey and the drug retrospective underestimate true use. Interviews were limited to households, thus excluding runaways and those who live on military bases, in college dormitories and in prison, all of whom are probably higher-use groups.

Much of the 1979 survey concentrates on marijuana, the third most frequently used drug in the United States following alcohol and cigarettes. It shows that marijuana use is related to age and sex. Marijuana use peaks between ages 18 and 25 and is used more by men than women.

Following are some of the major findings from the survey:

Marijuana
The 1979 survey again confirms the correlation between age and marijuana use. At ages 12 and 13, only 8 percent have tried

it; by ages 14 and 15, the percentage has jumped to 32 percent; and by ages 16 and 17, 51 percent have used it. Use peaks between 18 and 25 at 68 percent. A sharp decline is then seen between ages 26 and 34 with 48 percent reporting use. Only 10 percent of those over 35 years of age reported having used the drug.

Since the last survey in 1977, experience with marijuana increased in all age categories. However, current use stablilized among youth.

In the 12 to 17-year-old group, 31 percent report they have tried marijuana, up from 14 percent in 1972. Current use of marijuana in this age group is at 17 percent—the same as in 1977. In 1972, however, this group reported only 7 percent were current users.

In the 18 to 25-year-old age category, 68 percent report they have used marijuana in their lifetime, up from 60 percent in 1977 and 48 percent in 1972. Current use is also up from 27 percent in 1977 to 40 percent in 1979.

Four in 10 of the 18 to 25-year-olds who have tried marijuana report they have used it 100 or more times in their lives. Of the current users, two-thirds report they use it 5 or more days a month.

Men have consistently used marijuana more than women over the past decade. However, the new survey shows that use by women is increasing rapidly. If current trends continue, over the next few years sex differences in marijuana use may disappear.

Cocaine
Cocaine is second only to marijuana in its

increasing popularity. Since 1972 the rate of increase for cocaine use across all age groups has been noticeably larger than the rate of increase for marijuana.

Young adults show the highest rates of use and the most significant increases since 1977: 28 percent have tried the drug, a significant increase from the 19 percent rate in 1977. Current use is now 9 percent, up from 4 percent in 1977.

Of those young adults who have tried cocaine, one-third have used it 11 to 99 times, another third three to 10 times, and about a fourth have used it once or twice.

Hallucinogens
The number of people who have tried hallucinogens has increased significantly for all ages. Among youth, 7 percent have tried hallucinogens, young adults report 25 percent use and those over 25 years report 5 percent use. During the last two years current use by young adults has more than doubled.

Self-reported use of PCP or Angel Dust in the 12 to 17-year-old group shows a decrease since 1977 from 6 percent to 4 percent. The number of users between ages 18 and 25 has changed significantly; 15 percent report having tried it.

Source: Excerpted from U.S. Department of Health and Human Services, *A Drug Retrospective: 1961–1980* (Washington, D.C.: Government Printing Office, June 20, 1980).

WAYS OF VALIDATING SELF-REPORTS

Critics of self-report studies frequently suggest that it is not feasible to expect young people to admit illegal acts candidly. None have anything to gain, and those taking the greatest risk are the ones with official records. On the other hand, some young people may exaggerate their delinquent acts, or forget some of them, or be confused.[45]

We cannot be certain how valid self-report studies are because we have nothing reliable against which to measure them. Correlation with official reports is expected to be low because their inadequacies were largely responsible for the practice of asking youths themselves about their delinquency in the first place. Therefore, researchers have struggled to develop scientific methods to estimate the accuracy of self-report studies. This section will review some of the more important efforts.

Official Record Comparisons

The most common technique for validating self-reports is to compare the answers that youths give on them with the youths' official police records. A typical approach is to ask youths if they have ever been arrested for or convicted of a delinquent act and then check their official records against their self-reported responses. A number of studies using this method have found a remarkable degree of uniformity between self-reported answers and official records.[46]

There are two problems with the method, however. First, youths may be more willing to admit to offenses that they realize can be verified with official records than to offenses that they know went undetected. On the other hand, it has been shown time and time again that official delinquents admit much more delinquent activity than their records show. The second problem involves youths who are officially nondelinquent. Although critics had voiced the strongest doubts about the honesty of those at risk, it is possible that those least at risk—the presumed nondelinquents—may be the least willing to admit delinquent behavior. Official delinquents have no image to lose by admitting delinquency. In fact, the admission may improve their images. Others, however, may lose a great deal by admitting delinquent behavior. James Hackler and Melanie Lautt tested the following: (1) that the most delinquent males (those at risk) will self-report less delinquency than the officially nondelinquent and (2) that two groups, blacks and older youths, will underreport the most serious.[47] Hackler and Lautt correlated a sample of self-report questionnaires with four other measures of delinquency: (1) juvenile court and police referral records in which they used four levels of seriousness; (2) the head counselor's rating of the males based on the degree to which they were a disciplinary problem; (3) the teacher's grading of the youths as discipline problems and their future chances of getting into trouble with the law; and (4) the number of the subjects' friends who had contact with the police. The researchers found that, in fact, the most seriously delinquent boys did not underreport their delinquent activity. The most seriously delinquent seventeen-year-old blacks and whites and fifteen-year-old whites reported the most delinquency. The only underreporters were the fifteen-year-old blacks. In sum, comparing self-reports of delinquency with the official records of the subjects tends to uphold the general validity of the self-report studies.

Other Validity Tests

The following methods are also used to test the validity of self-reports. The known group method compares incarcerated youths with "normal" groups to see whether the former report more delinquency.[48] Peer informants—friends who can verify the honesty of a subject's answers—are used.[49] Subjects are tested twice to see if their answers remain the same (testing across time).[50] The questions used are designed to select those who are lying on the exam—for example, "I have never done anything wrong in my life."[51] In general, these efforts have validated self-report studies.

John Clark and Larry Tifft used an unusual and important method to test the validity of self-report studies.[52] They administered a questionnaire to forty-five university students, requesting information on delinquent acts that the students may have committed. Two weeks later, they requested a personal interview, which was scheduled by telephone contact. During the interview, the respondent "was informed that our primary interest was in the accuracy of his questionnaire. In asking for his utmost cooperation in making his responses accurate, we strongly alluded to the likelihood of inaccurate responses being given on questionnaires administered in group situations." Clark and Tifft informed respondents at this point that the accuracy of the questionnaire would be checked with a polygraph (lie detector) test. The respondents then selected their anonymous questionnaires from the pile, using their known respondent number, and added whatever changes they felt were necessary to make them truthful. Clark and Tifft had previously noted the subjects' original responses. The subjects were then examined on a polygraph to verify the validity of their responses. Clark and Tifft found that the original responses on the self-report questionnaire were 81.5 percent accurate, with an average of 6.5 changes. Some changed the reported number of admissions on a particular item, for example, from two to three. The accuracy rate of admissions, from zero to any number, was 92 percent.

Conclusions

None of the above methods can assure the validity of self-report studies. However, the original criticism—that the most delinquent youths will underreport—appears to be unfounded. One of the few validity checks that showed official delinquent youths to be the main underreporters also found that the relationship was not significant.[53] In fact, the major problem now appears to be the honesty of youths who are officially nondelinquent.[54]

What these validity tests have not measured is the notion that middle-class youths may be more articulate and more familiar with social science research. The forty-five undergradute students in Clark and Wenninger's study all held positive evaluations of social science research; and the more positive the evaluation, the lower the reporting error. On the other hand, lower-class youths may mistrust research because they do not understand its purposes, and this may affect their responses.

Despite inherent problems, criminologists generally accept self-report measures as tools for measuring and understanding delinquent behavior. The following chapters, which analyze the theoretical constructs of delinquent behavior, will cite many studies that use the self-report approach extensively.

VICTIMIZATION SURVEYS

A number of factors reduce the accuracy of the FBI's Uniform Crime Reports and all other official statistics. Many people simply refuse to report criminal and delinquent behavior to law enforcement authorities, and even when crimes are reported, inadequate record-keeping and deliberate falsification by police agencies create potentially misleading impressions of the annual delinquency rate.

In an effort to improve existing knowledge of the nature and extent of delinquent and criminal behavior, the Law Enforcement Assistance Administration of the U.S. Department of Justice, in conjunction with the U.S. Census Bureau, has undertaken a massive house-to-house survey, called the National Crime Survey (NCS), of the victims of criminal behavior.[55] A more accurate measure of criminal and delinquent behavior in the United States can benefit the planning and budgeting of prevention and treatment programs on the local, state, and federal levels of government. This section will analyze some findings relevant to youth and delinquent behavior.

Victimization in the United States

The National Crime Survey provides yearly estimates of the total amount of personal contact crimes (such as assault, rape, and robbery), household victimizations (such as burglary, larceny, and vehicle theft), and business-related crimes (robbery and burglary).[56] Table 3-2 (p. 56) contains estimates of criminal activity in America for the years 1973 to 1976. The figures are truly astounding. Approximately 40 million serious crimes occur annually (a number four times greater than that reported by the FBI), and this pattern is consistent from year to year. Personal larceny appears to be the most common criminal activity, followed by household larceny and burglary.

The differences between the NCS data and official statistics are particularly significant. As the last column in Table 3-2 indicates, a majority of citizens do not report their victimization to police. These data raise even greater doubts about the validity of official statistics than existed before the onset of the NCS.

Extent of Delinquent Behavior

The NCS city data include cases of personal victimization and business robberies in which the age of the assailant is known. Thus, it is possible to estimate the total number of criminal acts involving youths. Table 3-3 (p. 57) presents this information for lone offenders, and Table 3-4 (p. 58) presents data for multiple offenders.

Table 3-2. Estimated Number of Personal, Household, and Business Victimizations and Percent Not Reported to Police, by Type of Victimization, United States, 1973-76.

	1973		1974		1975		1976	
Type of victimization	Estimated number of victim- izations	Percent not reported to police	Estimated number of victim- izations	Percent not reported to police	Estimated number of victim- izations	Percent not reported to police	Estimated number of victim- izations	Percent not reported to police
Personal victimizations:								
Rape and attempted rape	152,740	51	161,160	47	151,055	44	145,193	47
Robbery	1,086,700	46	1,173,980	46	1,121,374	46	1,110,639	46
Robbery and attempted robbery with injury	376,000	35	383,470	37	353,493	34	360,700	36
Serious assault	208,800	28	215,000	32	207,114	33	175,660	32
Minor assault	167,200	42	168,400	44	146,380	37	185,041	39
Robbery without injury ...	396,740	43	466,400	41	467,595	41	453,867	40
Attempted robbery without injury	313,960	64	324,120	63	300,285	69	296,071	67
Assault.....................	4,001,820	55	4,063,680	54	4,176,056	54	4,343,201	52
Aggravated assault	1,616,700	47	1,695,440	46	1,590,080	44	1,694,941	41
With injury	490,960	39	545,990	39	543,175	34	588,672	37
Attempted assault with weapon...................	1,197,740	51	1,149,450	49	1,046,905	49	1,106,269	43
Simple assault	2,365,120	61	2,368,240	61	2,585,976	60	2,648,320	59
With injury	603,500	51	582,190	54	687,352	51	601,534	53
Attempted assault without weapon.........	1,781,610	64	1,786,050	63	1,898,624	63	1,956,786	60
Personal larceny with contact	495,590	66	511,480	65	513,952	65	497,056	63
Purse snatching	103,280	51	90,230	36	119,096	36	91,595	32
Attempted purse snatching................	71,260	84	62,830	77	60,912	82	55,535	76
Pocket picking	321,050	68	358,410	71	333,943	72	349,926	70
Personal larceny without contact	14,635,655	77	15,098,118	75	15,455,660	73	16,021,110	73
Household victimizations:								
Burglary...................	6,432,350	52	6,655,070	51	6,688,964	51	6,663,422	51
Forcible entry.............	2,070,950	29	2,190,330	28	2,251,869	27	2,277,063	29
Unlawful entry without force	2,956,830	62	3,031,080	62	2,959,734	62	2,826,599	60
Attempted forcible entry	1,404,560	68	1,433,660	64	1,477,361	67	1,559,760	66
Larceny	7,506,400	74	8,866,060	74	9,156,711	72	9,300,854	72
Under $50	4,824,900	84	5,641,160	84	5,615,914	84	5,601,954	84
$50 or more..............	1,884,280	47	2,351,490	51	2,707,605	46	2,745,097	47
Amount not ascertained ...	263,750	77	296,000	77	277,922	81	299,350	78
Attempted	533,560	80	577,410	75	555,270	76	654,454	73
Vehicle theft	1,335,410	31	1,341,890	32	1,418,725	28	1,234,644	30
Completed	884,710	13	855,680	11	910,253	8	759,816	11
Attempted	450,710	67	486,210	68	508,472	63	474,828	61
Business victimizations:								
Robbery	264,113	14	266,624	10	261,725	9	279,516	12
Burglary...................	1,384,908	21	1,555,304	19	1,518,339	18	1,576,242	25

Source: Table constructed by SOURCEBOOK staff from data provided by the National Criminal Justice Information and Statistics Service of the Law Enforcement Assistance Administration, *Sourcebook of Criminal Justice Statistics* (Washington, D.C.: Government Printing Office, 1978). All tables in this section came from the Sourcebook.

Table 3-3. Estimated Number of Personal Victimizations and Business Robberies, by Perceived Ages of Multiple Offenders and Type of Victimization, United States, 1976

It must be stressed that this table reflects the victim's perception of the offenders: how accurate these perceptions are has not been extensively studied in the NCS developmental work.

Type of victimization	Total		Perceived age of lone offender							
			Under 12		12 to 20		21 or older		Don't know or not ascertained	
	Number	Percent	Number	Percent	Number	Percent	Number	Percent	Number	Percent
Personal victimizations:										
Rape and attempted rape	121,900	100	0	0	23,266	19	97,476	80	1,158	1
Robbery	493,663	100	3,465	1	190,964	39	279,856	57	19,379	4
Robbery and attempted robbery with injury	135,416	100	0	0	42,252	31	87,278	64	5,886	4
Serious assault	59,335	100	0	0	13,545	23	42,263	71	3,527	6
Minor assault	76,082	100	0	0	28,707	38	45,016	59	2,359	3
Robbery without injury	197,322	100	2,235	1	77,403	39	108,466	55	9,219	5
Attempted robbery without injury	160,925	100	1,230	1	71,310	44	84,111	52	4,274	3
Assault	3,005,616	100	16,410	1	975,851	32	1,965,123	65	48,233	2
Aggravated assault	1,088,844	100	4,641	0	317,442	29	742,770	68	23,991	2
With injury	364,810	100	3,499	1	111,161	30	243,537	67	6,613	2
Attempted assault without weapon	1,389,243	100	8,386	1	469,525	34	892,305	64	19,028	1
Personal Larceny with contact	183,595	100	1,241	1	85,517	47	68,187	37	98,650	16
Purse snatching	50,068	100	0	0	35,864	72	10,575	21	3,629	7
Attempted purse snatching	31,892	100	1,241	4	16,213	51	10,882	34	3,555	11
Pocket picking	101,635	100	0	0	33,440	33	46,731	46	21,465	21
Business victimizations:										
Robbery	136,490	100	381	0	26,539	19	93,122	68	16,448	12

[a]Subcategories may not sum to total because of rounding.

Source: Table constructed by SOURCEBOOK staff from data provided by the National Criminal Justice Information and Statistics Service of the Law Enforcement Assistance Administration, *Sourcebook of Criminal Justice Statistics* (Washington, D.C.: Government Printing Office, 1978).

The figures represented in these tables are astounding. In a single year, more than 450,000 young people under age twenty engage in robbery, 27,000 in rape, 1.5 million in assault, 125,000 in personal larceny (such as purse snatching), and 60,000 in business robberies. In all over 2 *million* serious criminal acts involve youthful participants either in groups or alone. Moreover, these figures do not include crimes involving mixed age groups. And of course the NCS data do not include crimes in which the assailant's age could not be determined or guessed.

It is evident when we combine the findings of the NCS data with those of self-report studies that an overwhelming number of American young people are engaging in serious crimes. Also, these recently developed figures cast grave doubts on the ability of official statistics to accurately portray the actual occurrence of delinquent behavior.

Analysis of Victim Surveys

Victim surveys are an important addition to our knowledge about crime and delinquency. They may be more objective than official delinquency statistics

Table 3-4. Estimated Number of Personal Victimizations and Business Robberies, by Perceived Age of Lone Offender and Type of Victimization, United States, 1976

It must be stressed that this table reflects the victim's perception of the offender: how accurate these perceptions are has not been extensively studied in the NCS developmental work.

Type of victimization	Total		Perceived ages of multiple offenders									
	Number	Percent	All under 12		All 12 to 20		All 21 or older		Mixed[b]		Don't know or not ascertained[b]	
			Number	Percent	Number	Percent	Number	Percent	Number	Percent	Number	Percent
Personal victimizations:												
Rape and attempted rape	22,065	100	0	0	4,399	20	15,011	68	2,655	12	.0	0
Robbery	590,498	100	1,190	0	259,015	44	172,706	29	116,407	20	41,179	7
Robbery and attempted robbery with injury	213,015	100	1,190	1	97,448	46	44,867	21	51,101	24	18,409	9
Serious assault	108,379	100	0	0	40,894	38	24,137	22	36,933	34	6,415	6
Minor assault	104,635	100	1,190	1	56,554	54	20,730	20	14,168	14	11,993	11
Robbery without injury	243,475	100	0	0	81,054	33	104,990	43	39,686	16	17,745	7
Attempted robbery without injury	134,007	100	0	0	80,513	60	22,849	17	25,619	19	5,026	4
Assault	1,222,334	100	9,132	1	573,997	47	317,170	26	253,498	21	68,536	6
Aggravated assault	527,247	100	2,789	1	204,711	39	162,012	31	124,711	24	33,024	6
With injury	208,602	100	1,650	1	79,843	38	63,504	30	52,612	25	10,994	5
Attempted assault with weapon	318,645	100	1,140	0	124,868	39	98,508	31	72,100	23	22,030	7
Simple assault	695,087	100	6,343	1	369,287	53	155,158	22	128,787	19	35,512	3
With injury	159,021	100	1,245	1	90,971	57	41,395	26	21,309	13	4,101	3
Attempted assault without weapon	536,066	100	5,098	1	278,315	52	113,764	21	107,478	20	31,411	6
Personal Larceny with contact	105,713	100	1,220	1	46,523	44	40,860	39	8,964	8	8,145	8
Purse snatching	31,101	100	0	0	21,550	69	7,085	23	1,266	4	1,201	4
Attempted purse snatching	22,488	100	1,220	5	12,497	56	3,700	16	3,800	17	1,271	6
Pocket picking	52,123	100	0	0	12,476	24	30,076	58	3,898	7	5,673	11
Business victimizations:												
Robbery	116,381	100	886	1	33,711	29	51,267	44	17,275	15	13,243	11

[a]Subcategories may not sum to total because of rounding.
[b]"Mixed" cases are those in which the victim reported that there were offenders from more than one age group. "Don't know/not ascertained" include cases in which the victim did not know any of the ages, or in which the victim did not know whether more than one age group was involved.

Source: Table constructed by SOURCEBOOK staff from data provided by the National Criminal Justice Information and Statistics Service of the Law Enforcement Assistance Administration, *Sourcebook of Criminal Justice Statistics* (Washington, D.C.: Government Printing Office, 1978).

since they do not rely on potentially biased law enforcement agencies to record and disseminate information. Moreover, a crime does not have to be reported to the police in order for it to be recorded as an official statistic. It comes as no surprise that delinquency and crimes are far more prevalent than what is reported to police. The NCS data highlight the need for a vast improvement in criminal statistics and record keeping.

Victimization studies do have critical limitations, especially in identifying youthful misbehavior. For one thing, most delinquent acts, as suggested by self-report studies, are victimless crimes—for example, smoking marijuana, using a false I.D., and getting drunk. For other acts, the age of the assailants cannot be identified. Obviously, victimization surveys cannot record these acts accurately. Other youthful misbehavior is directed against impersonal victims; for example, a school is vandalized, or a large department store is ripped off. Again, these acts are not recorded in a victimization survey. Furthermore, few victims are positive about the age of their assailants. Thus, even when there is contact between criminal and victim, it is difficult for victimization surveys to determine which acts are committed by legal juveniles and which by adults. And of course, the same fear and mistrust that prevent people from reporting crime to police can also prevent their truthful participation in surveys.

Nevertheless, the NCS provides valuable additional information with which to estimate youthful participation in personal injury crimes. By all indications, the level of their participation is far greater than previously imagined, and it may be two to four times as great as the level that is reported in the official statistics.

OBSERVATION AND BIOGRAPHICAL DATA

The final major source of unofficial information on delinquency comes from personal observation of delinquents and their daily activities. Sometimes these records are provided by social scientists who participate in the activities of youth, interviewing them, and thereby gaining a feeling for their lives. The classic example of this type of research is *Street Corner Society* by William F. Whyte.[57] Whyte observed and recorded the activities of a youth gang in a lower-class neighborhood—the Norton Street Gang—over a year's time. His sensitive observations allow us to better understand the daily lives of marginal youth—their activities, values, fears, and aspirations.

Another type of observation takes the form of biographical life histories written by former delinquents and criminals. Sometimes these stories are told to academic researchers. Examples of "as Told To" accounts include Clifford Shaw's *The Natural History of a Delinquent Career*,[58] and Edwin Sutherland's *Professional Thief*,[59] and R. Lincoln Keiser's *The Young Lords: Warriors of the Streets*.[60]

The benefits of this method are manifold. It enables criminologists to get a personal glimpse of the life of youthful law violators that mere statistics cannot hope to provide. Direct observation provides information about the delinquents' thoughts, about their family life, peer group relationships, attitudes toward school, success, the law, and so on. It can uncover how delinquents feel about their illegal acts as well as their fears, hopes, and concerns. This information is neither precise nor quantitative, but it is extremely useful for theory development and policy formulation.

The approach has its drawbacks. Often, the information cannot be verified and therefore must be interpreted with caution. Personal biases, opinion, and perception can color first person accounts and even supposedly neutral observations. Certain information may be covered up to present the central figure in a better light, or events may be interpreted according to personal taste and attitudes. Despite these drawbacks, observations and life histories are still unique testimonials with which every criminologist should become familiar.

To better understand the value of first person accounts, Highlight 3-3 presents an excerpt from a recent work, *Manny: A Criminal Addict's Story*.

Highlight 3–3.   "I Was Eleven and Getting Kind of Wild."

I was eleven and getting kind of wild. At first I wasn't into much of anything wrong, but I had a real temper and when I said no you had to beat me over the head to change my mind. And Mom just didn't have the power to stay with me. So, I started cutting a lot of classes and lying about it until I got caught. I used to have this broad, Becky, write excuses for me and just skip school for days at a time. When they started hassling my mother she'd get real upset. So, I'd promise to do good and stay in school, but I never did.

When we moved over to Third Avenue, that's when I really started hitting the skids. Not stealing anything, but I joined a fighting gang. I became a member of the Young Stars.

Me and my brother had a lot of fun in the gang, I remember that. Me and Bobby were always together. When you saw one, you knew the other was somewhere around. My brother was known as the Undertaker in the Young Stars. And I was the warlord. I remember, I became the warlord in a full council meeting on my thirteenth birthday. And it was my job to arrange fights with gangs like the Scorpions, the Mau Maus, the Seven Devils, and the other gangs.

Remember, this was in the early fifties. It was the beginning of the youth rebellion in this country. Kids in my neighborhood really began to emphasize toughness. Gang rumbles were a way to be tough and a way to demonstrate how to be smarter than

others and "outwit the enemy." Also, our gangs gave us the opportunity to be on our own. What went on in the clubhouse was our business. And we made sure it was the most important business for every member.

Sometimes it got really rough. We used to fight in school. I mean, I'd be walking down the hall in school with a sweater on saying "Young Stars." Another guy would be in the hall with a sweater saying "Scorpions." And I'd see him and we'd start fighting. We would fight on sight all the time. This wasn't like black against white, Chicano against nigger, or orange against green. It was neighborhood against neighborhood, territory against territory. My neighborhood against all other neighborhoods. If you belonged to some gang and you came into my neighborhood around Third Avenue and 178th Street, we would fight.

You invaded our territory and it was war. It made no difference if you were rich or poor, friend or foe. For instance, I had friends from the old days who were from really wealthy families, and I'd been over to their houses to parties and for dinner, maybe even fooled around a little with their sisters or cousins. Then, a couple of years later I would fight them "to the death" because they were in a rival gang—guys that used to be good friends of mind.

Source: *Manny: A Criminal Addict's Story*
(Boston: Houghton-Mifflin, 1978), pp. 16–17.

CHAPTER SUMMARY

This chapter reviewed three sources of unofficial delinquency statistics: self-report studies, victimization surveys, and life histories. Though each is quite different, they all supply important information about delinquent behavior in America.

Self-report surveys ask youths to tell researchers about their violations of the law. Self-report data have been used to answer basic questions about the age, sex, race, socioeconomic status, and peer relations of delinquent youth. They are essential tools for most of today's delinquency research efforts.

National Crime Survey data have been used to study the teenage victims of crime as well as the teenage perpetrators of crime. They help us better understand the true proportions of crime in America and the role of minors in the crime problem.

Life histories help us get the flavor of delinquent behavior through the eyes of its participants. While not a precise measure of the personality or behavior of delinquent youth, life histories and other biographical data help fill in the gaps that other sources leave open.

Unofficial sources of delinquency indicate that youthful misbehavior is much more widespread than police and juvenile court records indicate. Victim reports show that incidents of serious juvenile delinquency occur millions of times each year. Similarly, self-report studies suggest that sometime during their lives almost all youths participate in some type of illegal behavior.

In addition to presenting us with a picture of the actual or perceived occurrence of delinquency, unofficial statistics enable us to better understand who juvenile delinquents are. They can be male or female, rich or poor, white, Hispanic, or black. Although official sources paint a picture of the delinquent as a poor minority youth, self-report studies indicate that delinquent behavior is not the product of any one race, nationality, or social class. Moreover, some self-report studies suggest that police handling of juveniles may reflect racial and economic bias.

When we trace the development of theoretical models of delinquency in the next four chapters, the influence of these various sources on delinquent behavior will be readily apparent. Early theories were based on official statistics and therefore viewed delinquency as a property of lower-class youth cultures (Chapters 4 and 5). Later theoretical models (Chapters 6, 7, and 8) reflect the picture of delinquency portrayed in self-report studies. They attempt to explain the occurrence of delinquent behavior in all social classes.

DISCUSSION QUESTIONS

1. Would you honestly tell a researcher about your delinquent activities?
2. What factors would cause teenagers to lie to university researchers?
3. Are victimization studies useful? If so, why?
4. If a self-report survey were conducted in a high school, who do you think would be unlikely to answer it?

SUGGESTED READINGS

Blackmore, John. "The Relationship between Self-Reported Delinquency and Official Convictions amongst Adolescent Boys." *British Journal of Criminology* 14 (1974): 172–176.

Bowers, William. *Question Sequencing Effects on Response to Sensitive Questions in the Self-Administered Questionnaire.* Boston: Russell B. Stearns Research Center, 1971.

Erickson, Maynard L. "The Group Context of Delinquent Behavior." *Social Problems* 19 (1975): 115–129.

———."Group Violations and Official Delinquency: The Group Hazard Hypothesis." *Criminology* 11 (1973): 127–160.

Gold, Martin. "On Social Status and Delinquency." *Social Problems* 15 (1967): 114–116.

———."Undetected Delinquent Behavior." *Journal of Research in Crime and Delinquency* 3 (1966): 27–46.

Hardt, Robert, and Peterson-Hardt, Sandra. "On Determining the Quality of the Delinquency Self-Report Method." *Journal of Research in Crime and Delinquency* 14 (1977): 247.

Hindelang, Michael. "With a Little Help from Their Friends: Group Participation in Reported Delinquent Behavior." *British Journal of Criminology* 16 (1976): 109–125.

———."Variations in Personality and Attributes of Social and Solitary Self-Report Delinquents." *Journal of Consulting and Clinical Psychology* 40 (1973): 452.

Kaplan, Howard B. "Self-Attitudes and Deviant Responses." *Social Forces* 54 (1976): 788–801.

REFERENCES

1. Roger Hood and Richard Sparks, *Key Issues in Criminology* (New York: McGraw-Hill, 1970), p. 72.

2. A pioneering effort of self-report research is A. L. Porterfield, *Youth in Trouble* (Fort Worth, Texas: Leo Potishman Foundation, 1946). For a review, see Robert Hardt and George Bodine, *Development of Self-Report Instruments in Delinquency Research: A Conference Report* (Syracuse, N.Y.: Syracuse University Youth Development Center, 1965). See also Fred Murphy, Mary Shirley, and Helen Witmer, "The Incidence of Hidden Delinquency," *American Journal of Orthopsychiatry* 16 (1946): pp. 686–696.

3. Hood and Sparks, *Key Issues in Criminology*, p. 46.

4. James Short and F. Ivan Nye, "Reported Behavior as a Criterion of Deviant Behavior," *Social Problems* 5 (1958): pp. 207–213.

5. For example, the following studies have noted the great discrepancy between official statistics and self-report studies: Maynard Erickson and LaMar Empey, "Court Records, Undetected Delinquency and Decision-Making," *Journal of Criminal Law, Criminology and Police Science* 54 (1963): pp. 456–469; Martin Gold, "Undetected Delinquent Behavior," *Journal of Research in Crime and Delinquency* 3 (1966): pp. 27–46; James Short and F. Ivan Nye, "Extent of Unrecorded Delinquency, Tentative Conclusions," *Journal of Criminal Law, Criminology and Police Science* 49 (1958): pp. 296–302.

6. In addition to the studies listed above, see David Farrington, "Self-Reports of Deviant Behavior: Predictive and Stable?" *Journal of Criminal Law and Criminology* 64 (1973): pp. 99–110; Michael Hindelang, "Causes of Delinquency: A Partial Replication and Extension," *Social Problems* 20 (1973): pp. 471–487.

7. See notes 5 and 6.

8. Research in the following sections was provided with the aid of Janie M. Burcart. Some sections were adapted, with her permission, from *Measuring Delinquency through Self-Report Instruments: A Bibliographic Essay* (Eugene, Ore.: Institute of Policy Analysis, 1977).

9. Albert Cohen, *Delinquent Boys* (New York: Free Press, 1955), p. 42.

10. Richard Cloward and Lloyd Ohlin, *Delinquency and Opportunity* (New York: Free Press, 1960), p. 13.

11. James Short and F. Ivan Nye, "Reported Behavior as a Criterion of Deviant Behavior," *Social Problems* 5 (1958): pp. 207–213.

12. Martin Gold, "Undetected Delinquent Behavior," *Journal of Research in Crime and Delinquency* 3 (1966): pp. 27–46.

13. Jay Williams and Martin Gold, "From Delinquent Behavior to Official Delinquency," *Social Problems* 20 (1972): pp. 209–229.

14. Short and Nye, "Reported Behavior as a Criterion of Deviant Behavior."

15. Ibid., p. 212.

16. Ivan Nye, James Short, and Virgil Olsen, "Socio-Economic Status and Delinquent Behavior," *American Journal of Sociology* 63 (1958): pp. 381–389.

17. Robert Dentler and Lawrence Monroe, "Social Correlates of Early Adolescent Theft," *American Sociological Review* 26 (1961): pp. 733–743.

18. John Clark and Eugene Wenninger, "Socio-Economic Class and Area as Correlates of Illegal Behavior Among Juveniles," *American Sociological Review* 27 (1962): pp. 826–834.

19. Chapter 5 will discuss the work of Albert Cohen (see note 10) and Richard Cloward and Lloyd Ohlin (note 11), who stress delinquent behavior as a product of minority youth culture.

20. William Arnold, "Continuities in Research: Scaling Delinquent Behavior," *Social Problems* 13 (1965): pp. 59–66.

21. LaMar Empey and Maynard Erickson, "Hidden Delinquency and Social Status," *Social Forces* 44 (1966): pp. 546–554.

22. Ibid., p. 549.

23. This finding results from differential law enforcement. A serious offense committed by a middle-class youth is less likely to result in probation or incarceration than one committed by a lower-class youth. Hence, the incarcerated middle-class youth should have committed much more and much more serious delinquency than that of his or her lower-class counterpart.

24. Ronald Akers, "Socio-Economic Status and Delinquent Behavior: A Retest," *Journal of Research in Crime and Delinquency* 1 (1964): pp. 38–46.

25. Harwin Voss, "Ethnic Differentials in Delinquency in Honolulu," *Journal of Criminal Law, Criminology and Police Science* 54 (1963): pp. 322–327.

26. Gold, "Undetected Delinquent Behavior."

27. Williams and Gold, "From Delinquent Behavior to Official Delinquency."

28. Richard Johnson, "Social Class and Delinquent Behavior," *Criminology* 18 (1980): pp. 86–93.

29. Delbert Elliott and Suzanne Ageton, "Reconciling Race and Class Differences in Self-Reported and Official Estimates of Delinquency," *American Sociological Review* 45 (1980): pp. 95–110.

30. Cohen, *Delinquent Boys*, pp. 140–142.

31. Gary Jensen and Raymond Eve, "Sex Differences in Delinquency: An Examination of Popular Sociological Explanations," *Criminology* 13 (1976): pp. 427–448.

32. Michael Hindelang, "Age, Sex, and the Versatility of Delinquent Involvements," *Social Problems* 18 (1979): pp. 522–535.

33. Short and Nye, "Extent of Unrecorded Juvenile Delinquency."

34. Williams and Gold, "From Delinquent Behavior to Official Delinquency."

35. Short and Nye, "Extent of Unrecorded Juvenile Delinquency," p. 300.

36. Leroy Gould, "Who Defines Delinquency: A Comparison of Self-Report and Officially-Reported Indices of Delinquency for Three Racial Groups," *Social Problems* 16 (1969): pp. 325–336.

37. Voss, "Ethnic Differentials in Delinquency in Honolulu."

38. Michael Hindelang, "Race and Involvement in Common Law Personal Crimes," *American Sociological Review* 43 (1978): pp. 93–109.

39. Elliott and Ageton, "Reconciling Race and Class Differences," pp. 108–110.

40. Sheldon Glueck and Eleanor Glueck, *One Thousand Juvenile Delinquents* (Cambridge, Mass.: Harvard University Press, 1934); and Thorsten Sellin and Marvin Wolfgang, *The Measurement of Delinquency* (New York: Wiley, 1964).

41. Martin Gold, *Delinquent Behavior in an American City* (Belmont, Calif.: Brooks/Cole, 1970).

42. Maynard Erickson, "The Group Context of Delinquent Behavior," *Social Problems* 19 (1971): pp. 115–129.

43. Michael Hindelang, "With a Little Help from Their Friends: Group Participation in Reported Delinquent Behavior," *Briti sh Journal of Criminology* 16 (1976): pp. 109–125.

44. Walter Miller, *Violence by Youth Gangs and Youth Groups as a Crime Problem in Major American Cities* (Washington, D.C.: Government Printing Office, 1975).

45. See, for example, Spencer Rathus and Larry Siegel, "Crime and Personality Revisited: Effects of MMPI Sets in Self-Report Studies," *Criminology* 18 (1980): pp. 245-251.

46. Voss, "Ethnic Differentials in Delinquency in Honolulu"; Erickson and Empey, "Court Records, Undetected Delinquency and Decision Making"; H. B. Gibson, Sylvia Morrison, and D. J. West, "The Confession of Known Offenses in Response to a Self-Reported Delinquency Schedule," *British Journal of Criminology* 10 (1970): pp. 277–280; and John Blackmore, "The Relationship between Self-Reported Delinquency and Official Convictions amongst Adolescent Boys," *British Journal of Criminology* 14 (1974): pp. 172–176.

47. James Hackler and Melanie Lautt, "Systematic Bias in Measuring Self-Reported Delinquency," *Canadian Review of Sociology and Anthropology* 6 (1969): pp. 92–106.

48. Farrington, "Self-Reports of Deviant Behavior."

49. Gold, "Undetected Delinquent Behavior."

50. Dentler and Monroe, "Social Correlates of Early Adolescent Theft"; and Farrington, "Self-Reports of Deviant Behavior."

51. F. Ivan Nye and James Short, "Scaling Delinquent Behavior," *American Sociological Review* 22 (1957): pp. 326–331.

52. John Clark and Larry Tifft, "Polygraph and Interview Validation of Self-Reported Deviant Behavior," *American Sociological Review* 31 (1966): pp. 516–523.

53. Gold, "Undetected Delinquent Behavior."

54. Erickson and Empey, "Court Records, Undetected Delinquency and Decision Making."

55. The National Crime Survey data used in this section come from Criminal Justice Research Center, *The Sourcebook of Criminal Justice Statistics* (Washington, D.C.: Government Printing Office, 1978).

56. Ibid., pp. 380–395.

57. William F. Whyte, *Street Corner Society* (Chicago: University of Chicago Press, 1955).

58. Clifford Shaw, *The Natural History of a Delinquent Career* (Chicago: University of Chicago Press, 1931).

59. Edwin Sutherland, *The Professional Thief* (Chicago: University of Chicago Press, 1937).

60. R. Lincoln Keiser, *The Vice Lords,* (New York: Holt, Rinehart and Winston, 1969).

PART II

THEORIES OF
DELINQUENT
BEHAVIOR

Chapter 4

Chapter Outline

Introduction
Individualistic Theories of Delinquency
Classical Theory
Positivist Theory
Critique of Individualistic Theories
Chapter Summary

Key Terms, Names, and Cases

social theory
scientific method
atavism
somatotypes
endo-, ecto-, and mesomorphs
sociobiology
I.Q.
nature vs. nurture
id — ego — superego
extroversion — neuroticism
M.M.P.I.
Cesare Beccaria
Jeremy Bentham
James Q. Wilson
Cesare Lombroso
Sheldon and Eleanor Glueck
C. Ray Jeffery
Arthur Jensen
Sigmund Freud
Hans Eysenck

Individualistic Theories of
Delinquent Behavior

INTRODUCTION

The next five chapters will analyze theories of delinquent behavior in detail. Chapter 4 will discuss theories based on the assumption that the personal characteristics and attributes of individuals cause their delinquent behavior. Subsequent chapters will review theories based on the idea that social forces such as poverty and lower-class cultural values or social-psychological factors such as alienation from society are the true cause of delinquency. Before beginning the discussion of this topic, the chapter will briefly discuss the concept of social science theory in general so that its purpose will be better understood.

When social scientists use the term *theory*, they refer to their efforts to take previously observed but as yet uncoordinated facts and order them so that they can be used to logically explain human behavior.[1] Criminological theory is a type of social theory directed at explaining why people become involved in crime and delinquency. Social theory has two purposes: (1) to explain the occurrence of *current* behavior trends and actions and (2) to predict *future* behavior patterns. A simple example can help illustrate this concept. Let us say that government statistics reveal that a disproportionate number of men who are currently serving prison sentences have divorced or separated parents. From this brief set of facts, we can logically derive a tentative *theoretical model*, which states: The strain of growing up in a broken home causes youngsters to eventually become delinquents and, later, adult criminals. This model satisfies both goals of social theory. It explains current behavior (the high percentage of prisoners who have divorced parents), and it predicts future behavior (children of divorced parents will be more likely to engage in illegal behavior than children with stable families).

Once a tentative theoretical model has been proposed, the criminologist must test its validity or accuracy. Criminological theories must be continually evaluated under all sorts of social conditions and in many different environments. To test the theory we have constructed we would have to determine whether the relationship between criminal behavior and broken homes applies to men and women; whites, blacks, Hispanics, and other ethnic group members; people in various geographic locales; and so on. We would also have to know why some youths from broken homes *do not* become criminals and why some youths from stable families do. Such issues would have to be explored before the proposed theory could become an accepted explanation of current behavior and a predictor of future behavior.

Once formulated, the propositions of criminological theory must be tested, using the *scientific method*. First, research questions, or *hypotheses*, are logically drawn from the theory and then investigated, using field (empirical) research. Research findings are expected to support the propositions of the original theory. Again, using our example to illustrate, we could logically hypothesize that youths whose parents are divorced or separated will self-report greater amounts of illegal behavior than youths whose parents are currently living together. To test this hypothesis, we could select random samples of youths, perhaps from a local school system, separate them according to family status (divorced versus intact), and have them respond to a self-report questionnaire. If the experimental group (from broken homes) reported a higher delinquency rate than the control group (from stable homes), the original theory would indirectly be supported. If both groups reported equal amounts of delinquency, or if the youths living in stable homes were actually more delinquent, the validity of the original theoretical model would be undermined. This process is the empirical testing of a theoretical hypothesis. If research data do not support a hypothesis derived from a theory, then the theory cannot be accepted as a valid explanation of behavior.

Unfortunately, all too often criminologists neglect to test their theoretical models thoroughly before they propose them. This is probably one of the important reasons why no single theory of delinquent behavior has yet been universally accepted as a satisfactory explanation of current delinquency and a predictor of future delinquency. As soon as a theory of delinquency is proposed, critics are quick to find flaws or logical inconsistencies in it. Although some of the theoretical models we will discuss are valid explanations of particular types of delinquency among special classes of delinquents (for example, lower-class gangs), a grand theory of delinquency that accurately explains all facets of youthful criminality has yet to be developed.

INDIVIDUALISTIC THEORIES OF DELINQUENCY

Individualistic theories of delinquency hold that people engage in illegal or antisocial behavior because of some facet of their own personal makeup. Such theories maintain that while most people living under similar conditions are subject to the same frustrations, desires, and social pressures, only a small minority become seriously delinquent or criminal. Therefore, some personal trait must separate the deviant members of society from the nondeviant. These personal differences account for the fact that, faced with the same life situations, one youth commits crimes but another attends school, church, and neighborhood functions.

Individualistic theories of delinquent behavior have a number of different branches. Yet they are linked together because of their focus on the individual actor. The earliest, *classical theory*, maintains that most people have equal potential for committing deviant acts, and only the fear of law and punishment keeps their criminal natures in check. A second position, *biological determinism theory*, maintains that delinquents and criminals are unique in their physical and mental makeup, that certain biophysical traits promote delinquent behavior, and that in some instances such characteristics can be passed down from one generation to the next. A more recent development is sociobiology theory, which maintains that the interaction of biological and ecological factors controls human behavior.

A third type of individualistic theory focuses on the *psychological and mental* aspects of deviant behavior. Advocates of this position argue that delinquency is caused by mental illness and psychological imbalance or improper learning, lack of moral development, and so on.

Some individualistic theories of delinquency recognize that social and environmental conditions influence behavior. However, in most instances, sociological issues are given secondary importance. It follows from this position that if we are to eliminate crime and delinquency, efforts must be directed more at individuals than at the social conditions in which they live.

CLASSICAL THEORY

In the early history of English and European jurisprudence, punishment for criminal acts was extremely severe. Capital punishment by hanging, flogging, and even more gruesome means was used for many common crimes. Little attention was paid to the age or sex of offenders. Even young boys and girls were liable to receive the death penalty for minor thefts. Some courts even employed torture to force confessions from those accused of crime. Equality before the law did not exist, and treatment of the accused depended on their station in life and the influence of family and friends.[2] Punishment was viewed as a deterrent; the harsher the punishment the more likely people would be deterred. Against this backdrop of repression and barbaric punishment, the classical theory of crime and delinquency was first formulated.

Classical theory assumes that human behavior is rational, logical, and a product of free will. People act the way they do after evaluating the consequences their actions will have on themselves and others.

Being rational, humans will try to maximize pleasure and minimize pain. Confounding this simple paradigm is the human urge to taste the forbidden fruits of life. Since people are naturally hedonistic, opportunistic, and undisciplined, law and punishment must control their behavior.

While this simple paradigm is the heart of classical theory, its adherents also maintain that a reasonable balance can be found between crime and punishment. They argue that punishment need not be severe; it should be merely adequate to fit the crime.

The two most prominent members of the classical school were Cesare Beccaria and Jeremy Bentham. To better understand classical values, we will focus on their work in some detail.

Cesare Beccaria

Born in Milan in 1738, Cesare Beccaria is best known for his essay *Dei delitti e delle pene (On Crime and Punishment)*, published in 1764, when he was twenty-six years old.[3] Beccaria's treatise views the law as necessary to restrain people from interfering with the freedom of their fellows. Without law, societies could not exist. When people became weary of living in anarchy and war, they accepted a rule of law because it guaranteed them tranquility and peace even at the expense of a portion of their freedom.[4]

In Beccaria's view, punishment is legitimate only when it is applied to protect a majority of citizens from the transgressions of a few.[5] Advocating the social contract principles of philosophers such as Voltaire, Rousseau, and Montesquieu,[6] Beccaria shares their belief that the right to be free from government restraint is to be abrogated only under the most extreme circumstances. Laws must therefore be applied systematically and fairly to all citizens and must be equally binding on all members of society. These procedures, Becarria believes, will ultimately reduce crime and delinquency. To meet this obligation, the state's criminal code must be simply written so that all can understand and obey it, and then the law must be fairly administered and applied.

To prevent crime and delinquency, Beccaria accepts the necessity of punishment. However, he also believes that punishment must be weighed against the importance of a crime to society. The more threatening the crime, the more severe the punishment.[7] Speaking against capital punishment, Beccaria warns that a punishment should not be so severe that it becomes itself an act of violence and barbarity.[8]

Jeremy Bentham

The work of the English philosopher Jeremy Bentham (1748–1832), is also closely associated with classical theory.[9] Bentham's philosophy is based on the concept of *utilitarianism*. An act has utility "if it tends to produce benefit, advantage, good or to prevent the happening of mischief, pain, evil, or unhappiness to the party whose interest is considered."[10] Criminologist Clayton Hartgen summarizes Bentham's application of this principle to criminal and delinquent behavior in Highlight 4–1.

Highlight 4–1. Clayton Hartgen on Utilitarianism.

The human being is basically a rational animal possessing a will that enables the individual freely to choose courses of action. Criminal conduct must, therefore, be the result of a deliberate, rational decision to break the law. Since human beings were also believed to possess the desire to achieve pleasure and avoid pain, this deliberate choice must represent a calculated move to gain that goal — crime, in other words, must provide some kind of pleasure to the criminal. It therefore follows that to deter a person from criminal ways, one must administer pain of an appropriate amount and kind to counterbalance the pleasure derived from crime.

Source: Clayton Hartgen, *Crime and Criminalization* (New York: Praeger, 1974), p. 89.

Legacy of Classical Theory

Classical theory still influences the nature and functions of juvenile law. Most state statutes are designed to eliminate delinquency and other illegal behaviors by ensuring that the pain of punishment far outweighs the benefits of illegal activity. Although reformers have long condemned a harsh penal system, some experts believe that more stringent prison sentences and severe punishment are actually the best deterrents to crime and delinquency.

Political scientist James Q. Wilson, a leading advocate of harsh punishment as a crime deterrent, suggests that there is little evidence to support a position that would-be law violators are immune to the risks associated with their crimes. If harsher punishment increases the cost of crime, without a corresponding increase in the value that can be expected from committing the crime, then, Wilson predicts, the crime rate will drop.[11]

This principle has special application to juvenile delinquency. Current delinquency rehabilitation programs, Wilson argues, are usually based on treating the *cause* of juvenile crime and are rarely concerned with its control. Therefore, they are doomed to failure, since they cannot eliminate the *benefits* of delinquent behavior for the crime-prone juvenile. Wilson further claims that a careful evaluation of modern delinquency prevention programs will reveal that no single approach based on rehabilitation has succeeded in reducing juvenile crime.

Another well-known modern classicist who views punishment as a solution to the problems of delinquency is sociologist Ernest van den Haag.[12] A national magazine asked van den Haag his plan to reduce violence in our society. Highlight 4-2 contains his answer.

Highlight 4-2. Ernest van den Haag on Controlling Violence.

Q. What do you think should be done to restore order?

A. Our law-enforcement agencies unfortunately are hamstrung at present. If you have a group of people bent on social violence, it's impossible—no matter how many policemen you have to stop them unless you have informers within the group, and the courts have made it very difficult to have such informers. These curbs should be eased.

We should also restore the death penalty—especially for terrorists. I'm not saying the death penalty is a panacea, but

our reluctance, particularly among the
educated, to use it is part of the general
reluctance to punish anyone for anything.

Source: *U.S. News & World Report*, December
11, 1976, p. 25.

Modern proponents of classical theory such as Wilson and van den Haag advocate the use of harsh punishment as a deterrent to delinquency. Has this belief actually influenced the current treatment of juvenile offenders? Many people support the need for longer periods of incarceration for some youths, especially those who commit violent crimes.[13] Although the number of institutionalized youth decreased steadily during the 1970s, this trend may reverse itself during the 1980s. A return to classical theory principles to deter delinquency is a distinct possibility.

POSITIVIST THEORY

During the latter part of the nineteenth century, positivist theory came to the forefront of criminological thought. This position suggests that the free will assumption of classical theory is in error and that human behavior is actually determined by internal and external forces. A person's ability to choose right from wrong is not solely a matter of personal conscience or discretion. Instead, it is controlled by forces beyond the individual such as biological makeup, psychological factors, or environment and culture. Positivists stress the empirical testing of social theory and try to maintain an objective, value-free attitude toward the subjects they study.

This section will review the position of positivist theory on individual factors such as genetic and biological makeup, family traits, and intelligence. Subsequent chapters will address positivist views on social factors such as the environment, the family, and cultural values.

Biological Determinism

Biological determinism theories suggest that biological and physical factors determine human behavior. These factors include body type, traits of the born criminal, genetic makeup, body build, and so on. Biological determinists maintain that the physical conditions people inherit or develop may cause them to violate the law. Physical makeup separates the deviant from the nondeviant, so deviant behavior is beyond an individual's control.

THEORIES OF PHYSICAL ANOMALIES

Cesare Lombroso   Cesare Lombroso (1835–1909), known as the father of criminology, was a doctor who served much of his career in the Italian army. His army experience gave him the opportunity to study human physical characteristics and note their relationship to behavior. Later he studied inmates at institutes for the insane in Pavia, Pesaro, and Reggio Emilia.[14]

Lombroso put his many years of research to use in his theory of *criminal atavism*. In this theory he suggests that delinquents manifest physical anomalies which make them biologically and physiologically similar to our primitive ancestors. These atavistic individuals are savage throwbacks to an earlier stage of human evolution. Lombroso's thought is illustrated in Highlight 4–3, which describes the autopsy of a well-known criminal.

Lombroso also identifies other criminal types, such as criminals by passion, occasional criminals (who are influenced by their environment), and criminaloids (who participate in less serious crimes). However, he is most famous for the concept of the atavistic, born criminal.

Responses to Lombroso: Charles Goring Lombroso's pioneering work received quite a bit of attention from the scientific community of his time. Soon a staunch group of admirers gathered about him. Nonetheless, a number of scholars, including the English criminologist, Charles Goring, challenged the validity of Lombroso's research.

Goring (1870–1919) found that Lombroso's methods were imprecise and inadequate.[15] In his study of three thousand English convicts, *The English Convict*, published in 1913, Goring uses the biometric method to study the criminal.[16] This method applies precise statistical tests to the study of human characteristics.

Goring rejected Lombroso's claims of biological determinism. In measuring such traits as distance between the eyes, head circumference, weight, hearing, and hair and eye color, he found little difference in the physical characteristics of criminals and noncriminals. Goring discovered, however, that delinquent behavior bore a significant relationship to a condition he referred to as "defective intelligence."[17] Consequently, Goring believed that delinquent behavior was inherited and could therefore best be controlled by regulating the

---

Highlight 4–3. Lombroso's Concepts of the Criminal Man.

This was not merely an idea, but a revelation. At the sight of that skull, I seemed to see all of a sudden, lighted up as a vast plain under a flaming sky, the problem of the nature of the criminal—an atavistic being who reproduces in his person the ferocious instincts of primitive humanity and the inferior animals. Thus were explained anatomically the enormous jaws, high cheek-bones, prominent superciliary arches, solitary lines in the palms, extreme size of the orbits, handle-shaped or sessile ears found in criminals, savages, and apes, insensibility to pain, extremely acute sight, tatooing, excessive idleness, love of orgies, and the irresistible craving for evil for its own sake, the desire not only to extinguish life in the victim, but to mutilate the corpse, tear its flesh, and drink its blood.

Source: Cesare Lombroso, "Introduction," in *Criminal Man According to the Classification of Cesare Lombroso, 1911,* by Gina Lombroso-Ferrero (Montclair, N.J.: Patterson Smith, 1972), pp. xiv.

reproduction of families exhibiting such traits as "feeble-mindedness, epilepsy, insanity, and defective social instinct."[18]

Raffaele Garofalo   A contemporary of Lombroso and Goring, Raffaele Garofalo (1852–1934), occupies a theoretical middle ground between them.[19] On the one hand, he shares Lombroso's belief that certain physical characteristics indicate a criminal or delinquent nature.[20] He suggests, for example, that enlarged mandibles are a sign of brutality and violence.[21]

Despite his respect for Lombroso, Garofalo argues that proof of a criminal or delinquent "type" has never actually been produced and that murderers and other serious criminals manifest many different physical traits. Garofalo explains deviant behavior with his concept of *psychic* or *moral anomaly*. This term refers to the criminal's lack of compassionate and altruistic feelings, a lack that has an organic root. The moral anomaly is a psychic force found more frequently in so-called inferior races and transmitted through heredity.[22] Though environment plays a role in the development of criminality, internal factors predominate. They include the "instincts" that are congenital or inherited or that are acquired in early infancy and thereafter become inseparable from the "psychic organism."[23]

Finally, Garofalo recognizes the differences existing among individual delinquents and suggests that delinquents be classified as murderers, who are totally lacking in humanity, and as lesser criminals, who in turn should be classified into violent criminals, thieves, and lascivious criminals (sexual offenders).

Enrico Ferri   Enrico Ferri (1856–1929) is identified along with Lombroso and Garofalo as part of "the holy three of criminology."[24] A student of Lombroso, Ferri believed that a number of biological, social, and organic factors caused delinquency and crime. These factors are described in Highlight 4–4. Thus, while Ferri accepted the validity of the biological approach to criminal activity, he attempted to interweave physical, anthropological, and social factors into his explanation of the causes of illegal behavior.[25]

Highlight 4–4.   Ferri's Crime-Producing Factors.

The organic constitution of the criminal comprises all anomalies of the skull, the brain, the vital organs, the sensibility, and the reflex activity, and all the bodily characteristics taken together, such as the physiognomy, tattooing, and so on.

The mental constitution of the criminal comprises anomalies of intelligence and feeling, especially of the moral sense, and the specialties of criminal writing and slang.

The personal characteristics of the criminal comprise his purely biological

conditions, such as race, age, sex; bio-social conditions, such as civil status, profession, domicile, social rank, instruction, education, which have hitherto been regarded as almost the exclusive concern of criminal statistics.

The physical factors of crime are climate, the nature of the soil, the relative length of day and night, the seasons, the average temperature, meteoric conditions, agricultural pursuits.

The social factors comprise the density of

population; public opinion, manners and religion; family circumstances; the system of education; industrial pursuits; alcoholism; economic and political conditions, public administration, justice and police; and in general, legislative, civil and penal institutions.

Source: Enrico Ferri, *Criminal Sociology* (New York: D. Appleton, 1897), p. 53.

THEORIES OF HEREDITY Another branch of biological determinism focuses on human heredity and its relationship to deviant behavior. This position holds that physical traits may indeed produce delinquent or criminal behavior and that possession of physical abnormalities can be transmitted genetically from one generation to the next. The result is delinquent-producing, "crimogenic" families.

Advocates of the psychobiological, or inheritance, theory studied the family trees of criminal and delinquent offenders. They traced the activities of several generations of families believed to have an especially large number of criminal members. The most famous of these studies involved the Jukeses and the Kallikaks. Richard Dugdale's book, *Crime, Pauperism, Disease and Heredity* (1895), and Arthur Estabrook's later work, *The Jukes in 1915*, traced the history of the Jukes, a family responsible for a disproportionate amount of crime. Dugdale concentrated his efforts on one branch of the family tree, the offspring of Ada Jukes, whom he labeled the "mother of criminals." Dugdale succeeded in locating over 1,000 of her descendants and found that they included 280 paupers, 60 thieves, 7 murderers, 140 criminals, 40 persons with venereal diseases, 50 prostitutes, and other assorted deviants.

Estabrook studied the Jukes family even more closely and accumulated data on 2,000 members. He found an additional 170 paupers, 118 criminals, 378 prostitutes, and assorted other deviants. In an associated effort, Henry Goddard studied the offspring of Martin Kallikak, who lived during the time of the American Revolution. Kallikak first had an illegitimate son by a woman of "low-born" family and then married into a "good" family. Goddard located 480 relations of the illegitimate offspring and 496 descendants of Kallikak's marriage. The former group contained substantially more deviant and criminal members than the latter group. The immediate implication of these studies was that undesirable hereditary characteristics, even in distant relatives, were enough to condemn succeeding generations of a family to a life of criminal degeneracy. Again, criminals were seen as being "born and not made."[26]

Studies like these were taken quite seriously in their time. Of course, the writings of the heredity school are no longer considered valid. Even if more families like the Jukeses or Kallikaks were located, this alone would not prove that psychodegeneracy is a cause of delinquency. Considering the thousands of family bloodlines within the United States, it would be expected that a few would produce a disproportionate number of deviants. Furthermore, many of the "best" families have produced murderers and thieves. Finally, there is no explanation as to why many members of psychodegenerate families live perfectly normal lives and become productive members of their communities.[27]

BODY-BUILD THEORIES   Another separate branch of biological determinism theory is the body-build, or *somato type* school. Advocates of this approach argue that delinquents and criminals manifest distinct physiques that make them susceptible to particular types of delinquent behavior.

One of the first criminologists to link body type with delinquency was Ernst Kretschmer. He identifies two distinct types, the *cyclothyme* and the *schizothyme*. Cyclothymes are spontaneous and lack sophistication. They are soft-skinned, with little muscle, and are kindhearted, tractable, sociable, talkative, and sometimes rash. Schizothymes have strong reactions and are apathetic and wayward in their nature. Their build is either tall and flat or wide, muscular, and strong.[28] Kretschmer believed that cyclothymes were less serious delinquents and criminals and that schizothymes were more serious ones.

Following Kretschmer, William H. Sheldon linked body type to delinquency.[29] In his analysis of youth, Sheldon discovered the existence of three basic body types. *Mesomorphs* have well-developed muscles and an athletic appearance. They are active, aggressive, and sometimes violent and are the most likely to become delinquents. *Endomorphs* have heavy builds and are slow moving. They are known for lethargic behavior. *Ectomorphs* are tall and thin and less social and more intellectual than the other types.

Recent studies of the relationship of body build and delinquency were conducted by Sheldon Glueck and Eleanor Glueck. The Gluecks used Sheldon's three body types and added a fourth, "balanced type," which includes boys with no discernible dominant body type. In a lengthy research effort involving large samples of delinquent and nondelinquent boys, the Gluecks found that mesomorphs were disproportionately represented among delinquent boys (60.1 percent versus 30.7 percent). Conversely, only 14.4 percent of the delinquents were ectomorphic, but 39.6 percent of the nondelinquents were ectomorphic.[30]

To summarize the Gluecks' findings on physique and delinquency:

1. The basic . . . difference of the physique types is accompanied by differences in the incidence among them of certain traits, some of which have been found . . . to be actually associated with delinquency, others potentially or indirectly so.
2. Differences in the physical and temperamental structure of body types bring about some variation in their response to environmental pressures.
3. Differences in the incidence of certain traits among the physique types, as well as divergences in their reactions to the environment, are reflected in certain differences in the etiology of deliquency among body types.[31]

The Gluecks' claim that a disproportionate number of delinquent youths may be mesomorphs because their strength and agility enable these boys to carry out the demands of the delinquent role. Endomorphs may be too slow and clumsy, and ectomorphs too fragile, to be successful delinquents. Recently, however, B. R. McCandless and his associates found no significant relationship between body build and self-reported delinquency.[32] The link between physique and delinquency seems tenuous at best.

LEGACY OF BIOLOGICAL DETERMINISM—SOCIOBIOLOGY   One of the most important recent developments in the study of criminology is sociobiology theory, which attempts to explain delinquent and criminal behavior from a biological and environmental viewpoint.[33] Sociobiology differs from earlier theories of biological determinism in that it stresses that biological and genetic conditions affect the perception and learning of social behaviors, which in turn are linked to existing environmental structures. Sociobiologists view biology, environment, and learning as mutually interdependent factors. Thus, problems in one area can possibly be altered by efforts in another. For example, a youth with a learning disability can be placed in a special environment and provided with beneficial learning techniques.

Sociobiologists charge that traditional criminologists ignore the biological basis for human behavior. Sociologically trained criminologists disregard all the advances made in the sciences of biology and experimental psychology. Furthermore, traditional criminologists seem content to study reports of behavior, either through surveys or self-reports rather than to observe the actual human behaviors they are allegedly concerned with.[34]

Sociobiology theory has a number of key principles. First, it rejects the traditional assumptions that all humans are born with equal potential to learn and achieve (equipotentiality) and that thereafter their behavior is controlled by social forces. While traditional criminologists suggest (either explicitly or implicitly) that all people are born equal and their parents, schools, neighborhoods, and friends control their subsequent development, sociobiologists argue that no two people (with rare exceptions such as identical twins) are alike and that the combination of human genetic traits and the environment produces individual behavior patterns.

A second critical focus of sociobiology is its position on learning. All social behavior, including criminal behavior, is learned. Each individual organism is believed to have a unique potential for learning. The physical and social environment interact to either limit or enhance an organism's capacity for learning. People learn through a process involving the brain and central nervous system. Learning is not controlled by social interactions but by biochemistry and cellular interaction. Learning can occur only if there are physical changes in the brain. In Highlight 4–5, C. Ray Jeffrey, a leading proponent of the sociobiological approach, provides a model to explain behavior.

Highlight 4–5. Jeffrey on Sociobiology.

Genetic Code $\times$ Environment = Brain Code $\times$ Environment = BEHAVIOR Genetic codes and brain codes are of a biochemical nature, involving the biochemical structure of genes and of neutral transmission in the brain. The type of behavior (response) exhibited by an organism depends on the nature of the environment (stimulus) and the way in which the stimulus is coded, transmitted, and decoded by the brain and nervous system. . . .

We do not inherit behavior any more than we inherit height or intelligence. We do inherit a capacity for interaction with the environment. Sociopathy and alcoholism are not inherited, but a biochemical preparedness for such behaviors is present in the brain which, if given a certain type of environment, will produce sociopathy or alcoholism.

Source: C. R. Jeffrey, "Criminology as an Interdisciplinary Behavioral Science," *Criminology* 16 (1978): 161–162.

Finally, sociobiologists are particularly concerned with the biological environment as a means of preventing crime and delinquency. Oscar Newman, for example, has contributed the concept of "defensible space," suggesting that environmental areas can be constructed or modified to prevent criminal activity.[35] In essence, the sociobiological position is that urban design, environmental psychology, and social ecology can be melded to reduce the crime problem.

Sociobiologists have evaluated the biological aspects of criminal and delinquent behavior from many different perspectives, including nervous system damage, brain injuries, epilepsy, blood chemistry, and chromosome error. For example, sociobiologists have examined males who have an xyy chromosome complement (xy is normal). Early indications suggested that men with this trait were aggressive and antisocial, but additional research has called into question the validity of the methodology used in the studies.[36] Today, many researchers believe that there is no relationship between xyy chromosome levels and delinquent behavior. With respect to delinquency, however, two sociobiological perspectives are extremely important—learning disabilities and intelligence (I.Q.). The former will be discussed in Chapter 10, when we evaluate the role that school plays in causing and preventing delinquency. The following sections will discuss the IQ controversy and review its history and current status.

Mental Ability and Delinquency

Since sociobiology is particularly concerned with how people learn, it is not surprising that its advocates have investigated the issue of mental ability (intelligence, or IQ) and its relationship to criminal and delinquent behavior. Although this type of investigation began well before sociobiology theory reached its current prominence, it is especially relevant in today's world.

Alfred Binet produced the first scale of general intelligence in 1905, and social scientists rapidly adopted the testing of mental ability. As designed by Binet and Theodore Simon and subsequently modified for general use, IQ (intelligence quotient) tests measured the ratio between an individual's mental age and chronological age. The higher the IQ score, the brighter the person; the lower the IQ, the more mentally deficient the person was believed to be. A basic assumption of these tests was that intelligence remained constant throughout life, although an individual's store of knowledge could increase.

With the outbreak of World War I, social scientists, in particular L. M. Terman and Arthur Otis, had an opportunity to administer IQ tests on a mass scale.[37] The tests were organized as the Army Alpha Examination and were used to screen recruits and to determine candidates for officer candidate school. In 1916, Terman wrote *Measurement of Intelligence* and helped convince public school systems on the East Coast to use his examinations for pupil classification, guidance, and college admissions.[38] Within five years, IQ test technology became immensely popular. Millions of schoolchildren were given the tests and were tracked by the school systems according to their IQ scores.

Paralleling the use of IQ tests as tracking devices was their use as mechanisms to determine potential delinquent behavior. Early criminologists felt that low intelligence was a major cause of delinquency. If one could determine which individuals had low IQs, one might identify potential delinquents before they committed socially harmful acts.[39] Since social scientists had a captive group of subjects in training schools and penal institutions, studies began to appear that measured the correlation between IQ and crime by testing adjudicated juvenile delinquents. Delinquent juveniles were believed to be inherently substandard in intelligence and thus naturally inclined to commit more crimes than more intelligent persons. Thus, juvenile delinquents were used as a test group around which numerous theories about intelligence were built, leading ultimately to the *nature-nurture* controversy that is still with us today. These concepts are discussed in some detail in the following sections.

NATURE THEORY The nature theory argues that intelligence is largely determined genetically, that ancestry determines IQ scores, and that low intelligence as demonstrated by low IQ is linked to delinquency.

When the newly developed IQ tests were administered to inmates of prisons and juvenile training schools in the first decades of the century, the nature position gained support because a very large proportion of the inmates scored low on the tests. Henry Goddard found in his studies in 1920 that many institutionalized persons were what he considered "feeble-minded" and thus concluded that at least half of all juvenile delinquents were mental defectives.[40] Goddard's results were challenged in 1931, when Edwin Sutherland evaluated IQ studies of criminals and delinquents and noted significant variation in their findings.[41] The discrepancies were believed to reflect refinements in testing methods and scoring rather than differences in the mental ability of criminals.

In 1926, William Healy and Augusta Bronner tested a group of delinquents in Chicago and Boston and found that 37 percent were subnormal in intelligence.[42] They concluded that delinquents were five to ten times more likely to be mentally deficient than normal boys.

In the 1930s and 1940s, a major study was undertaken by Cyril Burt in England that resulted in the establishment of the three-tiered tracking system in the schools.[43] Burt administered IQ tests to groups of identical twins who had been separated at birth and raised in different environments. His results indicated that twins had the same IQs regardless of the conditions under which they were raised. Burt's study strengthened the argument that intelligence was determined by heredity. Recently, Leon Kamin has seriously challenged Burt's data. Kamin found that the correlation between the twins' IQ scores remained remarkably similar in three of Burt's separate studies. Specifically, the results of twenty statistical tests were found to be identical. The odds against this happening are millions to one.[44] Furthermore, Burt's two research assistants, J. Conway and M. Howard, may never actually have existed, calling into question the entire validity of Burt's landmark study.

These and other early studies were embraced as proof that low IQ scores indicated potentially delinquent children and that a correlation existed between innate low intelligence and deviant behavior. IQ tests were believed to measure the inborn genetic makeup of individuals, and many criminologists accepted the predisposition of substandard individuals toward delinquency.

NURTURE THEORY The rise of culturally sensitive explanations of human behavior in the 1930s (see Chapters 5 and 6) led to the *nurture school* of intelligence. This theory states that intelligence must be viewed as partly biological but primarily sociological. Nurture theorists discredit the notion that persons commit crimes because they have low IQ scores. Instead, they postulate that environmental stimulation from parents, relatives, social contacts, schools, peer groups, and innumerable others create a child's IQ level, and that low IQs result from an environment that also encourages delinquent and criminal behavior. Thus, if low IQ scores are recorded among delinquents, it may reflect their cultural background, not their mental ability.

Studies challenging the assumption that persons automatically committed delinquent acts because they had below-average IQs began to appear as early as the 1920s. John Slawson studied 1,543 delinquent boys in New York institutions and compared them with a control group of New York City boys in 1926.[45] Slawson found that although 80 percent of the delinquents achieved lower scores in abstract verbal intelligence, delinquents were about normal in mechanical aptitude and nonverbal intelligence. These results indicated the possibility of cultural bias in portions of the IQ tests. He also found that there was no relationship between the number of arrests, the types of offenses, and IQ. In 1928, Barbara Burks discovered that children of mentally deficient parents could achieve average intelligence scores when placed in foster homes that provided a stimulating environment. This finding cast doubt on the hypothesis that intelligence is linked to heredity.[46] According to a 1935 study by Otto Klineberg, black children who transferred from southern schools to New York City schools showed a considerable increase in IQ levels.[47] These studies called into question the belief that IQ level remained constant throughout a person's life.

Kenneth Eels and his associates found that tests used in the 1950s systematically underestimated the abilities of children of the working class. They argued that traditional intelligence tests predict who will succeed in a school system that makes use of abstract ideas and experiences that only middle-class children are likely to have: "There are reasoning abilities in the lower class that schooling could capitalize on if it were redesigned to be less verbal and culture-laden."[48] Robert Rosenthal and Lenore Jacobsen, in *Pygmalion in the Classroom,* further debunked the notion that academic success and IQ scores were linked.[49] They handed teachers in California schools a list of pupils who supposedly had shown exceptional promise on a test but who had in fact been picked at random. When these "labeled" children were later reported to be exceptional academic performers, the use of IQ tests as predictors was called into question. Environment, in the form of teacher expectations and support, seemed to be more significant than native intelligence. Unfortunately, most scholars have rejected *Pygmalion*'s results because the study, as one critic put it, "is so defective technically that one can only regret that it ever got beyond the eyes of the original investigators."[50] Gradually, IQ scores have been accepted as tools to measure the degree to which an individual's intelligence developed environmentally according to traditional middle-class values.

The use of IQ tests to predict potential delinquents fell into disfavor throughout the 1960s. Social scientists recognized low IQ scores as one of many variables that could potentially contribute to delinquency and recommended social rehabilitation such as preschool programs to eliminate the IQ gap between lower- and middle-class youths. Compensatory education, with its emphasis on improving the learning environment of intellectually deprived children, was designed and implemented. The notion that intelligence was determined by heredity was discarded in favor of the idea that environment determined how bright a child could become.

RECENT IQ RESEARCH: NATURE THEORY RETURNS The contention that IQ scores are strongly related to delinquency has received recent support from Travis Hirschi and Michael Hindelang.[51] After reexamining a number of important research studies, Hirschi's own 1969 effort (see Chapter 5), the 1972 work of Marvin Wolfgang et al. (see Chapter 2), and research conducted in 1973 by Joseph Weis,[52] Hirschi and Hindelang conclude that "the weight of evidence is that IQ is more important than race and social class" for predicting delinquent involvement.[53] Furthermore, they reject the notion that IQ tests are race- and class-biased (favoring middle-class whites) and therefore invalid. They find major differences between delinquents and nondelinquents within *similar racial and socioeconomic class* categories. Their major contention is that low IQ increases the likelihood of delinquent behavior through its effect on school performance. That is, youths with low IQs do poorly in school, and school failure and academic incompetence are highly related to delinquency.

Thus, in the 1970s and the 1980s, attributing low IQ and delinquent behavior to genetics has once again gained support. The debate is no longer over whether heredity or environment causes low IQ but over which factor is proportionally more important and to what degree the proportions can be measured. The debate takes the following form:

1. Delinquents are generally poor academic achievers.
2. IQ scores are useful for predicting academic success.
3. Black children nationally score lower on IQ tests and perform less well in school.
4. A disproportionate number of adjudicated delinquents are black.
5. IQ scores are therefore accurate instruments to predict delinquency.
6. Blacks in particular are genetically inferior as illustrated by the failure of compensatory education programs to raise their IQ scores and prevent them from becoming juvenile delinquents.

The new heredity theorists, particularly Arthur Jensen and Richard Herrnstein, argue that genetic factors account for much of the variability in intelligence as measured by standard IQ scores, and environmental factors account for little.[54] Jensen argues that race is the key to IQ differences; Herrnstein believes that social class is the determining factor. Both agree that the observable gap in intelligence between blacks and whites and lower- and middle-class groups will remain fixed as long as the environmental conditions with which heredity interacts do not change. Thus, although both men believe that intelligence has a genetic basis, this does not preclude the influence of environmental factors. They believe further that making conditions wholesome and uniform for everyone will, over the course of generations, change the gene pool and make the distribution of inherited characteristics more equitable. Similarly, they argue that if cultural environment does not change, nothing but heredity or luck can influence the social status of the underprivileged. Blacks and the poor suffer more malnutrition, more premature births, more brain-damaged children, and more of the other environmental factors that produce children with lower intelligence. The hereditary theorists argue that unless conditions change, such factors will continue to affect the gene pool and low intelligence will continue to be transmitted from generation to generation.

Recently, however, a number of social scientists have countered arguments based on heredity. In their study of black children adopted by white families, Sandra Scarr and Richard Weinberg found that social environment plays the dominant role in determining the average IQ level of the black children.[55] Black adoptees scored as highly on IQ tests as white adoptees in other studies. They conclude, "The dramatic increase in the IQ mean and the additional finding that placement and adoptive family characteristics account for a major portion of the IQ differences . . . suggest that the IQ score of these children is malleable."[56] Thus, while the nature-heredity view of IQ has received recent support, there is no clear-cut evidence that either position is totally acceptable.

ANALYSIS OF MENTAL ABILITY THEORIES   Whether one accepts the nature-heredity or nurture-environmental arguments about the origins of intelligence, the fact remains that juvenile delinquents quite often score poorly on standard IQ tests. As a result, these exams continue to be used to screen children who fail to conform to the traditional middle-class values of academic success and high intelligence. Society views children with low IQ scores as potentially disruptive persons who have neither the capability nor the opportunity to support the system. The belief that low intelligence results in delinquent behavior is still with us, as is illustrated by the continued development of IQ tests claiming to predict potential juvenile delinquents. A great deal of federal money has been distributed to school systems and juvenile institutions for research to find the IQ test that will pinpoint young criminals. Gradually, social scientists had come to recognize intelligence as one of a multitude of variables in the causes of crime. The rebirth of heredity theories under the rubric of sociobiology indicates that the search for a link between genetics, socialization, and intelligence is still alive.

Psychological Theories of Delinquency

Psychological theories of delinquency hold that elements of the personality cause deviant modes of behavior. The clinical personality approach maintains that most delinquency is actually an abnormal behavior pattern caused by psychological maladjustment. Delinquent youths are viewed as neurotic (dominated by feelings of anxiety, compulsive behavior, and obsessional thoughts), psychotic (suffering severe behavior disorder), sociopathic (asocial, aggressive, impulsive, lacking guilt feelings), and schizophrenic (emotionally unstable and disordered, confused, disassociated). Youths suffering from emotional disorders are believed to engage in delinquent behaviors in order to satisfy some unconscious personality need. Their behaviors, therefore, can be controlled only by treating the symptoms of their abnormality.

Behaviorism is another major branch of psychological theory. Behaviorists believe that children learn behavior through childhood experiences and training. Youths become delinquent because they have not learned to respond in appropriate ways to everyday events. Advocates of the behaviorist approach stress such issues as social learning, modeling, and positive and negative reinforcers. They attempt to identify the relationship of these factors to delinquent behavior.

The following section will briefly examine the history of the psychological approach to delinquency, focusing on the work of Henry Maudsley and Sigmund Freud. Next, it will review a few currently popular psychological theories that can be applied to delinquency. Finally, the section will evaluate personality testing as a means of determining the delinquency-proneness of youth.

HEREDITARY INSANITY: HENRY MAUDSLEY The first psychological theories suggested that mental illness and insanity were inherited and that deviants were inherently mentally damaged by reason of their inferior genetic makeup.

One of the earlier pioneers of the concept of insanity was the English physician, Henry Maudsley (1835–1918).[57] Maudsley believed that insanity and delinquent behavior were strongly linked: "Crime is a sort of outlet in which their unsound tendencies are discharged; they would go mad if they were not animals, and they do not go mad because they are criminals."[58]

Maudsley was a firm believer that delinquency-producing mental traits were inherited, leading to long lines of crime-prone *mental degenerates*. He stated that children who become juvenile criminals do not have the "aptitude of the higher industrial classes" and that they are "deficient in the power of attention . . . have bad memories and make slow progress in learning."[59] Furthermore, Maudsley found delinquents to be "inherently vicious," to "steal and lie with a skill hard to believe," to be "hopeless pupils," and to come from "families in which insanity or some allied neuroses prevailed."[60] In sum, Maudsley believed insanity to be a condition passed from one generation to the next that rendered the affected incapable of controlling their aggressive behavior.

SIGMUND FREUD Psychological explanations of delinquency took a great step forward with the revolutionary work of Sigmund Freud, which still influences psychological thinking today.[61]

Briefly, Freud argues that the human personality contains three major components. The id is the unrestrained, primitive, pleasure-seeking component with which each child is born. The ego develops through the reality of living in the world and helps manage and restrain the id's need for immediate gratification. The superego develops through interactions with parents and other significant people and represents the development of conscience and the moral rules that are shared by most adults.

Freud suggests that unconscious motivations for behavior come from the id's action to account for two primal needs—sex and aggression. Human behavior is often marked by symbolic actions that reflect hidden feelings about these needs. For example, stealing a car may reflect a person's unconscious need for shelter and mobility to escape from hostile enemies (aggression) or perhaps an urge to enter a closed, dark, womb-like structure that reflects the earliest memories (sex).

All three segments of the personality are in simultaneous operation. The id dictates needs and desires; the superego counteracts the id by fostering feelings of morality and righteousness, and the ego evaluates the reality of a position between these two extremes. If these components are properly balanced, the individual can lead a normal life. If, however, one aspect of the personality becomes dominant at the expense of the others, the individual exhibits neurotic or even psychotic personality traits.

Freud also suggests that every person goes through a series of life stages that shape the personality. The first, experienced by the newborn infant, is the *oral stage*. This period is marked by receiving pleasure through eating, sucking, and chewing. In the second, the *anal stage*, occurring between one and three years of age, urinary and bowel movements replace sucking as a major source of pleasure. During this period, toilet training occurs, and for the first time, pressure is put on the child to conform to social rules.

The third influential stage is the *phallic,* in which children from ages three to six receive pleasure from fondling their genitals. During this period, the male child develops great unconscious feelings for his mother (Oedipus complex) and the female child for her father (Electra complex). Freud also identifies two later stages, genital and latency, but these are considered less important for human development since, for all intents and purposes, the personality is formed by age five.

Any trauma that occurs during any of these early life stages may have a lasting effect on the child's personality. For example, premature weaning during the oral stage may cause an individual to be fixated on oral pastimes such as smoking cigarettes and drinking alcohol. If toilet training is a frightening or frustrating experience, the child's superego may be damaged, and sometimes a sadistic and cruel anal personality will develop.

Furthermore, Freudian theory suggests that an imbalance in personality traits caused by a traumatic early childhood can produce a damaged adolescent personality. That is, deep-rooted problems developed early in childhood will cause long-term psychological problems. For example, if neglectful parents fail to develop a child's superego adequately, the id may become the predominate personality force. Later, the youth may demand immediate gratification, may lack compassion and sensitivity for the needs of others, may disassociate feelings, may act aggressively and impulsively, and may demonstrate other psychotic symptoms. As a result, delinquent activity may become an outlet for violent and antisocial feelings. Thus, to explain violent behavior, Freudian thought focuses on traumas developed during early developmental stages and the resulting personality imbalances.

Today, many clinical psychiatrists still recognize Freud's concepts as valid explanations of human behavior. Delinquency behavior can be viewed as impulsive acts filled with symbolic, unconscious motivation. A gun or knife is a penis substitute, drinking and drug use are substitutes for inadequate breast-feeding, and so on.[62]

LEGACY OF PSYCHOLOGICAL THEORY   Today, psychological theories are still used to identify the causes of individual delinquency and to plan treatments. It is beyond the scope of this text to discuss all the notable contributions of leading psychologists and psychiatrists, but a few of the most well-known clinicians and behaviorists whose work has been used to treat delinquents are mentioned below.

Hans Eysenck   Eysenck's theory of behavior posits three personality dimensions: extroversion (E), neuroticism (N), and psychoticism (P).[63] Highly extroverted people are sociable, active, optimistic, outgoing, and impulsive. (The opposite of the extrovert is the introvert, who has opposite characteristics.) The highly neurotic person is subject to mood swings, is overly sensitive, easily hurt, anxious, restless, and rigid. (The opposite of the neurotic is the stable individual.) Psychotics are likely to be solitary individuals who do not fit in well with others, are hostile, insensitive, and so on. Eysenck believes that these personality types may have a biological basis.

According to Eysenck, early childhood learning experiences condition human behavior, most notably the reaction to parental withdrawal of love and affection for misbehavior (as opposed to learning conditioned by physical discipline). Eysenck suggests that those with highly extroverted personalities are unlikely to learn proper socialization responses since they respond less well to conditioning. In a similar vein, people with highly neurotic personalities have trouble learning and are therefore likely to violate social rules and norms. People with psychotic traits are also likely to be offenders. Eysenck views the stable introvert as the least likely to become delinquent or criminal.

Numerous studies have attempted to test Eysenck's theoretical model, usually employing self-report surveys containing scales designed to measure E, N, and P. Although many of these studies show a consistently significant relationship between high scores on these three personality measures and criminal behavior, Eysenck's theory has not received sufficient experimental support to warrant its unqualified acceptance.

Jean Piaget   Piaget developed a theory holding that human action and behavior evolves through distinct stages of moral development.[64] They include egocentrism (ages two to seven), in which children see themselves as the center of all attention; concrete operations (seven to adolescence), in which children learn to relate discrete events to one another; and cognitive operations (adolescence and beyond), in which children's thinking becomes formalized and more abstract. In this final stage, children must learn to master abstract moral values to adjust to society successfully. Young children develop a sense of justice, and as they mature, they begin to relate punishment to the damage their acts have caused others. Piaget's work is not directly related to delinquency, but it is clear that improper moral development in children can lead to behavior transgressions in adults.

Lawrence Kohlberg   Kohlberg's theory of moral development projects the following six stages of personal growth:
A. The premoral period
Stage 1. Moral behavior is largely predicated on the basis of avoiding punishment.
Stage 2. The hedonistic stage. Each person seeks the maximum return to himself largely irrespective of the return to the other.
B. The period of conventional conformity to rules.
Stage 3. Persons conform and adjust to others.
Stage 4. There is respect for a duty to authority, such as social and religious authority, and an avoidance of censure by authority.
C. The morality of self-accepted principles. The period of autonomy.
Stage 5. The primacy of contracts, individual rights, democratically derived and self-accepted principles and laws.
Stage 6. The full development of a morality of individual and universal principles which may transcend those of the existing legal systems (e.g., the concept of an "illegal military order," such as to shoot women and children).[65]

According to Kohlberg, youths at the premoral stage refrain from delinquent behavior because they are afraid of the consequences. At the conventional-conformity stage, youths refrain because they obey legal rules. At the period of autonomy they refrain because they believe delinquent behavior is morally wrong and someone can get hurt. Using a Kohlberg's analysis involves helping deviant youth learn the value of stage six development and make mature behavior decisions that consider the rights of others.

Erik Erikson   Erikson's work also focuses on the various life stages through which people pass.[66] Unique psychological processes mark each stage. Erikson's stages of youth include infancy, early childhood, childhood, school age, and adolescence. When transitions are not smooth, the individual may experience an "identity crisis." Highlight 4–6 presents Erikson's application of this concept to delinquency.

Highlight 4-6. Erik Erikson on the Psychology of Delinquency.

On a somewhat larger scale, an analogous turn toward a negative identity prevails in the delinquent (addictive, homosexual) youth of your larger cities, where conditions of economic, ethnic and religious marginality provide poor bases for any kind of positive identity. If such "negative identities" are accepted as a youth's "natural" and final identity by teachers, judges, and psychiatrists, he not infrequently invests his pride as well as his need for total orientation in becoming exactly what the careless community expects him to become.

Similarly, many young Americans from marginal and authoritarian backgrounds find temporary refuge in radical groups in which an otherwise unmanageable rebellion-and-confusion receives the stamp of universal righteousness within a black-and-white ideology. Some, of course, "mean it," but many are merely drifting into such association.

... Schizoids and delinquents have in common a mistrust of themselves, a disbelief in the possibility that they could ever complete anything of value. This, of course, is especially marked in those who, for some reason or other, do not feel that they are partaking of the technological identity of their time. The reason may be that their own gifts have not found contact with the productive aims of the machine age or that they themselves belong to a social class (here "upper-upper" is remarkably equal to "lower-lower") that does not partake of the stream of progress.

Source: Erik Erikson, *Identity, Youth and Crisis* (New York: Norton, 1968), pp. 88 and 185.

Albert Bandura　　Albert Bandura is a well-known learning theorist who has specialized in delinquent behavior. Like most learning theorists, he views all behavior as the product of a reaction to a stimulus. The key issue in delinquency is learning illegal behavior patterns, not developing unconscious personality traits or life stages.[67]

Simply put, learning theorists such as Bandura suggest that people learn through being subjected to positive (reward) or negative (punishment) reinforcements. They also learn if their behavior is ignored, which can lead to its extinction. For example, if a young child exhibits an undesirable behavior such as biting, his parents can attempt to stop it by the negative reinforcement of slapping. Parents may also positively reward with a treat if a child goes a whole day without biting anyone. Finally, they can ignore the biting entirely and hope that it stops (extinction). Unfortunately, this relationship is not as simple as it seems. For example, the biting may actually be a means of getting parental attention, and punishing the child has the hidden reward of gaining the desired attention.

Learning theorists also suggest that people learn by *modeling* their behavior after others and imitating them. Thus, aggressive and destructive children may have repeatedly seen their parents acting that way themselves. Furthermore, modeling interacts with reinforcements to produce behavior. For example, a boy with a tough, aggressive father who rewards him with parental approval for being tough, violent, and brave will be likely to continue to employ aggressive behavior in all aspects of his life.

Using a learning approach, Bandura suggests that delinquent behavior can be extinguished if the punishments given delinquents outweigh the benefits they receive from their activities and if legitimate opportunities are opened up to increase the behavior options of delinquents so that they are not limited to antisocial behavior. Punishment alone, no matter how severe, is not enough to extinguish delinquency unless legitimate behavior opportunities are supplied.

PERSONALITY TESTING AND DELINQUENCY　　In the early history of clinical psychology and psychiatry human personality was evaluated through techniques that have become universally familiar because of their frequent portrayal in television, movies, and theater. A patient would relax on a couch and then discuss with a therapist his or her problems, fears, anxieties, and life history in a process called free association. The clinician would then make inferences about the nature of the client's personality and problems. Patterns would emerge that could be classified into various personality syndromes such as neuroses, paranoia, schizophrenia, hypochondria, and so on. Personality traits could then be related to behaviors such as delinquency.

The clinical process is time-consuming and consequently quite expensive. Therefore, psychiatrists and psychologists have developed *personality tests* designed to measure and analyze human personality traits quickly and efficiently. Personality tests have become a significant tool in the effort to derive a psychological profile of the delinquent.

Two types of personality tests predominate in the evaluation of the delinquent personality—projective techniques and personality inventories. Projective techniques require a subject to react to an ambiguous picture or shape by describing what it represents or by telling a story about it. The Rorschach Inkblot Test and the Thematic Apperception Test (TAT) are examples of two widely used projective tests.[68] Projective tests are given by clinicians trained to interpret client responses and categorize them according to established behavioral patterns. However, such tests must be given individually by highly trained clinicians, and the analysis of responses is sometimes subject to individual interpretation.

The second frequently used method of psychological testing is the personality inventory. These tests require subjects to agree or disagree with groups of questions in a self-administered survey. Survey items are designed to measure specific personality traits. Answers on individual items are then grouped into personality scales. Subjects receive scale scores based on their answers. Questions are usually vague so that subjects cannot guess their true intent and meaning. Scale items might include such ambiguous questions as: "Sometimes I wake up cold and frightened," "Loud noises scare me," and "I like mechanics magazines." Psychologists suggest that the way subjects answer these questions can be used to determine personality traits such as hypochondria, schizophrenia, and so on. Personality inventories are widely used because they measure a large variety of personality characteristics, are easily and uniformly administered, and can be scored by nonprofessionals. However, they have some limitations. It is uncertain why subjects answer particular questions the way they do. For example, subjects may deliberately try to give what they believe to be socially acceptable answers rather than tell the truth. Also, there is some question about the validity of subscales. For example, is it certain that a scale proporting to measure schizophrenia actually does so?

The most widely used psychological test is the Minnesota Multiphasic Personality Inventory, commonly called the MMPI.[69] Developed by R. Starke Hathaway and J. Charnley McKinley, the MMPI has subscales that purport to measure many different personality traits, including Psychopathic Deviation (Pd scale), Schizophrenia (Sc), and Hypomania (overactivity, Ma).

Elio Monachesi and R. Starke Hathaway pioneered the use of the MMPI to predict delinquent behavior.[70] They concluded that scores on some of the MMPI subscales, especially the Pd scale, predicted delinquency. In one major effort, they administered the MMPI to a sample of ninth grade boys and girls in Minneapolis and found that Pd scores had a significant relationship to later delinquent involvement.[71] Similar studies have been conducted by Hathaway, Monachesi, Lawrence Young, Dora Capwell, and (more recently) Michael Hindelang, Joseph Weis, and Spencer Rathus and Larry Siegel.[72]

Despite the time and energy put into using MMPI scales to predict delinquency, the results have proved inconclusive. Two surveys of the literature of personality testing, one by Karl Schuessler and Donald Cressey (covering the pre-1950 period) and the other by Gordon Waldo and Simon Dinitz (covering 1950–1965), found little evidence that personality traits could indeed predict delinquent involvement.[73]

In a recent study by Spencer Rathus and Larry Siegel, the exaggeration of the subjects significantly affected the relationship between delinquent behavior and MMPI scale scores.[74] By controlling for subject lying and exaggeration with scales built in to the MMPI, Rathus and Siegel found that the relationship between self-reported delinquent behavior and the schizophrenia subscale of the MMPI was completely eliminated, and the relationship between delinquency and psychopathic deviation and hypomania was significantly reduced.

EVALUATION OF PSYCHOLOGICAL THEORIES   Psychological theories can help explain the behavior of deeply disturbed, impulsive, or destructive youth. However, they are limited as general explanations of delinquency. For one thing, the phenomenon of juvenile delinquency is so widespread that to claim that all delinquents are psychologically disturbed is to make that claim against a vast majority of American youth.

Second, the relationship between personality tests and delinquent behavior has not been established, and this has done little to increase the credibility of psychological theory. Even when psychologists find that a large percentage of court-adjudicated youths suffer from personality problems, these young people represent only a small sample of the delinquent population (those who have been caught). It is conceivable that their emotional problems actually compelled them to desire apprehension and subsequent punishment. Or perhaps the shock of capture by police is so great that it causes abnormal behavior symptoms to develop. Most theory on the psychological basis of crime has been developed with research conducted with known criminals. Therefore, it cannot satisfy the need of a true theory to predict future behavior.

Psychological theories cannot explain why crime and delinquency rates vary. If we assume that official statistics have some validity, how can we explain the fact that some environments have higher crime rates than others? Is it possible that more psychological abnormality exists in a large city than in a middle-class suburb?

CRITIQUE OF INDIVIDUALISTIC THEORIES

What are the drawbacks to individualistic theory? Three drawbacks to individualistic theories stand out prominently. First, empirical research has not supported individualistic models to the extent that they can be used to predict future delinquent behavior accurately. This is quite important. For example, if we find that individual condition X is related to delinquency, we cannot be sure that all youths who experience X will eventually become delinquent. Even if 70 percent of those with X are delinquent, how can we account for the 30 percent who still remain law-abiding and stable?

Second, individualistic theories have difficulty accounting for the fact that most delinquents do not become adult criminals. As self-report studies show, almost all youths commit some delinquent acts. If individual abnormality causes crime, how can we account for delinquents who stop breaking the law when they become adults? Can we suggest that the abnormality simply went away?

Finally, many criminal acts seem "normal" responses to social conditions. People steal when they are hungry and fight to relieve social frustration. These seem to be reactions of almost anyone experiencing oppressive and unchanging social conditions. It seems too simple to classify delinquent youths as "abnormal" rather than to recognize the social conditions that may have caused their behavior. On the other hand, psychologically based theories have potential merit as explanations of the fact that, given the same set of social circumstances, one youth becomes a delinquent while another rejects antisocial behavior.

CHAPTER SUMMARY

Individualistic theories of delinquency focus on the personal characteristics of offenders as the cause of antisocial behavior.

Classical theory assumes the existence of free will and views crime as a matter of choice for all people. Laws and punishments deter most people from committing illegal acts. Classical theorists believe that increasing punishment will reduce crime.

Biological determinism suggests that delinquents have physical traits that cause their antisocial behavior. These traits include particularly their body builds, genetic code, chemical balance, and so on. A recent trend, sociobiology theory, argues that the interaction of human biology and the social environment determines the learning of acceptable or unacceptable behavior responses. One key issue in sociobiology is human intelligence, which is currently measured with IQ tests. There is considerable controversy over whether a relationship exists between IQ level and delinquency and whether the basis of this relationship is heredity or environment.

A third form of individualistic theory is psychologically based. It alleges that offenders have chronically abnormal personalities or suffer impaired development. Personality tests have been used to link personality traits with delinquency, but once again the results have been inconclusive.

Individualistic theories seem to have potential merit as explanations of delinquency since they are directed at answering the perplexing question: Why, given the same set of social circumstances, does one youth become a delinquent while another one works hard, obeys rules, and becomes a productive member of the community? None of the socially based theories to be discussed in the following chapter answer this question accurately. Even if we know that 80 percent of the youths in a community commit crime, we are still not sure why the other 20 percent do not. This is the single greatest flaw in sociological theories. With few exceptions, they are theories of delinquency *rate*, not delinquency *cause*.

DISCUSSION QUESTIONS

1. Is there such a thing as the "criminal man"?
2. Is crime psychologically abnormal? Can there be "normal" crimes?
3. Apply Freud's theory to such delinquent acts as shoplifting and breaking and entering a house?

SUGGESTED READINGS

Eysenck, Hans. Crime and Personality. 3d ed. London: Routledge and Kegan Paul, 1977.

Feldman, M. P. Criminal Behavior: A Psychological Analysis. New York: Wiley, 1977.

Hare, R. D., and Schalling, S. Psychopathic Behavior. New York: Wiley, 1978.

Hindelang, Michael. "The Relationship of Self-Reported Delinquency to Scales of the CPI and MMPI." Journal of Criminal Law, Criminology, and Police Science 63 (1972): 75–81.

Jeffrey, C. Ray. Crime Prevention through Environmental Design. Rev. ed. Beverly Hills, Calif.: Sage Publications, 1977.

Jeffrey, C. Ray, ed. Biology and Crime. Beverly Hills, Calif.: Sage Publications, 1979.

Lewis, D. O., and Balla, D. A. Delinquency and Psychopathology. New York: Grune and Stratton, 1976.

Van Den Berghe, P. V. Man in Society: A Biosocial View. New York: Elsevier, 1978.

Wilson, E. O. Sociobiology: The New Synthesis. Cambridge, Mass.: Harvard University Press, 1975.

REFERENCES

1. See, for example, Fred Kerlinger, Foundations of Behavioral Research, 2d ed. (New York: Holt, Rinehart and Winston, 1973), chaps. 1 and 2.

2. See Graeme Newman, The Punishment Response (New York: Lippincott, 1978).

3. See Elio Monachesi, "Cesare Beccaria," in Pioneers in Criminology, ed. Herman Mannheim (Montclair, N.J.: Patterson Smith, 1972), pp. 36–49.

4. Ibid., p. 40.

5. Ibid., p. 44.

6. Ibid., p. 39.

7. Ibid., pp. 43–45.

8. Ibid., pp. 45–46.

9. See, for example, Coleman Philipson, Three Criminal Law Reformers: Beccaria, Bentham, Romilly, reprint ed. (Montclair, N.J.: Patterson Smith, 1970).

10. Jeremy Bentham, An Introduction to the Principles of Morals and Legislation (New York: Hafner, 1948), p. 2.

11. James Q. Wilson, Thinking about Crime (New York: Vintage, 1977).

12. See, for example, Ernest van den Haag, Punishing Criminals: Concerning a Very Old and Painful Question (New York: Basic Books, 1975).

13. For a discussion of increased penalties for youth, see Wilson, Thinking about Crime, pp. 58–59.

14. Marvin Wolfgang, "Cesare Lombroso," in *Pioneers in Criminology*, ed. Herman Mannheim (Montclair, N.J.: Patterson Smith, 1970), pp. 232–271.

15. Edwin Driver, "Charles Buckman Goring," in Mannheim, ed., *Pioneers in Criminology*, pp. 429–442.

16. Charles Goring, *The English Convict: A Statistical Study, 1913* (Montclair, N.J.: Patterson Smith, 1972).

17. Driver, "Charles Buckman Goring," pp. 434–435.

18. Ibid., p. 440.

19. See, generally, Francis Allen, "Raffaele Garofalo," in Mannheim, ed., *Pioneers in Criminology*, pp. 318–339.

20. Raffaele Garofalo, *Criminology*, trans. Robert Miller (Montclair, N.J.: Patterson Smith, 1968), p. 71.

21. Ibid., p. 67.

22. Ibid., p. 79.

23. Ibid., p. 95.

24. See, generally, Thorsten Sellin, "Enrico Ferri," in Mannheim, ed., *Pioneers in Criminology*, pp. 361–384.

25. Stephen Schafer and Richard Knudten, *Juvenile Delinquency* (New York: Random House, 1970), p. 57.

26. These studies are described in Stephen Schafer, *Introduction to Criminology* (Reston, Va.: Reston Publishing, 1976), pp. 60–61.

27. Later in this chapter we will discuss a modern variation of heredity—sociobiology.

28. Cited in Schafer and Knudten, *Juvenile Delinquency*, p. 63.

29. William Sheldon, *Varieties of Delinquent Youth* (New York: Harper & Bros., 1949).

30. Sheldon Glueck and Eleanor Glueck, *Of Delinquency and Crime* (Springfield, Ill.: Charles C Thomas, 1974), p. 2.

31. Ibid., p. 73.

32. B. R. McCandless, W. S. Persons, and A. Roberts, "Perceived Opportunity, Delinquency, Race and Body Build among Delinquent Youth," *Journal of Consulting and Clinical Psychology* 38 (1972): 281.

33. See, generally, L. Hippchen, *The Ecologic-Biochemical Approaches to Treatment of Delinquents and Criminals* (New York: Van Nostrand Reinhold, 1978).

34. See C. R. Jeffrey, "Criminology as an Interdisciplinary Behavioral Science," *Criminology* 16 (1978): 149–167.

35. Oscar Newman, *Defensible Space* (New York: Macmillan, 1972).

36. S. Mednick and K. O. Christiansen, *Biosocial Bases of Criminal Behavior* (New York: Gardner, 1977). For studies of aggression, see Edwin Magargree, "The Production of Dangerous Behavior," *Criminal Justice and Behavior* 1 (1976): 3–21; Stephen Van Dine, Simon Dinitz, and John Conrad, "The Incapacitation of the Dangerous Offender: A Statistical Experiment," *Journal of Research in Crime and Delinquency* 14 (1977): 22–34.

37. L. M. Terman, "Research on the Diagnosis of Pre-Delinquent Tendencies," *Journal of Delinquency* 9 (1925): 124–130.

38. L. M. Terman, *Measurement of Intelligence* (Boston, Mass: Houghton-Mifflin, (1916).

39. For example, see M. G. Caldwell, "The Intelligence of Delinquent Boys Committed to Wisconsin Industrial School," *Journal of Criminal Law and Criminology* 20 (1929): 421–428; and C. Murcheson, *Criminal Intelligence* (Worcester, Mass.: Clark University, 1926), pp. 41–44.

40. Henry Goddard, *Efficiency and Levels of Intelligence* (Princeton, N.J.: Princeton University Press, 1920).

41. Edwin Sutherland, "Mental Deficiency and Crime," in *Social Attitudes*, ed. Kimball Young (New York: Henry Holt, 1973), chap. 15.

42. William Healy and Augusta Bronner, *Delinquency and Criminals: Their Making and Unmaking* (New York: Macmillan, 1926).

43. See, for example, Cyril Burt, "Evidence for the Concept of Intelligence," *British Journal of Educational Psychology* 25 (1955): 1; and C. C. Brigham, "Intelligence Tests of Immigrant Groups," *Psychological Review* 37 (1930): 158–165.

44. See J. Gaylin, "I.Q. and Heredity: Fraud?" *Science* 6 (1977): 194.

45. John Slawson, *The Delinquent Boys* (Boston: Budget Press, 1926).

46. Barbara Burks, "The Relative Influence of Nature and Nurture upon Mental Development," *Yearbook, National Society for the Study of Education*, Part I, 1928.

47. Otto Klineberg, *Negro Intelligence and Selective Migrations* (New York: Columbia University Press, 1935).

48. K. Eels et al., *Intelligence and Cultural Differences* (Chicago: University of Chicago Press, 1951), p. 181.

49. Robert Rosenthal and Lenore Jacobsen, *Pygmalion in the Classroom* (New York: Holt, 1968).

50. R. L. Thorndike, "revue of *Pygmalion in the Classroom*, by R. Rosenthal and L. Jacobson," *American Educational Research Journal* 5 (1968): 708.

51. Travis Hirschi and Michael Hindelang, "Intelligence and Delinquency: A Revisionist Review," *American Sociological Review* 42 (1977): 471-586.

52. Joseph Weis, "Delinquency among the Well-to-do" (Ph.D. Diss., University of California, Berkeley, 1973).

53. Hirschi and Hindelang, "Intelligence and Delinquency," p. 577.

54. See, generally, Arthur Jensen, *Bias in Mental Testing* (New York. Free Press, 1979). See also A. Jensen, "How Much Can We Boost IQ and Scholastic Achievement?" *Harvard Educational Review* 39 (1969): 1-123.

55. Sandra Scarr and Richard Weinberg, "I.Q. Test Performance of Black Children Adopted by White Families," *American Psychologist* 31 (1976): 726–739.

56. Ibid., p. 737.

57. See, generally, Peter Scott, "Henry Maudsley," in Mannheim, ed., *Pioneers in Criminology*, pp. 208–232.

58. Cited in ibid., p. 212.

59. Ibid., p. 227.

60. Ibid.

61. See, generally, Sigmund Freud, *An Outline of Psychoanalysis*, trans. James Strachey (New York: Norton, 1963).

62. Seymour Halleck, *Psychiatry and the Dilemmas of Crime* (Berkeley, Calif.: University of California Press, 1971).

63. See, generally, Hans Eysenck, *Crime and Personality* (London: Routledge and Kegan Paul, 1964); and H. J. Eysenck, "Crime and Personality: An Empirical Study of the Three Factor Theory," *British Journal of Criminology* 10 (1970): 225-227. For an extensive review of Eysenck's work, see N. Philip Feldman, *Criminal Behavior: A Psychological Analysis* (New York: Wiley, 1977), pp. 139–160.

64. See, generally, Jean Piaget, *The Moral Judgment of the Child* (London: Kegan Paul, 1932).

65. Adapted from Feldman, *Criminal Behaviour: A Psychological Analysis*, pp. 34–35.

66. See, generally, Erik Erikson, *Identity, Youth and Crisis* (New York: Norton, 1968).

67. See Albert Bandura and Frances Menlove, "Factors Determining Vicarious Extinction of Avoidance Behavior through Symbolic Modeling," *Journal of Personality and Social Psychology* 8 (1965): 99–108; and Albert Bandura and Richard Walters, *Social Learning and Personality Development* (New York: Holt, Rinehart and Winston, 1963).

68. See, generally, Spencer Rathus, *Psychology* (New York: Holt, Rinehart and Winston, 19), chap. 9.

69. See, for example, S. R. Hathaway and E. D. Monachesi, "The M.M.P.I. in the Study of Juvenile Delinquents," in *Mental Health and Mental Disorder*, ed. A. M. Rose (London: Routledge, . 1956).

70. R. Starke Hathaway and Elio Monachesi, *Analyzing and Predicting Juvenile Delinquency with the M.M.P.I.* (Minneapolis: University of Minnesota Press, 1953).

71. Ibid.

72. S. R. Hathaway, E. D. Monachesi, and Lawrence Young, "Delinquency Rates and Personality," *Journal of Criminal Law, Criminology, and Police Science* 51 (1960): 443–460; Michael Hindelang, "The Relationship of Self-Reported Delinquency to Scales of the CPI and MMPI," *Journal of Criminal Law, Criminology, and Police Science* 63 (1972): 75–81; M. Hindelang and Joseph Weis, "Personality and Self-Reported Delinquency: An Application of Cluster Analysis," *Criminology* 10 (1972): 268; Spencer Rathus and Larry Siegel, "Crime and Personality Revisited: Effects of MMPI Response Sets in Self-Report Studies," *Criminology* (1980, in press); and Dora Capwell, "Personality Patterns of Adolescent Girls," *Journal of Applied Psychology* 29 (1945): 289–300.

73. Karl Schuessler and Donald Cressey, "Personality Characteristics of Criminals," *American Journal of Sociology* 55 (1950): 476–484; Gordon Waldo and Simon Dinitz, "Personality Attributes of the Criminal: An Analysis of Research Studies 1950–1965," *Journal of Research in Crime and Delinquency* 4 (1967): 185–201.

74. Rathus and Siegel, "Crime and Personality Revisited."

Chapter 5

Chapter Outline	Key Terms, Names, and Cases
Introduction	cultural transmission
Cultural Transmission Theory	transitional areas
Strain Theory	lower class focal concerns
Sub-cultural Strain Theory	anomie
Middle-class Delinquency	delinquent subculture
Policy and Social Structure Theory	status frustration
Chapter Summary	middle class measuring rods
	blocked opportunities
	short-run hedonism
	Clifford R. Shaw
	Henry D. McKay
	Walter Miller
	Robert Merton
	Albert K. Cohen
	Rochard Cloward
	Lloyd Ohlin
	Ralph England

Social Structure Theories

INTRODUCTION

This chapter discusses theories that relate delinquent behavior to the social environment in which children live. Social structure theories are linked together because they all attempt to account for the cultural disparities found in official delinquency statistics. They reflect the fact that most official sources of delinquent behavior indicate that lower-class, inner-city youth commit a disproportionate amount of crime. If biological or psychological factors alone could account for delinquency, we would expect a more even distribution of delinquent behavior throughout the social structure (since individual pschological and biological factors are assumed to be normally distributed regardless of socioeconomic class). Since, according to official statistics, delinquency seems preponderant in lower class areas, social structure theorists maintain that forces must be operating in lower-class cultures that account for the relatively high crime and delinquency rates in these areas. Social structure theories suggest that the unique cultural norms, rules, and conditions in lower-class areas are so powerful that they actually influence or even force youths to violate the law.

In the following sections, we will discuss various social structure theories. First, we will review the cultural transmission approach of Clifford Shaw and Henry McKay and the similar work of sociologist Walter R. Miller. We will then turn to a separate branch of the social structure approach, strain theory, as exemplified by the theoretical models of Robert Merton, Albert Cohen, and Richard Cloward and Lloyd Ohlin. Finally, since these various theoretical models relate primarily to urban lower-class delinquency, we will offer a brief analysis of theories of middle-class delinquency.

CULTURAL TRANSMISSION THEORY

Cultural transmission theory is most widely associated with the work of Clifford R. Shaw and his colleague, Henry D. McKay.[1] Later theoretical efforts involving cultural transmission were conducted by sociologist Walter Miller.[2] Simply put, cultural transmission theories suggest that slum youths violate the law because they adhere to the unique, independent value system existing within lower-class areas—a value system that places them in conflict with middle-class norms and rules. Delinquent traditions are believed to be transmitted from one generation of youths to the next; as a result, stable pockets of delinquency are created and maintained.

Clifford Shaw and Henry McKay: Delinquency in Transitional Areas

Clifford Shaw and Henry McKay began their pioneering work on delinquency in Chicago during the early 1920s. This period in the city's history was typical of the transition taking place in many other urban areas. Chicago had experienced a mid-nineteenth century population expansion, fueled by a dramatic influx of foreign-born immigrants and, later, migrating southern black families. Congregating in the central city, the newcomers occupied the oldest housing and therefore faced numerous health and environmental hazards. Physically deteriorating sections of the city soon developed.

This condition prompted the city's wealthy, established citizens to become concerned about the moral fabric of society. There existed the widespread belief that foreign immigrants and blacks were crime-prone and morally dissolute. In fact, local groups were created with the very purpose of "saving" the children of poor families from moral decadence.[3] It was popular to view delinquency as the property of inferior racial and ethnic groups. (See Chapter 13 for a discussion of the childsavers.)

Based in Chicago, Shaw and McKay sought to explain delinquency within the context of the changing urban environment. They rejected the racial and cultural explanations of delinquency then popular and instead viewed the ecological conditions of the city itself as the real culprit in the creation of delinquent behavior. They saw that Chicago had developed into distinct neighborhoods, some marked by wealth and luxury and others by overcrowding, poor health and sanitary conditions, and extreme poverty. These slum areas were believed to be the spawning grounds of delinquency.[4]

Shaw and McKay viewed delinquency as a product of the decaying *transitional neighborhood*, which manifested social disorganization and maintained conflicting values and social systems. In this environment, teenage gangs developed as a means of survival, economic gain, defense, and friendship. Also, gangs maintained a unique set of cultural norms and values that differed sharply from those of the general society. The gang leaders soon recruited younger members into their midst, thus passing on delinquent traditions and ensuring the survival of the gang from one generation to the next. This view of delinquent behavior is known as *cultural transmission*.

MEASURES OF DELINQUENCY   Shaw and McKay collected extensive statistics on delinquency rates in the Chicago area. Included in their data were the records of almost 25,000 alleged delinquents brought before the Juvenile Court of Cook County, Illinois, during the period from 1900 to 1933. A later collection of data updated their survey through 1965. In addition, the researchers evaluated samples of youth committed to correctional schools and boys handled by police-probation officers.

Using this impressive array of data, Shaw and McKay identified the domicile of youthful delinquents in Chicago. They noted that distinct ecological areas had developed in the city, comprising a series of five concentric circles, or zones, and that some of the zones had more delinquent behavior than others. The areas of heaviest delinquency concentration appeared to be the transitional, inner-city zones of the city, where large portions of foreign-born citizens had recently immigrated.[5] The zones that were farthest from the city's center were less prone to delinquency. Analysis of these data indicated a surprisingly stable pattern of delinquent activity in the five ecological zones over a sixty-five-year period.

CAUSES OF DELINQUENCY   Shaw and McKay sought to explain the difference in the delinquency rates of slum and suburban communities through an analysis of the social values and social organization present in local communities. They found that clear-cut differences in social values existed in high and low delinquency areas. Areas with low delinquency rates were marked by "uniformity, consistency, and universality of conventional values and attitudes."[6] These areas followed middle class child-rearing practices and conformed to the legal code. On the other hand, the areas with high delinquency rates were marked by conflicting moral values and powerful attractions to deviant modes of behavior.[7] In these areas, delinquency provided a means for financially deprived youths to gain prestige, economic achievement, and other human satisfactions.[8]

Shaw and McKay viewed parent-child relationships as having an important influence on the development of social values. In zones with low delinquency rates, parents stressed such values as attendance at school, church, and community organizations. In high-rate transitional areas, a diversity of values existed. Some youths were taught to strive for basic middle-class goals; others were exposed to the rackets and illegitimate activities such as theft.[9]

Shaw and McKay concluded that in the transitional neighborhoods, deviant and conventional values compete side by side with one another. Boys exposed to both value systems are often forced to choose between them and consequently may align themselves with groups that share similar ideas and behavior. Thus, the development of teenage law-violating groups and gangs is an essential element of youthful misbehavior in slum areas. (See Chapter 9 for a detailed discussion of gang behavior.)

Because of their deviant values, slum youths often come into conflict with existing middle-class norms, which demand strict obedience to the legal code. Consequently, a value conflict occurs that sets the delinquent boy and his peer group even father apart from conventional society. The result is a fuller acceptance of deviant goals and behavior. Shut out of the "normal" stream of society, neighborhood street gangs become fixed institutions, recruiting new members and passing on delinquent traditions from one generation to the next. (See Highlight 5-1.)

In addition to social values, social organization differentiates high-rate from low-rate delinquency areas. In high-rate sections, conflicting social values help neutralize the benefits of what otherwise would be delinquency-resisting institutions. For example, a close-knit family, which should serve as a buffer against delinquency, actually loses its delinquency-resisting potential. So many families in transitional areas have adult members profiting from illegal activities that family ties can actually encourage delinquency. Even social control and crime prevention agencies, such as schools and community centers, have only limited utility since they are staffed and funded by outsiders who are not trusted by neighborhood residents.

CONCLUSIONS OF SHAW AND McKAY   After extensive analysis of their data, Shaw and McKay reached the following conclusions about ecology and delinquency:

1. Delinquency rates vary widely throughout the city. The probability of adolescents becoming delinquent and getting arrested and later incarcerated depends on their living in one of these high-rate areas.
2. Delinquency is a product of the socialization mechanisms existing within a neighborhood. Unstable neighborhoods have the greatest chance of producing delinquents.
3. High delinquency rates indicate the breakdown of social institutions and of the ability of society to care for and control its citizens.

Highlight 5-1. Shaw and McKay on Cultural Transmission.

From the data available, it appears that local variations in the conduct of children . . . reflect the differences in social values, norms, and attitudes to which the children are exposed. In some parts of the city, attitudes which support and sanction delinquency are . . . sufficiently extensive and dynamic to become the controlling forces in the development of delinquent careers among a relatively large number of boys and young men. . . .

In the low-income areas, where there is the greatest deprivation and frustration, where in the history of the city, immigrant and migrant groups have brought together the widest variety of divergent cultural traditions and institutions, and where there exists the greatest disparity between social values to which the people aspire and the availability of facilities for acquiring these values in conventional ways, the development of crime as an organized way of life is most marked.

Source: Clifford R. Shaw and Henry D. McKay, *Juvenile Delinquency and Urban Areas* (Chicago: University of Chicago Press, 1972), pp. 315–316, 319.

4. Delinquency is not the property of any one ethnic or racial group. Members of any racial or ethnic group will be delinquent if they live in the high-rate areas. Their crime rate will be reduced once they leave these areas.
5. Delinquency rates correlate highly with economic and social conditions such as poverty, poor health, and deteriorated housing.
6. Areas disrupted and in transition are the most likely to produce delinquency. After the transition has ended, a drop in the delinquency rate occurs.
7. Since the community is the major source of delinquency, it is evident that control of delinquency should be community-based.[10]

ANALYSIS OF SHAW AND McKAY   Most prominent among Shaw and McKay's many achievements was their finding that the ecology of the city actually influences delinquents behavior. The Shaw-McKay model replaced the view that delinquents were either biological throwbacks, intellectually impaired individuals, or psychologically damaged youths. Moreover, their research refuted the assumption that delinquency is a property of any one minority or ethnic group.

Since the basis of their theory was that neighborhood disintegration and slum conditions are the primary causes of delinquent behavior, Shaw and McKay paved the way for the many community action and treatment programs developed in the last half century. Shaw himself was the founder of one very influential community-based treatment program, The *Chicago Area Project*, which will be discussed later in this chapter.[11]

Another important feature of Shaw and McKay's work was that it depicted delinquent gang membership as a "normal" response to the adverse social conditions existing in urban slum areas. Their argument seems quite plausible today in light of what we know about delinquent behavior. Delinquent behavior helps provide the social and economic advantages that would otherwise be denied disadvantaged youth. One prominent mechanism for distributing social and financial gain is the delinquent gang, which facilitates illegal activity. Shaw and McKay, and other Chicago-based theorists, such as Frederick Thrasher (see Chapter 9), viewed gang members as neither troubled nor depressed.[12] Their illegal behavior was merely a way of achieving excitement, social success, and financial gain when all other avenues seemed closed. Some questions have been raised about the solidarity and cohesiveness of delinquent gangs, which may not be the close-knit groups that Shaw and McKay suggested they were. But their prevalence and importance in slum areas have been well documented in recent national surveys.[13] Thus, current evidence lends support to the Shaw-McKay view that teenage gangs frequently arise in the deteriorated sections of large cities and provide important outlets for their young members.

Despite these noteworthy achievements, Shaw and McKay's cultural transmission theory ignores a number of important methodological issues. This factor seriously damages the potential value of their theory. Most importantly, their heavy reliance on police and court records undermines the accuracy of the research findings. Many valid reasons exist to question the accuracy of official police and court statistics (see Chapters 2 and 3). Even if accurate, official statistics may merely reflect the current law enforcement practices operating in the city's various ecological zones. That is, a zone's high delinquency rate may be a result of diligent and extensive police surveillance in selected areas of the city and therefore may not reflect actual rates of delinquent activity. Numerous studies indicate that police use extensive discretion when arresting youths and that social status is one factor that influences their decisions.[14] Thus, it is likely that youths in middle-class neighborhoods commit numerous delinquent acts that never show up in official statistics because of police practices in these areas. On the other hand, children in lower-class areas face a far greater chance of arrest and court adjudication.

Shaw and McKay also fail to account for the relatively high delinquency rates that self-report studies have uncovered in suburban areas. Cultural transmission theory suggests that a relatively low delinquency rate exists in these zones. Yet, despite the maintenance of middle-class social values, the studies reviewed in Chapter 3 suggest that suburban youths are as prone to delinquency as youths living in inner-city neighborhoods. Though differences in delinquency rates may, in fact, be a function of law enforcement practices, Shaw and McKay's failure to inspect this issue thoroughly seems a serious oversight.

These criticisms aside, the Shaw-McKay theory provides a valuable addition to our understanding of the causes of delinquent behavior. By introducing a new variable—the ecology of the city—into the study of delinquency, the authors paved the way for a whole generation of criminologists to focus upon the social influences on delinquent behavior.

Miller's Theory of Lower-Class Culture Conflict

Sociologist Walter Miller's theory of lower-class culture conflict is another important attempt to explain the gang activity found in lower-class environments. Instead of viewing delinquency as a psychological aberration or the product of a diseased personality, Miller also portrays delinquent behavior as a "normal" reaction to the norms and values of a unique lower-class culture.[15]

Miller generally takes a cultural transmission approach, but his work differs markedly from that of Shaw and McKay. Most notably, Miller views delinquency as a product of the values and attitudes that are ingrained in all elements of lower-class culture. In contrast, Shaw and McKay suggest, first, that delinquent behavior is a product of the unsupervised youth groups and gangs that form in lower-class areas in order to gain financial and social privileges and, second, that many families in lower-class areas actually espouse middle-class values.[16] Both approaches characterize delinquency as a neighborhood tradition passed down from one generation to the next.

CHARACTERISTICS OF LOWER-CLASS CULTURE Miller studied the daily activities of working-class citizens while conducting a delinquent gang control program in a major eastern city.[17] He found that slum areas manifest a distinct cultural climate that remains stable over long periods of time. Citizens in these areas are on the fringe of the established economic system with little chance for success within the legitimate social order. Consequently, they seek to achieve personal satisfaction in their own neighborhoods and culture.

The family unit undergoes constant strain in this environment. Often, fathers are either sporadic visitors to their children or are totally absent from the home. As a result, lower-class families tend to be female dominated, according to Miller. This provides the essential dynamic for lower-class culture. Females tend to be protective and to encourage their male offspring to reject the carefree, deviant life that their fathers live. In opposition to this feminine ethic is the excessively macho climate of the ghetto streets ruled by delinquent groups and gangs. In late adolescence, the moral dilemma posed by the conflict between these two sets of values is solved when most young males join a one-sex peer group unit that replaces the family as the chief social reference point and provides a range of essential functions, including education and psychological support.[18]

Among adolescents, the orientation toward one-sex peer groups results in street corner hanging out, cliques, and their direct offshoot, the teenage gang. Miller found that these groups are actually critical elements in the maturation process of lower-class youths, providing youths with the ability to learn essential aspects of the male role.[19] Thus, Miller describes the lower-class culture as initially female-dominated but eventually controlled by single-sex groups that provide a family substitute and define the male role for adolescent boys.

LOWER-CLASS FOCAL CONCERNS   According to Miller, a unique group of value-like "focal concerns" dominate life among the lower class. These concerns do not necessarily represent a rebellion against middle-class values. They have evolved specifically to fit conditions in slum areas. The major focal concerns that Miller identifies are set out in more detail below.[20]

Trouble   Getting into and staying out of trouble is a major concern of lower-class citizens. Trouble includes such behavior as fighting, drinking, and sexual misconduct. In lower-class communities, people are evaluated in terms of their actual, or potential, involvement in trouble-making activity. The attitude toward trouble is not always clear-cut. Sometimes it confers prestige, for example, when a man gets a reputation for being able to handle himself well in a fight. However, getting into trouble and *having to pay the consequences* can make a person look foolish and incompetent. In most instances, trouble-making escapades are designed with a goal in mind, such as stealing an automobile when the money to buy one is unobtainable. They are usually not examples of unplanned, destructive behavior.

Toughness   Lower-class males want local recognition of their physical and spiritual toughness. They refuse to be sentimental or soft, and instead value physical strength, fighting ability, and athletic skill. Miller attributes the concern for toughness to a reaction to the female-dominated household. Fearing an accusation of homosexuality, lower-class men react strongly to any indication that they are female-dominated and therefore strive for a macho identity. Toughness involves a high tolerance of pain, disdain of fear, fighting skill, and the willingness to accept all manner of hardships without complaint. Lower-class males who cannot meet these standards risk getting a reputation for being weak, inept, and effeminate.

Smartness Another critical concern of lower-class citizens is the maintenance of an image of streetwise savvy, which carries with it the ability to outfox and outcon the opponent. This, of course, does not mean that intellectual brilliance is admired; in fact, ivory-tower types are disdained. Smartness to the lower-class citizen means knowing essential survival techniques like gambling, conning, and outsmarting the law. One unique example of smartness especially prevalent among teenage boys is a verbal repartee sometimes called sounding or ranking. During these exchanges, boys try to outdo each other in producing half-serious putdowns and insults to prove their quick wit and ingenuity. Youths who fail to attain a reputation for smartness may find themselves instead with the odious reputation of dupe or sucker.

Excitement Another important feature of the lower-class life-style is the search for fun and excitement to enliven an otherwise drab existence. The search for excitement may lead to gambling, fighting, getting drunk, sexual adventurism, and so on. Going out on the town looking for excitement may eventually lead to that other focal concern, trouble. Excitement is not sought all the time. In between, the lower-class citizen may simply "hang out" and "be cool." Those who do not seek excitement are known as deadheads. They are safe and passive.

Fate Lower-class citizens believe that their lives are in the hands of strong spiritual forces that guide their destinies. Getting lucky, finding good fortune, hitting the jackpot are all dreams that are present daily in each slum dweller's life. Getting lucky can mean a trip out of the ghetto and into the world of luxury and excitement. The belief in fate is behind the interest in playing the numbers, the horses, and the other forms of gambling that are so prevalent in the lower-class world.

Autonomy A general concern exists in lower-class cultures about personal freedom and autonomy. Being in the control of authority figures such as the police, teachers, and parents is an unacceptable weakness, incompatible with toughness. Conflicts arise when the lower-class citizen is confronted with rigidly controlled environments like schools, hospitals, the military, courts, and prisons. The usual manner of dealing with these authoritarian regimes is to actively disdain them, a behavior response that frequently results in a continuing relationship with them. For example, the behavior of youths can result in their getting left back in school.

In addition to the focal concerns listed above, Miller finds the following two concerns, which are unique to gang youths.

Belonging Lower-class youths find it essential to belong to a structured group and to be a well-thought-of, in-member of that group. One achieves this coveted membership by excelling at the general focal concerns, for example, toughness and smartness.

Status   Status is achieved and maintained by demonstrating excellence in the five generalized focal concerns. By achieving status, lower-class adolescents are able to feel grown up. Therefore, they can participate in adult activities such as gambling and drinking. Furthermore, when some members of a peer group or a gang achieve status, the group as a whole develops a significant reputation ("rep") in the community.

FOCAL CONCERNS AND DELINQUENCY   Miller argues that by strictly satisfying the behavioral demands imposed by lower-class focal concerns, an adolescent is drawn into an ever expanding pattern of delinquent behavior.[21] By adhering to the cultural values, rules, and norms with which they are in close personal contact, lower-class youths often find that they are in conflict with representatives of the legal code. For example, proving their toughness may demand that lower-class youths engage in constant fighting, both individually and in groups. Smartness may lead them into theft schemes and con games. Excitement causes them to gamble, drink, and engage in premarital sex. Thus, obedience to unavoidable cultural demands, not a sense of alienation or anger, precipitates lower-class delinquent behavior.

ANALYSIS OF FOCAL CONCERN THEORY   Miller's theoretical model has been praised as a sensitive attempt to view delinquent behavior from the perspective of its youthful participants, avoiding the middle-class bias that tarnishes some other theories of delinquency. In Highlight 5-2, noted criminologist Clarence Schrag comments on the importance of Miller's work.

Highlight 5-2. Schrag on Lower-Class Culture Conflict Theory.

Miller's work is detailed ethnography of lower class culture, attempting to document life as it is experienced by the inhabitants of our city slums. Instead of giving interpretations from a middle class point of view, a practice common in research on deviance, it reports the cognitive and affective orientations of the residents themselves. The result is a fresh perspective which indicates that many lower class offenders have little interest in middle class manners or middle class definitions of economic, social, and political success. Lower class ambitions are often aimed in another direction, involving such personal goals as excitement, enjoyment, freedom, and leisure. Reconciled to a world of dull, intermittent, and unrewarding employment, these people may seek their pleasures in expressive activities and in the consumption of goods and services. It therefore should not be surprising if the earnings from illicit activities (gambling, drug traffic, numbers and other rackets, graft, prostitution, loan sharking, and the like) along with welfare assistance are the chief sources of financial support in some of the slums of our large cities.

Source: Clarence Schrag, *Crime and Justice, American Style* (Washington, D.C.: Government Printing Office, 1971), p. 7.

Miller draws attention to the emergence of lower-class culture as a stable condition in American life. He maintains that this culture contains its own unique rules, values, and norms—all quite different from those of upper- and middle-class societies. Delinquency is a functional response to these values rather than a violation of existing community rules. This statement, of course, is the key to the validity of Miller's view. If we believe an isolated, unique lower-class culture exists, then it logically follows that the demands of this culture actually produce delinquency. Yet, it is the necessity of maintaining this belief that presents the greatest challenge to the validity of Miller's theory. It is difficult to imagine that an isolated lower-class community exists that totally shuns generally held values and concerns such as education, religion, and family and instead substitutes excitement, toughness, and fate for them.

Miller's focal concerns may be elements of a lower-class culture, but they certainly do not seem to be the only ones operating in these communities. Nor, considering the impact of the media, government agencies, and private charities, does it seem likely that lower-class citizens are insulated from at least a minimal awareness of middle-class values and goals. Yet Miller chooses to ignore the impact of middle-class values on lower-class communities and the possible influence this interaction can have.

Miller's theory fails to account for the delinquent behavior encountered in middle-class areas. In a similar vein, his work has been contradicted by a number of empirical studies that indicate that lower-class delinquents actually share many of the same values and attitudes as nondelinquents.[22]

Despite such criticism, Miller's efforts are directed primarily at explaining lower-class gang behavior. Viewed in this light, his focal concern theory makes an important contribution to our understanding of this phenomenon.

STRAIN THEORY

Strain theories constitute another branch of social structure theory. Collectively, they view crime and delinquency as a result of the frustration and anger people experience over their inability to achieve legitimate social and financial success. Strain theorists agree that most people originally share similar values and goals but that the ability to achieve them is stratified by socioeconomic class. In middle- and upper-class communities, strain does not exist, since education and prestigious occupations are readily obtainable. In lower-class slum areas, strain occurs because legitimate avenues for success are all but closed to young people. When acceptable means for obtaining success do not exist, individuals may either use deviant methods to achieve their goals or reject socially accepted goals and substitute others for them. This latter point is quite important because it distinguishes strain theories from cultural transmission theories. The former hold that everyone desires middle-class goals, but the frustration of achieving them causes lower-class youths to substitute delinquent behavior. The latter maintain that many, if not all, lower-class youths have a separate value system that places them in conflict with middle-class social control agents. In the following sections, we will examine the most significant strain theories in greater detail.

Robert Merton and the Theory of Anomie

Strain theories probably owe their popularity to the distinguished American sociologist, Robert Merton.[23] In 1938 Merton proposed a revised version of the concept of anomie, which has proved to be one of the most durable theoretical concepts in twentieth century social thought.[24] In his theory, Merton attempts to adapt the abstract concept of anomie to conditions that exist in American society. The French sociologist, Emile Durkheim, had previously employed the concept of anomie to describe the "normlessness" and social malaise that occur during a breakdown of existing social rules, laws, and values.[25] According to Durkheim, anomie can be brought about by man-made or natural disasters, such as war, plagues, or famine, that place strain on the social system. In addition, anomie can occur when societies undergo a period of transition—for example, when a tribal or feudal state evolves into a complex modern industrial system. Durkheim believed that an anomic condition results when the existing social structure can no longer establish and maintain controls over an individual's wants and desires. It is a breakdown of the rule of law. Under these conditions, crime can be considered a "normal" response to existing social conditions.

Merton adapts Durkheim's abstract concept to fit the conditions of modern American society. He believes that two elements of modern culture interact to produce potentially anomic conditions—culturally defined goals and socially approved means for obtaining them. Our society stresses the goals of acquiring wealth, success, and power. Socially permissible means include hard work, education, and thrift. Merton argues that every social system maintains a unique combination of goals and means. At one extreme are the social systems that place undue emphasis on goals to the exclusion of an interest in means.[26] In such an instance, attaining a desired goal permits the use of any available means, illicit or otherwise. At the other extreme are the social systems that seem so enamored with the means of attaining goals that the means become ritualistic and an end in themselves. An example is feudal society, which maintained an elaborate and nonfunctional system of manners and etiquette for members of royalty. And, of course, there are the intermediate systems, where a balance between cultural goals and institutional means is maintained.[27]

Merton's position is that the legitimate means to acquiring wealth are stratified across class and status lines. Those with little formal education and few economic resources soon find that they are denied the ability to acquire money and other success symbols legally.[28] Since socially mandated success goals are uniform throughout any society and access to legitimate means is bound by class and status, the resulting strain produces an anomic condition among those who are locked out of the legitimate opportunity structure. Consequently, they develop criminal or delinquent solutions to the problem of attaining goals.[29]

SOCIAL ADAPTATIONS Merton identifies five possible modes of adaptation or adjustment an individual can take when presented with the various combinations of culturally defined goals and means. Each one, listed below, represents a possible way of coping with either a balance or an imbalance of goals and means.

Conformity   Conformity occurs when an individual adheres to social goals and also can attain them legitimately (balanced system). This is the most common form of adaptation and signals the absence of an anomic condition (and deviant behavior as well).

Innovation   Innovation occurs when an individual accepts the goals of society but refects or is incapable of following legitimate means of attaining them. For example, when youths desire automobiles but lack money, the resulting conflict forces them to adopt an innovative solution to the problem. They steal cars.

Of the five adaptations, innovation is most closely associated with delinquent behavior. The inescapable demand to succeed that pervades American culture places such an enormous burden on those lacking economic opportunity that delinquent modes of adaptation are not a surprising result. This condition accounts for the high rate of delinquency in poverty areas where access to legitimate means is severely limited. However, innovative adaptations can occur in any social class when members perceive the lack of appropriate means to gain social success. For example, witness the stock frauds and tax evasion schemes of the rich.

Ritualism   Ritualism results from the diminution of goals and a rigid adherence to means. The maintenance of a strict set of manners and customs that serve no particular purpose is an example of ritualism. Such practices often exist in religious services, feudal societies, clubs, college fraternities, and organizations. Ritualists gain pleasure from the practice of traditional ceremonies that have neither a real purpose nor a goal.

Retreatism   Retreatism entails a rejection of both the goals and means of society. Merton suggests that people who adjust in this fashion are "in the society but not of it."[30]

Included in this category are "psychotics, psychoneurotics, chronic autists, pariahs, outcasts, vagrants, vagabonds, tramps, chronic drunkards, and drug addicts."[31] Often, this posture results when an individual accepts socially acceptable goals but is denied the means to attain them. Because such people are also morally or otherwise incapable of using illegitimate means, they attempt to escape their lack of success by withdrawing—either mentally or physically.

Rebellion   A rebellious adaptation involves the substitution of alternative sets of goals and means for the accepted ones of society. This adaptation is typical of revolutionaries, who wish to promote radical change in the existing social structure and who call for alternative life-styles, goals, and beliefs. For many years, revolutionary groups have abounded in our country, some espousing the violent overthrow of the existing social order and others advocating the use of nonviolent, passive resistance to change society. The revolutionary orientation can be used as a reaction against a corrupt and hated regime or as an effort to create alternate opportunities and life-styles within the existing system.

Merton's adaptations apply to both deviant and nondeviant behavior. In our

culture, innovation, retreatism, and rebellion seem most relevant to the understanding of delinquent behavior. Considering the apparent inequality in the social distribution of legitimate means, it is not surprising that large segments of
our population react to the resulting anomic condition with innovations such as
theft or extortion, with retreat into drugs or alcohol, or with rebellion by joining
revolutionary or cultist groups.

Analysis of Anomie Theory   Since its publication, Merton's theoretical model
has received praise for its scope and precision. It is more sophisticated than the
earlier cultural transmission approach since it raises the possibility of differing
types or styles of both deviant and nondeviant behavior and offers explanations
for the existence of each. Furthermore, by linking deviant behavior to the success goals that control our social behavior, anomie theory attempts to pinpoint
the cause of the conflict that produces personal frustration and consequent
criminality.

Merton's theory does not actually concern itself with the reason why any particular individual becomes delinquent. Instead, it attempts to explain the delinquency *rates* that exist in society. By acknowledging that our society unfairly
distributes the legitimate means to achieving success, anomie helps explain the
existence of high delinquency areas and the apparent predominance of delinquent and criminal behavior among particular social and ethnic groups in our
culture. By suggesting that social conditions, not individual personalities, produce crime, Merton together with Shaw and McKay, Miller, and other social
theorists, has greatly influenced the directions we have taken to reduce and
control delinquency during the latter half of the twentieth century.

Despite its preeminence in the field as an explanation of deviant behavior,
anomie theory has also received its share of criticism. In an important article,
the distinguished criminologist, Albert Cohen, poses some major questions
about the validity and value of the theory.[32]

For one thing, Cohen questions the comprehensiveness of Merton's model.
He insists that human goals, aspirations, and beliefs are not fixed. Instead, they
are constantly being influenced by social conditions and by relationships with
influential people such as family and peers. With respect to delinquency,
Cohen argues, personal relationships must certainly influence the ability to reconcile goals and means. If their close and admired associates engage in illegitimate activities, youths may emulate them. If, on the other hand, family and
friends practice conformity, this may influence youths to practice self-
discipline and restraint to achieve social goals.

In a similar vein, Cohen also charges that Merton fails to respond to the concept of social feedback, or interpersonal interaction, in the development of a
delinquent career. He suggests that societal responses to a youth's misbehavior
may dramatically affect subsequent conforming or illegitimate activities.
Among the possible effects caused by social feedback are the following.

Open up Legitimate Opportunities   Society may make special efforts to help
apprehended offenders conform. For example, delinquents are provided with
job training and educational opportunities.

Open up Illegitimate Opportunities   Influential members of society may actually aid delinquents in their illegitimate behavior. Examples include the police officer who takes bribes and the judge who fails to enforce the law.

Close off Legitimate Opportunity   By labeling delinquents as outcasts, society may exclude them from legitimate opportunities and enhance the relative attractiveness of delinquent behavior.

Close off Illegitimate Opportunities   As a response to criminal activity, social control agencies may resort to "increasing surveillance, locking the door, increasing the certainty and severity of punishment, cutting off access to necessary supplies, knocking out the fix."[33] This reaction would promote conformity. Thus, Cohen maintains that deviance can be reduced or increased by social reactions and that failure to sufficiently recognize the importance of interpersonal relationships is a major deficiency of Merton's theory.

Merton's theory also fails to account for a number of other issues. It fails to account for nonutilitarian acts of delinquency, such as violence or damage, which seem unrelated to the attainment of success goals. It also fails to explain the specific content of individual delinquent acts. In other words, why does one youth choose to steal, another to commit rape, and still another to set a fire? Finally, anomie theory seems lacking in internal consistency. It never fully explains why some people with full access to legitimate means engage in deviant behavior and why others who lack personal opportunity are able to avoid it. Although anomie theory was expressly designed to explain general trends rather than individual deviance, this oversight still seems to leave unanswered the basic question: Why does one person avoid crime and another fall prey to it?

SUBCULTURAL (STRAIN) THEORY

Subcultural (strain) theories are an extension of Merton's earlier work on anomie. Subcultural advocates share Merton's view that our society maintains generally accepted success goals, such as education, wealth, and power, and that the means for acquiring these goals are unequally distributed among the social classes. However, they differ from Merton by insisting that youths who live in poverty areas and who lack access to legitimate means reject socially approved goals and means and substitute for them a unique set of cultural values and standards of their own. The strain between upper-class goals and lower-class means eventually produces an independent lower class *subculture* that provides the ghetto youth with avenues for obtaining alternate forms of success and self-esteem.

In this section, we will review the two most important forms of subcultural strain theory—Cohen's theory of delinquent subculture and Cloward and Ohlin's opportunity theory.

Albert Cohen and the Theory of Delinquent Subculture

Albert Cohen first articulated the theory of delinquent subculture in his 1955 book, *Delinquent Boys.*[34] Cohen's main purpose is to explain the disproportionate amount of official delinquent behavior found in lower-class slum neighborhoods. His central position is that delinquent behavior of lower-class youths is actually a protest against the norms and values of the middle-class American culture. Because social conditions make them incapable of achieving success in a legitimate fashion, lower-class youths experience a form of culture conflict that Cohen labels "status frustration." As a result, many of them join together in teenage gangs and engage in behavior that is *nonutilitarian, malicious,* and *negativistic.*[35] Cohen views delinquents as forming a separate subculture and possessing a value system directly in opposition to that of the larger society. He describes the subculture as one that takes "its norms from the larger culture but turns them upside down. The delinquents conduct is right, by the standards of his subculture precisely because it is wrong by the norms of the larger cultures."[36]

CAUSES OF DELINQUENCY   According to Cohen, the development of the delinquent subculture is a function of the social and familial conditions children experience as they mature in the ghetto or slum environment. Delinquency is not a product of inherent class inferiority. Rather, it is a function of the social and economic limitations suffered by members of the less fortunate groups in our society. The numbing burden of poverty is the real villain in the creation of delinquent careers.[37]

A critical element of lower-class life, one that directly influences later delinquent behavior, is the nature of the child's family structure. Cohen argues that the relative position of a child's family in the social structure determines the quality of experiences and problems that the child will encounter later in life.[38] By implication, Cohen suggests that lower-class families are incapable of teaching their offspring proper socialization techniques for entry into the dominant middle-class culture. Lower-class families, permanently cut off from the middle-class way of life, produce children who lack the basic skills necessary to achieve social and economic success in our demanding society. Developmental handicaps produces by a lower-class upbringing include lack of educational training, poor speech and communication skills, and inability to delay gratification.[39]

MIDDLE-CLASS MEASURING RODS   One of the more significant handicaps that lower-class children face is the inability to positively impress authority figures such as teachers, employers, or supervisors. In our society, these positions tend to be held by members of the middle or upper class, who have a tough time relating to the lower-class youngster. Cohen calls the standards these authority figures set "middle-class measuring rods," and the conflict lower-class youths feel when they fail to meet these standards is a primary cause of delinquency. In Highlight 5–3, criminologist Clarence Schrag presents the essence of the middle-class measuring rod concept.

Highlight 5–3. Schrag on Middle-Class Measuring Rods.

Cohen maintains that people are everywhere evaluated in institutional settings—in school, on the job, under the law, and so on—that are largely dominated by representatives of the middle class. This means that everyone is rated, without regard to his social or ethnic background, in terms of traditional criteria, such as intelligence and verbal skill, ambition, sense of responsibility, ability to delay gratification in the interest of long-run goals, neatness and cleanliness, common courtesy, and rational control over physical impulses or agressive tendencies. These traits are commonly interpreted as hallmarks of the middle class way of life, the measuring rod to be used in ascertaining a person's worth.

People, of course, are given other evaluations, both formal and informal, in a variety of situations. The most important for teenagers and young adults, however, may be the authoritative judgements made by their superiors under the auspices of our major social institutions. Institutional judgements are part of an official record and are often certified for public use by means of diplomas, degrees, honors, awards, grants, promotions, performance ratings, credit ratings, police blotters, court reports, and other kinds of documents. Such records and documents may be consulted when a person seeks to improve his education, enter a profession or another occupation, join a social organization, get married, purchase a home, make a legal contract or change his status in any other significant manner.

Moreover, the ratings are reviewed, revised, magnified, or deprecated by the periodic updating of records and by the informal exchanges of information that commonly occur among the leaders of institutions, who frequently are also the pillars and the decision-makers of the community. From this we may conclude that a person's status and esteem in the community are largely determined by the judgements of his elders, which judgements reflect the traditional values of American society and are therefore regarded as binding on the middle class and on "respectable" members of the lower class as well.

Source: Clarence Schrag, *Crime and Justice, American Style* (Washington, D.C.: Government Printing Office, 1971), p. 74.

REACTIONS TO MIDDLE-CLASS MEASURING RODS Cohen's position is that lower-class boys who suffer the rejection of middle-class decision makers become deeply affected by their lack of social recognition.[40] In the typical case, they may elect to adopt one of three alternative behaviors: the "corner boy" role, the "college boy" role, or the "delinquent boy" role.

The stable corner boy role is the most common response to middle-class rejection. The corner boy is not overtly delinquent but behaves in a way that is sometimes defined as delinquent. For example, he is a truant.[41] He hangs out in the neighborhood, engages in gambling, athletics, and other group activities, and eventually obtains a menial job. His main loyalty is to his peer group, which he depends on for support, motivation, and interest. His values, therefore, are those of the group with which he is in close personal contact. The corner boy, well aware of his failure to achieve the standards of the American dream, retreats into the comforting world of his lower-class peers and eventually becomes a stable member of his society.

The college boy embraces the cultural and social values of the middle class. Rather than scorning middle-class measuring rods, he actively strives to be successful by middle-class standards. Cohen views this type of youth as one who is embarking on an almost hopeless path, since he is ill-equipped academically, socially, and linguistically to ever achieve the long deferred rewards of middle-class life.

The delinquent boy adopts a set of norms and principles in direct opposition to middle-class society. Cohen describes a number of general properties of the delinquent subculture. For one thing, its members often manifest "short-run hedonism."[42] Delinquents are believed to live for today and let tomorrow take care of itself. Although Cohen believes short-run hedonism is a characteristic of lower-class culture as a whole, he finds it especially applicable to delinquent groups.

Members of the delinquent subculture are also careful to maintain *group autonomy*. They resist efforts by family, school, or other sources of authority to control their behavior. Although some individual delinquents may respond to direction from others, the gang itself is autonomous, independent, and the focus of "attraction, loyalty, and solidarity."[43]

While members of the delinquent subculture often manifest negativistic and malicious behavior, Cohen believes they are still controlled to some degree by the norms and values of the generalized culture. They really want to be successful at school, jobs, and so on. To deal with the conflict inherent in this frustrating dilemma, the delinquent resorts to a process Cohen calls "reaction formation."[44] Symptoms of reaction formation include an overly intense response that seems disproportionate to the stimulus that triggers it. For the delinquent boy, this takes the form of "irrational," "malicious," "unaccountable" hostility to the enemy within the gates as well as without—the norms of respectable middle-class society.[45]

ANALYSIS OF COHEN'S THEORY OF DELINQUENT SUBCULTURE

Cohen carries the work of cultural transmission theorists a step further by explaining the factors that promote and sustain a delinquent subculture. By introducing the concepts of *status frustration, failure to meet middle-class measuring rods*, and *family disability*, Cohen makes a clear presentation of the factors that cause lower-class delinquency. Furthermore, by introducing the corner boy–college boy–delinquent boy triad, he attempts to explain why some lower-class youths are able to avoid entry into the delinquent subculture.

Despite its merits, Cohen's work is also open to a number of significant criticisms. For one thing, he does not present any rigorous empirical evidence to support his contentions; and, as we saw in Chapter 3, self-report studies have uncovered data indicating that delinquent behavior may be unrelated to social status or status frustration. Thus, while Cohen's theory seems plausible, he does not present enough evidence to support its validity unequivocably.

The internal consistency of Cohen's theory has also been brought into question. In a much-cited article, John Kitsuse and David Detrick note some of the ambiguity that runs through Cohen's statements.[46] For example, at some points Cohen claims that delinquent boys value the opinion of middle-class persons; at others he presents the opposite viewpoint—that they care little for middle-class opinions.[47] Kitsuse and Detrick also question the way Cohen uses the term *reaction formation*. It is difficult to test the validity of this theory scientifically. Kitsuse and Detrick object to the categorization of delinquency as nonutilitarian, malicious, and negativistic. They point to evidence that delinquent behavior is often rational, calculated, and utilitarian. It is, they conclude, a serious mistake to categorize all delinquents as being similarly engaged in destructive and thoughtless behavior.

Responding to these and other criticisms, Cohen (in conjunction with James Short) presented a refined version of his original theory.[48] In this paper, Cohen and Short recognize that the original formulation of the delinquent subculture may have been too simplistic and that a more complex model is called for. They therefore describe the following five delinquent orientations:

1. Parent male subculture—the negativistic subculture originally identified in *Delinquent Boys*.
2. The conflict-oriented subculture—the culture of a large gang that engages in collective violence.
3. The drug addict subculture—groups of youth whose life revolves around the purchase, sale, and use of narcotics.
4. Semiprofessional theft—youths who engage in the theft or robbery of merchandise for the purpose of later sale and monetary gain.
5. Middle-class subculture—delinquent groups that rise because of the pressures of living in middle-class environments.[49]

Thus, upon reflection, Cohen has attempted to broaden the behavior that can be explained by his original subcultural strain model.

Cloward and Ohlin's Theory of Opportunity

In their well-known 1960 work, *Delinquency and Opportunity*, Richard Cloward and Lloyd Ohlin added significantly to the knowledge of delinquent subcultures.[50]

In their synthesis, Cloward and Ohlin first agree with Robert Merton that socioeconomic class membership controls access to the legitimate means of achieving social goals.[51] However, they maintain that Merton's theory pays scant attention to the fact that even *illegitimate* means are unevenly distributed in the class structure. Cloward and Ohlin argue that some lower-class neighborhoods actually provide more opportunity for illegal gain than others do. These opportunities come in the form of access to rackets, organized crime, theft, and other high payoff illegal activities. Cloward and Ohlin's view, therefore, is that in a particular urban area or neighborhood, both legitimate and illegitimate opportunities are differentially available.

GANG SUBCULTURES   A key element in opportunity theory is the assumption that a strong relationship exists between the environment youths live in, its economic structure, and their subsequent behavior choices. For example, in wealthy or middle-class areas, educational and vocational opportunity abound, and youths can avail themselves of conventional means of getting ahead, such as going to college. However, in low-income areas, legitimate means are harder to come by, and therefore youths must seek illegitimate avenues of success.

Cloward and Ohlin propose that even illegitimate means for success are blocked to some youths. In fact, they are available only to children growing up in areas where "stable patterns of accommodation" exist between the criminal world and conventional society.[52] In these areas, adult criminals have worked out relationships with businesses, police, and court officials through bribery and corruption, so that they are almost immune from prosecution. Their criminal activity—organized crime, drug trafficking, gambling—provides a stable income and an alternative avenue to legitimate success. Under adult tutelage, youths fit right into this model and form a *criminal subculture*. To prepare for adult crime, they join gangs specializing in theft, extortion, and other profitable criminal activities. Later, they become part of the even more profitable adult crime organizations.

Of course, not all youths join criminal gangs. Some lower-class youths remain loyal to the values and rules of conventional society. Furthermore, some youths are incapable by temperament of following either criminal or conventional rules. They take drugs and alcohol and stress playing it cool and being high and strung out. Cloward and Ohlin call their world the *retreatist subculture*.

Finally, opportunity theory recognizes that some poverty areas are so unstable and disorganized, that even illegitimate means to success are blocked. Youths in these areas become members of the *conflict subculture*.[53] They form fighting gangs that provide the opportunity for success and ego gratification by enabling their members to show their bravery and strength and by allowing them to display fighting prowess. These gangs are the famed "bopping" gangs of the 1950s.[54]

In sum, Cloward and Ohlin view urban delinquency as a function of the differential opportunity youths have to gain both *legitimate* and *illegitimate* goals. Where opportunities for legal gain are blocked, criminal activity is attempted. When even criminal gain is unobtainable, then drug use (retreatist gangs) or violence (conflict gangs) will ensue.

ANALYSIS OF OPPORTUNITY THEORY   Cloward and Ohlin's theory integrates the three main streams of delinquency theory: anomie, subculture, and social learning. Their work has the distinct advantage of avoiding the pitfalls of previous theoretical models. It is neither so broad as to lack precision nor so narrow as to be unimportant. Their recognition that different types of delinquent gang cultures—conflict, retreatist, and criminal—exist seems to be a more realistic appraisal of the actual world of the delinquent than Cohen's original view of purely negativistic, destructive delinquent youths who oppose all social values. It is difficult to believe, as Cohen originally had it, that the majority of delinquent acts are purposeless and destructive when statistics show that teenagers engage in many profit-related offenses, such as burglaries and robberies. Cloward and Ohlin's model seems to fit existing data more closely.

Cloward and Ohlin's tripartite model of urban delinquency also relates directly to the treatment and rehabilitation of delinquents. While other theorists, such as Cohen, Miller, Shaw, and McKay, see delinquent youths maintaining values and attitudes in opposition to middle-class culture, Cloward and Ohlin suggest that many delinquents actually share the same goals and values of the general society but lack the means to obtain them. This position is an argument for rehabilitation programs because preventing delinquency does not involve changing basic attitudes and beliefs of delinquent youth. Rather such programs have the somewhat simpler task of providing youths with the means for obtaining the success they truly desire.

Several studies have been conducted to test opportunity theory. Judson

Landis and Frank Scarpitti made use of the Gough Socialization Scale of the California Personality Inventory and developed two new scales, one to measure middle-class value orientation and the other to measure perception of limited opportunity.[55] The latter scales employed such items as "good manners are for sissies" and "people should only keep promises when it is to their benefit." A questionnaire containing these scales was given to 1,030 white and black public school youths in Columbus, Ohio. It was also administered to 515 white and black boys ranging in age from thirteen to eighteen at the Boy's Industrial School in Lancaster, Ohio. The industrial school boys exhibited greater perception of limited opportunity than did the public school boys. The authors considered the possibility that this result was an outgrowth of the institutional climate of the training school. However, an examination of scores among the public school youths suggested that those who scored high on delinquency proneness scales also held perceptions of limited opportunity. Thus, the findings of this study would appear to support Cloward and Ohlin's hypothesis. However, Landis and Scarpitti's study also reveals that values are different in different social classes. Boys with a lower-class background in both samples tended to *reject* middle-class values, a finding that contradicts Cloward and Ohlin's presumption that all elements of society embrace the values of the dominant culture.

James Short, Ramon Rivera, and Ray Tennyson conducted a similar study in Chicago with a group of gang boys, a group of nongang boys from the same lower-class neighborhood, and a group of middle-class nongang boys.[56] They found that both gang and nongang boys attributed a high value and a high degree of legitimacy to middle-class values such as hard work and achievement in school. However, the gang boys also possessed positive attitudes toward delinquent images such as toughness and drug use. The study also found that the perception of limited access to legitimate opportunity was more likely to be associated with delinquency than the perception of access to illegitimate opportunity. Thus, Short, Rivera, and Tennyson support Cloward and Ohlin's proposition that perception of blocked legitimate opportunities is a predictor of delinquency.

Despite this evidence, some research has produced results that conflict with opportunity theory. For example, when testing samples of lower- and middle-class delinquents, Leon Fannin and Marshall Clinard found that subjects differed in their attitudes and values.[57]

Lower class boys felt themselves to be . . . tougher, more powerful, fierce, fearless, and dangerous than middle class boys. Middle class delinquents . . . conceived of themselves as being more loyal, clever, smart, smooth and bad. . . . The lower class would like to be (ideal self) tougher, harder and more violent than the middle class, while the latter would like to be more loyal, lucky, and firm.[58]

In a similar vein, Maynard Erikson and LeMar Empey studied delinquent peer associations among lower-, middle-, and upper-class youths. Upper-class youths were significantly less committed to delinquent associations then lower- *and* middle-class youths. Both of the latter groups had equal numbers of delinquent peers. The same pattern was maintained for peer commitment, which the authors measured by such items as, "Suppose you were planning to go to church one Sunday morning and your friends called and wanted you to do something else with them, would you go with them?"[59] This finding also contradicts Cloward and Ohlin.

Moreover, some recent surveys of gang delinquency have called into question Cloward and Ohlin's work (see Chapter 9). Briefly, this work suggests that gangs are more pervasive than was previously expected, more than one type of gang (conflict, violent, and so on) exists in a particular area, and the commitment of gang boys to one another is less intense than opportunity theory would suggest. Moreover, gangs do not seem to specialize in any particular type of behavior.

In sum, the work of Cloward and Ohlin is probably one of the most influential theoretical pronouncements of the twentieth century. Its complexity and sophistication successfully blends the work of such theorists as Cohen, Merton, and Sutherland. However, the theory of blocked opportunity has not received overwhelming empirical support, and, as we have seen, treatment programs based on its premises have not been totally successful.

MIDDLE-CLASS DELINQUENCY

A discussion of sociocultural theory would not be complete without some mention of middle-class juvenile delinquency. This phenomenon first came to the attention of authorities during the early 1960s, when the publication of self-report studies revealed a shockingly high delinquency rate in middle- and high-income areas (see Chapter 3). These findings surprised some criminologists who had long associated delinquent behavior with poor youths living in urban ghettos. In fact, the existence of large numbers of middle-class delinquents seriously compromised existing theories of youth crime, thereby helping promote the development of some of the more recent trends in delinquency research (see Chapters 6 and 7).

A number of reasons have been given to explain the prevalence of middle-class delinquency. On the one hand, the postwar baby boom produced a disproportionate number of teenage youths in the late 1950s and the 1960s. Many were members of families enjoying the newly won prosperity of that period. Many of these affluent families left their traditional urban neighborhoods and moved to the suburbs. Traditional family ties and patterns changed, and long-held concepts of obedience and control broke down. Teenagers with time on their hands and money in the bank no longer felt the constraining hand of family, clan, and neighborhood and began to seek new forms of excitement and experience. In this search, delinquent behavior played no small part.

Moreover, child-rearing practices themselves changed in the postwar period. The so-called permissive school of thought led by Dr. Benjamin Spock ·influenced the disciplinary practices of many families.[60] Schools began to try out innovative educational programs that stressed self-starting and self-discipline. At the same time, more than ever before, young people entered colleges and universities and delayed the period of entry into the work force. The period of adolescent inactivity was prolonged. Thus, middle-class youths were given more freedom than they had ever enjoyed before, but social norms constrained them from participating in meaningful social activity. The youth problem therefore extended to the very reaches of adult life.

Theories of Middle-Class Delinquency

Of the many attempts to document and explain middle-class delinquency, Ralph England's work is among the most well-known.[61] England argues that American youngsters have gradually been removed from functional roles in the economy through restrictive apprenticeship codes, protective labor legislation, the compulsory education movement, and the growth of urbanization.[62] Youths are no longer supposed to engage in productive labor, but they are also required not to loaf. They are discouraged from early marriages but allowed to engage in intense courtship experiences. They cannot vote but are expected to be civic-minded. They are given freedom but are not bound by the social ties that prevent privilege and freedom from deteriorating into license.[63]

The tension produced by these conflicting demands and experiences helps create a teenage culture that maintains its own brand of values and behavior. Adults seeking teenage consumers for their products fuel and sustain this independent life-style. Advertising compaigns forcefully sell records, cosmetics, movies, and clothes specifically to teens. Adult identification of the teenage life-style, including such phenomena as recognizing teenage leaders and spokespersons who are familiar with teenage concerns, helps to solidify the existence of this subculture.

England characterizes middle-class teenage culture as hedonistic, intent on short-run gratification from fast cars, early sexual experience, parties, and so on. The relationship between these needs and delinquency is complex, but essentially: "If the teenager's urgent need for status affirmation is met by the teenage culture, then it becomes necessary for him to reject influences from the adult world which threaten it and to accept only those giving it support."[64]

The threatening influences include any adult values, such as hard work and self-denial, running counter to short-run, irresponsible hedonism. Thus, England characterizes the middle-class delinquent as one engaging in illegal hedonistic acts such as drinking, drug use, premarital sex, and petty theft.

A number of other authorities on middle- and upper-class delinquency share England's theoretical framework. For example, sociologist Marvin Wolfgang has cited changes in the socialization of youth. Some of his most pertinent suggestions are contained in Highlight 5–4.

Another influential author, Thomas Vaz, has conducted research indicating that upper-class youths attending exclusive private schools, as well as middle-class youths, frequently engage in such behavior as gambling, drinking, theft, and property damage.[65] Vaz also suggests the existence of a hedonistic youth culture that controls and influences adolescent behavior.

The following causes are often given for middle- and upper-class delinquency: (1) anxiety regarding sex role identification in female-dominated households, (2) delay in achieving adult status, (3) feelings of status deprivation caused by lack of academic and other skills, (4) weakening of the middle-class principle of delayed gratification, (5) inadequate parent-child relationships, (6) ineffective performance in school, (7) the influence of deviant peer groups, and (8) capricious experimentation with deviant behavior.

Recent research indicates the existence of surprisingly large amounts of middle-class delinquency. Theorists have viewed this as a function of a hedonistic teenage culture fueled by too much freedom, leisure, and wealth as well as a lack of adult control.

Highlight 5-4. Marvin Wolfgang on the Culture of Youth.

Our youth in general are richer today than they have ever been and have more alternatives of action and more privileges. The list of privileges usurped by youth has not only increased but has shifted downward in age. The high school student of today has the accoutrements of the college student of yesteryear—cars, long pants, money, and more access to girls. This downward shift in privileges, precocious to younger ages, is a phenomenon well known to every parent whose own youth subculture was devoid of them.

This extended socialization is accompanied by the problem of poor adult models. Throughout the social classes, it appears that the search for the adult to be emulated is often a desperate and futile quest. Part of the reason for this futility is due to the very rapid social and technological changes occurring in our society which make it more difficult for the adult to perform his traditional role of model and mentor to youth.

Many youth feel forced into detachment and premature cynicism because society seems to offer youth today so little that is stable, relevant, and meaningful. They often look in vain for values, goals, means, and institutions to which they can be committed because their thrust for commitment is strong. Youth can be a period of fruitful idealism, but there are few of what Erik Erikson would call "objects of fidelity" for our youth; so that "playing it cool" is more than an ephemeral expression—it becomes a way of avoiding demaging commitments to goals and life-styles of the parent generation which may be outmoded tomorrow. Times and viewpoints shift rapidly, and many of our children resemble world-weary and jaded adults at age 14. The social isolation, social distance, alienation, and retreat from the adult world are increased by many social and technological mechanisms operating to encourage a youth subculture. As the numbers and intensity of value sharing in the youth subculture increase, the process of intergenerational alienation also escalates.

: Source: Marvin Wolfgang, "The Culture of Youth," in *The Task Force Report of the President's Commission of Law Enforcement and the Administration of Justice* (Washington, D.C.: Government Printing Office, 1967), pp. 147-148.

POLICY AND SOCIAL STRUCTURE THEORY

Social structure type theories have had an important impact on strategies to prevent delinquency. The idea behind such strategies is to pierce the delinquent subculture by organizing community-based programs that provide legitimate alternatives to the opportunities provided by delinquent gangs.

One of the first practical applications of the approach was the Chicago Area Project begun by Clifford R. Shaw in 1933.[66] The goal was to induce communities to adopt programs to combat the social disorganization and conflicting values that existed in Chicago's slums. Community control was believed essential so committees were organized to select a resident as leader of the project.[67] The leader and the committee then worked together to coordinate a variety of social services and activities, including recreation, clubs, hobby groups, groups to deal with school-community relations, and discussion groups. In all, twenty centers serving 10,000 youngsters were set up. This effort at community prevention of delinquency has met with mixed reviews; yet a number of research efforts conclude that it had a generally beneficial influence on its youthful participants.

Walter Miller began another similar project in Boston. The Mid-City Program helped reduce the gang problem by promoting intensive street work with youths.[68] Still another program, begun in 1962 in New York City, sought to provide opportunities to 107,000 people living in a sixty-seven-block area on the Lower East Side.[69] Based directly on Cloward and Ohlin's work, the Mobilization for Youth (MFY) focused on work training, community organization, counseling, education, and family counseling. The program leaders became active in championing the rights of the poor, causing a political backlash that resulted in the cutting off of agency funds and a subsequent shift in the program toward a more traditional counseling group work model. A similar, heavily funded program, Haryou-Act (Harlem Youth Opportunities Unlimited), met practically the same fate.

These programs probably failed because of their bandaid approach to the crushing problems of poverty, disrupted families, poor education, and racism. Although some noteworthy social programs have been in operation, they are often insufficient to counteract the heavy weight of social disability suffered by lower-class youths. The government still supports settlement houses, job training, and education programs, but they have not been especially successful in preventing delinquency.

In the future, delinquency subcultures will continue to be fought with such social programs as school desegregation, urban renewal, improved educational programs, and improved community services to the family.

CHAPTER SUMMARY

Social structure theories hold that delinquent behavior is an adaptation to the conditions that predominate in lower-class environments. While originally directed at explaining lower-class male gang delinquency, some social structure theoretical models are now aimed at explaining upper- and middle-class juvenile crime.

Social structure theory has two main branches. The first, cultural transmission, suggests that deviant values develop in deprived areas and become institutionalized as substitutes for legally acceptable middle-class ideals. Shaw and McKay view this development principally as a property of youthful street gangs, but a later work by Walter Miller argues that almost all lower-class citizens maintain separate value systems.

The second branch of social structure theory is strain theories. These hold that lower-class youths may actually desire legitimate goals, but their unavailability causes rage, frustration, and the substitution of deviant behavior. Sociologists Richard Cloward and Lloyd Ohlin have taken this idea one step further by suggesting that some neighborhoods even deny their residents the opportunity for illegal gain, thereby creating the rise of violence and drug-related subcultures.

Although these theoretical models seem quite powerful at first reading, especially considering the prevalence of delinquency in the nation's slum areas, they have been criticized on a number of methodological points. As a group, they rely on official police statistics, which generally suggest that the lower class is truly the most delinquent. They do not use self-report surveys, which suggest that delinquency is as prevalent in the middle and upper classes. If it is, the basis for the social structure approach is undermined.

DISCUSSION QUESTIONS

1. Is there a "transitional" area in your town or city?
2. Is it possible that a distinct lower-class culture exists? Do you know anyone who has the focal concerns Miller talks about?
3. Have you ever perceived anomie? What causes anomie?
4. Do middle-class youths become delinquent for the same reasons as lower-class youths?

SUGGESTED READINGS

Cohen, Albert. Delinquent Boys: The Culture of the Gang. New York: Macmillan, 1955.

Cohen, Albert, and Short, James. "Research in Delinquent Subcultures." *Journal of Social Issues* 14 (1958): 20–37.

Cloward, Richard, and Ohlin, Lloyd. *Delinquency and Opportunity*. New York: Macmillan, 1960.

Kobrin, Solomon. "The Chicago Area Project—A Twenty-five-Year Assessment." *Annals of the American Academy of Political and Social Science* 322 (1959): 20–29.

Miller, Walter. "The Impact of a Total-Community Delinquency Control Project." *Social Problems* 10 (1962), 168–191.

Polk, Kenneth. "Urban Social Areas and Delinquency." *Social Problems* 14 (1967): 320–325.

Quinney, Richard. "Crime, Delinquency and Social Areas." *Journal of Research in Crime and Delinquency* 1 (1964): 145–154.

Schrag, Clarence. *Crime and Justice—American Style*. Washington, D.C.: Government Printing Office, 1971.

Shaw, Clifford, and McKay, Henry D. *Juvenile Delinquency and Urban Areas*. Chicago: University of Chicago Press, 1969.

Thrasher, Frederick. *The Gang*. Chicago: University of Chicago Press, 1927.

REFERENCES

1. Clifford R. Shaw and Henry D. McKay, *Juvenile Delinquency and Urban Areas*, rev. ed. (Chicago: University of Chicago Press, 1972).

2. Walter Miller, "Lower Class Culture as a Generating Milieu of Gang Delinquency," *Journal of Social Issues* 14 (1958): 5–19.

3. See, for example, Anthony Platt, *The Child Savers: The Invention of Delinquency* (Chicago: University of Chicago Press, 1968).

4. Shaw and McKay, *Juvenile Delinquency and Urban Areas*.

5. Ibid., p. 52.

6. Ibid., p. 170.

7. Ibid.

8. Ibid.

9. Ibid., p. 171.

10. Ibid., pp. 38–389.

11. Solomon Kobrin, "Chicago Area Project—A Twenty-five-Year Assessment," *Annals of the*

American Academy of Political and Social Science 322 (1959): 20–29.

12. Frederick Thrasher, *The Gang* (Chicago: University of Chicago Press, 1927).

13. Walter Miller, *Violence by Youth Gangs and Youth Groups as a Crime Problem in Major American Cities* (Washington, D.C.: Government Printing Office, 1975).

14. See, for example, Larry Siegel, Dennis Sullivan, and Jack Greene, "An Analysis of Police Discretion Utilizing Decision Matrix Techniques," *Journal of Criminal Justice* 2 (1974): 131–146.

15. Miller, "Lower Class Culture as a Generating Milieu of Gang Delinquency," p. 5.

16. For a similar view, see LaMar Empey, *American Delinquency* (Homewood, Ill.: Dorsey Press, 1978) p. 264.

17. Miller, "Lower Class Culture as a Generating Milieu of Gang Delinquency," p. 6.

18. Ibid., p. 5.

19. Ibid., p. 14.

20. Ibid.

21. Ibid., p. 17.

22. See, for example, Larry Siegel, Spencer Rathus, and Carol Ruppert, "Values and Delinquent Youth: An Empirical Reexamination of Theories of Delinquency," *British Journal of Criminology* 6 (1973): 135–140.

23. See, for example, Robert Merton, *Social Theory and Social Structure* (Glencoe, Ill.: Free Press, 1957).

24. Robert Merton, "Social Structure and Anomie," *American Sociological Review* 3 (1938): 672–682.

25. For samples of his work, see Emile Durkheim, *The Rules of Sociological Method*, 8th ed. (Glencoe, Ill.: Free Press, 1950); *Suicide* (Glencoe, Ill.: Free Press, 1951).

26. Merton, "Social Structures and Anomie," p. 673.

27. Ibid., pp. 67-675.

28. Ibid., p. 680.

29. Ibid.

30. Robert Merton, "Social Structure and Anomie," in *The Sociology of Crime and Delinquency*, ed. M. Wolfgang, L. Savitz, and N. Johnston (New York: Wiley, 1970), p. 242.

31. Ibid.

32. Albert Cohen, "The Sociology of the Deviant Act: Anomie Theory and Beyond," *American Sociological Review* 30 (1965): 5–14.

33. Ibid., p. 11.

34. Albert Cohen, *Delinquent Boys* (New York: Free Press, 1955).

35. Ibid., p. 25.

36. Ibid., p. 28.

37. Ibid., pp. 73–74.

38. Ibid.

39. Ibid., p. 86.

40. Cohen, *Delinquent Boys*, p. 128.

41. Ibid., p. 129.

42. Ibid., p. 30.

43. Ibid., p. 31.

44. Ibid., p. 133.

45. Albert Cohen and James Short, "Research on Delinquent Subcultures," *Journal of Social Issues* 14 (1958): 20.

46. John Kitsuse and David Detrick, "Delinquent Boys: A Critique," *American Sociological Review* 24 (1959): 208–215.

47. Ibid., p. 210.

48. Cohen and Short, "Research on Delinquent Subcultures," p. 22.

49. Ibid., pp. 25–31.

50. Richard Cloward and Lloyd Ohlin, *Delinquency and Opportunity* (New York: Free Press, 1960).

51. See Edwin Sutherland, *Principles of Criminology*, 4th ed. (Philadelphia: Lippincott, 1947).

52. Cloward and Ohlin, *Delinquency and Opportunity*, p. 159.

53. Clarence Schrag, *Crime and Justice, American Style* (Washington, D.C.: Government Printing Office, 1971), p. 67.

54. See, for example, Irving Spergel, *Racketville, Slumtown and Haulburg* (Chicago: University of Chicago Press, 1964).

55. Judson Landis and Frank Scarpitti, "Perceptions Regarding Value Orientation and Legitimate Opportunity: Delinquents and Non-delinquents," *Social Forces* 84 (1965): 57–61.

56. James Short, Ramon Rivera, and Ray Tennyson, "Perceived Opportunities, Gang Membership and Delinquency," *American Sociological Review* 30 (1965): 56–57.

57. Leon Fannin and Marshall Clinard, "Differences in the Conception of Self as a Male among Lower and Middle-Class Delinquents," *Social Problems* 13 (1965): 205–215.

58. Ibid., p. 210.

59. LaMar Empey and Maynard Erickson, "Class Position, Peers, and Delinquency," *Sociology and Social Research* 40 (1965): 260–202.

60. Benjamin Spock, *Baby and Child Care*, (New York: Wallaby, 1977).

61. Ralph England, "A Theory of Middle-Class Juvenile Delinquency," *Journal of Criminal Law, Criminology, and Police Science* 50 (1960): 535–540.

62. Ibid., p. 537.

63. Ibid.

64. Ibid., p. 539.

65. Edmund Vaz, *Middle-Class Juvenile Delinquency* (New York: Harper & Row, 1967).

66. Described in National Institute for Juvenile Justice and Delinquency Prevention, *Preventing Delinquency, A Comparative Analysis of Delinquency Prevention Theory* (Washington, D.C.: Government Printing Office, 1977).

67. Ibid., p. 28.

68. Walter Miller, "The Impact of a 'Total Community' Delinquency Control Project," *Social Problems* 10 (1962): 168–191.

69. Described in Barry Krisberg and James Austin, *Children of Ishmael* (Palo Alto, Calif.: Mayfield Publishing, 1978), p. 37.

────────────Chapter 6═

Chapter Outline

Introduction
Differential Association Theory
Neutralization Theory
Control Theory
Containment Theory
Policy Implications of Social Process
   Theories
Chapter Summary

Key Terms, Names, and Cases

differential association
definitions toward delinquency
techniques of neutralization
drift
subterranean values
social bond
attachment
inner and outer containments
Edwin Sutherland
Donald Cressey
Gresham Sykes
David Matza
Travis Hirschi
Walter Reckless

Social Process Theories

INTRODUCTION

Social process theories examine the various sociocultural organizations, relationships, and processes that influence human behavior. In contrast to social structure theories, they suggest that most youngsters share common values, beliefs, and goals, but that certain conditions, which can exist in any economic strata, push some youths into delinquent behavior. Although lower-class youths may be more susceptible to delinquency-producing processes than middle- or upper-class youths, the latter are by no means immune.

Social process theories developed as a result of the important questions that social structure theories left unanswered. Criminologists had long puzzled over the fact that many lower-class youths, despite their exposure to the cultural conditions that presumably produce delinquency, do not become delinquent. In a similar vein, recent self-report studies indicate that many middle- and upper-class youths, who should have every reason to reject delinquent activity, actively engage in it. Thus, theories that explain delinquent behavior solely on the basis of position in the social structure do not take into account the self-report data indicating that delinquency is spread almost evenly throughout the social classes.

Another salient feature of social process theories is their suggestion that a majority of people in all social classes share similar goals, values, and beliefs. While many individuals actually have the *potential* to become delinquents or criminals, they are constrained by legal and moral rules. According to the social process approach, delinquents are either youths who learn to overcome (or ignore) social rules or individuals whose bond to society is so weakened that they are free from its constraining moral forces. Thus, unlike social structure theories, process theories attempt to identify the factors within any social setting that cause a youth to become involved in criminal behavior or remain stable and law-abiding.

125

Social process theories can also be contrasted with individualistic theories of delinquency. They categorically reject the notion of the born criminal, and instead they recognize that youths are deeply influenced by processes contained within their social world.

This chapter will first review differential association theory, one of the most influential models of crime and delinquency and one that stresses the *learning* of delinquent behavior. Next, it will discuss neutralization theory, which stresses the use of behavior rationalizations in the performance of delinquent acts. The chapter's following section will view control theory, the widely acclaimed work of criminologist Travis Hirschi. Finally, it will discuss containment theory, which attempts to add a social-psychological dimension to the explanation of delinquency.

DIFFERENTIAL ASSOCIATION THEORY

Edwin H. Sutherland, long considered the preeminent American criminologist, first formulated the theory of differential association in 1939 in his text, *Principles of Criminology*.[1] The final form of the theory appeared in 1947. Differential association was then applied to all criminal and delinquent behavior patterns, and its final form has remained unchanged ever since. Since Sutherland's death in 1950, his work has been continued by his long-time associate, Donald Cressey. Cressey has been so successful in explaining and popularizing his mentor's efforts that differential association remains one of the most enduring explanations of delinquent behavior.

Principles of Differential Association

An explanation of the basic principles of differential association is contained in the statements below:[2]

1. *Criminal behavior is learned.* This statement differentiates Sutherland's theory from prior attempts to classify delinquent behavior as an inherent characteristic of the born criminals. By suggesting that delinquent and criminal behavior is actually learned, Sutherland implies that it can be classified in the same manner as any other learned behavior, such as writing, painting, or reading.

2. *Criminal behavior is learned in interaction with other persons in a process of communication.* Sutherland believes that delinquent behavior is learned actively. An individual does not become a delinquent simply by living in a crimogenic environment or by manifesting personal characteristics, such as low IQ and family problems, associated with delinquency. Instead, criminal and other deviant behavior patterns are learned. Youths actively participate in the process with other individuals who serve as teachers and guides to delinquent behavior. Thus, delinquency cannot appear without the aid of others.

3. *The principal part of the learning of criminal behavior occurs within intimate personal groups.* Children's contacts with their most intimate social companions—family, friends, and peers—have the greatest influence on their learning of deviant behavior and attitudes. Relationships with these individu-

als color and control the interpretation of everyday events. Consequently, they help youths to overcome social controls so that they can embrace delinquent values and behavior. The intimacy of these associations far outweighs the importance of any other form of communication, for example, movies or television. Even on those rare occasions when violent motion pictures seem to provoke mass delinquent episodes, these outbreaks can be more readily explained as a reaction to peer group pressure than as a reaction to the films themselves.

4. *The learning of criminal behavior includes techniques of committing the crime, which are sometimes very complicated, sometimes very simple; and the specific direction of motives, drives, rationalizations, and attitudes.* Since delinquent behavior is similar to other learned behavior, it follows that the actual techniques of criminality must also be acquired and learned. For example, young delinquents learn from their associates the proper way to pick a lock, shoplift, and obtain and use narcotics. In addition, delinquents must learn to use the proper terminology for their acts and then acquire the proper personal reactions to them. For example, as Howard Becker points out, getting high on marijuana and learning the proper way to "smoke a joint" are behavior patterns usually acquired from more experienced companions.[3] Moreover, delinquents must learn how to react properly to their criminal acts—when to defend them, rationalize them, show remorse for them.

5. *The specific direction of motives and drives is learned from various favorable and unfavorable definitions of the legal codes.* Since the reaction to social rules and laws is not uniform across society, youths constantly come into contact with people who maintain different views on the utility of obeying the legal code. When definitions of right and wrong are extremely varied, people experience what Sutherland calls *culture conflict.* The attitudes toward criminal behavior of the important people in young people's lives influences the attitudes that they themselves develop. The conflict of social attitudes is the basis for the concept of differential association.

6. *A person becomes delinquent if definitions favorable to violating the law exceed definitions unfavorable to it.* According to Sutherland's theory, individuals will become delinquent when they are in contact with persons, groups, or events that produce an excess of definitions toward delinquency and, concomitantly, when they are isolated from counteracting forces.

A definition toward delinquency occurs, for example, when a youth is exposed to friends sneaking into a theater to avoid paying for a ticket or friends talking about the virtues of getting high. A definition against delinquency occurs when friends or parents demonstrate their disapproval of crime. Of course, neutral behavior, such as reading a book, exists. It is neither positive nor negative with respect to law violation. Cressey argues that it is important "especially as an occupier of the time of a child so that he is not in contact with criminal behaviors during the time he is so engaged in the neutral behavior."[4]

7. *Differential associations may vary in frequency, duration, priority, or intensity.* Whether a child learns to obey the law or to disregard it is influenced by the quality of social interactions. Those of lasting duration will have greater influence than those that are briefer. Similarly, frequent contacts have greater effect than rare and haphazard contacts. Sutherland did not specify what he meant by *priority,* but Cressey and others have interpreted the term to mean the

age of children when they first encounter definitions toward criminality.[5] Contacts made early in life will probably have a greater and more far-reaching influence than those developed later on. Finally, *intensity* is generally interpreted to mean the importance and prestige attributed to the individual or groups from whom the definitions are learned. For example, the influence of a father, mother, or trusted friend will far outweigh the effect of more socially distant figures.

8. *The process of learning criminal behavior by association with criminal and anticriminal patterns involves all of the mechanisms that are involved in any other learning.* This statement suggests that the learning of criminal behavior patterns is similar to the learning of nearly all other patterns and is not a matter of mere imitation.

9. *While criminal behavior is an explanation of general needs and values, it is not explained by those needs and values, since noncriminal behavior is an explanation of the same needs and values.* By this principle, Sutherland suggests that the motives for delinquent behavior cannot logically be the same as those for conventional behavior. He rules out such motives as a desire to accumulate money or social status, a sense of personal frustration, a low self-concept, or any other similar motive as causes of delinquency. They are just as likely to produce noncriminal behavior such as getting a better education or working harder on a job. It is only the learning of deviant norms through contact with an excess of definitions toward criminality that produces delinquent behavior.

Empirical Research on Differential Association

Despite its importance, less than adequate research has been devoted to testing the assumptions of differential association theory. It is difficult to conceptualize the principles of the theory in a way that lends itself to empirical measurement. For example, social scientists find it difficult to evaluate such vague concepts as *definition toward delinquency*. However, a number of notable research efforts have been undertaken to test the validity of Sutherland's approach.

James Short tested a sample of 126 boys and 50 girls incarcerated in state training schools in order to measure the relationship between frequency, duration, priority, and intensity of interaction with delinquent peers and exposure to crime and delinquency.[6] Short used such measures as the number of friends a youth had who were delinquent, the degree to which a youth associated with criminals, and the intimacy of friendships with delinquents. Short found that a consistent relationship existed between delinquent behavior and delinquent associations and that such associations were highly significant for both boys and girls. However, since the study was conducted with institutionalized youths regarded as seriously delinquent, it may not be applicable to the "average" law-violating child.

In a similar study, Albert Reiss and A. Lewis Rhodes attempted to determine whether delinquent behavior was associated with maintaining delinquent friendship patterns.[7] Using a sample of 378 white males grouped into friendship cliques, Reiss and Rhodes found that a boy's chance of committing a specific delinquent act depended on whether other members of his friendship group committed that same act. This pattern was related to social class. Delinquent boys from blue-collar families maintained delinquent friendship patterns. Among youths from white-collar backgrounds, this relationship held true only for less serious offenses. Moreover, Reiss and Rhodes did not interpret their results to be clear-cut support for differential association.

In a study of the self-reported delinquent behavior of a sample of teenage boys, Travis Hirschi developed data that can also be used to test critical assumptions of differential association theory.[8] Included among Hirschi's many findings is the fact that boys with strong attachments to criminally oriented parents are *as likely* to commit crimes as boys attached to conventional, law-abiding parents—a finding that seems to contradict differential association.[9] However, Hirschi also found that boys with delinquent friends are more likely to be delinquent themselves, a finding in support of Sutherland's theory.[10]

In a controlled experiment, Reed Adams measured the effect that social variables like friendship and nonsocial variables like the desire for monetary gain had on the commission of delinquent acts.[11] Adams found that nonsocial variables were considerably more powerful in causing delinquency than social variables. Therefore, Adams is generally critical of differential association theory.[12]

In general, attempts to measure the validity of differential association have proved inconclusive, inadequate, and marked by ineffective methodologies. This has led critics such as Robert Burgess and Ronald Akers to state: "The attempts to subject the theory to empirical test are marked by inconsistent findings both within the same study and between studies, as well as by highly circumscribed and qualified findings and conclusions."[13]

Analysis of Differential Association Theory

Since Sutherland's death, the leading advocate and interpreter of differential association theory has been his associate, Donald Cressey. Cressey has attempted to reply to critics of the theory and has compiled a list of the most severe criticisms directed against it. Cressey suggests that a number of misconceptions about differential association theory exist and that they produce unwarranted criticism of it. For example, some criminologists mistakenly claim that the theory is solely concerned with the number of personal contacts and associations a delinquent has with other criminal or delinquent offenders.[14] If this assumption were true, those most likely to become criminals would be police, judges, and correctional authorities, since they are constantly associating with criminals. Cressey argues that Sutherland stressed "excess definitions toward criminality," not mere association with criminals. Personnel of the juvenile justice system do have extensive associations with criminals, but these are more than counterbalanced by their associations with law-abiding citizens.

Another misconception is that delinquent behavior is learned only by contact with delinquents and criminals. Cressey claims, however, that even though differential association stresses an excess of definitions toward delinquency, it does not specify that they must come solely from criminal sources. For example, seemingly law-abiding parents can encourage delinquent behavior by telling their children that it is OK to cheat on a test if that's the only way to get ahead. Another example of this phenomenon is society's open admiration of law violators who consistenly flaunt social norms yet remain immune to legal sanctions—gamblers, white-collar criminals, organized crime chieftans, and so on.

Cressey does acknowledge that Sutherland's theory fails to explain why one youth who is exposed to delinquent definitions eventually succumbs to them while another, living under the same conditions, avoids them. According to Cressey, however, the validity of differential association theory does not rest on *why* particular individuals have the associations they do. He argues that the great number of human personality traits have yet to be explored in their entirety and that this complex endeavor is an independent concern for future research. In fact, as one criminologist states, "Sutherland was probably not trying to devise a theory that would explain individual criminal behavior, but rather to develop a theory that would bring some order to the understanding of crime rates."[15]

These misconceptions aside, Cressey recognizes a number of legitimate criticisms that can be directed at differential association. For one thing, the fourth principle listed above, which discusses the learning of criminal techniques, fails to account for the origin of these techniques. How did the first "teacher" learn delinquent techniques and definitions in order to pass them on? Another apparently valid criticism of differential association is that it assumes criminal and delinquent acts to be rational and systematic. This ignores spontaneous and wanton acts of violence and damage that appear to have little utility or purpose, such as the isolated, psychopathic killing, which is virtually unsolvable because of the killer's anonymity and lack of delinquent associations.

Perhaps the most serious criticism of differential association theory concerns the vagueness of its terms. This vagueness makes it very difficult to test its assumptions. For example, what constitutes an "excess of definition toward criminality?" How can we determine whether an individual actually has a prodelinquent imbalance of these definitions? It is simplistic to assume that, by definition, all delinquents have experienced a majority of definitions toward delinquency and all nondelinquents a minority of them. Unless the terms employed in the theory can be defined more precisely, its validity remains a matter of guesswork.

Despite these criticisms, differential association theory still maintains an important place in the study of delinquent behavior. For one thing, it provides a consistent explanation of *all* types of delinquent and criminal behavior. Unlike the social structure theories discussed previously it is not limited to the explanation of a single facet of antisocial activity, for example, lower-class gang activity. The theory can account for the extensive delinquent behavior found in middle- and upper-class areas. Even in these cultures, youths may be exposed to a variety of prodelinquent definitions from such sources as overly opportunistic parents and friends. Thus, it has greater application than the subcultural strain theory discussed earlier. In Highlight 6–1, criminologist Clarence Schrag discusses the importance of differential association theory.

Highlight 6–1. Clarence Schrag on Differential Association.

Instead of regarding crime as a product of personal inadequacies or of abnormal learning experiences, differential association implies that a society's norms may include criminal as well as noncriminal prescriptions, and that criminal behavior is to be expected of those individuals who have internalized an excess of definitions favoring law violations sufficient to prevail over their noncriminal definitions. Furthermore, it denies that law violators are the only sources of criminal skills and motivations, maintaining that persons who have never been arrested may serve as carriers of criminal definitions and rationalizations. Since these definitions, skills, and rationalizations are by no means restricted to the city slums or to the lower classes, it follows that criminal behavior may be indigenous to all segments of society, including our most hallowed institutions. In this way the theory brings a sharper focus on some of the social and cultural factors involved in crime causation.

The importance of this focus is apparent when the theory's claims are compared with the relevant empirical evidence. Criminal statistics suggest that offenses such as vagrancy, disorderly conduct, and most violations of vice laws are mainly concentrated in the lower classes; but homicide, assault, and many street crimes are distributed throughout the social spectrum, even though their greatest frequencies are usually found in highly urbanized and socially heterogeneous areas. Malfeasance, illegal fee-splitting, and certain other kinds of political and economic infractions, by contrast, are found almost exclusively in the more privileged groups and classes.

Source: Clarence Schrag, *Crime and Justice, American Style* (Washington, D.C.: Government Printing Office, 1971), p. 48.

In sum, despite the many criticisms leveled against it, differential association theory remains the most influential and well-known explanation of crime and delinquency in operation today.

NEUTRALIZATION THEORY

Neutralization theory, sometimes referred to as drift theory, is identified with the writings of David Matza and his associate, Gresham Sykes.[16] Like Sutherland, Sykes and Matza view the process of becoming a delinquent as a learning experience. However, their approach differs on some critical issues. Sutherland suggests that youths learn the techniques, values, and attitudes necessary for delinquent behavior. Sykes and Matza maintain that delinquents hold attitudes and values similar to those of law-abiding citizens. However, they learn techniques that enable them to neutralize these values and attitudes temporarily and *drift* back and forth between legitimate and delinquent behavior.

In his major work, *Delinquency and Drift*, Matza explains this position more fully. He suggests that most individuals spend their lives behaving on a continuum somewhere between total freedom and total restraint. "Drift" is the process by which an individual moves from one extreme of behavior to another, behaving sometimes in an unconventional, free, or deviant manner and at other times with constraint and sobriety.

The existence of a subculture of delinquency, in which criminal behavior is regularly supported, encourages drift among young people. Matza views the subculture as relatively amorphous and without formal rules of values (except those that are bestowed upon it by sociologists). He characterizes it as an informal, relatively inarticulate oral tradition. Members of the subculture infer the behavior they are to follow from the behavior cues of their comrades, including slogans and actions.[17]

Subsequently, writing with Gresham Sykes, Matza rejected the notion that the subculture of delinquency maintains an independent set of values and attitudes that place the delinquent in direct opposition to the values of the dominant culture. Rather, Matza and Sykes point to the existence in our society of a complex pluralistic culture that is both deviant and ethical. Juveniles are particularly susceptible to *subterranean values* since society does not provide them with specific goals or role orientations.

In a later paper, Matza, writing alone, further defines his concept of the teenage subculture as a conventional version of the delinquent's traditional behavior. It emphasizes fun and adventure, and its members are persistently involved in status offenses like smoking, drinking, gambling, and making out. They disdain school work and scholars and are overly concerned with proving masculinity or feminity.[18]

Techniques of Neutralization

Sykes and Matza suggest that juveniles develop a distinct set of justifications for their behavior when it violates accepted social norms. These "neutralization techniques" allow youths to temporarily drift away from the rules of the normative society and participate in subterranean behaviors. Sykes and Matza base their theoretical model on the following observations.[19]

In the first place, delinquents sometimes voice a sense of guilt over their illegal acts. If a stable delinquent value system existed in opposition to generally held values and rules, it would be unlikely that delinquents would exhibit any remorse for their acts, other than regret at being apprehended.

Second, juvenile offenders frequently respect and admire honest, law-abiding persons. "Really honest" persons are often revered, and if for some reason they are accused of misbehavior, the delinquent is quick to defend their integrity. Those admired may include sports figures, priests and other clergy, parents, teachers, and neighbors.

Third, delinquents draw a line between those whom they can victimize and those whom they cannot. Members of similar ethnic groups, churches, or neighborhoods are off limits as far as crime goes. This practice implies that delinquents are aware of the wrongfulness of their acts. Why else limit them?

Finally, delinquents are not immune to the demands of conformity. Most delinquents frequently participate in many of the same social functions as law-abiding youths, for example, school, church, and family activities.

Sykes and Matza argue that the evidence stated above substantiates the fact that delinquents operate as part of the normative culture and adhere to its values and standards. How, then, do they account for delinquency? They suggest that delinquency is a result of the neutralization of accepted social values through the employment of a standard set of rationalizations for illegal behavior. Thus, most youths generally adhere to the rules of society but learn techniques to temporarily release themselves from their moral constraints. Specifically, these techniques are as follows.[20]

THE DENIAL OF RESPONSIBILITY   Delinquents sometimes claim that their unlawful acts were simply not their fault. Delinquent acts were due to forces beyond their control, or they were an accident.

DENIAL OF INJURY   By denying the wrongfulness of an act, delinquents are able to rationalize their illegal behavior. For example, stealing is viewed as "borrowing"; vandalism is considered mischief that has gotten out of hand. Society often agrees with delinquents, labeling their illegal behavior "pranks" and thereby reaffirming that delinquency can be socially acceptable.

DENIAL OF VICTIM   Delinquents sometimes rationalize their behavior by maintaining that the victim of crime "had it coming." Thus, vandalism may be directed against a disliked teacher or neighbor, or homosexuals may be beaten up by a gang because their behavior is offensive.[21] Denying the victim may also take the form of ignoring the rights of an absent or unknown victim, for example, the unseen owner of a department store. It becomes morally acceptable for delinquents to commit crimes, such as vandalism, when the victims cannot be sympathized with or respected because of their absence.

CONDEMNATION OF THE CONDEMNERS   The delinquent views the world as a corrupt place with a dog-eat-dog moral code. Since police and judges are on the take, teachers show favoritism, and parents take out their frustrations on their kids, it is ironic and unfair for these authorities to turn around and condemn youthful misconduct. By shifting the blame to others, delinquents are able to repress the feeling that their own acts are wrong.

APPEAL TO HIGHER LOYALTIES   Delinquents argue that they are caught in the dilemma of being loyal to their own peer group while at the same time attempting to abide by the rules of the larger society. The needs of the group take precedence over the rules of society because the demands of the former are immediate and localized.[22]

In sum, the theory of neutralization presupposes a condition in which such slogans as "I didn't mean to do it," "I didn't really hurt anybody," "They had it coming to them," "Everybody's picking on me," and "I didn't do it for myself," are used by youths to rationalize accepted social norms and values so that they can enter or "drift" into delinquent modes of behavior.

Empirical Research on Neutralization Theory

A number of attempts have been made to verify the assumptions of neutralization theory empirically. Unfortunately, the results have been inconclusive. For example, Robert Ball created a neutralization inventory and used it with a sample of institutionalized and noninstitutionalized youth of high school age.[23] His inventory showed that institutionalized youths and self-reported delinquents accept excuses for deviant behavior to a significantly greater degree than noninstitutionalized youths and self-reported nondelinquents. These findings support Sykes and Matza. However, Ball's research data were gathered after delinquent behavior had already occurred. It cannot be inferred that delinquents also call upon justifications before they commit crimes or that these justifications cause the delinquent to drift.

In a study that generated opposing data, Michael Hindelang evaluated the self-reported delinquent behavior of a sample of high school youths.[24] Hindelang found that participation in delinquent activities is associated with greater approval of such activities. He concluded that delinquents do not subscribe to the same moral code as nondelinquents. Therefore, they have no real reason to neutralize societal constraints. This finding contradicts Sykes and Matza. However, Hindelang's sample was rather small (sixty-nine subjects), and he measured approval and disapproval of delinquent behavior after it had occurred.

In a recent study, Robert Regoli and Eric Poole updated Hindelang's work by testing the attitudes incarcerated youths hold toward their misdeeds. They found that the attitudes of those engaging in serious delinquent activity do not differ from those refraining from such activity.[25] They concluded that it is indeed possible that delinquents drift in and out of delinquent behavior. Unfortunately, Regoli and Poole's research suffers from methodological problems since it fails to include a truly nondelinquent comparison group.

A number of studies have attempted to test the validity of neutralization theory by comparing the values of delinquents to those of nondelinquents. If neutralization theory is valid, these groups should *not* differ in their values and attitudes. Robert Gordon and his associates assessed the attitudes of delinquent gang members and other youths toward social goals, leisure activities, and ethical orientations, as well as their degree of participation in delinquent behavior.[26] They found that gang youth value such middle-class behavior as "working for grades," "reading good books," and "saving one's money" as highly as nondelinquent youth, a finding that supports neutralization theory. Nonetheless, gang youths also value "pimps" and "fences" more highly than nongang youths, a finding that contradicts neutralization theory.

Larry Siegel and his associates found that delinquents do not value middle-class concepts like "the law," "saving money," and "education" as highly as nondelinquents.[27] However, Siegel did find that delinquents have generally favorable attitudes towards middle-class values, a finding that supports neutralization theory.

These representative studies illustrate the inconclusive evidence that has been generated in empirical tests of neutralization theory. Some research studies indicate that delinquents generally approve of social values; others reach the opposite conclusion. Some studies indicate that delinquent youths approve of criminal behavior; still others have found evidence that they oppose illegal bahavior. If neutralization theory is become a valid and practical explanation of delinquency, further research aimed at testing its assumptions is needed.

Analysis of Neutralization Theory

The theory of neutralization is a major contribution to the literature of crime and delinquency. Considered as a theoretical model, it avoids many of the pitfalls that beset earlier attempts to explain delinquent behavior.

One important feature of the theory is that it accounts for the fact that many teenage delinquents do not evolve into adult criminals. Neutralization theory implies that youths can forego criminal behavior when they reach their majority because in reality they never really rejected the morality of normative society. Once the needs and pressures of the postteenage world exert themselves—marriage, family, and job—delinquents are more likely than ever to drift into legitimate modes of behavior.

Second, unlike the social structure theories, neutralization theory does not presuppose that delinquents reject most middle-class attitudes, beliefs, and values. It is difficult to believe and harder to prove that delinquent youths do not share at least some of the same values and attitudes of other citizens. After all they belong to the same churches, attend the same schools, and share other facilities.

Finally, the concept of neutralization provides a logical explanation of many delinquent activities that defy other theoretical explanations. For example, the use of "soft" drugs such as marijuana, LSD, and cocaine seems particularly amenable to neutralization techniques like "everybody's doing it," "no one is really hurt," and so on.

Neutralization theory also has its drawbacks. As Travis Hirschi asks: Do delinquents neutralize law-violating behavior *before* or *after* they engage in it?[28] If in fact they neutralize their guilt after engaging in illegal activity, then neutralization theory loses its power as an explanation of the *cause* of delinquency and becomes a theory describing the *reactions* of juveniles to their misdeeds.

Even if neutralization techniques are actually used before the commission of delinquent acts, the theory fails to distinguish why some youths consistently drift into delinquency and others do not. Unless we can understand why drift occurs, the theory will remain too abstract and vague to be of practical use.

CONTROL THEORY

Control theory, the product of criminologist Travis Hirschi, links delinquent behavior to the bond an individual maintains with society. When that bond weakens or breaks, the constraints that society puts on its members are lifted, and an individual may violate the law.[29] Unlike some of the other theoretical models discussed here, Hirschi's control theory assumes that all individuals are potential delinquents and criminals and that social controls, not moral values, maintain law and order. Without controls and in the absence of sensitivity to and interest in others, a youth is free to commit criminal acts.[30]

Hirschi speculates that a consistent value system exists and that all people in society are exposed to it. Delinquents defy this moral code because their attachment to society is weak. In contrast to Sykes and Matza who believe that delinquents share the same values and attitudes as nondelinquents, Hirschi views the youthful law violator as someone who rejects social norms and beliefs. The major elements of his argument are: (1) there is a "variation in belief in the moral validity of social rules,"[31] (2) this variation is brought about by a weakening of the attachment of the individual to elements of society, and (3) this condition produces delinquent behavior.

Elements of Control Theory

Hirschi argues that the *social bond* a person maintains with society is divided into four main elements. They are detailed below.

ATTACHMENT   Attachment refers to a person's sensitivity to and interest in others. Psychologists believe that without a sense of attachment, a person becomes a psychopath and loses the ability to relate coherently to the world. The acceptance of social norms and the development of a social conscience depend on attachment to and caring for other human beings. Hirschi views parents, peers, and schools as the most important social institutions with which a person should maintain ties. Attachment to parents is the most important. Even if a family is shattered by divorce and separation, a child must retain a strong attachment to one or both parents. Without attachment to one's family, it is unlikely that feelings of respect for others in authority will develop.[32]

COMMITMENT   Commitment involves the time, energy, and effort expended in pursuit of conventional lines of action. It embraces such activities as getting an education and saving money for the future. Control theory holds that if people build up a strong involvement to life, property, and reputation, they will be less likely to engage in acts that will jeopardize their position. Conversely, lack of commitment to conventional values may foreshadow a condition in which risk-taking behavior, such as delinquency, becomes a reasonable behavior alternative.

INVOLVEMENT   An individual's heavy involvement in conventional activities does not leave time for illegal behavior. Hirschi believes that involvement — in school, recreation, and family — insulates a youth from the potential lure of delinquent behavior that idleness encourages.

BELIEF   People who live in common social settings often share a similar moral doctrine and revere such human values as sharing, sensitivity to the rights of others, and admiration for the legal code. If these beliefs are absent or weakened, individuals are more likely to share in antisocial acts.[33]

Hirschi further suggests that the interrelationship of elements of the social bond influences whether an individual pursues delinquent or conventional activities. For example, boys or girls who feel kinship and sensitivity to parents and friends should be more likely to desire and work toward legitimate goals. On the other hand, youths who reject social relationships will probably lack commitment to conventional goals. In a similar fashion, youths who are highly committed to conventional acts and beliefs will be more likely to be involved in conventional activities.

Empirical Research on Control Theory

One of Hirschi's most significant contributions to delinquency research is his attempt to test the principal hypothesis of control theory. He administered a complex self-report survey to a sample of over 4,000 junior and senior high school students in Contra Costa County, California.[34] In a detailed analysis of the data, Hirschi found considerable evidence to support the control theory model. A few of his more important findings are discussed in detail below.

ATTACHMENT Hirschi measured attachment to society with such survey items as, "Would you like to be the kind of person your father is?" and "When you come across things you don't understand, does your mother (father) help you with them?" Hirschi found that youths who were strongly attached to their parents were less likely to participate in delinquent behavior. This relationship also existed when race, social class and the parents own values were controlled.

With regard to this point, Hirschi found that lower-class parents, even those who themselves are committing criminal acts, express allegiance to the law and conventional society. Thus, attachment to the parents counteracts delinquent behavior even when the parents themselves are deviant.[35]

Hirschi also found that lack of attachment to the school and to education, measured by items such as, "Do you care what teachers think of you" and "It is none of the school's business if a student wants to smoke outside the classroom" is a strong predictor of delinquent behavior. Poor school performance and academic incompetence affect this relationship significantly. Youths with poor basic academic skills are likely to become detached from school and involved in delinquency. Hirschi traces this important relationship as follows: "The causal chain runs from academic incompetence to poor school performance to disliking of school to rejection of the school's authority to the commission of delinquent acts."[36]

Hirschi also examined the attachment of youths to their friends and other peers, using such questions as "Would you like to be the kind of person your best friends are?" He found that youths who maintain close associations with friends are less likely to commit delinquent acts. Delinquent youths, on the other hand, often maintain weak and distant relationships with their peers. Hirschi did find that boys with a high stake in conformity who maintain delinquent friends are more likely to commit delinquent acts than boys with a high stake in conformity without delinquent friends. However, this relationship does not immediately contradict the control approach. First, only 22 percent of the high stake boys had delinquent friends. Second, the greater a youth's stake in conformity, the less likely he was to maintain delinquent companions.

Among Hirschi's most important discoveries are:

1. Contrary to subcultural strain theories, the gang rarely recruits "good" boys or influences them to turn "bad."

2. Boys who maintain middle-class values are relatively unaffected by the delinquent behavior of their friends.
3. The idea that delinquents have warm, intimate relationships with one another is a myth.
4. "The child with little stake in conformity is susceptible to prodelinquent influences in his environment; the child with a large stake in conformity is relatively immune to these influences."[37]

COMMITMENT   Hirschi examined commitment to both deviant and conventional activities with questionnaire items dealing with frequency of smoking, drinking, and dating behavior, level of educational aspiration (desire for a college education, for example), and level of vocational expectation (blue-collar, white-collar, professional). Again, Hirschi found evidence that commitment to conventional values is related to rejection of delinquent behavior. On the other hand, youths who drink and cruise around in cars are often involved in delinquency. He states, "The picture of the delinquent as a striver, either in word or deed, simply does not fit the data."[38]

INVOLVEMENT   Involvement in conventional activities was defined as time spent on homework, and involvement in unconventional activities was defined as hours a week spent riding around in cars. Again, Hirschi found that involvement in school inhibits delinquency. On the other hand, youths who smoke, drink, date, ride around in cars, and find adolescence "boring" are more prone to delinquency.[39] However, this relationship is not as strong as Hirschi expected, and he found that boys who are involved in unconventional activities (smoking, drinking, and so on) are more likely to engage in delinquent acts regardless of their commitment to education and their involvement in school activities.

BELIEF   Hirschi measured a large variety of commonly held beliefs and values. Not surprisingly, he found that youths who expressed respect for the police and the law were less likely to commit delinquent acts. In general, there was little difference in the beliefs of delinquents and nondelinquents. In fact, delinquents often respected middle-class attitudes. For example, Hirschi reports that children who do not personally care about good grades still believe that youths who do care about school and get good grades are taking a path preferable to their own.[40]

Hirschi's data lend important support to the validity of control theory. While the statistical significance of his findings is sometimes less than he expected, his research data are extremely consistent. Only in very rare instances do his findings contradict the theory's most critical assumptions.

There have been other attempts to corroborate Hirschi's findings, most notably a 1973 study by Michael Hindelang.[41] Using subjects in the sixth through twelfth grades in a rural New York State school system, Hindelang replicated a number of Hirschi's most important results. With few exceptions, Hindelang's evidence supported Hirschi's control theory principles. The major difference between the two studies was in the area of attachment to peers. Hindelang found that close identification with peers was directly related to delinquent activity, while Hirschi's research produced the opposite result.

In sum, unlike many other theoretical models, control theory has stood the test of rigorous empirical research designed to evaluate its most significant assertions. It therefore presents an important arena for future research designed to validate its assumptions.

Analysis of Control Theory

Hirschi's control theory is a broad, far-reaching theory of delinquent behavior. It avoids the narrow focus of sociocultural theories, since it is applicable to youths in high, middle, and low socioeconomic groups. For example, in lower-class settings, the social bond may weaken because of limited access to legitimate activities, lack of attachment to a poor school system, and an impaired commitment to unobtainable future goals. Middle- and upper-class youths may find that their bond to their parents is weak, that their academic abilities fall below what is expected of people in their cultural circumstances, or that their relatively secure financial status interferes with a true commitment to long-term goals. Thus, control theory is neither culture-bound not limited to explaining delinquency among youths in a particular social class.

Another strength of control theory is its adaptability to empirical measurement. Many of the theoretical models discussed previously rely heavily on ambiguous concepts such as anomie, definitions toward delinquency, and drift, but Hirschi defines elements of the bond in simple, straightforward terms. For example, a youth's involvement can be measured by actual participation in school activities, community programs, and religious services.

Despite its relative power, control theory has some theoretical deficiencies. It fails to describe the chain of events that weaken the social bond. For example, is the weakening of one particular element of the bond—attachment, belief, commitment, or involvement—the principle cause of delinquency? When it is weakened, does it trigger deficiencies in the other elements, or are they all weakened simultaneously? Control theory also fails to explain whether a youth can maintain a strong bond to society and still be delinquent. In addition, Hirschi does not take into account periodic weakening of the social bond. Once weakened, is it possible for the bond to strengthen itself? Is delinquency episodic, or are delinquents perpetually involved in illegal behavior? Since most delinquents do not become adult criminals, can we assume that somehow their social bonds eventually are strengthened? How is this possible? Control theory does not adequately answer these and similar questions.

CONTAINMENT THEORY

Containment theory is a clear departure from sociological theories that fail to devote any attention to the individual characteristics of delinquents.[42] It is directed at answering the questions: "How is it possible for a youth living in a high crime and poverty area to resist engaging in delinquent activity" and "What personal properties *insulate* a youth from otherwise delinquent-producing influences." Criminologists advocating containment theory argue that sociological theories that ignore individual characteristics of offenders are insufficient as explanations of individual or group delinquency.[43]

Briefly, containment theory contends that society produces a series of pushes and pulls toward delinquency. These in turn are counteracted by internal and external containments, which help insulate the individual from delinquency. The elements of the theory are discussed in greater detail below.

INNER CONTAINMENTS   Inner containments consist of the inner strength of an individual personality—for example, good self-concept, ego strength, high frustration tolerance, goal orientation, and tension-reducing capabilities.

OUTER CONTAINMENTS   Outer containments are the normative constraints that societies and social groups ordinarily use to control their members. They consist of such factors as a sense of belongingness, consistent moral front, reinforcement of norms, goals, and values, effective supervision, discipline, and meaningful social role.[44]

INTERNAL PUSHES   Internal pushes involve such personal factors as restlessness, discontent, hostility, rebellion, mental conflict, anxieties, and need for immediate gratification.

EXTERNAL PRESSURES   External pressures are adverse living conditions that influence deviant behavior. They include relative deprivation poverty, unemployment, insecurity, minority status, limited opportunities, and inequalities.[45]

EXTERNAL PULLS   External pulls are represented by deviant companions, membership in criminal subcultures or other deviant groups, and influences such as mass media and pornography.

Simply put, containment theory suggests that the two containments act as a defense against a person's potential deviation from legal and social norms and work to insulate a youth from the pressures and pulls of crimogenic influences. If, in fact, social causes of crime exist, the containments act as buffers against them. Walter Reckless, who developed containment theory, suggests that of the two, inner containment is the more important in our society because individuals spend much of their time away from the family and other supportive groups that can contain them. They must therefore rely on their internal (inner) strengths to control their delinquent (push) urges.[46]

Nevertheless, youths subjected to both containments are less likely to become delinquent than those subjected to only one. Those with weak inner and external containments are the most prone to delinquency.

Empirical Research on Containment Theory

Walter Reckless has made an extensive effort to validate the principles of containment theory. In one early study, Reckless and his associates asked high school teachers in a high crime area to nominate boys who in their opinion would neither commit delinquent acts nor experience police and juvenile court contact.[47] The 125 boys included in Reckless's final sample of "good boys" scored very high on social responsibility scales and very low delinquency proneness scales. On self-evaluation items, the "good boys" reported themselves to be rather law-abiding and obedient. They attempted to avoid trouble at all costs and conformed to expectations of parents and teachers. In addition, their home life and relationships with parents were excellent. These findings led the researchers to conclude that insulation against delinquency is an ongoing process reflecting an "internalization of non-delinquent values and conformity to the expectations of significant others."[48] Whether nondelinquent boys are able to maintain their conventional status will depend on their ability to maintain their positive self-image in the face of environmental pressures toward delinquency.

In a follow-up study, Reckless and his associates compared "insulated" boys with those nominated as potential delinquents by their teachers. When the two groups were compared, significant differences in parental relations, self-image, and social responsibility were found. The "good boys" did better in each category.[49] Four years later, Simon Dinitz, Frank Scarpitti, Walter Reckless, and Ellen Murray followed up the original sample in order to measure any changes that had occurred.[50] The researchers found remarkable stability in self-image and personal behavior. "Good boys" maintained their superiority in self-image, behavior, and future optimism.

Despite their varied research efforts, the work of Reckless and his associates has been criticized for its lack of methodological rigor.[51] Questions have been raised about the adequacy of Reckless's measures of self-concept, the confusing definitions of terms, the unexplained differences in the number of "good" and "bad" boys contained in follow-up samples (more "good" boys than "bad" boys were located), and the fact that "good" and "bad" boys were measured one year apart.[52] In addition, using teacher nominations of "good" and "bad" boys seems to invalidate all of Reckless's research findings. On the one hand, teachers may nominate as "good" those boys who perform and behave well in school. Thus, school ability and performance rather than internal or external containment may be the true predictor of delinquency (a suggestion that supports Hirschi's control theory). On the other hand, once teachers have picked boys as "good" or "bad," it is possible that their selection influences further teacher-student relationships and consequently helps maintain the existing climate in the classroom. Thereafter, "good boys" may continue to receive favorable responses from teachers, and "bad boys" may get negative ones. This reaction certainly can help explain the stability of self-perception and proneness to delinquency that Reckless and his colleagues found in follow-up studies.

Analysis of Containment Theory

The major strength of containment theory is its ability to account for both delinquent and nondelinquent youths in high crime areas. It is a clear departure from prior theoretical models that focus solely on delinquent behavior and fail to explain the ability of some youths to conform to socially approved behavior despite their exposure to crimogenic influences. Another salient feature of containment theory is that it unifies sociological and psychological approaches to crime. Also, as Clarence Schrag contends, containment theory avoids presenting the societal effect on delinquency as homogenous. Instead, it portrays delinquent behavior as being affected by competing forces, some of which have a positive and some a negative influence.[53]

Schrag has also found a number of shortcomings of containment theory.[54] He contends that it does not lend itself to empirical testing. For example, Reckless provides few hints as to how to measure the relative strength of "inner" and "outer" containments. Also, the definitions of key terms such as *pushes* and *pulls* are ambiguous. In addition, Schrag finds that containment theory neglects to distinguish between types of delinquent behavior. That is, it fails to explain why one youth joins a gang, why another uses narcotics, why another damages property, and so on.

In sum, while containment theory presents a fresh approach to the study of delinquency, its methodological problems interfere with the acceptance of its most critical assumptions.

POLICY IMPLICATIONS OF SOCIAL PROCESS THEORIES

Social process theories have been used as a basis for delinquency prevention in a number of different areas. The basic assumption is that certain social processes and institutions are responsible for delinquent behavior and must be reversed or counteracted to impede youthful misbehavior and promote attachment to the conventional social order.

Some early programs attempted to marshall the forces of the community to provide support for potential delinquents. In one well-known project, the Cambridge-Somerville Youth Study,[55] teachers and police referred children between six and eleven years of age to a committee that then predicted whether they would eventually become delinquents. This predelinquent group was then assigned to a treatment schedule that involved intensive personal counseling over an average of five years. Nonetheless, comparison of this group with control groups led to the conclusion that the program had no significant benefit for delinquency prevention.[56] A similar program conducted by the New York City youth board met with equivalent disappointing results.[57]

Social process theory concepts have also been used to promote delinquency prevention through treatment. For example, differential association theory has been applied in treatment programs in which delinquent youth are subjected to "definitions toward delinquency" by formerly delinquent peers who have come to adopt legitimate behavior definitions themselves.[58] These programs will be discussed more formally in Chapters 17 and 18.

Perhaps the most important impact that social process theory has had on delinquency prevention policy has involved organizing the various agencies in the community—health, education, religion—to combat the forces promoting delinquency and strengthen the bond to the legitimate social order.

Highlight 6–2, a selection from a working paper of the National Advisory Commission on Criminal Justice Standards and Goals, discusses the concept of organizing community resources to prevent delinquency.

Highlight 6–2. Human Services and Delinquency Prevention.

Human Services and
Delinquency Prevention
Public action in delinquency prevention generally is restricted to improvements in the quality of human services provided to community members. This limitation does not negate individual responsibility and choice as a factor in the prevention of delinquency, but rather emphasizes that governments can influence personal action through educational, developmental, and supportive programming. Thus, although suggestions about child-rearing practices or child-teacher relations could have been offered, these would have overlooked the organization of service necessary to insure broad impact of such advice. The standards generally are cast in terms of specific recommendations to units of government or public agencies, but these programmatic ideas also are aimed at citizens who wish to evaluate the quality of the environment for child development in their own communities. . . .

The Health System
The health system refers to the network of people and facilities that is organized to provide care for the physical and mental health needs of the community. It includes doctors, nurses, medical technicians, and paraprofessionals, and the various equipment and technologies they employ. The health system is connected to delinquency most directly in the area of drug abuse, but there is increasing evidence that adequate health care can be of substantial help in preventing certain biologically related problems, such as hyperactivity or specific learning disabilities. Emphasis in the health area is on early identification of medical problem problems that might lead to behavioral

conflicts that contribute to delinquency. Recommendations in the area of mental health are aimed at helping individuals and families who face personal difficulties cope with societal and interpersonal tension.

The major issue in the provision of health care is the growing expense of providing adequate systems of health service. Good health care is becoming too expensive for most citizens to afford. Less affluent segments of the population are in particularly bad positions, because often they are more prone to illness due to nutritional deficiencies and have limited funds to purchase health services.

Currently there is national debate on alternative methods for financing health service, and there is increased concern for improving delivery of preventive health care services. The standards proposed in the health system area describe a minimum system for providing mental and physical health services. The thorny issue of funding such efforts through national health insurance or a private plan must be considered as part of the overall approach to providing good health services to families and children who desperately need such care.

Family Services
It is ironic that, despite a longstanding national dedication to the ideal of family life, so little concrete action has been taken to promote the wellbeing of families. Family services are among the least developed in social work practice, and few localities offer a comprehensive program in this area. Particular problems in the family area include the outdated system of welfare, which often works to destroy family ties rather than preserve them; the tax structure, which often penalizes families; and

changing sex role definitions, which are causing many persons to reevaluate the traditional forms of family life. It is not difficult to perceive that family life is going through a significant transformation within our society, in which old forms of family arrangements are being reexamined and new forms tried. Under such conditions of flux, it is important that positive steps be taken to support those families who are struggling to stay together.

To advocate one particular form of family life would be to make the same error as earlier national commissions, which supported one family style. The concept of family defined here is that of a living unit that provides care and nurturant support for its members in the context of mutual respect and love. This is the kind of family that can promote strong positive self-images among the young and perform the needed task of promoting the moral development of children.

The Educational System
Many observers have commented on the importance of the school in child development. The educational area is crucial to any comprehensive program for delinquency prevention. The central theme of the standards in this area is the need for a more thorough collaboration of the school system with the community. Schools must be integrated with the family and with other features of children's lives to provide meaningful educational experiences. The content and process of learning must be enriched by the diversity and support of community persons, who have much to contribute to the educational enterprise.

The question of financing is central to the educational area. School districts across the Nation are attempting to develop more equitable methods for securing educational revenues and distributing them fairly. The question of resources also is linked to the issue of school performance. The public is demanding higher levels of educational results commensurate with increased public expenditures. There is serious debate over the adequacy of current methods for

evaluating both teachers and students. One reasonably might expect that the educational system will continue to be a focus of public attention, because Americans have so much faith in it.

Manpower Development and the Employment System
A number of delinquency theorists have stressed the role of employment in assisting the child in the successful transition to adulthood. Indeed, many of one's social relationships develop from the work environment. Work is a crucial component of individual assessments of self-worth, as well as one method for accomplishing personal objectives. Unfortunately, the national record with respect to the employment of youth is not good; at present, nearly two-thirds of the Nation's teenagers are unemployed. Unemployment rates among inner-city minority youth are even higher. If this continues, the Nation faces the dismal prospect, and, indeed, the social disgrace of having an entire generation of disadvantaged youngsters who may never hold a steady job in their adult lives. . . .

Criminal/Juvenile Justice System
The quality of justice exhibited by the criminal and juvenile justice systems is critical in developing pro-legal attitudes among the young. Juvenile justice personnel must take some responsibility for prevention activities, without seeking to dominate community-wide approaches. The main component of successful law enforcement work in the prevention area is the development of cooperative working relationships with citizens and community groups who are concerned about the problems of crime and delinquency. Collaboration in the areas of diversion programs, the organization of citizen crime prevention efforts, and the dissemination of prevention information are examples of proven positive efforts in which criminal justice personnel help prevent delinquency.

Just as there are demands that the educational system become more receptive to community input, so too, citizens are calling for greater opportunities to scrutinize the juvenile justice system. Public confidence and support for law enforcement will come only from an informed public that is able to participate meaningfully in juvenile justice policies. Juvenile justice practitioners must be more open to citizen involvement in the same way that educators or health care professionals must be more open to public dialogue in their fields.

Criminal and juvenile justice agencies must be public examples of the principles of honesty, justice, and fair treatment. Lingering discriminatory practices in recruitment or selection of new personnel must end. Law must be enforced according to the principles which are cherished in a democracy. Anything less than the pursuit of justice surely will foster cynicism and apathy among the young.

Recreation
In times of scarce financial resources, it might seem logical to view recreation as a luxury item that can be ignored easily for the present. This view, however, grossly underestimates the role of recreation in the process of child development. Recreation permits children to learn new skills and to practice the social attitudes of cooperation and fair play. Recreation programs also can offer the individual an opportunity to express aspects of behavior not properly valued in other settings. Cultural enrichment programs are especially helpful in building positive self-images among the young and in developing their stake in conformity.

Many observers believe that the rising costs of recreation are out of control. Public space is at a premium and units of local government are pressured to make the most effective use possible of available space. One partial solution to this problem is to promote greater sharing of recreational facilities between the public and private sectors. Too often, resources are made available without proper coordinated planning, resulting in duplicative services. Public use of school and private recreational programming should be expanded, and

special emphasis should be placed on the neglected recreational needs of low-income neighborhoods. Innovative solutions for funding of recreational programming must be sought, so that the costs are kept within the means of all.

Housing
There are several ways in which adequate housing can be an effective component of a community program for delinquency prevention. First, decent housing would provide an environment that would foster normal and healthy children.

Principles of environmental design can be used to increase safety from crime in streets, public areas, and housing units. Environmental programs to promote safety often encourage increased use of public space in order to discourage law violators. Part of the answer in the housing area is to provide good living conditions that support community life in which neighbors take responsibility for one another.

This country faces a shortage of housing at the same time that there are thousands of abandoned living units in its major cities. The critical priority of all levels of government is to develop programs to recycle current housing resources. Housing is one area that local government can effectively act on, and action in the housing area is often beneficial in stimulating the local economy and providing needed jobs.

Religion
A child's development usually involves the inculcation of a set of moral beliefs that lead in the direction of socially approved behavior. Religious institutions traditionally have played a central role in the area of delinquency prevention, and many religious leaders remain forceful spokespersons for delinquency prevention in their communities. Religious organizations may sponsor programs themselves or they may become vehicles for public education about the subject of juvenile justice. Members of the religious community can be mobilized in support of necessary youth programming. Moreover, the religious community can

facilitate the participation of the private sector in delinquency prevention efforts.

Media
People are becoming increasingly aware of the impact of the mass media on their lives and the lives of their children. Television, radio, and the press are sources of education as great as or greater than the more traditional educational institutions of the community. The media constitute a very large national industry, dependent in large part on the patronage of the young. It is important to examine the collective effect of this industry on the development of young people. What values are they being taught by the media? What images of adult social roles do they see? Are they being prodded by media advertising into becoming conspicuous consumers at early ages? These are serious questions and the answers are sobering, especially when we consider the rise in drug abuse among the young and

media advertising campaigns that encourage alcohol consumption.

There has been considerable controversy surrounding violence and the media, and increasingly, the evidence has pointed to the detrimental impact television violence has on children. We know through research the effect wars and civil strife have in promoting youthful crime, and it is not hard to understand the impact the violence portrayed nightly on television can have on children. Although it would be wrong to hold the media solely responsible for the rising rates of delinquency, it would be equally wrong to imagine that the powerful communications industry does not exert a strong influence on youthful behavior.

Source: Adapted from National Advisory Commission of Criminal Justice Standards and Goals, *Juvenile Justice and Delinquency Prevention* (Washington, D.C.: Government Printing Office, 1977), pp. 80–83.

CHAPTER SUMMARY

Social process theories explain delinquency as a function of the human interactions that occur daily in society. As a group, they reject the view that delinquents are born criminals or that they are intellectually and psychologically impaired. In a similar vein, social process adherents take a dim view of theoretical models that blame delinquent behavior on the socioeconomic structure of society or on any of its class, racial, or social groupings.

Social process theories often stress the learning of delinquent or antidelinquent behavior. For example, Sutherland's theory of differential association suggests that delinquency is almost purely a learning process. Reckless's containment theory stresses the development of personal defenses that insulate youths against delinquency.

While Hirschi's control theory does not stress learning per se, it is evident that the weakening of the social bond is a long-term development that involves delinquent youths in an escalating process of antisocial behavior accompanied by a continuous diminution of their attachment to society.

Social process theories emphasize the active participation of youths in choosing their delinquent orientations. Delinquency is not a status that is simply conferred on a youth. It must be learned, practiced, and sought after. Furthermore, social process theories suggest that delinquent modes of adaptation are not the sole property of lower-class or disturbed youths. These theories predict that delinquency can occur in all social classes. Finally, social process theories recognize and account for a selectivity factor in delinquency. Not all youths living in an area become delinquent; not all delinquents become adult criminals.

However, social process theories do not account for the "aging out" factor in delinquency. This is a fault of the earlier social structure approach as well. Most delinquent youths stop violating the law once they mature and take on adult responsibilities such as marriage, family, and job. How is it possible for youths drawn into delinquency by social processes (or structures) to eventually withdraw from it? And, conversely, why do some youths become adult criminals? Perhaps the answer lies not so much in why youths become delinquents but in what happens to them once society recognizes their violations of law. It is to thoughts such as these that we turn in the next chapter.

DISCUSSION QUESTIONS

1. Identify the "processes" that produce delinquent behaviors?
2. Have you ever rationalized your deviant acts? What neutralization techniques did you use?
3. Discuss your "inner" and "outer" containments? Does self-esteem really influence behavior?
4. Comment on the statement "Delinquents are made, not born."

SUGGESTED READINGS

Bordua, David. "Recent Trends: Deviant Behavior and Social Control." *Annals of the American Academy of Political and Social Science* 369 (1967): 149–163.

Briar, Scott, and Irving Piliavin. "Delinquency: Situational Inducements and Commitment to Conformity." *Social Problems* 13 (1965): 35–45.

Cressey, Donald. "Differential Theory and Compliance Crime." *Journal of Criminal Law, Criminology and Police Science* 45 (1954): 29–40.

——"Application and Verification of the Differential Association Theory." *Journal of Criminal Law, Criminology, and Police Science* 43 (1952): 44.

Hindelang, Michael. "Causes of Delinquency: A Partial Extension and Replication." *Social Problems* 20 (1973): 47-487.

Hirschi, Travis. *Causes of Delinquency.* Berkeley: University of California Press, 1969.

Matza, David. *Delinquency and Drift.* New York: Wiley, 1964.

Reckless, Walter, *The Crime Problem.* 4th ed. Englewood Cliffs, N.J.: Prentice-Hall, 1967.

Short, James. "Differential Association and Delinquency." *Social Problems* 4 (1957): 233–239.

Sutherland, Edwin, and Cressey, Donald. *Criminology.* 8th ed. Philadelphia: Lippincott, 1970.

REFERENCES

1. Edwin Sutherland, *Principles of Criminology* (Philadelphia: Lippincott, 1939).

2. Edwin Sutherland and Donald Cressey, *Criminology,* 8th ed. (Philadelphia: Lippincott, (1970), pp. 75–77.

3. Howard Becker, *Outsiders* (New York: Free Press, 1963).

4. Sutherland and Cressey, *Criminology,* pp. 77–79.

5. Ibid.

6. James Short, "Differential Association as a Hypothesis: Problems of Empirical Testing," *So-*

cial Problems 8 (1960): 14–25.

7.   Albert Reiss and A. Lewis Rhodes, "The Distribution of Delinquency in the Social Class Structure," *American Sociological Review* 26 (1961): 732.

8.   Travis Hirschi, *Causes of Delinquency* (Berkeley: University of California Press, 1969).

9.   Ibid., p. 95.

10.   Ibid., p. 99.

11.   Reed Adams, "The Adequacy of Differential Association Theory," *Journal of Research in Crime and Delinquency* 11 (1974): 1–8.

12.   Ibid., p. 7.

13.   Robert Burgess and Ronald Akers, "A Differential Association-Reinforcement Theory of Criminal Behavior," *Social Problems* 14 (1966): 128–147.

14.   Donald Cressey, "Epidemiologies and Individual Conduct: A Case from Criminology," *Pacific Sociological Review* 3 (1960): 47–58.

15.   Sue Titus Reid, *Crime and Criminology*, 2d ed. (New York: Holt, Rinehart and Winston, 1979), p. 234.

16.   Gresham Sykes and David Matza, "Techniques of Neutralization: A Theory of Delinquency," *American Sociological Review* 22 (1957): 664–670; and David Matza, *Delinquency and Drift* (New York: Wiley, 1964).

17.   Matza, *Delinquency and Drift*, p. 51.

18.   David Matza, "Subterranean Traditions of Youth," *Annals* 378 (1961): 116.

19.   Sykes and Matza, "Techniques of Neutralization" p. 664-670.

20.   Ibid.

21.   See, for example, John Kitsuse, "Societal Reaction to Deviant Behavior," *Social Problems* 9 (1962): 247–256.

22.   For a vivid example of these values, see William F. Whyte, *Street Corner Society* (Chicago: University of Chicago Press, 1955).

23.   R. A. Ball, "An Empirical Exploration of Neutralization Theory," *Criminologica* 4 (1966): 22–32. See also M. William Minor, "The Neutralization of Criminal Offense," *Criminology* 18 (1980): 103–120.

24.   Michael Hindelang, "The Commitment of Delinquents to Their Misdeeds: Do Delinquents Drift?" *Social Problems* 17 (1970): 50–509.

25.   Robert Regoli and Eric Poole, "The Commitment of Delinquents to Their Misdeeds: A Reexamination," *Journal of Criminal Justice* 6 (1978): 261–269.

26.   Robert Gordon, James Short, Desmond Cartwright, and Fred Strodtbeck, "Values and Gang Delinquency: A Study of Street Corner Groups," *American Journal of Sociology* 69 (1963): 109–128.

27.   Larry Siegel, Spencer Rathus, and Carol Ruppert, "Values and Delinquent Youth: An Empirical Reexamination of Theories of Delinquency," *British Journal of Criminology* 13 (1973): 237–244.

28.   Hirschi, *Causes of Delinquency, p. 208.*

29.   Ibid.

30.   Ibid., p. 8.

31.   Ibid., p. 26.

32.   Ibid., p. 231.

33. Ibid., pp. 25–26.

34. Ibid., pp. 66–74.

35. Ibid., p. 108.

36. Ibid., p. 132.

37. Ibid., pp. 160–161.

38. Ibid., p. 185.

39. Ibid., p. 195.

40. Ibid., p. 224.

41. Michael Hindelang, "Causes of Delinquency: A Partial Replication and Extension," *Social Problems* 21 (1973): 471–487.

42. Among the many research reports by Reckless and his colleagues are Walter Reckless, Simon Kinitz, and Ellen Murray, "The Good Boy in a High Delinquency Area," *Journal of Criminal Law, Criminology, and Police Science* 48 (1957): 18–26; W. Reckless, S. Dinitz, and E. Murray, "Self-Concept as an Insulator against Delinquency," *American Sociological Review* 21 (1956): 744–746; W. Reckless and S. Dinitz, "Pioneering With Self-Concept as a Vulnerability Factor in Delinquency," *Journal of Criminal Law, Criminology, and Police Science* 58 (1967): 515–523; Walter Reckless, Simon Dinitz, and Barbara Kay, "The Self-Component in Potential Delinquency and Potential Non-delinquency," *American Sociological Review* 22 (1957): 566–570.

43. See Walter Reckless, *The Crime Problem* (New York: Appleton-Century-Crofts, 1967), pp. 469–483.

44. Schrag, *Crime and Justice, American Style*, p. 85.

45. Ibid.

46. Walter Reckless, "Containment Theory," in *The Sociology of Crime and Delinquency*, ed. Marvin Wolfgang, Leonard Savitz, and Norman Johnston, 2d ed. (New York: Wiley, 1970), p. 402.

47   Reckless, Dinitz, and Murray, "Self-Concept as an Insulator against Delinquency."

48. Ibid., p. 746.

49. Reckless, Dinitz, and Kay, "The Self-Component in Potential Delinquency and Potential Non-delinquency."

50. Frank Scarpitti, Ellen Murray, Simon Dinitz, and Walter Reckless, "The Good Boy in a High Delinquency Area: Four Years Later," *American Sociological Review* 23 (1960): 555–558.

51. Michael Schwartz and Sandra Tangri, "A Note on Self-Concept as an Insulator against Delinquency," *American Sociological Review* 30 (1965): 922–926.

52. Ibid.

53. Schrag, *Crime and Justice, American Style*, p. 84.

54. Ibid., pp. 84–85.

55. Edwin Powers and Helen Witmer, *An Experiment in the Prevention of Delinquency* (New York: Columbia University Press, 1961).

56. Ibid., p. 337.

57. Maude Craig and Selma Glick, "Ten Years' Experience with the Glueck Social Prediction Table," *Crime and Delinquency* 9 (1963): 249–261.

58. Donald Cressey, "Epidemiology and Individual Conduct," *Pacific Sociological Review* 3 (1960): 37–54.

Chapter 7

Chapter Outline

Introduction
Labeling Theory
Conflict Theory
Policy Implications of Social Reaction
   Theory
Chapter Summary

Key Terms, Names, and Cases

labeling theory
self-labeling
symbolic interaction
falsely accused
primary and secondary deviance
secret deviant
moral entrepreneur
demystification
conflict theory
Marxist thought
dialectic method
proletariat-bourgeoisie

Social Reaction Theories

INTRODUCTION

Social reaction theories suggest that delinquency results from the reactions of politically powerful individuals and groups, especially government social control agencies, to society's less fortunate members. These theoretical models view delinquents not as inherently wrong or evil people but rather as individuals who have a deviant status conferred upon them by those holding economic, political, and social power. A delinquent status therefore results from interpersonal interactions in which youths are made to feel inferior or outcast because of their socially unacceptable behavior. Some social reaction theorists maintain that the behavior of the economically and politically powerful is actually more deviant and criminal than the behavior of the youths they oppress. Police officers take bribes, businesses use unfair labor practices, politicians peddle their influence, and so on. Thus, it is not the quality of the delinquent act itself that is important to social reaction theorists; instead it is the way society and its institutions react to the act. The purpose of social reaction and control is, of course, to maintain the status quo, thereby ensuring that those in power will stay there indefinitely.

In this chapter, we will first review labeling theory, which maintains that official reactions to delinquent acts help label youths as "criminals," "troublemakers," and "outcasts" and helps lock them into a cycle of escalating delinquent acts and social sanctions. Then, we will turn to conflict theory, which holds that delinquent and criminal behavior is a product of the capitalist system of economic production and its destructive influence on human behavior.

LABELING THEORY

Proponents of labeling theory argue that being processed and labeled by the police, courts, and other agencies of justice becomes a critical determinant in the subsequent behavior of the suspected delinquent.[1] Labeling theory has been employed to explain juvenile and adult illegal behavior, as well as other forms of social deviance. However, our discussion will focus on delinquent behavior.

The way in which labels are applied and the nature of the labels themselves are likely to have important future consequences for the delinquent. The degree to which youngsters are perceived as criminals may affect their treatment at home, at work, and at school. Young offenders may find that their parents consider them a detrimental influence on younger brothers and sisters. Their teachers may place them in classes or tracks reserved especially for behavior problems, thus minimizing future chances of obtaining higher education.[2] The delinquency label may also restrict eligibility for employment and negatively affect the attitudes of society in general. And, of course, depending on the severity of the label, the youthful offender will be subjected to official sanctions ranging from a mild reprimand to incarceration.

Beyond these immediate results, labeling theory argues that, depending on the visibility of the label and the manner and severity with which it is applied, youths will have an increasing commitment to delinquent careers.[3] As the negative feedback of law enforcement agencies, parents, friends, teachers, and other figures, strengthens the commitment, delinquents may begin to reevaluate their own identity and come to see themselves as criminals, trouble-makers, or screw-ups.[4] Thus, through a process of identification and sanctioning, reidentification and increased sanctioning, the identity of young offenders becomes transformed. They are no longer children in trouble; they are *delinquents*, and they accept that label as a personal identity—a process called self-labeling.[5] (We employ this term to mean personal acceptance and acknowledgment of a negative label.)

A number of sources support labeling theory, including the President's Commission on Law Enforcement and the Administration of Justice, which states:

> The affixing of that label (delinquency) can be a momentous occurrence in a youngster's life. Thereafter he may be watched; he may be suspect; his every misstep may be evidence of his delinquent nature. He may be excluded more and more from legitimate activities and opportunities. Soon he may be designated and dealt with as a delinquent and will find it very difficult to move into a law-abiding path even if he can overcome his own belligerent reaction and self-image and seeks to do so.[6]

If the above statements are valid, the labeling process will be of great importance to those concerned with juvenile justice policy in America. Yet, relatively little empirical research has been carried out to test these assumptions or to measure the form and substance of the labeling process. The following sections will focus on a general overview of the labeling approach and then determine its specific relationship to delinquent behavior.

General Overview of Labeling Theory

Labeling theory traces its theoretical antecedents to the *symbolic interaction* school of sociology, whose proponents define self-concept as a function of the cues and reactions a person perceives from others.[7] Labeling theory focuses largely on social interactions that produce deviance. Its adherents claim that these interactions are of utmost importance in defining acts and individuals as deviant.

Labeling theory advocates view deviant behavior as a reaction of social sanctioning mechanisms to an individual act rather than a function of the act itself. "Deviance is not a property inherent in certain forms of behavior," argues sociologist Kai Erikson. "It is a property conferred upon those forms by the audiences which directly or indirectly witness them."[8]

This definition has been amplified by Edwin Schur, who states:

Human behavior is deviant to the extent that it comes to be viewed as involving a personally discreditable departure from a group's normative expectation and it elicits interpersonal and collective reactions that serve to "isolate," "treat," "correct" or "punish" individuals engaged in such behavior.[9]

Thus, the labeling approach focuses primarily on the social audience's reaction to persons and their behavior and the subsequent effects of that reaction rather than on the cause of the deviant behavior itself. Furthermore, labeling theorists allege that the treatment of offenders in the labeling process depends far less on their behavior than on the way others view their acts. This is not to say that the labeled person is a totally passive participant in an encounter whose onset and direction is controlled solely by the whim of capricious social control agencies. On the contrary, labeling theorists hold that people are given deviant labels because they actually participate in illegal or outlawed behavior.[10] The labeling perspective suggests that the offender is deviant as a matter of choice. Deviant behavior is not a semiautomatic response to social pressure or psychological conditions as early positivist theories suggest.[11] This behavior has been characterized as "risk-taking" behavior that the offender decides on.

The decision to engage in behavior that eventually may be labeled deviant is influenced by an individual's place in the social structure. Adherence to societal norms, especially legal rules, is predicated upon the relationship of the individual to the group whose particular values the norms have been designed to give dominance. Where personal allegiance is accorded to the established power structure, the probability of taking the risk of engaging in illegal behavior is reduced; on the other hand, members of outcast subgroups may frequently engage in illegal behavior as a means of acquiring group approval or obtaining material goods, where other avenues for achieving such goals are closed.[12] Thus, members of minority groups and individuals in the lower socioeconomic classes are much more likely to be labeled and sanctioned than the rich and powerful.

Societal Response to Labeling

In response to social transgressions, society assigns formal labels, such as "delinquent," or "homosexual," or "ex-con."[13] Often, labels are bestowed during ceremonies designed to redefine the deviants' identity and place them apart from the normative social structure.[14] The net effect of this legal and social process is a *durable negative label and accompanying loss of status*. The labeled deviant becomes a social outcast who is prevented from enjoying higher education, well-paying jobs, and other societal benefits.

Who is to be labeled and the forms labeling takes depend on social forces that vary considerably within cultural and temporal boundaries. What may be negatively labeled in culture X or time A may be ignored or even promoted in culture Y or time B. For example, during our own lifetimes, we have witnessed the legalization of abortions, the banning of school prayer, and, in some states, the decriminalization of marijuana. By recognizing the relationship between labels and culture, labeling theory remains more culturally relative than previously discussed theoretical models, which hold that certain criminal behavior is always immoral and should be consistently outlawed.

Finally, labeling theorists consider public identification of the offender as a necessary condition of deviant behavior. Without societal reaction, acts do not enter the realm of deviance. They remain relatively isolated, unimportant incidents of "different" or "unusual" behavior. Thus, the deviant label implies more than a person's mere participation in antisocial behavior. It signifies that the process had made a lasting mark on the person's self-image. Being cast as a deviant in turn amplifies the offender's "need" to commit illegal or otherwise negatively sanctioned behavior. The labeling process acts not merely to identify deviance; it also works to amplify it.[15]

Lemert's Model of Deviance

Edwin Lemert first articulated much of what we today regard as the fundamental assumptions of the labeling approach in his formulation of the primary-secondary deviance model.[16] Lemert argues that deviant acts actually form two distinct classes, primary and secondary, each of which comprises a specific role orientation of the individual. Primary acts can be rationalized by the offender or considered to be a function of a socially acceptable role, such as a youngster's getting drunk at an older sibling's wedding party. Although the acts may be considered serious, they do not materially affect self-concept. Primary deviants are not recognized by others as deviant; nor do they recognize themselves in these terms. Lemert attaches little importance to this category of offense, but he argues that deviations become significant (secondary) when they are organized into active roles that become the social criteria for assigning status.[17] Lemert suggests that deviant role reorganization, although dependent to some extent on cultural and psychological factors, is controlled mostly by the labeling that results from a negative social interaction. When discussing secondary deviant identity, he states that if a person's behavior is repetitive, highly visible, and subject to severe social reaction, it is likely that the person will incorporate a deviant identity into his or her psyche. Thereafter, all life roles will be predicated upon this new, deviant model.[18] Highlight 7-1 illustrates the process for a delinquent youth.

Highlight 7-1. Mark - How the Labeling Process Works

Mark is on the run. He cautiously peers around the store's corner onto the dark street. His tattered brown jeans and white T-shirt are all that protect him from the cold North wind. The tennis shoes on the bottom of his long legs are damp and muddy. His

---

brown eyes scan the street furtively in the hope of recognizing the car of a friend. Mark reaches down and fingers the switchblade in his pocket. He looks around the corner into the lighted store and waits.

Mark first began getting in trouble when he was eight years old, when he would steal money from his mother's purse. She tried to discipline him as best she could, but most of the time she was alone because her husband had to travel a lot on his job. One Sunday afternoon, when Mark was ten, the minister of their church and the Sunday school director came by to visit. They informed Mark's mother that her son had stolen the Sunday school collection money. Mark, hiding behind the corner of the living room, listened intently. When his mother saw him, he grinned sheepishly at her and darted back into his room. At first, the church officials said they would not let Mark come to Sunday school anymore. But Mark's mother said she would get help for her son at the local child guidance center.

At the first meeting with the social worker, Mark's parents were told that it was their fault that their son was in trouble, that he felt rejected by them and was stealing just to get their attention. Mark's father blew up at the social worker and walked out. His mother, on the verge of tears, remained. Upon the social worker's advice, the parents reluctantly became more lenient with Mark and took him on fun outings even when his behavior did not warrant such rewards. For three weeks, everyone thought that Mark was doing better. Then on Friday night, when Mark's father got in from a week on the road, there was a police car with its lights flashing in front of his house. Mark and a boy two years older had broken into a neighbor's house, stolen everything of value, and then proceeded to tear the house apart.

The neighbor was furious. Not only would the house have to be repainted and recarpeted, but the jewelry that had been stolen had been handed down for four generations. The police turned Mark over to the juvenile probation authorities, where he was found guilty by the local juvenile judge. When Mark's parents asked him why, at

first he gave them his usual grin. After repeated confrontation, he began to cry, saying he didn't know why. The older boy was sent to the state training school, while Mark was placed on probation for one year. It was only six weeks later, however, that Mark was caught burglarizing a local grocery store at midnight, when his parents had been sure he was in bed asleep.

The juvenile probation officer, who had used individual counseling with Mark, decided that what he needed was a different home placement. He was held in the detention center for six weeks. Mark, who now was almost twelve years old, was placed in a home with a truck driver and his wife. They were very friendly to Mark, and he was beginning to do better in school. The husband drank a lot, however; and one night when he was dead drunk and out, his wife made sexual advances to Mark and seduced him. The next night, when a similar situation began to develop, Mark ran away and hitchhiked to a city 100 miles away. The truck driver and his wife did not report Mark's leaving for six days; they "thought sure he would come back any day."

Even though the police put out a statewide pickup notice on Mark, it was six months before he was found, and then it was only because a night watchman caught him and another boy burglarizing a tool shop. Mark was returned to his home community, where he was found guilty of burglary again. The town and his family were getting somewhat fed up with Mark and his behavior. But the local juvenile judge rejected commitment to the state training school. In a private talk with the judge, Mark, unlike other boys, had not tried to deceive or "con" the judge. Instead, he admitted everything, but seemed confused and worried about his own behavior. Mark was only twelve, and the judge thought the community should do better for the youngster. This time he was placed in a group home that had recently been organized. He attended school in the day and participated in a confrontive form of group therapy at night. Mark did well in school during the day, but always seemed upset or withdrawn after the group therapy sessions at night. Then one night, during a session in which the group was especially critical of his best friend, he picked up a chair and attacked the boys.

This time the judge had no choice. Mark was committed to the state training school for an indefinite period of time. When Mark arrived, he took one look at the place and decided this was one place he wanted to get out of as quickly as possible. He talked to the boys in his dormitory and found out that if you smiled and spoke to all the staff, did not fight, and really acted like the program was helping you, you could get out in five to six months. So Mark did as the boys suggested. Between classes and activities he greeted all the staff. During group counseling he confessed to all the bad things he had done and promised that he would never do them again. He told the vocational counselor that if he could start learning a trade, it would help him stay out of trouble when he got out of the school.

Mark was then placed in an auto mechanics class, where, though he was interested, he could not understand what was going on. Rather than admitting that and perhaps being kept at the training school longer, Mark hung around the teacher, smiled and looked interested, and ran errands for him. At the five-month point, Mark's case was brought up at the progress review meeting. The caseworker detailed Mark's progress in individual and group counseling. The auto mechanics teacher reported that he had Mark with him most of the school day and he was a model student. When asked how Mark did on the tests, the teacher replied that he did not believe in tests. But through his observations, he knew Mark was doing well. The dormitory supervisor stated that the boy had not been in any trouble in the residence hall. Only the recreation supervisor voiced any concern that Mark was holding back and not really showing his true self. The caseworker, with her master's degree, countered by explaining that according to the psychiatrist, Mark had gone through an adolescent adjustment reaction and that was the cause of the former delinquency. The

committee voted 3 to 1 in approval of Mark's release.

When the family heard that Mark was coming home, they were initially shocked that he could have improved so fast. With somewhat disbelieving and subdued pleasure they agreed to have him return home. They were informed that through a recent federal grant, Mark would receive more intensive parole supervision than that given most youth on parole. When Mark arrived home, the family greeted and hugged him, glad that he was home and hoping that what the training school staff had said was true. Mark just sheepishly grinned and settled back into his home.

Things went along well for Mark, because it was still summer and all Mark had to do was lay around the house, watch TV, and hang around with his friends. When school started, his parole officer made sure that he was placed in a slower, special education classroom. The first week was fine because the teacher, who was a young attractive woman, tried to build positive attitudes about school by providing games and entertainment. It was during the second week, when school really started, that Mark began arguing with his teacher and the other students. Then one day he did not show up at school or at home. He had run away again. His parents were frustrated and felt the situation was hopeless. Not only did they not have their son, but every time they looked for help, they met only disappointment and failure.

It is at this point, a few weeks later, that we find Mark hiding around the corner of the all-night grocery store. Mark is scared. He doesn't know how he got where he is. He knows only that he is tired and hungry and has to get some money. He could call his parents, but he knows they will just call the cops. He shivers as the cold wind blows across his shirt. The people with whom he had last slept kicked him out because he didn't have any money for food. He doesn't want to rob the store. He walks back toward the alley. But he knows he has to get some money, just a little money; he will ask the old man nicely.

He walks into the store and slowly goes up and down the aisles looking at different items, nervously glancing toward the cash register. The store is empty. The old shopkeeper begins to stare at Mark. Now he is really scared. He has to make a move. Now! He walks hurriedly up to the shopkeeper, pulls out his knife, and demands the money. The shopkeeper looks attentive, but does not seem afraid. He tells Mark to put the knife down and walk out. Mark only gets more agitated and shakes the knife at the old man. The shopkeeper opens the cash register and hands Mark the dollar bills. Mark quickly turns to leave. The shopkeeper quietly and efficiently pulls out a gun and tells Mark to stop. Mark sees the gun and reaches frantically for the door. The gun fires! Mark feels the hot seering pain go through his back into his heart. As he slumps to the floor in his last gasps of breath, he looks up at the old shopkeeper with tears in his eyes—and then he falls over, dead.

Source: Denis Romig, *Justice for Our Children* (Lexington, Mass.: Lexington Books, 1978), pp. xix–xxii. Reprinted by permission of the publisher.

To further define and clarify the process of secondary deviance, Lemert suggests that stigmatization, punishment, segregation, and social control are each contributing factors in the transformation of personal roles and identity. That is, secondary deviance is a product of resocialization in which the deviant role becomes the central fact of existence and a person is transformed into one who "employs his behavior (deviant) or a role based upon it as a means of defense, attack, or adjustment to the overt and covert problems created by the consequent societal reaction to him."[19]

Thus, an important part of secondary deviance involves the labeled person maintaining behavior and beliefs that society considers deviant. Yet, this behavior enables offenders to cope with the subsequent negative social reactions to their label. Personal acceptance of this behavior and beliefs comprises label internalization or in other words, "successful" self-labeling.

Lemert's model highlights the deviance-producing properties of the labeling process. The model portrays immersion into a deviant identity as a cycle of events (Figure 7–1) in which a deviant act (A), leads to a social reac-

Figure 7–1. Representation of Lemert's Model of Primary-Secondary Deviance

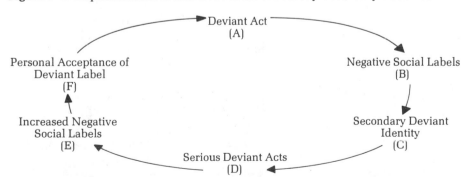

Lemert's conceptualization of the labeling process and his description of the primary-secondary deviance dichotomy are major theoretical underpinnings of the labeling approach.

tion (B), to self-conception as a "deviant" (C), to increased, more serious deviant acts (D), and to greater and more severe social reactions, including legal reprisals (E), until identification with a deviant identity, which increases the probability of future deviant acts, has become complete (F).

Thus, secondary deviance (or self-labeling) is a function of both prior deviant behavior and social labels, and at the same time it causes future misconduct.

Becker's Four-Fold Model of Deviance

Following Lemert, Howard Becker focuses on social interaction and its relationship to deviant careers.[20] While not as precise or technical as Lemert, Becker follows the same general theoretical pattern. He believes that legal and social rules are created by people he calls "moral entrepreneurs," who then apply them to those who violate their social standards. He states:

> Deviance is not a quality of the act the person commits, but rather a consequence of the application by others of rules and sanctions to an "offender." The deviant is one to whom that label has successfully been applied; deviant behavior is behavior that people so label.[21]

Although Becker devotes his primary attention to the role of social stigma in the label-producing process, he finds that social interaction is actually not a requirement for labeling. There are other ways of acquiring deviant status—for example, by becoming a "secret deviant" or "falsely accused." Becker discovered these conditions by cross-tabulating the dimensions of deviant behavior with social perceptions of that behavior, as illustrated in Figure 7–2.

Figure 7.2 Becker's Sequential Model of Deviant Behavior and Identity.

Types of Deviant Behavior

	Conventional Behavior	Illegal Behavior
Viewed as deviant	*Falsely accused*	*Pure Deviant*
Ignored as deviant	*Conformist*	*Secret deviant*

"Secret deviants" participate in deviant behavior but are never apprehended or labeled. Rapists, for example, are relatively immune to official labeling because many women are unwilling to report sexual attacks and also because it is difficult to acquire sufficient evidence to prosecute rape cases (see Chapter 2).[22]

Becker argues that these individuals label themselves by analogy. Most people are certainly aware of the labels that would befall them if they were caught. "Secret deviants" therefore suffer some of the same labeling effects they would suffer if they were apprehended.[23]

On the opposite end of the spectrum are the falsely accused. These individuals are subject to the same exclusion, sanctions, and stigma as actual perpetrators of deviant acts (pure deviants), although they have not personally participated in sanctioned behaviors. A number of different categories of falsely accused exist, including suspects and incorrigible delinquents.

Suspects are labeled diviant because they exhibit behavior that is normally associated with deviants, though they themselves are innocent of deviant behavior. Incorrigible delinquents are youths who have fallen under the catchall status of wayward youth, PINS, CHINS, and so on (see Chapter 1). Their label exists because parents or guardians refer them to the juvenile court as ungovernable or unmanageable, and they are adjudicated under a loosely defined statute governing this type of behavior. Often this procedure serves as a convenient way for neglectful parents to rid themselves of unwanted children who are otherwise innocent of misbehavior.

Becker's work has been most influential in popularizing the labeling approach. He is considered, along with Lemert, one of the founders of labeling theory.

The Juvenile Justice Process and Labeling

The labeling hypothesis has received some strong support from the literature of crime and delinquency. Frank Tannenbaum first suggested that social typing, which he called "dramatization of evil," transforms the offender's identity from a doer of evil to an "evil person."[24] Tannenbaum emphasized the role of the juvenile justice system in this scheme: "The entire process of dealing with young delinquents is mischievous insofar as it identifies him to himself and to the environment as a delinquent person."[25]

Modern theorists have built upon the work of Tannenbaum, continuing to describe the impact of juvenile justice processing on delinquent labeling and consequent illegal behavior. For example, Aaron Cicourel contends that delinquents are in reality the finished products of the juvenile justice "assembly line."[26] Although they enter as children in trouble, they emerge as individuals transformed by decision makers into bearers of criminal histories, which are likely to reinvolve them in criminal activity. The causes of this transformation, Cicourel argues, are the "encounters, oral and written reports, prospective reading, retrospective readings of 'what happened,' and the practical circumstances of settling matters in every day agency business."[27]

Arguing from a similar perspective, David Matza concludes that apprehension of delinquents will lead sanctioning bodies to anticipate further illegal actions on their part.[28] Apprehended offenders are invested with all the behavioral characteristics associated with their labels, and although they have not necessarily demonstrated these characteristics by their own behavior, they become "perennial suspects."[29] As a result, labeled youthful offenders may begin to reconsider their own self-concepts. This reconsideration, Matza explains, relates directly to their interaction with the system and the treatment they receive at its hands.

These statements imply that labeling by the juvenile justice system turns the self-perception of a youthful suspect into that of a delinquent.[30] Processing by the juvenile authorities may cause a youth to enter into a delinquent career and be committed to criminal activity. Sociologist Harold Garfinkel has provided a concise analysis of this process in his description of the interactions that occur when the public identity of an offender is transformed via a "successful" degradation ceremony into "something looked on as lower in the social scheme of social types."[31] Garfinkel concludes that this process may be similar in form and function to what is currently practiced in juvenile court.

In summary, theoretical statements concerning the label-producing experience argue that the more frequent, prolonged, or decisive the contacts with the juvenile justice system, the more likely it is that an offender will ultimately accept the delinquency label as a personal identity and enter into a life of crime.

Empirical Investigation in Juvenile Justice

Empirical evidence has not consistently confirmed the labeling phenomenon with regard to youthful offenders. The results of few studies to measure delinquents at the onset and conclusion of official contact have been contradictory and inconclusive. For example, Paul Lipsett developed a fairly comprehensive study of the effect of the juvenile court experience on the self-perceptions of youthful defendants.[32] The design involved the measurement of 265 male delinquents in three metropolitan courts before and after their trials. The boys were asked to evaluate such concepts as "self" and "judges," using a questionnaire constructed by Lipsett.[33] Lipsett expected that the effect of labeling would cause the boys to lower their ratings of themselves and others, thereby increasing their chances of continuing their delinquent careers. The study found instead that the boys raised these ratings after their trials were over, and this improvement was maintained even when independent variables such as social class, age, perception of judges' fairness, and presence of counsel were held constant. Unfortunately, Lipsett controlled for neither disposition outcome nor prior offense, two variables that may have influenced his findings. In any event, his data generally contradicted commonly held views of labeling advocates.

In a similar vein, Eloise Snyder studied the impact of the juvenile court hearing upon forty-three boys who had been placed on probation.[34] The boys themselves were interviewed a few weeks after their court hearings had been completed. Snyder found that they remembered feeling a great deal of fear over the outcome of their hearings and felt relieved that they were put on probation rather than institutionalized. However, none of the boys felt any shame, and what labeling they perceived diminished over time.[35]

One possible interpretation of Snyder's findings is that official labeling via a court appearance is transient, but actual labeling involves the reaction of friends and parents. Also, Snyder used only probationers in her sample. It is possible that disposition outcome plays an important role in labeling. For example, children whose cases are dismissed may report quite different labeling outcomes from those of youths who are sent to institutions.

Gary Jensen measured the interrelationship of officially recorded delinquency, self-reported delinquency, self-evaluation as a delinquent, and self-esteem.[36] He found that official labels are strongly related to self-definition of a delinquent and that white youths are much more likely than black youths to be self-labeled after official labeling. Whites are more likely than blacks to feel that others label them as delinquent. Also, lower-class youths are more likely than upper- or middle-class youths to personally accept delinquent labels. Jensen found that official labeling via a police contact was a more important determinant of deviant identity than a youth's own self-reported delinquency or the delinquency of peers. Yet Jensen did not show that self-perceptions as a delinquent actually increase after police contact. Thus, the relationship between these two variables is only implied rather than established. For example, youths who are already labeled may be more prone to arrest than nonlabeled youths, and this factor may account for the interrelationship that Jensen discovered.

In a similar vein, Susan Ageton and Delbert Eliot found in a longitudinal study of 2,616 youths in California that the self-concept of white youths who had police contact declined. This was not the case with peers who had avoided police contact.[37] Ageton and Eliot discovered, however, that police contact was not a significant factor in changing the self-concept of Hispanic, black, or other minority youths. Also, lower-class youths were more likely to be negatively affected by their experience with the law than were middle- or upper-class youths, a finding similar to Jensen's. Nonetheless, Ageton and Eliot concluded that, in general, police contact was a more important factor in measuring decreasing self-concept than factors such as self-reported delinquent behavior and the influence of a deviant peer group.

A number of studies have focused on the effects of institutionalization on variables that indicate delinquent labeling. In a comparative study of incarcerated youths, David Street, Robert Vinter, and Charles Perrow discovered a measurable change in self-concept in boys serving time in three training schools.[38] Moreover, they found that the style of the institution, whether it was punishment- or treatment-oriented, played an important role in the youths' adaptations. Youths in the higher security settings tended to sharpen their delinquency skills, stressing "playing it cool" and conforming to the demands of custodial care. In contrast, youths in the treatment-oriented facilities conformed to the institutions' goals of change and rehabilitation and developed a more positive self-concept.[39] Studies of youths held in training schools[40] and detention centers[41] have uncovered similarly inconclusive evidence of the effect of the labeling process.

One of the few studies focusing directly on labeling and juvenile justice was conducted by Jack Foster, Walter Reckless, and Simon Dinitz.[42] Their paper is important for a number of reasons. It examines an early stage of juvenile justice processing, and it suggests that labeling by the system does not produce important changes in personal image and consequent delinquent behavior.

The sample in the study consisted of 196 boys involved in activities definable as crimes and brought to the attention of police and courts. The boys were interviewed in their homes a week to ten days after the disposition of their cases, some with parents present. The researchers found, surprisingly, a general disregard for official labels. Most subjects did not perceive any personal conflict with parents or friends after their official labeling. Similarly, most boys did not feel that teachers or other school officials would be aware of their difficulties. They perceived only two significant areas of social liability. Fifty-four percent expected police to keep an eye on them, and 40 percent felt that future employers would hold the incident against them. Finally, the boys felt that the outcome of the disposition and the number of their previous offenses would prejudice future employers. In conclusion, the evidence that labeling transforms identities and produces subsequent delinquent behavior is insufficient.

Evaluation of Labeling Theory

Although the validity of labeling theory is widely accepted, it is by no means unanimous. Not enough studies have been conducted to reach conclusions about its properties. Among the theoretical failures of the approach is its inability to distinguish between deviance and nondeviance—that is, to specify the conditions that must occur before an act or individual is labeled deviant. Another criticism of labeling theory is directed toward its alleged cultural relativism. For example, Jack Gibbs argues that labeling theory is limited as a functional explanation of deviance since most social and legal rules are applied within a narrow boundary, depending upon the community and the policies of law enforcement agencies within it.[43] In a similar vein, Gibbs states that labeling theorists fail to explain the variation in crime and delinquency rates that occurs between communities having similar definitions of illegal behavior and similar law enforcement policies.[41]

Edwin Schur argues that labeling theory fails to consider the delinquent's motivation in committing an initial illegal act, knowing full well the high probability of being labeled.[45] Labeling theorists contradict themselves in proposing that the delinquent is at the mercy of social processes, and, at the same time, capable of significantly shaping personal projects and lines of action.[46] Ronald Akers offers a similar criticism, stating, "One sometimes gets the impression from reading the literature that people go about minding their own business and then—'wham'—bad society comes along and slaps them with a stigmatized label."[47] Akers questions the casual disregard with which labeling theorists treat the initial cause of deviance. He suggests that when a deviant is labeled, there is usually a good reason for it. "One may say," Akers comments, "that, in a sense, the behavior creates the label."[48]

On another level, David Bordua claims that the theory lacks empirical verification. Therefore, its pronouncements should be considered with caution.[49] Peter Manning underscores this point, claiming that labeling theory has failed to provide the conceptual tools to evaluate its theoretical premises accurately. As a result, it lacks the "detailed analysis of the conditions . . . under which a given tenet of labeling might hold."[50]

Sociologist Charles Wellford questions the validity of a number of the premises that are essential to the labeling approach.[51] He takes particular issue with the labeling assumption that no act is intrinsically criminal. Wellford points to the fact that some crimes, such as rape and homicide, are almost universally sanctioned. He says, "Serious violations of the law are universally understood and are, therefore, in that sense, intrinsically criminal."[52] Furthermore, he suggests, the labeling theory proposition that almost all law enforcement is biased against the poor and minorities is equally spurious: "I contend that the overwhelming evidence is in the direction of minimal differential law enforcement, determination of guilt and application of sanction."[53]

According to Wellford, this means that law enforcement officials more often than not base their arrest decisions on such factors as the seriousness of the offense, and they pay less attention to such issues as the race, class, and demeanor of the offender—factors that labeling theorists often link to the labeling decision.[51]

Finally, Wellford challenges the whole self-labeling perspective. Even though labeling may indeed affect self-attitudes, there is little evidence that attitudes are related to actual behavior change. Wellford believes instead that delinquent behavior is situationally motivated and depends upon ecological and personal conditions.

Some researchers have begun to explore the conditions that generate labeling, but most research lacks the methodological rigor needed to test the effects of labeling conclusively. Problems of instrumentation and experimental design have led critics such as Bordua and Wellford to question the validity of the entire labeling approach. Furthermore, this paucity of empirical information has left a number of major questions unanswered. Are labels actually generated by processing offenders through the justice system, and, if so, which interactions are most responsible? Does label acceptance (self-labeling) result? Are self-labeled offenders more likely to commit deviant acts? Can a person be immune to labels? If self-labeling does occur, and it is produced by the criminal and juvenile justice systems, can something be done about it? Does labeling really prevent an individual from achieving eventual success? Does labeling produce criminal careers? These and other similar questions must be answered adequately before labeling theory can be accepted as a valid theory of delinquent behavior.

CONFLICT THEORY

While not a criminological theory in a formal sense, conflict theory, sometimes known as critical theory, Marxist theory, or the new criminology, is a perspective on the causes of crime and delinquency that has found many adherents among scholars concerned with the political factors that influence illegal behavior.

Unlike traditional theoretical perspectives, which try to explain why an individual violates the law, conflict theory focuses on why governments make and enforce rules of law and morality. Conflict criminologists therefore neither seek explanations for lower- or middle-class delinquent behavior nor attempt to devise innovative ways of controlling youthful misbehavior. Their interests lie in other areas: (1) identifying "real" crimes in our society, such as profiteering, sexism, and racism; (2) evaluating how the criminal law is used as a mechanism of social control; and (3) turning the attention of citizens to the inequities in our society.

It is not accidental that the emergence of conflict theory as an explanation of deviant behavior had its roots in the widespread social and political upheavals of the 1960s.[55] These forces included the Vietnam War, the counterculture movement, and various forms of political protest. Conflict theory flourished within this framework, since it provided a theoretical basis to challenge the legitimacy of the government's creation and application of law.

Another influence that helped bring conflict theory to the forefront was the apparent failure of more traditional theories of deviance to explain the challenges to government authority.[56] Experts on the causes of deviant behavior were at a loss to explain such phenomena as the increase in illicit drug use among middle-class students; campus, prison, and urban rioting; and civil rights demonstrations and other political protests against the government.

At the same time, critical thinkers hurled challenges at the academic world, the center of most theoretical thought in criminology. They claimed that it was archaic, conservative, and out of tune with recent changes in society.[57] Critical criminology began to challenge the fundamental role criminologists play in uncovering the causes of crime and delinquency. At a time of general turmoil in society, conflict theorists called for sweeping innovation in academic settings—including changes in the way courses were taught, grading, and tenure. Criminologists were asked to evaluate their own lives and activities in order to understand their personal role in the crime problem. Was it possible that they were acting as agents of the state, taking money from government agencies to achieve more effective repression of the poor and laboring classes?[58] These theorists called for a reappraisal of the entire field of law and criminology.[59]

Marxist Thought

The foundation of conflict theory can be traced to the political and economic philosophy of Karl Marx (1818–1883).[60]

Marx believes that the character of every civilization is determined by its mode of production—the way its people develop and produce material goods. This concept has two components: (1) productive forces, which include such things as technology, energy sources, and material resources; and (2) productive relations, which are the relationships that exist between the people producing goods and services. The most important relationship in industrial culture is between the owners of the means of production, the capitalist bourgeoisie, and those who do the actual labor, *the proletariat*. Throughout history, society has been organized this way—master-slave, lord-serf, and now capitalist-proletarian.

The political and economic philosophy of the dominant class influences all aspects of life. Consciously or unconsciously, artists, writers, and teachers bend their work to the whims of the capitalist system. Thus, the economic system controls all facets of human life, and, consequently, people's lives revolve around the means of production.

Marx holds that the laboring class produces goods that exceed wages in value. The excess value then goes into the hands of the capitalists as profit. While some of this profit is spent on personal luxuries, most is spent on acquiring an ever-expanding capitalist base that relies on advanced technology for efficiency. Thus, capitalists are in constant competition with each other to maintain market position. To compete they must produce goods more efficiently and cheaply, a condition that requires them either to pay workers the lowest possible wages or to replace them with labor-saving machinery. Soon the supply of efficiently made goods outstrips the ability of the laboring classes to purchase them, a condition that precipitates an economic crisis. During this period, weaker enterprises go under and are consequently incorporated in ever-expanding, monopolistic mega-corporations that are strong enough to further exploit the workers. Marx believes that in the ebb and flow of the business cycle, the capitalist system contains the seeds of its own destruction and that from its ashes will grow a socialist state in which the workers themselves own the means of production.

In his analysis, Marx uses the dialectic method based on the analysis developed by philosopher George Hegel (1770–1831). Hegel argues that for every idea or *thesis* there exists an opposing argument or *antithesis*. Since neither position can ever be truly accepted, the result is a merger of the two ideas, or *synthesis*. Marx adapted this analytic method for his study of class struggle. History, argues Marx, is replete with examples of two opposing forces whose conflict promotes social change. When conditions are bad enough, the oppressed will eventually rise up to fight the owners and eventually replace them. Thus, in the end, the capitalist system will destroy itself.[61]

This brief discussion on Marxist thought is, of course, only the barest outline of a complex, highly technical topic. However, it provides a glimpse of the thought patterns that underpin conflict theory.

Elements of Conflict Theory

Based on Marx's theories of economic analysis, the primary goal of conflict theory is to examine the relationship between the ruling class and the process by which deviance is defined and controlled in capitalist society. By broadening the search for an explanation of deviance to include its defining process, conflict theorists depart from the narrower focus of earlier positivist models of deviant behavior (Chapters 4, 5, and 6).

The most important of these concerns is the nature and purpose of social control. Conflict theorists believe that the state creates laws and rules designed to maintain the power and position of the power elite. Critical criminologist Robert Meier has suggested that the new criminology centers around a view of society in which an elite class uses the criminal law as a means of meeting and controlling threats to its status. Meier views the ruling class as a self-interested lot whose primary interest is self-gain.[62] Another well-known critical criminologist, Richard Quinney, argues, "Capitalist justice is by the capitalist class, for the capitalist class, and against the working class."[63]

As articulated by Gresham Sykes, conflict theory views the criminal law and criminal justice system as a vehicle for controlling the poor, have-not members of society. It helps the powerful and rich to:

1. Impose their particular morality and standards of good behavior on the entire society.
2. Protect their property and physical safety from the depredations of the have-nots, even though the cost may be high in terms of the legal rights of those it perceives as a threat.
3. Extend the definition of illegal or criminal behavior to encompass those who might threaten the status quo.[61]

Sykes further asserts that the ruling elite draws the middle class into this pattern of control, leading it to believe that it also has a stake in maintaining the status quo.

The poor, according to conflict theory, may or may not commit more crimes than the rich, but they certainly are arrested and punished more often. Sykes argues that the poor are driven to crime for the following reasons:

1. The rules imposed from above have little relationship to the dictates of the cultural norms of the poor.
2. A natural frustration exists in a society where affluence is well-publicized but unattainable.
3. There is a deep-rooted hostility generated among members of the lower class toward a social order that they are not allowed to shape or participate in.[65]

Herman Schwendinger and Julia Schwendinger suggest that the nature of the conflict view of society, law, and deviant behavior can be summarized in the following way:

1. Legal relations in the United States secure an economic infrastructure that centers around a capitalist mode of production. The legal system is designed to guard the position of the owners (bourgeoisie) at the expense of the workers (proletariat).
2. Legal relations maintain the family and school structure so as to secure the labor force. Even common law crimes such as murder and rape are implemented to protect capitalism.
3. The capitalist state is made up of a civil society in which the dominance of the bourgeoisie is challenged by the antagonistic rural and urban proletariat.
4. The class interests that underlie the basic laws of the land (such as constitutional laws) are based on the conditions that reproduce the class system as a whole. Laws are aimed at securing the domination of the capitalist system.
5. Legal relations in the capitalist system may at times secure the interests of the working class, for example, laws protecting collective bargaining and personal income.
6. Due to the inherent antagonisms built into the capitalist system, all laws generally contradict their stated purpose of producing justice. Legal relations maintain patterns of individualism and selfishness and in so doing perpetuate a class system characterized by anarchy, oppression, and crime.[66]

Conflict theorists seriously contradict the long-held presumption that the American system of law and justice is humane and fair to all citizens. Conflict theory asks us to reevaluate many basic beliefs. For example, the fact that laws protecting private property may actually be designed to preserve the dominance of a ruling elite seems to strike at the very heart of our moral beliefs. For this reason alone, conflict theory has had a profound effect on mid-twentieth century criminological thought.

Demystification

Conflict theorists consider it essential to demystify law and science. This rather complex concept entails a number of different actions. For one thing, radical criminologists charge that an inordinate amount of scientific effort is devoted to unmasking the social conditions of lower-class citizens with the ostensible purpose of improving their lives. Such studies include views of lower-class family life, IQs, school performance, and so on. However, conflict criminologists argue that these efforts actually serve to keep the lower classes down by "proving" that they are more delinquent and less intelligent and that they have poorer school performance than the middle-class. All the while, the tests and instruments used to conduct these studies are biased and inaccurate.[67] Thus, in one sense, demystification entails uncovering the real reasons behind scientific research.

Another aspect of demystification involves identifying the historical development of criminal law. By drawing attention to the "real" reasons laws such as tax codes and statutes prohibiting theft and drug use were created, people will understand the purpose and intent of these laws. If it is found that theft laws, for example, were originally created to maintain the wealth and capital of the rich, then those who violate the law should not perceive themselves as evil, immoral, or wrong but rather as victims of an unjust system.

Finally, the demystification of capitalist society reveals the controlling nature of the "professional mystique."[68] It is alleged that our society grants inordinate power to professionals to judge and control the population. When teachers, doctors, lawyers, and psychologists judge persons to be "crazy," "stupid," "sick," "unfit," "delinquent," or "criminal," that label becomes their social identity. Radical criminologists charge that professionals often suppress and distort the truth, "unmasking" powerless people so that their position of social inferiority is maintained. The system quickly condemns those who speak against it as "subversive," "traitorous," or "mentally ill."

Conflict Concept of Delinquency

Conflict theorists view delinquency as a normal response by youth to the social conditions created by capitalist society.[69] In fact, the very creation of a unique legal category, delinquency, is a function of the class-consciousness that occurred around the turn of the century.[70] In his book *The Child Savers*, Anthony Platt documents the creation of the delinquency concept and the role played by wealthy childsavers in forming the philosophy of the juvenile court. In a later work, Platt claims:

The child-saving movement tried to do for the criminal justice system what industrialists and corporate leaders were trying to do by the economy—that is, achieve order, stability and control while perserving the existing class system and distribution of wealth.[71]

Thus, the roots of the juvenile delinquency concept can be traced to nineteenth century efforts of powerful and wealthy citizens to control the behavior of weak and disenfranchised youth.[72]

Herman Schwendinger and Julia Schwendinger describe today's delinquent behavior as a function of the capitalist system. They argue that capitalism accelerates the trend toward replacing living labor with machines so that youths are removed from a useful place in the labor force.[73] This process prolongs their dependency and forces them to be controlled by socialization agencies such as the family and, most importantly, the school. These social control agencies prepare youths for placement in the capitalist system by presenting them with behavior models that will help them conform to later job expectations. For example, rewards for good school work correspond to the rewards a factory supervisor uses with subordinate employees. In fact, most schools are set up to reward and nurture those youths who show early promise in areas such as self-discipline, achievement, and motivation and who are therefore judged likely to perform well in the capitalist system. Youths who are judged inferior as potential job prospects (the Schwendingers refer to them as prototypic marginals) become known to the school community by such titles as "greasers," "dudes," and "hoods" and eventually wind up in delinquent roles.[71]

The Schwendingers also view the juvenile justice system as creating and sustaining delinquency. They claim that the capitalist state fails to control delinquents because it is actually in the state's own best interest to maintain a large number of outcast deviant youths.[75] These youths can then be employed as low-paid factory labor in jobs no one else wants. Thus, it behooves capitalist managers to maintain an underclass of cheap labor to be employed in its factories and to buy inferior goods.

The capitalist system affects youths in each element of the class structure differently. In the lowest classes, youths form delinquent gangs, which can be found in the most desolated ghetto areas of the country. These violent street gangs serve outcast youths as a means of survival in a system that offers no other reasonable alternative. Other lower-class youths, who live in more stable areas, are usually on the fringe of criminal activity since the economic system excludes them from meaningful opportunity. Conflict theory also acknowledges middle-class delinquency. The alienation of individuals from one another, the never-ending competitive struggle, and the absence of human interest and feeling—all inherent qualities of capitalism—contribute to middle-class delinquency. Since capitalism is such a dehumanizing system, it is not surprising that even middle-class youths turn to drugs, gambling, and illicit sex to find escape and excitement. Thus, conflict theory explains the various forms of delinquent behavior in our society.

Evaluation of Conflict Theory

The major achievement of conflict theory is its call to reevaluate the institutions and processes of society and government. Barry Krisberg and James Austin state that the social turmoil of the 1960s and 1970s—including Vietnam, Watergate, FBI and CIA plots, civil rights, and worldwide revolutionary struggles—has led many Americans to question conventional values and social arrangements. Official wisdom is simply not accepted without question any longer.[76]

Conflict theory does indeed question the many instances of misguided "official wisdom" that pervade our society, but despite lofty goals and ideals, it suffers from a serious lack of empirical verification. Most research has been by necessity historical and theoretical. Even when a specific Marxist theory of deviance has been attempted, such as Stephen Spitzer's "Toward a Marxian Theory of Deviance,"[77] it lacks the specific propositions sociologists require to test theories properly.[78]

In a similar vein, Jackson Toby argues that conflict theory is a simple rehash of the old tradition of helping the underdog.[79] He likens the ideas behind Marxist criminology to the ideas of such literary works as *Robin Hood* and Victor Hugo's *Les Miserables* in which the poor stole from the rich to survive. In reality, Toby claims, most theft is for luxury, not survival. Moreover, he disputes that the crimes of the rich are more reprehensible and less understandable than those of the poor. Criminality and immoral behavior occur on every social level, but Toby believes that the relatively disadvantaged contribute disproportionately to the crime and delinquency rates.

Measuring the hypotheses of conflict theory is difficult because of the inadequacy of methodological tools for studying society from a critical perspective. Conflict theorists believe that current sociological methods are inadequate since the methods themselves are tools of repression. Thus, the evaluation of the conflict approach requires new tools of analysis specifically designed to measure broad social trends and relations.

POLICY IMPLICATIONS OF SOCIAL REACTION THEORY

Social reaction theories, especially the labeling approach, imply that any intervention of the justice system into the life of a juvenile offender is potentially harmful. Intervention imposes on youths an official record that may be a burden for the rest of their lives (especially in today's world of computerized records). In addition, the juvenile justice process identifies youthful offenders as deviants or outcasts to themselves, thereby increasing the possibility of their future identification with a delinquent self-image.

The acceptance of social reaction theories by policy makers has had a dramatic influence on juvenile justice operations in the 1070s and 1900s. A massive effort has been made on the local, state, and federal levels to limit the interface of youth with the juvenile justice system. One approach has been to *divert* youths from official processing channels at the time of their initial contact with police authorities (see Chapter 14). The usual practice is to have police refer children to community treatment facilities and clinics rather than to the juvenile court.

In a similar vein, children who have been petitioned to juvenile court are eligible for an additional round of court-based diversion programs. For example, *restitution* allows children to pay back the victims of their crimes for the damage (or inconvenience) they have caused instead of receiving an official delinquency label. (See Chapter 18.)

Delinquent youths have been relieved from the stigma associated with harsh court-ordered dispositions. For example, some states have banned the housing of status offenders with delinquents. Others have severely curtailed the use of secure facilities for adjudicated minors. Massachusetts is the first state to "deinstitutionalize" its juvenile justice system and rely entirely on nonsecure, community-based corrections for all adjudicated delinquents (see Chapter 19).

These efforts have met with varying degrees of success. While the number of youths in pretrial detention or secure institutions has markedly decreased, juvenile crime has increased. Consequently, the diversion movement has met

with the severe and vocal criticism of citizens demanding harsher, more punitive treatment for delinquent youth. These issues will be discussed in greater
detail in Chapters 13 and 16.

CHAPTER SUMMARY

Social reaction theories view delinquent behavior as a function of the influence
that powerful members of society have on less fortunate youths. Two main
branches of the theory are currently popular. Labeling theory views deviant behavior as a product of the deviant labels society imposes on its least powerful
citizens. Deviant labels mark people as social outcasts and create barriers between them and the general social order. Eventually, deviant labels transform
the offenders' own personalities, so that they come to accept their new "criminal or delinquent" identities as personal ones.

Labeling theorists suggest that delinquent labels lock individuals outside the
mainstream of society, thereby assuring that they will turn to additional illegal
behavior for survival. Who is to be labeled and the quality the labeling takes depends on a youth's position in the social structure; the poor and powerless are
much more likely to be labeled than the wealthy and powerful.

Conflict theory goes one step farther, suggesting that the capitalist system
itself produces delinquency. In fact, conflict theorists have condemned the labeling approach for being too conservative and overly concerned with the powerless members of society. In a famous article criticizing labeling theory,
Alexander Liazos argues that the labeling approach ignores the deviance of the
powerful while focusing on "nuts, sluts, and preverts."[80] By studying such outlawed behavior as delinquency, prostitution, and homosexuality, labeling theorists ignore what Liazos calls "covert institutional violence" such as racism,
sexism, war, poverty, and corruption.

Labeling theorists have tried to answer these charges and to justify their theoretical concerns. Erich Goode, for example, denies that labeling theory ignores
the power structure and its relationship to the defining of deviance. He finds
that the less powerful, economically deprived members of society are the ones
most often forced to suffer labeling. Therefore, labeling theory parallels the
study of powerlessness espoused by Marxist theorists.[81]

Both positions are extremely provocative, but research testing their basic
premises has been inadequate. In fact, the empirical research that has been
conducted to test labeling theory has generally not supported the theory's basic
hypotheses. However, more theoretical and empirical work is certainly called
for.[82]

DISCUSSION QUESTIONS

1. What are some common labels used in the school setting? How can these
hurt youths?
2. Can labels be beneficial to a person? What are some positive effects of
labeling?

3. Is it possible to overcome labels? What methods could a person employ to counteract labels?

4. Are there laws that seem to be designed to protect the rich? Is it possible that laws are actually applied fairly?

5. Are there factors in our economy that make Marx's predictions about capitalism obsolete?

6. Discuss examples of the blind obedience we give to professionals such as doctors, lawyers, and teachers.

SUGGESTED READINGS

Becker, Howard. *The Other Side: Perspectives of Deviance.* New York: Free Press, 1964.

_____*Outsiders: Studies in the Sociology of Deviance.* New York: Free Press, 1963.

Goode, Erich. "On Behalf of Labeling Theory." *Social Problems* 22 (1973): 570–583.

Lemert, Edward. *Human Deviance, Social Problems and Social Control.* 2d ed. Englewood Cliffs, N.J.: Prentice-Hall, 1972.

_____*Social Pathology.* New York: McGraw-Hill, 1951.

Liazos, Alexander. "The Poverty of the Sociology of Deviance: Nuts, Sluts, and Perverts." *Social Problems* 20 (1972): 103–121.

Mahoney, Anne R. "The Effect of Labeling upon Youths in the Juvenile Justice System: A Review of the Evidence." *Law and Society Review* 8 (1974): 583–614.

Spitzer, Stephen. "On the Marxian Theory of Social Control: A Reply to Horowitz." *Social Problems* 24 (1977): 364–365.

"Toward a Marxian Theory of Deviance." *Social Problems* 22 (1975): 000–051.

Wellford, Charles. "Labelling Theory and Criminology: 'An Assessment.'" *Social Problems* 22 (1975): 331–345.

FOOTNOTES

1. For a review of this position, see Anne R. Mahoney, "The Effect of Labeling upon Youths in the Juvenile Justice System: A Review of the Evidence," *Law and Society Review* 8 (1974): 583–614.

2. For an analysis of the track system, see Chapter 10.

3. John Hepburn, "Official Deviance and Spoiled Identity," paper presented at the meeting of the Society for the Study of Social Problems, Montreal, Canada, 1974 (mimeo).

4. For analysis of this concept, see David Matza, *Becoming Deviant* (Englewood Cliffs, N.J.: Prentice-Hall, 1974).

5. The self-labeling concept originated in Edwin Lemert, *Social Pathology* (New York: McGraw-Hill, 1951). See also Frank Tannenbaum, *Crime and the Community* (Boston: Ginn, 1936).

6. President's Commission on Law Enforcement and Administration of Justice, *Task Force Report: Juvenile Delinquency and Youth Crime*, p. 43.

7. Herbert Blumer, *Symbolic Interactionism: Perspective and Method* (Englewood Cliffs, N.J.: Prentice-Hall, 1969).

8. Kai Erickson, "Notes on the Sociology of Deviance," *Social Problems* 307-314 (1962).

9. Edwin Schur, *Labeling Deviant Behavior* (New York: Harper & Row, 1972), p. 21.

10. William Payne, "Negative Labels," *Crime and Delinquency* 19 (1973): 36-38.

11. Edwin Lemert, *Human Deviance, Social Problems and Social Control* (Englewood Cliffs, N.J.: Prentice-Hall, 1967), p. 10.

12. Ibid., p. 11.

13. For example, see studies of delinquent subcultures, such as Milton Yinger, "Contraculture and Counterculture and Delinquent Behavior," *American Sociological Review* 28 (1968): 625-635.

14. Harold Garfinkle, "Conditions of Successful Degradation Ceremonies," *American Journal of Sociology* 61 (1956): 420-424.

15. Lemert, *Human Deviance, Social Problems and Social Control*, p. 44.

16. Lemert, *Social Pathology*.

17. Ibid., p. 73.

18. Ibid.

19. Ibid., p. 75.

20. Howard Becker, *Outsiders: Studies in the Sociology of Deviance* (New York: Macmillan, 1963).

21. Ibid., p. 9.

22. Ibid., p. 20.

23. Schur, *Labeling Deviant Behavior*, p. 14.

24. Tannenbaum, *Crime and the Community*.

25. Ibid., p. 27.

26. Aaron Cicourel, *The Social Organization of Juvenile Justice* (New York: Wiley, 1968).

27. Ibid., p. 202.

28. David Matza, *Becoming Deviant* (Englewood Cliffs, N.J.: Prentice-Hall, 1969).

29. Ibid., p. 78.

30. S. Wheeler and L. Cottrell, "Juvenile Delinquency: Its Prevention and Control," in *Delinquency, Crime and Social Processes*, ed. Donald Cressey and David Ward (New York: Harper & Row, 1969), p. 609.

31. Garfinkel, "Conditions of Successful Degradation Ceremonies," p. 424.

32. Paul Lipsett, "The Juvenile Offender's Perception," *Crime and Delinquency* 14 (1968): 49.

33. The questionnaire design was in the form of a semantic differential. See C. Osgood, G. Suci, and P. Tannenbaum, *The Measurement of Meaning* (Urbana: University of Illinois Press, 1957).

34. Eloise Snyder, "The Impact of the Juvenile Court Hearing on the Child," *Crime and Delinquency* 17 (1971): 180-182.

35. Ibid.

36. For an opposing view, see John Hepburn, "The Impact of Police Intervention upon Juvenile Delinquents," *Criminology* 15 (1977): 235-262. See also Gary Jensen, "Labeling and Identity," *Criminology* 18 (1980): 121-129.

37. S. Ageton and D. Elliott, "The Effect of Legal Processing on Self-Concept" (Institute of Behavioral Science, University of Colorado, 1973). This paper is cited in Mahoney, "The Effect of Labeling upon Youths in the Juvenile Justice System," pp. 607-608.

38. David Street, Robert Vintner, and Charles Perrow, *Organization for Treatment* (New York: Free Press, 1966).

39. See T. Enyon and J. Simpson, "The Boy's Perception of Himself Delinquents," in *Becoming Delinquent*, ed. Peter Garabedian and Donald Gibbons (Chicago: Aldine Publishing, 1970), p. 210.

40. Ibid.

41. Gerald O'Connor, "The Effect of Detention upon Male Delinquency," *Social Problems* 18 (1970): 194-197.

42. Jack Foster, Simon Dinitz, and Walter Reckless, "Perception of Stigma Following Public Intervention for Delinquent Behavior," *Social Problems* 20 (1972): 202.

43. Jack Gibbs, "Conceptions of Deviant Behavior: The Old and the New," *Pacific Sociological Review* 9 (1966): 11-13.

44. Ibid., p. 13.

45. Schur, *Labeling Delinquent Behavior*, p. 14.

46. Ibid.

47. Ronald Akers, "Problems in the Sociology of Deviance," *Social Forces* 46 (1968): 463.

48. Ibid.

49. David Bordua, "On Deviance," *Annals* 312 (1969): 121.

50. Peter Manning, "On Deviance," *Contemporary Sociology* 2 (1973): 697.

51. Charles Wellford, "Labeling Theory and Criminology: An Assessment," *Social Problems* 22 (1975): 335.

52. Ibid.

53. Ibid., p. 337.

54. Ibid.

55. Gresham Sykes, "The Rise of Critical Criminology," *Journal of Criminal Law and Criminology* 65 (1974): 211.

56. Robert Meier, "The New Criminology: Continuity in Criminological Theory," *Journal of Criminal Law and Criminology* 67 (1976): 461.

57. See, for example, D. Sullivan, L. Tifft, and L. Siegel, "Criminology, Science and Politics," in *Criminal Justice Research*, ed. Emilio Viano, (Lexington, Mass.: Lexington Books, 1978).

58. Ibid., p. 10.

59. Meier, "The New Criminology," p. 463.

60. The ideas in this section are taken in part from C.D. Kerning, ed. *Marxism, Communism, and Western Society* Vol. 5 (New York: Herden and Herden, 1972), pp. 342-360.

61. Stephen Spitzer, "Toward a Marxian Theory of Deviance," *Social Problems* 22 (1975): 638.

62. Meier, "The New Criminology," p. 463.

63. Richard Quinney, *Class, State and Crime* (New York: Longman, 1977), p. 3.

64. Sykes, "The Rise of Critical Criminology," pp. 211-213.

65. Ibid.

66. Herman Schwendinger and Julia Schwendinger, "Delinquency and Social Reform: A Radical Perspective," in *Juvenile Justice*, ed. LaMar Empey (Charlottesville: University of Virginia Press, 1979), pp. 246-290.

67. Sullivan, Tifft, and Siegel, "Criminology, Science and Politics," p. 11.

68. Ibid.

69. Robert Gordon, "Capitalism, Class and Crime in America," *Crime and Delinquency* 19 (1973): 174.

70. Quinney, *Class, State and Crime*, p. 52.

71. Anthony Platt, "The Triumph of Benevolence: The Origins of the Juvenile Justice System in the United States," in *Criminal Justice in America: A Critical Understanding*, ed. Richard Quinney (Boston: Little, Brown, 1974), p. 367. See also Anthony Platt, *The Child Savers* (Chicago: University of Chicago Press, 1969).

72. Barry Krisberg and James Austin, *Children of Ishmael* (Palo Alto, Calif.: Mayfield Press, 1978), p. 2.

73. Schwendinger and Schwendinger, "Delinquency and Social Reform," p. 250.

74. Ibid., p. 252.

75. Ibid., p. 256.

76. Krisberg and Austin, *Children of Ishmael*, p. 4.

77. Spitzer, "Toward a Marxian Theory of Deviance" pp. 638-651.

78. Alan Horowitz, "Marxist Theory of Deviance and Teleology: A Critique of Spitzer," *Social Problems* 24 (1977): 362.

79. Jackson Toby, "The New Criminology Is the Old Sentimentality," *Criminology* 16 (1979): 516-526.

80. Alexander Liazos, "The Poverty of the Sociology of Deviance: Nuts, Sluts and Perverts," *Social Problems* 20 (1972): 250.

81. Erich Goode, "On Behalf of Labeling Theory," *Social Problems* 22 (1975): 579.

82. Lauren Wollan, "After Labeling and Conflict," *Social Problems* 26 (1979): 546.

Chapter 8

Chapter Outline

Introduction
The Inherent Nature of Female
  Delinquency
Developmental Theories of Female
  Delinquency
Theories of Economic and Social
  Determinism
Delinquent Girls and the Juvenile
  Justice System
Chapter Summary

Key Terms, Names, and Cases

female mind
atavistic anomalies
unadjusted girls
katabolic-anabolic
The Four Wishes
penis envy
women's movement
economic determinism
sexualization
Otto Pollak
W. I. Thomas
Gisela Konopka
Cesare Lombroso
Sigmund Freud
Rita James Simon
Freda Adler

Female Delinquency

INTRODUCTION

Criminologists have traditionally devoted insufficient attention to the study of female delinquency. Attempts to explain the causes of youth crime have been devoted primarily to male delinquency. A few of the theoretical models discussed previously may have some application to female delinquency—for example, labeling theory—but the majority are male-oriented. Only in the past decade have the nature and extent of female delinquency emerged as an issue of principal interest to professional criminologists.

What has caused this sudden interest in female delinquency? Most important has been the self-reported delinquency and official arrest rate of female delinquents, which has actually increased at a rate faster than that of male delinquents. Girls today may be committing more serious crimes than ever before, and this development mandates careful consideration (though, as we shall see later in this chapter, some experts dispute that a rapid increase in female delinquency is underway).

In addition, the beliefs previously held about the nature of female delinquency have changed markedly. Traditionally, girls have been viewed as sexual delinquents for engaging in prostitution, having sexual relations while still in their minority, and engaging in acts that imply that sexual misconduct has occurred or soon will occur, such as running away from home, staying out late at night, and associating with older boys. Consequently, girls have been considered neither violent nor responsible for major theft. Their delinquency has been viewed as moral, emotional, or family-related; and such problems have not been an important concern of traditional criminologists. In fact, the few "true" female delinquents have been considered aberrations whose criminal or delinquent activity was a function of their abandoning accepted feminine roles and taking on masculine characteristics.[1]

Today, as their social role is expanding and women are beginning to take their rightful place in the economic and professional mainstream of society, our conceptions of female delinquency are being altered. Women appear to be involved in many traditionally male crimes—theft, embezzlement, fraud; and in a similar vein, the stereotype of the female delinquent as a purely sexual deviant is being challenged.[2] Thus, the study of female delinquency is beginning to take on greater importance.

Historically, studies of the nature and cause of delinquency among girls can be classified into three main groupings: (1) those that focus on the inherent nature of the female; (2) those that point to the social and psychological development of girls; and (3) those that view the economic and social roles of women and girls in our society. Although they occasionally overlap, these are relatively independent concepts and will be analyzed separately. In addition, the special relationship of female delinquents to the juvenile justice system will be reviewed.

THE INHERENT NATURE OF FEMALE DELINQUENCY

A number of prominent early theorists suggest that female delinquency is a function of inherent female psychological and biological traits. These authorities believe that the interplay between the biological characteristics of women and girls, the psychology of the "female mind," and the social order produces female delinquency. Their views are antiquated today, but they were quite influential when they first appeared in print.

Lombroso's View of Female Delinquency

With the publication in 1895 of his book, *The Female Offender,* Cesare Lombroso extended his pioneering work on criminality to the study of female crime.[3] Lombroso, as noted previously in Chapter 4, believed that criminals can be distinguished from noncriminals by their multiple physical abnormalities, which he labeled *atavistic* anomalies. These signified the criminal's link to people's subhuman or savage past and the criminal's moral brotherhood with apes and modern savages. Through autopsies of convicted criminals, Lombroso, a physician, was able to distinguish many physical traits that he believed were characteristics of the "born criminal," including twisted nose, prominent ears, and excessive jaw.

Lombroso noted that women were lower on the evolutionary scale than men, more childlike, less sensitive, and less intelligent.[4] Women who committed crimes (most often prostitution and other sex-related offenses) could be distinguished from "normal" women by physical characteristics—excessive body hair, wrinkles, crow's-feet, and abnormal cranium, for example.[5] In physical appearance, delinquent females appeared closer to both criminal and noncriminal men than to other women.

Lombroso's belief that women are lower on the evolutionary scale than men is puzzling when we consider that he viewed atavism or primitivism as the key element in producing criminal behavior and that the crime rate of females is lower than that of males. Lombroso explained this apparent inconsistency by arguing that most girls are restrained from committing delinquent acts by counterbalancing traits such as "piety, maternity, want of passion, sexual coldness, weakness, and undeveloped intelligence."[6] The delinquent female lacks these traits and is therefore unrestrained in her childlike, unreasoned passions. Lombroso also believed that much female delinquency was masked and hidden.[7]

Lombroso did recognize, however, that there were actually far fewer female than male delinquents. He suggested that this was a function of the relative homogeneity and uniformity among females; the female "born criminal" was indeed a rare creature. However, he also believed that if a girl did become a delinquent, her behavior might become even more vicious than that of males. Highlight 8-1 presents some of his views.

The Unadjusted Girl

In the 1923 work, *The Unadjusted Girl,* W. I. Thomas added a psychological dimension to the inherent biological nature of female delinquency.[8] Thomas believed that there are basic biological differences between men and women. In an earlier work, *Sex and Society,* he argued that males are "katabolic," having an animal force that is destructive and aggressive and that produces creativity, while females are "anabolic," storing energy, being conservative, and being lethargic.[9]

Thomas also suggested that human behavior is a function of wish fulfillment that can be grouped into four independent categories:

1. Desire for experience—new sensations, excitement and adventure.
2. Desire for security—fear of death, caution, conservatism.

Highlight 8-1. Lombroso on the Female Delinquent and Criminal.

What terrific criminals would children be if they had strong passions, muscular strength, and sufficient intelligence; and if, moreover, their evil tendencies were exasperated by a morbid physical activity! And women are big children; their evil tendencies are more numerous and more varied than men's, but generally remain latent. When they are awakened and excited they produce results proportionately greater.

Moreover, the born female criminal is, so to speak, doubly exceptional as a woman and as a criminal. For criminals are an exception among civilized people, and women are an exception among criminals, the natural form of retrogression in women being prostitution and not crime. The primitive woman was impure rather than criminal.

As a double exception, the criminal woman is consequently a monster. Her normal sister is kept in the paths of virtue by many causes, such as maternity, piety, weakness, and when these counter influences fail, and a woman commits a crime, we may conclude that her wickedness must have been enormous before it could triumph over so many obstacles.

Source: Cesare Lombroso, *The Female Offender* (New York: Appleton, 1920), pp. 150-152.

---

3. Desire for response—love, approval, appreciation.
4. Desire for recognition—social status, fame, and luxury.[10]

According to Thomas, attempts to fulfill one's wishes can lead one down a path of good or a path of evil, depending on the opportunities available, individual temperaments, individual definitions of situations, and social pressures.[11] Unfortunately, in the individualistic society in which we live, many poor girls who have not been socialized under middle class controls can become thrill seekers while attempting to satisfy their wishes. Thus, delinquency in girls is the result of their impulse to get amusement, adventure, pretty clothes, and so on, and their falling prey to the allurements of the larger world.[12]

Thomas also believed that a girl's delinquent behavior is linked with her sexuality. He did not equate female delinquency with sex, but he believed that granting sexual favors may become a young girl's leverage for attaining her "wishes." In some cases, she uses it to ensnare men into committing crimes for her gain; if she becomes pregnant, she may also force them into marriage.[13] When these schemes backfire, the girl may be ruined and turned into a prostitute. This unfortunate turn of events is likely to occur when a young girl becomes enmeshed in the clutches of a "pimp" who will break her spirit in a brutal way and force her, out of fear, to continue to be a prostitute.[14]

However, Thomas saw hope for the unadjusted girl through rehabilitation. Society can transform the maladjusted female by altering the way her wishes are fulfilled.[15]

The Devious Female

Otto Pollak published his most significant work, *The Criminality of Women*, in 1950.[16] Pollak's thesis is that females are actually more delinquent than is usually believed, but their delinquency is often masked and therefore goes unreported.[17] Pollak offers a number of reasons for this phenomenon. He suggests that the police and courts forgive a girl for the same delinquent acts for which they will arrest and convict a boy.[18] Girls get away with delinquency because of a sense of misplaced gallantry or chivalry on the part of public officials.[19]

Pollak also claims that male victims of female delinquents will not complain to law enforcement authorities because of their culturally defined role as protectors of women and girls. Furthermore, girls are believed to be the instigators rather than the perpetrators of illegal behavior. It is often the case that a male will suffer arrest and conviction for illegal acts originally thought up by his female companion.[20] Finally, Pollak suggests that women and girls are inherently more deceitful creatures than men and boys, and their delinquency goes undetected because they are unusually cunning.[21]

Pollak suggests that two factors influence particular females to become juvenile delinquents. The first is excessively early physical growth and sexual maturity. Since our sexual mores demand that a girl must be "propositioned" before she can engage in sexual behavior, the overly developed girl simply has more opportunity to engage in immoral or delinquent behavior.[22] The "opportunity resulting from the fact of overdevelopment" is one of the important causes of female delinquency, according to Pollak.[23]

The second factor is related to a girl's home life. If a young girl comes under the influence of criminal parents or if she grows up in a broken home, she may seek outside substitutes for her poor home life. In the company of other lonely maladjusted girls, she will hang out, wander about, and eventually fall into a life of petty crime.[24]

In Highlight 8-2, Pollak suggests that female criminality has three distinct stages, each influenced by the onset of critical biological changes — menstruation, pregnancy, and menopause.

DEVELOPMENTAL THEORIES OF FEMALE DELINQUENCY

Developmental theorists posit that the social and psychological growth of a young girl, influenced and controlled by her family, her peers, and society, may be the key to understanding her delinquent behavior. If she experiences psychological impairment, trauma, family disruption, and so on, a young woman will eventually be forced to engage in delinquent associations and criminality. Let us examine a few key elements of this view.

Sigmund Freud

Sigmund Freud's analysis of psychological development and its influence on delinquency in general was reviewed in Chapter 4. With respect to female delinquency, Freud posits that psychological impairment is linked to sexuality and sexual jealousy developed early in childhood.

According to Freud, girls view their lack of a visible penis as a sign that they have been punished. Boys fear that they also can be punished by having their penis cut off and thus learn to fear women. From this conflict comes penis-envy and the girl's wish to become a boy.[25] Penis envy often produces an inferiority complex in girls, forcing them to make an effort to compensate

---

Highlight 8-2. Pollak on Life Stages and Feminine Crime.

Thefts, particularly shoplifting, arson, homicide, and resistance against public officials seem to show a significant correlation between the menstruation of the offender and the time of the offense. The turmoil of the onset of menstruation and the puberty of girls appears to express itself in the relatively high frequency of false accusations and—where cultural opportunities permit—of incendiarism. Pregnancy in its turn is a crime-promoting influence with regard to attacks against the life of the fetus and the newborn. The menopause finally seems to bring about a distinct increase in crime, especially in offenses resulting from irritability such as arson, breaches of the peace, perjury, and insults.

Source: Otto Pollak, *The Criminality of Women* (Philadelphia: University of Pennsylvania Press, 1950), p. 158.

for their defect. One way is to identify with their mother and accept a maternal role as wife and childbearer. Also, girls may become narcissistic and attempt to compensate for their lack of a penis by dressing well and beautifying themselves.[26]

If a young girl does not overcome her penis envy, neurotic episodes may follow: "If a little girl persists in her first wish—to grow into a boy—in extreme cases she will end as a manifest homosexual, and otherwise she will exhibit markedly masculine traits in the conduct of her later life, will choose a masculine vocation, and so on."[27]

The delinquent girl, according to Freudian theory, is attempting to be a man. Her subsequent aggression, whether sexual or violent, is the expression of her hopeless search for a penis.

The Troubled Adolescent Girl

Gisela Konopka's view of the female delinquent in *The Adolescent Girl in Conflict* (1966), incorporates many of the principles expounded by Freud but also emphasizes the influence of peers and socialization in causing deviant behavior.[28] Konopka suggests that delinquency has its roots in a girl's feeling of uncertainty and loneliness.[29]

During her adolescence a girl's major emotional need is to be accepted by members of the opposite sex. If normal channels for receiving such approval—family, friends, relatives—are impaired, she may fight isolation by joining a "crowd" or engaging in gratuitous sexual relationships. This behavior eventually leads to "rejection by the community, general experience of having no recognized success . . . and more behavior which increases the feeling of worthlessness."[30] Konopka identifies four major influences on loneliness and consequent delinquent behavior of girls:[31]

1. The onset of puberty in girls is traumatic because of the often cruel way in which it is received by parents and the fear it creates in the girl.
2. The social identification process can be dramatic and difficult because of a girl's competitiveness with her mother. In fatherless homes, girls have an especially hard time since "the road to a healthy development toward womanhood through affection for the male and identification with the female simply does not exist."[32]
3. Changing the pattern of females' cultural position can create problems. Delinquent girls are believed to suffer from a lack of training and education. This locks them into low-paying jobs with little hope for advancement. These conditions lead girls to relieve their thwarted ambition by aggressive or destructive behavior.
4. The world presents a hostile picture to some young girls. Adult authority figures tell them what to do, but no one is there to listen to their needs.

Konopka emphasizes the effect of the family and society on female emotions as a primary influence on a girl's delinquent behavior. A number of authorities have shared Konopka's views since the publication of her study. One significant work by Clyde Vedder and Dora Somerville, *The Delinquent Girl* (1970), also suggests that the delinquent behavior of girls is usually a problem of adjustment to family and social pressure.[33] In fact, the authors estimate that 75 percent of institutionalized girls have family problems. They also suggest that girls have serious problems in a male-dominated culture with rigid and sometimes unfair social practices.[34]

Research Support for Developmental Theory

Some empirical research lends support to developmental theories of female delinquency. For example, Ames Robey and his associates studied the background and behavior of adolescent girls in a suburban juvenile court clinic.[35] In their analysis of girls manifesting rebellious behavior, they often found sexual conflicts with both parents, sometimes marked by an erotic entanglement between father and daughter.[36]

William Wattenberg and Frank Saunders found a pattern of broken or disrupted homes in the backgrounds of female delinquents.[37] In their analysis of a sample of 4,533 youths contacted by the Youth Bureau of the Detroit Police Department, they found that girls were much more likely than boys to be charged with sex offenses, incorrigibility, and truancy. Girls were also likely to be described as aimless and nonenergetic. More revealing was the fact that girls often came from broken homes; and when police took them home, they were more likely than boys to be rejected by their parents.

Don Gibbons and Manzer Griswold had similar findings in their study of the delinquency referrals of an urban juvenile court.[38] More delinquent girls than boys were charged with ungovernable behavior, running away, and sex offenses (9.81 versus 4.7 percent). The girls were also more likely than boys to come from broken homes. This led Gibbons and Griswold to conclude that girls were more likely than boys to come before the court because of maladjustment.[39]

Gordon Barker and William Adams compared boys and girls in another setting, a state training school. They found that most of the male delinquents were incarcerated for burglary, robbery, and other theft-related offenses, but the girls tended to be involved in incorrigibility, sex offenses, and truancy.[40]

Barker and Adams concluded that the boys were delinquent to gain status and to demonstrate their masculinity by adventurous behavior. On the other hand, the girls were delinquent because of hostility toward parents and a consequent need to obtain gratification and attention from others.

In *Five Hundred Delinquent Women*, Sheldon Glueck and Eleanor Glueck examined the life histories of institutionalized female offenders.[41] A significant majority of 76 subjects had been involved in sexual deviance that began early in their teens. The Gluecks concluded that sexual delinquency and general behavior maladjustment developed in girls simultaneously with unstable home lives.[42]

In sum, the developmental approach to female delinquency posits that family interaction and child-parent relations are the key to understanding the antisocial behavior of girls. If a girl grows up in an atmosphere of sexual tension, where hostility exists between her parents or where the parents are absent from the home, it is likely that she will turn to outside sources for affection and support. Unlike boys, girls have very narrowly defined behavioral patterns that they must follow. If their reaction to loneliness, frustration, and parental hostility is sexual activity, running away, staying out late at night, and so on, they are likely to be defined as delinquent or wayward. The developmental approach holds that the psychological pressure of a poor home life is likely to have an even more damaging effect on females than males. Since girls are less likely than boys to have the support of close-knit peer associations, they are more likely to need close parental relationships in order to retain emotional stability. In fact, girls may become sexually involved with boys in order to receive support from them, a practice that only tends to magnify their problems.

THEORIES OF ECONOMIC AND SOCIAL DETERMINISM

All of us, despite our differences, are constantly growing and trying to understand each other's oppression, be it as working class women, black or brown women, gay women or middle class women. We are, by struggling, finding new ways of caring about each other, and it is this that gives us hope of having a movement, finally, which will provide for all of our needs.[43]

This statement represents the sentiments of women who are active participants in the social revolution that is commonly called the women's liberation movement.[44] Feminist leaders such as Betty Friedan of the National Organization for Women (NOW) have fought for more than a decade to allow women to break away from their traditional role of homemaker and mother and secure for themselves economic, professional, educational, and social advancement. There is little question that the women's movement has revised the way many women perceive their roles in society, and it has also significantly altered the relationship of women to many important social institutions.

It is not surprising that this rapid social change has influenced thinking about the nature and extent of female criminality too. A number of scholars, including Rita James Simon and Freda Adler, have drawn national attention to the changing pattern of female criminality and have offered new explanations for its cause.[45] Their position, simply put, is that society's economic and social conditions influence female crime. As these conditions change in the latter part of the twentieth century, so too will the criminal behavior of women and girls.

Freda Adler

Freda Adler's book, *Sisters in Crime,* has been an influential source of information on how changing roles have influenced female crime and delinquency.[46] Adler's major thesis is that by striving for social and economic independence, women have begun to alter social institutions, which, until fairly recently, protected males in their position of power. "The phenomenon of female criminality," she claims, "is but one wave in this rising tide of female assertiveness."[48]

Adler argues that the increase in female delinquency is affected by the changing patterns of females' behavior.[49] Girls are becoming increasingly involved in traditionally masculine crimes such as stealing, gang activity, and fighting.[50] Furthermore, Adler predicts that in the future the women's liberation movement will produce even steeper increases in the rate of female delinquency since it creates an environment in which the social roles of girls and boys converge. Boys, she argues, have traditionally entered puberty ill prepared for the world of aggression and competition they encounter in the activities of their peer groups. The consequent emotional strain leads them to engage in delinquent activities. Girls, on the other hand, have always maintained traditional, relatively static behavior patterns. These patterns have protected young girls from the pressures of transition into the adult world. However, Adler claims, "the modern girl . . . is passing from childhood to adulthood via a new and uncharted course. . . . She is partly pushed and partly impelled into fields previously closed to women. . . . Clearly, the developmental difficulties which encouraged male delinquency in the past are exerting a similar influence on girls."[51]

In Highlight 8–3, Adler proclaims that the changing female role will eventually produce female delinquents and criminals who are quite similar to their male counterparts.

Research Support for the Determinist View

A number of recent research studies have supported the determinist view of female delinquency. Most notable may be Rita James Simon's 1975 effort, *The Contemporary Woman and Crime.*[52] While not specifically devoted to youth crime, Simon's effort points to the consistent increase in the crime rate of females in general. Her comparison of arrest rates for the years 1953, 1963, and 1972 indicates that (1) women's crime rates have increased dramatically and (2) the type of female criminality has changed. Simon suggests that women commit significantly more larceny, fraud, forgery, and embezzlement—all business and economic related crimes. Their violent crime rate has remained somewhat static. In Highlight 8–4, Simon explains that her findings are a function of women's changing role.

Highlight 8–3. Adler on the Changing Role of Women and Crime.

Women are no longer behaving like subhuman primates with only one option. Medical, educational, economic, political and technological advances have freed women from unwanted pregnancies, provided them with male occupational skills, and equalized their strengths with weapons. Is it any wonder that once women were armed with male opportunities, they should strive for status, criminal as well as civil, through established male hierarchial channels.

In the cities . . . young girls are now taking to the streets just as boys have traditionally done. It has now become quite common for adolescent girls to participate in muggings, burglaries, and extortion rings which prey on schoolmates.

Source: Freda Adler, *Sisters in Crime* (New York: McGraw-Hill, 1975), pp. 10–11.

Highlight 8–4. Simon on Opportunity and Female Crime.

The same factors and conditions that explain women's increased participation in property offenses also serve to explain the slight decline or lack of increase in violent offenses during the same time period. The fact that women have more economic opportunities and more legal rights (divorces and abortions are easier to obtain) and that in recent years they have been developing a rhetoric which legitimizes their newly established socio-legal-economic status seems to lessen the likelihood that they will feel victimized, dependent, and oppressed. The diminishment of such feelings means that they will be less likely to attack their traditional targets: their husbands, lovers, pimps (that is, men with whom they are emotionally involved and dependent upon), and their babies (those recently born and those not yet delivered).

Source: Rita James Simon, "Women and Crime Revisited," *Social Science Quarterly* 56 (1976): 660–661.

As noted in Chapter 3, a number of self-report studies have been devoted specifically to the female delinquent, and their findings seem to support the determinist position. Michael Hindelang, for example, compared the self-reported delinquent behavior of 319 male and 444 female high school students.[53] The students were each given a confidential questionnaire that listed twenty-four delinquent acts, including drinking, theft, and drug use, and they were asked to indicate how many times in the past year they had engaged in each act.

Boys reported significantly more participation in each act except hit and run accidents and drug use other than marijuana smoking. Nonetheless, the reported delinquent behavior of the girls in the sample had a pattern similar to that of the boys. That is, the delinquent acts committed most and least often among the girls were nearly identical to those of the boys. Hindelang's findings led him to reject the belief that females are primarily sexual delinquents because females reported that they were actually engaging in many traditionally male crimes.

Martin Gold presents similar evidence in his 1970 study of delinquent behavior in a midwestern American city.[54] From interviews with more than 500 boys and girls, Gold found that the concept of the female as a sexual delinquent is misleading. He concluded that female delinquency was quite similar to male delinquency, only less extensive. Girls trailed boys in every offense category except running away from home and hitting their parents, but the mixture of girls' offenses was not very different from that of boys.[55]

John Clark and Edward Haurek took a sample of 1,116 public school students, aged eleven to nineteen, living in four diverse communities (industrial, urban, suburban, and rural).[56] They listed forty-six delinquent acts, such as theft, drinking alcohol without permission, and gang fights; and they discovered that the ratio of male to female delinquency was much lower than expected. For only four of the acts (three involving property damage and the fourth hanging around a bar or poolroom) was male delinquent behavior four times as great as female, a much lower figure than was originally expected.

A similar study by Nancy Wise found an overall delinquency ratio of 1.7 to 1 between the offenses of boys and those of girls, indicating that Clark and Haurek's findings were not unusual.[57] Further evidence is supplied in the study of Gary Jensen and Raymond Eve, who analyzed the self-report questionnaires of more than 4,000 California high school students. Their study revealed substantial female participation in such delinquent acts as theft, fist fights, and vandalism.[58]

Notwithstanding the evidence in the studies described above, Darrell Steffensmeier and Renee (Hoffman) Steffensmeier reached very different conclusions:

1. Arrest data and juvenile gang studies show little increase in female violence or gang related acts. Young female offenders do not seem to be catching up with males in terms of violent or serious crimes.
2. Gains in serious crimes by female offenders (as measured by the UCR) have leveled off. Earlier crime reflected the general increase in the overall crime rate occurring in the 1970s.
3. Self-report studies show that female participation in most crime patterns has remained stable for the past ten years. Increases have come in the area of drug use and alcohol abuse.
4. The future of female criminality seems uncertain. If anything, adult females should increase their participation in larceny offenses.[59]

Thus, some evidence suggests that the delinquency pattern of young girls is similar (if not as extensive) as that of boys and that the rate of female delinquency is increasing. However, from analyzing existing data sources, some researchers have reached the opposite conclusion.

DELINQUENT GIRLS AND THE JUVENILE JUSTICE SYSTEM

Authorities generally agree that the juvenile justice system treats girls and boys differently. However, by no means do they agree about the direction that difference takes—more lenient or more severe. For many years, it was believed that male-dominated police and courts were likely to be "chivalrous" towards girls and treat them benignly and compassionately. Recently, more experts have held the opposite to be true. Girls may actually be subject to closer control and more exacting discipline than boys. Let us examine each of these positions in some detail.

Deferential Treatment of Girls

Over twenty-five years ago, Otto Pollak tried to explain the lower female crime rate by suggesting that women benefited from a "double standard." Police tended to treat the minor offenses of young girls unofficially in order to save them from the social stigma attached to a court appearance.[60]

Pollak further suggested that, even if arrested, females were more likely to be acquitted. He went so far as to suggest that district attorneys were actually apologetic to their female cases, expressing remorse at what they considered a personally distasteful, yet unavoidable, duty.

The belief that deferential treatment exists is quite common. Feminist Freda Adler has suggested recently that police may sometimes be less suspicious of and more open with female criminals and delinquents, eventually developing a paternalistic attitude toward them.[61] Those who share this view believe that women are generally protected in a male-dominated society.[62]

The belief that agents of the juvenile justice system treat girls more leniently rests on the assumption that many police officers and court personnel come from working class, male-dominated backgrounds. Therefore, they have protective and paternalistic attitudes toward girls. Though research evidence for this position is incomplete, some studies have supported it. For example, Jay Williams and Martin Gold found in their national study of juvenile offenders that younger teenagers and females commit fewer and less serious offenses; if caught, they are less likely to have their offenses recorded by police.[63]

Thus, some experts believe that the juvenile justice system is more tolerant of female delinquency. However, those holding this position have become a distinct minority.

Girls as Victims of the Justice System

Evidence is growing that girls are actually more vulnerable than boys to being arrested for illegal acts and subsequently disciplined and punished; that is, "to be minor and female is to be doubly vulnerable."[64] This somewhat surprising conclusion is based on the following three assumptions:

1. The police and the courts generally believe girls to be sexual delinquents and therefore psychologically disturbed or impaired. They are thus in need of immediate and concerted treatment.
2. Police and courts are likely to intervene in cases involving a teenage girl since they believe that her home environment is the cause of her problems and to return her to that environment would be harmful and damaging.
3. The delinquency of boys can often be tolerated since the prevalent attitudes are that "boys will be boys" and that occasional law violation is normal. Any delinquent behavior by girls is so unusual that it must be considered a serious problem.[65]

A number of different sources in the literature of crime and delinquency support these statements. For example, Jean Strouse suggests that it is common for juvenile court judges to place delinquent girls in confinement for even minor offenses since they almost always suspect that sexual activity has taken place. Boys who have engaged in the very same behavior are believed to be undergoing normal adolescent growing pains and are therefore treated lightly.[66]

In a similar vein, Theodore Ferdinand and Elmer Luchterhand suggest that police and juvenile courts are often overly sensitive to the family problems that may have precipitated female delinquency. Returning a young girl who has engaged in sexual misbehavior to her home is considered to be more detrimental to her well-being than utilizing some other form of treatment, such as placement in a foster home or institution.[67]

Freda Adler points out that the juvenile court's role as arbiter of family problems forces it into a position of strictly controlling the behavior of girls, whose acts are viewed as sexual in nature and therefore either threaten the social fabric or undermine the authority of the family.[68] Thus, concludes Adler, boys are prosecuted for stealing and various sorts of mischief; however, the majority of girls brought before the juvenile court have committed no crime but are thought to be sexually incorrigible.[69]

Further evidence of discrimination in the handling of female delinquents was found by Yona Cohn in her study of the disposition recommendations of probation officers.[70] Judges often rely on these recommendations in making their decisions in juvenile cases. In her study, Cohn found that, as expected, girls had a much lower arrest rate than boys. Girls constituted only one-sixth of her sample of youths in a metropolitan court. Yet, they constituted nearly one-half of the youths sentenced to some sort of institutional care. Of thirty-five girls in her sample, thirty were considered to need institutional sentences or psychiatric care. Cohn attributes this high percentage to the fact that girls frequently violate the sexual taboos of the middle-class probation officer.

In an analysis of more than 9,000 youths apprehended by police in a midwestern city, Robert Terry found evidence that girls were more prone to be referred to state authority than boys; and if actually petitioned to juvenile court, they were more likely to receive an institutional sentence (76.7 percent of the girls and 59.7 percent of the boys were institutionalized).[71] Terry argued that the appearance of a girl in juvenile court is taken quite seriously because it indicates that she has failed to heed what must have been numerous warnings about her behavior. The misbehavior of girls was taken more seriously than that of boys since it was less compatible with the female role.[72]

In a recent study, Meda Chesney-Lind found that police in Honolulu, Hawaii, were likely to arrest female adolescents for sexual activity and ignore the same behavior among male delinquents.[73] Seventy-four percent of the females in her sample were charged with sexual activity or incorrigibility, but only 27 percent of the boys suffered the same charges. Moreover, the court ordered physical examinations in over 70 percent of the female cases, but only about 15 percent of the males were forced to undergo this embarrassing procedure.[74] Girls were also more likely to be sent to a detention facility before trial, and the length of their detention averaged three times that of the boys'. Finally, between 1929 and 1950, three times as many females as males were institutionalized; from 1954 to 1964, the ratio was "reduced" to two females to one male.

Chesney-Lind explains her data by suggesting that female adolescents have a much narrower range of acceptable behavior than male adolescents. Therefore, any sign of misbehavior in young girls is seen as a substantial challenge to authority and to the viability of the double standard of sexual inequality.[75] Female delinquency is viewed as relatively more serious than male delinquency and therefore more likely to be severely sanctioned.

Discrimination against female delinquents has been corroborated by a number of other research studies. For example, data compiled by Rosemary Sarri for the National Assessment of Juvenile Corrections indicate that treatment of female juveniles is consistently more punitive than that of males. The arrest ratio of males to females is four to one, but the secure, pretrial detention ratio is only three to one.[76]

In a similar study, Kenneth Wooden describes a government-sponsored survey that found that, of the 44,104 boys and 13,099 girls held in institutions in the United States, two-thirds of the girls are status offenders, as compared with one-third of the boys.[77] Many of the girls, the study revealed, were there only because they had engaged in sexual intercourse. In a survey of the institutional practices of the juvenile justice systems of two states, Wooden discovered that much the same pattern existed in each: "In Nebraska only seven percent of the boys were locked up for noncriminal acts compared with 53 percent of the girls. In Arkansas it was 22 percent for males; females totaled 78 percent."[78]

Not only are girls sent to institutions more often than boys; they also remain there longer. This occurs largely because status offenders are given indeterminate sentences, but youths who commit crimes are given specific sentences. As one study put it, "A girl whose behavior is considered to be promiscuous can be legally detained longer than a boy . . . who has committed a felony."[79]

Thus, there is evidence that the law treats girls more harshly than boys; and although girls may commit fewer serious criminal offenses, they are more likely to be arrested, processed to court, and institutionalized. At the root of this official sex discrimination is the belief that girls are sexual delinquents in need of care and custody. If such care is not promptly received, they will be led to pregnancy, prostitution, or worse.

How can we square the idea that girl's delinquency is increasing at a faster rate than boys in the crime statistics because they are treated more harshly with the idea that they show up more frequently because they are actually committing more crimes as a result of their changing social role? After a careful review of official and unofficial delinquency statistics, Darrell Steffensmeier and Renee Hoffman Steffensmeier showed that gains in the rate of serious female delinquency may have abated and that any further gain may reflect increasing adolescent arrest rates for both males and females.[80]

CHAPTER SUMMARY

Female delinquency has become a topic of considerable interest to criminologists and other experts interested in youth crime. It is believed that the nature and extent of female delinquent activities has changed, and it appears that girls are now engaging in more frequent and serious illegal activity.

Attempts to discover the cause of female delinquency can be placed in a number of different categories. Early efforts by Cesare Lombroso and W. I. Thomas and a somewhat later effort by Otto Pollak place the blame for female crime on the inherent biological nature of the female. Later, developmental theorists viewed a girl's psychological makeup and family environment as important factors in her misbehavior. Recently, socioeconomic factors have been suggested as playing a pivotal role in causing female delinquency.

Descriptions of the treatment female delinquents receive after they have been apprehended have changed. Initially, experts believed that girls were treated more leniently than boys because the agents of the juvenile justice system had a chivalrous, protective attitude toward girls. Today, most experts believe that the juvenile justice system treats girls more harshly and that girls charged with (noncriminal) status offenses are sometimes punished more severely than boys charged with delinquent offenses.

Despite our most persistent efforts to alleviate sexual discrimination in law and justice, true equality for males and females before the law will not be easily achieved. It has taken many decades for sexual discrimination to become so deeply rooted in America's legal processes, and it will take considerable time for those same attitudes to release their hold on our system of juvenile justice.

DISCUSSION QUESTIONS

1. Are girls delinquent for different reasons than boys? Do they have a unique set of problems?
2. Are girls the victims of unfairness at the hands of the justice system, or do they benefit from "chivalry"?
3. Comment on Pollak's charge that women and girls are sneaky and cunning?

SUGGESTED READINGS

Anderson, Etta. "The 'Chivalrous' Treatment of the Female Offender in the Arms of the Criminal Justice System." Social Problems 23 (1976): 350–357.

Armstrong, Gail. "Females under the Law: Protected but Unequal." Crime and Delinquency 23 (1977): 109–120.

Chesney-Lind, Meda. "Judicial Enforcement of the Female Sex Role: The Family Court and the Female Delinquent." Issues in Criminology 8 (1973): 51–59.

_____"Judicial Paternalism and the Female Status Offender." Crime and Delinquency 23 (1977): 12-130.

_____"Juvenile Delinquency: The Sexualization of Female Crime." Psychology Today 8 (1974): 43–46.

Conway, Allan, and Bogdan, Carol. "Sexual Delinquency: The Persistence of a Double Standard." Crime and Delinquency 23 (1977): 131–135.

Crites, Laura, ed. The Female Offender. Lexington, Mass.: D. C. Heath, 1976.

Giallombardo, Rose. The Social World of Imprisoned Girls. New York: Wiley, 1974.

Price, Ray. "The Forgotten Female Offender." Crime and Delinquency 23 (1977): 101–108.

Scott, Jocelynne. "Liberation of the Female Lawbreaker." International Journal of Criminology and Penology 6 (1978): 5–18.

REFERENCES

1. Cesare Lombroso, The Female Offender, trans. (New York: Appleton, 1920).

2. Rita James Simon, The Contemporary Woman and Crime Washington, D.C.: Government Printing Office, 1975).

3.   Lombroso, *The Female Offender*.

4.   Ibid., p. 122.

5.   Ibid., pp. 51–52.

6.   Ibid., p. 151.

7.   Ibid., p. 156.

8.   W. I. Thomas, *The Unadjusted Girl* (New York: Harper & Row, 1923).

9.   W. I. Thomas, *Sex and Society* (Boston: Little Brown, 1907).

10. Thomas, *The Unadjusted Girl*.

11. Ibid., p. 241.

12. Ibid., p. 109.

13. Ibid., p. 140.

14. Ibid., p. 141.

15. Ibid., pp. 232–233.

16. Otto Pollak, *The Criminality of Women* (Philadelphia: University of Pennsylvania Press, 1950).

17. Ibid., p. 1.

18. Ibid., p. 2.

19. Ibid., p. 4.

20. Ibid., pp. 2–3.

21. Ibid., p. 8.

22. Ibid., p. 125.

23. Ibid.,

24. Ibid., p. 139.

25. Sigmund Freud, *An Outline of Psychoanalysis*, trans. James Strachey (New York: W. W. Norton, 1949), p. 278.

26. Dorie Klein, "The Etiology of Female Crime: A Review of the Literature," in *The Criminology of Deviant Women*, ed. F. Adler and R. Simon (Boston: Houghton Mifflin, 1979), pp. 69–71.

27. Freud, *An Outline of Psychoanalysis*, p. 12.

28. Gisela Konopka, *The Adolescent Girl in Conflict* (Englewood Cliffs, N.J.: Prentice-Hall, 1966).

29. Ibid., p. 40.

30. Ibid.

31. The following four paragraphs are adapted from Peter and Lucille Kratcoski, *Juvenile Delinquency* (Englewood Cliffs, N.J.: Prentice-Hall, 1979), pp. 146–147.

32. Konopka, *The Adolescent Girl in Conflict*, p. 50.

33. Clyde Vedder and Dora Somerville, *The Delinquent Girl* (Springfield, Ill.: Charles C. Thomas, 1970).

34. Ibid., p. 153.

35. Ames Robey, Richard Rosenwalk, John Small, and Ruth Lee, "The Runaway Girl: A Reaction to Family Stress," *American Journal of Orthopsychiatry* 34 (1964): pp. 763–767.

36. Ibid., p. 764.

37. William Wattenberg and Frank Saunders, "Sex Differences among Juvenile Offenders," *Sociology and Social Research* 39 (1954): pp. 24–31.

38. Don Gibbons and Manser Griswold, "Sex Differences among Juvenile Court Referrals," *Sociology and Social Research* 42 (1957): pp. 106–110.

39. Ibid., p. 110.

40. Gordon Barker and William Adams, "Comparison of The Delinquencies of Boys and Girls," *Journal of Criminal Law, Criminology and Police Science* 53 (1962): pp. 470–475.

41. Eleanor Glueck and Sheldon Glueck, *Five Hundred Delinquent Women* (New York: Knopf, 1934).

42. Ibid., p. 90.

43. Deborah Babcox and Madeline Belken, *Liberation NOW* (New York: Dell Publishing, 1971), p. 5.

44. Leaders of the women's movement include Gloria Steinem, Germaine Greer, and Kate Millett. Earlier revolutionaries include Simone de Beauvoir and Gertrude Stein.

45. Simon, *The Contemporary Woman and Crime*; Freda Adler, *Sisters in Crime* (New York: McGraw-Hill, 1975).

46. Adler, *Sisters in Crime*.

47. Ibid., p. 1.

48. Ibid., p. 2.

49. Ibid., p. 89.

50. Ibid., p. 95.

51. Ibid., p. 104.

52. Rita James Simon, "Women and Crime Revisited," *Social Science Quarterly* 56 (1976): 658–663.

53. Michael Hindeling, "Age, Sex, and the Versatility of Delinquency Involvements," *Social Forces* 14 (1971): 552–534.

54. Martin Gold, *Delinquent Behavior in an American City* (Belmont, Calif.: Brooks/Cole, 1970).

55. Ibid., p. 118.

56. John Clark and Edward Haurek, "Age and Sex Roles of Adolescents and Their Involvement in Misconduct: A Reappraisal," *Sociology and Social Research* 50 (1966): 495–508.

57. Nancy Wise, "Juvenile Delinquency in Middle-Class Girls," in *Middle Class Delinquency*, ed. E. Vaz (New York: Harper & Row, 1967), pp. 179–188.

58. Gary Jensen and Raymond Eve, "Sex Differences in Delinquency: An Examination of Popular Sociological Explanations," *Criminology* 13 (1976): 427–448.

59. Darrell Steffensmeier and Renee Hoffman Steffensmeier, "Trends in Female Delinquency," *Criminology* 18 (1980): 62–85. See also Steffensmeier and Steffensmeier, "Crime and the Contemporary Woman: An Analysis of Changing Levels of Female Property Crime, 1960–1975," *Social Forces* 57 (1978): pp. 566–584; and Joseph Weis, "Liberation and Crime: The Invention of the New Female Criminal," *Crime and Social Justice* 1 (1976): pp. 17–27.

60. Pollak, *The Criminality of Women*, p. 14.

61. Adler, *Sisters in Crime*, p. 49.

62. Walter Reckless, "A New Theory of Delinquency and Crime," *Federal Probation* 25 (1961): pp. 42–46.

63. Jay Williams and Martin Gold, "From Delinquent Behavior to Official Delinquency," *Social Problems* 20 (1972): p. 226.

64. Jean Strauss, "To Be Minor and Female: The Legal Rights of Women under Twenty-One," *Ms.* 1 (1972): -84.

65. Theodore Ferdinand and Elmer Luchterhand, "Intercity Youth, the Police, the Juvenile Court and Justice," *Social Problems* 17 (1970): pp. 510-526.

66. Strauss, "To Be Minor and Female."

67. Ferdinand and Luchterhand, "Intercity Youth, the Police, the Juvenile Court and Justice," p. 310.

68. Adler, *Sisters in Crime,* p. 92.

69. Ibid., p. 89.

70. Yona Cohn, "Criteria For 'Probation Officer's Recommendations to 'Juvenile Court," *Crime & Delinquency* 1 (1963): 272-275.

71. Robert Terry, "Discrimination in the Police Handling of Juvenile Offenders by Social Control Agencies," *Journal of Research in Crime and Delinquency* 14 (1967): p. 218.

72. Ibid.

73. Meda Chesney-Lind, "Judicial Enforcement of the Female Sex Role: The Family Court and the Female Delinquent," *Issues in Criminology* 8 (1973): pp. 51–59.

74. Ibid., p. 56.

75. Ibid., p. 54.

76. Rosemary Sarri, *Under Lock and Key: Juveniles in Jail and Detention* (Ann Arbor, Mich.: National Assessment of Juvenile Corrections, 1975), p. 62.

77. Kenneth Wooden, *Weeping in the Playtime of Others: America's Incarcerated Children* (New York: McGraw-Hill, 1976).

78. Ibid., p. 119.

79. Alan Conway and Carol Bogdan, "Sexual Delinquency: The Persistence of a Double Standard," *Crime and Delinquency* 23 (1977): p. 133.

80. Steffensmeier and Steffensmeier, "Trends in Female Delinquency."

PART III

ENVIRONMENTAL
INFLUENCES ON
DELINQUENCY

Chapter 9

Chapter Outline

Introduction
Definition of Gangs
History of Gangs
Gang Structure
Causes of Gang Delinquency
Types of Gangs
Extent of the Gang Problem
Chapter Summary

Key Terms, Names, and Cases

interstitial area
near group
law violating youth group
street corner society
bopping gangs
detached street worker
sociopathic youth
gang typologies
the violent gang
Walter Miller
Frederick Thrasher
Lewis Yablonsky
Malcolm Klein
William F. Whyte
Herbert Block
Arthur Niederhoffer

Juvenile Gangs ————————————— in America

INTRODUCTION

The delinquent gang is a topic of considerable interest to many American citizens. A powerful mystique has grown up around gangs, so that mere mention of the term gang evokes images of black-jacketed youths who roam the streets at night in groups bearing such colorful names as the Egyptian Kings, the Cobras, and the Savage Skulls. Films, television shows, and novels such as *The Warriors, Blackboard Jungle, The Wanderers, Amboy Dukes,* and *West Side Story* have popularized the teenage gang.[1]

Considering the importance and threat of gang violence, information about gangs is surprisingly lacking. We are not sure how many gangs actually exist, how many gang members there are, or how much crime is gang related. The secretive, constantly changing nature of the juvenile gang is probably one reason for this lack of knowledge; the danger of collecting the information is another.

This chapter will explore much of the literature currently available on the gang problem. First, it will define *delinquent gang* and explore the gangs' components. Then, it will look at the history of gangs and gang behavior and view the nature of today's gangs. It will also explore the varying formats, or typologies, of gangs and will explain theories of gang formulation. Finally, it will survey the extent of today's gang activity.

DEFINITION OF GANGS

One of the more serious problems social scientists face in their efforts to study delinquent gangs is the lack of consensus on what defines a gang. Sometimes the term *gang* is used broadly to describe any congregation of youths who have joined together to engage in delinquent acts. Some police departments use the term narrowly, designating as gangs only those groups that hold and defend territory, or turf.[2] Frederick Thrasher is one of many who have attempted to define the juvenile gang:

A gang is an interstitial group originally formed spontaneously and then integrated through conflict. It is characterized by the following types of behavior: meeting face to face, milling, movement through space as a unit, conflict and planning. The result of this collective behavior is the development of tradition, unreflective internal structure, espirit de corps, solidarity, morale, group awareness and attachment to local territory.[3]

Thrasher's definition first appeared in 1927, and it seems to capture the essence of group *cohesiveness* and *solidarity* that is still the prevailing view of gangs. Thrasher uses the term *interstitial* to mean a break in the social fabric, a foreign element in normal society.[4]

Malcolm Klein provides a more recent definition of the gang:

Any denotable adolescent group of youngsters who (a) are generally perceived as a distinct aggregation by others in their neighborhood; (b) recognize themselves as a denotable group (almost invariably with a group name); and (c) have been involved in a sufficient number of delinquent incidents to call forth a consistent negative response from neighborhood residents and/or enforcement agencies.[5]

Klein's definition highlights the gang's threat to the community and the negative image it maintains in its own neighborhood. Desmond Cartwright's definition also includes the element of danger:

An interstitial and integrated group of persons who meet face to face more or less regularly and whose existence and activities are considered an actual or potential threat to the prevailing social order.[6]

Cartwright goes on to suggest that the gang concept involves such normal and standard group processes as recruiting new members, goal setting, assigning goals, and status development.[7]

The Delinquent Gang as a Near Group

Sociologist Lewis Yablonsky makes an important contribution to the understanding of gang behavior with his definition of the *gang* as a near group. According to Yablonsky, human collectives tend to range from highly cohesive, tight-knit organizations to mobs with anonymous members who are motivated by emotion and disturbed leadership. Teenage gangs fall somewhere in between the two extremes. Therefore, they can be characterized as *near groups*. They usually have the following characteristics:

1. Diffuse role definition.
2. Limited cohesion.
3. Impermanence.
4. Minimal consensus of norms.
5. Shifting membership.
6. Disturbed leadership.

7. Limited definition of membership expectations.[8]

In Yablonsky's view, the gang maintains only a small core of totally committed members, who need the gang for satisfaction and other personal reasons. These core members work constantly to keep the momentum of the gang going. On a second level are *affiliated* youths, who participate in gang activity only when the mood suits them. At a third level are *peripheral* members, who participate in a particular situation or fight but who usually do not identify with the gang. The size of the gang may therefore vary considerably, based on need and situation. For example, an impending "rumble" with a rival gang may bring out loosely affiliated or peripheral gang members if they believe it is in their interest to join with the gang in the fight.

In sum, Yablonsky differs with the majority of other experts on teenage gangs. They view gangs as stable units with emotionally secure leaders who excel at a variety of skills such as fighting, athletics, and verbal prowess.[9]

Walter Miller's "Law Violating Youth Group"

In a recent paper, sociologist Walter Miller suggests that the restrictive definitions used to classify gangs have caused the amount of delinquent behavior attributed to youth groups to be radically underestimated.[10] From data collected in a federally sponsored survey of collective youth crime in twenty-four major cities, Miller decided that *law violating youth* group is a more appropriate term than teenage gang to identify collective youth crime. He says, "A law-violating youth group is an association of three or more youths whose members engage recurrently in illegal activities with the cooperation and/or moral support of their companions."[11]

Miller does not use the term *delinquency* in his definition. Instead, he employs the term *law violation* to underscore the fact that collective youth crime is an activity of *social adolescents*, aged twelve to twenty-one, rather than of *legal adolescents*, aged seven to seventeen or eighteen. He suggests that unrestricted use of the term *delinquent gang* erroneously implies that youth gang members are all legal minors. Moreover, Miller recognizes the loose affiliations found in many youth groups. He employs such terms as *cooperation* and *moral support* to convey the idea that collective activities rarely include all group members. In many instances, gang delinquency is a cooperative venture in which only a few members play a part.

Miller also recognizes the existence of "formal" delinquent gangs. However, he believes that formal gangs represent only one element of collective youth crime, which also includes cliques, networks, bands, corner groups, and so on. Miller defines the *gang* as follows: "A Youth-Gang is a self-formed association of peers, bound together by mutual interests, with identifiable leadership, well-developed lines of authority, and other organizational features, who act in concert to achieve a specific purpose or purposes which generally include the conduct of illegal activity and control over a particular territory, facility, or type of enterprise." [12] Miller's conception of the gang as only one of a variety of law violating youth groups enables us to maintain a more accurate perspective of collective youth problems in America.

HISTORY OF GANGS

Gangs developed quite early in the nation's history. In Highlight 9–1, sociologist James Inciardi describes the formation of the earliest American gangs.

Highlight 9–1. The Earliest History of Gangs in America.

The earliest gangs consisted almost entirely of Irishmen. The Irish, emigrating to this country in vast numbers and lacking funds, education, and skills, were met with contempt by native New Yorkers and were forced into the city's worst slum—the Five Points district. This section of lower Manhattan was formed by the intersection of five streets—Anthony, Orange, Cross, Little Water, and Mulberry—and it became the core of what ultimately grew into the largest Irish community outside of Dublin. The housing was composed of clapboard tenements, built on the former site of the old Collect, or Fresh Water Pond, a marshy area of wetland and meadow extending from present day Chambers Street to Canal Street, east of Broadway. The marsh had been poorly drained and filled with garbage, and by 1820 the inadequate foundations of the tenements had begun to slowly sink into the moist soil. The Irish clustered by the thousands in the Five Points, and lacking other means of earning a living, many developed criminal careers.

The first of the city's organized gangs had their genesis in the tenements of the Five Points, yet their actual structuring into working units followed the opening of the *green-grocery speakeasies* which sprang up along those streets which formed the Points. The first of these speakeasies was opened by one Rosanna Peers on Center Street, just south of Anthony. Piles of decaying green vegetables were displayed outside the doors of Rosanna's establishment, but her chief source of revenue came from the potent liquor sold in her back room at prices lower than those in recognized saloons. This speakeasy quickly became the resort of thugs, pickpockets, murderers, and thieves. "The Forty Thieves," which history suggests was the first New York gang with a definite,

acknowledged leadership, appears to have been formed in Rosanna's jaded emporium, and her back room was used as the gang's traditional meeting place. The Forty Thieves were predominantly muggers and pickpockets, and operated on the Lower East Side of Manhattan from the early 1820s to just prior to the Civil War. Like many other gangs succeeding them, they encouraged a submob of juveniles, dubbed the "Forty Little Thieves," from which they recruited new talent.

Following the Forty Thieves Gang, the "Kerryonians" were organized in 1825 and were also headquartered at the Rosanna Peers grocery store. The members of the Kerryonians Gang had all been born in County Kerry, Ireland, and much of their time was devoted to mugging Englishmen. Other gangs of note which developed in this area were the "Roach Guards," "Dead Rabbits," "Chickesters," "Plug Uglies," and "Shirt Tails." The Dead Rabbits were originally part of the Roach Guards, organized to honor the name of a Five Points liquor dealer. There was internal dissension within the gang, and at one of their meetings a dead rabbit was thrown into the room. It was accepted as an omen by one of the opposing factions, which withdrew and formed an independent unit under the banner of the maligned animal. The Plug Uglies were formed in the mid-1820s and took their name from the giant plug hats which each member filled with rags and straw to protect their heads during gang battles. The Shirt Tails were so called because they wore their shirts on the outside of their trousers, like Chinamen. Little is known of the origins of the Chickesters, yet their claim to immortality comes from their persistence in outliving all of the original Five Points gangs and in spawning the more murderous gangs of the post-Civil War era.

From the Bowery, directly north of the Five Points, came such gangs as the "American Guards," "Atlantic Guards," "True Blue Americans," and the "Bowery Boys;" and from Hell's Kitchen on New York's middle West Side came the "Hudson Dusters," "Potashes," and "Gophers." These gangs of the Five Points, Bowery, and Hell's Kitchen, which often included hundreds of men and boys, consisted of many small gangs grouped together and led by a supreme chieftain who commanded absolute loyalty. Gangsters were regularly dispatched by their leaders to nearby areas to steal, rob and kill, or to wage street battles against rival gangs. And with violence and theft as patterned activities, the gangs of New York proceeded to terrorize the city for some one hundred years. Furthermore, they represented the first enduring criminal organizations and established the subcultural systems from which later racketeers descended.

While Five Points, Hell's Kitchen, and Bowery gangs were operating within the directives of street crime and with members most frequently thieves and murderers, the criminal groups who settled in the Fourth Ward of New York confined their activities to alternate types of predatory behavior. The Fourth Ward, lying east and south of the Five Points along the East River, had been the finest residential section of New York during the eighteenth century. Its streets were lined with splendid mansions inhabited by the first families of the city, the wealthy merchants, and the political heroes. John Hancock's home was located here, as was George Washington's at the time of his inauguration. But the wave of immigration which broke upon the American continent soon after the Revolution forced the aristocracy northward, and by the 1840s the old mansions had given way to rows of tenements housing a population steeped in poverty and vice.

Gangsterism in the Fourth Ward was initially devoted to theft along the East and Hudson River piers, followed by piracy in the grand manner of Blackbeard and Henry Morgan. The river thieves included the "Charlton Street Gang," the "Hookers," "Daybreak Boys," "Swamp Angels" and the "Old Border Gang," and in all, there were some 500 river pirates organized into more than 50 active gangs. The Charlton Street Gang included a collection of bandits who operated from a small sloop which sailed along the Hudson from the Harlem River as far north as Poughkeepsie, some 70 miles above Manhattan Island. With the Jolly Roger flying from the masthead, they robbed riverside farmhouses and mansions and held men, women, and children for ransom. The Daybreak Boys were the best organized of the gangs. They prowled about the docks and along the rivers in rowboats and became notorious during the 1850s for their success in scuttling ships throughout the New York port. Manhattan waters were also regularly invaded by the gangs of Irishtown, a sparsely settled region between Brooklyn and Williamsburg. Other river bandits were also expert sneak thieves, and as masked burglars they plundered the small towns along both shores of Long Island Sound.

The gangs of youthful and young adult criminals who made war on one another and terrorized the streets of New York were also evident in other cities. Philadelphia had its "Buffaloes," "Blood Tubs," "Rugs," and "Copper Heads;" Baltimore had its "Stringers;" and a group known as the "Crawfish Boys" plagued the streets of Cincinnati. Other urban areas developed later than the large cities in the east, but they, nevertheless, had their exposure to street gangsterism. In 1837 when New York was a major metropolis and its Five Points area had already developed as a center for street crime, Chicago was just a settlement of some 500 buildings with a population of only 4,100. Within a few decades, however, Chicago's underworld had emerged with an active criminal class. Similarly, it was not until 1835 that the first dwelling appeared along the beach of Yerba Buena Cove, the present site of San Francisco, but with the discovery of gold along the nearby American River in 1848, the Barbary Coast

quickly grew as a leading American
underworld.

Source: James Inciardi, *Reflections on Crime: An*

Introduction to Criminology and Criminal Justice
(New York: Holt, Rinehart and Winston, 1978),
pp. 34-37. Footnote omitted. Reprinted by
permission of Holt, Rinehart and Winston.

Frederick Thrasher and William F. Whyte

Frederick Thrasher initiated study of the modern gang in his analysis of more
than 1,300 youth groups in Chicago. His report on this effort, *The Gang*, was
first published in 1927.[13]

Thrasher found that the social, economic, and ecological processes that
affect the structure of great metropolitan cities create *interstitial areas*, or
cracks in the normal fabric of society, characterized by weak family controls,
poverty, and social disorganization. According to Thrasher, spontaneous
youth groups develop in interstitial areas to meet childhood needs such as
play, fun, and adventure—activities that sometimes lead to delinquent acts.[14]

The slum area presents many opportunities for conflict between youth
gangs and between youth gangs and adult authority. If this conflict continues,
the group becomes more solidified and its activities become primarily illegal.
The group thus develops into a gang, with a name and a structure oriented toward delinquent behavior.

To Thrasher, the gang provides the young lower-class boy with an opportunity for success. Since adult society does not meet the needs of slum dwellers,
the gang solves the problem by offering what society fails to
provide—excitement, fun, and opportunity. The gang is not a haven for disturbed youth but rather an alternative life-style for normal boys.[15]

Since its publication, Thrasher's work has had an important influence on
the accepted view of the gang. Some recent and sophisticated studies of delinquent gang behavior (discussed previously in Chapters 5 and 6), such as
Cloward's and Ohlin's opportunity theory and Miller's focal concerns theory,
seem similar to Thrasher in their emphasis on the gang as a means for lower-
class boys to achieve advancement and opportunity as well as to defend
themselves and attack their rivals.

Thrasher's work has also influenced the research methods used to observe
gangs. For example, William F. Whyte employed Thrasher's technique of
personal observation and his humanistic approach in his classic work, *Street
Corner Society*.[16] Whyte actually hung out for three years with a group of Italian youths called "The Norton Street Gang" in a Boston neighborhood.
Whyte found that the members of this group sought comfort, mutual support,
and prestige from the gang because opportunities for employment were limited and future success was uncertain.

Whyte approached his study in much the way an anthropologist researches
a native culture. His careful observations give us a clear picture of the daily
activities, conversation, beliefs, values, and hopes of gang youth.

Gangs in the 1950s, 1960s and Beyond

In the 1950s and early 1960s, the threat of gangs and gang violence swept the public consciousness. It was unusual for a week to go by without a major city newspaper featuring a story on the violent behavior of "bopping gangs" and their colorful leaders and names—the Egyptian Kings, the Young Lords, the Blackstone Rangers. Social service and law enforcement agencies directed major efforts to either rehabilitating or destroying the gangs. Movies, such as *The Wild Ones* and *Blackboard Jungle,* were made about gangs, and the play *West Side Story* romanticized violent gangs. However, by the 1960s, the gang menace seemed to have disappeared. Some experts attribute the decline of gang activity to successful gang control programs. For example, in the detached street worker project, a social worker was attached directly to an individual gang to rechannel the energies of gang boys in useful directions.[17] Others believe that gangs were eliminated because police gang control units infiltrated gangs, arrested leaders, and constantly harassed members.[18] Another explanation for the decline in gang activity is the increase in political awareness that developed during the 1960s. Many gang leaders were directed away from crime and into the social or political activities of groups such as the Black Panther Party, civil rights groups, and anti-Vietnam War groups. In addition, many gang boys were drafted. Still another explanation is that gang activity diminished during the 1960s because many gang boys became active users of heroin and other drugs, which curtailed their group-related criminal activity.[19]

Gang activity began anew in the early 1970s. As Walter Miller comments on the New York scene:

All was quiet on the gang front for almost 10 years. Then, suddenly and without advance warning, the gangs reappeared. Bearing such names as Savage Skulls and Black Assassins, they began to form in the South Bronx in the spring of 1971, quickly spread to other parts of the city, and by 1975 comprised 275 police-verified gangs with 11,000 members. These new and mysteriously emerging gangs were far more lethal than their predecessors—heavily armed, incited and directed by violence-hardened older men, and directing their lethal activities far more to the victimization of ordinary citizens than to one another.[20]

Gang activity has also reemerged in other major cities, especially Philadelphia, Los Angeles, and Chicago. There is growing evidence that the teenage gang is today an important and ever-growing phenomenon on the American scene.

GANG STRUCTURE

This section will focus on such issues as gangs' age and sex structure, ethnic composition, location, and leadership patterns.[21]

Age

The ages of gang members range widely. In his description of gangs, Thrasher included young adolescent boys as well as adult criminals. Whyte and Solomon

Kobrin and his associates reported on both delinquent and young adult gangs whose members were in their twenties.[22] However, most gangs studied have consisted mainly of teenagers. Some of the age ranges include: ten to twenty-five, reported by David Kantor and William Bennett;[23] twelve to twenty-two, reported by the New York City Youth Board;[24] eleven to twenty-five, reported by Charles Cooper;[25] and twelve to the early twenties, reported by Malcolm Klein.[26]

The majority of gang members are in the sixteen to eighteen year old bracket. Small gangs are more likely to have restricted age ranges, with all members being within two to three years of each other. Larger gangs sometimes have youthful cliques and therefore have a much larger age range.

In his recent national study, Walter Miller found that many criminal justice experts believe gangs are being formed of older members than they used to be.[27] Two major factors are cited for this trend. The first is based on the assumption that gang activity is largely a product of returning Vietnam veterans, who have resumed their former gang membership, bringing to it their increased knowledge of combat and weapons. The second argument is that older men are now directing the gang activities of younger members, who are less liable to receive severe criminal penalties if apprehended by law enforcement agents. However, in a subsequent analysis of 807 gang-related arrests in four of the nation's largest cities (New York, Chicago, Los Angeles, and Philadelphia), Miller found that 93 percent of the arrested youths fell within the fourteen to twenty-one age span and that 82.2 percent fell within the fourteen to nineteen age range. Only 6 percent of the arrestees were under thirteen or over twenty-three. Since Miller did not use a large sample in his analysis, the preliminary statistical evidence does not immediately contradict the notion of an expansion of the traditional age range of gang members.

Sex

Of the more than 1,000 groups included in Thrasher's original survey, only half a dozen were female gangs. This may have been an accurate portrayal of gang membership in the 1920s, but a change has taken place today. Though female gangs may not function independently, female units or auxiliaries of boys' groups seem quite common in major cities. For example, Klein reports on one or two such groups associated with each male gang he observed in Los Angeles.[28] Walter Miller cites two of seven groups he studied in Boston as female.[29]

Females are involved in gang activities in one of three ways: as auxiliaries, or branches, of male gangs; as part of sexually mixed gangs; or as autonomous gangs. Of these, the first form has been the most common. Often, the units will take on a feminized version of the male gang name, such as "Devil's Disciples" or "Lady Disciples."

Miller's recent survey seems to substantiate the rather limited representation of girls in gang activities. For example, New York police estimated that half of the city's gangs had female branches, but their members comprised only 6 percent of the total gang population. A general estimate that gangs are 90 percent or more male is probably accurate for all cities where gangs are active.[30]

Ethnic and Racial Composition

The ethnic and racial distribution of gangs reflects their inner-city locale. Gangs seem to be overrepresented by minority group members.

Most gangs seem to be racially exclusive. Though Lewis Yablonsky reports racially mixed violent gangs, the majority of gang observers—including Malcolm Klein, Walter Miller, James Short and Fred Strodtbeck, Irving Spergel, and Frederick Thrasher—view gangs as racially homogeneous groups—all white, all black, all Hispanic, and so on.[31] Moreover, most, though not all, intergang conflict appears to be among groups of the same ethnic and racial background.

Miller found that gangs can be divided into four main racial groupings: black (African origin), Asiatic origin (Chinese, Japanese, Korean, Taiwanese, Samoan, and American Indian), European origin (English, Italian, Irish, Slavic, and German), and Hispanic origin (Mexican, Puerto Rican, Panamanian, and others from Spanish-speaking countries).[32] The number of gang members in the various ethnic groupings in six cities that Miller surveyed is illustrated in Table 9-1.

As the data in Table 9-1 indicate, approximately half of the gangs in these cities are black, approximately one-third are Hispanic, and somewhat under one-tenth are Asian and non-Hispanic white. Furthermore, the various cities differ in the racial makeup of their gangs. For example, in Philadelphia and Detroit, the overwhelming number of gang members are black. In New York, Hispanic gangs predominate. San Francisco's small gang population is mostly Oriental.

Miller found that during the 1970s most gangs were ethnically homogeneous. However, some ethnic mixing could be found, including multinational (Italian, Irish, Polish) white Catholic gangs and Puerto Rican gangs with Afro-American members.

Table 9-1. Ethnic/Racial Background of Gang/Group Members in Six Gang-Problem Cities by Continent of Ancestral Orgin.

	Africa		Asia		Hispanic	Europe Africa America	Other Europe		Est. No. Gang Members	
	No.	%	No.	%	No.	%	No.	%	No.	%
NYC	10,150	(35)	1,450	(5)	14,500	(50)	2,900	(10)	29,000	(100)
Chicago	4,725	(60)	225	(3)	2,250	(30)	525	(7)	7,500	(100)
L.A.	9,000	(35)	2,700	(20)	4,725	(35)	1,350	(10)	13,500	(100)
Phila.	9,000	(90)	0		500	(5)	500	(5)	10,000	(100)
Detroit	745	(85)	0		45	(5)	85	(10)	875	(100)
San Fran.	15	(5)	235	(90)	15	(5)	5		250	(100)
Six Cities	29,135	(47.6)	4,610	(7.5)	22,035	(36.0)	5,360	(8.8)	61,125	(100)

Source: Walter Miller, *Violence by Youth Gangs and Youth Groups as a Crime Problem in Major American Cities* (Washington, D.C.: Government Printing Office, 1975), p. 25.

Location

The gang problem appears to be an urban, lower-class phenomenon. Though middle-class and suburban gangs exist, they are generally short-lived and are less likely than the others to indulge in serious delinquent activity. Two types of urban areas are gang-prone. The first was described by Frederick Thrasher as follows: "In nature, foreign matter tends to collect and cake in every crack, crevice, and cranny—interstices. There are also fissures and breaks in the structure of social organizations. The gang may be regarded as an interstitial region in the layout of the city."[33] By "interstitial," Thrasher means the shifting, changing, or transitional neighborhoods of the larger cities.

The second gang area is the "stable slum," a neighborhood where population shifts have slowed down, permitting patterns of behavior and traditions to develop over a number of years. Most typical of these areas are the slums in New York and Philadelphia and the Mexican-American *barrios* of the Southwest and California.

Saul Bernstein and others have pointed out that transitionary neighborhoods produce more spontaneous gangs. There, groups of different ethnic backgrounds are often pitted against each other.[34] The stable slum more often contains the large structured gang clusters that are the most resistant to attempts by law enforcement and social service agencies to modify or disband them. The transitional and the stable slums are not the sole environments that produce gangs, but the evidence shows that they do contain the majority of urban gangs.

In recent years, there has been a massive movement of people out of the central city into outlying communities and suburbs. Many of these people have been upper or middle class, but lower-income residents have also been affected. In some cities once-fashionable outlying neighborhoods have declined and downtown, central city areas have undergone extensive urban renewal. However, even though gang areas have shifted their locale, the ecological patterns that produce them remain unchanged.

In his national study, Miller found that the central, inner-city districts of major cities like New York and Chicago have become devoted to finance, retail stores, restaurants, and entertainment.[35] Two aspects of this development inhibit gang formation—first, few residential areas and thus few adolescent recruits, and second, a policy of intensive police patrol. According to Miller, slums or ghettos have shifted from the inner-city areas to outer-city, ring-city or suburban areas—that is, to formerly middle-class areas that are now in decay. Housing projects are also gang-prone. Thus, gangs are still located in ghettos, but today these ghettos are often at some distance from their traditional inner-city locations.[36]

Leadership

Most experts describe gang leaders as cool characters who have earned their position by a variety of abilities—fighting prowess, verbal ability, athletic distinction, and so on. For example, William Whyte describes the gang leader as:

[The] focal point for the organization of his group. In his absence, the members of the gang are divided into a number of small groups. There is no common activity or general conversation. When the leader appears, the situation changes strikingly. The small units form into one large group. . . . The members do not feel that the gang is really gathered until the leader appears. . . . The leader is the man who acts when the situation requires action. He is more resourceful than his followers. . . . The leader need not be the best baseball player, bowler, or fighter, but he must have some skill in whatever pursuits are of interest to the group.[37]

Other experts emphasize that gang leadership is not held by one person and that it varies with particular activities, such as fighting, sex, and negotiations. In fact, in some gangs, each age level of the gang has its own leaders. Older members may be looked up to, but they are not necessarily considered leaders by younger members. In his analysis of Los Angeles gangs, Malcolm Klein has observed that many gang leaders shrink from taking a leadership role and actively deny leadership. Klein overheard one gang boy claim: "We got no leaders, man. Everybody's a leader, and nobody can talk for nobody else."[38] The most plausible explanation of this ambivalence is the boy's fear that during times of crises, his decisions will conflict with those of other leaders and he will lose status and face.

Barry Krisberg studied gangs in Philadelphia and discovered that leaders stressed the concept of "hustling," emphasizing individual gain and success.[39] Krisberg found that many gang leaders were not even aware of outside philosophies, racial groups, leaders, or ideas. They did not plan actions in advance because announcing future goals would lock them into a position where their inability to achieve would be an overt admission of failure. Furthermore, gang leaders maintained a mirror image of the values of the larger society—for example, "Do unto others before they do unto you." The basic theme of the gang leader was survival in the urban jungle.

Thus, the experts do not agree about the nature of gang leadership. Some view it as transient in nature while others view it as steady and in the hands of the toughest, smartest, and most able boys.

CAUSES OF GANG DELINQUENCY

A number of attempts have been made to explain the development and maintenance of gangs. In this section, the most significant will be explained. These explanations have some similarities, but they differ enough to warrant independent discussion.

Block's and Niederhoffer's Anthropological View

Herbert Block and Arthur Niederhoffer have suggested that gangs provide a mechanism for bridging the gap between the freedom of childhood and the responsibilities of adulthood.[40] The young people of all societies go through an adolescent period in which they attempt to gain adult status. Societies vary in the amount of aid they grant adolescents during this period. When assistance from adults is inadequate, adolescents will provide their own, including the development of gangs. In America, upper- and middle-class youths are more easily able to identify with adults, and the transition to adulthood can be attained without gangs. Lower-class youths find the transition more difficult, since adult support is usually lacking.

The cornerstone of the Block-Niederhoffer theory is that gang processes and functions are quite similar to the puberty rites of primitive cultures, and like their primitive counterpart, they help the child bridge the gap between childhood and adulthood. Block and Niederhoffer cite a number of gang behavior patterns that they find similar to primitive puberty rites.[41]

DECORATIONS Many gang boys display tattoos and other identifying marks. Some gangs make tattooing an integrat part of the initiation ceremonies. Gangs also adopt uniforms—especially jackets with the name of the gang on it, motorcycle jackets, and boots. Another form of decoration is scars, which gang members view as measures of their toughness and recklessness. Some boys will scar themselves with the name of their girl friends as a show of solidarity with their mates.

ACQUISITION OF A NEW NAME AND A NEW LANGUAGE In the puberty rites of primitive societies, the novice theoretically emerges as a new person with a new name and language. New names are a badge of honor among street gangs, and gangs frequently create a unique jargon.

SECLUSION FROM WOMEN, BACHELOR HUTS, AGE GRADES The adolescent gang is preeminently a male sanctuary. Usually, girls are kept at arm's length from the group, which congregates nightly at the same poolhall or street corner.

BREAK FROM THE HOME AND ASSIMILATION BY A NEW GROUP Primitive societies have specific rights involving separation from home, transition to manhood, and incorporation into the adult world. The gang allows the adolescent to separate from his parents' control and helps bridge the gap to maturity.

SEXUAL AMBIVALENCE Gang members and adolescents in primitive societies share a degree of sexual ambivalence. Males add seemingly feminine articles to their clothing. Female gang members wear the shirt, jacket, and boots of males. Group sex is another form of sexual ambivalence. Girls are not sought for any other reason but sex.

HAZING AND ORDEAL Many gangs put new members through a period of hazing as an initiation to the gang to make sure they have "heart."[42] This feature is also quite similar to primitive tribal rites. Block and Niederhoffer use the following as an example of gang hazing:

A gang operating in East Harlem, NYC, uses as a test for membership an ordeal which they call "cramping." The youth applying for membership is held by two of the older boys while the rest of the gang pummel him in the abdominal region as hard as they can. If he "chickens-out" he cannot become a member of the gang.[43]

SEX AND FERTILITY THEME IN PUBERTY RITES   As lower-class youths reach their late teens, the gang allows them access to sexual contacts—girl gangs, female gang followers, hangouts to go to, and so on.

DEATH AND REBIRTH MYTH   In primitive society, initiation into a cult is viewed as the death of childhood. By analogy, younger boys in lower-class urban areas yearn for the time when they can join the gang and really start to live. Membership in the adolescent gang "means the youth gives up his life as a child and assumes a new way of life."[44] Gang names themselves, are suggestive of "primitive totemic ancestors" since they usually are symbolic Jaguars and Egyptian Kings, for example).

In conclusion, Block and Niederhoffer suggest that the gang transforms its members into something different from nonmembers. Because of their highly charged, explosive nature, gangs crystallize in visible and overt form the traits that are repressed or dormant in nongang teenagers.[45]

Social-Cultural View

The most widely-held view among sociologists is that sociocultural factors contribute to the formation of gangs. We have previously discussed the work on gangs of Thrasher (this chapter), of Cloward and Ohlin (Chapter 5), and of Cohen (Chapter 5).

In still another study of gang formation, Irving Spergel analyzed delinquent behavior in three cities: "Racketville," "Slumtown," and "Haulburg." Spergel found that Slumtown, the area with the lowest income and the highest population, also had the highest number of violent gangs.[46] According to Spergel, the gang gives lower-class youths a means for attaining personal reputations and consequent peer group status. Spergel's position is similar to Cloward's and Ohlin's and Cohen's.

Malcolm Klein's studies suggest that although there is much variation, the situation of the average gang member is not good. Members are poor and come from broken homes. They lack adequate educational and vocational role models, and they have family members with criminal histories.[47]

Also contributing to the development of gangs in lower-class areas is the unique set of cultural norms and values in these areas.[48] Walter Miller's analysis of the six focal concerns of lower-class culture is perhaps the most familiar recording of lower-class norms and beliefs. Miller's work suggests that the delinquent gang is a normal response to the culture of the lower-class environment.

In summary, the sociocultural view assumes that gangs are a natural and normal response to the privations of lower-class life and that gangs are a status generating medium for boys whose aspirations cannot be realized by legitimate means.

Psychological Views of Gang Creation

A minority position on the formation of gangs is that they serve as an outlet for psychologically diseased youth. The most notable proponent of this view is Lewis Yablonsky, whose theory of violent gang formation holds that violent gangs recruit their members among the more sociopathic youths living in disorganized slum communities.[49]

Yablonsky views the "sociopathic" youth as one who lacks "social feelings." He "has not been trained to have human feelings or compassion or responsibility for another."[50] Yablonsky supports this contention by pointing to the eccentric, destructive, and hostile sexual attitudes and behavior of gang youths, who are often violent and sadistic.[51] He sums up the sociopathic character traits of gang boys as:

1. A defective social conscience marked by limited feelings of guilt for destructive acts against others.
2. Limited compassion or empathy for others.
3. The acting out of behavior dominated by egocentrism and self-seeking goals.
4. The manipulation of others in a way possible for immediate self-gratification (for example, sexually exploitative modes of behavior) without any moral concern or responsibility.

Yablonsky's views are considered highly controversial and are by no means shared by all gang experts.

TYPES OF GANGS

The gang does not exist; rather gangs come in a wide variety of forms. While there is said to be a relationship between gang form and the level and type of gang delinquency, this relationship is somewhat ephemeral. Delinquency and violence, in one form or another, can be expected from any gang.[52]

The literature of juvenile delinquency has described a great diversity of gang types. No single type of gang is responsible for the totality of gang violence and delinquency. Discussion of some of the more popular gang typologies follows below:

The Structural Approach

Malcolm Klein identifies four major structural groupings among gangs: spontaneous, traditional, splinter clique, and horizontal.[53]

SPONTANEOUS   A spontaneous gang is a self-contained gang usually of ten to thirty members, with an age range of two to three years. The members reside in urban areas of transition. They can be splinter groups of larger gangs that have broken off to pursue their own needs. Spontaneous gangs tend to be organized around a particular pursuit—for example, theft—and are usually short-lived.

TRADITIONAL   Traditional gangs are also known as vertical, area, or cluster gangs. They have two to five independent age subgroups within the overall gang. Each group has a sense of self-identity and an individual name and identifies with both the overall gang and its own grouping.

SPLINTER CLIQUE   A splinter clique consists of three to twelve boys who have split off from a larger group to form an independent group. They have abandoned traditional roles and instead embrace criminal or drug related adult crime patterns.

HORIZONTAL   The horizontal pattern consists of temporary alliances across neighborhoods between boys' groups that are usually independent.[54]

Yablonsky's Behavioral Approach

Klein's concept of a gang typology is not unique, and a number of similar views are available in the literature of crime and delinquency. Another typology, which is based on gang behavior, has been formulated by Yablonsky. In his view, gangs follow one of three basic behavioral patterns: social, delinquent, and violent.[55]

THE SOCIAL GANG   The social gang is a relatively permanent group that hangs out at a specific location such as a candy store or street corner. Members develop a sense of comradeship and often engage in organized group activities including dancing, discussions, and athletic events. The group stays together because of mutual attraction among its members rather than through a need for protection or esteem. The general feeling is that the group will provide the means for a better, more enjoyable life and that group activities are superior to individual ones. This group is thus similar to Whyte's street corner gang.

The social gang is not likely to participate in serious delinquent activity and will engage in physical violence only if members are attacked and retaliation is unavoidable. Its members include the most stable boys in the neighborhood, those who have the closest association with the norms and values of the overall society.

DELINQUENT GANG   The delinquent gang is a cohesive group organized around the principle of monetary gain from delinquent activities. Its members depend on one another to carry out planned activities and to provide help if necessary. The leader who usually emerges is the most competent at stealing and is an excellent organizer and planner.

Members of this type of gang are emotionally stable and therefore able to organize their time and efforts for criminal activity. Gang activity is viewed as a way of getting ahead in the world. It is pursued not for enjoyment but as an avenue to wealth and prestige. The delinquent gang member accepts the goals of the larger society, such as wealth, success, and power, but rejects the legitimate means available for attaining them. However, delinquent gang membership is not viewed as a stepping-stone to adult criminal behavior. It exists to satisfy present needs.

THE VIOLENT GANG   The violent gang is organized to obtain the emotional gratification that violent activities can bring to youth. Members spend their time building arsenals and planning and carrying out violent acts.

Leaders tend to be emotionally unstable, and they have a need to control and direct others. Both leaders and followers tend to overestimate the importance, size, and power of their group.

The structure of violent gangs is constantly changing. Allies one day become enemies the next, according to gang leaders.

The violent gang is also identified by intragroup violence. Sometimes this is verbal in nature, with one member needling and insulting (sounding) another. At other times, hostility and aggression take on physical form.

Violent gangs appear to emerge almost spontaneously. They provide a vehicle for violent, hostile youths to act out their aggressions and personal problems.

Membership in violent gangs is fluid. There is a widespread belief that complex initiation rites take place before a youth can join a violent gang and that the rites often entail physical pain and proving one's courage. This may be a myth.

Other Typologies

A number of other authors have attempted to describe alternative forms taken by delinquent gangs.[56] We have previously noted Cloward's and Ohlin's concept of the criminal, conflict, and retreatist gangs.[57] In a similar fashion, Albert Cohen and James Short identify the theft, conflict, and addict gang.[58] New York City's Delinquency Evaluation Project divides gangs into problem, nonproblem, and conflict groups.[59] The New York City Youth Board labels gangs as vertical, horizontal, self-contained, and disintegrative.[60]

Walter Miller has identified three distinctive types of gangs—fighting gangs, turf gangs, and gain-oriented gangs.[61]

EXTENT OF THE GANG PROBLEM

How many gangs currently exist? How much crime do they commit? Much controversy surrounds these questions, and less than adequate data exist with which to accurately answer them. In the 1950s, gang activity was believed to be widespread throughout the nation; yet, by the mid-1960s, it seemed to all but disappear. The extent of gang activity and the population of gangs themselves are still not known today.

Much of what we do know about the gang problem comes from Walter Miller's recent survey of gang behavior.[62] According to Miller, gang delinquency is most serious in six cities: Chicago, New York, Los Angeles, Philadelphia, Detroit, and San Francisco. Using data from police, courts, and other agencies, Miller estimates that these cities contain anywhere between 760 and 2,700 gangs at any one time, with total memberships of 28,450 to 81,500 youths. The wide range of these statistics gives evidence of the difficulty in accurately estimating the extent of the gang problem.

In a subsequent analysis of his survey data, Miller reports on information gathered in twenty-four cities throughout the United States, which he groups into separate categories based on population. In one analysis of gang problems in a group of fifteen large cities, Miller discovered that 1,300 gangs existed. Five of the cities—Boston, Philadelphia, New York, Chicago, and Los Angeles—reported having at least 100 gangs in operation between 1973 and 1977. For the total group of fifteen cities, the number of gang members was estimated at 52,000 (or about 25 members per gang). Gang size ranged from 60 members in New York and Los Angeles to 10 to 15 in Boston and San Francisco. Furthermore, it was estimated that 3.5 percent of all males between the ages of ten and nineteen were active gang members.

In another analysis of his data, Miller examined the presence of law violating youth groups in thirteen medium-sized cities, ranging from St. Paul, Minnesota, with a population of 287,000, to Dallas, Texas, with a population of 816,000.

More than 8,000 youth groups were found in these cities—an average of 615 per city. They ranged in size from 23 members in Miami, Florida, to 9 in Cleveland, Ohio, and St. Louis, Missouri, with a national average of 15 members.

Miller extrapolates from these findings to estimate the existence of 120,000 law violating youth group members in the thirteen cities, making up 19 percent of the male population aged ten to nineteen. In the 900 American cities with populations of more than 25,000, Miller projects the existence of 105,000 youth groups, with a membership of 1.0 million. Nationally, he estimates the existence of 80 groups for every gang in his data and 30 group members for every gang member.

Miller found evidence that gang related killings are extremely high. The five largest cities with gang problems (New York, Chicago, Los Angeles, Philadelphia, and San Francisco) have almost 200 gang related killings a year.[63] In addition, gangs such as the "Brotherhood" in Detroit, "Savage Skulls" in New York, and "Hwa Ching" in San Francisco are using greater numbers of sophisticated weapons than ever before.[64]

In his more recent analysis of gang behavior between the years 1973 and 1977, Miller found little evidence that the gang problem is abating. In the three cities that take special notice of gang members arrested by police—New York, Los Angeles, and Chicago—13,000 yearly arrests occurred, 6,000 of them for serious crimes. During the six-year period 1972 to 1977, approximately 1,000 gang related killings were reported in the six largest cities. Miller also found that gangs and other law violating youth groups committed over half of all youth crimes, or 1.6 million criminal acts.[65]

CHAPTER SUMMARY

Gangs are a serious problem in many cities; yet, little is known about them. Most gang members are males, aged fourteen to twenty-one, who live in urban ghetto areas. Ethnic minorities make up the majority of gang members. Gangs can be classified by their structure, behavior, or status. Some are believed to be social; others are criminally oriented; still others are violent.

Gangs developed early in the country's history and reached their heyday in the 1950s and early 1960s. After a lull of ten years, gang operations seem to be on the rise. Millions of crimes, including hundreds of murders, are believed to be committed annually by gangs. Gang and delinquent group membership may be in the millions.

We are still not sure what causes gangs. One view is that they serve as a bridge between adolescence and adulthood in communities where adult control is lacking. Another view suggests that gangs are a product of lower-class social disorganization and that they serve as an alternative means of advancement for disadvantaged boys. Still another view is that some gangs are havens for psychotic and disturbed youths.

It is evident from the enormity of the gang problem and the insufficient knowledge available about gangs that further research on gangs is urgently needed.

DISCUSSION QUESTIONS

1. Do gangs serve a purpose? Differentiate between a gang and a fraternity.
2. Discuss the differences between violent, criminal, and drug oriented gangs.
3. How do gangs in suburban areas differ from inner-city gangs?

SUGGESTED READINGS

Block, Herbert, and Niederhoffer, Arthur. *The Gang: A Study in Adolescent Behavior.* New York: Philosophical Library, 1958.

Gannon, Thomas. "Dimensions of Current Gang Delinquency." *Journal of Research in Crime and Delinquency* 4 (1967): 119–131.

Klein, Malcolm. "Factors Related to Juvenile Gang Membership Patterns." *Sociology and Social Research* 51 (1966): 49–62.

———*Juvenile Gangs in Context: Theory, Research and Action.* Englewood Cliffs, N.J.: Prentice-Hall, 1967.

———"Impressions of Juvenile Gang Members." *Adolescence* 3 (1968): 53–78.

Kobrin, Solomon. "The Conflict of Values in Delinquency Areas." *American Sociological Review* 16(1951): 653–661.

Matza, David, and Sykes, Gresham. "Juvenile Delinquency and Subterranean Values." *American Sociological Review* 26 (1961): 712–719.

Myerhoff, Howard, and Myerhoff, Barbara. "Field Observations of Middle-Class Gangs." *Social Forces* 42 (1964): 328–336.

Short, James, ed. *Gang Delinquency and Delinquent Subcultures.* New York: Harper & Row, 1968.

Short, James, and Strodtbeck, Fred. *Group Process and Gang Delinquency.* Chicago: University of Chicago Press, 1965.

Spergel, Irving. *Racketville, Slumtown, Haulburg: An Exploratory Study of Delinquent Subcultures.* Chicago: University of Chicago Press, 1964.

Yablonsky, Lewis. *The Violent Gang.* New York: Macmillan, 1963.

REFERENCES

1. Other well-known gang-related media presentations include the motorcycle gangs depicted in the movies *The Wild Ones* and *Hell's Angels on Wheels* and the neighborhood street toughs in *Saturday Night Fever.* See also David Dawley, *A Nation of Lords* (Garden City, N.Y.: Anchor, 1973).

2. Walter Miller, *Violence by Youth Gangs and Youth Groups as a Crime Problem in Major American Cities* (Washington, D.C.: Government Printing Office, 1975).

3. Frederick Thrasher, *The Gang* (Chicago: University of Chicago Press, 1927), p. 57.

4. Ibid., p. 22.

5. Malcolm Klein, *Street Gangs and Street Workers* (Englewood Cliffs, N.Y.: Prentice-Hall, 1971), p. 13.

6. Desmond Cartwright, Barbara Tomson, and Hersey Schwarts, eds., *Gang Delinquency* (Monterey, Calif.: Brooks/Cole, 1975), pp. 149–150.

7. Ibid., p. 20.

8. Lewis Yablonsky, *The Violent Gang* (Baltimore: Penguin Books, 1966), p. 109.

9. Malcolm Klein, "Violence in American Juvenile Gangs," in *Crimes of Violence*, ed. Donald Mulvihill and Melvin Tumin with Lynn Curtis, National Commission on the Causes and Prevention of Violence, vol. 13 (Washington, D.C.: Government Printing Office, 1969), p. 1432.

10. Walter Miller, "Gangs, Groups and Serious Youth Crime," in *Critical Issues in Juvenile Delinquency*, ed. David Schioor and Delos Kelly (Lexington, Mass.: Lexington Books, 1980).

11. Ibid.

12. Ibid.

13. Thrasher, *The Gang.*

14. Ibid., p. 37.

15. Ibid., p. 172.

16. William F. Whyte, *Street Corner Society* (Chicago: University of Chicago Press, 1955).

17. Irving Spergel, *Street Gang Work: Theory and Practice* (Reading, Mass.: Addison-Wesley, 1966).

18. Miller, *Violence by Youth Gangs*, p. 2.

19. Ibid., pp. 1–2.

20. Ibid.

21. Material in the following sections was adapted in part from Miller, *Violence by Youth Gangs*; and Klein, "Violence in American Juvenile Gangs."

22. Solomon Kobrin, Joseph Puntel, and Emil Peluso, "Criteria of Status among Street Groups," *Journal of Research in Crime and Delinquency* 4 (1967): 98–118.

23. David Kantor and William Bennett, "Orientation of Street-Corner Workers and Their Effects on Gangs," in *Controlling Delinquents*, ed. Stanton Wheeler (New York: Wiley, 1968), pp. 271–286.

24. *Reaching the Fighting Gang* (New York: City Youth Board, 1960).

25. Charles Cooper, "The Chicago YMCA Detailed Workers: Current States of a Gibson Program," in *Juvenile Gangs in Context*, ed. Malcolm Klein (Englewood Cliffs, N.J.: Prentice-Hall, 1967), pp. 183–193.

26. Malcolm Klein, *The Ladino Hills Project* (Los Angeles: Youth Studies Center, University of Southern California, 1968).

27. Miller, *Violence by Youth Gangs*, pp. 21–22.

28. Klein, *The Ladino Hills Project*.

29. Walter Miller, "The Impact of a 'Total Community' Delinquency Control Project," *Social Problems* 10 (1962): 168–169.

30. Miller, *Violence by Youth Gangs*, p. 23.

31. Klein, "Violence in American Juvenile Gangs," p. 1429.

32. Miller, *Violence by Youth Gangs*, pp. 2-26.

33. Thrasher, *The Gang*, p. 20.

34. Saul Bernstein, *Youth in the Streets: Work with Alienated Youth Groups* (New York: Association Press, 1964).

35. Miller, *Violence by Youth Gangs*, pp. 17–20.

36. Ibid.

37. Whyte, *Street Corner Society*.

38. Malcolm Klein, "Impressions of Juvenile Gang Members," *Adolescence* 3 (1968): 59.

39. Barry Krisberg, "Gang Youth and Hustling: The Psychology of Survival," *Issues in Criminology* 9 (1974): 115–129.

40. Herbert Block and Arthur Niederhoffer, *The Gang: A Study in Adolescent Behavior* (New York: Philosophical Library, 1958).

41. Ibid., pp. 95–113.

42. For a similar view, see Thrasher, *The Gang*, p. 221.

43. Block and Niederhoffer, *The Gang*, p. 106.

44. Ibid., p. 112.

45. Ibid., p. 113.

46. Irving Spergel, *Racketville, Slumtown, and Haulburg: An Exploratory Study of Delinquent Subcultures* (Chicago: University of Chicago Press, 1964).

47. Klein, *Street Gangs and Street Workers*, pp. 12–15.

48. Malcolm Klein and Lois Crawford, "Groups, Gangs and Cohesiveness," *Journal of Research in Crime and Delinquency* 4 (1967): 67.

49. Yablonsky, *The Violent Gang*, p. 237.

50. Ibid.

51. Ibid., pp. 239–241.

52. Klein, *Street Gangs and Street Workers*, p. 80.

53. Ibid., pp. 64–70.

54. See also Hans Mattick and Nathan Caplan, *The Chicago Youth Development Project* (Ann Arbor, Mich.: Institute for Social Research, 1964), p. 28.

55. Yablonsky, *The Violent Gang*, pp. 187–193.

56. See, for example, Kobrin, Puntel, and Peluso, "Criteria of Status among Street Groups"; and Solomon Kobrin, "The Conflict of Values in Delinquency Areas," *American Sociological Review* 16 (1951): 653–661.

57. Richard Cloward and Lloyd Ohlin, *Delinquency and Opportunity* (Glencoe, Ill.: Free Press, 1960).

58. Albert Cohen and James Short, "Research in Development Subc ultures," *Journal of Social Issues* 14 (1958): 20–37.

59. *Dealing with the Conflict Gang in New York*, Interim Report No. 14 of the Juvenile Delinquency Evaluation Project of the City of New York, May 1960 (mimeo).

60. *Reaching the Fighting Gang.*

61. Miller, "Gangs, Groups and Serious Youth Crime."

62. Ibid., pp. 29–60.

63. Miller, *Violence by Youth Groups*, p. 37.

64. Ibid., p. 43.

65. Estimates taken from Miller, "Gangs, Groups and Serious Youth Crime."

Chapter 10

Chapter Outline

Introduction
The School in Modern American Society
Educational Factors and Delinquency
Delinquency in the Schools
The Role of the School in Delinquency
  Prevention
Chapter Summary

Key Terms, Names, and Cases

aspirations
learning disabilities
tracking
academic alienation
truancy
drop-out
vandalism
educational alternatives
prolonged childhood
verbal skills
self-fulfilling prophecy
student subculture
school discipline

Schools and Delinquency ═══════════════

INTRODUCTION

"Many of the underlying problems of delinquency, as well as their prevention and control, are intimately connected with the nature and quality of the school experience."[1] This statement, published in a 1977 report on school-related crime by the U.S. Senate Subcommittee on Delinquency, summarizes a long-held belief of many criminologists—that there is a link between the ever-increasing problem of juvenile crime and the nature of the educational process in the schools.

Since the schools are responsible for educating virtually everyone during most of the formative years, and since so much of an adolescent's time is spent in school, it seems logical to assume that there must be some relationship between the rising delinquency rate and what is happening—or not happening—in classrooms throughout the country.[2] This relationship was pointed out as early as 1939, when a study by the New Jersey Delinquency Commission found that, of 2,021 inmates of prisons and correctional institutions in that state, two out of every five had first been committed for truancy.[3] Numerous studies confirmed the initial hypothesis that schools and delinquency are somehow related. For example, a decade-long study of delinquent behavior, published in 1973, found school relationships to be a predictive factor of delinquency exceeded in importance only by family and peer group influences.[4] Delbert Elliot and Harwin Voss, considered to be among the most methodologically sound researchers on this topic, found that school-related variables are more important as contributing factors to delinquent behavior than the effects of either family or friends.[5] Although they differ in the type and degree of influence they ascribe to school-related factors, most researchers agree that the educational system bears some of the responsibility for the high rate of juvenile crime.

The Authors wish to express their appreciation to Elena Natalizia for her assistance in the research and development of this chapter.

THE SCHOOL IN MODERN AMERICAN SOCIETY

The school plays a significant role in shaping the values and norms of American children.[6] In contrast to earlier periods, when formal education was a privilege of the upper classes, the American system of compulsory public education has now made schooling a legal obligation.[7] One study has found that today 94 percent of the high school age population is in school, as compared with only 7 percent in 1890.[8] Thus, in contrast to the earlier, agrarian days of U.S. history, when most adolescents shared in the work of the family and became socialized into adulthood as part of the work force, today's young people, beginning as early as age three or four, spend most of their time in school.[9] Therefore, the school has become the primary instrument of socialization, the "basic conduit through which the community and adult influences enter into the lives of adolescents."[10]

The fact that young people spend a longer time in school prolongs the period of their adolescence. As long as students are still economically dependent on their families and have not entered the work world, they are not considered "adults," either in their own minds or in the estimation of the rest of society. The responsibilities of adulthood, come later to modern youth than to their ancestors, and some experts consider this "prolonged childhood" a contributing factor to the irresponsible, childish, often irrational behavior of many juveniles who commit delinquent acts.[11]

Another significant aspect of the educational experience of American youth is that it is overwhelmingly a peer experience. Children spend their school hours with their peers, and most of their activities after school take place with school friends. Young people rely increasingly on their school friends and consequently become less and less interested in adult role models. Often, the norms and values of the peer culture are at odds with those of adult society. Thus, a pseudo-culture with a distinct social system develops. It offers a united front to the adult world.[12] Law-abiding behavior or conventional norms may not be among the values promoted in such an atmosphere. Rather, the youth culture may admire bravery, defiance, and "having fun" much more.

In addition to its role as an instrument of socialization, the school has become a primary determinant of economic and social status in American society.[13] In this highly technological age, education is the key to a "successful" job. No longer can parents ensure the status of their children through social class origin alone. Educational achievement has become of equal, if not greater, importance as a determinant of economic success.

Schools, then, are fundamentally geared toward success defined in terms of academic achievement, which provides the key to profit and position in society. Kenneth Polk and Walter Schafer propose that "present day adolescents derive much of their identity out of what happens to them in the flows through school. It is the school that sets them into tracks or streams from which present and future social and economic status is derived."[14] Virtually all adolescents, therefore, must participate in the educational system not only because it is required by law but because the notion of success is defined very clearly in terms of possession of a technical or professional skill that can be acquired only through formalized education.

This emphasis on the value of education is fostered by parents, by the media, and by the schools themselves. Regardless of their social or economic background, most children grow up accustomed to believing that education is the key to success. In fact, contrary to popular belief, black and low-income youth place a higher value on education than do white and higher-income youth.[15] A national study of education, the *Coleman Report*, found that a significant majority of youths who were asked how they would feel about having to leave school said they would "try hard" or "do anything" to stay in school. Black students gave these answers as often as whites and were even more likely to respond that they wanted to be among the best students in the class.[16]

Despite their apparent acceptance of the value of education, many youths do not meet acceptable standards of school achievement. In addition, whether failure is measured by test scores, nonpromotion, or dropping out, its incidence is considerably higher among low-income and minority students than among white and upper-class students. A single school failure, furthermore, often leads to patterns of chronic academic failure.[17] The links between school failure, academic and social aspirations, and delinquency will be explored more fully in the following sections.

EDUCATIONAL FACTORS AND DELINQUENCY

There are several key factors within the educational setting which have been cited as contributing to the link between schools and delinquency. This section will focus on the most important of these factors, emphasizing their relevance to the study of delinquent behavior.

Aptitude and Achievement

One of the most oft-cited reasons for the school/delinquency relationship is that poor academic performance is directly linked to delinquent behavior. The fact that delinquents and nondelinquents differ in academic achievement has been corroborated by numerous studies which can be used as evidence that delinquency and school failure are correlated. For example, a 1907 report by the Task Force on Juvenile Delinquency revealed that boys who failed in school were seven times more likely to become delinquent than those who did not fail.[18] Many other studies confirm the relationship between academic performance and delinquency.[19] Students who are chronic underachievers in school are also the most likely to be delinquent. Many researchers do not conclude that delinquency is exclusively a lower-class problem. On the contrary, they indicate that delinquent behavior is more closely related to a poor school record than to minority or low socioeconomic status.[20]

A recent study by Frank Jerse and Ebrahim Fakouri confirms the relationship between academic achievement and delinquency. Based on a comparison of the academic records of delinquents and nondelinquents, including their scores on standardized tests of basic skills, Jerse and Fakouri found that delinquents are often academically deficient, a condition that may lead to their leaving school and getting involved in antisocial behavior.[21]

Some researchers have attempted to explain how poor academic performance and delinquency are related. Polk and Schafer, for example, contend that educational failure begins early in life and is often repeated. Failure elicits negative responses from important people in the child's life, and these reactions may lead the nonachieving student to delinquency. As early as 1945, William Kvaraceus claimed that youths receiving low grades are regarded as failures and treated accordingly, regardless of whatever other talents or abilities they have.[22]

An important result of academic failure is a loss of self-esteem. Studies using a variety of measures of academic competence and self-esteem clearly demonstrate that good students have a better attitude toward themselves than do poor students.[23] Moreover, several research efforts corroborate that low self-esteem contributes to delinquent behavior.[24]

School Failure, Social Class, and Delinquency

During the 1950s, research by Albert Cohen indicated that delinquency was fundamentally a phenomenon of working-class students who were poorly equipped to function in middle-class schools. Cohen referred to this phenomenon as a failure to live up to "middle-class measuring rods."[25] Jackson Toby reinforced this concept of class-based delinquency, contending that the disadvantages of lower-class children in school (for example, lack of verbal skills, lack of parental education, lack of motivation) are a direct result of their position in the social structure and implicitly foster their delinquency.[26]

Kenneth Polk, Dean Frease, and F. Lynn Richmond challenged this class-based explanation of delinquency. They found that boys who do poorly in school, regardless of their socioeconomic background, are more likely to be delinquent than those who perform well in school.[27] In addition, Arthur Stinchcombe showed that lack of correspondence between students' occupational goals and their present school positions is more important in determining delinquency than is social class position. Thus, according to Stinchcombe's articulation hypothesis: "The key fact is the future of students, not their origins. Since we know that origins partly determine futures, social class will be an important variable, but in an unusual way."[28]

Finally, Polk and Richmond further reinforced the notion that delinquency is affected far more strongly by differing levels of educational achievement than by social status. They found that for both poor and wealthy youth, delinquency is low where students have earned As and Bs and gets progressively higher as grade point average decreases.[29] It appears therefore, that the relationship between academic failure and delinquency holds as much for middle- and upper-class students as it does for lower-class students.[30] Yet, although students from all social strata who suffer academic failure appear equally prone to delinquency, lower-class students have a tendency to fail significantly more often than students from higher economic levels. Hence, they exhibit higher rates of delinquent behavior.

Some theorists contend that the high incidence of failure among lower-class youths is actually fostered by the schools themselves.[31] As Martin Gold describes the school experience, it is a frightening world in which conditions for success or failure are clear and ever-present. Constant testing and comparing and the threat of failure make it the most difficult experience for youngsters in American society.[32]

Polk and Schafer cite some of the specific defects in schools that increase the propensity to failure, especially among low-income and minority students:

1. Belief among teachers and administrators that disadvantaged pupils have limited potential.
2. Instruction that is irrelevant.
3. Teaching methods that are not appropriate.
4. Testing, grouping, and tracking of students.
5. Lack of adequate remedial education.
6. Inferior teachers, buildings, and equipment in low-income areas.
7. Lack of understanding and cooperation between the school and the community.
8. Inadequate integration of students of different racial and economic backgrounds.[33]

Polk and Schafer charge that the schools, by their failure to counterbalance the handicaps of low-income and minority children, actively contribute to their academic failure. Research data confirm not only that such children begin school at lower levels of achievement but that their performance progressively deteriorates the longer they are in school. Although these data do not quantify the exact amount of the school's negative impact, Polk and Schafer suggest that the effect "is probably considerable. If this is true, the school itself becomes an active force in the generation of delinquency insofar as it is linked to failure."[34]

In summary, then, many researchers corroborate that there is a definite correlation between delinquent behavior and academic achievement. Yet, as Gold makes clear, "correlation is not causation; the relationship supports but does not confirm the hypothesis of a causal link between the two."[35] Gold's clarification is particularly important for avoiding the tendency to label all underachieving students as "probable delinquents."[36]

Learning Disabilities

Much attention has been focused on the effects of learning disabilities (LD) on juvenile delinquency (JD). The "LD/JD link," as it is called, presumes that students with learning problems (not necessarily related to mental ability) will tend to become delinquent more often than students who do not have such problems. The Senate Subcommittee on Delinquency describes the sequence that operates with regard to the LD/JD link:

A learning disabled child has the mental capacity to master the material in school, but is prevented from doing so by the disorder. Since the child appears to have the ability to succeed the failure may be mistakenly traced to laziness or lack of interest despite the fact that the child may be putting a great deal of effort into the work. The resulting frustration, humiliation and resentment can lead to emotional problems and ultimately behavioral difficulties. As the pattern is continuously reproduced and reinforced throughout the school experience the individual may be viewed, and in fact begin to act, as a troublemaker. Thus the inability to successfully cope either on an academic or social level increases the chances of delinquency both in and out of school.[37]

Noting that the study of learning disabilities is a recent development and that there is a danger that the LD/JD link may be applied indiscriminately to many students who are neither learning disabled nor delinquent, the subcommittee urged the National Institute for Juvenile Justice and Delinquency Prevention to undertake a thorough study of this topic. Researchers have been unable to establish a definite causal relationship between learning disabilities and delinquency:

As of the end of 1975, the existence of a causal relation between learning disabilities and delinquency has not been established; *the evidence for a causal link is feeble.* On the basis of the sketchy data so far produced, the notion that many delinquents have become so *because* of learning disabilities cannot be accepted. The notion that programs to diagnose and treat learning disabilities clearly will actually *prevent* delinquency is not supported by any data at all. Far from being "studied to death," as proponents of the LD/JD link sometimes claim, the link has scarcely been studied at all. The existing work that meets normal minimal standards is fragmentary.[38]

One of the most recent and comprehensive studies in this area is a four-year project being conducted by the National Center for State Courts in conjunction with the Association for Children with Learning Disabilities. This research does not support a causal link between learning disabilities and delinquency. Data based on self-reports indicate that learning disabled children do not engage in more delinquent acts, and they are only slightly more likely to be caught committing delinquents acts. The study indicates, however, that learning disabled children are much more likely to be adjudicated delinquent. This finding has led these researchers to formulate the "different treatment" hypothesis:

This hypothesis suggests that learning disabled children are, for reasons other than their delinquent behavior, treated differently in the juvenile justice system. The result of this treatment . . . seems to be the overrepresentation of learning disabled children among those officially adjudicated delinquent. It is not possible from the data available in this study to determine exactly where in the juvenile justice system learning disabled children might be treated differently. The difference in rates of adjudications might result from differences in rates of prosecution, differences in results of disposition negotiations, or differences in the fact-finding processes. A precise determination requires an in-depth analysis of this question alone. But there does seem to be something happening somewhere in the processing of such juveniles in the justice system that is somehow related to learning disabilities.[39]

The overrepresentation of learning disabled children among those adjudicated delinquent may be due to one of the following two factors. First, consciously or not, judges, police, intake officers, and other juvenile justice personnel may be negatively influenced by the learning disabled child's record of academic failure. Second, children with learning disabilities may appear more in need of "protection" than other children because they are unable to present or defend themselves well before the court.[40] Learning disabilities alone are unable to account for delinquent behavior, but the "link" between learning disabilities and juvenile delinquency is more properly understood in combination with other factors, such as the effect of the learning disability on school personnel and juvenile justice administrators.

Tracking

"Placement in noncollege tracks of the contemporary high school means consignment to an educational oblivion without apparent purpose or meaning."[41] Many researchers have looked at the effects of academic tracking—that is, dividing the students into groups according to their ability and achievement level—as one of the contributors to student delinquency.[42] Studies overwhelmingly indicate that, compared with those in college prep tracks, noncollege preparatory students experience greater academic failure and progressive deterioration of achievement, participate less frequently in the extracurricular life of the school, have an increased tendency to drop out, engage in more frequent misbehavior in school, and commit more delinquent acts. Furthermore, these differences are at least partially caused by assignment to a low academic track, by which the student is effectively locked out of a chance to achieve educational success.

The following list shows some of the effects of tracking as it relates to delinquency:

1. *Self-fulfilling prophecy.* Low-track students, from whom little achievement and more misbehavior are expected, tend to live up to these often unspoken assumptions about their behavior.
2. *Stigma.* The "labeling" effect of placement in a low track leads to loss of self-esteem, which increases the potential for academic failure and troublemaking both in and out of school.
3. *Student subculture.* Students segregated in lower tracks develop a value system that often rewards misbehavior rather than the academic success they feel they can never achieve.
4. *Future rewards.* These students are less inclined to conform. Since they see no future rewards for their schooling, their futures are not threatened by a record of deviance or low academic achievement.
5. *Grading policies.* Low-track students tend to receive lower grades than other students, even for work of equal quality, based on the rationale that students who are not college bound are "obviously" less bright and do not need good grades to get into college.
6. *Teacher effectiveness.* Teachers of high-ability students make more of an effort to teach in an interesting and challenging manner than those who instruct lower-level students.

A tracking system locks certain students out of the possibility of academic success, thereby causing problems of lack of motivation, failure, and rebellion, which may provide fertile ground for delinquent behavior.

Alienation and Delinquency

Alienation of students from the educational experience is another primary factor in the link between schools and delinquency. Clearly, the two factors are closely related, for it is unlikely that a child who is doing poorly in school will perceive school as a rewarding or meaningful experience.

A major research study by Travis Hirschi indicates that intellectual ability is very closely related to whether children like school. (See Chapter 6 for a more detailed analysis of Hirschi's work.) He suggests that the following causal chain may lead to lack of attachment to school, which may then lead to delinquency:

Academic → Poor School → Dislike → Rejection → Commission of
Incompetence   Performance   of School   of School's   Delinquent
                                         Authority   Acts

Hirschi's analysis leads him to the following conclusions. The lower the grades and the scores on achievement tests, the more likely the students are to be delinquent. The less students like school and the less they care about their teachers' opinions of them, the more likely they are to reject school authority and become delinquent.[43] Hirschi's conclusions are supported by a number of other studies.[44]

Other factors not directly related to academic achievement may alienate many young persons—particularly high school students—from the educational experience. One such factor is the isolation and impersonality that result from the large size of many modern public schools. According to the Senate Subcommittee on Delinquency, although larger schools are more economical to construct, their climate is often impersonal, and relatively few students can find avenues for meaningful participation. The resulting resentment can breed an environment in which violence and vandalism are likely to occur.[45] Smaller schools offer a more personalized environment in which students can experience more meaningful interaction with the rest of the educational community. Furthermore, the subcommittee notes, teachers and other school personnel have the opportunity in a smaller school to deal with early indications of academic or behavior problems and thereby to act to prevent delinquency.

In addition to impersonality, students are alienated from the traditional student role that continues to operate in the schools. They are traditionally defined as passive, docile receivers of knowledge, and they are seldom encouraged to take responsibility for their own learning. In many schools, students have little voice in decision making. Some of them therefore feel excluded from the process of their education, and such alienation may at times result in withdrawal from or overt hostility toward the school and all that it represents.[46]

Still another cause of alienation among many students is their inability to see any relevance or significance to what they are taught in school. The gap between their education and the real world leads them to feel that the school experience is little more than a waste of time.[47]

Education and Future Goals

Many students, particularly those from low-income families, think that school has no payoff in terms of their future occupations. Since the legitimate channel appears to be meaningless, "the illegitimate alternative becomes increasingly more attractive and delinquency sometimes results."[48] Stinchcombe found this to be true among the male and female high school students he studied. He noted that rebelliousness in school was closely linked to the perception that school was irrelevant to future job prospects. He found that students who did not plan to attend college or to use their high school educations directly in their careers were particularly rebellious.[49] Likewise, Hirschi concluded that among both black and white students, expectations of a college education and commitment to long-term goals are associated with low rates of delinquency.[50]

Alienation is a problem particularly among low-income and minority students because American schools are predominantly white, middle-class institutions. Although all states have had compulsory education statutes for several decades, today's schools are oriented solely toward middle-class youths who plan to go to college, excluding lower-class youths, whose needs and values are ignored.[51]

This middle- and upper-class bias is clearly evident in the preeminent role given to the college prep curriculum and the second-class position of vocational and technical programs in many school systems. Furthermore, methods of instruction as well as curriculum materials reflect middle-class mores, language, and customs, and thus they have little meaning for the disadvantaged child. Polk and Schafer point out that the middle-class bias in schools relates not only to class and ethnic background but to intellectual style as well.[52]

For some students, then, school is alien territory—a place where they feel unwelcome, either because they lack academic skills or because they are "different" from the role models that the school holds out to them. Mihaly Czikszentmihalyi and Reed Larson hold that "disruption of classes, vandalism, and violence in schools are, in part, attempts . . . to obtain enjoyment in otherwise lifeless schools."[53] Hirschi's research seems to confirm this view, for he found that liking school was very highly correlated with nondelinquency. It was surpassed in importance only by having a low number of delinquent friends.[54] For the alienated student, delinquency often appears to be an attractive alternative to the hostile, or at best boring, atmosphere of the school.

One very important aspect of the process of alienation is that alienated students develop support groups that encourage the delinquent acts of their members. In fact, there is evidence that alienated youths form a subculture and work in concert to subvert the educational system in many schools. This subculture participates in a higher than normal amount of delinquent behavior.[55]

The problem, therefore, is not that individual students feel isolated from the educational process, but that a loosely-structured subculture of youths supporting each other's deviance exists. Individualized treatment efforts will have little effect if they discount these subcultural influences. As Polk and Schafer note, "An approach is needed that will counteract the system processes which generate this subcultural response."[56]

DELINQUENCY IN THE SCHOOLS

This section will discuss delinquency in school, including violence, vandalism, drug abuse, and truancy. In addition, it will deal with dropping out as it relates to delinquency rates. Finally, it will explore the effects of the school's response to deviant behavior.

Violence, Vandalism, and Drug Abuse

Although teenagers spend only 25 percent of their time in school, 40 percent of the robberies and 36 percent of the physical attacks involving this age group occur in school. Young persons between the ages of twelve and fifteen incur the highest risk, for in this group 68 percent of the robberies and 50 percent of the assaults take place on school grounds. The risk of being victimized is highest for minority students in largely white schools and for white students in minority-dominated s chools.[57] A report issued in 1976 by the National Education Association revealed that during that year there were 100 homicides in U.S. schools, 9,000 rapes, 12,000 armed robberies, and over $600 million in destroyed property.[58] The U.S. Office of Education, in its record of the offenses commited in schools, listed the following (in descending order of frequency): burglary, personal theft, drug abuse, disorderly conduct, assault, bomb threats or actual use of explosives, alcohol abuse, weapons offenses, arson, robbery, and rape.[59]

Crime in the schools has reached epidemic proportions, and educational institutions are rapidly turning into armed battlegrounds. One of the most significant recent studies of this phenomenon is the 1977 report of the Subcommittee on Juvenile Delinquency of the Senate Judiciary Committee. Highlight 10–1 is excerpted from this report.

Highlight 10–1. Report of the Senate Subcommittee on Delinquency.

Only a decade ago violence and vandalism in schools were considered troublesome but hardly critical problems in our educational system. Virtually every school in America had experienced problems involving an occasional fight or a broken window. Such occurrences have been viewed as more or less a fixture of school life from the beginning of organized educational activities. Recently, however, the situation has changed and what was once regarded as an unfortunate but tolerable fact of life for teachers and students has become a source of growing concern and even alarm for many members of the educational community. The Subcommittee's intensive investigation has found these concerns to be well-founded; acts of violence and vandalism are indeed occurring with more frequency and intensity than in the past. In some schools, these probably have escalated to a degree which makes the already difficult task of education almost impossible. . . .

It should be made clear, of course, that

not every elementary and secondary school in the country is staggering under a crime wave of violence and vandalism. However, while many school systems are able to operate on a relatively satisfactory basis in terms of the levels of school related crime, there is abundant evidence that a significant and growing number of schools in urban, suburban, and rural areas are confronting serious levels of violence and vandalism.

We should emphasize that this is not a problem found exclusively in large cities or solely involving less affluent school districts. Schools voicing a concern over the escalating rates of violence and vandalism along with the often attendant problems of weapons, drugs, and rampant absenteeism, can be found in any city, suburb or town regardless of geographical location or per capita income. Simply put, while not every school suffers from serious violence and vandalism problems, no school can afford to adopt the smug attitude that "it can't happen here." Unfortunately, it can, and has, been happening at all too many schools. . . .

It should be clearly understood that the figures produced by both district and nationwide studies are best viewed as estimates of the number of such incidents [of violence and vandalism]. . . . There is no uniform nationwide reporting system for school related crime and the accuracy of school and district level varies widely from place to place. . . .

Regardless of the difficulty, if not the impossibility, of precisely determining the exact number of crimes committed in our schools, it is beyond question that these problems are reaching serious proportions on a nationwide basis. The particular statistics in individual districts may vary from year to year but the overall trend points to an increasingly serious situation. Moreover, the range and type of violence and crime found to exist in our schools include virtually every type of crime found in the streets, including the rape of an elementary school teacher by an intruder in front of her entire class and the fatal stabbing of a young high school student in the middle of an afternoon math lesson. We can no longer assume our school buildings provide a safe and secure environment in which to learn. . . .

An attendant problem of this violence which carries with it potentially tragic consequences is the appearance of growing numbers of dangerous and even deadly weapons in schools across the country. The precise number of weapons in any particular school is, of course, difficult to determine since those persons who have them in their possession are obviously anxious to keep them concealed. Nevertheless the Subcommittee has received reports which indicate serious concern with the increasing prevalence of dangerous weapons in schools. . . .

It should be made clear, however, that firearms are not the most typical items found at schools in which there is a tendency to carry some form of weapon. More likely those who are so inclined will carry a small knife concealed on their person. . . .

The motivations for carrying such weapons are diverse and include reasons based on revenge or protection as well as a desire to affect symbols of status and power in the student body at large. . . .

Whatever the motivation, it is obvious that the presence of these weapons in schools is a threat to the safety of both students and teachers within these institutions. Their ready availability leaves open the very real possibility that a simple assault or fight could quickly escalate into a much more serious incident with potentially tragic and irreparable consequences. . . .

In addition to increasing incidents of violence the Subcommittee has found that our schools are experiencing significant and sometimes staggering levels of vandalism. At a time when school boards are under considerable pressure to reduce the budgetary expenditures, schools in America spend an estimated $590 million on vandalism each year. The combination of rising vandalism costs and reduced budget resources cannot but help to have an effect on our overall educational effort.

Some school boards are forced to divert literally millions of educational dollars to vandalism prevention and control. . . .

While it must be recognized that what takes place in the hallways and classrooms of a school is often a reflection of the streets and homes of the community, and that schools can have little immediate effect on whatever deficiencies might exist in the general society, there appear to be several factors intimately connected with violence and vandalism that are susceptible to some form of control by the schools. The Subcommittee believes that schools can contribute to solving these problems by formulating programs and policies that can effectively deal with these conditions. . . .

Another facet of contemporary education, which was repeatedly alluded to throughout the Subcommittee's investigation as a contributing factor to school problems, was the use of drugs, including alcohol, in schools and on school campuses. It is clear that the last several years have witnessed an increase in the use of drugs by young people in our society. As in the case of other societal trends this one has not stopped at the schoolhouse door. Data from the Subcommittee's 1970–73 survey showed that drug related offenses in schools increased by 37.5 percent over this period.

In some places drugs are considered a regular part of school life. . . . On a nationwide basis the National Education Association estimates that fully 30 percent of the 18 million students in the Nation's public schools, or 5.5 million youngsters, are using illegal drugs. . . .

It should be emphasized that the drug abuse affecting our schools is not limited to "hard drugs" such as heroin or cocaine, or "soft drugs" such as marijuana but also includes, to a growing extent, the favorite recreational drug of adult Americans—alcohol. . . .

The fact that most Americans are more tolerant of alcohol than other drugs should not obscure the fact that its use by underage students can lead to serious problems of abuse. A nationwide study of drinking behavior by junior and senior high school students in grades 7 through 12 found that 28 percent of these adolescents are problem drinkers. . . . Over 10 percent of students in these 6 grades drink large amounts of liquor at least once a week and an astounding 2.4 percent of them drink every day. More pointedly, 4.9 percent of these students reported that they in fact had become involved in altercations with principals or teachers as a direct result of their drinking. Although most statistical studies of the problems of alcohol and other drug abuse are directed at junior and senior high school students there are at least some indications that these problems are growing in the elementary grades as well. . . .

The detrimental effect of drug abuse on an individual's capacity to learn and function in an academic environment is obvious. There is just no way to teach a student who is sedated, high, drunk, or a combination of all three. Beyond the individual tragedies involved, however, there are disturbing indications of some parallels between substance abuse and incidents of violence and vandalism in the schools. There appears to be at least some link between the abuse of these substances and antisocial acts committed by those abusing them. A study of this phenomenon conducted by Daniel Yankelovich found that 62 percent of students who abused drugs in a survey group had intentionally destroyed school property and 70 percent of them had been suspended or expelled from school. . . .

Despite the problems presented by the presence of various drugs in schools, it is apparent that, in terms of potential for violent activities, the distribution of illegal drugs poses a greater danger than their simple personal possession or use. When students or other young people are involved in selling drugs in schools or are used as intermediaries by outside adult pushers the potential for serious trouble is dramatically heightened. Moreover illicit organizations geared to the distribution of drugs often find schools, and especially schools located in more affluent communities, particularly lucrative targets. They are of course, one of the main gathering places for large numbers of potential customers, and in wealthy areas the students often have little trouble finding sufficient money for transactions. In the suburbs of Chicago large volume distributors of heroin, cocaine, and other drugs arranged for special shipments of these substances to coincide with the opening of school in September of 1976.

The existence of a school based drug distribution system often carries with it all the competition, rivalry, and antagonism inherent in other illegal underground operations. . . . It is not exceptional to find a significant level of threats and physical violence present in situations involving drug traffic. As is normal in any enterprise which relies on the transfer of an illegal commodity, the preservation of the operation requires a host of ancillary illegal activities to insure the secrecy, payments and exclusivity required for its continued existence. . . .

The Subcommittee also investigated the possibility that acts of violence and vandalism may present a certain pattern traceable to factors such as the characteristics of a particular school or the time of day when the majority of incidents occur. There is some indication, for example, that larger schools are more likely to experience serious problems than schools of small or moderate sized enrollments.

This correlation between school size and school problems seems to prevail regardless of whether the school is located in urban, suburban or rural settings. Contrary to the beliefs of some people that violence and vandalism are problems found only in larger metropolitan areas, all indications are that the size of the school building itself is a more significant factor in this regard than the area in which it is located. . . .

. . . There appears to be at least some pattern to the timing and location of some incidents of violence and vandalism. It is generally agreed that the more costly acts of vandalism take place after school hours or on weekends when there are relatively few people in school. The majority of window breakage and serious acts of arson, for example, take place not when the school is filled with students but when it stands idle and empty. . . .

Although there may be more numerous incidents of window breakage than other acts of vandalism, the most costly offense is arson. In fact almost 40 percent of all vandalism costs can be attributed to fire damage. . . .

While acts of vandalism are somewhat predictable based on past experiences, situations involving violent confrontations are more random and less structured. Even here, however, certain areas of the school or certain situations appear to be more conducive to the possibility of such incidents occurring. When large numbers of students must rather quickly negotiate through narrow hallways or walkways with other students lounging in the same area, the tendency for a simple shoving and pushing altercation to escalate into a serious incident is increased. Moreover areas of the schools that are particularly isolated, such as the rear of stairwells or seldom used entrances or exit ways, provide a prime location for acts of violence toward unwary individuals.

Many students express a particular fear of school washrooms as being the site of significant numbers of assaults and extortion incidents.

Despite the existence of some patterns and predictability to these incidents, there is always a measure of randomness and arbitrariness in the occurrence of crime. Indeed part of the fear of crime is the inability to precisely forecast, and therefore the inability to absolutely prevent when, where and how a crime will occur. . . .

Violence also tends to spiral and fall through certain periods. An examination of assault data on students and teachers over a two year period in New York City revealed that more of these incidents occurred in the spring and particularly in March than at other times of the year. Some schools reported periods when they felt the worst was over and the numbers of violent incidents were falling only to witness an inexplicable return of the problems to dangerous heights.

Debates over the annual increase or decrease in the crime picture in a particular school district should not obscure the issue of primary importance—school related violence and vandalism is presenting the American education system with a serious problem that demands attention. A school board or administrator who views a seasonal leveling or decrease in incidents as an indication that the issue of school related crime is no longer important or deserving of attention may be making a mistake with tragic consequences. . . .

A panel of classroom teachers appearing before the Subcommittee reinforced the point that crime problems can be found in schools located in affluent suburbs as well as country crossroads. . . .

Perhaps one of the reasons urban areas are singled out as being uniquely beset by these problems is that some of the larger cities have made some effort to establish a reporting system designed to more accurately reflect the situation in their schools. Comparisons with other districts that have not made such efforts can leave a false impression. Morever most urban districts have a greater overall number of buildings, staff and students and they quite naturally reflect a larger cumulative figure for incidents of violence and vandalism than the moderate sized districts found more in the suburban and rural areas. Many urban districts are also beset by more serious community problems that tend to reflect high youth unemployment, poor housing conditions and higher overall crime rates. Nevertheless as Dr. Paul R. Salmon of the American Association of School Administrators has observed, "The difference between inner city and suburban schools is merely one of degree, not of kind." . . .

Recently . . . it has become apparent that the youth gangs are back [in schools] and they are bigger, better organized and far better armed than were their predecessors.

Serious problems arising from organized gang activities are not, for the most part, a pervasive phenomenon in many schools across the country. In the majority of schools in which violence and vandalism constitute problems incidents usually arise from un-organized and random acts committed by individuals or small groups. While it would not therefore be accurate to state that gangs are a significant contributing factor to school crime problems on a nationwide basis, it is clear that in those cities and suburban areas experiencing a resurgence of violent gang activities the schools are also feeling the effects of the return of the armies of the streets. In some areas the impact on the educational process has been devastating. . . .

The natural desire to reverse the alarming trend of violence and vandalism should not stampede schools into adopting a series of cure all fads, each of which promises to bring a speedy end to these problems, but each of which amounts to more promises than progress. The complex roots of these problems, the critical situation already exist-ing in numerous schools across the country, the precarious position of education budgets at local, State and Federal levels and the inevitable frustration which results from programs that fail and promises that go

unfulfilled, all argue against those who guarantee the easy solution and the quick repair. The policies instituted to confront these problems must be thoughtfully plan-ned and carefully implemented. Moreover, it should be clear that solutions cannot be found by simply passing a law or signing a bill. As Senator [Birch] Bayh pointed out during the Subcommittee's investigations:

"I am sure we can all agree that there is no Federal solution to problems such as these. The real answers to violence and vandalism in schools cannot be provided by the Government in Washington or by government at the State or local level. State, Local and Federal agencies can work together to insure that schools are receiving all the resources and assistance they need, but the ultimate solutions can only be found in the students, parents, teachers and administrators who make up the educational community of a school. . . ."

It is interesting to note that virtually every promising strategy which the Subcommittee studied contained elements of participations by administrators, students, teachers, par-ents and other members of the community. The involvement of diverse elements of the school community is the foundation for many of these programs and can in fact be determinative of their success or failure. . . .

In summary, the Subcommittee believes that the extent of violence and vandalism in schools represents serious and in some cases urgent problems for American education. While many schools in the country are not now confronted with uncontrollable levels of violence and vandalism, it is clear that an increasing number are in fact experiencing these problems at a level which threatens their ability to adequately educate our children. The trends in this area are not always inexorably upward in every district in the country, but on a nationwide basis the evidence is overwhelming that these prob-lems are increasing in size and seriousness.

Violence and vandalism are unacceptable forms of behavior in any sphere of society, but they are particularly inappropriate at institutions where the next generation of Americans are supposedly learning the basic skills necessary for healthy, satisfying, and useful lives as adult citizens.

Source: Senate Subcommittee on Delinquency, *Challenge for the Third Century: Education in a*

Safe Environment (Washington, D.C.: Government Printing Office, 1977), pp. 7–47. Footnotes omitted.

Another major research effort on school-related crime is the 1977 *Safe School Study* of the National Institute of Education. This report places strong emphasis on the social as well as the financial implications of school delinquency. Among large-city junior high school students surveyed in this study, 7 percent reported being afraid most of the time they were in school, while 8 percent admitted staying home at least one day a month because of fear of school crime; 33 percent of these students said that they avoided certain places in their schools because they feared attack, with restrooms being cited as the area most often avoided.[60]

Truancy

Truancy in itself is a form of delinquency, and at the same time it provides fertile ground for other, usually more serious, unlawful behavior. Obviously, the latter is the more critical problem, for many students are occasionally truant without ever engaging in serious delinquency. However, especially if it is habitual, truancy can put adolescents in situations that significantly increase their chances of becoming delinquent. Truancy itself may not cause delinquency, but it may indicate the inability to fit into an orderly, regulated pattern of life.[61]

One of the issues of concern to the Senate Subcommittee on Delinquency was the effect of the "intruder," frequently a truant, on violence and vandalism within the schools. This issue is discussed in Highlight 10–2.

Highlight 10–2. Findings of the Senate Committee on Delinquency.

One factor repeatedly brought to the Subcommittee's attention actually emcompasses several subsidiary issues of concern to educators: truancy, suspension, and expulsion. In the context of school violence and vandalism these . . . combine to present schools with one of the major contributing factors to these problems—the school intruder.

The intruder is a person, frequently of school age, who is not presently attending school, but will congregate with others around the building and occasionally enter the school without authorization. All too often the entrance is merely a prelude to more serious problems for the school community. Intruders account for a surprisingly large percentage of the violence inflicted on teachers and students within our schools. A study of crime problems in New York City schools, for example, found that over 23 percent of the total incidents were committed by intruders.

The Los Angeles school system estimates that a majority of violent crimes are caused not by attending students, but by young intruders, many of whom are former students either voluntarily out of class or suspended from the system. In New Orleans the public schools report that groups of intruders, again composed partially of former students who are truant or suspended, contribute to problems of extortion, vandalism, theft, narcotics traffic and assaults on school grounds. . . .

The President of the National Association of School Security Directors told the Subcommittee that intruders are a significant contributor to violence and vandalism problems on a nationwide basis and that schools often become focal points for large groups of class cutters, suspended students and truants.

Nonattending students appear to play a considerable role in vandalism as well as violence. Although most vandals are not apprehended, the Greenberg study of a West Coast school system found that of the small numbers that were, 72.2 percent had a history of truancy problems. . . .

Given the dimensions and the roots of the intruder phenomenon truancy cannot but help to have an effect on the overall problems of violence and vandalism. It should not be surprising, therefore, to find that increasing violence and vandalism rates have parallel increasing truancy rates. . . .

The reasons for such truancy rates are varied. Some students claim that their courses are boring or filled with information

they felt is useless to their needs. Others complain that the methods of presenting the materials are uninteresting and not stimulating. Many chronic truants are often the overlooked and educationally disenfranchised members of the school community. . . . An even more disturbing fact is that some students stay away from school because they are simply too afraid to go. . . .

Schools are also plagued by the in-school truant: students who arrive at school more or less on time but who do not attend classes. Often, rather than simply leaving the school, these students spend the day loitering in the halls, gambling or occasionally participating in illegal activities. . . .

Paradoxically, while these youngsters have opted out of regular school life there is a tendency among significant numbers of them to congregate around schools in order to seek out their friends or acquaintances. Few of them have other interests such as jobs or outside activities and, obviously, few have positive ties to a school community which for a variety of reasons has been unable to meet their societal or educational needs. The reduction of truancy rates, therefore, is one way of confronting the problems of the school intruder who contributes significantly to the overall increase in violence and vandalism.

Source: U.S. Senate Subcommittee on Delinquency, *Challenge for the Third Century: Education in a Safe Environment* (Washington, D.C.: Government Printing Office, 1977), pp. 22–24. Footnotes omitted.

The School's Response to Delinquency

Students who violate school regulations in such matters as smoking, truancy, tardiness, classroom behavior, and respect for authority are far more inclined to become delinquent than students who follow school rules. The pioneer studies of Sheldon Glueck and Eleanor Glueck indicate that the second greatest difference (after delinquency of their companions) between delinquent and nondelinquent boys was that the former had a history of school truancy. The third factor was their record of misbehavior in school. Conflict with school authority appears to be a reliable predictor of more serious delinquency outside the school.[62]

Of course, it would be logical to assume that delinquency both in and out of school reflects the same feeling of rebelliousness against the status quo and that this explains their often simultaneous occurrence. Data suggest, however, that misbehavior in school generally (though not always) precedes delinquency within the larger community. Polk and Schafer conclude, therefore, that the school itself may foster serious delinquency by its imprudent handling of behavior problems in school.[63]

Recent research indicates that school crime as well as other types of crime develop most often in families and schools that rely on severe, authoritarian methods of discipline.[64] Use of corporal punishment, for example, produces fear, anger, and aggression in the recipient, thereby leading to further behavior problems.[65] Schools that use this sort of discipline probably help to foster the very forms of school misbehavior that they are seeking to discourage. Therefore, schools should reevaluate their responses to delinquent behavior. Furthermore, schools should take care not to make it virtually impossible for students to reenter the mainstream of the school once they have committed deviant acts.[66]

Dropping Out

Delinquency is not the only alternative available to academically or socially alienated students. They can also drop out of school.

If factors in the school help foster student delinquency, then dropping out should significantly reduce the probability of continued delinquency among disaffected students. To test this hypothesis, Delbert Elliott and Harwin Voss studied about 2,600 male and female students during their four years in high school, and the evidence these researchers gathered led to the following conclusions:

1. The rate of delinquency is significantly higher among those who drop out of school than among those who do not.
2. The dropouts' reasons for becoming delinquent while still in school are often rooted in the school experience itself (limited academic achievement, feelings of alienation from school, association with delinquent classmates, for example).
3. The rate of delinquency for dropouts increases during the period immediately preceding their leaving school; but once they drop out, both police-recorded and self-admitted delinquency decline rapidly.[67]

Sociologist Daniel Glaser also notes that this phenomenon seems to cut across socioeconomic lines: "In *every* neighborhood and *every* socioeconomic class, most of those who are first arrested *while still in school* are less frequently arrested after they drop out."[68]

Several other research efforts are consistent with the results of the Elliott and Voss study. It has been observed, for example, that the arrest rates for property crimes decline substantially after age sixteen, and even more rapidly after ages seventeen and eighteen,[69] the ages of which students most frequently leave school. Similarly, in England, conviction rates for property offenses decline after the age of fifteen, when compulsory education ends and youths usually enter the world of work.[70] Additionally, research has shown a decrease in delinquency during the summer months, when school is not in session.[71]

Evidence that delinquency rates decline after some students leave school has caused a great deal of discussion among educators and juvenile justice personnel as to the wisdom of compulsory education statutes. Some argue that the effort to force unwilling teenagers to stay in school is counterproductive and that truancy and delinquency might be lessened by allowing them instead to assume a productive position in the work force. For many youths, leaving school can actually have the beneficial effect of allowing them to escape from a stressful, humiliating situation that has little promise of offering them any future benefits.[72] Nonetheless, the national mandate seems to be maintaining most youths in school at all costs and helping them to achieve some sort of academic success.

THE ROLE OF THE SCHOOL IN DELINQUENCY PREVENTION

The failure of schools to assume their share of the task of delinquency prevention was noted in 1975 by the National Advisory Commission on Criminal Justice Standards and Goals:

The conclusion of the Commission is that we are doing very little in the schools as a direct, intentional effort to discourage young people from criminal careers. Moreover, there is the strong suggestion that some of the basic conditions of schools which we take for granted actually create the animosities, frustrations, and despair that lead people eventually to violence.[73]

Furthermore, the Commission pointed out that this failure is due largely to the reluctance of educational structures to change to meet contemporary needs:

The school system shows an almost absolute imperviousness to change. Schools have changed little in the past hundred years. Although changes in values, customs, life styles, technology, and knowledge have been extensive, schools seem unable to adapt to people's needs. This inability must be considered a major contribution to the frustrations that breed crime. Jerrold Zacharias' contention that "it is easier to put a man on the moon than to reform the public schools" is a tragic historical fact.[74]

Some experts contend that no significant change in the lives of youths is possible through changing the schools alone. The entire social and economic structure of society must be altered if schools are truly to help students realize their full potential. Alexander Liazos, for example, asserts that schools are primarily perpetrators of the status quo and that delinquency in schools is simply a refusal to fit into the precast mold into which schools attempt to place students. "There are no possible solutions in schools," he contends, "as long as schools must prepare students for alienated work."[75] Therefore, in his view, it will take a restructuring of the entire society before delinquency can be dealt with effectively: "We cannot focus on schools as the problem or the solution. We need to change the economy and the society, and the ruling groups that control them. We must create a true democracy where the people control all institutions."[76]

It is more commonly believed, however, that schools can make a significant contribution to the reduction and prevention of delinquency among youths.

Various organizations, research groups, and individuals have suggested specific steps to accomplish this. Some examples of such proposals will be outlined in the following section.

Educational Alternatives

In its 1975 report, *A National Strategy to Reduce Crime,* the National Advisory Commission on Criminal Justice Standards and Goals made the following school-related recommendations for delinquency prevention:

1. Adopt teacher training programs for parents.
2. Adopt policies and practices to ensure that schools and classrooms reflect the best examples of justice and democracy in their organization and their operation and in the rules and regulations governing student conduct.
3. Guarantee literacy to elementary school students.
4. Provide special language services for bicultural students.
5. Develop career preparation programs in schools.
6. Provide effective supportive services in schools.
7. Offer alternative education programs for deviant students.
8. Open schools for community activities.

The report particularly noted the importance of the second recommendation, which pertains to the schools as a model of justice:

Children develop concepts of justice, law, and good citizenship primarily from continual first-hand experience with the realities those concepts embrace. School children should understand the reasons for law and order in their surroundings; students should have a part in formulating the rules of behavior derived from these reasons; and these rules should be in accord with practices of justice and fairness that students encounter outside the school.

To the extent that democratic practices are lacking in the formulation and enforcement of school rules and regulations, school authorities should design alternatives.[77]

Further, the National Advisory Commission took a strong stand in favor of the school's obligation to service the needs of the total community as part of its delinquency prevention efforts:

A school that fails to provide opportunity for people to participate actively in meaningful educational programs and in decisionmaking functions is obsolete, and does not deserve continued support.

School experiences must be relevant to life experiences and employment opportunities. Schools must become accessible to every resident, young and old, on a 7-day a week, year-round basis. The school is a public instrument and must be used to train and serve all the people. Since it is the principal training institution, it is imperative that the school be provided all the resources to operate on a full basis.[78]

At the conclusion of its report on school-related crime, the Senate Subcommittee on Delinquency recommended the following:

1. Alternative education programs for students who require them.
2. Community education programs.
3. Alternatives to suspension of troublesome students.

4. Codes of rights and responsibilities drawn up by all elements of the school community (students, teachers, parents, and administrators).

5. Curriculum reform, especially the use of apprenticeship programs and law-related education.

6. Police, school, and community liaison programs.

7. Teacher education in appropriate disciplinary techniques and sensitivity to special students.

8. Proper training of school security personnel.

9. Improved counseling and guidance programs.

10. Creation of a more personalized atmosphere in schools through architectural design and use of smaller buildings.

11. Student and parental involvement in programs to combat violence and vandalism in schools.

In addition, the subcommittee recommended that the educational community work together with juvenile authorities and child-serving institutions to promote a united effort at reducing delinquency. The report also called upon Congress to support these efforts with appropriate legislation and funds.[79]

After analyzing the data compiled in its years of research, the National Institute of Education drew up a description of a "safe school" to be used as a model for educational institutions in their efforts to prevent delinquency among students:

Throughout this analysis, the data point to the principal and the school administration as the key element. An effective principal who has developed a systematic policy of discipline helps each individual teacher to maintain discipline by providing a reliable system of support, appropriate in-service training for teachers, and opportunities for teachers to coordinate their actions. This means that the teachers themselves are in a more secure position and are more likely to take effective disciplinary actions to control their own classrooms. Teachers also are more likely to recognize that they have a responsibility in establishing school-wide discipline. Students will respond favorably when this occurs; they will see the system as fair, will understand better what the rules are, and will be less likely to feel that the school is capricious and despotic. The effective school also finds ways to provide positive incentives to all students. The honors of the school go to many students, regardless of social class or academic ability. The school is sufficiently comprehensive to offer something of value to all of its students.[80]

The report also cites the following factors as being likely to help schools effectively reduce the levels of violent crime within their walls:

(1) increasing efforts in student governance and rule-enforcement; (2) treating students fairly and equally; (3) improving the relevance of subject matter to suit students' interests and needs; and (4) having smaller classes, with teachers instructing a smaller number of different different students.[81]

Future Adjustments

A number of individual researchers have suggested improvements in the schools based on their studies of the relationships between school and delinquency. The following is only a short list of such suggestions, some of which reaffirm proposals mentioned earlier in this section:

1. Perhaps society in general, and school personnel in particular, should redefine the notion of acceptable behavior in broader terms, so that the term *delinquency* is reserved only for serious offenses. Although there must certainly be limits to the amount of adolescent misbehavior society will tolerate, these limits may have to be broadened in order to avoid the negative consequences of premature labeling.[82]

2. Special classes or schools with individualized educational programs that foster success rather than failure may be needed for nonadjusting students. Specific efforts should be made to help students learn to deal constructively with failure when it does occur in their academic experience.[83]

3. Provision should be made for more personalized student-teacher relationships. This effort to provide young persons with a caring, accepting adult role model will, it is hoped, strengthen the controls against delinquency.[84]

4. The use of home-school counselors to act as liaisons between the family and the school may be effective in preventing delinquency. These counselors would try to ensure cooperation between the parents and the school and secure needed services—academic, social, or psychological—for troubled students before serious delinquency becomes a problem.[85]

5. Experiments should be undertaken to integrate job training and experience with the usual classroom instruction, in order that students may see education as a meaningful and relevant prelude to their future careers. Job training programs could emphasize public service so that students could gain a sense of attachment to their communities while they are acquiring useful vocational training.[86]

Many experimental programs have attempted to prevent or reduce delinquency by manipulating factors in the learning environment. Studies evaluating these programs, some of which have taken place in correctional settings and others within the public schools, have indicated that certain educational approaches consistently achieve positive results in rehabilitating troubled youths. According to these studies, an effective educational program to prevent delinquency would include several of the following components:

1. Understanding teachers.
2. Individualized diagnosis.
3. Specific learning goals.
4. Individualized programs.
5. Basic academic skills.
6. Multisensory teaching.
7. High-interest material.
8. Sequential material.
9. Rewarding attention and persistence, initially.
10. Differential reinforcement of learning performance.

Maximizing educational effectiveness requires all of the above elements to be present in the schools.[87]

Schools may be unable to reduce delinquency singlehandedly, but a number of viable alternatives to their present operations could aid in a community-wide effort at lessening the problem of juvenile crime.

CHAPTER SUMMARY

For several decades, criminologists have attempted to explain the relationship between schools and delinquency. Although no clear causal relationship can be conclusively proved, research points to many definite links between the delinquent behavior of juveniles and their experiences within the educational system.

Contemporary youths spend much of their time in school because education has become increasingly important as a determinant of social and economic success. Educational institutions are one of the primary instruments of socialization, and it is believed that this role is bound to affect the amount of delinquent behavior among school-age children.

Those who claim a causal link between schools and delinquency cite two major factors in the relationship. The first is academic failure, which arises from a lack of aptitude or from learning disabilities and which results in tracking. The second factor is alienation from the educational experience, due to such realities as the impersonal nature of the schools, the traditionally passive role assigned to students, and students' perception of their education as irrelevant to their future lives.

Student misbehavior, which may have its roots in the school experience itself, ranges from minor infractions of school rules (for example, smoking and loitering in halls) to serious crimes such as assault, burglary, arson, drug abuse, and vandalism of school property. Truancy is another manifestation of students' dissatisfaction with the educational experience and frequently sets the stage for more serious forms of delinquency both in and out of school. Some dissatisfied students choose to drop out of school as soon as they reach the legal age, and research has shown a rapid decline in delinquency among those who do drop out.

Finally, although schools alone cannot control the problem of delinquency, they can take positive steps to prevent delinquency among the nation's youths.

DISCUSSION QUESTIONS

1. Was there a delinquency problem in your high school? If so, how was it dealt with?
2. Should disobedient youths be suspended from school? Does this solution hurt or help?
3. What can be done to improve the delinquency prevention capabilities of schools?

SUGGESTED READINGS

Crime and Delinquency 24 (1978). (Special issue on schools and delinquency).

Elliott, Delbert S., and Voss, Harwin L. *Delinquency and the Dropout.* Lexington, Mass.: Lexington, 1974.

Hirschi, Travis. *Causes of Delinquency*. Berkeley, Calif.: University of California Press, 1969.

Jerse, Frank W., and Fakouri, M. Ebrahim. "Juvenile Delinquency and Academic Deficiency." *Contemporary Education* 49 (1978): 106–109.

McCullough, B. Claire; Zaremba, Barbara A.; and Rich, William D. "The Role of the Juvenile Justice System in the Link between Learning Disabilities and Delinquency." *State Court Journal* 3 (1979): 24–26, 44–47.

National Institute of Education, U.S. Department of Health, Education and Welfare. *Violent Schools—Safe Schools: The Safe School Study Report to the Congress*. Vol. 1. Washington, D.C.: Government Printing Office, 1977.

Polk, Kenneth, and Schafer, Walter E. eds. *Schools and Delinquency*. Englewood Cliffs, N.J.: Prentice-Hall, 1972.

Schafer, Walter E., and Olexa, Carol. *Tracking and Opportunity*. Scranton, Pennsyvania: Chandler Publishing, 1971.

U.S. Senate Subcommittee on Delinquency. *Challenge for the Third Century: Education in a Safe Environment*. Washington, D.C.: Government Printing Office, 1977.

REFERENCES

1. U.S. Senate Subcommittee on Delinquency, *Challenge for the Third Century: Education in a Safe Environment* (Washington, D.C.: Government Printing Office, 1977), p. 1.

2. Ibid., p. 22.

3. *Justice and the Child in New Jersey*, report of the New Jersey Juvenile Delinquency Commission (1939), p. 110, cited in Paul H. Hahn, *The Juvenile Offender and the Law* (Cincinnati: Anderson Publishing, 1978).

4. J. Feldhusen, J. Thurston, and J. Benning, "A Longitudinal Study of Delinquency and Other Aspects of Children's Behavior," *International Journal of Criminology and Penology* 1 (1973): pp. 341–351.

5. Delbert S. Elliott and Harwin L. Voss, *Delinquency and the Dropout* (Lexington, Mass.: Lexington Books, 1974), p. 204.

6. See, for example, Sutherland and Cressey, *Criminology*, (Philadelphia, Pa.: Lippincott, 1978), pp. 248–249.

7. National Advisory Commission on Criminal Justice Standards and Goals, *A National Strategy to Reduce Crime* (New York: Avon Books, 1975), pp. 194–198.

8. U.S. Office of Education, *Digest of Educational Statistics* (Washington, D.C.: Government Printing Office, 1969), p. 25.

9. LaMar Empey, *American Delinquency: Its Meaning and Construction* (Homewood, Ill.: Dorsey Press, 1978), p. 59.

10. Kenneth Polk and Walter E. Schafer, eds., *Schools and Delinquency* (Englewood Cliffs, N.J.: Prentice-Hall, 1972), p. 13.

11. See the previous discussions on middle-class delinquency in Chapter 5.

12. James S. Coleman, *The Adolescent Society* (New York: Free Press, 1961), p. 4.

13. Material in this section is based in part on Polk and Schafer, *Schools and Delinquency*, pp. 10–14, 22, 68–69, 166–167.

14. Ibid., p. 14.

15. Albert J. Reiss, Jr., and Albert Lewis Rhodes, *A Socio-psychological Study of Adolescent Conformity and Deviation*, U.S. Office of Education Cooperative Research Project Number 501 (1959), cited in Polk and Schafer, *Schools and Delinquency*, p. 167.

16. Ibid.

17. Ibid., p. 68.

18. Task Force on Juvenile Delinquency, *Juvenile Delinquency and Youth Crime* (Washington, D.C.: Government Printing Office, 1967), p. 51; see also Alexander Liazos, "Schools, Alienation, and Delinquency," *Crime and Delinquency* 24 (1978): p. 355.

19. Sheldon Glueck and Eleanor Glueck, *Unraveling Juvenile Delinquency* (New York: Commonwealth Fund, 1950); Kenneth Polk and David S. Halferty, "Adolescence, Commitment, and Delinquency," *Journal of Research in Crime and Delinquency* 4 (1966): pp. 82–86; Travis Hirschi, *Causes of Delinquency* (Berkeley, Calif.: University of California Press, 1969); LaMar T. Empey and Steven G. Lubeck, *Explaining Delinquency* (Lexington, Mass.: D.C. Heath, 1971); and Polk and Schafer, *Schools and Delinquency*.

20. Empey, *American Delinquency*, p. 301.

21. Frank W. Jerse and M. Ebrahim Fakouri, "Juvenile Delinquency and Academic Deficiency," *Contemporary Education* 49 (1978): pp. 108–109.

22. William C. Kvaraceus, *Juvenile Delinquency and the School* (New York: World Book, 1945), p. 140, cited in Polk and Schafer, *Schools and Delinquency*, p. 169.

23. Martin Gold, "School Experiences, Self-esteem, and Delinquent Behavior: A Theory for Alternative Schools," *Crime and Delinquency* 24 (1978): pp. 294–295.

24. Ibid.

25. Albert K. Cohen, *Delinquent Boys* (New York: Free Press, 1955). See also Kenneth Polk, Dean Frease, and F. Lynn Richmond, "Social Class, School Experience, and Delinquency," *Criminology* 12 (1974): pp. 84–85.

26. Jackson Toby, "Orientation to Education as a Factor in the School Maladjustment of Lower-Class Children," *Social Forces* 35 (1957): pp. 259–266.

27. Polk, Frease, and Richmond, "Social Class, School Experience, and Delinquency," p. 92.

28. Arthur L. Stinchcombe, *Rebellion in a High School* (Chicago: Quadrangle Press, 1964), p. 70.

29. Kenneth Polk and F. Lynn Richmond, "Those Who Fail," in Polk and Schafer, *Schools and Delinquency*, p. 67.

30. Polk, Frease, and Richmond, "Social Class, School Experience, and Delinquency," p. 94; and Polk and Schafer, *Schools and Delinquency*, p. 172.

31. William Glasser, *Schools without Failure* (New York: Harper & Row, 1969).

32. Gold, "School Experience, Self-esteem and Delinquent Behavior," p. 292.

33. Polk and Schafer, *Schools and Delinquency*, pp. 185–209.

34. Ibid., pp. 183–185.

35. Gold, "School Experience, Self-esteem and Delinquent Behavior," pp. 296–297.

36. Jerse and Fakouri, "Juvenile Delinquency and Academic Deficiency," p. 109.

37. U.S. Senate Subcommittee on Delinquency, *Challenge for the Third Century*, p. 31.

38. Charles A. Murray, *The Link between Learning Disabilities and Juvenile Delinquency* (Washington, D.C.: Government Printing Office, 1976), p. 65.

39. B. Claire McCullough, Barbara A. Zaremba, and William D. Rich, "The Role of the Juvenile Justice System in the Link between Learning Disabilities and Delinquency," *State Court Journal* 3 (1979): p. 45.

40. Ibid., p. 46.

41. Kenneth Polk, "Class, Strain and Rebellion among Adolescents," in Polk and Schafer, *Schools and Delinquency*, p. 114.

42. Material in this section is based on Walter E. Schafer, Carol Olexa, and Kenneth Polk, "Programmed for Social Class: Tracking in High School," in Polk and Schafer, *Schools and Delinquency*, pp. 34–54.

43. Hirschi, *Causes of Delinquency*, pp. 113–124, 132.

44. Albert J. Reiss and Albert L. Rhodes, "The Distribution of Juvenile Delinquency in the Social Class Structure," *American Sociological Review* 26 (1961): pp. 720–732; Empey and Lubeck, *Explaining Delinquency*, pp. 96–97; and Michael J. Hindelang, "Causes of Delinquency: A Partial Replication," *Social Forces* 21 (1973): pp. 471–487.

45. U.S. Senate Subcommittee on Delinquency, *Challenge for the Third Century*, p. 33.

46. Ruth S. Cavan and Theodore N. Ferdinand, *Juvenile Delinquency* (Philadelphia: Lippincott, 1975), p. 256.

47. "Learning into the 21st Century," report of Forum 5, White House Conference on Children, Washington, D.C. (1970).

48. Polk and Schafer, *Schools and Delinquency*, p. 72.

49. Stinchcombe, *Rebellion in a High School*, p. 70; and Daniel Glaser, *Crime in Our Changing Society* (New York: Holt, Rinehart and Winston, 1978), pp. 162–163.

50. Hirschi, *Causes of Delinquency*, pp. 170–183.

51. Cavan and Ferdinand, *Juvenile Delinquency*, pp. 256–257.

52. Polk and Schafer, *Schools and Delinquency*, p. 23.

53. Mihaly Czikszentmihalyi and Reed Larson, "Intrinsic Rewards in School Crime," *Crime and Delinquency* 24 (1978): p. 322.

54. Hirschi, *Causes of Delinquency*, pp. 131–132, 156.

55. Polk and Richmond, "Those Who Fail," p. 69.

56. Polk and Schafer, *Schools and Delinquency*, pp. 20–29.

57. National Institute of Education, U.S. Department of Health, Education and Welfare, *Violent Schools—Safe Schools: The Safe School Study Report to the Congress*, vol. 1 (Washington, D.C.: Government Printing Office, 1977), cited in Robert J. Rubel, "Analysis and Critique of the HEW's *Safe School Study Report to the Congress*," *Crime and Delinquency* 24 (1978): p. 259.

58. *Cincinnati Enquirer*, September 5, 1976.

59. Report of the U.S. Office of Education, *Juvenile Justice Digest* 4 (1976). p. 29.

60. The preceding section is based on Rubel, "Analysis and Critique," pp. 263–264.

61. Cavan and Ferdinand, *Juvenile Delinquency*, p. 264.

62. Glueck and Glueck, *Unraveling Juvenile Delinquency*.

63. Polk and Schafer, *Schools and Delinquency*, p. 178.

64. See U.S. Senate Subcommittee on Delinquency, *Challenge for the Third Century*, pp. 21–27.

65. Ralph S. Welsh, "Delinquency, Corporal Punishment and the School," *Crime and Delinquency* 24 (1978): p. 336.

66. Polk and Schafer, *Schools and Delinquency*, pp. 162–163.

67. Elliott and Voss, *Delinquency and the Dropout*.

68. Glaser, *Crime in our Changing Society*, p. 164.

69. Daniel Glaser, *Strategic Criminal Justice Planning* (Washington, D.C.: Government Printing Office, 1975), Tables 3–2, 3–3, and 3–4, cited in Glaser, *Crime in our Changing Society*, p. 163.

70. I. J. McKissack, "The Peak Age of Property Crimes," *British Journal of Criminology* 7 (1967): pp. 184–197.

71. Kenneth Polk, "Delinquency and Community Action in Non-Metropolitan Areas," Appendix R in President's Commission on Law Enforcement and the Administration of Justice, Task Force Report, *Juvenile Delinquency and Youth Crime* (Washington, D.C.: Government Printing Office, 1967).

72. Cavan and Ferdinand, *Juvenile Delinquency*, pp. 265–266; see also Glaser, *Crime in our Changing Society*, p. 164.

73. National Advisory Commission on Criminal Justice Standards and Goals, *A National Strategy to Reduce Crime*, p. 195.

74. Ibid., p. 195.

75. Liazos, "Schools, Alienation, and Delinquency," p. 367.

76. Ibid.

77. National Advisory Commission on Criminal Justice Standards and Goals, *A National Strategy to Reduce Crime*, p. 197.

78. Ibid., p. 178.

79. U.S. Senate Subcommittee on Delinquency, *Challenge for the Third Century*, pp. 94-95.

80. National Institute of Education, *Violent Schools—Safe Schools*, pp. 137, A–13, A–14, cited in Rubel, "Analysis and Critique," pp. 264–265.

81. Ibid.

82. Winston M. Ahlstrom and Robert J. Havighurst, *400 Losers* (San Francisco: Jossey-Bass, 1971), p. 224.

83. Ibid.; Cavan and Ferdinand, *Juvenile Delinquency*, pp. 270–271.

84. Ahlstrom and Havighurst, *400 Losers*, p. 223.

85. Ibid., pp. 224–225.

86. Ibid., p. 225.

87. Dennis J. Romig, *Justice for Our Children: An Examination of Juvenile Delinquency Rehabilitation Programs* (Lexington, Mass.: D.C. Heath, 1978), pp. 3-35, 37.

=Chapter 11=

Chapter Outline

Introduction
Family and Delinquency
The Family's Influence on Delinquency
Child Abuse and Neglect: Definition and
    Scope
Causes of Abuse and Neglect
Philosophy and Practice of the Child
    Probation System
Disposition of Abuse and Neglect Cases
Abuse, Neglect, and Delinquency
Chapter Summary

Key Terms, Names, and Cases

Parents Anonymous
guardian *ad litem*
child protection
battered child syndrome
Child Abuse Act
parens patriae
intervention abandonment
neglect
abuse
child reporting statutes
Juvenile Justice Standards
Richard Gelles
C. Henry Kempe
David Gil

The Family and Delinquency: Child Abuse and Neglect

INTRODUCTION

One of the most important suspected causes of juvenile crime is the relationships within families. Today, the family is undergoing significant change. Traditional family arrangements are being reexamined, and new approaches are being tried. Numerous factors influence these changes, including changing roles for parents, the rising divorce rate, more women in the work force, more single parent homes, and more permissiveness in general.

Families today are faced with socioeconomic burdens, parental pressures, and family and cultural conflicts. Child rearing is probably the heaviest burden for families today. Many children in America grow up in below normal family circumstances. Consequently, many experts believe that family problems and failures have resulted in hundreds of thousands of children being neglected and abused each year. Although many in the field of juvenile justice concentrate on delinquents and status offenders, many others are concerned with abuse and neglect.

The abuse and neglect of children have become a widespread and serious problem in America. As many as a million children are being maltreated in a variety of ways, ranging from gross neglect and starvation to overt physical and mental cruelty. Each year, juvenile courts hear approximately 150,000 child neglect cases throughout the country. Children who are the victims of abuse suffer physical and psychological damage at the time the abuse takes place and later in life. Moreover, evidence supports a link between the abuse of young children and their subsequent violent and aggressive behavior as juvenile delinquents and status offenders.

This chapter explores the major issues surrounding the problem of family failure. First, it discusses the family and its relationship to delinquency. Next, it explains the various definitions of the term *child abuse*. Then, it reviews the extent and scope of the problem in detail. Following this analysis, it examines the factors that precipate abuse, particularly the relationship between abuse and delinquency.

THE FAMILY AND DELINQUENCY

Negative family environments and experiences contribute to the delinquent behavior of children chiefly because the family is the primary unit in which children learn the values, attitudes, and processes that guide their actions throughout their lives. Experts in the fields of juvenile delinquency, sociology, and psychology generally agree on the following:

It is the social interaction between the child and those in its immediate environment that constitutes the vast majority of the steps contributing to the production of a healthy and normal young person. ... The learning process is enhanced by environmental stimulation, ... but the central developmental relationship occurs within the family.[1]

Considering the significance of the family in the early development of children, therefore, it is not surprising that the National Advisory Commission on Criminal Justice Standards and Goals concluded in its 1976 report on juvenile justice and delinquency prevention:

Family life that is shattered by episodes of physical or emotional mistreatment may breed feelings of rejection among children and retard the youngsters' normal development. Thus, programs designed to insure that all children are raised in home situations beneficial to their healthy growth should be a major component of a community delinquency prevention plan.[2]

In addition to the physical and emotional mistreatment of children, other family factors are believed to be conducive to delinquency:

1. The immorality or criminality of parents or siblings.
2. The absence of one or both parents through death, divorce, or illegitimate birth.
3. Poor disciplinary practices, which may take the form of either extreme laxity or extreme severity.
4. Lack of love and harmony among family members, resulting in a tense atmosphere in the home.
5. Severe financial difficulties.
6. Mental illness or chemical dependency of one or both parents.[3]

The American family suffers from an increased amount of stress and breakdown in contemporary society. Although many families remain healthy and strong, trends such as the following remind us that many others have become severely disrupted:

1. Teenage alcoholism and drug abuse are becoming more and more prevalent.
2. Suicide is now the second leading cause of death for young persons between the ages of fifteen and twenty-four.

3. It is predicted that one out of every nine youngsters will have been involved with the juvenile court system by the age of eighteen.
4. One out of every six children is growing up in a single-parent home.
5. Fifty percent of mothers now work.
6. The tax and welfare systems often tend to penalize families rather than help them.
7. Public housing and urban renewal have disrupted neighborhoods and dislocated families.[4]

Thus, traditional American family life is disintegrating. The extended family, once widespread because of the economic necessity of sharing housing with many family members, is now for the most part an anachronism. It has been replaced by the nuclear family, which has been described as a "dangerous hothouse of emotions" because of the intensely close contact between parents and children, unrelieved by contact with other family members living nearby.[5]

Within the nuclear family are indications of breakdown. Much of the parental responsibility for child rearing is delegated to babysitters, television, and paraprofessionals. Despite such changes in structure, some families are able to adapt and continue functioning as healthy and caring units, producing well adjusted children. Others, however, have crumbled under the burden of such stresses, with severely damaging effects on the present and future lives of their children.[6] This is particularly true when child abuse and neglect become part of family life.

THE FAMILY'S INFLUENCE ON DELINQUENCY

Since a strong, intact family is a front-line defense against delinquency, it is possible that a disrupted family will encourage any preexisting forces that are operating in a child's life to produce delinquency. This statement seems in accord with a number of theoretical models, including the *social structural* view of delinquency (Chapter 5), which holds that the family is a barrier between children and the forces causing delinquency that operate in their communities. It also applies to the *social process* view (Chapter 6), which suggests that a secure family life and attachments to parents counterbalance the negative impact of any detrimental social process with which a youth may come in contact. Similarly, the *psychological* view of delinquent behavior stresses the importance of the family in a youth's development, whether the theory takes a developmental, life-stage, or learning perspective (Chapter 4).

The literature on the family's role in causing delinquency can be divided into two broad areas: family disruption and family relationships.

Family Disruption

It has long been believed that family disruption due to divorce, separation, death, or abandonment exerts a powerful influence on youthful misconduct. It almost seems self-evident that since a child is first socialized at home and from the beginning learns appropriate behavior, values, and beliefs from parents, any disjunction in an orderly family structure will have a negative impact on the child's life. Moreover, family breakups are often associated with discord, conflict, hostility, and aggression—factors that seem to foster a delinquent orientation (see, for example, the social learning approach of Bandura, discussed in Chapter 4).

Despite the strong hypothetical case linking broken homes to delinquency, the empirical research on the matter has been inconclusive. Early studies used the records of police, courts, and correctional instititions to establish a link between broken homes and delinquency.[7] However, these studies were usually flawed by their use of "official" data. Thus, youths from "broken homes" may get arrested, petitioned to juvenile court, and institutionalized more often than youths from intact families, but this does not necessarily mean that they actually engage in more frequent and serious delinquent behavior. Official statistics may reflect the fact that agents of the justice system treat children from disrupted households more severely because they cannot call on parents for support. Also, these children may be stereotyped as "problem children."

Clifford Shaw and Henry McKay were the first to provide important evidence that broken homes were not necessarily related to delinquency. In their analysis of youths in Chicago, their data revealed that 36.1 percent of a school sample and 42.5 percent of a delinquent sample came from disrupted families—a finding that caused them to look doubtfully on the contention that broken homes and delinquency were linked (see Chapter 5 for a discussion of their work).[8]

Numerous subsequent studies, using both official and self-report data, have failed to establish any clear-cut relationship between broken homes and delinquent behavior.[9] Relationships that have been uncovered tend to be difficult to generalize. For example, Martin Gold found a relationship between broken homes and juvenile delinquency but it held only for boys and girls who had nondelinquent friends. Youths with delinquent friends were likely to be delinquent whether or not they had both parents at home.[10] Interestingly, Gold found that youths living with stepfathers were more likely to be delinquent than youths raised solely by their natural mothers. Travis Hirschi found the same thing in his study of youth in California (see Chapter 6),[11] and Joan McCord, William McCord, and Emily Thurber had similar results with a sample of youth from Massachusetts.[12] (The latter two studies did not find a general relationship between parental absence and delinquency.)

It is possible that the very factors linking family dissolution to delinquency—conflict, lack of control, animosity, bitterness, and so on—are present in many intact families. Thus, many children whose parents were not divorced or separated suffer the same disabilities and pain that some youths experience in broken homes. Conversely, many youths who reside in single-parent homes get the same loving care and affection that are available in the best two-parent homes. Therefore, it may be the quality of parent-child relationships, whether with one parent or two, and not the mere presence of both parents in the home, that controls delinquent behavior.

Family Relationships

Evidence suggests that the quality of family relationships has a great bearing on the subsequent behavior of youths. Specific family problems that have been linked to delinquency include inconsistent discipline, marital discord, and parental criminality. For example, F. Ivan Nye found that mothers who threatened discipline but failed to carry it out were more likely to have delinquent children than those who were consistent in their discipline.[13]

Similarly, parental harmony has been related to delinquency. Studies show that families in which parents cannot function properly are more likely to have children who become delinquents (and even drug addicts) than either families in which parents provide proper role models or families where parents are absent.[14] Then, too, parents who themselves engage in criminal behavior are more likely to have children who become delinquent.[15]

These are but a few of the many research efforts that link the quality of a child's family life with delinquency.[16] The quality of the delinquent's home life tends to be more disrupted and to have more conflict than that of the nondelinquent's. Also, delinquent children are not close to their parents and do not communicate with them. What develops from the research on delinquency and family relationsips is a picture of family life that does little to support and much to hinder a growing child's development. The delinquent child has parents who may drink, participate in criminal acts, be harsh disciplinarians, be cold and unaffectionate, have marital conflicts, and be poor role models. Thus, the quality of a child's family life seems much more important than the simple fact of whether the home is intact.

Concern about the quality of family life has recently increased because of the disturbing reports that many children are physically abused and neglected by their parents and that this harsh treatment has serious consequences for their future behavior. Since this topic is one of great importance, we will devote the remainder of this chapter to the issue of child abuse and neglect.

CHILD ABUSE AND NEGLECT: DEFINITION AND SCOPE

Parental abuse and neglect is not solely a modern phenomenon. From infanticide to severe physical beatings for disciplinary purposes, maltreatment of children has occurred consistently throughout history. Some concern for the negative effects of such maltreatment was voiced in the eighteenth century in the United States, but concerted efforts to deal with the problem of endangered children did not begin until 1874.

In that year, residents of a New York City apartment building reported to a public health nurse that a child in one of the apartments was being abused by her stepmother. The nurse found a young child, named Mary Ellen, who was repeatedly beaten and chained to her bed and who was malnourished from a continuous diet of bread and water. The child obviously was seriously ill, but the police agreed with her parents that the law entitled them to raise Mary Ellen as they saw fit.

Since no child protection agencies existed at that time, Mary Ellen's removal from her parents had to be arranged through the Society for Prevention of Cruelty to Animals on the ground that she was a member of the animal kingdom, which the SPCA was founded to protect. The intervention of the SPCA resulted in a legal suit and a jail sentence for Mary Ellen's parents, but more importantly, it led to the founding of the Society for Prevention of Cruelty to Children the following year, marking the extension of humane organizations from animals to humans.[17]

In the twentieth century, little legal or medical research into the problems of maltreated children occurred prior to the work of Dr. C. Henry Kempe of the University of Colorado. In 1962, Dr. Kempe reported the results of a survey of medical and law enforcement agencies that indicated that the child abuse rate was much higher than had previously been thought. He coined a new term, *the battered child syndrome*, which he applied to cases of nonaccidental physical injury of children by their parents or guardians. Kempe's work sparked a flurry of research into the problems of the battered child, and a network of law enforcement, medical, and social service agencies was formed to deal with battered children.[18]

Professionals dealing with such children soon discovered the limitations of Kempe's definition, as they came face to face with a wide range of physical and emotional abuse inflicted on children by their parents. As Kempe himself recognized in 1976:

The term "battered child" has been dropped. . . . When coined 15 years ago, its purpose was to gain the attention of both physicians and the public. We feel, now, that enough progress has been made to move on to a more inclusive phrase—child abuse and neglect. The problem is clearly not just one of *physical* battering. Save for the children who are killed or endure permanent brain damage, . . . the most devastating aspect of abuse and neglect is the permanent adverse effects on the developmental process and the child's emotional well-being.[19]

Thus, the definition has expanded, and the term *child abuse* is now a generic one that includes neglect as well as overt physical beating. Specifically, the term now describes any physical or emotional trauma to a child for which no reasonable explanation, such as an accident or ordinary disciplinary practices, can be found. Child abuse is generally seen as a pattern of behavior rather than a single beating or act of neglect. The effects of a pattern of behavior are cumulative. That is, the longer the abuse continues, the more severe the effect on the child.[20]

Although the terms *child abuse* and *neglect* are sometimes used interchangeably, they represent different forms of maltreatment. Neglect is the more passive term, referring to deprivations that children suffer at the hands of their parents—lack of food, shelter, health care, and parental love. Abuse, on the other hand, is a more overt form of physical aggression against the child, one that often requires medical attention. Yet, the distinction between the two terms is often unclear. In many cases, both occur simultaneously in the same family.

Legally, each state jurisdiction has its own definition of child abuse. Despite the variety of these definitions, they all contain a combination of two or more of the following components:

1. Nonaccidental physical injury.

2. Physical neglect.
3. Emotional abuse or neglect.
4. Sexual abuse.
5. Abandonment.[21]

Physically harmful action by parents includes:

Throwing, shooting, stabbing, burning, drowning, suffocating, biting ... and deliberately disfiguring their own infants and children. By far, the greatest number of injuries resulted from beatings with various kinds of implements and instruments. Some children have been strangled or suffocated with pillows held over their mouths, or plastic bags thrown over their heads. A number have been drowned in bathtubs.[22]

Physical neglect results from parents' failure to provide adequate food, shelter, or medical care for their children as well as failure to protect them from physical danger. Emotional abuse or neglect frequently accompanies physical abuse; it is manifested by constant criticism and rejection of the child, who, as a result, loses self-esteem.[23] Sexual abuse refers to the exploitation of children through rape, incest, and molestation by parents or legal guardians. Finally, abandonment refers to the situation in which parents physically leave their children with the intention of completely severing the parent-child relationship.[24]

In light of the several types of mistreatment that parents inflict on their children, many have criticized the terms *child abuse* and *neglect and dependency* as being too limited. Vincent J. Fontana, chairman of the New York City Mayor's Task Force on Child Abuse and Neglect, proposes the term *maltreatment syndrome* to refer to the whole range of parental neglect and abuse, from the malnourished infant to the battered child.[25] Both the National Advisory Commission on Criminal Justice Standards and Goals and the Juvenile Justice Standards Project use the term *endangered children* to describe the many varieties of abuse and neglect that children suffer.[26]

Child abuse and neglect appear to have reached epidemic proportions in recent years. In Illinois, for example, reported cases of abuse have almost doubled since 1976, and other states report similar rates of increase.[27] Douglas J. Besharov, director of the National Center on Child Abuse and Neglect reports:

Approximately one million children are maltreated by their parents each year. Of these, as many as 100,00–200,000 are physically abused, 60,000–100,000 are sexually abused, and the rest are neglected. Each year, more than 2,000 children die in circumstances suggestive of abuse or neglect.[28]

A national survey conducted by sociologists Richard Gelles and Murray Straus updates and greatly expands these figures.[29] Gelles and Straus maintain that between 1.4 and 1.9 million children in the United States are subject in a given year to physical abuse from their parents.[30] Moreover, physical abuse is rarely a one-time act; the average number of assaults per year was 10.5, and the median was 4.5.[31]

In addition to parent-child abuse, Gelles and Straus found that 16 percent of the couples in their sample reported a violent act toward a spouse (husband or wife); 50 percent (of multi-child families) reported attacks between siblings, and 20 percent had incidents where children attacked parents.[32]

Children of all ages are victimized by abuse and neglect, but there is a greater incidence among children under three years old. A large percentage of abused children are infants six months old or younger. Generally, boys are abused more frequently until the age of twelve. Among teenagers, girls are more often the victims of abuse (see Highlight 11–1). Generally, one parent is the active abuser; the other parent passively tolerates the abuse.[33] Approximately 35 percent of the parents involved in child abuse cases have been involved in prior cases of abuse. Siblings of the most recent victim have also suffered from parental abuse in 27 percent of the families involved in abuse cases.[34]

True rates of abuse and neglect are not known at present, since current data are based only on cases that are recognized, diagnosed, and reported to authorities. Since much evidence indicates that reported cases represent only a fraction of the total amount of abuse and neglect, it seems certain that abuse rates are much higher than our present figures indicate. Sexual abuse is particularly underreported. Thus, the current assessment of the rate of abuse and neglect is, at best, tentative, because estimates are based on uncertain and limited information.[35] How much child abuse and neglect does exist, however, is directly related to what causes such behavior.

CAUSES OF ABUSE AND NEGLECT

Parental maltreatment of children is obviously a complex problem with neither a single cause nor a single solution. It cuts across racial, ethnic, religious, and socioeconomic backgrounds, affecting the entire spectrum of society. Abusive parents cannot be categorized by sex, age, or educational level. They are persons from all walks of life, with varying cultural and economic backgrounds. A number of general factors, however, do seem to occur with some frequency in abusive or neglectful families. These factors will be described in this section; yet, present research on the etiology of parental abuse is severely limited by a lack of research data on families in which abuse does not occur. Thus, efforts to isolate factors that either contribute to or lessen the incidence of abuse and neglect are hampered by an inability to make valid comparisons.[36]

In general, abusive and neglectful families suffer severe stress. The parents are unable to cope with it, and it may lead them to maltreat their children. As Fontana expresses it:

The lives of these parents are usually marked with divorce, paramour relationships, alcoholism, financial stress, poor housing conditions, recurring mental illness, mental retardation, and drug addiction. These stress factors all play leading roles that cause the potentially abusing parent to strike out at a child during a time of crisis.[37]

Many of these same stress factors have been shown to have a direct link to delinquent behavior among children.

Statistics show a high rate of reported abuse and neglect cases among lower economic classes, and this has led to the popular misconception that parental maltreatment of children is exclusively a "ghetto" problem.[38] Research indicates, however, that abuse and neglect occur among families of all socioeconomic levels, although low-income parents are often subject to greater

Highlight 11-1.   A Study of Abuse and Neglect.

Lisa—A Sexually Abused Child

Lisa is an 18 year old, white Protestant, with one older and one younger brother. Her childhood was spent in the southwest with her father, a skilled machinist, and her mother, a teacher. Lisa reports that as a child her mother was physically abusive to her, at one point assaulting her in the face and breaking several teeth. Alienated from her mother, she looked to her father for protection. When at the age of 12, he began having sex play with her, she reported she welcomed the attention despite the fact she felt it "wasn't right." Shortly after this, her parents divorced and her father began living with another woman. Lisa began running away from the mother's home until the courts granted her to the custody of her father, because her mother stated she could not control her.

The sexual play with the father continued when he was granted custody of her. At age 14, the father, while drunk, forced Lisa to have intercourse with him. Lisa told her stepmother about the situation, but the stepmother refused to believe her, stating she was misinterpreting his "fatherly affection." Thereafter, intercourse occurred at least monthly for approximately one year, usually when the father was drunk. Lisa sought escape by using drugs. At age 16, she was rescued by being arrested for possession and put in a juvenile home. She has not had to return home since then, but told no one of the reasons for her drug use until she entered this study.

Source: The Female Offender Resource Center, *Little Sisters and the Law* (Washington, D.C.: Government Printing Office, 1977), page 230. Footnote omitted.

---

levels of environmental stress and have fewer resources available to deal with such stress than parents with higher incomes.

Cases of abuse and neglect among poor families are more likely to be dealt with by public agencies. Therefore, they are counted among cases of reported abuse. Higher-income families can afford private treatment, which shields their problems from public view. Furthermore, courts and society in general are likely to look differently upon abuse cases that involve well educated suburban dwellers. Just as the majority of parents who live in poor, urban environments do not abuse or neglect their children, it is assuredly true that violent abuse and physical and emotional neglect occur in middle- and upper-income families.[39] The high rate of abuse and neglect among the poor does indicate, however, that programs aimed at eliminating the stresses of poverty—for example, welfare reform, increased funding for daycare, job training, and parent education—may well be central to preventing abuse, neglect, and possible future delinquency.

Two factors have a direct correlation with abuse and neglect. First, parents who themselves suffered abuse as children tend to abuse their own children; second, isolated and alienated families tend to become abusive. A cyclical pattern of family violence seems to be perpetuated from one generation to another within families. Evidence indicates that a large number of abused and neglected children grow into adolescence and adulthood with a tendency to engage in violent behavior. The behavior of abusive parents can often be traced to negative experiences in their own childhood—physical abuse, lack of love, emotional neglect, incest, and so on. These parents become unable to separate their own childhood traumas from their relationships with their children.

They also often have unrealistic perceptions of the appropriate stages of childhood development. Thus, when their children are unable to act "appropriately"—when they cry, throw food, or strike their parents—the parents may react in an abusive manner.[40] For parents such as these: "the axiom about not being able to love when you have not known love yourself is painfully borne out in their case histories. . . . They spend their days going around the house, ticking away like unexploded bombs. A fussy baby can be the lighted match."[41]

Parents also become abusive if they are isolated from friends, neighbors, or relatives who can provide a lifeline in times of crisis:

Potentially or actually abusing parents are those who live in states of alienation from society, couples who have carried the concept of the shrinking nuclear family to its most extreme form, cut off as they are from ties of kinship and contact with other people in the neighborhood.[42]

Many abusive and neglectful parents describe themselves as highly alienated from their families and lacking close relationships with persons who could provide help and support in stressful situations.[43]

It would be misleading to pinpoint any one factor as a definitive explanation of why abuse and neglect occur. It does seem, however, that a combination of the following elements is likely to result in parental maltreatment of children:

1. The parents have a history of having been abused, neglected, or deprived as children.
2. The parents are isolated, with no lifeline for help in a crisis.
3. The parents perceive their child as disappointing in some way.
4. A crisis precipitates the abuse.[44]

PHILOSOPHY AND PRACTICE OF THE CHILD PROTECTION SYSTEM

Although abusive parents are subject to prosecution in criminal courts under the traditional statutes against assault, battery, and homicide, they are most often dealt with in juvenile or family court. Specific neglect and abuse laws exist in each state, and they are generally more concerned with the care and protection of the child than the punishment of the parent. In 1974, Congress passed the Child Abuse Prevention and Treatment Act, which provides money to states to bolster their services to maltreated children and their parents.

Recently, partly because of the impetus of this act, most of the states have improved the legal framework behind their child protection systems. Many states now require the reporting of suspected neglect as well as abuse. State laws specifically prescribe procedures for investigation and prosecution of cases. Many states have established specialized agencies to protect children. Some statutes provide a guardian *ad litem* for the child (a lawyer appointed by the court to look after the interests of those who do not have the capacity to assert their own rights). States also ensure confidentiality of reporting and mandate professional training and public education programs.[45]

One of the major problems in enforcing abuse and neglect statutes is that maltreatment of children can easily be hidden from public view. Although state laws require doctors, teachers, and others who deal with children to report suspected cases to child protection agencies, many maltreated children are out of the law's reach because they are too young for school or because their parents do not take them to a doctor or a hospital. Parents abuse their children in private and, even when confronted, often accuse the child of lying or blame the child's medical problems on accidents or legitimate discipline.[46] Thus, legal and social service agencies must find more effective ways to locate abused and neglected children and to provide procedures to handle such cases once they are found.

Approximately 150,000 children are brought into court in the United States each year because of parental violation of abuse and neglect statutes.[47] Once the court establishes jurisdiction in these cases, it is likely that the child will be separated from the parents, either temporarily or permanently. Furthermore, parents may be subject to criminal prosecution or supervision by law enforcement and social service agencies. In light of the frequency of this type of legal intervention into family life and its potentially negative effects on both children and parents, there is much disagreement as to when courts have the right to intervene and declare a child abused or neglected.[48]

Juvenile or family courts are generally guided by three interests: (1) the role of the parents, (2) protection for the child, and (3) the responsibility of the state. Frequently, these interests conflict. In fact, at times even the interests of the two parents are not in harmony. Ideally, the state attempts to balance the parents' natural right to control their children's upbringing with the child's right to grow into adulthood free from severe physical or emotional harm. This is generally referred to as the balancing of the interests approach.[49]

The legal system in this country operates on a strong presumption of the autonomy of parents in matters affecting their children. Both common and statutory law have for centuries protected the primacy of the parental right to rear children free from the undue intervention of the state. The interests of children, on the other hand, are less clearly understood and generally have not been recognized as legal rights. As a result, in many cases children have been treated like the property of their parents because they have been unable to assert their rights.[50] Though some of the most recent legislation is weighted in favor of the child's need for protection rather than the rights of the parents, "the overwhelming weight of legal authority continues to support the rights of parents to control the upbringing of their children."[51]

Because it is presumed that parents act in the best interest of their children, doubtful cases are generally decided in favor of the parent. Only in rare circumstances, in cases of serious danger, does the state intervene under the doctrine of *parens patriae*.[52] Because the state has an interest in protecting children from harm and preventing future juvenile delinquency, it has removed children from their home, either temporarily or permanently, for neglect, extreme physical cruelty, lack of medical treatment, sexual abuse, drunkenness and debauchery, prostitution, adultery and cohabitation, mental illness, and the criminal conviction of a parent.[53]

Juvenile justice standards proposed in 1976 retain the concept of the supremacy of parental rights, except in extreme cases. These standards are based on "a strong presumption for parental autonomy in child rearing and the philosophy that coercive intervention is appropriate only in the face of serious

specifically defined harms to the child.''[54] Intervention under these standards is
the exception rather than the rule, and the focus of state interference in family
life shifts from parental fault to actual or imminent serious harm to the child.
The National Advisory Commission recognizes that coercive intervention is
sometimes necessary but that its costs often outweigh its benefits:

> Intervention disrupts family ties and can generate substantial psychological trauma for
> the child. Moreover, when a child is removed from his or her family and placed in foster
> care, society often lacks the ability to insure that placement is superior to his own home.
> Indeed, a careful examination of the state-of-the-art limitations indicates that, except in
> cases involving serious harm to the child (actual or imminent), society is generally
> unable to improve the situation through coercive intervention.[55]

The commission authorizes intervention only in the following statutorily prescribed cases: lack of a caretaker (parent or other adult) for the child, serious
nonaccidental physical injury to the child, physical injury resulting from inadequate supervision or protection, severe emotional damage or physical illness
that parents are unwilling to treat, sexual abuse, or delinquent activity that the
parents condone or encourage. Furthermore, the standards provide that it is
necessary but not sufficient for the courts to show that a child is endangered by
one of these situations. Before authorizing intervention, the courts must also
find that the intervention will be a less harmful alternative for the child than
lack of coercive state action.[56]

In 1977, the joint Juvenile Justice Standards Project of the American Bar Association and the Institute of Judicial Administration proposed a series of very
similar though more comprehensive standards on abuse and neglect. Like the
previous standards, the IJA/ABA norms are based on the premise that coercive
state intervention is to be used as a last resort and only in cases involving serious
specific harm. The major goals of these standards are:

> to allow intervention only where there is reason to believe that coercive intervention
> will in fact benefit the child; . . . to insure that when intervention occurs, every effort is
> made to keep children with their parents, or if this is impossible, to provide them with a
> stable living situation conducive to their well-being; to insure that procedures are
> followed which facilitate making appropriate decisions; and to insure that all decision
> makers are held accountable for their actions.[57]

Criticizing the often vague standards—such as the concept of ''the best interests of the child''—that allow judges wide discretion in neglect and abuse cases,
the IJA/ABA standards propose that the grounds for coercive intervention be
narrowly defined. They provide the same grounds for intervention as the National Advisory Commission. They also propose that procedural safeguards be
provided for all parties, including the child. Further, the standards require that
decision makers justify their choices and be held accountable for monitoring
the effects of their decisions. Although these standards reiterate a ''strong presumption for parental autonomy in child rearing'' (Standard 1.1), they also
specify that ''in cases where a child's needs, as defined in these standards,
conflict with his/her parents' interests, the child's needs should have priority.''[58]

The IJA/ABA standards recognize that interference with family ties is always a traumatic experience for a child, even if the home is abusive or

neglectful.[59] They recommend that children be removed from their families only when no other solution will protect them from danger. The burden of proof is on the intervening agency to show by "clear and convincing" evidence that removal is necessary. In addition, realizing that treatment programs and foster care are limited, the standards specify that the court must find that a placement is actually available before it authorizes the removal of a child from his or her home.[60]

At present, all fifty states have statutes requiring that persons suspected of abuse and neglect be reported. Although procedures vary from state to state, most follow a similar legal process once a social service agency files a petition in juvenile or family court alleging abuse or neglect.[61] Parents have the right to counsel in all cases of abuse and neglect, and many states require the court to appoint an attorney for the child as well. The child's attorney is usually called the "guardian *ad litem*" (attorney for the litigation in question) and often acts as an advocate for the child's welfare as well as providing legal assistance.

When an abuse or neglect petition is filed, an advisement hearing is held to notify the parents of the nature of the charges against them. If the parents admit the allegations, the court enters a consent decree, and the case is continued for disposition. Approximately half of all cases are settled by admission at the advisement hearing. If the parents deny the petition, an attorney is appointed for the child, and the case is continued for a pretrial conference.

At the pretrial conference, the attorney for the social service agency presents an overview of the case and summarizes the evidence. Such matters as admissibility of photos and written reports are settled. The parents' attorney also reviews the facts of the case and reveals the evidence that will be used. At this point in the process, the attorneys can plea bargain. As a result, about three-fourths of the cases that go to pretrial conference are settled by a consent decree. Thus, eighty-five out of every hundred petitions filed will be settled at either the advisement hearing or the pretrial conference. Of the fifteen remaining cases, five will generally be settled before trial. Usually, no more than ten cases out of every hundred will actually reach the trial stage of the process. These few cases are tried with the regular adversary process, and the allegation of abuse and neglect is almost always readily proved.

From the perspective of both the child and the parents, the most crucial part of an abuse or neglect proceeding is the disposition hearing, an entirely separate process held after the adjudication. The social service agency presents its case plan, which includes recommendations for returning the child to the parents, any conditions the parents must meet, a visitation plan if the child is to be taken from the parents, and so on. The plan is discussed with the parents, and an agreement is reached by which the parents commit themselves to following it.

Periodically, review hearings are held to determine if the conditions of the case plan are being met. Parents who fail to cooperate are warned that they may lose their parental rights. Most abuse and neglect cases are concluded within a year. Either the parents lose their rights and the child is given a permanent placement, or the child is returned to the parents and the court's jurisdiction ends.

DISPOSITION OF ABUSE AND NEGLECT CASES: TREATMENT AND TERMINATION

Just as there is widespread disagreement as to when state intervention into family life is appropriate, there is also considerable controversy over what forms of intervention are helpful in abuse and neglect cases. Most often, children are separated from their parents, usually on a temporary basis. Children are removed from their homes in approximately half of all neglect proceedings. Placement of these children in foster care is intended to be temporary, but half of the children are likely to remain in foster care for three years or more.[62] Furthermore, children are likely to be shifted from one temporary home to another during this period, which severely deprives them of their need for a stable family environment. The court's dilemma is whether to leave children at home, where they may continue to be seriously abused or even killed, or to risk the negative psychological impact of destroying the parent-child relationship.

Ultimately, the court has the power to terminate the rights of parents over their children on a permanent basis. Because the effects of destroying the family unit are serious and far-reaching, the court does so only in the most severe cases. Most states distinguish between procedures to authorize temporary deprivation of custody and those resulting in permanent termination of parental rights. In general, moreover, much stricter statutory requirements exist for permanent termination than for temporary loss of custody rights.[63]

In the vast majority of abuse and neglect cases, permanent removal of the child is not warranted. Parents and children are required to participate in treatment programs that seek to rehabilitate the family and prevent a recurrence of the maltreatment. Such programs attempt to alter the psychological, social, and environmental factors that are at the root of the problem. Social casework, mental health services, daycare centers, homemaker services, parent effectiveness training, group therapy, and foster grandparent programs are among some of the most frequently utilized efforts to help children and parents avoid potential abuse or neglect situations. One of the most important and most difficult goals of such treatment services is to reduce the isolation of parents by helping them improve their relationships with others (family, friends, professionals) who may be able to provide help and support in crisis situations.

A widely used self-help therapeutic technique for abusive parents is Parents Anonymous. PA groups are guided by professional therapists who help parents find more appropriate ways of dealing with explosive family situations. Both parents are encouraged to attend, even if only one is actively engaged in the abuse, and the group helps them recognize their potential to be good parents without resorting to abuse.[64]

Despite the treatment programs outlined above, much more help is needed to deal effectively with the problem of child abuse and neglect. Even today, more organized services are available in the United States to prevent cruelty to animals than to children.[65] Furthermore, the efficacy of treatment programs is questionable. A three-year evaluation of thirteen child abuse and neglect service programs concluded that the chance of future abuse was lessened in only 42 percent of the cases by the time the treatment ended. In addition, severe abuse or neglect recurred among 30 percent of the parents while they were in treatment.[66]

The question is: How strong a commitment is our society willing to make to provide the funds and the personnel necessary to deal with the problem of abuse and neglect at its roots? As Dr. Suzanne Steinmetz, a sociologist at the University of Delaware, told the 1978 Senate Subcommittee on Children and Youth:

Somewhere in our funding efforts aimed at eliminating domestic violence, we must make the same type of commitment that is made for the building of rockets—when something doesn't work properly—back to the drawing board, reevaluate, redesign, and replenish the funds. Surely people are as valuable as rockets and satellites.[67]

Child abuse is not only a serious problem in itself. It also has a direct bearing on efforts to prevent and control juvenile delinquency.

ABUSE, NEGLECT, AND DELINQUENCY

The immediate effects of abuse and neglect are evident—physical injury, malnutrition, emotional depression, death. Less obvious are the potential effects of maltreatment on its young victims. It encourages them to use aggression as a means of solving problems. It prevents them from feeling empathy for others. It diminishes their ability to cope with stress. It makes them vulnerable to the aggression and violence in the culture.[68]   Definitive support for a direct causal relationship between an abusive childhood and delinquency is lacking, but researchers generally agree that abuse and neglect may have a profound effect on behavior in later years. Exposure to excessive physical aggression and emotional chaos in early life provides a foundation for several varieties of violent and antisocial behavior.[69] In fact, sociologists Richard Gelles and Murray Straus state that "with the exception of the police and the military, the family is perhaps the most violent social group, and the home the most violent social setting, in our society."[70]

Ray Helfer and Henry Kempe contend:

The effects of child abuse and neglect are cumulative. Once the developmental process of a child is insulted or arrested by bizarre child rearing patterns, the scars remain. One should not be surprised, then, to find that the large majority of delinquent adolescents indicate that they were abused as children.[71]

Aggressive, delinquent behavior is the means by which many abused or neglected children act out their hostility toward their parents. Some join gangs, which furnish a sense of belonging and allow pent-up anger to be expressed in group-approved delinquent acts.[72]

A 1975 Philadelphia study found that 82 percent of the juvenile offenders in the sample were abused as children; 43 percent remembered being knocked unconscious by one of their parents. A research project among 200 juveniles in a detention center in Denver reported that 72 percent remembered being seriously injured by their parents. Statements of 100 of these juveniles, confirmed by their parents or other reliable sources, revealed that 84 percent were significantly abused before the age of six; 92 percent were bruised, lacerated, or fractured within one and one half years prior to their apprehension for delinquency.[73] Likewise, studies of persons convicted of murder reveal "a demonstrable association between homicide and maltreatment in early childhood."[74] Among children who kill or who attempt murder, the most common factor is said to be "the child's tendency to identify himself with aggressive parents, and pattern after their behavior."[75] Further, one study of several cases of murder and murderous assault by juveniles indicated that in all cases "one or both parents had fostered and condoned murderous assault."[76]

Jose Alfaro conducted a study for the New York State Assembly Select Committee on Child Abuse. It followed two separate samples of youth in order to evaluate the link between abuse and delinquency.[77] One sample consisted of all youths referred to child protection services in eight New York counties during the years 1952 and 1953. The other sample consisted of all youths referred to juvenile courts in the same counties in 1971 and 1972. The children in the first sample were traced forward for twenty years to determine their delinquent involvement. The youths in the second sample were traced backward to find if they had been abused as children. The researchers learned that 17.2 percent of the abused children had subsequent juvenile court experience, and 22.8 percent of the court referred sample had prior experience with child protection agencies. Thus, the study found strong, if not unqualified, evidence to support the juvenile delinquency–abuse link.

A similar project studied the records of 5,392 children referred to the Arizona State Department of Economic Security for child abuse or neglect. Of the total cases, 873, or 16.2 percent, had been referred to juvenile court, again indicating a substantial link between abuse and neglect and subsequent delinquency.[78] In addition, a study of incarcerated youths in Texas found that 29 percent of the sample had been physically abused. In a similar study in Arkansas, the figure was 86 percent.[79]

Another recent study compared the child abuse records of matched samples of 109 delinquent and nondelinquent youths in New Haven, Connecticut.[80] Looking at the records of the major hospital serving the area, the study found that 8.6 percent of the delinquents and only 1 percent of the nondelinquents had required hospital service for abuse. Furthermore, 36 percent of the delinquents as compared to 21.6 of the nondelinquents had received treatment for head and face injuries, which are considered instances of possible abuse.

One other large-scale study of the link between child abuse and delinquency bears noting. Richard Jenkins, a psychiatrist, evaluated the records of 1,500 youths referred to a mental health clinic in Chicago. Of these, 445 had been referred by the juvenile court for aggressive and assaultive delinquency. A second group of 231 youths had been sent by the court because of their records of property offenses.[81] Jenkins found that the assaultive and aggressive juveniles came from families that were punitive and rejecting and that used extreme and inconsistent measures of physical punishment. The property offenders generally had family backgrounds marked by poverty and by neglectful parents who were frequently alcoholic, promiscuous, and irresponsible.

Such research findings do not necessarily mean that most abused or neglected children eventually become delinquent. Many do not, and many seriously delinquent youths come from what appear to be "model homes." They do suggest, however, that youths who break the law, especially through acts of violence, often have a history of maltreatment as children. Certainly, more research is necessary to reach any reliable conclusions about the relationship between childhood abuse and neglect and subsequent delinquency. However, it seems likely that maltreatment of children may be one of the significant contributing factors in juvenile delinquency. Thus, efforts to combat maltreatment are vital not only in preventing the immediate harms of abuse and neglect but also in reducing the possibility that the victims will settle into patterns of violent, aggressive criminal behavior throughout their lives.

CHAPTER SUMMARY

Family relationships have long been linked to the problem of juvenile delinquency. Early theories viewed the broken home as a cause of youthful misconduct. However, more recent research indicates that divorce, separation or the death of parents play a less than imagined role in influencing delinquent acts. Other experts have suggested that it is the quality of family life which has the greatest influence on a child's behavior. Keeping this in mind, studies have explored the role of discipline, parental misconduct and family harmony has on youth crime. Concern over the relationship between family life and delinquency has been heightened by reports of widespread child abuse and neglect. Cases of abuse and neglect have been found in every level of the economic strata and it has been estimated that almost 2 million youth are subject to abuse each year from their parents.

Two factors are seen as causing child abuse: First, parents who themselves suffered abuse as children tend to abuse their own children; Second, isolated and alienated families tend to become abusive.

Local, State and Federal governments have attempted to alleviate the problem of child abuse. The major problem has been the issue of State interference in the family structure. At present, all 50 states have statutes requiring suspected cases of abuse and neglect to be reported.

A number of studies have linked abuse and neglect to juvenile delinquency. Studies show that a disproportionate number of court adjudicated youth had experienced child abuse or neglect. While the evidence so far is not absolutely conclusive, it suggests that there exists a strong relationship between child abuse and neglect and subsequent delinquent behavior.

DISCUSSION QUESTIONS

1. What is the meaning of the term *child abuse*? Of the term *child neglect*?
2. Social agencies, police departments, and health groups all indicate that child abuse and neglect are increasing. What is the incidence of such action by parents against children? Are the definitions of *child abuse* and *child neglect* the key elements in determining the volume of child abuse cases that exists in various jurisdictions?
3. What causes parents to abuse their children?
4. What is meant by the *child protection system*? Do courts act in the best interest of the child when they allow an abused child to remain with the

parents? Is it preferable for the state to act on *parens patriae* in such cases?
5. You are a juvenile police officer. You learn that a young girl's parents are not providing her with the necessary food, shelter, and clothing that represent proper care. What will you do to correct this situation?
6. The juvenile crime problem of young people committing robberies and murders is highlighted in the newspapers daily. To correct that problem, say juvenile justice practitioners, we need a strong, just, and effective justice system. Is it possible, however, to prevent youth crime by preventing child abuse and neglect?

SUGGESTED READINGS

Areen, Judith. "Intervention between Parent and Child: A reappraisal of the State's Role in Child Neglect and Abuse Cases." *Georgetown Law Review* 63 (1975): 887–937.

Besharov, Douglas J. "The Legal Aspects of Reporting Known and Suspected Child Abuse and Neglect." *Villanova Law Review* 23 (1978): 458–546.

Costa, Joseph J., and Nelson, Gordon K. *Child Abuse and Neglect: Legislation, Reporting, and Prevention.* Lexington, Mass.: D.C. Heath, 1978.

Fontana, Vincent J. *"The Maltreated Children of Our Times."* Villanova Law Review 23 (1978): 448–457.

Fraser, Brian G. "A Glance at the Past, a Gaze at the Present, a Glimpse at the Future: A Critical Analysis of the Development of Child Abuse Reporting Statutes." *Chicago-Kent Law Review* 54 (1977-78): 641–686.

Gil, David. *Violence against Children.* Cambridge, Mass.: Harvard University Press, 1971.

Helfer, Ray E., and Kempe, C. Henry, eds., *Child Abuse and Neglect: The Family and the Community.* Cambridge, Mass.: Ballinger Publishing, 1976.

Inglis, Ruth. *Sins of the Fathers: A Study of the Physical and Emotional Abuse of Children.* New York: St. Martin's Press, 1978.

Institute of Judicial Administration/American Bar Association Juvenile Justice Standards Project. *Standards Relating to Abuse and Neglect.* Cambridge, Mass.: Ballinger Publishing, 1977.

Justice, Blair, and Justice, Rita. *The Abusing Family.* New York: Human Sciences Press, 1976.

Kempe, Ruth S., and Kempe, C. Henry. *Child Abuse.* Cambridge, Mass.: Harvard University Press, 1978.

National Advisory Commission on Criminal Justice Standards and Goals. *Juvenile Justice and Delinquency Prevention.* Washington, D.C.: Government Printing Office, 1976.

REFERENCES

1. National Advisory Commission on Criminal Justice Standards and Goals, *Juvenile Justice and Delinquency Prevention* (Washington, D.C.: Government Printing Office, 1976), p. 78.

2. Ibid., p. 92.

3. See Edwin H. Sutherland and Donald H. Cressey, *Criminology* (Philadelphia: Lippincott, 1978), chapter 10; and Daniel Glaser, *Crime in Our Changing Society* (New York: Holt, Rinehart and Winston, 1978), pp. 165–169.

4. Walter F. Mondale, "The Burdened Family," *Trial* 10 (1974): pp. 12–18; and National Advisory Commission on Criminal Justice Standards and Goals, *Juvenile Justice and Delinquency Prevention*, p. 81.

5. Ruth Inglis, *Sins of the Fathers: A Study of the Physical and Emotional Abuse of Children* (New York: St. Martin's Press, 1978), p. 131.

6. See Joseph J. Costa and Gordon K. Nelson, *Child Abuse and Neglect: Legislation, Reporting, and Prevention* (Lexington, Mass.: D. C. Heath, 1978), p. xiii.

7. For a review of these early studies, see Thomas Monahan, "Family Status and the Delinquent Child: A Reappraisal and Some New Findings," *Social Forces* 35 (1957): pp. 250–258.

8. C. Shaw and H. McKay, *Report on the Causes of Crime*, vol. 2, *Social Factors in Juvenile Delinquency* (Washington, D.C.: Government Printing Office, 1931), p. 392.

9. Lawrence Rosen, "The Broken Home and Male Delinquency," in *The Sociology of Crime and Delinquency*, ed. M. Wolfgang, L. Savitz, and N. Johnston (New York: Wiley, 1970), pp. 489–495.

10. Martin Gold, *Delinquent Behavior in an American City* (Belmont, Calif.: Brooks/Cole, 1970), p. 128.

11. Travis Hirschi, *Causes of Delinquency* (Berkeley: University of California Press, 1971), p. 242.

12. Joan McCord, William McCord, and Emily Thurber, "Some Effects of Paternal Absence on Male Children," *Journal of Abnormal and Social Psychology* 64 (1962): pp. 361–369.

13. F. Ivan Nye, *Family Relationships and Delinquent Behavior* (New York: Wiley, 1938).

14. Richard Smith and James Walters, "Delinquent and Non-Delinquent Males' Perceptions of Their Fathers," *Adolescence* 13 (1978): p. 21.

15. Harriet Wilson, "Juvenile Delinquency, Parental Criminality, and Social Handicap," *British Journal of Criminology* 15 (1975): pp. 241–250. See also D. J. West, *Who Becomes Delinquent* (London: Heinemann, 1973).

16. Hirschi, *Causes of Delinquency*, pp. 90–92.

17. Glaser, *Crime in Our Changing Society*, p. 246. See also Lois Hochhauser, "Child Abuse and the Law: A Mandate for Change," *Harvard Law Journal* 18 (1973): p. 200; and Douglas J. Besharov, "The Legal Aspects of Reporting Known and Suspected Child Abuse and Neglect," *Villanova Law Review* 23 (1978): p. 458.

18. Vincent J. Fontana, "The Maltreated Children of Our Times," *Villanova Law Review* 23 (1978): p. 448.

19. Ray E. Helfer and C. Henry Kempe, eds., *Child Abuse and Neglect: The Family and the Community* (Cambridge, Mass.: Ballinger Publishing, 1976), p. xix.

20. Brian G. Fraser, "A Glance at the Past, a Gaze at the Present, a Glimpse at the Future: A Critical Analysis of the Development of Child Abuse Reporting Statutes," *Chicaco-Kent Law Review* 54 (1977–78): p. 643.

21. Ibid.

22. Vincent J. Fontana, "To Prevent the Abuse of the Future," *Trial* 10 (1974): p. 14.

23. See in particular Inglis, *Sins of the Fathers*, chapter 8.

24. Ruth S. Kempe and C. Henry Kempe, *Child Abuse* (Cambridge, Mass.: Harvard University Press, 1978), pp. 6–7.

25. Fontana, "The Maltreated Children of Our Times," pp. 448–449.

26. National Advisory Commission on Criminal Justice Standards and Goals, *Juvenile Justice and Delinquency Prevention*; and Institute of Judicial Administration/American Bar Association Juvenile Justice Standards Project, *Standards Relating to Abuse and Neglect* (Cambridge,

Mass.: Ballinger Publishing, 1977).

27.   Mark Miller and Judith Miller, "The Plague of Domestic Violence in the U.S.," *U.S.A. Today* 108 (1980): p. 26.

28.   Besharov, "The Legal Aspects of Reporting Known and Suspected Child Abuse and Neglect," p. 458.

29.   Richard Gelles and Murray Straus, "Violence in the American Family," *Journal of Social Issues* 35 (1979): pp. 15–39.

30.   Ibid., p. 24.

31.   Ibid.

32.   Ibid., pp. 26–27.

33.   Fontana, "The Maltreated Children of Our Times," p. 450. See also David Gil, *Violence against Children* (Cambridge, Mass.: Harvard University Press, 1971).

34.   Gil, *Violence against Children*, p. 114.

35.   Fontana, "To Prevent the Abuse of the Future," p. 14; and Kempe and Kempe, *Child Abuse*, p. 8.

36.   Fraser, "A Glance at the Past, a Gaze at the Present, a Glimpse of the Future," p. 644; and Costa and Nelson, *Child Abuse and Neglect*, pp. xii–xiv, 1.

37.   Fontana, "The Maltreated Children of Our Times," pp. 450–451. See also Blair Justice and Rita Justice, *The Abusing Family* (New York: Human Sciences Press, 1976); Brandt F. Steele, "Violence within the Family," in Helfer and Kempe, *Child Abuse and Neglect*, p. 12; and Nanette Dembitz, "Preventing Youth Crime by Preventing Child Neglect," *American Bar Association Journal* 65 (1979): pp. 920–923.

38.   David Gil, "Violence against Children," *Journal of Marriage and the Family* 33 (1971): pp. 644–648.

39.   Steele, "Violence within the Family," pp. 10–12.

40.   Fontana, "To Prevent the Abuse of the Future," p. 16; Fontana, "The Maltreated Children of Our Times," p. 451; and Brandt F. Steele and Carl B. Pollock, "A Psychiatric Study of Parents Who Abuse Infants and Small Children," in *The Battered Child*, ed. Ray Helfer and C. Henry Kempe (Chicago: University of Chicago Press, 1968), pp. 103–145.

41.   Inglis, *Sins of the Fathers*, p. 68.

42.   Ibid., p. 53.

43.   Steele, "Violence within the Family," p. 13.

44.   Kempe and Kempe, *Child Abuse*, p. 24; and Fraser, "A Glance at the Past, a Gaze at the Present, a Glimpse at the Future," p. 644.

45.   Besharov, "The Legal Aspects of Reporting Known and Suspected Child Abuse and Neglect," pp. 459–460; and Glaser, *Crime in Our Changing Society*, p. 246. For a survey of each state's reporting requirements, abuse and neglect legislation, and available programs and agencies, see Costa and Nelson, *Child Abuse and Neglect*.

46.   Dembitz, "Preventing Youth Crime by Preventing Child Neglect," p. 922; and Glaser, *Crime in Our Changing Society*, p. 247.

47.   Institute of Judicial Administration/American Bar Association Juvenile Justice Standards Project, *Standards Relating to Abuse and Neglect*, p. 1.

48.   Judith Areen, "Intervention between Parent and Child: A Reappraisal of the State's Role in Child Neglect and Abuse Cases," *Georgetown Law Review* 63 (1975): pp. 887–888.

49.   Ibid., p. 890; and Keith E. Galliher, Jr., "Termination of the Parent-Child Relationship: Should Parental I.Q. Be an Important Factor?" *Law and the Social Order* 1973: p. 856.

50. James J. Delaney, "New Concepts of the Family Court," in Helfer and Kempe, *Child Abuse and Neglect*, p. 339.

51. Areen, "Intervention between Parent and Child," pp. 89-892.

52. Ibid., p. 893; and Brian G. Fraser, "The Child and His Parents," in Helfer and Kempe, *Child Abuse and Neglect*, p. 325.

53. Galliher, "Thermination of the Parent-Child Relationship," pp. 857-858.

54. National Advisory Commission on Criminal Justice Standards and Goals, *Juvenile Justice and Delinquency Prevention*, p. 335.

55. Ibid.

56. Ibid., p. 369 (Standard 11.16).

57. Institute of Judicial Administration/American Bar Association Juvenile Justice Standards Project, *Standards Relating to Abuse and Neglect*, p. 3.

58. Ibid., pp. 37, 44 (Standard 1.5).

59. For a complete discussion on the psychological effects of removal from the home on children, see Joseph Goldstein, Anna Freed, and Albert J. Solnit, *Beyond the Best Interests of the Child* (New York: Free Press, 1973).

60. Institute of Judicial Administration/American Bar Association Juvenile Justice Standards Project, *Standards Relating to Abuse and Neglect*, p. 123.

61. The following explanation of court procedures is adapted from Delaney, "New Concepts of the Family Court," pp. 349-354. For a complete discussion of procedures used in neglect cases, see Michael S. Wald, "State Intervention on Behalf of 'Neglected Children': A Search for Standards for Placement of Children in Foster Care, and Termination of Parental Rights," *Stanford Law Review* 28 (1976): pp. 626-706.

62. Wald, "State Intervention on Behalf of 'Neglected Children,'" pp. 626-627.

63. Galliher, "Termination of the Parent-Child Relationship," pp. 855-859.

64. Brian G. Fraser, "A Pragmatic Alternative to Current Legislative Approaches to Child Abuse," *American Criminal Law Review* 12 (1974-75): p. 123; and Costa and Nelson, *Child Abuse and Neglect*, pp. xvi-xvii.

65. Miller and Miller, "The Plague of Domestic Violence in the U.S.," p. 28.

68. Steele, "Violence within the Family," p. 23.

69. See the work of Albert Bandura, discussed in Chapter 4.

70. Richard Gelles and Murray Straus, "Violence in the American Family," *Journal of Social Issues* 35 (1979): p. 15.

71. Helfer and Kempe, *Child Abuse and Neglect*, pp. xvii-xviii.

72. Kempe and Kempe, *Child Abuse*, p. 42.

73. National Center on Child Abuse and Neglect, Department of Health, Education and Welfare, *1977 Analysis of Child Abuse and Neglect Research* (Washington, D.C.: Government Printing Office, 1978), p. 29.

74. Steele, "Violence within the Family," p. 22.

75. L. Bender and F. J. Curran, "Children and Adolescents Who Kill," *Journal of Criminal Psychopathology* 1 (1940): p. 297, cited in Steele, "Violence within the Family," p. 21.

76. W. M. Easson and R. M. Steinhilber, "Murderous Aggression by Children and Adolescents," *Archives of General Psychiatry* 4 (1961): pp. 1-9, cited in Steele, "Violence within the Family," p. 22. See also J. Duncan and G. Duncan, "Murder in the Family: A Study of Some Homicidal Adolescents," *American Journal of Psychiatry* 127 (1971): pp. 1498-1502; C. King, "The Ego

and Integration of Violence in Homicidal Youth," *American Journal of Orthopsychiatry* 45 (1975): pp. 134–145; and James Sorrells, "Kids Who Kill," *Crime and Delinquency* 23 (1977): pp. 312–326.

77. New York State Assembly Committee on Child Abuse, *Report on the Relationship between Child Abuse and Neglect and Later Socially Deviant Behavior* (Albany, N.Y.: New York State, March 1978). This study and the following studies were originally reported in Charles Smith, David Berkman, and Warren Fraser, "The Shadows of Distress," *A Preliminary National Assessment of Child Abuse and Neglect and the Juvenile Justice System* (Washington, D.C.: Government Printing Office, 1980), pp. 129–149.

78. F. G. Bolton, J. Reich, and S. E. Guiterres, "Delinquency Patterns in Maltreated Children and Siblings," *Victimology* 2 (1977): pp. 349–359.

79. Chris Mouzakitis, *An Inquiry into the Problem of Child Abuse and Juvenile Delinquency* (Little Rock, Ark.: Graduate School of Social Work, University of Arkansas, n.d.); and Steven Charles Wick, *Child Abuse as Causation of Juvenile Delinquency in Central Texas* (Seattle, Wash.: URSA Institute, n.d.).

80. Dorothy Lewis, David Balla, Shelly Shanok, and Laura Snell, "Delinquency, Parental Psychopathology, and Parental Criminality: Clinical and Epidemiological Findings," *Journal of the American Academy of Child Psychiatry* 15 (1976): pp. 665–678.

81. Richard Jenkins, "The Varieties of Adolescent's Behavior Problems and Family Dynamics," *American Journal of Psychiatry* 124 (1968): pp. 1440–1445.

PART IV

JUVENILE JUSTICE
ADVOCACY

Chapter 12

Chapter Outline

Introduction
The Field of Study
The Definition of Juvenile Justice
The Development of Juvenile Justice
The System of Juvenile Justice
The Process of Juvenile Justice
Comparison of the Adult and Juvenile
   Systems
Early Efforts to Distinguish between
   the Juvenile and the Adult Systems
The Goals of Juvenile Justice
Current Issues in Juvenile Justice
   Administration
Chapter Summary

Key Terms, Names, and Cases

Juvenile Justice System
process
parens patriae
diversion
children in need of supervision
disposition
adjudication
rehabilitation
prevention
deterrence
detention
juvenile court
petition
intake
In re Gault
adult criminal justice system
delinquency
discretion

An Overview of the
Juvenile Justice
System

INTRODUCTION

Until recently, public concern over crime centered primarily around the rising tide of adult criminality. However, within the last decade, America has witnessed a phenomenal rise in crime by the young. The 1967 task force report on juvenile delinquency of the President's Commission on Law Enforcement and Administration of Justice called juvenile crime "the single most pressing aspect of the crime problem in the United States.'" The 1974 Juvenile Justice and Delinquency Prevention Act indicated that juveniles account for almost half the arrests for serious crime in America today.[2] In the fifteen years since the commission's report, juvenile lawlessness has become a critical national problem. Without question, this explosion in youth crime, identified statistically in earlier chapters, has turned up serious flaws in the juvenile justice system, and a search for ways to solve the growing problem of serious youth criminality is currently underway.

Part 5 of this text examines the entire juvenile justice system and the diverse ways of dealing with children in trouble. Throughout the discussion, it analyzes both the theories underlying the system and the reality of how it works. The first chapter in this part provides an overview of the contemporary juvenile justice system. It explores juvenile justice as a field of study and the agencies and organizations of the system. Then, it analyzes the different points at which decisions are made about children as they move through the juvenile justice system. Next, it discusses the goals and priorities of the system. The discussion focuses on how well the system has achieved its dual goals of preventing juvenile crime and rehabilitating juvenile offenders. This is followed by a review of critical issues that cut across the entire spectrum of the juvenile justice process, such as public policy and planning, civil rights for children, diversion, and dispositional reform.

The second chapter of this part deals with the history and philosophy of the juvenile justice system. It discusses the early development of the concept of childhood, the origin of youthful criminality, and the institutions concerned with juvenile neglect and delinquency from early times through the establishment of the modern juvenile court in Chicago, Illinois, in 1899.

The third chapter deals with the legal rights of juveniles. It reviews the major United States Supreme Court decisions regarding juvenile justice, the impact of lower court decisions in this area of law, and the organization and structure of the juvenile court system, including its jurisdiction.

THE FIELD OF STUDY

Since the early 1960s, many noteworthy national groups have explored the study of juvenile justice and delinquency. These groups include the President's Commission on Law Enforcement and Administration of Justice, the National Advisory Commission on Criminal Justice Standards and Goals, and the American Bar Association.[3] In addition, criminologists, sociologists, and penologists have published extensive amounts of material dealing with the problem of juvenile delinquency. Most agree that the present juvenile justice system has failed to achieve its twofold goal of preventing juvenile criminality and rehabilitating juvenile offenders, even though some of the major recommendations of these groups have been implemented. Most states, for instance, have delinquency prevention programs, improved court services, and additional community treatment programs. Numerous jurisdictions have reformed sections of their juvenile codes. In addition, legal decisions safeguarding the constitutional rights of juvenile offenders have increased the procedural formalities of the juvenile courts. However, rates of delinquency increase, rates of rehabilitation decrease, and children continue to be treated unfairly.

THE DEFINITION OF JUVENILE JUSTICE

The term *juvenile justice* refers to society's efforts to control juvenile crime through public and private crime prevention and social control agencies. It deals primarily with theories of child behavior, treatment, and delinquency and agencies of the juvenile justice system. The term encompasses many areas of study, including the etiology of crime, institutional and agency controls, methods of prevention and community services, and the legal methods required to deal with young people who violate the law.

As a field, juvenile justice has evolved from many disciplines. At one time, the study of delinquency was in the domain of sociology and was a subdiscipline of criminology. Today, juvenile justice and delinquency are studied not only in academic sociology departments but in colleges of criminal justice, schools of social work, and professional schools such as law, public policy, and administration.

Not surprisingly, individual fields discuss problems of juvenile crime control primarily from their own perspectives. The legal profession, for example, focuses on juvenile justice as a legal system where conduct is controlled by rules of law. The law is the formal means of preventing antisocial behavior in children through its investigation, apprehension, detention, adjudication, and disposition of the youthful offender.

Traditionally, the juvenile court treated juvenile offenders with leniency and tolerance instead of processing them through a system that resembled the adult criminal justice system. However, over the past twenty years, lawyers have become active participants in the juvenile justice process, and the constitutional framework within which the juvenile court functions has been redefined. Now, constitutional doctrines of fundamental fairness deriving from the due process clause of the Fourteenth Amendment require that juvenile court proceedings be similar to adult proceedings. Consequently, lawyers play a critical role in today's juvenile process.

Other professionals, particularly those in academic settings, such as sociologists and criminologists, concentrate on such theoretical issues as the definition of delinquency, its causes, and its prevention. Sociologists tend to theorize that the child's family, community, and environment contribute to deviant behavior, and they generally have only a peripheral interest in the juvenile justice process itself. Psychiatrists, psychologists, and social workers usually favor an individual treatment philosophy and believe that the offender's behavior is symptomatic of some emotional problem. Often, they ignore the organizational and institutional framework of juvenile justice and concentrate on their own individual treatment specialties.

A variety of other disciplines contribute to the field of juvenile justice. Political scientists, for example, explore the role of federal and state government in relation to urban problems. They also deal with the political implications of juvenile justice systems, examine legislation, and study how court decisions affect the civil liberties of children. The field of public administration has been helpful in its analysis of crime and juvenile justice theories of administration, organization, and management. Other fields, such as medicine, the physical sciences, and urban and social planning, also contribute ideas to the body of knowledge concerned with understanding juvenile justice and delinquency.

Lastly, information is gathered about the juvenile justice practices of police, courts, and correctional agencies, and this information is merged with the contributions of the various disciplines mentioned above. Juvenile justice personnel, for instance, emphasize the practical considerations of processing large groups of juveniles through an inadequate system with limited resources.

In summary, a great deal of information has been extracted from various disciplines and consolidated to serve as a fund of knowledge for juvenile justice. Without such knowledge, the juvenile justice system would be unable to develop the techniques required to help children in trouble.

THE DEVELOPMENT OF JUVENILE JUSTICE

The contemporary American system of dealing with children in trouble began in 1899 with the establishment of the first juvenile court in the state of Illinois.[4] As the National Advisory Commission on Criminal Justice Standards and Goals put it, the motivating principles of the Illinois reformers at the turn of the century were:

1. Children, because of their minority status, should not be held as accountable as adult transgressors;
2. The objective of juvenile justice is to help the youngster, to treat and rehabilitate rather than punish;
3. Disposition should be predicated on analysis of the youth's special circumstances and needs;
4. The system should avoid the punitive, adversary and formalized trappings of the adult criminal process with all its confusing rules of evidence and tightly controlled procedures.[5]

Briefly stated, the fundamental intention of the Illinois Juvenile Court Act of 1899 was to create a statewide special court for predelinquent and delinquent youths. In such a setting, children were to be segregated from adults, and individual treatment programs were to be adopted to prevent future delinquency. Programs were to be administered by a juvenile court judge and other staff, such as probation and social service personnel, utilizing individual and group rehabilitation techniques. This juvenile court was supposed to be a nonlegal social service agency providing care to delinquent and neglected children. In addition, the court and its personnel were to act under the concept of *parens patriae*, that is, in the child's best interest. The court's approach was to be paternalistic rather than adversary in nature. Diagnosis of the child's problem and of how it could be solved through programs of treatment was of primary importance.

These concepts about juvenile justice spread rapidly across the country during the early decades of the twentieth century. Statutes similar to the Illinois Juvenile Court Act were enacted in almost every state. In addition, juvenile courts became staffed by groups of probation officers, social workers, and treatment specialists.

However, the dream of trying to rehabilitate children in a benign court setting was not achieved. Individual treatment approaches failed, and delinquency rates soared. In many instances, the courts deprived children of their liberty and treated them unfairly. As a result, in the 1950s and early 1960s, the constitutionality of various juvenile court statutes was challenged. Such challenges changed the juvenile justice system significantly during the 1960s, when the United States Supreme Court expressed a new and deep concern for constitutional guarantees for criminal defendants and when it became clear that many juvenile courts failed to extend due process to juvenile offenders. As a result, a series of Supreme Court decisions (which will be discussed in subsequent chapters) mandated procedural guarantees at virtually every stage of the juvenile justice system.

Today, the juvenile justice system is very much a legal system. The Supreme Court has played a significant, if not monumental, role in the formulation of juvenile law and procedure over the past fifteen years. Notwithstanding this position, the courts have neither repudiated the goal of rehabilitating children nor subjected children to the procedures and philosophy of the adult criminal justice system.

THE SYSTEM OF JUVENILE JUSTICE

The American juvenile justice system exists within all states by statute. Each jurisdiction has a juvenile code and a special court structure to deal with children in trouble.

On a nationwide basis, the juvenile justice system consists of between 10,000 and 20,000 public and private agencies, with a total budget amounting to hundreds of millions of dollars and over 50,000 employees. Most of the 40,000 police agencies have a juvenile component, and more than 3,000 juvenile courts and about 1,000 juvenile correctional facilities exist throughout the country.[6]

There are thousands of juvenile police officers, more than 3,000 juvenile court judges, more than 6,500 juvenile probation officers, and more than 30,000 juvenile institutional employees.[7]

In 1978, there were more than 2 million juvenile arrests, almost 1.5 million delinquency cases disposed of by the courts, and 0.5 million children placed on formal or informal probation.[8] On any given day, approximately 12,000 children are in more than 300 detention units. More than 25,000 children are held in state institutions in a year.[9]

These figures do not take into account the vast numbers of children who are referred to community diversion programs. There are hundreds and possibly thousands of these programs throughout the country, and vast numbers of people are employed in them. This multitude of agencies and people dealing with juvenile delinquency and status offenses has led to the development of what professionals in the field view as an incredibly expanded and complex juvenile justice system.

Before proceeding, it is important to explain the meaning of the term system. It refers to groups or organizations with a formal structure and clearly stated goals. Often, a system is considered the ideal kind of formal organization. The idea that all these agencies of juvenile justice are actually a coordinated system has become increasingly popular among practitioners, academicians, and other professionals who deal with juvenile crime. The idea implies that interrelationships exist among the agencies concerned with juvenile delinquency prevention and control. The systems approach, as it is often called, sees a change in one part of the system affecting changes in other parts. It implies that a closely-knit, coordinated structure of organizations exists among various agencies of juvenile justice.[10] For example, broadening the arrest power of the police officer regarding juvenile offenders adds to the burdens of the juvenile court; changing dispositional procedures affects the juvenile correctional agencies; revising the juvenile code by eliminating status offenses decreases the number of children entering the system.

Unfortunately, the systems approach exists more in theory than in practice. The various elements of the juvenile justice system are all related, but only to the degree that they influence each other's policies and practices. They are not so coordinated that they operate in unison. In fact, many juvenile justice agencies compete for budgetary support, espouse different philosophies, and have personnel standards that differ significantly. It would be useful for all the agencies concerned with juvenile justice to be an integrated system. As the National Advisory Commission on Criminal Justice Standards and Goals has pointed out: "Even in the most disjointed system, police, prosecution, courts, and corrections function in a roughly interdependent fashion, linked, as if they are parts of a single system."[11] However, most program decisions are made without proper planning information or objective data, and effective evaluation is a rarity in the juvenile justice field. Consequently, the vast majority of states operate fragmented and generally uncoordinated juvenile justice systems.

Basically, the police, courts, and juvenile correctional agencies comprise the major components of juvenile justice. This is the official government system that exists in each community. It is also the primary system to handle delinquent and noncriminal behavior. However, in most jurisdictions, other institutions also handle juvenile antisocial behavior—the mental health system, the schools, and, of course, extensive networks of private social service programs. Furthermore, the workload of the juvenile justice system is directly related to the ability of the family and the community to resolve and contain juvenile problems.[12] Which of the various institutional systems children are sent to depends upon the community's ability to prevent juvenile misbehavior. Thus, a typical flowchart of a juvenile justice system often begins with the concept of prevention followed by police, judicial, and correctional intervention. Figure 12-1 illustrates the steps in the system of juvenile justice.

THE PROCESS OF JUVENILE JUSTICE

How are children processed by the agencies and organizations of the juvenile justice system? Most children come into contact with the police officer initially. When a juvenile commits a serious crime, the police are empowered to make an arrest. Less serious offenses may also require police action, but instead of being arrested, the child may be warned, or the parents may be called, or a referral may be made to a juvenile social service program. Fewer than half of all children arrested by the police are actually referred to the juvenile court.

When a police officer decides to take a child into custody, the child may be brought to the Juvenile Aid Bureau of the police department and then to a detention program or intake program prior to a court appearance. At this point, further referral to a social service agency may occur. However, if the crime is a serious one, the juvenile court prosecutor may initiate a petition against the child. This begins the trial process. After a petition is filed, the child can be released in the custody of parents until the court appearance, but sometimes the child may continue to be detained. When the child appears before the court, the court can decide to waive the case, to transfer it to an adult court, or to adjudicate it in juvenile court. If the adjudication or trial declares the child delinquent or in need of supervision, the court initiates a social study of the child's background. After this study, which is called a predisposition report, an appropriate disposition leading to a correctional and rehabilitation program is provided. The various stages in the juvenile justice system that were illustrated in Figure 12-1 are described in more detail in the following sections.

Figure 12–1. Juvenile Justice System.

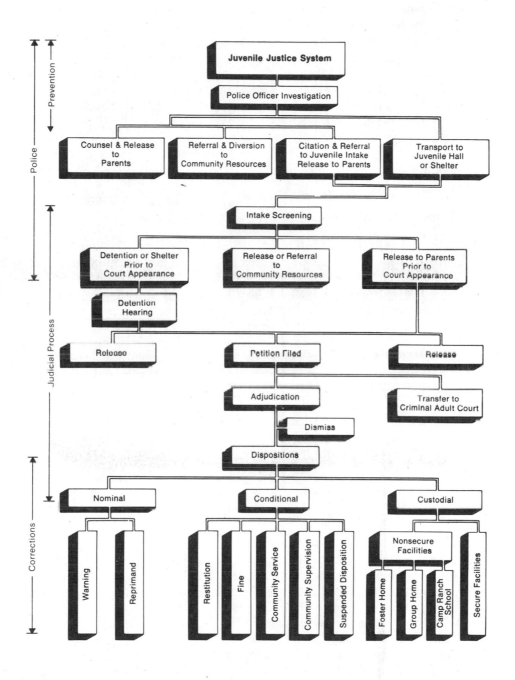

Source: National Advisory Commission on Criminal Justice Standards and Goals, *Report of the Task Force on Juvenile Justice and Delinquency Prevention* (Washington, D.C.: Law Enforcement Assistance Administration, 1976), p. 9.

Police Investigation

When juveniles commit crimes, police agencies have the authority to investigate the incidents and then to decide whether to release the children or detain them and refer them to the juvenile court. This is often a discretionary decision, based not only on the nature of the offense committed but also on the conditions existing at the time of the arrest. Such factors as the type and seriousness of the offense, the history of the child's past contacts with the police, and whether or not the crime is denied determine whether a petition is filed. While juveniles are in the custody of the police, they have basic constitutional rights similar to those of adult offenders. Children are protected against unreasonable searches and seizures under the Fourth and Fourteenth Amendments. Constitutional limitations are also placed on police interrogation procedures.

Intake Screening at the Court

If the police decide to file a petition, the child is taken to the juvenile court. The primary issue at this point is whether the child should remain in the community or be placed in a detention or shelter home. Also, it is essential to determine whether referral services should be obtained before any further court action. In the past, far too many children were routinely taken to court and held in detention facilities to await court appearances. Normally, there is a detention hearing, which results in a decision to remand the child to a shelter or to release the child. At this point, the child has a right to counsel and other procedural safeguards. A child who is not detained is usually released to the parent or guardian. Most state juvenile court acts provide for a child to return to the home to await further court action, except when it is necessary to protect the child, when the child presents a serious danger to the public, or when it is not certain that the child will return to court for further adjudication. In many cases, the police will refer the child to a community service program at intake instead of filing a formal charge.

Pretrial Procedures

If children admit to the crimes for which they were arrested, juvenile court rules of procedure normally require that they know of their right to a trial, that the plea or admission be voluntary, and that they understand the charges and consequences of the plea. Often, if a child admits to the crime, the case will not be adjudicated.

If the child denies the allegation of delinquency, an adjudicatory hearing or trial is held on the merits of the case. Under extraordinary circumstances, a juvenile who commits a serio us crime may be transferred to an adult court instead of being adjudicated. Today, most jurisdictions have laws providing for such transfers. Whether or not they occur depends on the type of offense, the child's prior record, the nature of past treatment efforts, the availability of treatment services, and whether it is likely that the child will be rehabilitated in the juvenile court.

Adjudication

If the child does not admit guilt and is not transferred to an adult court, an adjudication hearing is held to determine innocence or guilt. The court hears evidence on the allegations in the delinquency petition. As a result of the landmark Supreme Court case, *In re Gault,* at this stage of the proceeding the juvenile offender is entitled to almost all the procedural guarantees given adult offenders. These rights include the right to representation by counsel, freedom from self-incrimination, the right to confrontation and cross-examination of witnesses, and, in certain instances, the right to a jury trial. In addition, many states have their own procedures concerning rules of evidence, competence of witnesses, pleadings, and pretrial motions. At the end of the adjudicatory hearing, the court enters a judgment against the child.

Disposition

If the adjudication process finds the child delinquent, the court deliberates about what should be done to the child. Most juvenile court acts require a separate dispositional hearing. Here, the judge imposes a disposition on the juvenile offender in light of the offense, prior record, and family background. The judge has broad discretion and can prescribe a wide range of dispositions—from a simple warning or reprimand to community service or probation or more intense social control measures such as institutional commitment, including group home, foster care, or secure facility care. In theory, the judge's decision serves the best interests of the child, the family, and the community. The disposition is one of the most important stages in the juvenile process because it may be the court's last opportunity to influence the child's behavior. Disposition is concerned primarily with treating the child and controlling antisocial behavior.

Postdisposition

Some jurisdictions allow for a program of juvenile aftercare or parole. They also allow cases to be appealed. There may even be a review of the statutory basis under which the child is to receive treatment from the state.

A child can be paroled from an institution and placed under the supervision of a parole officer. This means that the child will complete the period of confinement in the community and receive assistance from the parole officer in the form of counseling, school referral, and vocational training. In some jurisdictions, the adjudication of a delinquency petition can b e appealed to a higher court. Provisions for such appeals vary greatly within each jurisdiction.

Finally, there is the question of whether juveniles who are committed to programs of treatment and control have a right to treatment. The right to treatment is a relatively new legal doctrine that has been recognized by some courts. It requires that states provide suitable treatment programs for children even if the states have to set them up. Appellate courts have ruled that if treatment is not provided, individuals must be released from confinement. Right to treatment suits ordinarily define treatment as a court-proposed rehabilitation plan pro-

viding services through probation, court programs, or various types of institutional care.

COMPARISON OF THE CRIMINAL
AND JUVENILE JUSTICE SYSTEMS

The components of the adult and juvenile criminal processes are similar. Both
include police investigation, arrest, administrative booking, preliminary hearings, bail, plea bargaining and admission of a plea, grand jury indictment,
formal arraignment, trial, verdict, sentence, and appeal. However, the juvenile
system has a separate, complementary (almost parallel) organization structure.
In many communities, juvenile justice is administered by people who are better
educated and who bring special skills to the task. Also, more facilities and services are available to juveniles than to adults. Correctional institutions have
separate programs for juveniles and emphasize probation over institutional
care.

The juvenile court, with its emphasis on individualized treatment, was originally conceived of as a social court, not a formalized court of law. This view has
encountered much criticism over the first sixty years of the twentieth century,
and it has resulted in the development of procedures and laws similar to those
that protect adult offenders. However, the purpose of the juvenile court is to
treat and rehabilitate children, not to punish them. The juvenile justice system
was designed not only to prevent juvenile crime and to rehabilitate juvenile
offenders but also to provide for abused children, neglected children, and incorrigible children. In essence, it was to provide services to promote the normal
growth and development of all children who came before it. One of the major
concerns of the juvenile court reform movement was to make certain that the
stigma attached to a person who became a convicted criminal offender would
not be attached to children in juvenile proceedings. Thus, even the language
used in the juvenile court differs from that used in the adult criminal court.
Children are not formally indicted for a crime. They have a petition filed
against them. Detention facilities are called shelter homes rather than jails. The
criminal court trial is a hearing or adjudication in the juvenile justice system.
Until recently, attorneys did not act as prosecutors or defenders. They acted on
behalf of parents and often decided a case informally with the court in terms of
what was best for the child rather than in terms of the legal merits of the case.
Table 12-1 compares the vocabulary used in the adult and juvenile criminal
justice systems.

EARLY EFFORTS TO DISTINGUISH BETWEEN
THE JUVENILE AND THE ADULT JUSTICE SYSTEMS

Highlight 12-1 contains materials written during the early history of the juvenile court movement in the twentieth century. It shows how the juvenile system
was to be distinguished from the adult system.

Table 12-1. Comparison of Terms Used in Adult and Juvenile Justice Systems

	Juvenile Terms	Adult Terms
The Person and the Act	Delinquent child Delinquent act	Criminal Crime
Preadjudicatory Stage	Take into custody Petition Agree to a finding Deny the petition Adjustment Detention facility, child care shelter	Arrest Indictment Plead guilty Plead not guilty Plea bargain Jail
Adjudicatory Stage	Adjudicatory or fact-finding hearing Adjudication	Trial Conviction
Post-Adjudicatory Stage	Dispositional hearing Disposition Commitment Residential child care facility Aftercare	Sentencing Hearing Sentence Incarceration Halfway house Parole

Highlight 12-1. Early Advocates of the Juvenile Justice System.

In 1927 Herbert Lou, in his classic treatise, *Juvenile Courts in the United States, stated:* "The traditional administration of criminal justice is characterized by the theories of retribution, of determent and of law as an inflexible body of rules. The juvenile court is conspicuously a response to the modern spirit of social justice. It is perhaps the first legal tribunal where law and science, especially the science of medicine and those sciences which deal with human behavior, work side by side. It recognizes the fact that the law unaided is incompetent to decide what is adequate treatment of delinquency and crime. It undertakes to define and readjust social situations without the sentiment of prejudice. The methods which it uses are those of social case work, in which every child is studied and treated as an individual. These principles upon which the juvenile court acts are radically different from those of the criminal courts. In place of

judicial tribunals, restrained by antiquated procedure saturated in an atmosphere of hostility, trying cases for determining guilt and inflicting punishment, we now have juvenile courts, in which the relations of the child to his parents and to the state or society are defined, and are adjusted according to the scientific findings about the child and his environment."

Source: Herbert Lou, *Juvenile Courts in the United States* (Chapel Hill: University of North Carolina Press, 1927), p. 9.

P. Flexner and N. Oppenheimer, in a 1922 Children's Bureau publication, stated: "While in some instances principles of juvenile court legislation have been greatly extended in America, their source is the common law, the juvenile court being a growth in rather than a departure from legal theory. The distinction between children and adults was sharply drawn in criminal cases. Children under 7 at common law were held incapable of committing a crime. By extending the age limit to 16 or 18 years, juvenile court legislation, as in the enforcement of the duties of parents and of the state, has merely widened the application of the British common law rule. But in doing so it has in effect built a new structure upon old foundations. The basic conceptions which distinguish juvenile courts from other courts can be briefly summarized. Children are to be dealt with separately from adults. Their cases are to be heard at a different time and preferably in a different place; they are to be detained in separate buildings and if institutional guidance is necessary they are to be committed to institutions for children. The procedure of the court must be as informal as possible. Its purpose is not to punish but to save. It is to deal with children not as criminals, but as persons in whose guidance and welfare the state is peculiarly interested. Save in the cases of adults, its jurisdiction is equitable, not criminal in nature."

Source: P. Flexner and N. Oppenheimer, *The Legal Aspects of the Juvenile Court*, no. 9 (Washington, D.C.: U.S. Children's Bureau, 1922), p. 21.

Julia Lathrop, in her introduction to *The Delinquent Child and the Home* (1917), stated: "The features of the Illinois Juvenile Code of 1899 which have attracted universal attention have been of course those of general application—the recognition of the delinquent child as a ward in chancery and not as an accused or convicted criminal, the separate court for children cases and the system of probation. Doubtless, none of these provisions was an original conception, but the combination of a separate court, a separate place of detention for children, and the system of returning the child to his home and providing probation officers to help him there was probably new and was certainly unprecedented in a city as large as Chicago."

Source: Julia C. Lathrop, "Introduction," in *The Delinquent Child and the Home: Study of Delinquent Wards of Juvenile Court of Chicago*, by S. Breckinridge and E. Abbott (New York: Russell Sage Foundation, 1917), p. 1.

Thus, the goal of the early reform movement was to create a juvenile justice system geared to treatment, not to punishment. The purpose of the court, in fact, was to keep children from criminal behavior by rehabilitating instead of punishing them.

One of the most important persons in the juvenile system was the judge. As a trained lawyer, the judge was asked to understand the child's point of view and to have the necessary legal information and understanding of social services to assist with the child's problems and design a plan for treatment. Through the early 1960s, the juvenile court system operated in such a way as to deny the child procedural rights normally available to adult offenders. The early case of *Ex Parte Sharp* in 1908 decided that children did not need such constitutional safeguards as counsel, a jury trial, freedom from self-incrimination, and freedom from unreasonable searches and seizures in the juvenile court system because the primary purpose of the system was not punishment but rehabilitation.[13]

In the mid-1960s, primarily because rehabilitation had failed and because the wide discretion allowed the employees of the juvenile justice system had produced injustice, procedural rules based on constitutional principles were instituted. Today, children receive as much procedural protection as adults. This does not necessarily conflict with the court's philosophy of treatment for children. The present goal is to rehabilitate children while giving them procedural safeguards. As the President's Commission on Law Enforcement and Administration of Justice stated:

What is entailed is not the abandonment of the unique qualities of the juvenile court or adoption of the precise model of the criminal trial but rather accommodation of the dual goals of due process and welfare by instituting procedures permitting the court to effectively pursue humane and rehabilitative aims within the framework of a system that recognizes the indispensability of justice to any coercive governmental venture into the lives of individuals.[14]

Tables 12-2 and 12-3 show the major similarities and differences between the adult and juvenile justice systems.

Table 12-2. Similarities between Juvenile and Adult Systems

1. Police officers, judges, and correctional personnel use discretion in decision making in both the adult and the juvenile systems.

2. Search and seizure law and the Fourth Amendment apply to juvenile and adult offenders.

3. The right to receive Miranda warnings applies to juveniles as well as adults.

4. Juveniles and adults are protected from prejudicial lineups or other identification procedures.

5. Similar procedural safeguards protect juveniles and adults when they make an admission of guilt.

6. Prosecutors and defense attorneys plan an equally critical role in juvenile and adult advocacy.

7. Juveniles and adults have the right to counsel at most key stages of the court process.

8. Pretrial motions are available in juvenile and criminal court proceedings.

9. Negotiations and the plea bargain exist for children and adult offenders.

10. Children and adults have a right to a hearing and and appeal.

11. The standard of evidence in juvenile delinquency adjudications, as in adult criminal trials, is that of proof beyond a reasonable doubt.

Table 12-3. Differences between Juvenile and Adult Systems

1. The primary purpose of juvenile procedures is protection and treatment. With adults, the aim is to punish the guilty.

2. Age determines the jurisdiction of the juvenile court. The nature of the offense determines jurisdiction in the adult system.

3. Juveniles can be apprehended for acts that would not be criminal if they were committed by an adult (status offenses).

4. Juvenile proceedings are not considered criminal; adult proceedings are.

5. Juvenile court procedures are generally informal and private. Those of adult courts are more formal and are open to the public.

6. Courts cannot release identifying information about a juvenile to the press but must release information about an adult.

7. Parents are highly involved in the juvenile process but not in the adult process.

8. The standard of arrest is more stringent for adults than for juveniles.

9. Juveniles are released into parental custody. Adults are generally given the opportunity for bail.

10. Plea bargaining is used in most adult cases. Most juveniles cases are settled by open admission of guilt.

11. Juveniles have no constitutional right to a jury trial. Adults have this right.

12. Juvenile dispositions are for indefinite terms. Adult sentences include proportionality and definiteness.

13. The procedural rights of juveniles are based on the concept of fundamental fairness; those of adults are based on the constitutional right to due process under the Bill of Rights and the Fourteenth Amendment.

14. Juveniles have the right to treatment under the Fourteenth Amendment. Adult offenders have no such right.

15. A juvenile's record is sealed when the age of majority is reached. The record of an adult is permanent.

THE GOALS OF JUVENILE JUSTICE

One of the reasons the juvenile justice system is so complex is that its goals are unclear. Consequently, it is difficult to reform the system and equally difficult to control and reduce juvenile criminality. Senator Birch Bayh, for example, discusses this problem of conflicting goals and points out that neither the total system nor any single agency within it has clear-cut, uniform objectives and priorities. He adds:

The nation's juvenile justice system is in the midst of reexamining its fundamental premises. It has suddenly been forced to recognize the conflict between the principles underlying the juvenile court and the reality of its performance. Seven decades after the Illinois legislature established the nation's first special system for juvenile justice, that system has clearly demonstrated its failure. Despite good intentions, it has probably produced more criminals than it has rehabilitated.[15]

Paul Nejelski and Judith LaPook emphasize the fact "that society has developed diverse and complex ways of dealing with children in trouble."[16] The different perspectives that have been adopted are suggested by the variety of labels attached to children being processed: delinquent, in need of supervision, neglected, dependent, abused, mentally ill, retarded, runaway, incorrigible, and truant.

The juvenile system is more complicated and diverse than the adult system. In addition to enforcing the law (the emphasis of the adult system), the juvenile system is faced with conflicting philosophies, problems of criminal responsibility, treatment approaches due to process rights, and a myriad of other issues. In addition, the legal arm of the juvenile system must rely on the educational, social service, and mental health systems for assistance. Thus, the multiplicity of goals and priorities and the interrelationship between juvenile justice and other institutional groups makes it controversial and often difficult to assess whether the system is meeting the needs of children in trouble.

What exactly are the goals of juvenile justice today? Experts continue to debate whether one goal should take precedence, whether the system should have multiple goals, and which goals, if any, should be given priority. Individuals in law enforcement claim that crime is best controlled if the goal is to deter children from committing antisocial acts. Those in prevention agencies argue that social reform, legislative progress, and programs leading to education, recreation, and employment are the necessary goals. Others in corrections argue that rehabilitation and treatment are most significant. Those in the juvenile court want to emphasize diverting children before the formal trial. Still others spend considerable time talking about how to respond to children with special needs—the uneducated, the mentally ill, and the mentally retarded.

Since the 1960s three major national reports have identified goals of juvenile justice and delinquency reform. In 1967, the President's Commission on Law Enforcement and Administration of Justice identified the following goals:

Society's efforts to control and combat delinquency may be seen as operating on three levels. The first and most basic involves provisions of a real opportunity for everyone to participate in the legitimate activities that in our society lead to a good life: education, recreation, employment, family life. Secondly, the pursuit of these goals is not inconsistent with the need to strengthen the system of juvenile justice. Some young offenders are dangerous repeaters responsible for hold-ups, muggings, and assaults. These measures depend upon an effective system of justice. Swift apprehension, thorough investigation, prompt disposition, are needed to maximize the system's deterent impact and the respect accorded the law it upholds. Furthermore, the system should operate with procedural formality necessary to safeguard the rights that any person has when he is subject to the application of coercive power. Thirdly, there should be a response to the special needs of youths with special problems. They may be delinquent, they may be law abiding but alienated and uncooperative, they may be behavior or academic problems in school or misfits among their peers or disruptive in recreation groups. For such youths, it is imperative to furnish help that is particularized enough to deal with their individual needs but not separate them from their peers and label them for life.[17]

In 1976, the *Report of the Task Force on Juvenile Justice and Delinquency Prevention*, authored by the National Advisory Commission on Criminal Justice Standards and Goals, identified twelve major themes that are central to the development of standards and goals for juvenile justice:

1. Increase family stability.
2. Develop programs for families needing service. These include families with children who are truant or who run away, families with children who disregard parental authority, and families with children who use intoxicating beverages or who are under ten years of age and commit delinquent acts.
3. Develop programs for children who are neglected or physically abused.
4. Develop programs for young people to prevent their delinquent behavior before it occurs.
5. Develop diversion activities whereby youths are processed out of the juvenile justice system.
6. Develop dispositional alternatives so that institutionalization can be used only as a last resort.
7. Extend due process to all juveniles.
8. Control the violent and the chronic delinquent.
9. Reduce the proportion of minorities who are victims of delinquent acts and who are clients in the juvenile justice system. Increase the proportion of

minority policymakers and operators in the juvenile justice system.

10. Increase the coordination among agencies to improve the operation of the juvenile justice system and to increase resources and knowledge about how to deal with juvenile offenders.

11. Improve research.

12. Allocate resources especially to the many states that do not have their own resources to deal with juvenile problems.[18]

Given these major themes, the task force report identified the following major goals:

1. Reduce juvenile violence.
2. Reduce the number of juveniles who repeatedly commit delinquent acts.
3. Provide due process for all children.
4. Integrate and coordinate the present fragmented juvenile justice system.
5. Provide protection for children who need it.[19]

In addition to these goals, other more practical goals have been suggested. In its major summary report, the Juvenile Justice Standards Project of the Institute of Judicial Administration and the American Bar Association lists the basic principles on which it bases its major recommendations for change in the juvenile justice system:

1. Sanctions for juvenile offenders should be proportional.
2. Sentences or dispositions should be determinate.
3. Decision makers should choose the least restrictive alternative when intervening in the lives of juveniles and their families.
4. Noncriminal misbehavior (status offenses and private offenses, victimless crimes) should be removed from juvenile court jurisdiction.
5. Open proceedings and accountability should replace closed proceedings and unrestrained official discretion.
6. All affected persons should have the right to counsel at all stages of the proceedings.
7. Juveniles should have the right to decide on actions affecting their lives and freedom unless they are incapable of making reasonable decisions.
8. The role of parents in juvenile proceedings should be redefined, with particular attention to possible conflicts of interest between parent and child.
9. Detention, treatment, and other intervention prior to adjudication and disposition should be limited.
10. Strict criteria should be established for the waiver of juvenile court jurisdiction in order to regulate the transfer of juveniles to adult criminal courts.[20]

Many of these goals are controversial. For example, the first three eliminate indeterminate commitments and discretion and recommend the criminal law approach of definiteness in sentencing. The fourth principle limits the jurisdiction of the court and eliminates status offenses from the court's responsibility. The sixth principle views hearings as adversarial rather than informal and requires representation by counsel at all critical points in the proceedings. The other principles limit the discretionary power to detain juveniles and to waive them to the adult court. They also call for a redefinition of the role of parents and an increase in the power of children to make decisions.

After an extensive review of the literature, the authors suggest that the juvenile justice system can be improved by seeking to achieve the following realistic goals:

1. *Juvenile Delinquency Prevention.*   Prevention seeks to divert individual children from antisocial behavior during the early stages of their lives. Building stronger family units, providing counseling in schools, and improving living conditions are all examples of prevention.

Prevention involves developing a comprehensive delinquency plan, collecting data about delinquency in local communities, clarifying delinquency goals, and providing an inventory of community resources and programs. Once that is accomplished, programs of prevention involving health, family, education, employment, recreation, housing, religion, and even the media can play an important role in thwarting juvenile delinquency.

2. *Diversion and Removal.*   Juvenile justice agents have often exercised discretion in excluding individuals from the system. A child can be diverted at any stage of the process. Basically, diversion has focused on certain groups—youths committing minor, noncriminal acts, first offenders, and youths committing minor crimes who might be more appropriately handled by social agencies. Diversion programs can exist at the police department level, at the intake level of the court system, at the petition-filing level, and even at the time an adjudication occurs.

In addition to diversion, the goal of removing noncriminal misbehavior, such as status offenses, from juvenile court jurisdiction should be seriously considered. School programs, counseling centers, and other activities within the mental health and educational systems might be more appropriate for children involved in problems of truancy. Those children who are incorrigible can be handled in mental health settings.

3. *Fairness and Justice.*   All children processed through the juvenile justice system should be treated fairly and humanely. No distinction should be made between white and minority juvenile offenders or between those in the lower classes and those in the middle and upper strata of society. Procedures to ensure due process should be present in all areas of the juvenile justice system. Investigation, arrest, diversion, detention, arraignment, adjudication, sentencing, and institutionalization must all be consistent with our democratic system. Recent Supreme Court decisions have made it clear that youths charged with delinquent acts and others brought into the juvenile justice system are entitled to most of the due process rights accorded adults.

4. *Efficiency and Effectiveness of Juvenile Justice.*   Juvenile justice agencies should be well-organized and well-managed. The efficient operation of juvenile services requires qualified personnel, adequate organizational structure, sound fiscal planning, and the development of successful programs. The general public has, for the most part, been unenthusiastic about providing money for the care and protection of children in the juvenile justice system. Often, facilities for juveniles are crowded, courts lack personnel, probation services are not sufficiently extensive, and educational and recreational programs are underfinanced and inadequate. Thus, resources must be developed to pro-

vide an efficient, effective juvenile justice program.

5. *Evaluation.*   Lastly, the goal of evaluation is vital to juvenile justice administration. Without constantly evaluating the juvenile delinquency problem, those in the field are incapable of developing realistic and effective programs and services. The lack of knowledge is even more critical than the lack of resources. The *Report of the Task Force on Juvenile Justice and Delinquency Prevention* noted "that the juvenile justice system continues to base its operations on scarce information."[21] The research results available in most areas of operation are so limited that practitioners are dealing with the virtually unknown. Thus, there is a need for the federal government and the states as well as the private sector to sponsor research to improve the quality of juvenile justice by finding answers about delinquency and its prevention. It remains for further research to determine which of the many diverse goals of the system can be achieved and which will have the most significant impact on the control and ultimate reduction of juvenile delinquency.

CURRENT ISSUES IN JUVENILE JUSTICE ADMINISTRATION

The juvenile justice system has taken few, if any, significant measures to effectively reduce juvenile crime in America. This failure is understandable in light of the country's heterogeneous culture, mixed political system, conflict over the causes of crime, and ever-changing values. Nonetheless, the general public is concerned about the crimes committed by young people. Citizens and juvenile justice practitioners such as lawyers, judges, and treatment personnel all recognize the destructive aspects of adult and juvenile crime. Consequently, they continue to commit large amounts of time and money to crime control. But, there appears to be no real solution to the problem of juvenile delinquency.

Of course, part of the problem results from the awesome complexity of the juvenile justice system itself. Financial limitations, political considerations, and labor needs, among others, create a complex and often antagonistic system. In addition, juvenile justice practitioners often disagree about statutes, court decisions, and agency practices as well as about the goals needed.

In spite of these problems, however, numerous programs, innovative ideas, and court decisions have affected the practices of the police and of judicial and correctional agencies. Among them are the development of procedural due process rights for children, the establishment of federal funding programs, the adoption of new juvenile justice programs, and the recognition by the general public of the need to reduce juvenile crime. Since it is impossible to identify all the major changes taking place within the juvenile justice system, attention is given here to a few of the major issues.

Public Policy in Planning

A major problem within the juvenile justice system has been the need to manage resources for effective decision making. Jurisdictions have often made policy decisions without proper planning information or data regarding the impact of existing services. Effective planning can assist in allocating resources and in delivering services to children on a federal, state, and local level.

The federal government has sought to update the criminal and juvenile justice systems since the mid-1960s with federal funding. Prior to that time, most juvenile justice agencies operated under the philosophy of state, independent, and local control. This left jurisdictions with fragmented and often uncoordinated systems. In addition, the major components of the system were generally understaffed and financially unable to cope with the escalating juvenile crime problem.

In 1968, Congress created the Law Enforcement Assistance Administration (LEAA) within the Department of Justice under Title I of the Omnibus Crime Control and Safe Streets Act.[22] The purpose of the LEAA was to provide the states with federal funds to combat crime. However, most LEAA funds were directed at the adult criminal justice system. Congress therefore passed the Juvenile Justice and Delinquency Prevention Act in 1974. This act was a major piece of legislation that sought to improve the juvenile justice system.[23] The Office of Juvenile Justice and Delinquency Prevention was established within the LEAA and was charged with the responsibility of implementing the new act. The major thrust of the legislation was to prevent inappropriate detention and placement of youths in jails, training schools, and other institutions because of the lack of community alternatives. In order for states to be eligible for federal assistance, however, state planning agencies were to develop annual comprehensive plans in each jurisdiction.

In addition to the federal government's role in developing policy direction and planning, such private groups as the American Bar Association and the National Council on Crime and Delinquency have developed detailed standards to help states improve their juvenile justice systems. These organizations have attempted to provide guidelines to govern the processing of juvenile offenders from the time of the initial petition through their eventual release from the system. The *Standards for Juvenile Justice* developed by the American Bar Association and the Institute of Judicial Administration, for example, consist of twenty-four volumes covering each stage of the juvenile process. They also cover abuse and neglect, the rights of minors, standards relating to schools and education, and standards dealing with the planning needs in juvenile justice.[24] All were prepared by leading lawyers, judges, and academicians in the field of juvenile justice administration.

The National Council on Crime and Delinquency (NCCD) is a private national agency that provides services to promote the rehabilitation of juvenile and adult offenders. It generally works to develop effective juvenile, family, and criminal courts and to improve probation, parole, and institutional programs. Its work includes the development of the Standard Family Court Act, the Standard Probation and Parole Act, Model Rules for Juvenile Courts, and other guidelines.

Efforts to implement the standards of both agencies have been made over the years. Although no jurisdiction is required to adopt them, they serve as reference points for states that wish to modify their current juvenile justice practices and procedures.

The ultimate goal of producing standards is to reform the juvenile justice system. The standards incorporate a comprehensive collection of data in the field of juvenile justice. As the American Bar Association stated in its *Standards for Juvenile Justice,* the purposes for formulating national standards are (1) to achieve uniformity, (2) to develop linkages within the system, (3) to reexamine concepts and premises, and (4) to codify relevant case law and administrative decisions.[25]

Civil Rights for Children

Today, the concept of due process is being applied increasingly to all groups in society. The trend toward a wider use of due process to prevent abusive power has spread to such fields as public welfare, juvenile justice, adult corrections, and mental health.

Prior to the 1960s, the judicial system generally refused to become involved in arbitrary administrative practices in human service agencies. Today, the courts have discarded the traditional hands-off doctrine; they readily review individuals' grievances in order to ensure equal protection and due process of law. The judicial system has clearly declared that persons on welfare, patients in mental hospitals, juveniles before a court, and inmates in correctional facilities have basic rights.[26]

What is meant by the term *due process of law*? It refers to a course of legal proceedings carried on regularly and in accordance with established rules and principles. Due process seeks to assure that no persons shall be deprived of life, liberty, or property without notice, counsel, a hearing, or the opportunity to confront their accusers. Basically, the term ensures what the Supreme Court refers to as fundamental fairness, which is guaranteed under the Fifth and Fourteenth Amendments to the Constitution.

Five Amendments have direct bearing on the procedural rights of children: the Fourth Amendment (search and seizure), the Fifth Amendment (double jeopardy, self-incrimination, and due process), the Sixth Amendment (speedy and public trial, right of confrontation and cross-examination, and right to counsel), the Eighth Amendment (bail and cruel and unusual punishment), and the Fourteenth Amendment (due process of law). Through continual interpretation of these Amendments, the courts have set guidelines for balancing the interests of the child and the state in the juvenile justice system.

Just what constitutes due process in a specific case depends on the facts in that case, on federal and state constitutional and statutory guarantees, on court decisions, and on the concepts that society considers important at a given time and place. For instance, in years past, due process did not require the right to counsel at juvenile adjudications, but today counsel is required by law. Years ago, due process did not require a formal hearing at transfer proceedings for juvenile offenders, but today due process requires such a hearing. Due process of law is not a fixed concept. It reflects what society deems fair and just at a particular time.

Furthermore, due process in juvenile justice as elsewhere involves various procedural safeguards such as notice of charges, a formal hearing, the right to counsel, an opportunity to respond to charges, cross-examination of witnesses, the determination of innocence or guilt on the basis of facts, and a written statement for the reasons for a decision. The degree of loss suffered by the child or adult indicates which requirements apply.

The Warren Court led the move toward due process of law in juvenile matters and in other areas as well during the 1950s and 1960s. It had its foundation in social movements that demanded the recognition of the needs of the poor, of minorities, and of ethnic groups for fair treatment under the law. Many legal scholars believe, however, that the Supreme Court's expansion of constitutional liberties has slowed considerably in the past decade under Chief Justice Warren Burger. Some say that the present court is less sympathetic to the plight of the accused—minority and child—and more receptive to prosecuting and law enforcement approaches. For instance, in recent years the Supreme Court has upheld capital punishment, cut back on Fourth Amendment protections against unreasonable searches and seizures, and validated strict sentencing statutes. On the other hand, the appellate courts have moved in case after case to increase rights for juvenile offenders and for children in general, to strike unfair abortion statutes, and to increase the rights of adult offenders in the areas of probation, parole, and institutional confinement.

Today, the trend toward judicial involvement continues in juvenile justice and in other fields as well. The federal courts have ordered busing to integrate public schools, have ruled certain jails to be in violation of the Eighth Amendment, have declared certain mental hospitals to be in violation of the due process clause, and have imposed new procedural rules on almost every kind of human service agency. Probably no other major North American or Western European country gives its judiciary as much power as America does. Consequently, it is important to consider the need to apply due process of law while at the same time maintaining effective social control. Too much due process hampers efforts to deal with crime and delinquency, but arbitrary practices of police, courts, and correctional agencies infringe on the juvenile's constitutional rights.

Diversion

Diversion—the use of alternatives to formal judicial action—is currently one of the more popular approaches to juvenile justice reform.[27] Presidential commissions, the American Bar Association, and the National Advisory Commission on Criminal Justice Standards and Goals have all supported this approach.

Diversion generally takes two different directions. On the one hand, after a child is screened by intake divisions in the juvenile court, formal juvenile proceedings can be ended and the child can be removed from the juvenile justice system. Often, referrals are made to parents and to social service agencies that are outside the juvenile justice system. More formal diversion programs, however, refer children to services available within the network of agencies that comprise the juvenile justice system. Whether a child will be prosecuted or referred to an alternative program is at the discretion of intake officials in the juvenile court and the police.

Diversionary programs have developed at all agency levels in the juvenile justice system. They provide counseling, education, training, and psychiatric treatment. In fact, in many instances, children are spared prosecution and may even have the records of their arrest and involvement in the court expunged.

Diversion rests on the assumption that formal processing of children in the juvenile court produces the negative effect of increased recidivism. Furthermore, most juvenile justice experts believe that certain groups of children, such as status offenders, runaways, and truants, should be removed from the court and helped in the community. On the other hand, some experts, for example LaMar Empey, believe that diversion programs are simply widening the net of the existing juvenile justice system.[28] Children are assigned to diversion programs instead of having their minor violations of the law overlooked.

The major benefit of diversion programs is that they broaden the existing resources that can be used to deal with children in trouble. Presently, diversion is used mainly for status offenders and children who commit minor violations of the criminal law. In years to come, children who commit more serious offenses will probably be referred to diversion programs. In order for this to be accomplished, our knowledge about the success of diversionary alternatives must increase.

Dispositional Reform

The juvenile justice system has been largely unable to rehabilitate the adjudicated child. This problem exists primarily because the juvenile court and correctional agencies have been unsuccessful with their dispositional and sentencing approaches. Lack of theoretical knowledge of human behavior is, of course, a constant problem. However, the dispositional process has been ineffective because the kinds of dispositions available to the court are limited. Most dispositions call for a period of court probation or some kind of institutionalization. At the discretion of the court, sentences are left open-ended so children can be kept under supervision until they are rehabilitated. Such a policy was supposed to fit the personal needs and characteristics of each child and serve the best interests of the child.

However benevolent this approach was supposed to be, it has not been successful. Disparity among sentences, lack of due process in dispositional hearings, sentencing decisions made without information, and lack of dispositional resources have all created a growing despair about dispositional effectiveness in the juvenile courts.

Consequently, efforts are being made to improve one of the most important phases of juvenile proceedings—the dispositional decision. One of the first steps is to reassess the purpose of disposition. Rehabilitation has been in vogue for most of the twentieth century, but today many groups are urging that juvenile delinquency dispositions protect society and deter crime as well as rehabilitate the criminal.

Indeterminant sentencing statutes often place children under dispositional authority until they reach their majority. This approach presupposes the continued need for rehabilitation and treatment until the child reaches majority. However, it is now felt that the court should impose a fair disposition that fits the crime and not be so concerned about the total rehabilitative effort.

The juvenile justice system has sought to remove children by diverting status offenders and minor offenders, but it has also sought to toughen sentences for serious juvenile offenders. Such groups as the National Advisory Commission on Criminal Justice Standards and Goals and the American Bar Association strongly advocate both types of disposition and the establishment of classes of delinquent acts for dispositional purposes. Types of dispositions suggested include warnings for minor infractions, conditional dispositions involving probation, and custodial dispositions where the child is removed from the home.[29] Adult offenses are classified according to their seriousness within the state's penal code, but few states classify delinquent acts. However, it is possible that future juvenile codes will include such categories as class 1 delinquent acts, comparable to misdemeanors, and class 2 delinquent acts, comparable to felonies.

In general, courts make dispositional decisions based on inadequate information about the children appearing before them. However, the process of investigating the crime and questioning the juvenile must preserve the child's legal rights. By the same token, details about the offense, the juvenile's age and identity, and the child's social and personal characteristics, including psychological and psychiatric information, are needed at the disposition for the court to make a proper decision.

The failure of traditional dispositional programs has inspired some new approaches to juvenile crime. Certainly, eliminating status offenders from the system is one possible approach.[30] Another, of course, is to remove children from formal institutional care and replace these facilities with community treatment programs.[31] A third approach involves efforts to amend juvenile laws to increase the number of dispositional alternatives and to change indeterminant sentencing provisions, particularly for violent juvenile offenders. Flat, determinant, or presumptive sentencing provisions have already been developed for the adult criminal justice system in such states as Maine, California, and Indiana.[32] Similar legislation is pending in numerous other jurisdictions.

The concept of rehabilitation for both juvenile and adult offenders is being attacked on all sides. Whether the efforts to legislate rehabilitation out of existence on the adult level will become more pronounced on the juvenile level is unclear at this time. Ernest Van den Haag goes so far as to suggest that juveniles who have committed acts that the adult criminal justice system defines as crimes should be tried and sentenced by adult courts under adult laws.[33] That approach may be extreme, but it should warn us that unless dispositional reform occurs, the philosophy of rehabilitation may return to a philosophy of punishment for children.

CHAPTER SUMMARY

In this chapter, we analyzed the system of juvenile justice as a group of public agencies and as a process for servicing children. The chapter discussed how juvenile justice operates in theory and in practice.

The chapter began with an analysis of juvenile justice as a field of study. Although the establishment of the first juvenile court in Cook County, Illinois, was considered a milestone of the twentieth century, juvenile justice as a field of study became prominent in the 1960s, when many noteworthy national groups explored the delinquency problem. Since then, a field of study has emerged using knowledge from various disciplines such as law, sociology, political science, and criminology to understand what causes young people to commit crimes and how to deal with their behavior. Juvenile justice, then, consists of the study of juvenile delinquency and antisocial behavior and the agencies concerned with its prevention, control, and treatment.

Juvenile justice was also explored as a process consisting of the steps that a child takes from the initial investigation of a crime through the appeal of the case. These steps are the police investigation, the intake procedure in the juvenile court, the pretrial procedures used for juvenile offenders, the adjudication, the disposition, and the postdispositional procedures.

The juvenile system was also compared to the adult criminal justice system to illustrate their interrelationship. This analysis included a discussion of how each system differs, the terminology used in the adult and juvenile agencies, the law, and the critical points in each process.

How the juvenile justice system deals with the child is also determined by the multiple goals of the system and its individual agencies. Thus, a detailed review was presented regarding the various goals of juvenile justice as stated by the National Advisory Commission on Juvenile Justice and Delinquency Prevention and the American Bar Association. The authors identified the following realistic goals for juvenile justice: (1) delinquency prevention, (2) diversion, (3) fairness and justice for children, (4) efficiency and effectiveness, and (5) evaluation and monitoring of juvenile justice programs. Juvenile justice is a very complex system whose many goals are often unrelated to day-to-day operations. Nonetheless, if the professionals responsible for the administration of juvenile justice are to make progress against delinquency, the quest for knowledge must be based on clearly stated goals for the system.

The chapter concluded with an analysis of the current trends in juvenile justice administration that are directly related to and influenced by the above goals. Such issues include the need for public policy and planning in juvenile justice, the continued implementation of diversion activity, dispositional reform, and the continual effort to improve civil rights for all children. As Senator Bayh has pointed out, it is imperative that this nation devote its resources and talents to resolving the legal and social issues confronting the juvenile justice system.[34] The chapters that follow describe and analyze this system and present the issues in detail.

DISCUSSION QUESTIONS

1. The terms *juvenile justice system* and *juvenile justice process* are often used synonymously. What is meant by each term, and how do they differ from each other?

2. The formal components of the criminal justice system are often considered to be the police, the court, and the correctional agency. How do these components compare with the major areas of the juvenile justice system? Is the operation of justice similar in the juvenile and the adult systems? What are the similarities and differences between these two major areas of social control?

3. How the juvenile justice system deals with the juvenile offender is often determined by the multiple goals of the system and its individual agencies. Discuss some of the major goals of juvenile justice. Has the system been successful in achieving any particular goal? Why or why not, and if so, how?

4. In the juvenile justice system, children are often filtered out, or diverted, from formal court processing. What types of cases are diverted? Why?

5. In juvenile justice, as in any changing field, it is often difficult to determine what trends and developments will persist and have a major impact. Discuss some of the major trends currently confronting the field of juvenile justice. Which issues do you believe will have a significant impact on juvenile crime control? What other basic unresolved issues exist in juvenile justice today?

SUGGESTED READINGS

American Bar Association and Institute of Judicial Administration. *Standards for Juvenile Justice: A Summary and Analysis.* Cambridge, Mass.: Ballinger Press, 1977.

Besharov, Douglas. *Juvenile Justice Advocacy—Practice in a Unique Court.* New York: Practicing Law Institute, 1974.

Blumberg, Abraham S. *Criminal Justice: Issues and Ironies.* 2d ed. New York: Watts, 1979.

Blumstein, Alfred. "Systems Analyses and the Criminal Justice System." *Annals of the American Academy of Political and Social Science* 374 (1967): 92–96.

Cavan, Ruth, and Ferdinand, Theodore. *Juvenile Delinquency.* Philadelphia: Lippincott, 1974.

Cicourel, Aaron V. *The Social Organization of Juvenile Justice.* New York: Wiley, 1968.

Cromwell, Paul; Killinger, George; Sarri, Rosemary; and Solomon, H. M. *Text and Readings—Introduction to Juvenile Delinquency.* St. Paul, Minn.: West Publishing, 1974.

Davis, Samuel. *Rights of Juveniles—The Juvenile Justice System.* New York: Clark Boardman, 1974.

Empey, LaMar T. "Juvenile Justice Reform: Diversion, Due Process, and Deinstitutionalization." In *Prisoners in America,* edited by Lloyd Ohlin. Englewood Cliffs, N.J.: Prentice-Hall, 1973.

Empey, LaMar T., and Lubeck, Steven. *Delinquency Prevention Strategies.* Washington, D.C.: Government Printing Office, 1970.

Hahn, Paul. *The Juvenile Offender and the Law.* Springfield, Illinois: Anderson, 1978.

Hall, Livingston; Kamisar, Yale; LaFave, Wayne; and Israel, Jerold. *Modern Criminal Procedure.* 4th ed. St. Paul, Minn.: West Publishing, 1974.

Kessenbaum, Gene. *Delinquency and Social Policy.* Englewood Cliffs, N.J.: Prentice-Hall, 1974.

Lerman, Paul. *Community Treatment and Control.* Chicago: University of Chicago Press, 1975.

National Advisory Commission on Criminal Justice Standards and Goals. *Report of the Task Force on Juvenile Justice and Delinquency Prevention.* Washington, D.C.: Law Enforcement Assistance Administration, 1976.

Piersma, Paul; Ganousis, Jeanette; Volnik, Adrienne; Swanger, Harry; and Connell, Patricia. *Law and Tactics in Juvenile Cases.* 3d ed. Philadelphia: American Law Institute–American Bar Association Committee on Continuing Professional Education, 1974.

Platt, Anthony M. *The Child Savers: The Invention of Delinquency.* Chicago: University of Chicago Press, 1969.

President's Commission on Law Enforcement and Administration of Justice. *Task Force Report: Juvenile Delinquency and Youth Crime.* Washington, D.C.: Government Printing Office, 1967.

Quinney, Richard. *Critique of Legal Order: Crime Control or Capitalist Society.* Boston: Little, Brown, 1974.

Reid, Sue Titus. *Crime and Criminology.* 2d ed. New York: Holt, Rinehart and Winston, 1979.

Remington, Frank; Newman, Donald; Kimball, Edward; Milli, Marygold; and Goldstein, Herman. *Criminal Justice Administration, Materials and Cases.* Indianapolis: Bobbs-Merrill, 1968.

Rubin, H. Ted., ed. *Juveniles in Justice—A Book of Readings.* Santa Monica, Calif.: Goodyear Publishing, 1980.

Senna, Joseph, and Siegel, Larry. *Introduction to Criminal Justice.* St. Paul, Minn.: West Publishing, 1978.

Wakin, Edward. *Children without Justice—A Report of the National Council of Jewish Women.* New York: National Council of Jewish Women, 1975.

Wheeler, Stanton, and Cottrell, Leonard S. *Juvenile Delinquency: Its Prevention and Control.* New York: Russell Sage Foundation, 1966.

REFERENCES

1. President's Commission on Law Enforcement and Administration of Justice, *Task Force Report: Juvenile Delinquency and Youth Crime* (Washington, D.C.: Government Printing Office, 1967).

2. See Public Law 93–415 of 1974.

3. See, generally, President's Commission on Law Enforcement and Administration of Justice, *The Challenge of Crime in a Free Society* (Washington, D.C.: Government Printing Office, 1967); National Advisory Commission on Criminal Justice Standards and Goals, *Report of the Task Force on Juvenile Justice and Delinquency Prevention* (Washington, D.C.: Law Enforcement Assistance Administration, 1976); and American Bar Association and Institute of Judicial Administration, *Standards for Juvenile Justice: A Summary and Analysis* (Cambridge, Mass.: Ballinger Press, 1977).

4. See Herbert Lou, *Juvenile Courts in the United States* (Charlotte: University of North Carolina Press, 1927).

5. National Advisory Commission on Criminal Justice Standards and Goals, *Report of the Task Force on Juvenile Justice and Delinquency Prevention,* p. 6.

6. N. Paris, M. Gottfredson, M. Hindelang, and T. Flanagan, eds., *Sourcebook of Criminal Justice Statistics—1978* (Washington, D.C.: Government Printing Office, 1979), pp. 187, 522–526.

7. See National Council of Juvenile and Family Court Judges, *Directory of Juvenile and Family Court Judges* (Reno: University of Nevada Press, 1979); and National Council on Crime and Delinquency, *Probation and Parole Directory,* 17th ed. (Hackensack, N.Y.: National Council on Crime and Delinquency, 1976).

8. *Uniform Crime Reports for the United States—1978* (Washington, D.C.: Government Printing Office, 1978), pp. 41–46.

9. Paris, Gottfredson, Hindelang, and Flanagan, *Sourcebook of Criminal Justice Statistics—1978.*

10. See, generally, Hubert Packer, *The Limits of the Criminal Sanction* (Stanford, Calif.: Stanford University Press, 1968).

11. National Advisory Commission on Criminal Justice Standards and Goals, *Report of the Task Force on Juvenile Justice and Delinquency Prevention,* p. 730.

12. Ibid., p. 720.

13. 15 Idaho 126, 96, p. 563 (1908).

14. President's Commission on Law Enforcement and Administration of Justice, *The Challenge of Crime in a Free Society,* p. 89.

15. Birch Bayh, "Juveniles and the Law: An Introduction," *American Criminal Law Review* 12 (1974): 1.

16. Paul Nejelski and Judith LaPook, "Monitoring the Juvenile Justice System: How Can You Tell Where You're Going, If You Don't Know Where You Are?" *American Criminal Law Review* 12 (1974): 9.

17. President's Commission on Law Enforcement and Administration of Justice, *The Challenge of Crime in a Free Society,* p. 88.

18. National Advisory Commission on Criminal Justice Standards and Goals, *Report of the Task Force on Juvenile Justice and Delinquency Prevention,* pp. 11-14.

19. Ibid. pp. 14-15.

20. David Gilman, "IJA-ABA Juvenile Justice Standards Project: An Introduction," *Boston University Law Review* 57 (1977): 622-623.

21. National Advisory Commission on Criminal Justice Standards and Goals, *Report of the Task Force on Juvenile Justice and Delinquency Prevention,* p. 253.

22. See Public Law 90-351, Title I—Omnibus Crime Control and S afe Streets Act of 1968. 90th Congress, June 19, 1968.

23. See Public Law 93-415, 1974.

24. American Bar Association and Institute of Judicial Administration, *Standards for Juvenile Justice.*

25. American Bar Association and Institute of Judicial Administration, *Standards for Juvenile Justice,* p. 0.

26. See "Towards Greater Fairness for All," *Time,* February 26, 1973, pp. 95-96.

27. See Paul Nejelski, "Diversion: The Promise and the Danger," *Crime and Delinquency* 22 (1976): 393-410; Wallace Loh, "Pretrial Diversion from the Criminal Process," and Raymond Nimmer, *Diversion: The Search for Alternative Forms of Prosecution* (Chicago: American Bar Foundation, 1974).

28. LaMar T. Empey, *American Delinquency—Its Meaning and Construction* (Homewood, Ill.: Dorsey Press, 1978), p. 541.

29. See National Advisory Commission on Criminal Justice Standards and Goals, *Report of the Task Force on Juvenile Justice and Delinquency Prevention* (Washington, D.C.: Law Enforcement Assistance Administration, 1976), pp. 452-456.

30. See Orman Ketcham, "Children's Rights: The Problem on Noncriminal Misbehavior," *State Court Journal* 3 (1979): 19-25.

31. Empey, *American Delinquency,* p. 533.

32. See Marvin Zalman, "The Rise and Fall of the Indeterminate Sentence," *Wayne Law Review* 24 (1978): 854-937; U.S. Department of Justice, National Institute of Law Enforcement and Criminal Justice, *Determinate Sentencing—Reform or Regression* (Washington, D.C.: Government Printing Office, 1978).

33. Ernest Van den Haag, "Punitive Sentences," *Hofstra Law Review* 7 (1978): 123-139.

34. Bayh, "Juveniles and the Law," pp. 1-7.

Chapter 13

Chapter Outline

Introduction
Care of Children in the Middle Ages
Child Care in the 15th and 16th Centuries
Early English Developments and the
   Chancery Court System
Children in Colonial America
19th Century Developments in Great Britain
19th Century Developments in America
Establishment of the Illinois Juvenile Court
   in 1899
The Modern Juvenile Court
Chapter Summary

Key Terms, Names, and Cases

Enoch Wines
Marcus Ames
primogeniture
dower
poor laws
apprenticeship
chancery court
Kent v. U.S.
New York Children's Aid Society
Wellesley v. Wellesley
child saving
house of refuge
parens patriae
Haley v. Ohio
middle ages
Ex parte Crouse
O'Connell v. Turner
cottage system
Illinois Juvenile Court Act

The History and Philosophy of Juvenile Justice

INTRODUCTION

This chapter analyzes the history of dealing with children in order to explain how and why the juvenile justice system exists in its present form.[1] How has the role of children changed from the Middle Ages to the present time? Where did the term *delinquency* originate? What are the historical developments that led to the juvenile court movement? These are some of the basic questions that this chapter seeks to answer.

The chapter begins with an analysis of the concept of childhood in the fifteenth century, for little information exists about the role of children prior to that time. It then turns its attention to the children's court movement in England during the period when adults and children were treated similarly under the criminal laws. Severe and often brutal punishments were inflicted on convicted offenders, with little regard for their age. The chapter reviews the role of the chancery courts and the extension of the doctrine of *parens patriae*. It then discusses the care and protection of children in colonial America. It details the historical developments of the nineteenth century that led to the creation of the first modern juvenile court in Chicago in 1899. These developments include a discussion of the social welfare movement, the notion of treating children separately, and the establishment of legislation to segregate delinquent children from adult criminal offenders. The chapter concludes with a look at the period from the turn of the century to the mid-1960s, including the actual operation of the contemporary juvenile court system.

CARE OF CHILDREN IN THE MIDDLE AGES

Between 700 A.D. and 1500 A.D., little is actually known about the day-to-day lives of children. During this period, the concept of childhood as we know it today did not exist. The concept of children as a distinct social group with unique needs and behaviors is for the most part relatively new.

In the early centuries of the Middle Ages, family life was paternalistic.[2] The father was the final authority on all family matters and exercised complete control over the social, economic, and physical well-being of his wife and children. Ordinarily, if the father's will was not obeyed, his children and wife were subject to the severest punishment, even death. The concept of the father's dominance had its roots in Roman law, which gave a father unlimited authority over his family. This included the right of life and death over all family members, and power to sell members of the family, the right to veto marriages, and the right to recover previously stolen children.

Much of what we know about family life in this period concerns upper-class, land-holding families. Here, the nuclear family—father, mother, and children—was viewed as a small segment of a larger clan. This larger group, or extended family, was made up of many loosely related families sharing a common heritage and tradition. In England, for example, the Yorks, Tudors, and Lancasters were all powerful congregate family groups. These families sought to expand their power and influence over rivals by intermarriage. The importance of improving and expanding the family influenced marriage, inheritance, and child-rearing practices. For example, marriages were not made for love or affection. They were made for family interest, to strengthen alliances, and to improve on one's possessions. Thus, love was subjugated to duty to family and relatives.

Other practices also greatly influenced the daily life of children during the Middle Ages. Primogeniture required that the eldest surviving male child inherit family lands and titles. He could then distribute them as he saw fit to younger siblings. However, there was no absolute requirement that he distribute portions of the estate. Thus, when this was not done, many youths were forced to fend for themselves. They entered religious orders, became soldiers, or sought wealthy patrons. Primogeniture often caused intense family rivalry that led to blood feuds and tragedy among family members. For example, a mother might die in childbirth, leaving behind an infant who was sole heir to a family estate and title. If the child's father remarried and produced offspring who had no hope of substantial inheritance, conflicts arose over the inheritance rights of the first-born infant and subsequent siblings. The considerable jealousy that existed would create feuds between individual family members.

The dower system was the custom that mandated a family to bestow money, land, or other wealth upon a potential husband or his family in exchange for securing his marriage to their daughter. In return, the young woman received a promise of financial assistance, called a jointure, from the groom's family. It provided her with a lifetime income in the event that she outlived her mate. The dower system had a significant impact on the role of the female in medieval society and consequently on the role of children. It ensured that marriages would be contracted only within a social class and not across classes. It gave the girl's father control over whom she married because he could threaten to withhold funds. It placed the female in the role of an economic drain on the family. A father with many daughters and few sons might find himself financially unable to obtain suitable marriages for his daughters. As a result, in many instances the youngest girls in families entered convents, became unwanted, or were left at home.

Little is known about the peasant family during the Middle Ages. It did not maintain the same ties to a powerful kinship group as did the wealthy families. Although it too had a patriarchal family structure, a great portion of the family's time was devoted to work and survival. Thus, the peasant father's influence was weaker than that of the wealthy landowner. Children were expected to assume adult roles early in life. They went into domestic or agricultural service on great estates or were apprenticed in trades or crafts. To some degree, this system of control over children lifted the burden from parents and placed the children in the care of wealthy families.

CHILD CARE IN THE FIFTEENTH AND SIXTEENTH CENTURIES

Medieval features of the family had an important effect on child-rearing practices during the fifteenth and sixteenth centuries. For instance, newborn children were almost immediately handed over to wet nurses, who breast fed and cared for them during the early years of their lives. These women often lived away from the family so that parents had little contact with the children. Even the wealthiest families employed wet nurses, because it was considered demeaning for a noblewoman to nurse. Swaddling, a common practice, entailed wrapping a newborn child entirely in bandages. The bandages prevented any movement and enabled the wet nurse to easily manage the child. It was thought that this practice protected the child, but, ironically, it most likely contributed to high infant mortality rates since the child could not be kept clean.

Discipline was severe during this period. Young children of all classes, both peasant and wealthy, were subjected to stringent rules and regulations. They were beaten severely for any sign of disobedience or ill-temper. Many children during this time would be considered abused if they lived in today's world. The relationship between parent and child was remote. Children were expected to enter the world of adults and to undertake responsibilities early in their lives, sharing in the work of their siblings and parents.

The roots of the nonpersonal relationship between parent and child can be traced to high mortality rates, which made sentimental and affectionate relationships risky. It would have been foolish for parents to invest emotional effort in relationships that could so easily be terminated by violence, accidents, or disease. Parents often thought that children must be toughened to ensure their survival in a hostile world. Close family relationships were viewed as detrimental to this process. Also, since the eldest male child was viewed as the essential and important element in a family's well-being, younger male and female siblings were considered economic and social liabilities. Often, children and others thought to be suffering from disease or retardation were abandoned to churches, orphanages, or foundling homes.[3]

In summary, then, lack of parental affection, physical and emotional remoteness, severe physical punishments and other discipline, rigid social class structure, and conflict, suspicion, hostility, and alienation among family groups all characterized child care in the Middle Ages. These conditions are the most significant features precipitating the children's court movement in Great Britain in the seventeenth and eighteenth centuries.

EARLY ENGLISH DEVELOPMENTS AND THE CHANCERY COURT SYSTEM

Throughout the seventeenth and eighteenth centuries, a number of developments occurring in England directly affected the juvenile legal system as it emerged in America. They include: (1) changes in family style and child care, (2) the effect of the English poor laws in America, (3) the apprenticeship movement, and (4) the role of the chancery court.[4]

Changes in Family Structure

Family structure and the role of children began to change after the Middle Ages as the influence of the great families began to wane. Such extended families as the Yorks and the Tudors, which were created over centuries, gave way to the nuclear family structure with which we are familiar today. It became more common for marriage to be based on love and mutual attraction between men and women than on parental consent and male dominance. Parents still kept their rigid discipline over children, however. The control of a child's actions was considered essential for proper maintenance of the family structure.

In an effort to provide more controls over children, schools began to flourish in many large cities during this time.[5] Their structure and subject matter were quite different from those that exist today. The subject matter included grammar, Latin, law, and logic. Children often began to study at an early age. During the later part of the seventeenth century, grammar schools and boarding schools emerged. Children were sent to school very early in England. The growth of this scholastic movement was directly related to the emphasis such philosophers as John Locke and Jean Jacques Rousseau put on the learning process. Teachers in these institutions often ruled by fear, and flogging was their main method of discipline. Students were often beaten for academic mistakes as well as moral lapses. Such brutal treatment involved both the rich and the poor and extended to all levels of educational life, including boarding schools and universities. Only toward the end of the eighteenth century, when the Enlightenment, stressing the rights of man, emerged did this treatment abate throughout the continent of Europe. However, it remained in full force in Great Britain. And although it may be difficult to understand this brutal approach to children, the child's position in society was that of a second-class citizen.

However, toward the close of the eighteenth century, the work of such philosophers as Voltaire, Rousseau, and Locke began to herald a new age for childhood and family.[6] The Enlightenment stressed a humanistic view of life, freedom, family, reason, and law. The philosophers suggested that the ideal person was sympathetic to others and receptive to new ideas. These new beliefs influenced the life-style of the family. The father's authority was tempered, discipline in the home became more relaxed, and the expression of love and affection became of deep concern to family members. Upper- and middle-class families began to devote attention to child-rearing.

As a result, toward the end of the eighteenth and beginning of the nineteenth centuries, children began to emerge, at least in the wealthier classes, as a readily distinguishable group with independent needs and interests. Parents often took greater personal interest in their upbringing. In addition, serious questions arose over the treatment of children in school. Public outcries led to a decrease in excessive physical discipline there. Restrictions were placed on the use of the whip. And in some schools, the imposition of academic assignments or the loss of privileges replaced corporal punishment. Nonetheless, not all customs underwent positive change. Girls were still undereducated, parents were still excessively concerned with the moral and religious development of their children, physical punishment was still primarily in use, and schools continued to mistreat children. Yet, the changes in England in this period paved the way for today's family structure of child care.

Poor Laws

While children of the upper classes were involved in educational programs, poor children in the cities and counties had different experiences. As early as 1535, the English passed statutes known as Poor Laws.[7] These laws allowed for the appointment of overseers to bind out destitute or neglected children as servants. The Poor Laws forced children to serve during their minority in the care of families who trained them in agricultural, trade, or domestic services. The Elizabethan Poor Laws of 1601 became a model for dealing with poor children for more than two hundred years. These laws created a system of church wardens and overseers who, at the consent of justices of the peace, identified vagrant, delinquent, and neglected children and took measures to put them to work. Often this meant placing them in poorhouses or workhouses or apprenticing them to masters.

Apprenticeship Movement

Apprenticeship in Great Britain existed through almost the entire history of the country.[8] It was a practice that placed children in the care of adults who trained them to discharge various duties and obtain different skills. Voluntary apprentices were bound out by parents or guardians who wished to secure training for their children. Involuntary apprentices were compelled to serve by the authorities until they were twenty-one or older. The master-apprentice relationship was similar to the parent-child relationship in that the master had complete responsibility for and authority over the apprentice. If an apprentice was unruly, a complaint could be made and the apprentice could be punished. Apprentices were often placed in rooms or workshops separate from other prisoners and generally were treated differently from those charged with a criminal offense. Even at this early stage, conviction was growing that the criminal law and its enforcement should be applied differently to children.

Chancery Court

The concept of *parens patriae* and the chancery court system played significant parts in shaping juvenile justice in Great Britain. Chancery court existed throughout the Middle Ages. It was concerned primarily with protecting property rights, although its authority extended to the welfare of children generally. However, the major issues in medieval cases that came before the chancery courts concerned guardianship, the uses and control of property, and the arrangement of people and power in relation to the monarchy. Agents of the chancery courts were responsible for controlling and settling problems involving rights to estates and guardianship interests in regard to the hierarchy of families and the state. These courts were founded on the proposition that children and other incompetents were under the protective control of the king. Thus, the Latin phrase, *parens patriae*, referred to the role of the king as the father of his country. As Douglas Besharov states, "The concept apparently was first used by English Kings to justify their intervention in the lives of the children of their vassals—children whose position and property were of direct concern to the monarch."[9] In the famous English case, *Wellesley v. Wellesley*, a duke's children were taken away from him in the name and interest of *parens patriae* because of his scandalous behavior.[10] Thus, the concept of *parens patriae* became the theoretical basis for the protective jurisdiction of the chancery courts acting as part of the crown's power.

As time passed, the crown used *parens patriae* more and more to justify its intervention into the lives of families and children by its interest in their general welfare. However, as Douglas Rendleman points out, "The idea of parens patriae was actually used to maintain the power of the crown and the structure of control over families known as feudalism."[11]

The chancery courts dealt with the property and custody problems of the wealthier classes. They never had jurisdiction over children charged with criminal conduct. Juveniles who violated the law were handled within the framework of the regular criminal court system. Nonetheless, the concept of *parens patriae*, which was established with the English chancery court system, grew to refer primarily to the responsibility of the courts and the state to act in the best interests of the child. The idea that the state—and particularly the juvenile court—in the twentieth century should act to protect the young, the incompetent, the neglected, and the delinquent subsequently became a major influence on the development of the American juvenile justice system.

CHILDREN IN COLONIAL AMERICA

While England was using its chancery courts and its Poor Law system to deal with unfortunate children, the American colonies were struggling with similar concepts. Initially, the colonies were a haven for poor and unfortunate people looking for religious and economic opportunities denied them in England and Europe. Along with early settlers, many children came not as citizens but as indentured servants, apprentices, or agricultural workers. They were recruited from the various English workhouses, orphanages, prisons, and asylums that housed vagrant and delinquent youths during the sixteenth and seventeenth centuries.[12]

At the same time, the colonies themselves produced illegitimate, neglected, abandoned, and delinquent children whose parents could not care for them. The colonies' initial response to caring for such unfortunate children was to adopt a court system and Poor Law system similar to the English one. Involuntary apprenticeship and the indenture and binding out of children became an integral part of colonialization in America. Poor Law legislation was passed, for example, in Virginia in 1646 and Massachusetts and Connecticut in 1673.[13] Poor and dependent children were required to serve apprenticeships.

The master in colonial America acted as a natural parent, and in certain instances, apprentices would actually become part of the nuclear family structure. If they disobeyed their masters, apprentices were punished by local tribunals. If masters abused apprentices, courts would make them pay damages, return the child to the parents, or find new guardians.

The apprenticeship system eventually eroded under the pressure of national growth prompted by the war of independence, the rise of the industrial revolution, and the ever-increasing European immigration. The concepts of *parens patriae* and the chancery court system came to be unacceptable in America because they represented the ideas of monarchy and feudalism that were being rejected in the establishment of the new country. Thus, after the American Revolution, many poor youths sought jobs in mills and factories and lived in boarding homes and industrial settlements provided by mill owners.

By the beginning of the nineteenth century, the apprenticeship system could no longer compete with the factory system. Yet the problems of how to deal effectively with growing numbers of dependent youths increased consistently. Early American settlers were firm believers in hard work, strict discipline, and education. Those principles were viewed as the only reliable method for salvation. A child's life was marked by work alongside parents, some schooling, prayer, more work, and further study.

As in England, moral discipline was rigidly enforced. It was not uncommon in the colonies for children who were disobedient or disrespectful to their families to be whipped or otherwise physically chastised. Children were often required to attend public whippings and executions because they served as important forms of moral instruction. Parents often referred their children to published works and writings on behavior and discipline and expected them to follow their precepts carefully. As in England, children in Colonial America were subject to adult criminal procedures and adult punishments.

In keeping with the family interest in hard work and discipline, the Factory Act of the early nineteenth century limited the hours children were permitted to work and the age at which they could begin work. It also prescribed a minimum amount of schooling to be provided by factory owners.[14] Often, these statutes were violated, and conditions of work and school remained troublesome issues well into the twentieth century. Nevertheless, the statutes were a step in the direction of reform.

DEVELOPMENTS IN GREAT BRITAIN IN THE NINETEENTH CENTURY

During the nineteenth century in Great Britain, delinquent, neglected, depen-

dent, and runaway children were not treated as separate groups.[15] Children
were often charged and convicted of crimes including capital offenses, and the
harsh sentences that were imposed were similar to those imposed on adults.
The adult criminal code also applied to children, and no actual juvenile court
was in existence before the end of the nineteenth century.

One of the major factors that influenced the development of the children's
court movement in Great Britain in the nineteenth century was a philosophical
shift in the understanding of crime and delinquency. Classical criminology was
based on the idea that people were hedonistic by nature but could freely choose
to behave morally.

By the middle and late nineteenth century, the criminal justice systems in
Great Britain and America came to assume that crime was an individual condition requiring scientific understanding. Also, steps were taken to deemphasize
the responsibility of children under the criminal laws. In Great Britain, children were removed from adult prisons. Separate institutions for training and
educating youths in need of care were established. The *Wellesley* case of 1827
established the principle that a court could remove a child from the custody of
its parents.

Throughout the early period of the nineteenth century, various pieces of legislation were introduced in parliament to soften the criminal procedures for
children. The concept of probation, which was introduced in Massachusetts in
1841, influenced criminal legislation in England and encouraged the treatment
of offenders within the community.[16] National conferences held in the mid-
nineteenth century in Great Britain further developed the concept that juvenile
offenders should be treated separately from adults. The many books and reports written during this time made the subject of juvenile child care one of intense public interest. By the turn of the century, Great Britain was examining
different ways of amending the criminal laws that treated and punished juvenile offenders. At the same time, developments were occurring in America that
laid the groundwork for the present juvenile justice system.

DEVELOPMENTS IN AMERICA IN THE NINETEENTH CENTURY

The American states in the nineteenth century did not distinguish among delinquent, neglected, and runaway children. Each was considered a member of the
same outcast group. No special facilities existed for the care of youths in trouble
with the law; nor were there separate laws or courts to control their behavior.
Youths who committed petty crimes such as stealing, gambling, or minor damage to property were viewed as wayward or as the victims of neglect and were
placed in community asylums or homes. Youths who were involved in serious
crimes were subject to the same punishments as adults—prison, whipping, or
death. The criminal laws of the late eighteenth and the nineteenth centuries in
both England and America provided severe and often brutal punishments for
convicted offenders, regardless of age.

To understand the contemporary juvenile justice system, we have to ask our-
selves what important factors in nineteenth century America led to reform in
the field of child care. Four significant events nourished and supported the

eventual development of the juvenile justice system in America—urbanization and childsaving, institutional care, the concept of *parens patriae*, and the reform school movement.

Urbanization and Childsaving

Especially during the first half of the nineteenth century, America experienced a rapid population growth. This was due primarily to an increase in the birthrate and to continuing increases in European immigration to America. The growing numbers of young people who were eligible for apprenticeship programs overwhelmed this system of work and training. In the south, slavery eliminated the need for field hands and servants. To accommodate groups of dependent and destitute youths, local jurisdictions developed systems of almshouses, poorhouses, and workhouses. In crowded, unhealthy conditions, they accepted the poor, the insane, the diseased, and vagrant and destitute children. The overseers who were responsible for them placed many children in institutions.

In addition, increased urbanization and industrialization led to the belief that certain segments of the population, namely youths in urban areas and immigrants, were particularly prone to criminal deviance and immorality. The children of these classes were considered a group that might be "saved" by state intervention.[17] Such intervention, primarily by organizations and groups of the middle class, created a childsaving movement. It became acceptable for wealthy, civic-minded citizens to help alleviate the burdens of the unfortunate urban classes and the immigrants. Such efforts included shelter care for youths, educational and social activities, and the development of settlement houses. Their main focus, however, was on extending government control over a whole range of youthful activities that had previously been left to private or family control, including idleness, drinking, vagrancy, and delinquency.

Prominent among those interested in the care of unfortunate children were penologist Enoch Wines, Judge Richard Tuthill, Lucy Flowers of the Chicago Women's Association, Sara Cooper of the National Conference of Charities and Corrections, and Sophia Minton of the New York Committee on Children.[18] These and other individuals became known as childsavers. They believed that poor children presented a threat to the moral fabric of American society and should be controlled because their behavior could lead to the destruction of the nation's economic system. Thus, as a result of the process of industrialization and immigration, shortcomings in the existing criminal justice system, and the development of the childsaving movement, special institutions for children began to emerge. These factors eventually led to significant involvement of the various states in expanding state jurisdiction over the care of children.

Childsaving Movement

While various legislatures enacted laws giving courts the power to commit children who were runaways, who committed criminal acts, and who were out of the control of parents, specialized institutional programs were also created. One of the most concrete examples of institutional care was the House of

Refuge in New York in 1825.[19] It was based on the concept of protecting youths by taking potential criminals off the streets and reforming them in a family-like environment.

When the New York House of Refuge opened, the majority of children admitted were status offenders who were placed there because of vagrancy or neglect. However, the institution was run more like a prison with a work schedule, study schedule, strict discipline, and absolute separation of the sexes. Such a harsh program led to runaways, with the result that the House of Refuge was forced to change its approach to a more lenient one. Children entered the House by court order, sometimes over parental objections, for vagrancy or delinquency. Their stay depended on need, age, and skill. Once there, youths were required to do piecework provided by local manufacturers or to work part of the day in the community.

Despite criticism of the program, the concept enjoyed expanding popularity. In 1826 the Boston City Council founded the House of Reformation for juvenile offenders in the city of Boston. Similar institutions were opened in Massachusetts and New York in 1847.[20] To these schools, which were both privately funded and publicly supported, the courts committed children found guilty of criminal violations, as well as those beyond the control of their parents. Because the childsaving movement regarded both convicted offenders and parents of delinquent children in the same category, they sought to have the reform schools establish control over the children. As Robert Mennel states, "By training destitute and delinquent children, and by separating them from their natural parents and adult criminals, refuge managers believed they were preventing poverty and crime."[21]

Parens Patriae and Its Legal Challenges

Refuge programs extended the philosophy of *parens patriae*, which gave such programs the right to have parental control over the committed child. Mennel has summarized this attitude: "The doctrine of parens patriae gave refuge managers the best of two worlds, familial and legal: it separated delinquent children from their natural parents and it circumvented the rigor of criminal law by allowing courts to commit children, under loosely worded statutes to specially created schools instead of jails."[22] Once a refuge received a child, procedures of criminal law no longer applied.

However, this process of institutional control over children in the name of the state and family did not proceed without some significant legal challenges. In 1838, in the case *Ex parte Crouse*, a young child's father attempted to free her from the Philadelphia House of Refuge, which claimed the right of parental control over her because of unmanageable behavior.[23] The girl's father argued that her commitment without a trial by jury was unconstitutional. In its decision, the court held that the House of Refuge was specifically planned to reform, restrain, and protect children from depraved parents or their environment. A statutory procedure without a trial in the interest of the child was legal. As a result, the *Crouse* case represented the idea that the state had almost complete authority to intervene in parent-child relationships. The court stated:

The right of parental control is a natural, but not an unalienable one. It is not accepted by the Declaration of Rights out of the subjects of ordinary legislation; and it consequently remains subject to the ordinary legislative power which, if wantonly or inconveniently used, would soon be constitutionally restricted, but the competency of which, as the government is constituted, cannot be doubted.[24]

The *Crouse* decision showed that children could be deprived of the constitutional liberties guaranteed to adults.

Another, more significant, case was decided in favor of the parent and child against the state. The case was *O'Connell v. Turner.*[25] In 1870, the Illinois courts committed Daniel O'Connell to the Chicago Reform School on the ground that he was a vagrant or destitute youth without proper parental care. The parents attacked the child's commitment because he was not convicted of a crime and had been apprehended and confined under a general grant of power to arrest for simple misfortune. The basic legal problem was whether children could be committed to reform schools in the absence of criminal conduct or because of gross misconduct on the part of their parents.

The law was held to be unconstitutional; and on subsequent appeal, the court ordered Daniel O'Connell discharged. As Justice Thornton noted in the case: "The warrant of commitment does not indicate that the arrest was made for a criminal offense. Hence, we conclude, that it was made under the general grant of power to arrest and confine for misfortune."[26] The fact that the court distinguished between criminal acts and those arising from misfortune was significant, for all legislation dealing with misfortune cases was subsequently appealed as a direct result of the *O'Connell* decision. Also, as Sanford Fox indicates, the *O'Connell* case changed the course of events in Illinois. The Chicago Reform School was closed in 1872, and the case encouraged procedural due process reform for committed youths.[27]

Reform School Movement of the Late Nineteenth Century

Despite the *Crouse* and *O'Connell* decisions, state intervention into the lives of children continued throughout the latter portion of the nineteenth century and well into the twentieth century. The childsavers influenced state and local governments, for example, to create institutions, called reform schools, exclusively devoted to the care of vagrant and delinquent youth. State institutions opened in Westboro, Massachusetts, in 1848 and in Rochester, New York, in 1849.[28] These were soon followed by institutional programs in other states—Ohio in 1850 and Maine, Rhode Island, and Michigan in 1860.[29] Children lived in congregate conditions and spent their days working at institutional jobs, learning a trade where possible and receiving some basic education. They were racially and sexually segregated, discipline was harsh and often involved whipping and isolation, and the physical care was of poor quality.

Some viewed houses of refuge and reform schools as humanitarian answers to poorhouses and prisons for vagrant, neglected, and delinquent youth, but many remained opposed to such programs. For example, as an alternative, New York philanthropist Charles Brace helped develop the Childrens Aid Society in 1853.[30] Brace's formula for dealing with neglected and delinquent youth was to rescue them from the harsh environment of the city and provide them with temporary shelter care. He then sought to place them in private homes throughout the country. This program was very similar to foster home care programs today. As Fox points out, "The great value to be placed on family life for deviant and crime-prone children was later explicitly set forth in the juvenile court act."[31]

Although the child reformers provided services for children, they were unable to stop juvenile delinquency. Most reform schools were unable to hold youthful law violators and reform them. Institutional life was hard. Large numbers of children needing placement burdened the public finances supporting such programs. Thus, while state control over vagrant, delinquent, and neglected children became more widespread after the Civil War, it also became more controversial. As the country grew, it became evident that private charities and public organizations were not caring adequately for the growing number of troubled youths.

Individual reform groups continued to lobby for government control over children, but the commitment of children under *parens patriae* without due process of law began to be questioned. Why should parents have their children taken away from them. What was in the best interest of the child in terms of proper parental care? Should minors be imprisoned for being vagrants? What right did the state have to place in reform school children who did not violate the criminal law? These and other questions began to plague reformers and those interested in the plight of children. Institutional deficiencies, the detention of delinquent children in adult jails and prisons, the handling of poor, dependent, ignorant, and noncriminal delinquents by inadequate private child welfare organizations without due process, and the religious segregation of children all formed the basis for the idea that a juvenile court should be established.

THE ESTABLISHMENT OF THE ILLINOIS JUVENILE COURT IN 1899

Against the background of the early reform efforts of the childsavers, the well-known Illinois Juvenile Court Act was passed in 1899. This was a major event in the history of the juvenile justice movement in this country. Its significance was such that by 1917 juvenile courts had been established in all but three states.

What exactly did the passage of the Illinois Juvenile Court Act mean? Not surprisingly, different commentators have explained it differently. The traditional interpretation is that the reformers had the highest motives and passed legislation that would serve the best interests of the child. Justice Abe Fortas takes this position in the *In re Gault* case (1967):

The early reformers were appalled by adult procedures and penalties and by the fact that children could be given long prison sentences and mixed in jails with hardened criminals. They were profoundly convinced that society's duty to the child could not be confined by the concept of justice alone. . . . The child—essentially good, as they saw it—was to be made to feel that he was the object of the state's care and solicitude, not that he was under arrest or on trial. . . . The idea of crime and punishment was to be abandoned. The child was to be treated and rehabilitated and the procedures from apprehension through institutionalization were to be clinical rather than punitive.[32]

The traditional interpretation was that the reformers were imbued with a positivistic philosophy and emphasized individual values and judgments about children and their care. Society was to be concerned with where children came from, what their problems were, and how these problems could be handled in the interests of the children and of the state.

On the other hand, revisionist commentators such as Anthony Platt have suggested that the reform movement actually expressed the vested interests of a particular group. According to Platt:

> The child savers should not be considered humanists: (1) their reforms did not herald a new system of justice but rather expedited traditional policies which had been informally developed during the nineteenth century; (2) They implicitly assume the natural dependence of adolescents and created a special court to impose sanctions on premature independents and behavior unbecoming to youth; (3) Their attitudes toward delinquent youth were largely paternalistic and romantic but their commands were backed up by force; (4) they promoted correctional programs requiring longer terms of imprisonment, longer hours of labor, and militaristic discipline, and the inculcation of middle class values and lower class skills.[33]

Thus, according to the revisionist approach, the reformers applied the concept of *parens patriae* for their own purposes, including the continuance of middle- and upper-class values, the control of political systems, and the furtherance of a child labor system consisting of marginal and lower-class skilled workers. Sanford Fox, in his classic article on the history of juvenile justice reform, describes what the juvenile court came to be after its initial establishment in 1899 in Illinois. According to Fox, the Illinois Act (1) restated the belief in the value of coercive prediction; (2) continued nineteenth century summary trials for children about whom the predictions were to be made; (3) made no improvements in the long-condemned institutional care furnished these same children; (4) codified the view that institutions should, even without badly needed financial help from the legislature, replicate family life; and (5) reinforced the private sectarian interest whose role had long been decried by leading child welfare reformers in the area of juvenile care.[34]

Interpretations of its motives and effects differ, but, unquestionably, the Illinois Juvenile Court Act established juvenile delinquency as a legal concept and the juvenile court as a judicial form. Sections of this act are quoted in Highlight 13-1.

Highlight 13-1. Illinois Juvenile Court Act of 1899.

Section 1. Definitions] This act shall apply only to children under the age of 16 years not now or hereafter inmates of a State institution, or any training school for boys or industrial school for girls or some institution incorporated under the laws of this State, except as provided in sections twelve (12) and eighteen (18). For the purposes of this act the words dependent child and neglected child shall mean any child who for any reason is destitute or homeless or abandoned; or dependent upon the public for support; or has not proper parental care or guardianship; or who habitually begs or receives alms; or who is found living in any house of ill fame or with any vicious or disreputable person; or whose home, by reason of neglect, cruelty or depravity on the part of its parents, guardian or other person in whose care it may be, is an unfit place for such a child; and any child under the age of 8 years who is found peddling or selling any article or singing or playing any musical instrument upon the streets or giving any public entertainment. The words delinquent child shall include any child under the age of 16 years who violates any law of this State or any city or village ordinance. The word child or children may mean one or more children, and the word parent or parents may be held to mean one or both parents, when consistent with the intent of this act. The word association shall include any corporation which includes in its purposes the care or disposition of children coming within the meaning of this act.   . . .

§ 3. Juvenile Court] In counties having over 500,000 population the judges of the circuit court shall, at such times as they shall determine, designate one or more of their number whose duty it shall be to hear all cases coming under this act. A special court room, to be designated as the juvenile court room, shall be provided for the hearing of such cases, and the findings of the court shall be entered in a book or books to be kept for that purpose and known as the "Juvenile Record," and the court may, for convenience, be called the "Juvenile Court."

§ 4. Petition to the Court] Any reputable person, being resident in the county, having knowledge of a child in his county who appears to be either neglected, dependent or delinquent, may file with the clerk of a court having jurisdiction in the matter a petition in writing, setting forth the facts, verified by affidavit. It shall be sufficient that the affidavit is upon information and belief.   . . .

§ 6. Probation Officers] The court shall have authority to appoint or designate one or more discreet persons of good character to serve as probation officers during the pleasure of the court; said probation officers to receive no compensation from the public treasury. In case a probation officer shall be appointed by any court, it shall be the duty of the clerk of the court, if practicable, to notify the said probation officer in advance when any child is to be brought before the said court; it shall be the duty of the said

probation officer to make such investigation as may be required by the court; to be present in court in order to represent the interests of the child when the case is heard; to furnish to the court such information and assistance as the judge may require; and to take such charge of any child before and after trial as may be directed by the court.

§ 7. Dependent and Neglected Children] When any child under the age of sixteen (16) years shall be found to be dependent or neglected within the meaning of this act, the court may make an order committing the child to the care of some suitable State institution, or to the care of some reputable citizen of good moral character, or to the care of some training school or an industrial school, as provided by law, or to the care of some association willing to receive it embracing in its objects the purpose of caring or obtaining homes for dependent or neglected children, which association shall have been accredited as hereinafter provided.   . . .

§ 9. Disposition of Delinquent Children] In the case of a delinquent child the court may continue the hearing from time to time and may commit the child to the care and guardianship of a probation officer duly appointed by the court and may allow said child to remain in its own home, subject to the visitation of the probation officer; such child to report to the probation officer as often as may be required and subject to be returned to the court for further proceedings, whenever such action may appear to be necessary, or the court may commit the child to the care and guardianship of the probation officer, to be placed in a suitable family home, subject to the friendly supervision of such probation officer; or it may authorize the said probation officer to board out the said child in some suitable family home, in case provision is made by voluntary contribution or otherwise for the payment of the board of such child, until a suitable provision may be made for the child in a home without such payment; or the court may commit the child, if a boy, to a training school for boys, or if a girl, to an industrial school for girls. Or, if the child is found guilty of any criminal offense, and the judge is of the opinion that the best interest requires it, the court may commit the child to any institution within said county incorporated under the laws of this State for the care of delinquent children, or provided by a city for the care of such offenders, or may commit the child, if a boy over the age of ten years, to the State reformatory, or if a girl over the age of ten years, to the State Home for Juvenile Female Offenders. In no case shall a child be committed beyond his or her minority. A child committed to such institution shall be subject to the control of the board of managers thereof, and the said board shall have power to parole such child on such conditions as it may prescribe, and the court shall, on the recommendation of the board, have power to discharge such child from custody whenever in the judgment of the court his or her reformation shall be complete; or the court may commit the child to the care and custody of some association that will receive it, embracing in its objects the care of neglected and dependent children and that has been duly accredited as hereinafter provided. ...

§ 11. **Children Under Twelve Years Not To Be Committed to Jail]** No court or magistrate shall commit a child under twelve (12) years of age to a jail or police station, but if such child is unable to give bail it may be committed to the care of the sheriff, police officer or probation officer. ...

Source: Illinois Statutes 1899, Section 131.

---

also

The Juvenile Court Act made a major distinction for the first time between children who were dependent and neglected and those who were delinquent. Delinquent children were those under the age of sixteen who violated the laws. The act also established a court specifically for children and an extensive probation program whereby children were to be under the responsibility of probation officers. In addition, the legislation allowed children to be committed to institutions and reform programs under the laws and control of the state.

Although this act can be seen as coercive and perpetuating state control over children, it also can be viewed as making the following positive contributions to the development of a juvenile justice system.

1. Without question, a separate court was established for delinquent, dependent, and neglected children.
2. Special legal procedures were to govern the adjudication and disposition of juvenile matters.
3. Children were to be separated from adults in courts and in institutional programs.
4. Probation programs to assist the court in making decisions in the best interests of the state and the child were to be developed.

Although such leading experts as Fox and Platt believe that the act was not a progressive child care statement, there is no question that it expanded the jurisdiction of the juvenile courts and the child care facilities that came into existence throughout the country.

THE MODERN JUVENILE COURT: 1899–1967

Following the passage of the Juvenile Court Act, similar legislation was enacted throughout the country. The courts created by this legislation became known as special courts. Predelinquent children (neglected, and dependent children) as well as delinquent children were brought before them. These juvenile courts segregated delinquents from adult criminals and attempted to use individual treatment programs to prevent further delinquency. Their jurisdiction during the twentieth century was based primarily on a child's actions and status—not strictly on the basis of violation of the criminal law. Furthermore, since the *parens patriae* philosophy predominated, a form of personalized justice developed, characterized by a procedural laxity and informality that did not provide juvenile offenders with the full panoply of constitutional protections. The court's process was paternalistic rather than adversary in nature. For example, attorneys were not required. Hearsay evidence, inadmissible in criminal trials, was admissible in the adjudication of juvenile offenders. Verdicts were based on a "preponderance of the evidence" instead of being "beyond a reasonable doubt," and children were often not granted any right to appeal their convictions. These characteristics allowed the juvenile court to function in a nonlegal manner and to provide various social services to children in need.

The major functions of the juvenile justice system were to prevent juvenile crime and to rehabilitate juvenile offenders. The function of the two most important actors, the juvenile court judge and the probation staff, was to diagnose the child's condition and prescribe programs to alleviate it. Until 1967, judgments about children's actions and consideration for their constitutional rights were secondary.

By the 1920s, noncriminal behavior in the form of incorrigibility and truancy from school was added to the jurisdiction of many juvenile court systems. Programs of all kinds—including individual counseling and institutional care—were used as methods to cure juvenile criminality. An entire group of new workers—criminologists, sociologists, social workers, probation officers, and psychologists—began to emerge to deal with delinquency and noncriminal behavior. Much of their effort was involved in seeking to rehabilitate children brought before the court.

By 1925, juvenile courts existed in virtually every jurisdiction in every state. Although the juvenile court concept expanded rapidly, it cannot be said that each state implemented the philosophy of the court thoroughly. Some jurisdictions established elaborate juvenile court systems. Others passed legislation but provided no services. Some courts had trained juvenile court judges; others had nonlawyers sitting in juvenile cases. Some courts had extensive probation departments; others had untrained probation personnel. Thus, there was and is great diversity in the practices and procedures of the juvenile justice system.

A number of significant events occurred during the 1960s and affected the development of the juvenile justice system. In 1962, the state of New York passed legislation creating a family court system.[35] The new family court was to assume the responsibility for all matters involving family life. Its particular emphasis was to be on delinquent, dependent, and neglected children and paternity, adoption, and support proceedings involving parents. In addition, the legislation established a separate classification—Person in Need of Supervision (PINS). This category, covering noncriminal behavior, was the forerunner of the legislative categories like Children in Need of Supervision (CHINS), Minors in Need of Supervision (MINS), and Families in Need of Supervision (FINS). These labels covered actions like truancy, running away, and incorrigibility. In using them to establish jurisdiction over children and their families, juvenile courts expanded their role as a social agency. Noncriminal children were now involved in the juvenile court system to a greater degree. Consequently, many juvenile courts had to improve their services as social agencies, and efforts were made to play down the authority of the court as a court of law and increase the personalized system of justice for children.

During the first half of the twentieth century, several constitutional challenges to informal juvenile court processes occurred without much success. In *Haley v. Ohio* in 1948 and *Gallegos v. Colorado* in 1962, the Supreme Court concerned itself with juveniles who were pressured to give statements to the police in violation of their Fourteenth Amendment due process rights.[36] Both Haley and Gallegos were delinquent children whom police had held in custody. Neither of the children had been allowed to see his parents or an attorney. The result was that both gave involuntary statements to the court. However, both cases dealt solely with the issue of self-incrimination, and neither significantly affected the overall informality and procedural inadequacy of the juvenile court system at that time.

Gradually, concern developed that children were not being given their legal rights and, at the same time, were not being rehabilitated. In 1966, the Supreme Court decided the case of *Kent v. United States*, which required regularity in the procedures by which children were transferred from juvenile to adult courts.[37] The decision gave official recognition to the punitive aspects of dealing with juvenile offenders. Furthermore, the task force report on delinquency of the President's Commission on Law Enforcement and Administration of Justice was published in 1967. It expressed deep concern about the ineffectiveness of the juvenile justice system and its lack of procedural safeguards for children. In 1967, the Supreme Court decision of *In re Gault* assured juveniles of due process of law and the right to counsel in the adjudication of their cases.[38] This decision is the latest reappraisal of the juvenile court since its establishment.

History, philosophical ideals, legal decisions, and scientific theories all have influenced the shape of the contemporary juvenile justice system. The characteristics of this system—legal social courts, unclear goals and objectives, abuses of discretion by police and judges, ineffective programs, and unqualified personnel—will be examined in future chapters. We are currently in the midst of a legal revolution in the juvenile justice system. The courts are applying constitutional doctrines of fundamental fairness under the due process clause of the Fourteenth Amendment to guarantee basic rights to juveniles involved in delinquency proceedings.

CHAPTER SUMMARY

This chapter focused on the historical development of juvenile justice from the Middle Ages to the beginning of the twentieth century and the development of the modern juvenile court. First, the chapter described the care of children and the early concepts of family life in the fifteenth and sixteenth centuries. In addition, it explored some of the early concepts of family living, such as dower, primogeniture, and punishment, in an attempt to understand how children and families lived during that period.

What followed was an analysis of the child care movement in the sixteenth, seventeenth, and eighteenth centuries in both Great Britain and colonial America. For Great Britain, the chancery court movement, the Poor Laws, and the apprenticeship programs had a great impact on the lives of children. For colonial America, many of the characteristics of English family living were adopted.

The chapter discussed in much detail developments in Great Britain and in America in the nineteenth century. In Great Britain, for example, neglected delinquent and dependent or runaway children were treated no differently from criminal defendants. Often, children were charged and convicted of crimes through procedures used with adults. However, during this time, because of philosophical shifts in the areas of crime and delinquency as well as a change in the emphasis of the concept of *parens patriae*, steps were begun to reduce the responsibility of children under the criminal law in both Great Britain and America. Some issues that had a strong effect on the development of the juvenile court were the childsaving movement, the development of reform schools, and the problems of urbanization in America.

At the end of the chapter was a summary of the original Illinois Juvenile Court Act and its specific characteristics and goals. Thus, this chapter presented a history of the juvenile justice movement, highlighting the main ideas and factors that led to the creation of the juvenile court movement in this country. The United States Children's Bureau in 1954 interpreted the historical development and philosophy of the juvenile justice system in the following way:

> The essential philosophy of the juvenile court has been called individualized justice. This in essence means that the court recognizes the individuality of the child and adapts its orders accordingly, that it is a legal tribunal where law and science, especially the science of medicine and those sciences which deal with human behavior, such as biology, sociology, and psychology, work side by side, and that its purpose is remedial and to a degree preventive, rather than punitive.[39]

DISCUSSION QUESTIONS

1. What is the relationship between the historical and philosophical approaches to caring for children in the fifteenth, sixteenth, and seventeenth centuries and the understanding of our present juvenile justice system?
2. What factors precipitated the development of the Illinois Juvenile Court Act of 1899? In Great Britain? In America?
3. Such terms as *apprenticeship, Poor Laws, chancery court*, and *parens patriae* exist in the early history of the juvenile court movement. What do these terms mean? Where did the term *delinquency* originate?
4. Throughout history, children have often been treated under the criminal law differently from adults. Prior to the twentieth century, were children held

responsible for criminal actions? Are children responsible for crimes they commit today? Are they liable for civil wrong?

5. One of the most significant reforms in dealing with the juvenile offenders was the opening of the New York House of Refuge in 1825. What was the social and judicial impact of this reform on the juvenile justice system?

6. Two notions about the creation of the juvenile justice system with regard to historical evidence exist today. One is referred to as the traditional interpretation; the other is called the revisionist position. Summarize the characteristics of both positions. What is the childsaving movement?

SUGGESTED READINGS

Baker, Harvey. "Procedure of the Boston Juvenile Court." *Survey* 23 (1910): 643.

Beemsterboer, Matthew. "The Juvenile Court: Benevolence in the Star Chamber." *Journal of Criminal Law, Criminology, and Police Science* 50 (1960): 464.

Bremmer, Robert, ed. Barnard, John; Hareven, Tamara; and Mennel, Robert, asst. eds. *Children and Youth in America: A Documentary History*. Vol. 1. *1600-1685*. Cambridge, Mass.: Harvard University Press, 1970.

Committee on the History of Child-Saving. *History of Child Saving in the United States*. Montclair, N.J.: Patterson Smith, 1971.

Commonwealth v. Fisher, 213 Pa. 48; 62 A. 198 (1905).

Fox, Sanford J. "Juvenile Justice Reform: A Historical Perspective." *Stanford Law Review* 22 (1970): 1187.

Hawes, Joseph M. *Children in Urban Society*. New York: Oxford University Press, 1971.

Ketcham, Orman. "The Unfulfilled Promise of the Juvenile Court." *Crime and Delinquency Journal* 7 (1961): 97.

Lou, Herbert. *Juvenile Courts in the United States*. Charlotte: University of North Carolina Press, 1927.

Mack, Julian. "The Juvenile Court." *Harvard Law Review* 23 (1909): 104.

Mennel, Robert M. *Thorns and Thistles*. Hanover, N.H.: University Press of New England, 1973.

Paulsen, Monroe G., ed. *The Problems of Juvenile Courts and the Rights of Children*. Philadelphia: American Law Institute-American Bar Association, 1975.

Pickett, Robert S. *House of Refuge—Origins of Juvenile Reform in New York State, 1815-1857*. Syracuse, N.Y.: Syracuse University Press, 1969.

Pinchbeck, Ivy, and Hewitt, Margaret. *Children in English Society*. Vols. 1 and 2. London: Routledge and Kegan Paul, 1969.

Platt, Anthony. *The Child Savers*. Chicago: University of Chicago Press, 1969.

————. "The Rise of the Child Saving Movement: A Study in Social Policy and Correctional Reform." *Annals of the American Academy of Political and Social Science* 381 (1969): 2-38.

Powers, Edwin. *Crime and Punishment in Early Massachusetts, 1620-1692*. Boston: Beacon Press, 1966.

President's Commission on Law Enforcement and Administration of Justice. *Task Force Report: Juvenile Delinquency and Youth Crime*. Washington, D.C.: Government Printing Office, 1967.

Rendelman, Douglas R. "Parens Patriae: From Chancery to the Juvenile Court." *South Carolina Law Review* 23 (1971): 205.

Schultz, Edwin. "The Cycle of Juvenile Court History." *Crime and Delinquency Journal* 19 (1973): 457.

Van Waters, Miriam. "The Socialization of Juvenile Court Procedures." *Journal of American Institute of Criminal Law and Criminology* 13 (1922): 61.

William, Amos, and Willford, Charles, eds. *Delinquency Prevention.* Englewood Cliffs, N.J.: Prentice-Hall, 1967.

REFERENCES

1. See Sanford J. Fox, "Juvenile Justice Reform: A Historical Perspective," *Stanford Law Review* 22 (1970): 1187.

2. See Lawrence Stone, *The Family, Sex, and Marriage in England: 1500-1800* (New York: Harper and Row, 1977).

3. See Philipe Fries, *Century of Childhood: A Social History of Family Life* (New York: Vintage Press, 1962).

4. See Douglas R. Rendleman, "Parens Patriae: From Chancery to the Juvenile Court," *South Carolina Law Review* 23 (1971): 205.

5. See Stone, *The Family, Sex, and Marriage in England;* see Stone, ed., Schooling and Society: Studies in the History of Education (Baltimore: Johns Hopkins University Press, 1970).

6. Ibid.

7. See Wiley B. Sanders, *Some Early Beginnings of the Children's Court Movement in England,* National Probation Association Yearbook (New York: National Council on Crime and Delinquency, 1945).

8. Rendleman, "Parens Patriae," p. 205.

9. Douglas Besharov, *Juvenile Justice Advocacy—Practice in a Unique Court* (New York: Practicing Law Institute, 1974), p. 2.

10. *Wellesley v. Wellesley,* 4 Eng. Rep. 1078 (1827).

11. Rendleman, "Parens Patriae," p. 209.

12. See Anthony Platt, "The Rise of the Child Saving Movement: A Study in Social Policy and Correctional Reform," *Annals of the American Academy of Political and Social Science* 381 (1969): 21–38.

13. Robert Bremmer, ed.; and John Barnard, Hareven Tamara, and Robert Mennel, asst. eds., *Children and Youth in America* (Cambridge, Mass.: Harvard University Press, 1970), p. 64.

14. Ibid.

15. Robert M. Mennel, "Origins of the Juvenile Court: Changing Perspectives on the Legal Rights of Juvenile Delinquents," *Crime and Delinquency* .

16. See, generally, Daniel Glaser, *The Effectiveness of a Prison and Parole System* (Indianapolis: Bobbs-Merrill, 1964); and Charles Newman, ed., *Sourcebook on Probation, Parole and Pardons,* 2d ed. (Springfield, Ill.: Charles C Thomas, 1964).

17. Anthony M. Platt, *The Child Savers: The Invention of Delinquency* (Chicago: University of Chicago Press, 1969).

18. Ibid.

19. Fox, "Juvenile Justice Reform," p. 1188.

20. See Robert S. Pickett, *House of Refuge—Origins of Juvenile Reform in New York State, 1815-1857* (Syracuse, N.Y.: Syracuse University Press, 1969).

21. Mennel, "Origins of the Juvenile Court," pp. 69–70.

22.   Ibid., pp. 70–71.

23.   4 Wharton 9 (1839).

24.   Ibid., p. 11.

25.   55 Ill. 280 (1870).

26.   Ibid., p. 283.

27.   Fox, "Juvenile Justice Reform," p. 1217.

28.   See U.S. Department of Justice, Juvenile Justice and Delinquency Prevention, *Two Hundred Years of American Criminal Justice: An LEAA Bicentennial Study* (Washington, D.C.: Law Enforcement Assistance Administration, 1976).

29.   Ibid., pp. 62–74.

30.   Fox, "Juvenile Justice Reform," p. 1229.

31.   Ibid., p. 1211.

32.   *In re Gault*, 387 U.S. 1, 87 S.Ct. 1428, 18 L.Ed. 2d 527 (1967).

33.   Platt, *The Child Savers*, p. 116.

34.   Fox, "Juvenile Justice Reform," p. 1229.

35.   See Family Court Act, State of New York, Article 7, Sec. 712.

36.   332 U.S. 596, 68 S.Ct. 302 (1948); 370 U.S. 49, 82 S.Ct. 1209 (1962).

37.   383 U.S., 86 S.Ct. 1045, 541 (1966).

38.   387 U.S. 1, 87 S.Ct. 1428 (1967).

39.   U.S. Children's Bureau, National Probation and Parole Association, *Standards for Specialized Courts Dealing with Children* (Washington, D.C.: Government Printing Office, 1954), p. 1.

Chapter 14

Chapter Outline	Key Terms, Names, and Cases
Introduction	waiver
Supreme Court Decisions	status offenders
The Juvenile Justice Process and Lower	Sheldon Glueck
Court Decisions	Judge Baker
Organization of Juvenile Courts	Margarite Warren
Juvenile Court Jurisdiction	*In re* Gault
Criticisms of Juvenile Court	Kent v. U.S.
Chapter Summary	*In re* Winship
	McKeiver v. Pennsylvania
	Breed v. Jones
	Morrissey v. Brewer
	jurisdiction
	Mapp v. Ohio
	Miranda v. Arizona
	Gideon v. Wainwright
	State v. Redeman
	In re Marsh
	In re Nelson
	People v. Lara
	CHINS
	West v. U.S.
	U.S. v. Wade
	Kirby v. Illinois
	Baldwin v. Lewis
	Doe v. State
	In re Roberts
	Lamb v. Brown

The Legal Rights
of Juveniles

INTRODUCTION

The purpose of this chapter is to review the legal aspects of the juvenile justice system and the rights of juveniles processed in it. The first section considers the major Supreme Court decisions concerning constitutional requirements for juvenile proceedings. The next section examines lower court decisions concerning constitutional issues of due process as well as statutory interpretations or changes in juvenile statutes. This section seeks to explain some of the constitutional issues being raised in juvenile courts.

Next, the chapter looks briefly at the organization of the juvenile courts. The modern juvenile court is a specialized court for children, but its form and structure are different in each jurisdiction. Some states have a family court system, others a juvenile court structure, and still others juvenile proceedings within the criminal court system. This section gives considerable attention to an analysis and critique of the juvenile court structure today. The chapter goes on to discuss the jurisdiction of the juvenile court. The juvenile court has extensive authority over children who commit delinquent acts as well as noncriminal behavior. This part of the chapter will review such issues as subject matter jurisdiction, age determination, and interstate jurisdiction. Finally, the chapter discusses criticisms of the juvenile court.

SUPREME COURT DECISIONS

In today's society a child is considered a person under the United States Constitution. When a state or the federal government moves against a child and threatens to take away his or her liberties, the child is entitled to due process rights and procedures under the Bill of Rights, as applied to the states through the Fourteenth Amendment. In many respects, the rights of children in the juvenile justice system are similar to those of adults in the criminal justice system. As Justice Hugo Black stated in the landmark case *In re Gault:*

When a person, infant or adult, can be seized by the state, charged and convicted, for violating a state criminal law, and then ordered by the state to be confined for six years, I think the Constitution requires that he be tried in accordance with the guarantees of all the provisions of the Bill of Rights, made applicable to the states by the Fourteenth Amendment. Appellants are entitled to these rights not because fairness, impartiality and orderliness, in short, the essentials of due process require them and not because they are the procedural rules which have been fashioned from the generality of due process, but because they are specifically and unequivocably granted by provisions of the Fifth and Sixth Amendments which the Fourteenth Amendment makes applicable to the states.

Undoubtedly, it would be a plain denial of equal protection of the laws—an invidious discrimination—to deny children, because they are children, the constitutional safeguards enjoyed by adults.

The Supreme Court has set forth the role of due process in juvenile justice through five major decisions made within the last two decades. In so doing, it has held that juveniles are entitled to a wide range of procedural safeguards that were previously denied them. The first of these cases was *Kent v. the United States,* decided in 1966.[2] In the *Kent* case, the juvenile court had waived its jurisdiction over the child, permitting his prosecution in a criminal court. Kent attacked the criminal conviction, alleging errors in the juvenile court's waiver proceeding. The Supreme Court reversed the conviction and held that the District of Columbia Juvenile Court Act Waiver Provisions were invalid. In so doing, the Court agreed that Kent had a right to a hearing on waiver to the adult court, access to social service reports, and a statement of reasons supporting a decision to waive jurisdiction to the adult court. Thus, in the *Kent* case, the Court held that a transfer proceeding was a critically important stage in the juvenile process and must hold to at least minimal due process and fair treatment standards as required by the Fourteenth Amendment.

In the case of *In re Gault,* which was decided in 1967, the Supreme Court further articulated the basic requirements of due process that must be satisfied in juvenile court proceedings. It held that a juvenile in an adjudicatory hearing must be afforded the following due process rights:

1. The child must be given adequate notice of the charges.
2. The child and the parent must be advised of the right to be represented by counsel.
3. The child has a constitutional privilege against self-incrimination.
4. The child has the right of confrontation and sworn testimony of witnesses available for cross-examination.

The *Gault* decision literally reshaped the constitutional and the philosophical structure of the juvenile court system. As a result, those working in the system—judges, social workers, attorneys, and the like—were faced with the problem of reaffirming the rehabilitative ideal of the juvenile court while ensuring that juveniles received proper procedural due process rights.

Following the *Gault* case, the Supreme Court decided *In re Winship* in 1970. This case considered the problem of the quantum of proof required in juvenile delinquency adjudications.[3] Prior to the *Winship* case, most juvenile courts judged the sufficiency of evidence in juvenile matters by applying a preponderance of the evidence, or clear and convincing evidence, test. In *Winship*, the Court rejected the idea that the juvenile system was a civil system and held that the Fourteenth Amendment due process clause required that delinquency charges in juvenile court be proved beyond a reasonable doubt.

This movement toward broader procedural protections for juveniles was temporarily halted in 1971 with the ruling in the case of *McKeiver v. Pennsylvania.*[4] In *McKeiver*, the Court decided that juveniles were not to be afforded the constitutional right to a trial by jury in a delinquency proceeding. The Court expressed its concern that juries in juvenile courts would impinge upon the interests of the state and the public in conducting juvenile court proceedings in an efficient, reasonably informal, and flexible manner. What the Court was saying was that a jury trial for juveniles was not essential to a fair and accurate fact-finding process in the juvenile court system.

Since the *McKeiver* case, however, the Court has redirected itself to expanding due process protection for juveniles. In the 1975 case of *Breed v. Jones*, the Court held that the double jeopardy provisions of the Fifth Amendment be used in a hearing where a juvenile is being considered for transfer to the criminal court as well as being adjudicated a delinquent.[5] Thus, the *Breed* decision forbids the criminal trial of a juvenile after he or she has been tried as a delinquent in the juvenile court for the same offense. Transfer for criminal prosecution must occur prior to any adjudication of the child in the juvenile court.

The future course of constitutional decisions affecting the rights of juveniles in the juvenile justice system is difficult to predict. Certainly the thrust of the Supreme Court has been clear over the past decade. Due process and fair treatment must be accorded juveniles throughout the entire juvenile justice process. Generally speaking, the Court's decisions and opinions have been confined primarily to the procedural aspects of the adjudicatory stages of juvenile proceedings. In the *Kent, Gault,* and *Winship* cases, the majority opinions expressed deep concern and skepticism about the rehabilitative promises of the juvenile court system. As a result, these opinions responded more to the need for procedural due process rights. However, the *McKeiver* decision reflected a shift back to the rehabilitative ideal and the informality and paternal protection of the juvenile court in preference to further formalizing court proceedings. The *Breed* decision sought to balance the juvenile's interest in procedural protections and the rehabilitative goals of the juvenile justice system.

Thus, with the exception of *McKeiver*, over the past fifteen years the Court has regularly granted to children due process guarantees that are similar to those of adult defendants in the criminal justice system. Whether that trend will continue remains to be seen. However, as Justice Harry A. Blackmun stated in the *McKeiver* case: "If the formalities of the criminal adjudicative process are to be superimposed upon the juvenile court system, there is little need for its separate existence. Perhaps that ultimate disillusionment will come one day, but for the moment we are disinclined to give impetus to it."[6] This statement implies that the Court intends to deal with juvenile rights on a case by case basis.

Obviously, many constitutional questions involving the rights of juveniles have not been decided. Such issues include the right to bail, the right to treatment in institutions, the right to counsel at lineup, the right to a jury trial, and the rights of juveniles in institutional programs. The Court will probably decide these and other issues separately and on the basis of principles enunciated in *In re Gault*. As Justice Abe Fortas stated in the *Gault* case:

Juvenile court history has again demonstrated that unbridled discretion, however benevolently motivated, is frequently a poor substitute for principle and procedure. . . . The absence of procedural rule based on constitutional principle has not always produced fair, efficient and effective procedures. Departure from established due process has frequently resulted not in enlightened procedure but in arbitrariness.[7]

Future Supreme Court decisions on juvenile matters will thus be decided on a case by case basis and will reflect the Court's determination that a particular practice violates the due process clause of the Fourteenth Amendment of the Constitution.

THE JUVENILE JUSTICE PROCESS AND LOWER COURT DECISIONS

Throughout the 1960s and 1970s, the Supreme Court significantly increased constitutional safeguards for the adult criminal offender. Nearly all the provisions of the Bill of Rights were made applicable to the states through the due process clause of the Fourteenth Amendment. Many of these decisions affected pretrial, trial, and posttrial constitutional rights of defendants. *Mapp v. Ohio*, for example, extended the exclusionary rule (preventing the admission of illegally obtained evidence at trial) to state court proceedings.[8] The case of *Escobedo v. Illinois* held that a state must afford the accused the right to counsel in a police station.[9] In the famous case of *Miranda v. Arizona*, the Court defined the defendant's Fifth Amendment privilege against self-incrimination when taken into custody.[10] In the case of *Gideon v. Wainwright*, the Court established the right of a defendant in a felony trial to have counsel in a state prosecution.[11] *Barker v. Wingo* decision set out the criteria by which to judge whether the Sixth Amendment right to a speedy trial is being violated.[12] As a result of these decisions and others affecting the adult process, children have been granted similar protections. In addition, the landmark juvenile decision of *In re Gault*, although specifically applicable to the trial process, served to extend constitutional guarantees of due process to juveniles during pre- and postadjudication proceedings.

Thus, the constitutional due process revolution in the adult system had a significant impact on the development of rights in the juvenile justice system. Particularly in the lower courts, it has produced a great deal of litigation, which is reviewing juvenile justice codes and practices in light of constitutional questions. What follows is a review of significant lower court decisions affecting juvenile rights during the pre-judicial, adjudicatory, and dispositional stages of the juvenile justice system.

The Arrest Stage of the Juvenile Process

Judicial limitations on police discretion in the investigation of offenses involving juveniles are similar to the limitations applied to adult offenders.

When a juvenile is apprehended, the police must decide whether to release the child or refer him or her to the juvenile court. Cases involving serious crimes against property or persons are often referred to court. On the other hand, minor disputes between juveniles, school and neighborhood complaints, petty shoplifting cases, runaways, and minor person-oriented assualts and batteries are diverted from court action. To make the decision, the police must investigate the juvenile as they would an adult. In the case of *In re Joseph S.*, a youth was spontaneously identified at the police station by one of the victims in an assault and battery case.[13] Later, the child was asked to sign a written confession and agreed to do so. The child's counsel subsequently filed motions to suppress the show-up identification and the confession. On appeal, the court denied the motion, arguing that the action in the police station neither resulted from the use of an illegal lineup nor affected the core identification of the child. However, the superior court granted the motion to suppress the confession, concluding that counsel was not present at the time of the confession and that the juvenile may not knowingly have waived his right to representation. This is an example of a lower court decision securing for juveniles a right that is extended to adults—the right to be protected during identification and interrogation.

The criteria for the lawful arrest of a juvenile are generally similar to those governing arrest procedures for adults. Some juvenile codes give broader legislative authority to take children into custody because it is believed to be for their general welfare. However, the courts often limit this jurisdiction. *In re Moten* deals with the issue of procedural due process during arrest.[14] Moten was taken into custody after an altercation with police officers who had entered her home to locate a runaway. When the officers attempted to take the runaway into custody, Moten protested and was in turn arrested herself. The arrest was overturned on appeal when the court found that the police had entered Moten's home without sufficient authority. On rehearing, the resisting arrest charge was upheld on the ground of reasonableness.

The case of *State v. Redeman* deals with the problem of showing sufficient probable cause before issuing arrest warrants for juveniles.[15] Redeman was picked up on a warrant that was issued because of the statements of an accomplice. He appealed on the ground that the warrant was improperly issued. The court agreed that probable cause must be shown in order to take a child into custody. Currently, lawyers are challenging many juvenile arrest statutes because of their vagueness. Common terms such as "out of control," "habitual," "ungovernable," or "loitering" do not really describe the conduct that the statutes are supposed to be controlling. Thus, it is often possible to challenge their vagueness.

Search and Seizure

Once juveniles have been taken into custody, they have the same constitutional right to be free from unreasonable searches and seizures as adults. The Fourth Amendment states:

The right of the people to be secure in their persons, houses, papers, and effects, against unreasonable searches and seizures, shall not be violated, and no Warrants shall issue, but upon probable cause, supported by Oath or affirmation, and particularly describing the place to be searched, and the person or things to be siezed.

Most courts have held in state jurisdictions that the Fourth Amendment ban against unreasonable searches and seizures applies to juveniles in delinquency proceedings and that illegally seized evidence is inadmissible in a juvenile trial. To exclude incriminating evidence, a child's attorney makes a pretrial motion to suppress the evidence—the same procedure used in the adult criminal process. The *In re Marsh* case was an appeal from a probation revocation order in which the petitioner, arrested on a firearms violation, charged that illegally seized evidence was used in error during the revocation hearing.[16] The case of *Ciulla v. State* takes up the question of what constitutes the seizure of inadmissible evidence. Here the court ruled Cuilla's arrest to be unlawful at the time of the search and declared the marijuana that the child had in his possession to be inadmissible. The court declared: "A minor has the same constitutional right to be secure in his person from all unreasonable seizures as has an adult. The Fourteenth Amendment and the Bill of Rights protect minors as well as adults."[17] Another Fourth Amendment issue involving juveniles is whether the juvenile can be searched for less than probable cause. Probable cause must be shown in order to arrest adults who commit felonies. In the case of *Moss v. Weaver*, the court warned against a lesser standard for juveniles. Mere suspicion alone does not justify police officers searching a juvenile.[18]

On of the most difficult search and seizure problems peculiar to juveniles is whether it is constitutionally valid for a school official to search children or their possessions. That issue is discussed in Chapter 15.

Custodial Interrogation and the Fifth Amendment

Normally, parents are contacted immediately after a child is taken into custody. In years past, the police often questioned juveniles without their parents or even an attorney present. Any incriminatory statements or confessions that the juveniles made could be used in evidence at their trials. However, in 1966 the landmark Supreme Court case *Miranda v. Arizona* placed constitutional limitations on police interrogation procedures used with adult offenders. *Miranda* held that persons in police custody must be given the following warnings:

1. They have the right to remain silent.
2. Any statements they make can be used against them.
3. They have the right to counsel.
4. If they cannot afford counsel, it will be furnished at public expense.[19]

These warnings, which secure the adult defendant's Fifth Amendment privilege against self-incrimination, have been made applicable to children taken into custody. The Supreme Court case of *In re Gault* stated that constitutional privileges against self-incrimination are applicable in juvenile as well as adult cases. *In re Gault* implies that *Miranda v. Arizona* applies to custodial interrogation of juvenile offenders in the pre-judicial stage of the juvenile process. State court jurisdictions seem to be applying the requirements of *Miranda* to juvenile proceedings as well.

In re Nelson discusses the interrogation of juveniles at the station house; it also touches on the application of *Miranda* under such circumstances.[20] The case of *U.S. v. Barfield* analyzes the use of verbal coercion by law enforcement agents in obtaining information from juveniles.[21] Here the court ruled that threats of long sentences, if cooperation was not given to the police by the child, are invalid where there was reasonable chance that the child would be physically harmed or otherwise punished. The 1948 Supreme Court case of Haley v. *Haley v. Ohio* illustrates the Court's initial effort to limit police discretion during interrogation procedures for juveniles.[22] The case concerned the admissibility of a confession taken from a fifteen-year-old boy on trial for first degree murder. The Court decided that there were no differences between children and adults threatened by the criminal process and that both should have the constitutional protection of due process.

One of the most difficult problems associated with the custodial interrogation of children has to do with their waiver of *Miranda* rights. This issue has resulted in considerable lower court litigation. The question is: Can juveniles knowingly and willingly waive the rights given to them by *Miranda v. Arizona* without the aid of counsel or parents? Some courts have concluded that it is not essential for parents or attorneys to be present for children to effectively waive their rights. Other courts require the presence of parents or attorneys. In *People v. Lara*, the court said that the question of a child's waiver is to be determined by the totality of the circumstances doctrine.[23] This means that the validity of a waiver rests not only on the age of the child but on a combination of other factors, including intelligence, education, and comprehension. *West v. U.S.* provides the most extensive list of such factors.[24] The general rule is that juveniles can intentionally waive their rights to protection from self-incrimination, but the validity of this waiver is a question of fact to be determined by the circumstances of each case. Highlight 1-1, the *Fare v. Michael C.* case, is the most recent example of this problem.

Highlight 14-1. Fare v. Michael C.

Facts: Michael C. was implicated in the murder of Robert Yeager, which occurred during a robbery of Yeager's home. A small truck registered in the name of Michael's mother was identified as having been near the Yeager home at the time of the killing, and a young man answering Michael's description was seen by witnesses near the truck and near the home shortly before Yeager was murdered.

On the basis of this information, the police of Van Nuys, California, arrested Michael at approximately 6:30 P.M. on February 4. He was then 16½ years old and on probation to the juvenile court. He had been on probation since the age of 12. Approximately one year earlier he had served a term in a youth corrections camp under the supervision of the juvenile court. He had a record of several previous offenses, including burglary of guns and purse snatching, stretching back over several years.

When Michael arrived at the Van Nuys station house, two police officers began to interrogate him. No one else was present during the interrogation. The conversation was tape recorded. One of the officers initiated the interview by informing Michael that he had been brought in for questioning

---

in relation to a murder. The officer fully advised him of his *Miranda* rights. The following exchange then occurred:

Q: Do you understand all of these rights as I have explained them to you?

A: Yeah.

Q: Okay, do you wish to give up your right to remain silent and talk to us about this murder?

A: What murder? I don't know about no murder.

Q: Do you want to give up your right to have an attorney present here while we talk about it?

A: Can I have my probation officer here?

Q: Well I can't get a hold of your probation officer right now. You have a right to an attorney.

A: (How I know you guys won't pull no police officer in and tell me he's an attorney?)

Q: Your probation officer is Mr. Christiansen.

A: Yeah.

Q: Well I'm not going to call Mr. Christiansen tonight. There's a good chance we can talk to him later, but I'm not going to call him right now. If you want to talk to us without an attorney present, you can. If you don't want to, you don't have to. But if you want to say something, you can, and if you don't want to say something you don't have to. That's your right. You understand that right?

A: Yeah.

Q: Okay, will you talk to us without an attorney present?

A: Yeah, I want to talk to you.

Michael thereupon proceeded to answer questions. He made statements and drew sketches that incriminated him in the Yeager murder.

Largely on the basis of Michael's incriminating statements, probation authorities filed a petition in juvenile court alleging that he had murdered Robert Yeager and that he should be made a ward of the juvenile court.

The California Supreme Court reversed the conviction, holding that Michael's request to see his probation officer negated any possible willingness on his part to discuss his case with the police and thereby invoked his Fifth Amendment privilege.

Decision: Michael alleged that statements had been obtained from him in violation of *Miranda* because his request to see his probation officer at the outset of the questioning invoked his Fifth Amendment right to remain silent, just as if he had requested the assistance of an attorney. Accordingly, Michael argued that since the interrogation did not cease until he had a chance to confer with his probation officer, the statements and sketches could not be admitted against him in the juvenile court proceedings.

The Supreme Court reversed and remanded in an opinion by Justice Blackmun. The *Miranda* rule that prior to interrogation the state must warn the accused of the right to an attorney and of the right to remain silent unless an attorney is present "has the virtue of informing police and prosecutors with specificity as to what they may do in conducting custodial interrogation, and of informing courts under what circumstances statements obtained during such interrogation are not admissible," the Court said. In this case, the California court had significantly extended the rule, it continued, and had ignored the basis of the *Miranda* rule, which is the "critical position" lawyers occupy in our legal system. Probation officers frequently are not trained in the law, and moreover they are employees of the state, duty bound to report wrongdoing by the juvenile. "In these circumstances," the Court said, "it cannot be said that the probation officer is able to offer the type of independent advice that an accused would expect from a lawyer retained or assigned to assist him during questioning."

The Court also rejected the contention that the youth's request constituted a request to remain silent. On the basis of the record, his replies show that he "voluntarily and knowingly waived his Fifth Amendment rights."

Significance of Case: The *Fare v. Michael*

C. case applied the "totality of the circumstances" approach to the interrogation of juveniles. The question of whether the accused waived his rights is one of substance, not form. Did the defendant knowingly and voluntarily waive the rights delineated in *Miranda*? The juvenile court was originally correct. The transcript of the interrogation took care to ensure that Michael understood his rights. The police fully explained that he was being questioned in connection with a murder. They informed him of all the rights delineated in *Miranda* and ascertained that he understood them. Nothing indicates that Michael failed to understand what the

officers told him. Moreover, after his request to see his probation officer had been denied, and after the police officer once more had explained his rights to him, he clearly expressed his willingness to waive his rights and continue the interrogation.

In addition, the Court held that the *Miranda* rule should not be extended to include a juvenile's request to see his or her probation officer. Such a request does not have the same effect as the request to see a lawyer.

Source: This material is a summary of the *Fare v. Michael C.* case, 442 U.S. 23, 99 S.Ct. 2560 (1979).

Identification from Lineups

Another important issue arises in the early police processing of juvenile offenders. Should the constitutional safeguards established for adult offenders to protect them during lineups and other forms of identification be applied to juvenile proceedings. In *U.S. v. Wade*, the Supreme Court held that the accused has a right to have counsel present at postindictment lineup procedures and that pretrial identification is inadmissible when the right to counsel is violated.[25] The Court further clarified this issue in *Kirby v. Illinois*, holding that the defendant's right to counsel at pretrial identification proceedings goes into effect only after the complaint for indictment has been issued.[26] Based on these decisions, courts have ruled that juveniles also have constitutional protection during lineup and identification procedures. They have a right to counsel at a police lineup once they are charged with a delinquent act, and if this right is violated, the pretrial identification is excluded. For example, in the case of *In re Holley*, a juvenile accused of rape did not have counsel during the lineup identification procedure. In reversing Holley's conviction, the appellate court said that absence of counsel during Holley's lineup precluded the child from having a fair trial.[27]

Pretrial Release and Juvenile Detention

For the most part, the Supreme Court has not examined the constitutional issues in the pre-judicial stage of the juvenile justice process, that is, the state when a decision is made either to release a child to the parent or guardian or to detain the child in shelter care pending trial. Issues here include juvenile detention, bail, and the admission of guilt by the child. There have been numerous state decisions, and all the states provide for such procedures in their statutes and appellate decisions. However, the case law and statutes vary widely. Most state statutes ordinarily require a hearing on detention if the initial decision is to keep the child in custody. The case of *In re William M.* arose because a California court failed to conduct a legislatively prescribed detention hearing.[28] At a detention hearing, the child has a right to counsel and is generally given other procedural due process safeguards, notably the privilege against self-incrimination and the right to confront and cross-examine witness. In addition, most state juvenile court acts provide criteria to be used in deciding to detain a child. These include: (1) the need to protect the child, (2) the likelihood that the child presents a serious danger to the public, and (3) the likelihood that the child will return to court for adjudication. Unlike the adult system, where the sole criterion for pretrial release is availability for trial, a child can be detained for other reasons.

If the child is to be detained, the question of bail arises. Here, the statutes and cases vary widely. Some states allow juveniles to be released on bail; others do not. Many states accept the release of the child to the parent as a substitute for bail. The laws are also unclear about whether juveniles have a state or federal constitutional right to bail. Some courts have found it unnecessary to rule on the issue because liberal release provisions act as an appropriate alternative to the bail process. The cases of *Baldwin v. Lewis* and *Rivera v. Freeman* represent such decisions.[29] On the other hand, in the case of *Doe v. State,* the supreme court of Alaska found that children have a right to remain free pending their adjudication.[30] This decision seems to imply that children have the same right to release on bail that adults have. *Doe v. State* is the state court decision that comes closest to the principle that the juvenile has a constitutional right to bail.

Pleas

A child can plead guilty or not guilty to a juvenile delinquency or noncriminal behavior petition. Some jurisdictions seek to minimize the use of adult criminal standards by using other terminology, such as *agree to a finding* or *deny the petition.* If the child pleads not guilty, the court ordinarily sets a date for trial. If juveniles admit to the charges against them, the juvenile court normally requires that they know of their right to a trial, that the plea or admission be made voluntarily, and that they understand the charges and consequences of the plea. These requirements are quite similar to those established for adult offenders.

Plea Bargaining

The majority of juvenile court cases that are not adjudicated seem to be the result of open admissions rather than actual plea bargaining. Unlike the adult system, where 70 to 90 percent of all charged offenders are involved in some plea bargaining, there is less plea bargaining in the juvenile court. In fact, the National Advisory Commission on Criminal Justice Standards and Goals recommends that plea bargaining in all forms be eliminated from both the adult and juvenile processes.[31]

The Transfer of Jurisdiction
to the Adult Criminal Justice System

Prior to the development of the first modern juvenile court in Illinois in 1899, juveniles were tried in adult criminal courts. The subsequent creation of the juvenile court systems eliminated this problem. However, the juvenile system did recognize that certain crimes required children to be tried as adults. Today, most jurisdictions provide by statute for waiver or transfer of juvenile offenders to the criminal courts. Because of the effect of the waiver decision on the child, a considerable amount of litigation has been heard before the various state courts and before the Supreme Court on this issue.

The case of *Kent v. U.S.* challenged the provisions of a District of Columbia code that stated that the juvenile court could waive jurisdiction after a full investigation. *Kent v. U.S.* was the first steps in establishing minimum requirements of due process of law in waiver proceedings. The Michigan case of *People v. Fields* reviewed the question of whether the legislature must establish suitable criteria when juveniles are to be treated as adults.[32] In this case the Court determined that a Michigan statute was unconstitutional because it supplied no criteria for the transfer of a child to the adult court.

Adjudication

If a child remains in the juvenile court, an adjudicatory or fact-finding hearing reviews the evidence on the allegations in the petition. The Court decided in *In re Gault* that the concept of fundamental fairness be made applicable to juvenile delinquency proceedings in the adjudication phase. In other words, it ruled that the due process clause of the Fourteenth Amendment requires procedural guarantees in the adjudication of delinquency cases. Such guarantees include the right to counsel, the right to fair notice of charges, the right to confrontation and cross-examination, and, of course, the right to refrain from self-incrimination. In addition, the Court has held that proof in a juvenile prosecution must be beyond a reasonable doubt.

On the other hand, in the area of the right to a trial by jury, the Supreme Court has declared in the case of *McKeiver v. Pennsylvania*, that the Fourteenth Amendment does not require the state to provide juveniles with a jury trial. The state courts continue to grapple with many legal issues in the area of adjudication. The issues include the need for an impartial judge, the right to effective counsel, the application of criminal rules of evidence in juvenile court proceedings, the right to a jury trial for juveniles, and, of course, the possibility of a public hearing in juvenile proceedings.

Disposition

After adjudication, the child is brought before the court for a disposition. The court decides what sentence should be imposed in light of the child's offense, prior record, and family background. Most jurisdictions have statutes that require a separate dispositional hearing. In the lower court case of *In re Roberts*, a

Maryland juvenile court did not hold a separate dispositional hearing for a child.[33] As a result of this procedural defect, the appeals court returned the case to the juvenile court. In the case of *In re Robert F.*, the appellate court found it necessary to vacate the placement because Robert's attorney was absent during the dispositional hearing.[34] In the case of *Cecilia R.*, the appellate court of New York decided that a dispositional hearing should not proceed in the absence of the juvenile herself.[35] Numerous cases deal with the actual disposition of the child to either probation or institutional care. In the case of *In re Stanley M.*, the court required that all community-based remedies and programs be explored and exhausted before a child is incarcerated.[36] In the *Ellery C.* decision, a child characterized as a Person in Need of Supervision was confined at a New York State training school.[37] The Legal Aid Society appealed the confinement, maintaining that PINS children are statutorily and constitutionally denied a right to treatment when confined with juvenile delinquents. The court concluded that appropriate supervision and treatment were not provided in the training school but that no viable programs were available for PINS children elsewhere either. Consequently, the distinction between PINS and delinquent children was useless. For Ellery C., the immediate result was release. The decision was expected to be a milestone in juvenile rights, but it has not resulted in any significant changes with respect to treatment and services provided to incarcerated juveniles.

Postdispositional Legal Problems

The lower courts have also litigated numerous issues in the postdispositional stage of the juvenile process. Such issues include: (1) the transfer of juveniles to adult institutions, (2) juvenile aftercare services, (3) provisions for appeals, and (4) the statutory or constitutional right to treatment. The early case of *In re Rich* forbade the transfer of a juvenile offender to ad adult facility.[38] However, other courts have taken the position that a child can be sent from a juvenile facility to a penal or a mental health institution if the transfer is in the child's best interest or if it is acceptable to the court.

In the area of juvenile aftercare, when a child is placed on parole, the courts have generally applied constitutional provisions similar to those of the adult system. For example, the case of *Morrissey v. Brewer* held that a parolee is entitled to due process rights upon revocation of parole.[39] Although the Supreme Court has not granted such due process rights to children, many states have adopted administrative regulations requiring juvenile agencies to incorporate similar due process procedures.

So far, the courts have not found that a constitutionally mandated right of appeal exists for a juvenile offender. The right of appeal for both juveniles and adults generally exists by legislative enactment.

Appeal procedures include the right to a free transcript, the need to have counsel present, and the availability of such legal devices as collateral attack of the judgment through the use of extraordinary writs, such as the writ of *certiorari* and the writ of *habeas corpus*.

Finally, there is the question of whether juveniles who are committed to institutions have a right to proper treatment. Numerous courts have dealt with the placement of juveniles in institutions and their right to treatment. This issue is discussed in detail in Chapter 19.

This section has reviewed the legal rights of juvenile offenders processed through the juvenile justice system from arrest to postdisposition. One of the primary questions remains: What standard will the courts adopt for applying rights to juvenile proceedings in the future? Up to now, the Supreme Court has applied the traditional due process standard of fundamental fairness in juvenile justice. Basic procedural rights have been measured against the essentials of due process and fair treatment and not necessarily carved directly out of the United States Constitution or the state constitutions.

The problem with this approach is that it does not clearly determine what rights truly apply to the juvenile process because the term *due process* is vague and does not have precise limits. For example, is a child in the juvenile justice system entitled to all the rights that an adult has in a criminal proceeding? That question generally remains unclear from the point of view of case decisions and statutory law. Furthermore, our research has found some major gaps in the procedural safeguards afforded children as compared to those afforded adult offenders.

One of the major areas requiring further legal clarification is the pretrial stage of the juvenile process. This area has many trouble spots, including detention, the concept of probable cause, the issue of waiver and preliminary types of hearings, pretrial disclosure of information, bail, and the right to an appointed effective counsel throughout all the early proceedings. Similarly, fair procedures are unclear at the disposition stage and need to be further developed. Other problems include the legal requirement for the use of presentence investigation, the establishment of more suitable dispositions, and the need for juvenile court judges to state their reasons for sentences openly.

THE ORGANIZATION OF THE JUVENILE COURT

Today's juvenile court is a specialized court for children. Its organizational structure varies within each state. Juvenile courts can be found as part of a high court of general trial jurisdiction, as a special session of a lower court of trial jurisdiction, as an independent statewide court, or even as part of a broader family court. The juvenile court staff includes a judge, probation people, government prosecutors and defense attorneys, and a variety of social service programs. The juvenile court functions in a sociolegal manner and seeks to promote the rehabilitation of the child within a framework of procedural due process.

As Sanford Fox states, it is important to understand that the juvenile court is part of the total juvenile justice system, a complex of law enforcement, judging, punishing, and helping functions carried on officially and unofficially by a variety of public offices.[40] Some of the court's major characteristics include: (1) a philosophy of rehabilitation; (2) procedural informality within the context of legal rights; (3) the use of social service agencies in dealing with children, particularly at the pre-judicial stages; (4) a heavy emphasis on the social sciences for both diagnosis and treatment at adjudication; (5) a significant deemphasis on incarceration as a method of social control; and (6) the development of postadjudication programs and services.

Most typically juvenile courts in the United States are established as sessions of lower or higher courts of limited or general jurisdiction. Most states establish the juvenile court as a lower court of limited jurisdiction where juvenile jurisdiction is part of a district court, city court, or recorder's court and where the jurisdiction is limited solely to juvenile delinquency matters. Salaries, physical facilities, and even the prestige of the court can all be directly affected by its jurisdictional location. These factors tend to limit the ability of the court to attract competent people (including judges) and to obtain necessary resources from the legislature. It is unclear why juvenile courts have been structured in lower trial courts in many states. Quite possibly it was to provide local attention to juvenile matters. In addition, legislators may have seen the juvenile court as an inferior court, relegated to the lowest level because of its jurisdiction over children. Massachusetts is an example of a state whose juvenile courts are placed in a special session of a lower court of limited trial jurisdiction.[41] It allows juvenile sessions to be heard in its district courts, and it has established special juvenile courts in major urban areas.

On the other hand, an increasing number of states, including California, Illinois, and Wisconsin, place juvenile matters at the highest court of general trial jurisdiction.[42] Here juvenile cases are tried in the more prestigious courts of general jurisdiction. Standard 8.1 of the report of the National Advisory Commission on Criminal Justice Standards and Goals recommends: "The court having jurisdiction over juvenile matters should be at the level of the highest court of general trial jurisdiction and should be a division of that court."[43]

States that deal with juvenile matters at the highest trial court level have an integrated organizational structure that results in more efficient and effective court administration. Such courts are better able to secure the funding they need to improve physical facilities and hire competent judicial and probation personnel.

One of the arguments against placing juvenile matters in the highest court of general trial jurisdiction is that most officials concerned with delinquency believe that a lower court relates more efficiently and effectively to the concerns of parents and young people in local areas. Others have suggested that large states with rural areas often need small localized court systems within their small communities. On the other hand, such states as Florida, Colorado, and even Alaska have placed juvenile matters within the highest courts of general jurisdiction.[44]

Some states have independent juvenile court systems. Often, such systems are referred to as statewide juvenile courts. Separately organized and independent juvenile courts exist in such states as Connecticut and Utah and in parts of other states, such as Georgia and Kansas. Even New York and Hawaii have organized their juvenile courts on a statewide basis, although the New York system is a family court system.[45] The major advantages to the statewide independent system are that it can generally service sparsely populated areas within a given jurisdiction, that it permits judicial personnel and others to deal exclusively with children's matters, and that it can obtain legislative funding far better than other court systems. On the other hand, the very reason for its

existence—obtaining legislative funding—can also act to its detriment. Separately organized juvenile courts encounter resistance from legislative funding
groups concerned with duplication of effort and unwilling to provide resources
for the control and prevention of juvenile delinquency.

The major disadvantage to implementing a family court structure is that it requires major reorganization of the present court system by the legislature. The
costs are substantial, especially in the first few years of the court's existence.
Where family court structures do exist, there is little statistical data to indicate
that they have reduced delinquency or improved family programs. However, it
has become more and more apparent to experts that to treat problems of
intrafamily crime, divorce, adoption, and neglect in separate courts is to encourage inconsistency in court administration and decision making and to
foster an ineffective method of case-flow management.

Thus, it would be preferable to deal with juvenile matters in a family court
system. Assigning such functions to inferior courts of limited jurisdiction leads
to limited resources, lack of credibility, and a questionable framework of legal
standards and safeguards.

JUVENILE COURT JURISDICTION

Juvenile court jurisdiction is established by state statute. Juvenile courts are created by state constitution or by state legislation. The New York family court, for
example, is part of the New York state constitution. Legislation is passed to implement the constitutional mandate and to specify the actual details of the state
court. More often, however, the juvenile courts are created by the authority of
the legislature. Thus, the jurisdiction itself is generally controlled by legislative
enactment. The major areas of juvenile court jurisdiction are discussed in the
following sections.

Age

One of the first factors controlling juvenile court jurisdiction is age. The states
differ over the age that brings children under the jurisdiction of the juvenile
court. Samuel Davis, in *The Rights of Juveniles: The Juvenile Justice System*,
lists all the state jurisdictional ages.[46] Many states, for example, Alaska,
California, Minnesota, and Wyoming, include all children under eighteen.
Others, including Louisiana, Massachusetts, and Michigan, set the upper limit
at under seventeen. Still other jurisdictions, for example, Alabama and
Connecticut, have established the juvenile age as sixteen or under.

In jurisdictions where the maximum age is on the low side, often the criminal
court can transfer persons between the ages of sixteen and eighteen to the juvenile court at its discretion. Some jurisdictions have established jurisdictional
ages that vary according to the sex or geographic location of the juvenile. Recently, however, statutes employing these distinctions have been held to be in
violation of the equal protection clause or due process clause of the Constitution. In the case of *Lamb v. Brown*, an Oklahoma statute that allowed females
under the age of eighteen the benefits of juvenile court proceedings while limit-

ing the same benefits to males under sixteen was held to be unconstitutional.[47]

A few state statutes describe juvenile court jurisdiction in terms of minimum age. Massachusetts, for example, defines the child as a person who is under seventeen but over seven years of age.[48] Normally, what operates is the common law understanding of the responsibility of children. Under the age of seven, children are deemed incapable of committing crimes. Between the ages of seven and fourteen, there is a rebuttable presumption that children do not have the capacity for criminal behavior. Over the age of fourteen, there is the belief that children are responsible for their actions. Thus, the jurisdictional age for children in the juvenile court varies from one state to another. Some states use nineteen, others use eighteen, some use seventeen, and a few use sixteen. As Davis says, by far the most common maximum jurisdictional age is eighteen; that age is accepted as the jursidictional age in more than two-thirds of the states and in the District of Columbia.[49]

Criminal and Noncriminal Behavior

Juvenile court jurisdiction is also based on the nature of the child's actions. If a child commits a crime, this conduct normally falls into the category of juvenile delinquency. Definitions of delinquency vary from state to state, but most are based on the common element of a maximum age as well as on the fact that delinquency is an intentional violation of the criminal law. The New York State Family Court Act defines *juvenile delinquent* as "a person over seven and less than sixteen years of age who does any act which, if done by an adult, would constitute a crime."[50] In New York, a delinquency petition must allege that the child requires supervision and treatment or confinement. Thus, the definition of delinquency is incomplete for jurisdictional purposes unless the petition indicates that the child needs court supervision. In Massachusetts, *juvenile delinquency* is defined as the behavior of children from age seven to age sixteen who violate state or local criminal laws.[51]

On the other hand, juvenile courts also have jurisdiction over status offenders, children whose offenses are not the type of activity for which an adult is normally prosecuted. Numerous juvenile delinquency statutes still include status offenses within their definition. However, many jurisdiction have also separated the PINS and CHINS statutes so that separate petitions and proceedings can be held for children who are runaways, unmanageable, truant, and incorrigible.

The position of the status offender within the juvenile justice system remains one of the most controversial topics today. One of the most difficult problems with such jurisdiction is the statutes themselves. For example, the behaviors common to these statutes—for example, "unmanageable," "unruly," and "in danger of leading an idle, dissolute, lewd or immoral life"—have been challenged in court for being unconstitutionally vague and indefinite. However, most courts that have addressed this issue have upheld the breadth of the statutes in view of their overall concern for the welfare of the child. *Commonwealth v. Brasher* and the *District of Columbia v. B.J.R.* are examples of cases involving hazily defined behavior where the appellate courts have upheld the definition of status offenses.[52]

As discussed in Chapter 1, the major concern with status offenders continues to be whether they should be eliminated from the juvenile court system. At the present time, the leading proponents for eliminating them include such groups as the National Commission on Criminal Justice Standards and Goals, the National Council on Crime and Delinquency, and the American Bar Association. Judge Orman Ketcham of the superior court of the District of Columbia summarizes the arguments in favor of removing status offenses from the juvenile justice system:

1. A juvenile's acts of misbehavior and unruliness that are not a violation of the criminal law do not constitute grounds for juvenile court jurisdiction.
2. Intervention by a juvenile court over such actions is an unprincipled use of judicial authority.
3. Intervention by a juvenile court in noncriminal behavior is an uneconomic use of public funds.
4. Juvenile court involvement with status offenders acts as a detriment to providing rehabilitation and socialization.
5. Involvement by the juvenile court in such behavior is possibly unconstitutional.[53]

On the other hand, Judge Lindsay Arthur of the juvenile division of the Hennepin County Court in Minnesota suggests that status offenders need a court of last resort for the following reasons:

1. Removing children who commit noncriminal behavior from the juvenile court system abandons those children most in need.
2. Insurmountable administrative problems involving treatment programs within the community will exist once children cannot be brought within the court's jurisdiction.
3. Children require unequal protection of the law and specialized programs that justify the use of statutes that are broad and concerned with the general welfare of the individual.[54] Without doubt, juvenile court intervention in the area of noncriminal behavior has proved ineffective. By the same token, the juvenile court does act as a last resort for parents who have no other alternative for children who are unmanageable, truant, or runaway. What approach will be taken in the future is unclear now, but there is no question that the issue of juvenile noncriminal misbehavior will receive considerable attention.

Waiver

Only a handful of states give their juvenile courts exclusive original jurisdiction for all offenses of children within the juvenile delinquency age categories and status offense category. Accepting the premise that the rehabilitative resources and protective processes of the juvenile court are not appropriate in cases of serious criminal conduct, various states have excluded capital offenses, offenses punishable by death or life imprisonment, and certain other offenses from the juvenile court's jurisdiction. This generally sets up a system of exclusive jurisdiction to the criminal court system. In other words, throughout the country, numerous states have given the criminal courts exclusive jurisdiction over certain offenses, usually serious ones, regardless of the desires of the juvenile court. In many other jurisdictions, the juvenile courts have overlapping or concurrent jurisdiction with the criminal court system.

CRITICISMS OF THE JUVENILE COURT

The juvenile court system in America has not succeeded significantly in treating and rehabilitating the delinquent child or the status offender. It has not reduced the rate of juvenile crime or brought justice and fairness to the child in court. Studies by experts in the fields of criminology, law, and sociology and national reports of all kinds have documented the practices and the failures of the juvenile court system. What are the reasons for such failure?

As the President's Commission on Law Enforcement and Administration of Justice so eloquently stated as early as 1967, one reason for the failure of the juvenile courts has been "the community's continuing unwillingness to provide the resources—the people and facilities and concerns—necessary to permit them [the juvenile courts] to realize their potential and prevent them from acquiring some of the undesirable features typical of lower criminal courts in this country."[55]

In some jurisdictions, for example, the juvenile court judgeship does not have high status and prestige. As a result, lawyers with outstanding ability and concern for children are not attracted to the position. Some juvenile court judges in this country have no undergraduate degrees, and others are not attorneys. Furthermore, many of these judges have little or no understanding of the social sciences and the application of diagnostic information to children handled by the court.

Another serious resource problem is the lact of probation personnel throughout the juvenile court system. Where juvenile probation officers are qualified and well-trained and where their caseloads are reasonable, they are in a position to carry out and implement the philosophy of the court. However, most courts operate with only a minimum number of probation officers to service children. Probation has become the predominant disposition of chioce in the juvenile court system, but at best it means only minimal supervision for children placed under its control. Some courts have no probation services at all. Where services do exist, caseloads are often very high, trained personnel are scarce, and referral programs are inadequate. When the probation officer has large caseloads, almost no time is left to provide individual treatment and counseling for the child. Time is often spent in court investigations, administrative detail, and field work.

In the area of institutionalization, the National Advisory Commission on Criminal Justice Standards and Goals has noted the scarcity of appropriate community institutional programs.[56] Programs for the treatment of children that involve some confinement are generally carried on in understaffed, security-type institutions where few educational, vocational, counseling, or job placement services are available. Other intermediate services, such as half-way houses, residential treatment centers, and a variety of diversified institutional programs with intensive community supervision, have been difficult to establish and even more difficult to operate effectively.

The fact that there are limited resources in the juvenile court, however, is not the only problem. In the past decade, the federal government, through the Law Enforcement Assistance Administration and the Juvenile Delinquency Prevention Act of 1974, has provided the states with millions of dollars to develop adult criminal and juvenile social control programs. Yet, delinquency rates increase and recidivism continues unabated. Thus, the problem does not necessarily revolve around the lack of resources alone.

The solution is much more complicated than simply the infusion of more resources into the juvenile court. The failure of the juvenile court to fulfill its rehabilitative and quasi-legal goal stems to a great degree from a lack of knowledge about the fundamental problem of juvenile delinquency and child care in this country. The President's Commission on Law Enforcement and Administration of Justice noted, "Experts in the field agree that it is extremely difficult to develop successful methods to prevent serious delinquent acts through rehabilitative programs for the child."[57]

Probably the most complex problem of all is to understand juvenile misbehavior and to determine its appropriate treatment. The knowledge to prevent delinquency is difficult to come by. The scientific information to carry out the treatment philosophy of the juvenile court does not exist to a great degree today. In addition, experts differ on the various theories underlying delinquency prevention and the approaches needed to deal with it. It is becoming clear, however, that delinquency is not so much an act of individual deviance as it is the result of a multitude of societal influences on families and children. Factors like discrimination, poor housing, unemployment, and poor education are beyond the direct treatment and control of the juvenile court judge, probation officer, or social service agent.

This direction can be observed in the theories of a variety of experts viewing delinquencys. Wheeler and L. Cottrell, in their work on the labeling process, indicate that "categorizing of a child as a delinquent increases the pressure from the community for the child to act as a delinquent."[58] Edwin Sutherland indicates that antisocial behavior results from the learning of deviant actions from others within the environment.[59] Other theorists, such as Richard Cloward and Lloyd Ohlin, as well as Albert Cohen and the most noted researcher on gangs, Walter Miller, all indicate that deviant behavior to some degree is a result of peer conflict and environmental influence.[60] Thus, both in theory and in practice, the juvenile justice system has fallen short. Its theories to some degree remain untested, and its rehabilitative treatment methods, programs, and practices remain unclear. In addition, it continues to be faced with the philosophy originally established in the Illinois Juvenile Court Act of 1899 that treatment within a benign setting is the goal of the juvenile court system.

Many of the answers we need to understand juvenile delinquency and control are not available today. Nevertheless, social science theory has played, and continues to play, a critical role in how society handles the juvenile offender. Over the years, numerous experts have documented the use and effectiveness of certain techniques, devices, and programs for controlling juvenile antisocial behavior. From the turn of the twentieth century up to the present time, this effort continues.

In 1906, for example, Judge Harvey Baker, the first justice of the Boston Juvenile Court, began his efforts to service children in a juvenile court setting. In a report of the first five years of the operations of the Boston Juvenile Court, Judge Baker noted, "A clinic for the intensive study of baffling cases which failed to respond to ordinary probationary treatment would enhance the efficiency of the court.[61] As a result, the Judge Baker Foundation and Clinic was established in 1917 and became the country's first organized clinic associated with a juvenile court.

Throughout the 1930s and 1940s, Sheldon Glueck and Eleanor Glueck studied the behavior of large groups of delinquent youths.[62] Social service workers like Gisela Konopka undertook studies of the case histories of young girls and documented the social work movement in the juvenile justice field.[63] Herbert Weeks demonstrated the effectiveness of the group-oriented treatment program and the benefits of short-term residential treatment.[64] LaMar Empey has shown the positive results of a variety of delinquency prevention strategies and programs.[65] John Martin and Joseph Fitzpatrick have dealth with delinquency in terms of race, class, and the sociocultural model inherent in urban ghettos as distinguished from the psychological aspects of delinquency.[66] Sherwood Norman has pioneered in the development of the youth service bureau as a key to delinquency prevention.[67] The work of Marguerite Warren with the community treatment program of the California Youth Authority has been widely acclaimed.[68] The development of these important programs and concepts of delinquency prevention and control rely to a great degree on scientific knowledge and are examples of how the justice system must use and depend on empirical information.

As Paul Nejelski and Judith LaPook state, "The price of failing to establish impartial means of monitoring system performance is to continue the inadequate performance of the past and present."[69]

CHAPTER SUMMARY

Over the past two decades, the courts have moved in case after case to eliminate the traditional view that a child brought into the juvenile justice system has no rights. Both the Supreme Court and the lower courts have granted children procedural safeguards and the protection of due process in the juvenile courts. This chapter began by considering the five major Supreme Court decisions that laid down the constitutional requirements for juvenile proceedings. Next, the chapter reviewed lower court decisions throughout the entire juvenile process, beginning with the arrest stage through search and seizure, custodial interrogation, identifications, pretrial detention, pleas, plea bargaining, adjudication, disposition, and appeal. It is important to recognize that in years past, the protections that are afforded to children today and that have been afforded to adults were not available to children.

After reviewing the legal rights of juveniles with particular emphasis on court decisions, the chapter discussed the juvenile court structure. The juvenile court is a specialized court that can be organized in jurisdictions on an independent basis, within a criminal court, or as a statewide family court.

Finally, the chapter analyzed the issue of jurisdiction within the juvenile court. It discussed such elements as age, both minimum and miximum; jurisdiction over conduct, including criminal behavior and children in need of supervision; and the idea of transferring children to adult courts.

Because of the growing recognition of juvenile rights, the traditional doctrine of *parens patriae* is becoming less important today in the juvenile courts. Guaranteeing the procedural due process rights of juveniles is replacing the court's belief that it can act arbitrarily in the best interest of the child. The future course of juvenile rights is difficult to determine. Most likely, the Supreme Court will decide each case and the applicability of each right independently and individually and on the basis of standards enunciated in the *Gault* case.

DISCUSSION QUESTIONS

1. Are the legal rights of juvenile offenders similar to those of adults charged with a crime? What is the Bill of Rights? Does it apply to children?
2. The Supreme Court has made a number of major decisions in the area of juvenile justice. What are these decisions? What is their impact on the juvenile justice system? Is the effect of the decisions influenced by how local jurisdictions carry out the law set forth by the courts?
3. What is the meaning of the term *procedural due process of law*? Explain why and how procedural due process has had an impact on juvenile justice.
4. The juvenile court is considered a specialized court for children. How is it organized, and why?
5. What factors determine the jurisdiction of the juvenile court? Can the term *jurisdiction* mean that a child of any age under majority can be brought to the juvenile court? Does the concept of jurisdiction differ for male and female juvenile offenders?

SUGGESTED READINGS

Alexander, Paul. "Constitutional Rights in the Juvenile Court." In *Justice for the Child*, edited by Margaret K. Rosenheim. Chicago. University of Chicago Press, 1962.

American Bar Association. Project on Standards for Juvenile Justice. *Standards Relating to Counsel for Private Parties*. Cambridge, Mass.: Ballinger Press, 1977.

Arthur, Lindsay G., ed. *National Bench Book for Juvenile Courts*. National Council for Juvenile and Family Court Judges. St. Paul, Minnesota, 1979.

Bazelon, David L. "Beyond Control of the Juvenile Court." *Juvenile Court Judges Journal* 21 (1970): 42.

Besharov, Douglas J. *Juvenile Justice Advocacy—Practice in a Unique Court*. New York: Practicing Law Institute, 1974.

Buss, W. "The Fourth Amendment and Searches of Students in Public Schools." *Iowa Law Review* 59 (1974): 739.

Children's Bureau, U.S. Department of Health, Education and Welfare. *Standards for Juveniles and Family Courts*. Washington, D.C.: Government Printing Office, 1966.

Davis, Samuel. *Rights of Juveniles—The Juvenile Justice System.* New York: Clark Boardman, 1974.

———."Jurisdictional Dilemma of the Juvenile Court." *North Carolina Law Review* 51 (1972): 195-217.

Duffee, David, and Siegel, Larry. "The Organization Man: Legal Counsel in Juvenile Court." *Criminal Law Bulletin* 7 (1971): 6-15.

Fox, Sanford. *Modern Juvenile Justice: Cases and Materials.* St. Paul, Minn.: West Publishing, 1972.

Juvenile Justice and Delinquency Prevention Act of 1974, 18 U.S.C., Section 5031.

National Conference of Commissioners on Uniform State Laws. *Uniform Juvenile Court Act.* Philadelphia: Note. "Juveniles—Interrogation—Parens Patriae and Miranda: Conflicting Interests." *Seton Hall Law Review* 3 (1972): 482-496.

Note. "Right to Bail for Juveniles." *Chicago-Kent Law Review* 48 (1973): 99-115.

Piersma, Paul; Ganousis, Jeanette; and Kramer, Prudence. "The Juvenile Court: Current Problems, Legislative Proposals, and a Model Act." *St. Louis University Law Journal* 20 (1975): 1-99.

Polier, Justice W. *A View from the Bench: The Juvenile Court.* New York: National Council on Crime and Delinquency, 1964.

Popkin, Alice; Lippert, Fred; and Keiter, Jeffrey. "Another Look at Role of Due Process in Juvenile Court." *Family Law Quarterly* 6 (1973): 233-269.

Senna, Joseph, and Siegel, Larry. *Juvenile Law Cases and Comments.* St. Paul, Minn.: West Publishing, 1976.

of the Juvenile Justice Process: An Siegel, Larry; Senna, Joseph; and Libby, Therese. "Legal Aspects Overview of Current Practices and Law." *New England Law Revie' American Criminal Law Review* 12 (1974): 1-249.

Boston University Law Review 57 (1977): 617-795.

———."A Symposium—Juveniles and Law.'

———."A Symposium—Juvenile Justice."e, 1966.

REFERENCES

1.　387 U.S. 1, 87 S.Ct. 1428 (1967).

3.　397 U.S. 358, 90 S.Ct. 1068 (1970).

4.　403 U.S. 528, 91 S.Ct. 1976 (1971).

5.　421 U.S. 519, 95 S.Ct. 1779 (1975).

6.　*McKeiver,* 403 U.S. 528 at 538 (1971).

7.　*Gault,* 387 U.S. 1 at 7 (1967).

8.　367 U.S. 643, 81 S.Ct. 1684 (1961).

9.　378 U.S. 478, 84 S.Ct. 1758 (1964).

10.　384 U.S. 436, 86 S.Ct. 1602 (1966).

11.　372 U.S. 335, 83 S.Ct. 792 (1963).

12.　407 U.S. 514, 92 S.Ct. 2182 (1972).

13.　308 N.Y.S.2d 943 (1969).

14.　242 So.2d 849 (La. 1970); 89 Nev. 564, 517 P.2d 183 (1973).

15.　485 P.2d 655, 6 Or. App. 205 (1971).

16.　Ill., 237 N.E.2d 529 (1968).

17.　434 S.W.2d 948 (Tex. Civ. App. 1968).

18. 383 F.Supp. 130 (D.C. Fla. 1974).

19. *Miranda v. Arizona,* 384 U.S. at 478–479.

20. 296 N.Y.S.2d 472, 58 Misc. 2d 748 (1969).

21. 507 F.2d 53 (5th Cir. 1975).

22. 322 U.S. 596, 68 S.Ct. 302 (1948).

23. 67 Cal.2d 365, 62 Cal. Rptr. 586, 432 P.2d 202 (1967).

24. 399 F.2d 467 (5th Cir. 1968).

25. 388 U.S. 218, 87 S.Ct. 1926 (1967).

26. 406 U.S. 682, 92 S.Ct. 1877 (1972).

27. 107 R.I. 615, 268 A.2d 723 (1970).

28. 3 Cal.3d 16, 89 Cal. Rptr. 33, 473 P.2d 737 (1970).

29. 300 F.Supp. 1220 (E.D.Wis. 1969); 469 F.2d 1159 (9th Cir. 1972).

30. 487 P.2d 47 (Alaska 1971).

31. National Advisory Commission on Criminal Justice Standards and Goals, *Task Force Report: Courts* (Washington, D.C.: Government Printing Office, 1973).

32. 388 Mich. 66, 199 N.W.2d 217 (1972).

33. 13 MD. App. 644, 284 A.2d 621 (1971).

34. 293 N.Y.S.2d 873, 30 A.D.2d 933 (1968).

35. 36 N.Y.2d 317, 237 N.E.2d 812 (1975).

36. 332 N.Y.S.2d 125, 39 A.D.2d 746 (1972).

37. 337 N.Y.S.2d 936, 40 A.D.2d 862 (1972). See *The Ellery C. Decision: A Case Study of Judicial Regulation of Juvenile Status Offenders* (New York: Institute of Judicial Administration, 1975).

38. 125 Vt. 373, 216 A.2d 266 (1966).

39. 408 U.S. 471, 92 S.Ct. 2593 (1972).

40. Sanford Fox, *Juvenile Courts in a Nutshell* (St. Paul, Minn.: West Publishing, 1972).

41. Mass. Gen. Laws, Ann. Chapter 119.

42. National Advisory Commission on Criminal Justice Standards and Goals, *Report of the Task Force on Juvenile Justice and Delinquency Prevention* (Washington, D.C.: Law Enforcement Assistance Administration, 1976), p. 277.

43. Ibid.

44. Ibid.

45. See New York Family Court Act, Section 712.

46. Samuel Davis, *Rights of Juveniles: The Juvenile Justice System* (New York: Clark Boardman, 1975).

47. *Lamb v. Brown,* 456 F.2d 18 (1972).

48. Mass. Gen. Laws, Chapter 119, Section 53.

49. Davis, *Rights of Juveniles,* p. 233.

50. Family Court Act, State of New York, Section 712, Article 7, Part 1.

51. Mass. Gen. Laws, Chapter 119, Section 53.

52. 359 Mass. 550 (1971); 322 A.2d 58 (1975).

53. Orman Ketcham, "Why Jurisdiction over Status Offenders Should Be Eliminated from Juvenile Courts," *Boston University Law Review* 57 (1977): 645–662.

54. Lindsay Arthur, "Status Offenders Need a Court of Last Resort," *Boston University Law Review* 57 (1977): 63–644.

55. President's Commission on Law Enforcement and Administration of Justice, *The Challenge of Crime in a Free Society* (Washington, D.C.: Government Printing Office, 1967).

56. National Advisory Commission on Criminal Justice Standards and Goals, *Corrections* (Washington, D.C.: Government Printing Office, 1973).

57. President's Commission on Law Enforcement and Administration of Justice, *The Challenge of Crime in a Free Society*, p. 80.

58. S. Wheeler and L. Cottrell, "Juvenile Delinquency: Its Prevention and Control," in *Delinquency, Crime and Social Processes*, ed. Donald Cressey and (New York: Harper & Row, 1969).

59. Edwin Sutherland and Donald Cressey, *Criminology* (Philadelphia: Lippincott, 1970), p. 78.

60. Richard Cloward and Lloyd Ohlin, *Delinquency and Opportunity* (New York: Free Press, 1960); Albert Cohen, *The Culture of the Gang* (New York: Free Press, 1955); and Walter Miller, *Violence by Youth Gangs in American Cities* (Washington, D.C.: Government Printing Office, 1975).

61. See Judge Baker Foundation, *Harvey Baker—Upbuilder of Juvenile Court* (Boston, Mass., 1920) pp. 2-3.

62. See, for example, Eleanor T. Glueck, "Efforts to Identify Delinquents," *Federal Probation* 24 (1960): 49–56.

63. Gisela Konpka, *Adolescent Girls in Conflict* (Englewood Cliffs, N.J.: Prentice-Hall, 1966).

64. Herbert Ashley Weeks, *Youthful Offenders at Highfields* (Ann Arbor: University of Michigan Press, 1958).

65. See, for example, LaMar T. Empey and Steven Lubeck, *The Silverlake Experiment: Testing Delinquency Theory and Community Intervention* (Chicago: Aldine Publishing, 1971).

66. See John Martin and Joseph Fitzpatrick, *Delinquent Behavior: A Redefinition of the Problem* (New York: Random House, 1966).

67. Sherwood Norman, *The Youth Service Bureau—A Key to Delinquency Prevention* (Hackensack, N.J.: National Council on Crime and Delinquency, 1975).

68. See Ted Palmer, "California's Community Treatment Program for Delinquent Adolescents," *Journal of Research in Crime and Delinquency* 8 (1971): 71.

69. Paul Nejelski and Judith LaPook, "Monitoring the Juvenile Justice System: How Can You Tell Where You're Going, If You Don't Know Where You Are?" *American Criminal Law Review* 12 (1974): 31.

PART V

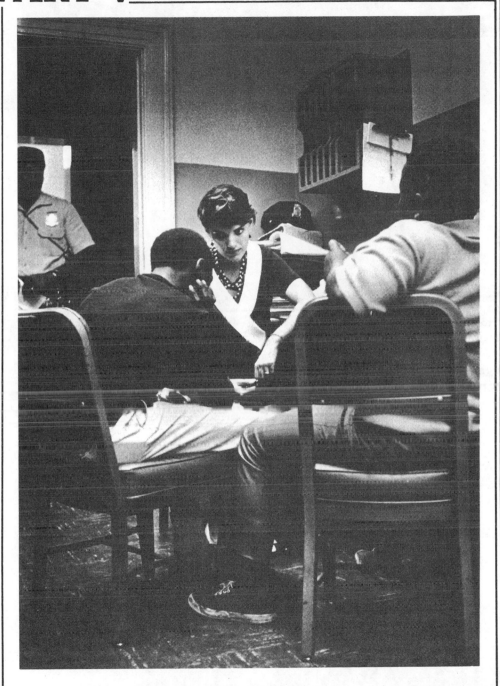

PROCESSING THE JUVENILE OFFENDER

Chapter 15

Chapter Outline	Key Terms, Names, and Cases
Introduction	juvenile police officer
The Role of the Police and Juvenile Offenders	pretrial procedure
	American Bar Association
Organization of Police Services for Juveniles	O.I.C.
Recruitment and Training of Juvenile Police Officers	I.A.C.P.
	discretion
Legal Aspects of Police Work with Juveniles	August Vollmer
Police Discretion with Juveniles	juvenile unit
Factors Affecting Police Discretion	Uniform Juvenile Court Act
Police Work and Delinquency Prevention	Kenneth C. Davis
Directions in Police Work with Children	youth service bureau
Chapter Summary	police organization
	crime prevention

Police Work With Juveniles

INTRODUCTION

No formula has yet been established to prevent crime among people of any age. Various segments of society make efforts to control antisocial behavior. The modern juvenile justice system is the primary source of effort to control juvenile crime. Other segments of society—the political system, the schools, and religious institutions—also play a role; however, the focal point of social control rests with the modern police agency. When individuals or groups are upset about rising crime rates, the police are generally the first to be called to the task of solving the problem.

Traditionally, the primary responsibility of the police has been to protect the public. That has been, and continues to be, in the minds of most citizens, their most serious and important responsibility. In years past, the rights of individuals were considered subordinate to the general needs of the community. The first and foremost duty of the police was law enforcement.

During the past half century, however, as society has become more complex, so have the problems of police officers. For example, according to the FBI Uniform Crime Reports, juvenile offenders now account for nearly 50 percent of the arrests for serious crimes in the United States.[1] Many more young people are breaking the law, and more resources are needed to cope with this problem.

Every state has laws aiming at the rehabilitation of juvenile offenders. Rehabilitation has been, and continues to be, a goal of the juvenile justice system. Children are considered different from adults and thus entitled to special care. Therefore, when the police deal with the juvenile offender, it is necessary for them to recognize this rehabilitative ideology.

The problems of the police officer have become more complex because the police are the first to come into contact with the juvenile offender. Even the most casual meeting between a police officer and child can have a profound effect on the child. Police officers represent the authority of the community. How the child reacts to this authority often depends on the police officer's response to the child's behavior. This does not ignore the issue that many police officers are faced with delinquent children who exhibit violent criminal behavior. The fact remains that the police first come into contact with more than three-fourths of young people who enter into the juvenile court system. In addition, the police have initial contact with runaways, abused children, and, of course, truants.

Furthermore, the role of the police officer in dealing with children and adults has become more complex since the establishment of clear-cut procedural and due process rights for people who violate the law. The police are required to follow fair procedures and practices in handling young people.

Lastly, the behavioral sciences have offered various theories of delinquency that affect the methods of the police, the judiciary, and the correctional agencies. The importance of these theories, which have been discussed in previous chapters, cannot be overemphasized. They are the basis for many programs for treatment and control in the juvenile justice system.

The police play a critical role in preventing and controlling delinquent behavior. Furthermore, their responsibilities and operating procedures are constantly changing vis-a-vis theoretical information about delinquency.

The material in Part 5 of this text deals with an analysis of the juvenile justice process, the police, the pretrial system, juvenile trial, community treatment, and institutionalization. Chapter 15 focuses on police work in juvenile justice and delinquency prevention. It outlines the role and responsibilities of the police, covers the organization and management of police-juvenile operations, discusses the legal aspects of police work, discusses the concept of police discretion, and explores the relationship between the police and the community's efforts to prevent crime.

THE ROLE OF THE POLICE AND JUVENILE OFFENDERS

How do juvenile officers spend their time, and what roles do they perform in the overall police and criminal justice system? Juvenile officers either operate alone as specialists within a police department or work as part of the juvenile unit of a police department. Their role is similar to that of officers working with adult offenders—to intervene if the actions of a citizen produce public danger or disorder. Most officers regard the violations of juveniles as nonserious unless they are committed by a troublemaker or involve significant damage to persons or property. Juveniles who misbehave are generally ignored or treated informally. Police encounters with juveniles generally result from reports made by citizens, and the bulk of such encounters pertain to matters of minor legal consequence.[2]

In a Children's Bureau Report in 1962, Richard Myren and Lynn Swanson suggested that the juvenile police officer has the following role:[3]

1. To provide staff assistance to the chief of police.
2. To provide line operations of the juvenile unit.

3. To provide control functions by formulating and disseminating juvenile policy within the police department.

4. To form a liaison with other agencies in the community that deal with children.

In its *Standards Relating to Police Handling of Juveniles*, the American Bar Association is more specific about the role of juvenile officers. It suggests that they have a major responsibility for the diversion and referral of juvenile problems.[4]

In general, the police role in dealing with juveniles involves:

1. Handling children who commit minor offenses where arrest rarely occurs. In this instance, the police act as social service agents, referring the children and their families to appropriate community services.

2. Arresting children who commit serious crimes

3. Handling cases of child abuse and neglect. The police are often called on to intervene in such cases even though these problems are generally outside their competence and jurisdiction. Here, too, juvenile officers function as social service agents.

4. Dealing with children who commit status offenses—that is, runaways, truants, and those who are incorrigible.

ORGANIZATION OF POLICE SERVICES FOR JUVENILES

In years past, the problem of juvenile delinquency and youth crime received relatively little attention from most municipal police departments. Even when juvenile crime continued to increase during the 1960s and 1970s, police resources were generally geared to adult offenders. However, the alarming increase in serious juvenile crime in the past few years has made it obvious that the police can no longer neglect youthful antisocial behavior. They need to assign resources to the problem and to have the proper organization for coping with it. The theory and practice of police organization has undergone many changes in recent years. As a result, police departments are giving greater emphasis to the juvenile function.

The organization of juvenile work depends on the size of the police department, the kind of community in which it is located, and the amount and quality of resources available in the community.[5] Today, most police agencies recognize that juvenile crime requires special attention. Specialized police work with children goes back to the establishment of the first juvenile court in 1899 in the state of Illinois, and its importance has been recognized for many years.[6]

The police who work with juvenile offenders ordinarily have special skills and talents that go beyond those generally associated with regular police work. In large urban police departments, juvenile services are often established through a specialized unit. Ordinarily, this unit is the responsibility of a command-level police officer. The unit commander assigns officers to deal with juvenile problems throughout the police department's jurisdiction. Police departments with very few officers have little need for an internal division with specialized functions. Most small departments assign one officer the responsibility of handling juvenile matters for the entire community. It cannot be assumed in either large or small departments that only those police officers assigned to work with juveniles will be involved in juvenile offenses. When officers on patrol encounter a youngster committing a crime, they are initially responsible for dealing with the problem. However, they generally refer the case to the juvenile unit or juvenile police officer to follow up. In working with adult offenders, most police officers are concerned primarily about the type of offense the suspect has committed. When working with young people, the juvenile officer is concerned with what to do in cases that cannot be handled with on-the-scene referrals to families or social agencies.

The Task Force Report on Juvenile Justice and Delinquency Prevention of the National Advisory Committee on Criminal Justice Standards and Goals suggests the following in Standard 7.1:

Every police agency having more than 75 sworn officers should establish a juvenile investigation unit and every smaller police agency should establish such a unit if community conditions warrant.

This unit should be functionally centralized to the most effective command level; and should be assigned responsibility for conducting as many juvenile investigations as possible, assisting field officers in juvenile cases, and maintaining liaison with other agencies and organizations interested in juvenile matters.[7]

Most large urban police departments with juvenile units are organized in a military-like hierarchy, as illustrated in Figure 15-1. The number of police officers assigned to juvenile work has increased in recent years. The International Association of Chiefs of Police found that approximately 500 departments of the 1,400 surveyed had juvenile units in 1960. By 1970, the number of police departments with a juvenile specialist had doubled. Today, most departments with a few hundred or more police officers have a juvenile specialist.[8] The amount of personnel allocated for juvenile work varies widely—between 2.5 and 7.5 percent of departmental personnel.[9] Each police department should establish for itself how many people it needs to cope with juvenile problems.

RECRUITMENT AND TRAINING OF JUVENILE POLICE OFFICERS

If police departments are to substantially improve their performance, particularly in specialized areas, they must be able to attract qualified young men and women whose backgrounds, intelligence, and capabilities give them the potential to be effective law enforcement agents. In recent years, police careers have become more attractive, and the growing number of criminal justice programs in colleges has attracted a pool of educated young people seeking law enforcement degrees. In many communities, educational pay incentives and adequate salaries have made police careers even more inviting.

Most juvenile officers are appointed after they have some general patrol experience. A desire to work with juveniles and a basic understanding of human behavior is generally considered essential to appointment. Sometimes, juvenile officers are assigned on the basis of written and oral examinations as well as general experience. In some instances, women, younger officers, and minority

Figure 15-1.   ORGANIZATION OF A METROPOLITAN POLICE DEPARTMENT.

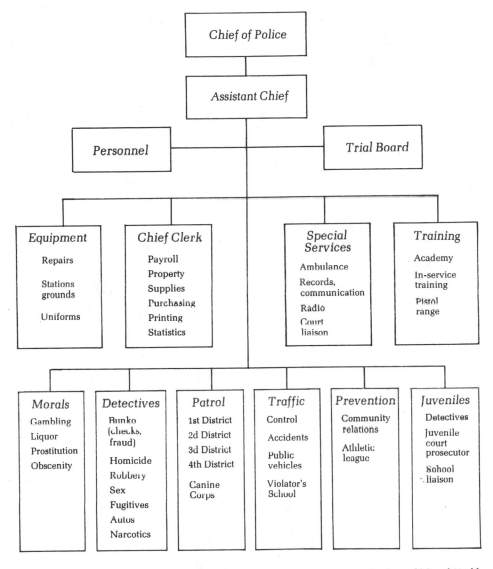

Source: Adapted from Clarence Schrag, *Crime & Justice American Style*, National Institute of Mental Health (Washington, D.C.: Government Printing Office, 1971), p. 142.

officers are made juvenile officers in order to develop proper relationships with youths in particular areas. Of course, juvenile officers should have an aptitude and an interest in working with young people.

In some instances, it is advantageous to assign new officers with special educational backgrounds in the social sciences to the juvenile unit. For example, in 1967 the President's Crime Commission suggested a three-level police force to include community service officers, police officers, and police agents. The community service officers would be in uniform but unarmed. Their function would be simply to assist in looking for crime-breeding areas. Police officers would be armed and uniformed and handle routine calls. Police agents would have three years of college study in the social sciences and would be specialists in such areas as police and community relations or juvenile delinquency. Thus, a new officer with mature judgment, some college education, and some experience in social service might be a better candidate for a juvenile officer position than an officer with patrol experience but little desire to work with juvenile offenders.[10]

Police departments cannot operate to their fullest potential without effective training at all levels. Training programs depend on local resources and the kind of problems that require solution. The FBI provides training at the National Police Academy in Virginia. Other national agencies interested in promoting police training are the Law Enforcement Assistance Administration and the International Association of Chiefs of Police. On the local level, colleges and universities sponsor training courses in juvenile justice. On the state level, training academies run by the civil service, the state police, or a major metropolitan police department provide regular career development sessions for improving police leadership skills in all areas, including juvenile justice. In Standard 7.7, the National Advisory Committee on Criminal Justice Standards and Goals makes the following personnel training recommendations:

1. All police recruits should receive at least 40 hours of mandatory training in juvenile matters;
2. Every police department and/or state or regional police training academy should train all officers and administrators in personnel in crisis intervention techniques;
3. All officers selected for assignment to juvenile units should receive at least 80 hours of training in juvenile matters either before beginning their assignment or within a one-year period; and
4. All police juvenile officers should be required to participate in at least one 40-hour in-service training program each year.[11]

Training programs for juvenile officers should include information on the overall scope of the juvenile justice system. Training should be designed to keep experienced officers abreast of new developments in the field of juvenile law. Additional material should include the history of juvenile justice, the juvenile offender, and the juvenile court system; the role of the police officer in dealing with noncriminal behavior; the serious violent juvenile offender; and services and programs in the police department's local jurisdiction. Also, information should be provided on students and teachers, and on ethnic, cultural, and minority relations. As the American Bar Association states in its *Standards Relating to Police Handling of Juveniles*, recruitment, in-service, and promotional training should explore juvenile policy guidelines and the philosophy behind them.[12]

LEGAL ASPECTS OF POLICE WORK WITH JUVENILES

The jurisdiction of the juvenile officer and the juvenile court is based on legislation identifying what conduct the states want to regulate regarding children. Prior to the advent of juvenile court statutes, however, the common law gave special consideration to children. Over the years, numerous changes have been made in the laws that determine juvenile responsibility, and each state determines by its own statutes the age level for juvenile court jurisdiction.[13]

Many state statutes dealing with juveniles are modeled on the Uniform Juvenile Court Act of the National Conference of Commissioners on Uniform State Laws. The act suggests the following statutory grounds for taking children into custody:

Section 13. Taking into Custody.

A. A child may be taken into custody
  1. pursuant to an order of the court under this act;
  2. pursuant to the laws of arrest;
  3. by a law enforcement officer if there are reasonable grounds to believe the child is suffering of illness or injury or is in immediate danger from his surroundings and that his removal is necessary;
  4. by a law enforcement officer if there are reasonable grounds to believe that the child has run away from parents, guardian, or other custodian.[14]

When the police investigate juveniles, the basic question confronting them and the courts is whether juveniles at this stage of the juvenile justice process have constitutional rights similar to those of adults. Today, procedural safeguards for children are similar in many respects to those for adults. The American Bar Association suggests the following:

Standard 3.2 Police Investigation into criminal matters should be similar whether the suspect is an adult or a juvenile. Juveniles, therefore, should receive at least the same safeguards available to adults in the criminal justice system. This should apply to:
  a) Preliminary investigations;
  b) The arrest process;
  c) Search and seizure;
  d) Questioning;
  e) Pretrial identification;
  f) Pre-hearing detention and release.[15]

Consistent with the meaning of the due process clauses of the Fifth and Fourteenth Amendments and the various provisions of the Bill of Rights made applicable to the states through the Fourteenth Amendment, constitutional safeguards are available to youths taken into custody by the police. Although court decisions vary from state to state, most opinions on juvenile law provide for procedural due process for children on the basis of the concept of fundamental fairness and of standards established in the adult criminal justice system.[16]

The precise extent to which juvenile procedures should parallel adult procedures continues to be the source of some debate. Some experts suggest that the juvenile justice system requires less due process because of its protective and social nature. Others emphasize that the *Gault* decision virtually imposes adult due process on the juvenile justice system.

When a police officer arrests a juvenile or an adult, the procedure must be consistent with the provisions of the Fourth Amendment. Juveniles are taken into custody with an authorized warrant issued by a neutral and detached magistrate or without a warrant when the offense is committed in the presence of a police officer. In addition, police officers can make an arrest if they have probable cause to believe that a crime has been committed and that the person arrested has committed it. In many jurisdictions, juveniles can be taken into custody under a variety of other circumstances. These circumstances are specified by state statutes, and the purpose of the statutes is to protect the juveniles.

Before interrogations, juveniles are generally given *Miranda* warnings and promptly notified of their constitutional rights. Police procedures for taking a juvenile into custody on juvenile delinquency charges are essentially similar to those employed in adult arrests. When a child is arrested, most jurisdictions require prompt notification of the parents or guardians that the child is in custody. Often, a juvenile is questioned following arrest only after being given the opportunity to confer with an attorney. Juveniles, like adults, have the right to waive counsel, but generally they should do so only after conferring with parents or an attorney.

Investigations of juvenile suspects often involve a search. When the child gives consent, it must be completely voluntary. Virtually the same requirements that apply to adult offenders concerning exceptions to the warrant requirement—stop and frisk law, searches incident to an arrest, and automobile searches—apply to juveniles under the protection of the Fourth Amendment.

Although the Supreme Court has not ruled on the issue of pretrial identification for juveniles, most police departments apply identification procedures that have been developed for adult offenders. This means that children have basically the same right as adults to counsel at line-ups.

The Report of the Task Force on Juvenile Justice and Delinquency Prevention has suggested the following guidelines for taking a juvenile into custody:

Juveniles should also be fully informed of their constitutional rights. In questioning youths about crime or delinquent acts they may be involved in, police should give the warnings required by the Miranda decision. Overall the police should treat juveniles with fundamental fairness, safeguarding their rights at every step of the proceedings. Police should not accept any attempt by the juveniles to waive their constitutional rights without first consulting their attorney.[17]

As has been noted in the *Kent* and *Gault* cases, the basic criteria determining the legality of police procedures for dealing with children is whether the police show fundamental fairness under the law that guarantees the rights of the child. Applying this concept today, most states have procedures for arrests, custodial interrogations, search and seizures, and pretrial identifications that for all practical purposes are the same for adults and children. Even more care should be taken to protect the constitutional rights of children because they are more vulnerable than adults.

POLICE DISCRETION WITH JUVENILES

The authority of a juvenile officer who arrests a child is not exercised in every case. Police discretion is defined as the selective enforcement of the law by duly authorized police agents. Roscoe Pound defined discretion as the authority conferred by law to act in certain conditions or situations in accordance with an official's or agency's own considered conscience or judgment.[18] Discretion operates in the twilight zone between law and morals. According to Kenneth Culp Davis, discretion gives officers a choice among possible courses of action within the effective limits on their power.[19] Goldstein has termed the exercise of police discretion a prime example of low visibility decision making in the criminal justice system.[20] Low visibility decision making refers to decisions made by public officials in the criminal or juvenile justice systems about which information is not available or decisions which the public is not in a position to understand, regulate, or criticize.

Police discretion is probably one of the most controversial and important of all police practices. It exists not only in the police area but in prosecutorial decision making, judicial judgments, and corrections. Discretion results in the law being applied differently in different situations. For example, two teenagers are caught in a stolen automobile. One is arrested; the other is released. Two youths are drunk and disorderly. One is sent home; the other is booked and sent to juvenile court. A group of youngsters are involved in a gang fight. Only a few are arrested; the others are released.

Regardless of what enforcement style they employ, all police officers in both the adult and the juvenile justice systems use a high degree of personal discretion in carrying out their daily tasks. In particular, much discretion is exercised in juvenile work because of the informality that has been built into the system to individualize justice. Often decisions by the police and others are vague and lack checks and balances. According to Victor Streib, arbitrary discretion is a characteristic of the informal juvenile justice system.[21] Furthermore, Streib says, police intake officials, prosecutors, judges, and correctional administrators make final, largely unreviewed, decisions about children that are almost totally unsupervised in any meaningful way.

The daily procedures of juvenile justice personnel are not subjected to administrative scrutiny or judicial review, except when they clearly violate a child's constitutional rights. As a result, discretion sometimes deteriorates into discrimination, violence, and other abusive practices on the part of the police. As Herbert Packer has stated, the real danger in discretion is that it allows the law to discriminate against precisely those elements in the population—the poor, the ignorant, the unpopular—who are the least able to draw attention to their plight and to whose sufferings the vast majority of the population is not the least bit responsive.[22]

The problem of discretion in juvenile justice has two extremes. On the one hand, too much discretion allows for open-ended, unchecked decisions and possibly unfair decisions. On the other hand, too little discretion ties the hands of decision makers and does not provide flexibility in dealing with individual juvenile offenders. Guidelines and controls are needed to structure the use of discretion.

The first contact a child has with the juvenile justice system is with the police. Studies indicate that a large majority of police decisions at this initial contact involve discretion. Paul Strasburg, for example, found that only about 50 percent of all the children who come in contact with the police ever get past the initial stage of the process.[23] Nathan Goldman examined the arrest records for over 1,000 juveniles from four communities in Pennsylvania to determine what factors operated in police referrals of juveniles to the court.[24] He concluded that over 64 percent of police contacts with juveniles were handled informally without court referral. Irving Piliavin and Scott Briar observed the behavior of thirty officers in the juvenile bureau of a large industrial city. Their study documented further the informality of police discretion in the initial arrest decision.[25] In 1966, D. Black and A. Reiss recorded descriptions of 280 encounters between juveniles and the police in efforts to discover discriminatory decision making. They found an unusually low arrest rate.[26]

These studies indicate that the police use a large amount of discretion in their decisions regarding juvenile offenders. The research generally does not prove that racial discrimination exists in handling juveniles. Instead it shows that differential decision making goes on without clear guidance and uniformity.

FACTORS AFFECTING POLICE DISCRETION

How does a juvenile officer decide what to do about a child who is apprehended? The general environment in which the officer works affects the decision. For instance, some officers work in communities that tolerate a fair amount of personal freedom. In liberal environments the police may be inclined to release children into the community rather than to arrest them. Other officers may work in extremely conservative communities that expect a no-nonsense approach to police behavior. Here, police may be more inclined to arrest a child.

The policies, practices, and customs of the local police department also provide a source of environmental influence. For example, juvenile officers may be pressured to make more arrests or refrain from making arrests under certain circumstances. Directives and orders instruct officers to be alert to certain types of violations on the part of juveniles. The chief of police and political officials of a community might initiate policies governing the arrest practices of the juvenile department.

Another source of influence is the pressure that individual superiors such as police supervisors or juvenile parole officers exert. The sergeant, for example, may initiate formal or informal directives regarding the handling of youth in a given community. Some supervising officers may personally believe that it is important to curtail disorderly conduct, drinking, or drug use. In addition, certain officers are influenced by the way their peers handle discretionary decision making.

A final environmental factor affecting the performance of officers is their perception of community alternatives to police intervention. Police officers may use arrest because they believe that nothing else can be done and that arrest is the best possible example of good police work. On the other hand, juvenile officers may refer a large number of juveniles to social service agencies, particularly when they believe that a community has a variety of good resources.

In addition to the environment, a variety of situational factors affect a police officer's decision making. Situational influences are those attached to a particular crime. It is difficult to identify every factor influencing police discretion, but a few factors stand out as having major significance. Studies have found that police officers rely heavily on the demeanor of a child in making decisions. In other words, the child's attitude and appearance play a serious role in the decision making process. Goldman discovered that community attitudes, political pressures, and the bias of the individual police officer may also influence whether an offender is arrested, taken into custody, or released.[27] Aaron Cicourel found that the decision to arrest is often based on information regarding the offender's overall demeanor, including dress, attitude, speech, and level of hostility toward the police.[28] Piliavin and Briar found that police perceptions of the attitudes of offenders toward the police, the law, and their own behavior were the most important factors in the decision to process or release an offender.[29]

Whether they deal with juvenile or adult offenders, most studies conclude that the following variables are important to decisions made by police officers:

1. The attitude of the complainant.
2. The type and seriousness of the offense.
3. The race and sex of the offender.
4. The age of the offender.
5. The attitude of the offender.
6. The history of the offender's prior contacts with the police.
7. In the case of a child, the perceived willingness of the parents to assist in disciplining the child and solving the problem.
8. The setting or location in which the incident occurs.
9. In the case of a child, whether the child denies the actions or insists on a court hearing.
10. The likelihood that a child can be serviced by a referral agency in the community.

Because it is unlikely that the above criteria will operate fairly under all conditions, a number of leading organizations have suggested the use of guidelines to control police discretion. The American Bar Association states, "Since individual police officers may make important decisions affecting police operations without direction, with limited accountability, and without any uniformity within a department, police discretion should be structured and controlled."[30] The ABA noted further "that there is almost a unanimous opinion that steps must be taken to provide better control and guidance over police discretion in street or station house adjustments of juvenile cases."[31] In addition, the National Advisory Committee on Criminal Justice Standards and Goals in its Standard 4.4 suggests the following:

> To stimulate the development of appropriate administrative guidance and control over police discretion in juvenile operations, legislatures and courts should actively encourage or require police administrative rule-making.[32]

One of the leading exponents of police discretion is Kenneth Culp Davis, who has done much to raise the consciousness of criminal justice practitioners about discretionary decision making. Davis recommends controlling administrative discretion (1) through the use of statutorial definition, (2) through the development of written policies, and (3) through the recording of decisions by criminal justice personnel.[33] Such practices would provide fair criteria for arrests, adjustment, and police referral of juvenile offenders and would help eliminate largely personal judgments based on the race, the attitude, or the demeanor of the juvenile. Highlight 15–1 presents two actual cases requiring discretionary decisions on the part of juvenile police officers.

Highlight 15–1.   Discretionary Decision Making in Juvenile Police Work.

The Case of Wayne W.

Wayne W. is a fourteen year old white boy who was caught shoplifting with two friends of the same age and sex. Wayne attempted to leave a large department store with a $12 shirt and was apprehended by a police officer in front of the store. From talking to Wayne and his parents and checking around the neighborhood, the officer determined the following facts:

1. Wayne seemed quite remorseful about the offense. He said several times that he did not know why he did it and that he had not planned the act. He seemed upset and scared and, while admitting the offense, did not want to go to court.

2. Wayne had three previous contacts with the police: one for malicious mischief when he destroyed some property, another involving a minor assault on a boy, and a third involving another shoplifting charge. In all three cases, Wayne promised to refrain from ever committing such acts again, and as a result he was not required to go to court. The other shoplifting involved a small baseball worth only $3.

3. Wayne appeared at the police department with his mother because his parents are divorced. She did not seem overly concerned about the case and felt that her son was not really to blame. She argued that he was always getting in trouble and she was not sure how to control him. She blamed most of his troubles with the law on his being in the wrong crowd.

4. The store had left matters in the hands of the police and would support their decision one way or the other.

5. The other two boys did not steal anything and claimed that they had no idea that Wayne was planning anything when they entered the store. Neither had any criminal record.

Should Wayne be sent to court for trial? What other remedy might be appropriate?

The Case of John M.

John M. is a fifteen year old youth who was picked up with a group of friends for unauthorized use of a motor vehicle. John is the son of a local doctor.

The crime occurred at midnight on a Saturday night, and the boys were apprehended when the automobile went out of control and hit a telephone pole. At the police station, John appeared contrite and explained that the car had been "borrowed" from a neighbor as a prank. The other boys agreed with his story. No liquor or drugs were found at the scene.

John's parents were very upset at the incident. They claimed to have enough problems with a daughter who had quit school and was now living as a hippie in California. The parents presented a good appearance.

John attends an exclusive private school, where he is described as an average, if uninterested student. John has no previous record, aside from being at a teenage party where liquor was served. His parents promised closer supervision in the future.

How should the police officer working on John's case proceed? What alternatives are available from dealing with John?

POLICE WORK AND DELINQUENCY PREVENTION

If the police are to work effectively in providing services to children and in enforcing the law, they need to develop relationships and programs with social service systems. Then, they can play an important role in implementing policies to control delinquency and to prevent it. Since the police decide what happens to a juvenile taken into custody, it is essential that they work closely with social service groups on a day-to-day basis. In addition, the police need to assume a leadership role in identifying the needs of children in the community and to help the community provide for such needs. In helping develop delinquency prevention programs, the police need to work closely with organizations like youth service bureaus, the schools, recreational facilities, and employment programs.

As early as 1967, the President's Crime Commission recommended that communities establish neighborhood agencies to serve youth—youth service bureaus—located in comprehensive neighborhood community centers. Such bureaus were to work with juveniles—both delinquent and nondelinquent—referred by the police, the juvenile court, parents, schools, and other sources.[34] Since 1967, a wide variety of youth service bureaus has been established. These bureaus use organizational structures that are tailored for the needs of their particular jurisdiction. Sherwood Norman defines a youth service bureau as a noncoercive, independent public or private agency established to divert children and youth from the justice system by (1) mobilizing community resources to solve youth problems, (2) strengthening existing youth resources and developing new ones, and (3) promoting positive programs to remedy delinquency-breeding conditions.[35]

According to Norman, the youth service bureau is organized to divert children and youth from the juvenile justice system. While doing so, it makes services available to parents and children on the verge of trouble and in need of help, thus helping to prevent delinquency.[36]

Most youth service bureaus are not part of the juvenile justice system. They accept children who are to be diverted from that system. Although there is no particular prototype for such agencies, the President's Crime Commission suggests that their relationship to the juvenile justice system should be the relationship illustrated in Figure 15–2.

Using community services to deal with delinquent and nondelinquent children has many advantages. First, such services allow children to avoid the stigma of being processed by a police agency. Second, they improve the community's awareness of the need to help children. Third, through the involvement of local residents' help they give a greater recognition to the complexity of the delinquent's problem, thus developing a sense of public responsibility and support for such programs. Fourth, they restrict court referral by the police to cases involving serious crimes.

To play a role in delinquency prevention, the police should maintain relationships with other agencies, for example, numerous mental health clinics, recreational organizations, church groups, and welfare agencies.

One of the most important institutions to play a role in delinquency prevention is the school. Chapter 10 discussed the role of the school and its relationship

Figure 15-2. Proposed Juvenile Justice System.

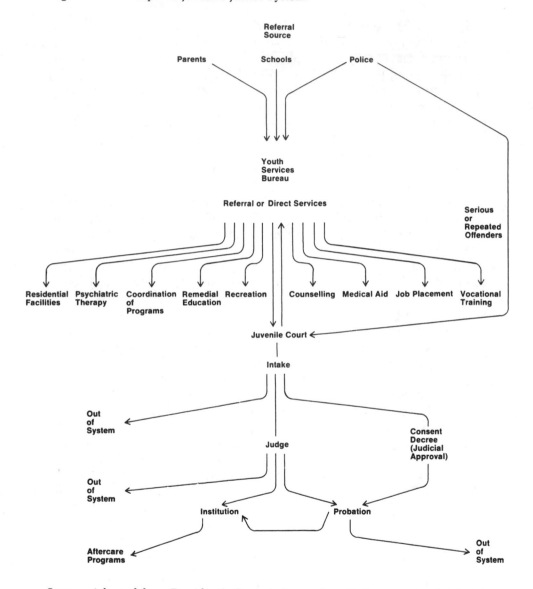

Source: Adapted from President's Commission on Law Enforcement and Administration of Justice, *The Challenge of Crime in a Free Society* (Washington, D.C.: U.S. Government Printing Office, 1967), p. 89.

to delinquency. The emphasis here is on the need for the police to develop effective relationships with schools in order to deal with predelinquent children. The educational process is a primary source of socialization for children. In recent years, the courts have granted children more due process rights in the schools, and children have been allowed greater freedoms. Peer groups pressures, youth gangs, and and ghetto values have led to delinquent and antisocial behavior within school settings. In addition, conflict over discriminatory forms of public education in recent years has led to racial and minority problems in many public schools systems across the country. The *Brown v. the Board of Education* decision in the 1950s has led courts to use busing to ensure equal education for all children.[37] These conflicts within the schools have often resulted in problems of communication and delinquent behavior by young people.

Linking the school with the police in the community is one way to help prevent delinquency. Liaison programs between the police and the schools have been implemented in many communities throughout the United States. Liaison officers from schools and police departments serve in educational and counseling roles to prevent and identify juveniles committing offenses during school hours on school property. They also protect children from persons loitering in or near schools, and they handle large school crowds. Juvenile police liaison officers should have some experience and training in juvenile and community relations work.

Another contribution that police departments can make to delinquency prevention involves police participation in recreation programs. Over the years, police departments have played a leadership role in developing recreational programs for juveniles. In some instances, they have actually operated such programs. In others, they have encouraged community support for recreational activities, including little league baseball, athletic clubs, camping programs, police athletic league programs, and scouting programs.

Perhaps one of the most important areas in delinquency prevention involves the development of employment opportunities for young people. Although all levels of government are involved in expanding job opportunities for youth, the juvenile police program is in a position to support such efforts. Many researchers indicate that youth unemployment is a major factor contributing to delinquent behavior. In addition, numerous sociological and cultural theories of delinquency indicate that employment is a significant variable in causing such behavior. Thus, the police should make an effort to develop employment opportunities for young people in the community. Contacts can be made with groups running programs like the National Job Corps, Opportunities Industrialization Center, and the National Urban League. The practices of both the police and employers can have a significant effect on delinquency prevention.

DIRECTIONS IN POLICE WORK WITH CHILDREN

Most of the important decisions in the juvenile justice system are made by police officers on the street. They have the first contact with juveniles, and their discretionary judgment determines if a child reaches the court system. Thus, the importance of the role of police officers cannot be overemphasized because their contact is society's first effort to prevent delinquency. Discretion often leading to unfair results, characterizes many police decisions in the juvenile justice system. Often, the actions of the police reflect the society's uncertainty about how to handle youth. If the police were to implement the law fully, the courts would be overwhelmed with both juvenile and adult offenders. Large numbers of youths are referred out of the juvenile justice system. Although this approach is encouraged, its effectiveness in reducing delinquency is questionable. Thus, it seems likely that many states will reduce the broad authority in their juvenile codes for taking children into custody and narrow police action to utilize the formal juvenile justice process. In addition, many police departments will probably develop specific procedures to handle children who violate the law, as well as those who are status offenders and those who are neglected and abused. Furthermore, with the continued increase in youth crime, it is expected that the police will exercise greater leadership in encouraging communities to provide more resources in the police department and in the area of social services for handling juvenile offenders.

Underlying these future directions of police work with young people is the fact that police departments are not predominantly juvenile organizations. Their primary role is to control adult crime. However, to accomplish that task they must control youthful criminality. Thus, police departments in the future will have to increase their commitment to their juvenile units. Debate about the direction of the juvenile justice system will continue, but the fact is that police policy in dealing with children will determine the well-being of both the children and society. What ultimately happens to a youth who is apprehended by the police may be most importantly determined by the police decision-making process. Police practices before and after custody—involving release of the child, referral to nonjudicial agencies, and referral to the juvenile court—are essential ingredients in any effort to control and prevent juvenile delinquency.

CHAPTER SUMMARY

As society has become more complex and rates of delinquency and noncriminal behavior have soared, the police have become more important than ever before to the juvenile justice system. It is almost always the police officer who has the initial contact with the large proportion of young people committing antisocial acts. Thus, the importance of the juvenile police officer cannot be overemphasized.

This chapter has focused on the role of police with juvenile offenders. Numerous factors influence the decisions that the police make about children. They include the seriousness of the offense, the harm inflicted on the victim, and the likelihood that the child will break the law again.

Attention was also given to the organization of police services, with particular emphasis on the management of juvenile police services. The recruitment, selection and training of juvenile police officers is essential to good police organization. Information regarding the legal aspects of police work with children, including the details of arrest, custodial interrogation, and line-ups is also covered.

One of the most important issues is police discretion in dealing with juvenile offenders. Discretion is a low visibility decision made in the administering of adult and juvenile justice. Discretionary decisions are made without guidelines or policy statements from the police administrator. Discretion is essential in providing individualized justice, but such problems as discrimination, unfairness, and bias toward particular groups of children must be controlled. The chapter concluded with an analysis of the role of the police in the area of delinquency prevention and the need of the police organization to develop and maintain programs with social service agencies.

DISCUSSION QUESTIONS

1. The term *discretion* is often defined as selective decision making by police and others in the juvenile justice system who are faced with alternative modes of action. Discuss some of the factors affecting the discretion of the police when dealing with juvenile offenders.

2. You are a police officer interested in working with juvenile offenders. What are some of the basic requirements that will help you be assigned to working with juveniles?

3. What role should police organizations play in delinquency prevention and control? Is it feasible to expect police departments to provide social services to children and families? How should police departments be better organized to provide for the control of juvenile delinquency?

4. Discuss some of the major techniques used by the police to investigate juvenile antisocial behavior. Why have the courts established rules and procedures for police investigations? Does the *Miranda* rule apply to juveniles arrested for both criminal and noncriminal behavior?

SUGGESTED READINGS

American Bar Association. *Project on Standards for Criminal Justice: Standards relating to Urban Police Function.* New York: Institute of Judicial Administration, 1972.

——Project on Standards for Juvenile Justice: Standards Relating to Police Handling of Juvenile Problems. Cambridge, Mass.: Ballinger Press, 1977.

Bordua, David J., ed. *The Police: Six Sociological Essays.* New York: Wiley, 1967.

Cavan, Ruth Stonle. *Juvenile Delinquency.* Philadelphia: Lippincott, 1969.

Chevigny, Paul. *Police Power: Police Abuses in New York City.* New York: Vantage Books, 1969.

Davis, Kenneth C. *Discretionary Justice: A Preliminary Inquiry.* Baton Rouge, La.: Louisiana State University Press, 1969.

Davis, Samuel. "Justice for the Juvenile: The Decision to Arrest and Due Process." *Duke Law Journal*—(1971): 913–920.

Eldefonso, Edward. *Law Enforcement and the Youthful Offender: Juvenile Procedures.* New York: Wiley, 1967.

Ferdinand, Theodore N., and Luchterhand, Elmer G. "Inner-City Youths, the Police, Juvenile Court, and Justice." *Social Problems* 17 (1970): 510–528.

LaFave, Wayne R. *Arrest: The Decision to Take a Suspect into Custody.* Boston: Little, Brown, 1965.

Niederhofer, Arthur. *Behind the Shield.* Garden City, N.Y.: Doubleday, 1967.

Packer, Herbert L. *The Limits of the Criminal Sanction.* Stanford, Calif.: Stanford University Press, 1968.

Piliavin, Irving, and Briar, Scott. "Police Encounters with Juveniles." *American Journal of Sociology* 70 (1964): 206–214.

National Advisory Commission on Criminal Justice Standards and Goals. *Police.* Washington, D.C.: Government Printing Office, 1973.

President's Commission on Law Enforcement and Administration of Justice. *Task Force Report: Juvenile Delinquency and Youth Crime.* Washington, D.C.: Government Printing Office, 1967.

Skolnick, Jerome H. *Justice without Trial: Law Enforcement in Democratic Society.* New York: Wiley, 1966.

Sterling, James. *Changes in the Role Concepts of Police Officers.* Washington, D.C.: International Association of Chiefs of Police, 1972.

Terry, Robert M. "Discrimination in the Handling of Juvenile Offenders by Social Control Agencies." *Journal of Research in Crime and Delinquency* 4 (1967): 218–226.

Weiner, Norman L., and Willie, Charles V. "Decisions by Juvenile Officers." *American Journal of Sociology* 76 (1971): 199–210.

Wilson, James Q. *Varieties of Police Behavior: The Management of Law and Order in Eight Communities.* Cambridge, Mass.: Harvard University Press, 1968.

REFERENCES

1. Uniform Crime Reports for the United States, 1978 (Washington, D.C.: U.S. Government Printing Office, 1978).

2. Donald Black and Albert J. Reiss, Jr., "Police Control of Juveniles," *American Sociological Review* 35 (1970): p. 63; Richard Lundman, Richard Sykes, and John Clark, "Police Control of Juveniles—A Replication," *Journal of Research on Crime and Delinquency* 15 (1978): p. 74.

3. Richard Myren and Lynn Swanson, *Police Work with Children—Perspectives and Principles* (Washington, D.C.: Government Printing Office, 1962), p. 9.

4. American Bar Association, *Standards Relating to Police Handling of Juvenile Problems* (Cambridge, Mass.: Ballinger Press, 1977), p. 1.

5. Ibid., p. 83.

6. See August Vollmer, *The Police and Modern Society* (Berkeley: University of California Press, 1936): O. W. Wilson, *Police Administration,* 2d ed. (New York: McGraw-Hill, 1963).

7. National Advisory Commission on Criminal Justice Standards and Goals, *Task Force Report on Juvenile Justice and Delinquency Prevention* (Washington, D.C.: Law Enforcement Assistance Administration, 1973), p. 245.

8. Ibid.

9. Bernard Greenblatt, *Staff and Training for Juvenile Law Enforcement in Urban Police Departments,* Children's Bureau Publication 13 (Washington, D.C.: Government Printing Office, 1960).

10. President's Commission on Law Enforcement and Administration of Justice, *The Challenge of Crime in a Free Society* (Washington, D.C.: Government Printing Office, 1967), p. ix.

11. National Advisory Commission on Criminal Justice Standards and Goals, *Task Force Report on Juvenile Justice and Delinquency Prevention,* p. 258.

12. American Bar Association, *Standards on Police Handling of Juvenile Problems,* p. 109.

13. Samuel Davis, *Rights of Juveniles: The Juvenile Justice System* (New York: Clark Boardman, 1974), Appendix B.

14. National Conference of Commissioners on Uniform State Laws, *Uniform Juvenile Court Act* (Philadelphia: American Law Institute, 1968), Sec. 13. See also National Council on Crime and Delinquency, *Standard and Family Court Act* (New York: NCCD, 1959); Paul Piersma, Jeanette Ganousis, and Prudence Kramer, "The Juvenile Court: Current Problems, Legislative

Proposals and a Model Act," *St. Louis University Law Journal* 20 (1975): pp. 1:99.

15. American Bar Association, *Standards on Police Handling of Juvenile Problems*, p. 54.

16. Joseph Senna and Larry Siegel, *Introduction to Criminal Justice* (St. Paul, Minn.: West Publishing, 1978), Chapter 5.

17. National Advisory Commission on Criminal Justice Standards and Goals, *Task Force Report on Juvenile Justice and Delinquency Prevention*, p. 207.

18. See Roscoe Pound, "Discretion, Dispensation and Mitigation: The Problem of the Individual Special Case," *New York University Law Review* 35 (1960): p. 926.

19. Kenneth C. Davis, *Discretionary Justice: A Preliminary Inquiry* (Baton Rouge: Louisiana State University Press, 1969).

20. Joseph Goldstein, "Police Discretion Not to Invoke the Criminal Process: Low Visibility Decisions in the Administration of Justice," *Yale Law Journal* 69 (1960): p. 544.

21. Victor Streib, *Juvenile Justice in America* (Port Washington, N.Y.: Kennikat Press, 1978).

22. Herbert Packer, *The Limits of the Criminal Sanction* (Stanford, Calif.: Stanford University Press, 1968).

23. See Paul Strasburg, *Violent Delinquents: Report to Ford Foundation from Vera Institute of Justice* (New York: Monarch, 1978): p. 11; see also Robert Terry, "The Screening of Juvenile Offenders," *Journal of Criminal Law, Criminology and Police Science* 58 (1967): p. 173:181.

24. Nathan Goldman, *The Differential Selection of Juvenile Offenders for Court Appearance* (Washington, D.C.: National Council on Crime and Delinquency, 1963).

25. Irving Piliavin and Scott Briar, "Police Encounters with Juveniles," *American Journal of Sociology* 70 (1964): pp. 206:214; also Theodore Ferdinand and Elmer Luchterhand, "Inner-City Youth, the Police, Juvenile Court and Justice," *Social Problems* 8 (1970): pp. 510;526.

26. Black and Reiss, "Police Control of Juveniles"; see also Richard J. Lundman, "Routine Police Arrest Practices," *Social Problems* FALL (1974): pp. 127:141.

27. Goldman, *The Differential Selection of Juvenile Offenders for Court Appearance*, p. 25; also Norman Werner and Charles Willie, "Decisions of Juvenile Officers," *American Journal of Sociology* 77 (1971): pp. 199:214.

28. See Aaron Cicourel, *The Social Organization of Juvenile Justice* (New York: Wiley, 1968).

29. Piliavin and Briar, "Police Encounters with Juveniles," p. 215.

30. American Bar Association Project on , *Standards for Criminal Justice: Standards Relating to Urban Police Function* (New York: Institute of Judicial Administration, 1972), Standard 4.2., p. 121.

31. American Bar Association, *Standards Relating to Police Handling of Juvenile Problems*, p. 45.

32. National Advisory Commission on Criminal Justice Standards and Goals, *Task Force Report on Juvenile Justice and Delinquency Prevention*, Standard 4.4, p. 189.

33. Kenneth C. Davis, *Police Discretion* (St. Paul, Minn.: West Publishing, 1975).

34. President's Commission on Law Enforcement and Administration of Justice, The Challenge of Crime in a Free Society, p. 89.

35. Sherwood Norman, *The Youth Service Bureau—A Key to Delinquency Prevention* (Hackensack, N.J.: National Council on Crime and Delinquency, 1972), p. 8.

36. Ibid.

37. See National Advisory Commission on Criminal Justice Standards and Goals, *Community Crime Prevention* (Washington, D.C.: Government Printing Office, 1973); see also *Brown v. Board of Education*, 347 U.S. 483 (1954).

Chapter 16

Chapter Outline	Key Terms, Names, and Cases
Introduction	diversion
The Concept of Detention	transfer proceedings
How a Child Enters Detention	intake
Current Detention Problems	Kent v. The United States
Standards for Detention Care	Breed v. Jones
The Intake Process	petition
Diversion	detention
Illustrations of Diversion Programs	jail
The Petition	Martarella v. Kelly
Bail for Children	601 Project
The Plea and Plea Bargaining in Juvenile Justice	bail
	shelter care
Transfer Proceedings	plea
Chapter Summary	plea bargain
	Santobello v. New York
	due process
	double jeopardy
	neglected children
	lockup

Early Court Processing

INTRODUCTION

One of the most important periods in the juvenile process is the time between the child's arrest and trial. After the juvenile has been taken into police custody, decisions as to the disposition of the case need to be made under police and judicial discretionary authority. By this point the child has been told of the right to counsel and the right to remain silent during questioning. In addition, the child's parents have probably been notified. At this time, the child may be faced with involuntary placement in a detention or shelter care facility. Detention, even if only for a short period, may have a serious effect on the child. For those children who are confined unnecessarily, it may contribute to future antisocial and delinquent behavior.

During this period, the child either retains his or her own attorney or is assigned counsel by the court. In addition to detention, the juvenile, the family, and the attorney must also consider diversion, bail, plea bargaining, and, in serious cases, the transfer of the child to the adult court. The family may seek to work with the police department and the courts to avoid formal judicial proceedings and seek help through a diversion program. Or, after an interview, the intake probation officer in the court may recommend that no further action be taken against the juvenile. Alternatively, the juvenile might be supervised by the intake section of the court without a judicial determination.

If the decision is to file a petition initiating formal judicial action against the juvenile, the child's attorney will find it necessary to seek pretrial release through bail or some other release measure and possibly to enter into plea bargaining discussions.

Thus, the period between the time a juvenile is arrested and the time he or she goes to trial is one of the most critical points in the juvenile justice system. It is then that decisions are made about what to do with the child. Because the steps in this process are so important, this chapter will examine how the child is handled during this period. First, it will look at the detention system, which takes children out of the community. It will define detention and review its many ramifications. Second, it will explore the relationship between detention and intake in the juvenile court. Intake procedures serve as a means of screening and diverting certain juvenile offenders from judicial proceedings. The chapter will then give considerable attention to the trend in juvenile intake and detention that emphasizes diversion, including the review of a variety of community-based alternatives to judicial processing. Lastly, the chapter will examine the function of bail and plea bargaining for children.

THE CONCEPT OF DETENTION

Detention is the temporary care of children in physically restricted facilities pending court disposition or transfer to another agency.[1] Traditional detention facilities for children are designed as secure environments. They have locked doors, high fences or walls, screens or bars, and other obstructions designed to prevent an accused juvenile from leaving the facility at will.

Detention facilities of this kind normally handle juveniles at different stages of the juvenile justice process. Some juveniles are kept in detention to await their court hearings. Other children in detention are those who have had a trial but who have not been sentenced or who are awaiting the imposition of their sentences. A third group of children are those whose sentences have been imposed but who are awaiting admittance to a correctional training school. Thus, as the American Bar Association states, "The term 'pre-trial detainee' is inaccurate to describe the many juveniles in detention whose cases have already been adjudicated but whose disposition remains implemented."[2] Regardless of when the child enters detention, detention is not a form of punishment. A juvenile is not a sentenced offender when placed in detention. In other words, a detention facility is not to be used as a permanent correctional facility. It operates as a placement between the police and the courts, providing temporary care for children who require secure custody. However, a 1975 report by the National Council of Jewish Women entitled *Children without Justice* found that "the care in detention was of varying degrees, the custody was a matter of lock and key, and the instructive experience was more the exception than the rule. ... Repeatedly, detention emerged as a form of punishment without conviction—and often without crime."[3]

Other than the secure facility, there are different types of residential care programs that should be distinguished from detention. Shelter care, for example, is the temporary care of children in physically unrestricting facilities. The secure detention facility is normally used for children who have been charged with delinquent acts. Shelter care programs, including receiving homes, group homes, foster care homes, and temporary care facilities, are normally used for dependent and neglected children and status offenders. As the National Council on Crime and Delinquency states in its *Standards and Guides for the Detention of Children and Youth*, "Children who require detention are for the most part disturbed adolescents who have been apprehended for serious violations of the law. Those that require shelter care are for the most part infants, toddlers, pre-school children and school-age children usually in the lower grades."[4] Most experts in juvenile justice advocate that detention be limited to alleged delinquent offenders who require secure custody for the protection of themselves and others. All too often, however, children who are neglected and dependent as well as children in need of group homes and treatment centers are placed in secure detention facilities. As a result, in many jurisdictions, laws have been passed that bar sending status offenders and neglected children to detention facilities for juvenile delinquents. In addition, alternatives to detention centers—for example, temporary foster homes, detention boarding homes, and programs of neighborhood supervision—have been developed in numerous jurisdictions. They enable youths to live in homes while the courts dispose of their cases.

HOW A CHILD ENTERS DETENTION

The majority of children taken into custody by the police are released to their parents or guardians. Some are detained overnight in a detention facility until their parents can be notified of the arrest. Police officers normally take a child to a place of detention only after other alternatives have been tried. Many juvenile courts in large urban areas have staff members, such as intake probation officers, on duty to screen detention admittance twenty-four hours a day. Thus, if a child is not released to parents, the police normally take the child to the detention facility or to the juvenile court.

Children who are apprehended for juvenile delinquency are normally detained if they are inclined to run away while awaiting their trials, if it appears that they will commit an offense dangerous to themselves or to the community, or if they are violators from other jurisdictions. Children who are not runaways or dangerous to themselves generally should not be placed in a detention facility. In addition, neglected and dependent children and status offenders should not be placed in a secure facility.

A child who is placed in a detention facility or shelter care unit should not be kept there longer than twenty-four hours. Most jurisdictions require the filing of a formal petition against the child invoking the jurisdiction of the juvenile court within the twenty-four-hour period. Since the Kent v. The United States case, and the awareness that enormous discretion governs decisions at different stages in the juvenile justice system, many juvenile codes have established criteria for detaining juveniles. To detain a juvenile, clear evidence must be established of probable cause to believe that the child has committed the offense and that he or she will flee the area if not detained. Furthermore, once a child has been detained and a petition filed, the child should not continue in detention without a detention hearing. Although there is considerable variation among the states about detention hearings, most jurisdictions require them almost immediately after the child's admission to a detention facility.[5]

The American Bar Association's Standards Relating to Interim Status, Standard 7.6, suggests the following in regard to detention hearings:

(a) Timing. An accused juvenile taken into custody should, unless sooner released, be accorded a hearing in court within 24 hours of the filing of the petition for a release hearing required by Standard 6.5(b)2. (b) Notice. Actual notice of the detention review hearing should be given to the accused juvenile, the parents and their attorneys immediately upon intake officials' decision that the juvenile will not be released prior to the hearing. (c) Rights. An attorney for the accused juvenile should be present at the hearing in addition to the juvenile's parents, if they attend.[6]

The intake probation department of the juvenile court decides whether to keep a child in detention when the police file a petition. Usually a probation officer in the intake department assists the court in making a decision about the child's release. This decision is part of the intake procedure of the juvenile court. It is described in the following section.

In sum, whether children enter detention depends on the nature of the actions they have committed, whether they are a danger to themselves or others, and whether or not their parents or lawful guardians can be reached quickly to take them home. If children are to be kept longer than twenty-four hours, a formal petition must be filed against them and their parents must be notified so the children can possibly be released in their custody. Furthermore, criteria for detention must be established, and a formal detention hearing must be held. Cooperation between the police and the juvenile court is essential in the development of a sound policy of detention intake.

CURRENT DETENTION PROBLEMS

Use of Jails

Almost all experts in the field of juvenile justice agree that placing children under the age of eighteen in any type of jail facility should be prohibited. Arguments against the use of jails for juveniles were clearly stated in the National Council on Crime and Delinquency's *Standards and Guides for the Detention of Children and Youth*:

The case against the use of jails for children rests on the fact that youngsters of juvenile court age are still in the process of development and are still subject to change, however large they may be physically or however sophisticated their behavior. To place them behind bars at a time when the whole world seems to turn against them, and belief in themselves is shattered or distorted, merely confirms the criminal role in which they see themselves. Jailing delinquent youngsters plays directly into their hands by giving them delinquency status among their peers. If they resent being treated like confirmed adult criminals, they may—and often do—strike back violently at society after their release. The public tends to ignore the fact that every youngster placed behind bars will return to the society which placed him there.[7]

Based on the latest reliable information from the National Jail Census, a total of 7,800 juveniles were reported in 4,037 jails on a given day in 1970. Of the total number of juveniles detained in jails, 66 percent had not been adjudicated.[8] The *Report on Corrections* of the National Advisory Commission on Criminal Justice Standards and Goals estimated in 1973 that at least 50,000 and possibly more than 100,000 children of juvenile court age are held in jails and police lockups each year.[9] Rosemary Sarri, in a well-documented report entitled *Under Lock and Key: Juveniles in Jail and Detention*, reported that it is probable that up to 500,000 juveniles are processed through local adult jails each year in the United States.[10]

Without question, jailing of juveniles is a substantial problem in the United States. Large numbers of juveniles continue to be held in jail prior to their adjudication today. Even though they are usually held in separate areas of the jail, the same physically restrictive and unhealthy conditions exist for the child and the adult suspect.

Over the years, jails have been the least progressive of all correctional institutions in America. Most jails were constructed in the nineteenth century. Few have been substantially improved in the twentieth century, and many are in poor physical condition. Many jails throughout the country are overcrowded, have no rehabilitation programs, provide little or no medical attention, and make no effort to provide adequate plumbing, ventilation, or heating. Many jails are fire hazards. Courts throughout the country have ruled that conditions in particular jails make incarceration there a cruel and unusual punishment and this is a violation of the Eighth and Fourteenth Amendments to the United States Constitution. However, in 1972, only five states explicitly prohibited jailing children under all circumstances, although most statutes recommend that the practice be stopped.[11]

Overuse of Detention

The most recent available data indicate that approximately 500,000 juveniles enter detention each year in the United States. In 1971, a total of 11,748 youths were counted in 303 detention units.[12] Since every indication is that these data have remained reasonably constant over the past decade, it can be assumed that over half a million children enter detention each year and that about 12,000 are in a short-term detention facility on any given day, with the average length of stay about eleven days per youth. Since approximately 100,000 more children are admitted to all types of juvenile correctional facilities, detention is the most widely used form of placement for children. Five out of every six children in all juvenile facilities are held in detention.[13] Thus, the importance of detention as a critical point in the juvenile justice process cannot be overstated.

Detention has many major problems:

1. Appropriate facilities may be unavailable or not used.
2. Detention may be ordered for the administrative convenience of law enforcement personnel who desire access to the juvenile.
3. Detention may be used as punishment.
4. Adult facilities may be used.
5. The length of detention may be unfair and detrimental to the child.[14]

Certainly, many jurisdictions use the traditional detention in a secure setting where foster homes, family homes, group homes, or boarding facilities are not available. Also, where administrators, police officials, and prosecutors are more concerned about custody and adjudication, the secure detention home provides a suitable place for administrative control over the child awaiting trial. Many judges believe that detention has some therapeutic value. They see confinement as a deterrent to further delinquency. Such an approach is a major obstacle in reducing the number of children sent to detention facilities.

Many jurisdictions continue to place in detention children who have committed no crimes (they are truant, incorrigible, or runaway) as well as children who are neglected or abused. An estimated 50 percent of the population in most detention homes is drawn from these groups.[15] While this policy continues, it will act as a major obstacle to goals of delinquency prevention and treatment, particularly for status offenders. Highlight 16–1 is a vivid illustration of the problems in juvenile detention in America.

Highlight 16–1. DYS urged: Shut 3 centers.

Study cites cost of juvenile detention facilities

By Jerry Taylor
Globe Staff

The state Department of Youth Services (DYS) should close three of its seven detention centers for juvenile delinquents, cutting the number of cells in these "juvenile jails" in half, the Massachusetts Advocacy Center says.

"Each year they house nearly 2300 youngsters, many of whom present no security risk, at a cost to Massachusetts taxpayers of nearly $4 million," the advocacy center, a private nonprofit organization, said in a 154-page report issued today after a one-year study of "secure" juvenile detention.

"The great majority (at least 70 percent) of these youngsters are not awaiting trial. They have already been found delinquent by a court and committed to DYS."

The report calls for closing the boys' detention center in Boston's Roslindale section, which it described as "a building in which decent programs and humane care cannot take place," and two of the three girls' centers, in the Charlestown YMCA and the Old Colony YMCA, Brockton. It suggests that the money made available from these shutdowns be spent on expanding community-based residential programs.

DYS Comr. Edward M. Murphy, in a letter included in the report, argued against closing Roslindale. He called the center "far from perfect," but asserted it is superior to the other six and "one of the few physical plants within the department's control that offers adequate recreational, educational and food service space."

The report entitled "Delinquent Justice: Juvenile Detention Practice in Massachusetts," recommends keeping detention centers in Westfield and at Danvers and Taunton State Hospitals, all for boys, and the girls' center on the grounds of Madonna Hall in Marlboro, a girls' boarding school run by the Sisters of the Good Shepherd.

Closing the three detention facilities would reduce DYS's capacity for "secure" pretrial custody from 122 youths — 90 boys and 32 girls — to 67 youths — 55 boys and 12 girls.

The advocacy center defended its proposals by citing statistics showing a decline since 1975 in serious crime by juveniles (youths 16 and younger) in Massachusetts.

It said the DYS detention centers, costing $61 to $113 a day per inmate, now keep behind locked doors, bars, or barbed wire fences a high proportion of offenders and suspects who either should be in rehabilitation programs or in a less expensive and confining place awaiting trial.

"Why are they there?" the report asked.

The report then went on to state that "Some are there because they disrupt community programs; some are there because they are chronic runaways; some are there because they have emotional problems; and some are there simply because judges and other officials consider their homes to be 'unfit.'

"But the major reason that committed children are locked up in secure detention is rarely acknowledged: They are there because the beds are there. These are the leftover institutions, the vestiges of an earlier era when children were imprisoned out of a misguided benevolence, in order to 'reform' them.

Two major reasons for overuse of detention, the report found, are that the seven DYS regional offices have a financial incentive to place teenagers there and that some privately-run treatment programs refuse "difficult" youths referred by DYS.

The report includes a breakdown of the 103 youths in DYS detention centers on Aug. 21, 1979. Eighty-five had been convicted of various offenses, 28 for violent crimes, and were awaiting transfer to DYS treatment programs. Eighteen, including 12 girls, were awaiting trial. Of the 18, two, both males, were accused of major crimes against persons.

The study took exception to what it called an over-representation of girls in detention. One-fourth of the DYS detention beds today are for girls while they account for only 10 percent of all juveniles committed to DYS.

"Girls are locked up at a more frequent rate than boys for reasons that have less to do with their delinquency than with the notion that they must be 'protected' from unhealthy families or unwholesome environments," the report, written by Elizabeth W. Vorenberg and Sharland Trotter of the advocacy center's staff, said.

Recommendations for juvenile detention centers

The Massachusetts Advocacy Center makes the following recommendations for juvenile detention centers of the state Department of Youth Services:

• Close the Roslindale center for boys and the detention centers for girls in the Charlestown YMCA and the Brockton

YMCA, reducing capacity for boys from 90 to 55 and for girls from 32 to 12.

• Minimize institutional aspects of any new or renovated centers.

• Amend state law to give an independent hearing officer the power to revoke a center's license.

• Department of Public Health should refer violations of its regulations to state attorney general's office.

• Office for Children should restrict waivers of its licensing standards.

• Equalize pay of detention workers and DYS regional caseworkers.

• Strip-search only those juveniles suspected of carrying contraband.

• Prohibit isolation except in cases of imminent danger or bodily injury or property damage.

• Directors of centers should give written justifications for isolation and strip searches to DYS headquarters.

• Create a citizen advisory committee for each detention center.

• All judges and others involved in detention decisions should visit every two months the centers where they send youths.

• Massachusetts Bar Assn. should name a commission to explore bail and other pretrial procedures for juveniles and report findings to the Legislature in one year.

• DYS should identify all its juveniles by race to permit evaluation of role that color plays in detention placements.

• Judges setting bail for juveniles should document their reasons in writing.

• DYS should help every juvenile to have his or her bail reviewed by a higher court.

Reprinted courtesy of *The Boston Globe*, June 25, 1980.

STANDARDS FOR DETENTION CARE

The typical detention facility in America is operated by a county government and is located in an urban area. The building is usually an institutional facility with a physically secure custody. It has minimal program activities and few professionally trained staff members. The National Advisory Commission on Criminal Justice Standards and Goals reported in 1973 that only 44 percent of all workers in detention facilities had college degrees in social work, psychology, or education. Salaries were low, and few programs were operated on a civil service or merit system. Also, few facilities provided programs of recreation, education, group discussion, individual guidance, or religious services.[16] To understand the present state of detention in the juvenile justice system and recognize the need for improvement, one need only review the case of *Martarella v. Kelly*.[17] This case contended that the incarceration of noncriminal children in maximum-security detention facilities in New York under conditions described as punitive, hazardous, unhealthy, and lacking in rehabilitative treatment constituted cruel and unusual punishment and violated due process under the Eighth and Fourteenth Amendments. The *Kelly* case challenged the detention of children identified as persons in need of supervision in three maximum-security facilities without treatment and under cruel and unusual conditions. The court held that one of the facilities was so deplorable that it violated the Eighth Amendment. A second facility was closed prior to the court decision, and conditions in the third facility were found to be correctable. The court also found that the treatment of long-term detainees was inadequate and recommended the development of both educational and recreational programs for children, maximum ratios of staff to children, and provisions for medical and psychiatric treatment.[18]

Juvenile detention programs throughout the country vary significantly, and many fail to provide adequate services to children. Traditionally, detention has been based on the concept of secure custody. In recent years, however, efforts have been made to improve services in secure detention facilities. Programs such as reception and diagnosis, community contact involving legal services and family visiting, and counseling, recreational, and educational programs are important aspects of secure detention. In addition, new types of residential facilities are being created. Young persons who cannot return home are being held in dormitories and multiple residential dwellings. Many states, for example, have established programs for children as alternatives to detention.[19] Detention in boarding homes and foster homes is being given greater emphasis, particularly with nondelinquent children.

For children who commit serious delinquent acts, certain standards are recommended. The American Bar Association, for example, suggests: (1) that the use of adult jails be prohibited; (2) that states develop policies favoring nonsecure detention centers; (3) that juveniles not charged with a crime not be held in secure detention facilities with accused juvenile offenders; (4) that population limits be placed on detention homes; (5) that juveniles held in interim detention be given educational programs; and (6) that juveniles in detention be given basic constitutional rights, including the right to privacy, the right to an attorney, the right to appropriate visitation, and telephone and mail privileges.[20]

THE INTAKE PROCESS

When the police department believes a child needs a court referral, the police become involved in the intake division of the court. The term *intake* refers to the screening of cases by the juvenile court system. It involves the review and initial screening of a child and family by intake probation officers to determine if the child needs the services of the juvenile court. The intake process serves the following important functions:

Intake reduces the considerable demands on limited court resources to manageable levels; it screens out cases that are not within the court's jurisdiction; and most importantly it obtains assistance from community agencies when court authority is not necessary for referral.[21]

In addition, the intake stage is a time when the child can receive treatment in a most efficient and timely manner. It represents an opportunity to place the child in informal programs operated by the court and the community. The intake process is critically important because more than half of the referrals to the juvenile courts never go beyond that stage.

Juvenile court intake—which seeks to screen out cases not within the court's jurisdiction and to handle cases not serious enough to court intervention—is now provided for by statute in the majority of states.[22] Also, most of the model acts and standards in juvenile justice suggest the development of juvenile court intake proceedings.[23]

Intake procedures are desirable for the following reasons:

1. Filing complaints against children in a court may do more harm than good, because rehabilitation often fails in the juvenile court system.
2. Processing children in the juvenile court labels them delinquent, stigmatizes them, and thus reinforces their antisocial behavior.
3. Nonjudicial handling of children gives them and their families an opportunity to work with a voluntary social service agency.
4. Intake screening of children helps conserve already overburdened resources in the juvenile court system.
5. Intake screening allows juvenile courts to enter into consent decrees with juveniles without filing petitions and without formal adjudication. (The consent decree is basically a court order authorizing the disposition of the case without a formal finding of delinquency. It is based on an agreement between the intake department of the court and the juvenile who is the subject of the complaint.)[24]

Notwithstanding all the advantages of intake, it also has some problems:

1. Since half of all juveniles who are arrested and brought to court are handled nonjudicially, intake sections are constantly pressured to provide available services for a large group of children. Intake programs also need to be provided twenty-four hours a day in many urban courts so dispositions can be resolved quickly on the day the child is referred to the court.
2. The key to good intake service is the quality of the intake probation staff in the court. Poorly qualified employees in intake are a serious flaw in many court systems.
3. Although almost three-quarters of all state juvenile court statutes provide intake and diversion programs, the criteria and procedures for selecting children for such nonjudicial alternatives have not been established.

Normally, the intake probation officer undertakes a preliminary investigation to obtain information about the child and the family prior to making a decision. Written guidelines are needed to assist intake personnel in their duties and to alert juveniles and their families to their procedural rights.

4. A number of legal problems are associated with the intake process. Among them are whether the child has a right to counsel at this stage, whether juveniles are protected against self-incrimination at intake, and to what degree the child needs to consent to nonjudicial disposition as recommended by the intake probation officer.

DIVERSION

One of the most important alternatives chosen at intake is nonjudicial disposition, or, as it is variously called, nonjudicial adjustment, handling or processing, informal disposition, adjustment, or diversion.[25] *Diversion* is probably the most common term used to refer to screening out children from the juvenile court without judicial determination.

Numerous national groups, commentators, lawyers, and criminal justice experts have sought to define the concept of diversion since its inception in the mid-1960s. We suggest that diversion is primarily the early court process of placing offenders, both adult and juvenile, into noncriminal programs prior to their formal trial or conviction.[26] Paul Nejelski defines diversion as "the channeling of cases to noncourt institutions, in instances where these cases would ordinarily have received an adjudicatory hearing by a court."[27] The National Advisory Commission on Criminal Justice Standards and Goals' Task Force on Courts suggests that there is a distinction between diversion and screening. Diversion encourages an individual to participate in some specific program or activity by express or implied threat of further prosecution. Screening, on the other hand, involves abandoning efforts to apply any coercive measures to a defendant.[28]

Whatever formally accepted definition is used, diversion generally refers to formally acknowledged and organized efforts to process juvenile and adult offenders outside the justice system. As LaMar Empy states, "Diversion suggests that more first-time and petty, as well as status, offenders, should be channeled away from legal processing and into community institutions.[29]

Diversion has become one of the most popular reforms in juvenile justice since it was recommended by the President's Crime Commission in 1967. Arguments for the use of diversion programs include the following:

1. It keeps the juvenile justice system operating; without it, the system would collapse from voluminous caseloads.
2. It is preferable to dealing with the inadequate juvenile justice treatment system.
3. It gives legislators and other government leaders the opportunity to reallocate resources to programs that may be more successful in the treatment of juvenile offenders.
4. Its costs are significantly less than the per capita cost of institutionalization.

As Nejelski states: "There is much that is new about juvenile diversion—new screening procedures, new programs, and new incentives from federal funding. It is the overture to the new corrections, with its emphasis on de-institutionalization and purchase of services."[30]

Many diversion programs exist throughout the United States today. Since the mid-1960s, the Law Enforcement Assistance Administration, the now disbanded Youth Development and Delinquency Prevention Administration of the U.S. Department of Health, Education, and Welfare, and the U.S. Department of Labor have greatly expanded funding for diversion programs. These programs vary in size and emphasis but generally possess the same goal—to constructively bypass juvenile adjudication by providing reasonable alternatives in the form of treatment, counseling, employment, or education programs.

There are police-based diversion models that include family crisis intervention projects, referral programs, and youth service bureaus. In addition, there are numerous court-based diversion models. These have been used extensively for status offenders, minor first offenders, children involved in family disturbances, and children involved in offenses such as shoplifting, minor assault, and battery. Court-based diversion programs include intervention projects involving employment, referral for educational programs, and placement of juveniles who are involved with drugs in drug-related programs.

ILLUSTRATIONS OF DIVERSION PROGRAMS

Highlight 16-2 provides detailed descriptions of three unique juvenile diversion projects.

Highlight 16-2. Diversion Projects.

The 601 Diversion Project. The Sacramento County Probation Department created an experimental diversion project designed to give children family crisis therapy on a short-term basis. The name of the project, *601 Diversion,* is derived from Section 601 of the state welfare and institutions code, which deals with juveniles and with delinquent problems. Cases generally involve conflict and lack of communication between youths and their families. The diversion project experimented to determine whether juveniles charged with offenses such as refusing to obey their parents or being habitually truant could be better handled through short-term family therapy administered at the intake department by specially trained probation officers rather than through traditional court

procedures. The program identified a particular kind of problem—the problem of children beyond the control of their parents—and provided a referral service for treatment. When a "601" child is referred by the police, school, or parents, the specialized unit of the probation department arranges to see if special counseling can be of assistance. Thus, instead of the child proceeding through the juvenile court, the child and the family receive immediate family counseling services.

Los Angeles County Regional Diversion Program. Since 1974, a regional diversion network has served more than 25,000 troubled and delinquent youngsters in sixty-four cities in Los Angeles County. Over thirteen diversion programs covering 80 percent of the county work with law

---

enforcement agencies, schools, probation departments, and other social service agencies to identify youngsters and their families who can profit from diversion programs rather than judicial services. Funds are provided through the Law Enforcement Assistance Administration and the Los Angeles Regional Criminal Justice Planning Board. Both public and private agencies provide the service, which include crisis intervention, counseling, mental health programs, legal assistance, and vocational training. Clients range from troubled youths referred by the schools to hard-core juvenile offenders and adjudicated by the courts.

Bronx Neighborhood Youth Diversion Program. The Bronx Neighborhood Youth Diversion Program deals with youths between twelve and fifteen years of age. It is primarily a community-run program. Cases

are generally referred by probation officers and family court judges. The program has a staff of counselors and advocates, and it works on a one-to-one basis. The advocate counselor directs the child and supervises his or her overall activities, including work, school, and home relationships. In addition, the program has a "forum," which is a panel of community residents. The forum deals with offenses that neighborhood children commit and acts as a resolution group between parents and children.

Sources: Roger Baron, Floyd Feeney, and Warren Thornton, "Preventing Delinquency through Diversion: The Sacramento County 601 Diversion Project," *Federal Probation* (March 1973), pp. 13–18; and U.S. Department of Justice, *Exemplary Projects* (Washington, D.C.: Government Printing Office, 1978), pp. 19–21.

These, then, are some of the varied approaches to diversion programs for youth in the United States. Others include Project De Novo in Minneapolis, Minnesota, which offers counseling, employment placement, and educational opportunities to juveniles and adult offenders except those accused of violent crime.[31] In San Diego, California, the County Probation Department runs a juvenile narcotics project. It offers drug education in lieu of juvenile prosecution.[32] Philadelphia, Pennsylvania, has a pre-indictment probation program that concentrates on diverting first offenders charged with nonviolent crimes.[33] The Baltimore Pre-Trial Intervention Project is a ninety-day project specifically designed for juveniles between the ages of fifteen and seventeen.[34] It offers an in-house education program in addition to counseling and job placement services.

Many states have created statutory diversion programs for juvenile and adult offenders, but most of the diversion programs operating today are informal and not mandated by law. They are the result primarily of federal project funding. Legislation is needed for the true implementation of such programs if diversion is to perform the services intended.

Some commentators have raised questions about the effectiveness of the various diversion approaches. Don Gibbons and Gerald Blake, for example, found that a review of diversion programs in Los Angeles County provided little factual evidence in support of such programs.[35] Nejelski has pointed out the lack of evaluation procedures in the four diversion programs he evaluated.[36] Richard Lundman takes the position that diversion will probably not reduce recidivism or correct existing treatment abuses.[37] Nonetheless, most juvenile justice experts believe that diversion provides great hope for the prevention and control of juvenile and antisocial behavior. Highlight 16–3 presents the position of the National Advisory Commission on Criminal Justice Standards and Goals.

Highlight 16–3. Ramifications of Diversion.

It is obvious that diversion is both a new idea and a very old practice. It is also obvious that prevention, diversion, screening, and minimizing penetration are closely related concepts that become easily confused by those attempting to deal with alternatives to criminal justice processing. Each, however, is predicated on the assumption that the existing system is often destructive and that it is better to direct many offenders to programs that are less stigmatizing, less restricting, less punitive, than it is to escalate them through the justice system. Unfortunately, however, diversion may be used as an excuse for not addressing the very real problems associated with the development of effective preventive, correctional, differential care, custody, and treatment programs. Many programs that are labeled diversion did not originate as formal efforts to divert people from the criminal justice process but came about through ambiguities in the law or the discretionary practices of individual agents of the justice system. Real programs of diversion specify objectives, identify a target group, outline means and activities for achieving the goals, implement programs, and produce evidence of a plan to at least attempt to evaluate whether or not the means employed are successful in achieving the goals desired. Because of the variety of diversionary methods, it is essential that the community obtain reliable information concerning their effectiveness in crime control. Information is needed regarding diversion's impact on the justice system, the role diversion plays in crime prevention, and the relative rates of success on cases diverted from the system at different stages as compared with cases subjected to varying degrees of criminalization. Such information is not now available, nor will it be available until records are kept on diversion as well as on cases processed officially.

When two or more control methods appear to be about equally effective, researchers need to decide between them. Research involves experimental design and random assignment of cases to alternative treatment or control methods, and it requires most of all that judgments of authorities be assessed in terms of their empirical consequences, not their intended effects.

In the absence of research and experimentation, the assessment of correctional policies is largely a matter of guesswork. But the evidence that does exist suggests that diversion may warrant consideration as the preferred method of control for a far greater number of offenders. Moreover, it appears that diversion plays a significant role in crime prevention and in maintaining the justice system so that it is not swamped by its own activity.

Diversion provides society with the opportunity to begin the reordering of the justice system, by redistributing resources to achieve justice and correctional goals—to develop truly effective prevention, justice, control, and social restoration programs.

Perhaps the single greatest contribution that diversion can make during the next decade is to make society more conscious and sensitive to the deficiencies of the justice system, and hence to force radical changes within the system so that appropriate offenders are successfully diverted from the system while others are provided with programs within the system that offer social restoration instead of criminal contamination.

Source: National Advisory Commission on Criminal Justice Standards and Goals, *Corrections* (Washington, D.C.: Government Printing Office, 1978), pp. 93–94.

THE PETITION

A complaint is the report that the police or some other agency makes to the court to initiate the intake process. Once the agency makes an intake decision that judicial disposition is required, a formal petition is filed. The petition is the formal legal complaint that initiates judicial action against a juvenile charged with actions alleging juvenile delinquency or noncriminal behavior. The petition includes such basic information as the name, age, and residence of the child, the parents' names, and the facts alleging the child's delinquency. The police officer, a family member, or a social service agency can bring a petition. If, after being given the right to counsel, the child admits the allegation in the petition, a hearing is immediately scheduled for the child to make the admission before the court, and information is gathered to develop a plan.

If the child does not admit to any of the facts in the petition, a date for a scheduled hearing on the petition is set. This hearing, whose purpose is to determine the merits of the petition, is similar to the adult trial. Once a hearing or adjudication date has been set, the probation department, which is the agency providing social services to the court, is normally asked to prepare a social study report. This report, often known as the social investigation or the predisposition investigation, collects relevant information about the child and recommends treatment and service.

When a date has been set for the hearing on the petition, parents or guardians and other persons associated with the petition, such as witnesses, the arresting police officer, and victims, are notified of the hearing. On occasion, the court may issue a summons—a court order requiring the juvenile or others involved in the case to appear for the hearing. The statutes or the juvenile code in a given jurisdiction govern the contents of the petition.[38] Some jurisdictions, for instance, require that a petition be filed on information and belief of the complainant alone. Others require that the petition be filed under oath or even that an affidavit accompany the petition. Some jurisdictions authorize only one official, such as a probation officer or prosecutor, to file the petition. Others allow numerous officials, including family and social service agencies, to set forth facts in the petition.

BAIL FOR CHILDREN

Bail is money or some other security provided to the court to ensure the appearance of a defendant at every subsequent stage of the justice process. Its purpose is to obtain the release from custody of the person charged with the crime. Once the amount of bail is set by the court, the defendant is required to pay a percentage of the entire amount in cash or securities or to pay a professional bail bondsman to submit a bond as a guarantee for returning to court. If a person is released on bail but fails to appear in court at the stipulated time, the bail deposit is forfeited. The person is then confined in a detention facility until the court appearance.

With a few exceptions, persons other than those accused of murder are entitled to reasonable bail, as stated in the Eighth Amendment of the United States Constitution. There is some controversy today as to whether a constitutional right to bail exists or whether the court can impose excessive bail resulting in a person's confinement. In most cases, a defendant has a right to be released on reasonable bail. Many jurisdictions require a bail review hearing by a higher court when a person is detained because the initial judge sets excessive bail.

Whether a defendant will appear at the next stage of the juvenile or criminal proceeding is a key issue in determining bail. Bail cannot be used to punish an accused; nor can it be denied or revoked at the discretion of the court. Many experts believe that money bail is one of the worst aspects of the criminal justice system. It has plagued the system for decades. It is discriminatory because it works against the poor. It is costly because the government must pay to detain those offenders who are unable to pay bail and who could otherwise be in the community. It is believed that people who await trial in jail have a higher proportion of subsequent convictions than people who are released on bail. The detention of individuals who cannot pay has a dehumanizing effect on them.[39]

Over the years, few have realized that the same issues are involved in the detention of juveniles. Juvenile detention prior to adjudication is one of the most serious problems facing the juvenile justice system. Large numbers of juveniles are incarcerated at this critical stage. Poor conditions exist in the detention facilities where they are held, and there are harmful aftereffects of the detention process. Despite these facts, many states refuse juveniles the right to bail. They argue that juvenile proceedings are civil, not criminal, and that detention is rehabilitative, not punitive. In addition, juveniles do not need a constitutional right to bail because statutory provisions allow children to be released in parental custody. Furthermore, it is suggested that detention facilities and the number of children in them should be reduced instead of developing a bail program.[40]

In view of the recognized deficiency of the adult bail system, some experts believe that alternative release programs should be developed for the juvenile justice system. These programs include release on recognizance, release to a third party, and the use of station-house summonses or citation programs in lieu of arrest.

Some states do provide bail programs for children. Massachusetts, for example, applies the same standard in deciding bail for children and adults.[41] Bail is used only to assure the presence of the accused at trial. A presumption exists that the accused should be released solely on this promise.

Many jurisdictions, however, are unclear whether a child has the constitutional right to be released on bail. Some courts have stated that bail provisions do not apply to juveniles. Others rely on the Eighth Amendment or on state constitutional provisions or statutes and conclude that juveniles do have a right to bail.

In a bail hearing for a child, the court reviews such factors as the charge, the history of the parents' ability to control the child's behavior, the child's school participation, psychological and psychiatric evaluations, and the child's desire to go home and the parents' interest in continuing to take care of the child while awaiting the trial.

THE PLEA AND PLEA BARGAINING IN JUVENILE JUSTICE

In the adult criminal justice system, the defendant normally enters a plea of guilty or not guilty. More than 90 percent of all adult defendants plead guilty before the trial stage. A large proportion of those pleas involve what is known as plea bargaining. Plea bargaining is the exchange of prosecutorial and judicial concessions for guilty pleas.[42] It permits a defendant to plead guilty in exchange for a less serious charge or an agreement by the prosecutor to recommend a reduced sentence to the court.

Few juvenile codes require a guilty or not guilty plea when a petition is filed against a child in the juvenile court. In most jurisdictions, the child either submits to a finding of the facts or denies the petition.[43] When the child admits to the facts, the court determines an appropriate disposition and treatment plan for the child. When the allegations in the petition are denied, the case normally proceeds to the trial or adjudication stage of the juvenile process. When a child enters no plea, the court imposes a denial of the charges for the child.

A high percentage of juvenile offenders enter guilty pleas or admissions in the juvenile court. How many of these pleas involve plea bargaining between the prosecutor or probation officer and the child's attorney is unclear. In the past, it was believed that plea bargaining was unnecessary in the juvenile justice system because the court had the flexibility to dispose of cases in the best interest of the child. However, in recent years, with the increase of violent juvenile crime, attorneys have begun to see some advantage to negotiating a plea rather than accepting the so-called good interests of the court regarding the child's offense. Also, the reality of the juvenile system is that it is a legal system almost identical to the adult criminal process. The extension of the adversary process for children has led to an increase in plea bargaining. Other factors in the trend toward juvenile plea bargaining include the use of prosecutors rather than probation personnel and police officers in juvenile courts and the ever-increasing caseloads in such courts. Plea bargaining negotiations generally involve the reduction of a charge, the changing of the proceedings from delinquency to noncriminal behavior, the elimination of possible waiver proceedings to the criminal court, and suggested agreements between the government and defense regarding dispositional programs for the child.

Court decisions and national commissions and lawyers throughout the country have recognized the propriety of plea bargaining in the adult system. In particular, the case of *Santobello v. New York* in 1971 explicitly recognized the validity of the plea bargaining process.[44] The case of *McKeiver v. Pennsylvania* recognized plea bargaining as a tool in the juvenile justice system.[45] Where the plea bargaining process is largely informal, lacking in guidelines, and having excessive discretionary power, efforts have been made to control the decision making in many courts where it is used. We have explored the various uses of information in making prosecutorial decisions to accept plea bargaining. Such factors as the offense, the defendant's prior record, and the type and strength of admissibility of evidence are considered important in the plea bargaining process. Similar types of information are also used to make decisions about plea bargaining in juvenile justice.

Plea bargaining has grown extensively in recent years. Because of overcrowded court caseloads, it has become an essential yet controversial part of the administration of justice. Although little clear evidence indicates how much plea bargaining there is in the juvenile justice system, it is apparent that such negotiations do exist and seem to be increasing.[46]

TRANSFER PROCEEDINGS

One of the most significant actions that occurs in the early court processing of a juvenile offender is the transfer process. Otherwise known as waiver or bindover, this process involves transferring a juvenile from the juvenile court to the criminal court. Most state statutes allow for this kind of transfer.

Historically, the American justice system has made a fundamental distinction between children and adults. The juvenile justice system emphasizes rehabilitation, and the criminal justice system emphasizes deterrence, punishment, and social control.

Proponents of the transfer process claim that children who commit serious offenses and who may be hardened offenders should be handled by the criminal court system. In fact, so the argument goes, these children cannot be rehabilitated. Others suggest that the transfer process is applied to children unfairly and is a half-hearted effort at implementing the treatment philosophy of the juvenile court. Furthermore, some children tried in the adult criminal court may be incarcerated under conditions so extreme that the children will be permanently damaged.

In reality, however, some juveniles take advantage of decisions to transfer them to the adult court. Often, although the charge against a child may be serious in the juvenile court, the adult criminal court will not agree, and a child will have a better chance for dismissal of the charges or acquittal after a jury trial. One of the most serious disadvantages to transferring a child is the stigma that may attach to a conviction in the criminal court. Labeling children as adult offenders early in life may seriously impair their further education, employment, and other opportunities.

Statutory Criteria in Transfer

In every jurisdiction, statutes set the standards for transfer procedures. Age, of course, is of particular significance. Some jurisdictions allow for transfer between the ages of fourteen and seventeen years. Others restrict waiver proceedings to mature juveniles and specify particular offenses. In a few jurisdictions, any child can be sentenced to the criminal court system regardless of age.

The Massachusetts General Laws, Chapter 119, Section 61, establish the following criteria:

1. Only juveniles between the ages of fourteen and seventeen are eligible for transfer.
2. A child can be transferred only if he or she has previously been committed to the Department of Youth Services or has committed an offense involving infliction or threat of serious bodily harm.

If the above conditions are met, a transfer hearing must be held to determine whether it is in the public interest to transfer the child. The court must consider the seriousness of the alleged offense; the child's family, school, and social history; the general protection of the public; the nature of past treatment efforts for the child; and the likelihood of the child's rehabilitation in the juvenile court.[47]

Thus, the waiver process is a statutory one, and the criteria that affect the decision to transfer the child to the criminal court are found in each of the state juvenile court acts. Many states, however, favor keeping children in juvenile court rather than transferring them to criminal court. Certainly, the ineffectiveness of the criminal justice system is itself an adequate argument for keeping children in juvenile court.

Due Process in Transfer Proceedings

Since 1966, the Supreme Court and other federal and state courts have evaluated the constitutionality of numerous transfer statutes. Many of them have been declared invalid.

Two Supreme Court decisions, *Kent v. United States* in 1966 and *Breed v. Jones in 1975*, are set out in Highlight 16-4 because of their significance.[48] The *Kent* case declared a District of Columbia transfer statute unconstitutional and attacked the subsequent conviction of the child by granting him specific due process rights. In *Breed v. Jones*, the Supreme Court declared that the child was granted the protection of the double jeopardy clause of the Fifth Amendment after he was tried as a delinquent in the juvenile court for the same offense.

Highlight 16–4. Two Supreme Court Cases about Transfer Procedure.

Kent v. United States
383 U.S. 541, 86 S.Ct. 1045, 16 L.Ed. 2d 84(1966)

Facts Morris Kent was arrested at the age of sixteen in connection with charges of housebreaking, robbery, and rape. As a juvenile he was subject to the exclusive jurisdiction of the District of Columbia Juvenile Court. The District of Columbia statute declared that the court could transfer the petitioner "after full investigation" and remit him to trial in the United States District Court. Kent admitted his involvement in the offenses and was placed in a receiving home for children. Subsequently, his mother obtained counsel, and they discussed with the social service director the possibility that the juvenile court might waive its jurisdiction. Kent was detained at the receiving home for almost one week. There was no arraignment, no hearing, and no hearing for petitioner's apprehension. Kent's counsel arranged for a psychiatric examination, and a motion requesting a hearing on the waiver was filed. The juvenile court judge did not rule on the motion and entered an order stating, "after full investigation, that the court waives its jurisdiction and directs that a trial be held under the regular proceedings of the criminal court." The judge made no finding and gave no reasons for his waiver decision. It appeared that the judge denied motions for a hearing, recommendations for hospitalization for psychiatric observation, requests for access to the social service file, and offers to prove that the petitioner was a fit subject for rehabilitation under the juvenile court.

After the juvenile court waived its jurisdiction, Kent was indicted by the grand jury and was subsequently found guilty of housebreaking and robbery and not guilty by reason of insanity on the charge of rape. Kent was sentenced to serve a period of thirty to ninety years on his conviction.

Decision Petitioner's lawyer appealed the decision on the basis of the infirmity of the proceedings by which the juvenile court waived its jurisdiction. He further attacked the waiver on statutory and constitutional grounds, stating: "(1) no hearing occurred, (2) no findings were made, (3) no reasons were stated before the waiver, and (4) counsel was denied access to the social service file." The Supreme Court found that the juvenile court order waiving jurisdiction and remitting the child to trial in the district court was invalid. Its arguments were based on the following:

1. The theory of the juvenile court act is rooted in social welfare procedures and treatments.

2. The philosophy of the juvenile court, namely *parens patriae*, is not supposed to allow procedural unfairness.

3. Waiver proceedings are critically important actions in the juvenile court.

4. The juvenile court act requiring full investigation in the District of Columbia should be read in the context of constitutional principles relating to due process of law. These principles require at a minimum that the petitioner be entitled to a hearing, access to counsel, access by counsel to social service records, and a statement of the reason for the juvenile court decision.

Significance of the Case This case examined for the first time the substantial degree of discretion associated with a transfer proceeding in the District of Columbia. Thus, the Supreme Court significantly limited its holding to the statute involved but justified its reference to constitutional principles relating to due process and the assistance of counsel. In addition, it said that the juvenile court waiver hearings need to measure up to the essentials of due process and fair treatment. Furthermore, in an appendix to its opinion, the Court set up criteria concerning waiver

of the jurisdiction. These are listed below:

1. The seriousness of the alleged offense to the community.

2. Whether the alleged offense was committed in an aggressive, violent, or willful manner.

3. Whether the alleged offense was committed against persons or against property.

4. The prosecutive merit of the complaint.

5. The desirability of trial and disposition.

6. The sophistication and maturity of the juvenile.

7. The record and previous history of the juvenile.

8. Prospects for adequate protection of the public and the likelihood of reasonable rehabilitation.

Breed v. Jones
421 U.S. 519, 95 S.Ct. 1779, (1975)

Facts In 1971, a petition in the juvenile court in the state of California was filed against Jones, who was then seventeen, alleging that he had committed an offense which, if committed by an adult, would constitute robbery. Petitioner was detained pending a hearing. At the hearing, the juvenile court took testimony and found that the allegations were true and sustained the petition. The proceedings were continued for a dispositional hearing, at which point Jones was found unfit for treatment in the juvenile court. It was ordered that he be prosecuted as an adult offender. At a subsequent preliminary hearing, the petitioner was held for criminal trial, an information was filed against him for robbery, and he was tried and found guilty. He was committed to the California Youth Authority, over objections that he was being subjected to double jeopardy.

Petitioner Jones sought an appeal in the federal district court on the basis of the double jeopardy argument that jeopardy attaches at the juvenile delinquency proceedings. The writ of *habeas corpus* was denied.

Decision The Supreme Court held that the prosecution of Jones as an adult in the

California Superior Court after an adjudicatory finding in the juvenile court that he had violated a criminal statute and a subsequent finding that he was unfit for treatment as a juvenile violated the double jeopardy clause of the Fifth Amendment of the United States Constitution as applied to the states through the Fourteenth Amendment. Thus, Jones's trial in Superior Court for the same offense as that for which he was tried in the juvenile court violated the policy of the double jeopardy clause even if he never faced the risk of more than one punishment, since double jeopardy refers to the risk or potential risk of trial and conviction, not punishment.

Significance of the Case The *Breed* case provided answers on several important transfer issues:

1. *Breed* prohibits trying a child in an adult court when there has been a prior adjudicatory juvenile proceeding.

2. Probable cause may exist at a transfer hearing, and this does not violate subsequent jeopardy if the child is transferred to the adult court.

3. Because the same evidence is often used in both the transfer hearing and subsequent trial in either the juvenile or adult court, a different judge is often required for the different hearing.

Today, as a result of *Kent* and *Breed,* nearly every state provides specific requirements for transfer proceedings in its juvenile code. For the most part, when a transfer hearing is conducted today, due process of law requires (1) a legitimate transfer hearing, (2) a sufficient notice to the child's family and defense attorney, (3) the right to counsel, and (4) a statement of the reason for the court order regarding transfer. These rights recognize what *Kent v. the United States* indicated—namely, that the transfer proceeding is a critically important action in determining the statutory rights of the juvenile offender.

CHAPTER SUMMARY

Generally, many important decisions about what happens to a child occur prior to the adjudication. Detention in secure facilities for those charged with juvenile delinquency and involuntary placement in shelter care for those involved in noncriminal behavior place a severe limitation on the rights of the child and the parents and are important decisions at the early court stage of the juvenile process. The intake stage is essentially a screening process to make decisions about what action should be taken regarding matters referred to the court. The law enforcement officer is required to make hard decisions about court action or referral to social agencies. In addition, it is important for law enforcement agencies and the juvenile courts to have a sound working relationship. Their objective is basically similar—the protection of the child and the community.

Throughout the early court stage of the juvenile process, the issue of discretion plays a major role. In the last decade, juvenile justice practitioners have made efforts to remove as many children as possible from the juvenile courts and place them in other programs. This approach is called diversion from the juvenile justice system. It is one of the newest and most popular of delinquency prevention and control strategies. Since only a small percentage of juvenile cases eventually go to a complete trial, many children make admissions and are placed in these programs. Those who are held for trial generally are released to their parents or released on bail or through other release alternatives, such as release on recognizance. The juvenile justice system, like the adult system, is not able to try every child accused of a crime or a status offense. There are not enough judges, prosecutors, defense attorneys, and courts in existence for this purpose. In addition, diversion programs seem to hold a better hope for the prevention and control of delinquency. As a result, subsystems such as diversion, statutory intake proceedings, some amount of plea bargaining, and other informal adjustments are essential ingredients in the administration of the juvenile justice system.

DISCUSSION QUESTIONS

1. Why has the use of jails and detention facilities for children been considered one of the greatest tragedies in the entire juvenile justice system?
2. Processing juvenile cases in an informal manner—that is, without filing a formal petition—is a common practice in the juvenile court system. Mention some methods of informally handling cases in the juvenile court.
3. The use of diversion programs in the juvenile justice system has become commonplace as an effort to channel cases to noncourt institutions. Discuss the advantages and disadvantages of diversion. Describe diversion programs and their common characteristics.
4. What is the purpose of bail? Do children as well as adults have a constitutional or statutory right to bail? What factors are considered in the release of a child prior to formal adjudication?
5. Under extraordinary circumstances, once juvenile proceedings have begun, the juvenile court may seek to transfer a juvenile to the adult court. This is often referred to as a transfer proceeding. Is such a proceeding justified? Under what conditions? Does the juvenile court afford the public sufficient protection against serious juvenile offenders?

SUGGESTED READINGS

Alschuler, Albert W. "The Prosecutor's Role in Plea Bargaining." *University of Chicago Law Review* 36 (1968): pp. 52–104.

American Bar Association. *Project on Standards for Juvenile Justice: Standards Relating to Interim Status of Juveniles.* Cambridge, Mass.: Ballinger Press, 1977.

American Bar Association. *Project on Standards for Juvenile Justice: Standards Relating to Juvenile Probation Function.* Cambridge, Mass.: Ballinger Press, 1977.

American Bar Association. *Project on Standards for Juvenile Justice: Standards Relating to Pre-Trial Court Procedures.* Cambridge, Mass.: Ballinger Press, 1977.

Bail Reform Act of 1966, 18 U.S.C.A. 2146.

Baldwin v. Lewis, 300 F. Supp. 1220 (E.D. Wis. 1969), reversed on other grounds, 442 F. 2nd 29 (7th Cir., 1971).

Besharov, Douglas. *Juvenile Justice Advocacy—Practice in a Unique Court.* New York: Practicing Law Institute, 1974.

Cohen, Lawrence E. "Pre-Adjudication Detention in Three Juvenile Courts." Law Enforcement Assistance Administration. Washington, D.C.: Government Printing Office, 1975.

Comment. "Juvenile Right to Bail." *Journal of Family Law* 2 (1971).

In re Macedon, 240 Cal. App. 2nd 600; 49 Cal. Rptr. 861 (1966).

Sumner, Helen. *Locking Them Up: A Study of Juvenile Detention Decisions in Selected California Counties.* New York: National Council on Crime and Delinquency, 1971.

Vinter, Rober D., ed. *Time Out: A National Study of Juvenile Correctional Programs.* Ann Arbor, Mich. University of Michigan Press, 1976.

REFERENCES

1. National Council on Crime and Delinquency, *Standards and Guides for the Detention of Children and Youth* (New York: NCCD, 1961), p. 1.

2. American Bar Association, *Standards Relating to Interim Status of Juveniles* (Cambridge, Mass.: Ballinger Press, 1977), p. 4.

3. Edward Wakin, *Children without Justice—A Report by the National Council of Jewish Women* (New York: National Council of Jewish Women, 1975), p. 43.

4. National Council on Crime and Delinquency, *Standards and Guides for the Detention of Children and Youth,* p. 12.

5. The National Council on Crime and Delinquency, *Standard Juvenile and Family Court Act* (New York: NCCD, 1965); National Advisory Commission on Criminal Justice Standards and Goals, *Corrections* (Washington, D.C.: Department of Justice, 1973); and William Sheridan, *Model Acts for Family Courts* (Washington, D.C.: Department of Health, Education and Welfare, Office of Human Development, 1975) all state that children should receive a detention hearing within a short period after admission.

6. American Bar Association, *Standards Relating to Interim Status of Juveniles,* p. 86.

7. National Council on Crime and Delinquency, *Standards and Guides for the Detention of Children and Youth,* p. 3.

8. U.S. Bureau of the Census, *National Jail Census* (Washington, D.C.: LEAA, 1971).

9. National Advisory Commission on Criminal Justice Standards and Goals, *Corrections,* p. 251.

10. Rosemary C. Sarri, *Under Lock and Key—Juveniles in Jails and Detention* (Ann Arbor, Mich.: National Assessment of Juvenile Corrections, 1974), p. 5.

11. Ibid.

12. U.S. Department of Justice, Law Enforcement Assistance Administration, *Children in Custody: A Report on the Juvenile Detention and Correctional Facility Census of 1974* (Washington, D.C.: Government Printing Office, 1974).

13. Ibid.

14. See Margaret Rosenheim, ed., *Justice for the Child* (New York: Free Press, 1962).

15. U.S. Department of Justice, Law Enforcement Assistance Administration, *Children in Custody: Advance Report on the Juvenile Detention and Correctional Facility Census of 1975* (Washington, D.C.: Government Printing Office, 1977), pp. 28–29.

16. National Advisory Commission on Criminal Justice Standards and Goals, *Courts* (Washington, D.C.: Government Printing Office, 1973), p. 27.

17. 349 F. Supp. 575 (1972).

18. Ibid., p. 584.

19. See Donnell Pappenfort, Dee Morgan Kilpatrick, and Robin Roberts, eds., *Detention Facilities and Temporary Shelters in Child Caring: Social Policy and the Institution* (Chicago: Aldine Publishing, 1978).

20. American Bar Association, *Standards Relating to Interim Status of Juveniles,* pp. 97–101.

21. President's Commission on Law Enforcement and the Administration of Justice, *Task Force Report: Juvenile Delinquency and Youth Crime* (Washington, D.C.: Government Printing Office, 1967), p. 147.

22. American Bar Association, *Standards Relating to Juvenile Probation Function* (Cambridge, Mass.: Ballinger Press, 1977), p. 25.

23. National Council on Crime and Delinquency, *Standard Family Court Act*, Section 12; William Sheridan, *Model Acts for Juvenile and Family Courts*, Section 13; National Conference of Commissioners on Uniform State Laws, *Uniform Juvenile Court Act*, Section 9.

24. American Bar Association, *Standards Relating to Juvenile Probation Function*, p. 53.

25. Ibid., p. 2.

26. Joseph Senna and Larry Siegel, *Introduction to Criminal Justice* (St. Paul, Minn.: West Publishing, 1978), p. 257.

27. Paul Nejelski, "Diversion: The Promise and the Danger," *Crime and Delinquency Journal* 22 (1976) pp. 393–410.

28. National Advisory Commission on Criminal Justice Standards and Goals, *Courts*, p. 20.

29. LaMar T. Empey, *American Delinquency—Its Meaning and Construction* (Homewood, Ill.: Dorsey Press, 1978), p. 532.

30. Nejelski, "Diversion," p. 394.

31. See Raymond T. Nimmer, *Diversion—The Search for Alternative Forms of Prosecution* (Chicago, American Bar Foundation, 1974), pp. 58–59.

32. Ibid.

33. Ibid.

34. Ibid.

35. Don C. Gibbons and Gerald F. Blake, "Evaluating the Impact of Juvenile Diversion Programs," *Crime and Delinquency Journal* 22 (1976), pp. 411–419.

36. Nejelski, "Diversion," p. 393.

37. Richard J. Lundman, "Will Diversion Reduce Recidivism?" *Crime and Delinquency Journal* 22 (1976), pp. 428–437.

38. Sanford Fox, *Juvenile Courts in a Nutshell* (St. Paul, Minn.: West Publishing, 1977), p. 145.

39. See, generally, Daniel Freed and Patricia Walk, *Bail in the United States, 1964*, working paper for National Conference on Bail and Criminal Justice (New York: Vera Institute of Justice and U.S. Department of Justice, 1964).

40. Paul Piersma et al., *Law and Tactics in Juvenile Cases* (Philadelphia: American Law Institute—American Bar Association Committee on Continuing Education, 1977), pp. 195–199.

41. Mass. Gen. Laws, Chapter 276.

42. Albert W. Alschuler, "The Prosecutor's Role in Plea Bargaining," *University of Chicago Law Review* 36 (1968): 50: 112.

43. Fox, *Juvenile Courts in a Nutshell*, pp. 195–196.

44. 395 U.S. 238, 89 S.Ct. 1709, 23 L.Ed. 2d 274 (1969).

45. 403 U.S. 528, 91 S.Ct. 1976, 29 L.Ed. 2d 647 (1971).

46. Douglas J. Besharov, *Juvenile Justice Advocacy—Practice in a Unique Court* (New York: Practicing Law Institute, 1974), p. 311.

47. Mass. Gen. Laws, Chapter 119 61.

48. 383 U.S. 541, 86 S.Ct. 1045, 16 L.Ed. 2d 84 (1966); 421 U.S. 519, 95 S.Ct. 1179, 44 L.Ed. 2d 346 (1975).

Chapter 17

Chapter Outline

Introduction
The Prosecutor in the Juvenile Court
Functions of the Juvenile Prosecutor
Role of the Juvenile Court Judge
Selection and Qualifications of Juvenile
  Court Judges
The Defense Attorney in the Juvenile Justice
  System
Public Defender Services for Children
Adjudication
Constitutional Rights at Adjudication
Dispositions
Trends in Juvenile Sentencing
Predisposition Report
The Child's Right to Appeal in the Juvenile
  Court
Chapter Summary

Key Terms, Names, and Cases

McKeiver v. Pennsylvania
adjudication
disposition
In re Gault
prosecutor
Gideon v. Wainwright
Argersinger v. Hamlin
appeal
bifurcated hearing
public defender
pre-disposition report
certiorari
collateral review
jury trial
de novo
In re Winship
writ of habeas corpus
prosecutorial discretion
juvenile court judge
defense attorney
Powell v. Alabama

The Juvenile Trial and Disposition

INTRODUCTION

This chapter will begin with a description of the important legal actors in the trial and disposition process—the juvenile court prosecutor, the juvenile court judge, the defense attorney, and the probation officer. Next, it will look at the constitutional rights of the child, particularly the rights to counsel and to a jury trial, through an analysis of the landmark *In re Gault* case and *McKeiver v. Pennsylvania*. In addition, it will review the various procedural rules that apply at the adjudicatory and dispositional hearings. The chapter will conclude with an analysis of the social study report. This report, otherwise known as the preliminary investigation or presentence report, is an essential part of the juvenile court's operating procedures. On the basis of the social study, facts are presented to the court and dispositions regarding the child's treatment are made.

THE PROSECUTOR IN THE JUVENILE COURT

The juvenile prosecutor is the government attorney responsible for representing the interest of the state. The prosecutor brings the state's case against the accused child. Depending on the level of government and the jurisdiction, the prosecutor can be called a district attorney, a county attorney, a state attorney, or a United States attorney. He or she is a member of the bar and becomes a public prosecutor through political appointment or popular election.

Ordinarily, the juvenile prosecutor is a staff member of the local prosecuting attorney's office. If the office of the district attorney is in an urban area and of sufficient size, the juvenile prosecutor may work exclusively on juvenile and other family law matters. If the caseload of juvenile offenders is small, the juvenile prosecutor also has criminal prosecution responsibilities.

For the first sixty years of its existence, the juvenile court did not include a prosecutor as representative of the state in court proceedings.[1] The concept of advocacy and the adversary process were seen as inconsistent with the philosophy of diagnosis and treatment in the juvenile court system. The court followed a social service helping model with informal and noncriminal proceedings believed to be in the best interests of the child.

These views changed dramatically with the Supreme Court decisions of *Kent v. United States, In re Gault,* and *In re Winship.*[2] These decisions ushered in an era of greater formality and due process rights for children in the juvenile court system. Today, many jurisdictions require by law that a prosecutor be present in the juvenile court. A survey conducted by the Department of Justice in 1973 found that approximately 40 percent of the sixty-eight major American cities surveyed had public prosecutors at detention hearings and over 75 percent had prosecutors at pretrial motions, probable cause hearings, bind-over hearings, and, adjudication hearings.[3]

In addition, the major legislation in the field of juvenile justice over the past decade has recommended the incorporation of a state juvenile attorney. For instance, the Uniform Juvenile Court Act of 1968 provides for a prosecuting attorney to be involved at adjudication.[4] The Model Rules for Juvenile Courts of the National Council on Crime and Delinquency recommend the use of an attorney in complex juvenile cases.[5] The Children's Bureau's legislative guide for drafting family and juvenile court acts prescribes the mandatory use of an attorney to handle juvenile matters.[6] Numerous jurisdictions, such as Vermont, Massachusetts, Minnesota, and California, have incorporated a state attorney to prosecute juvenile matters. In the words of the American Bar Association, "An attorney for the state, hereinafter referred to as the juvenile prosecutor, should participate in every proceeding of every stage of every case subject to the jurisdiction of the family court in which the state has an interest."[7] Including a prosecutor in juvenile court balances the interests of the state, the defense attorney, the child, and the judge in their respective roles. The independence of their respective functions and responsibilities is preserved.

The *Gault* decision has expanded the rights of children in other pretrial and postdispositional areas of the juvenile justice system. The complicated legal requirements of the Fourth, Fifth, and Sixth Amendments regarding arrest, search and seizure, and custodial interrogation, now apply to juvenile delinquency cases. All these proceedings use lawyers. In 1964, juvenile prosecutors appeared in no more than 15 percent of court cases. Today, state representation in juvenile matters is much higher.[8]

FUNCTIONS OF THE JUVENILE PROSECUTOR

A prosecutor enforces the law, represents the government, maintains proper standards of ethical conduct as an attorney and court officer, participates in programs and legislation involving legal changes in the juvenile justice system, acts as a spokesperson for the field of law, and takes an active role in the community in preventing delinquency and protecting the rights of juveniles. Of these responsibilities, representing the government while presenting the state's case to the court is the prosecutor's most frequent task. In this regard, the prosecutor performs many of the following duties:

1. Investigates possible violations of the law.
2. Cooperates with the police, intake officer, and probation officer regarding the facts alleged in the petition.
3. Authorizes reviews and prepares petitions for court.
4. Plays a role in the initial detention decision.
5. Represents the state in all pretrial motions, probable cause hearings, and consent decrees.
6. Represents the state at transfer hearings.
7. If necessary, recommends physical or mental examinations for children brought before the court.
8. Seeks amendments or dismissals of filed petitions if appropriate.
9. Represents the state at the adjudication of the case.
10. Represents the state at the disposition of the case.
11. Enters into plea bargaining discussions with the defense attorney.
12. Represents the government on appeal and in *habeas corpus* proceedings.
13. Is involved in hearings dealing with violation of probation.

The power to initiate formal petitions against a child is the key to prosecutorial responsibility. The ability to either initiate or discontinue delinquency or status offense allegations represents the control and power a juvenile prosecutor has over a child. Prosecutors have broad discretion in the exercise of their duties. Because due process rights have been extended to juveniles, the prosecutor's role in the juvenile court has in some ways become similar to the role of the attorney in the adult court. In the case of *State v. Grayer*, for example, a Nebraska court upheld the validity of the discretionary power of the juvenile prosecutor to decide whether to prosecute the child as a juvenile or as an adult.[9]

Such an approach demonstrates the judicial movement toward developing procedures for juveniles that are similar to those for adult offenders. However, it is important for the juvenile prosecutor not only to represent the government but also to remain cognizant of the philosophy and purpose of the juvenile court. In that regard, the following general principles for juvenile prosecution have been established. They are presented in Highlight 17–1.

Highlight 17–1. Prosecution Guidelines for Boston Juvenile Court.

A. *GENERAL PRINCIPLES FOR JUVENILE PROSECUTION*
1.1 The prosecutor is an *advocate* of the State's interest in juvenile court. The "State's interest" is complex and multivalued, and may vary with the type of proceeding and the nature of the particular case. Foremost, it includes: (a) protection of the community from the danger of harmful conduct by the restraint and rehabilitation of juvenile offenders; and (b) concern, shared by all juvenile justice system personnel, as *parens patriae*, with promotion of the best interests of juveniles.
1.2 To the extent that the State's interest in community protection may conflict with its interest as *parens patriae* in promoting the well-being of a particular child, the prosecutor will be required to balance the interests based upon the nature and facts of

the particular case. For example, to the extent that interests have to be balanced in given cases, the balance might be struck in favor of community protection when the juvenile presents a substantial threat to community security but of promoting the well being of a child for most other types of situations.

1.3. In his role as *advocate*, the prosecutor has responsibility to ensure adequate preparation and presentation of the State's case, from the stage of police investigation through post-disposition proceedings. He is also committed generally to the advancement of legitimate law enforcement and child welfare goals by the participation of his office, together with other agencies such as the public defender's office, in drafting court rules and legislation, in appellate litigation, and in other activities which shape development of the law.

1.4. Commitment to the rehabilitative philosophy of the juvenile court bars the use of certain penal objectives to achieve community security and protection. Retribution, for example, is not a proper goal of juvenile court prosecution.

1.5. Since unnecessary exposure to juvenile court proceedings and to formal labeling and treatment in the juvenile court process is often counter-productive for many juveniles, the prosecutor's duty to promote both the community's long-term security and the best interest of particular juveniles requires him to encourage and stimulate early diversion of cases from the court and to strive for imposing the least restrictive alternative available in dealing with a juvenile throughout the juvenile justice process. It also requires that a prosecutor proceed only on legally sufficient

complaints or petitions even though a juvenile may require treatment or other types of assistance. Responsibility in this area is exercised by such means as issuing enforcement guidelines to the police, screening out deficient, insufficient, or trivial complaints, and actively encouraging and participating in efforts to refer juveniles to other agencies or reach agreement on other acceptable dispositions in cases where court handling is not the best means for either protecting the community or helping the juvenile.

1.6. The prosecutor shares the responsibility with other juvenile court personnel to ensure that rehabilitative measures undertaken as alternatives to court handling or pursuant to court-ordered disposition are actually carried out, and that facilities and services for treatment and detention meet proper standards of quality.

1.7. The prosecutor has a duty to *seek justice* in juvenile court by insisting upon fair and lawful procedures. This entails the responsibility to ensure, for example, that baseless prosecutions are not brought, that all juveniles receive fair and equal treatment, that liberal discovery of the State's case is available to defense counsel, that exculpatory evidence is made available to the defense, and that excessively harsh dispositions are not sought. It also entails the responsibility to oversee police investigative behavior to ensure its compliance with the law.

Source: U.S. Department of Justice, Prosecution in The Juvenile Court: Guidelines for the Future (Washington, D.C.: LEAA, National Institute of Law Enforcement and Criminal Justice, 1973), p. 89.

ROLE OF THE JUVENILE COURT JUDGE

The judge is the central character in a court of juvenile or family law. His or her responsibilities are quite varied and have become far more extensive and complex in recent years.[10] Following *Kent* and *Gault*, new rulings have probed the basic legal aspects of the juvenile justice system. Furthermore, most juvenile courts are faced with an ever-increasing volume of proceedings because of the substantial increase in juvenile crime. In addition, juvenile cases are far more complex today and represent issues involving social change, such as truancy, alcoholism, the use of drugs by children, juvenile prostitution, and violent juvenile crime. Such cases involve problems of both public safety and individualized treatment for children.

Juvenile or family court judges perform the following functions. They rule on pretrial motions involving such legal issues as arrest, search and seizure, interrogation, and lineup identification. They make decisions about the continued detention of children prior to trial. They determine the child's right to bail. They make decisions about plea bargaining agreements and the informal adjustment of juvenile cases. They handle bench and jury trials, rule on the appropriateness of conduct, settle questions of evidence and procedure, and guide the questioning of witnesses. They assume the responsibility for holding dispositional hearings and deciding on the treatment accorded the child. They handle waiver proceedings. They handle appeals where allowed by statute, and where no prior contact has been made with the case.

In addition, the judge often has extensive control and influence over other service agencies of the court—probation, the court clerk, the law enforcement officer, and the office of the juvenile prosecutor. Of course, courts differ organizationally and procedurally. Larger courts have more resources to handle the volume of juvenile cases. They may have specialized approaches to juvenile problems, including varied caseloads, diversion programs, and a whole host of special social services. Smaller courts may have no more than a judge, clerk, and probation staff.

The juvenile court judge exercises considerable leadership in developing services and solutions to juvenile justice problems. Judges participate in efforts to reform juvenile law, and they serve in organizations devoted to juvenile delinquency prevention.

Finally, it is always incumbent upon juvenile court judges to follow the code of judicial conduct, which requires their highest ethical and moral behavior.

SELECTION AND QUALIFICATIONS OF JUVENILE COURT JUDGES

The National Advisory Commission on Criminal Justice Standards and Goals views the selection of juvenile court judges as one of the most important aspects of the juvenile system:

Effective operation of the entire system of juvenile justice rests, in large measure, on the competency of judges in the family court. Obviously, skilled judges cannot guarantee sound administration of justice in the absence of carefully considered laws. But meticulous reforms of laws and procedural rules are of little value unless the bench is staffed by competent jurists. In the final analysis, no single factor weighs so heavily in the success of the juvenile system as the provision of qualified judges.[11]

In the criminal and the juvenile justice systems, judges are selected by election, merit appointment, or a combination of election and appointment. Most judges in the United States are elected. Over thirty-five states select all or most of their judges by a partisan or nonpartisan election.[12] In a minority of states judges are appointed by the governor, who selects them from a list of candidates chosen by a nominating commission.

In some jurisdictions, juvenile court judges handle family-related cases exclusively. In others, they handle criminal and civil cases as well. Traditionally, juvenile court judges have been relegated to a lower status than other judges, with less prestige, responsibility, and salary. Judges assigned to juvenile courts have not ordinarily been chosen from the highest levels of the legal profession. Groups like the President's Commission on Law Enforcement and the American Judicature Society have noted that the field of juvenile justice has often been shortchanged by the appointment of unqualified judges and staff. In some jurisdictions, particularly major urban areas, juvenile court judges may be of the highest caliber, but many courts throughout the country continue to function with mediocre judges.

Most states have no statutory provisions regulating qualifications. Basically, juvenile court judges should have the following qualifications:

1. They should be members of the bar in their jurisdictions and have some experience practicing law.
2. They should be deeply concerned about the rights of people.
3. They should be keenly interested in the problems of children and families.
4. They should be aware of the contributions of the fields of psychology, psychiatry, social work, and the social sciences to the field of juvenile justice.
5. They should be able to evaluate legal evidence and make dispositions uninfluenced by personal concepts of child care.
6. They should be good administrators.
7. They should conduct hearings in a kindly manner and relate well to children.

As the Advisory Council of Judges of the National Council on Crime and Delinquency has stated, "Juvenile court has been brilliantly conceived; its legal and social facets are not antithetical, but the preservation of equilibrium between them, which is the key to their successful fusion, depends upon the legal knowledge, social perspective, and eternal vigilance of one person, the judge."[13]

Inducing the best legally trained individuals to accept juvenile court judgeships is a very important goal. Where the juvenile court is part of the highest general court of trial jurisdiction, the problem of securing qualified personnel is not as great a problem. However, if it is of limited or specialized jurisdiction and it has the authority to try only minor cases, it may attract only poorly trained and poorly qualified personnel. The juvenile court has a negative image to overcome because even though what it does is of great importance to parents, children, and society in general, it has been placed at the lowest level of the judicial hierarchy.

In addition to judges, many family courts have referees who assist the judges in handling juvenile cases. Ordinarily, referees or commissioners are lawyers who meet the same qualifications as the judges and who are selected by them. Referees are ordinarily under the supervision of the judge rather than the probation department. When there are judicial vacancies or there is an unexpected volume of cases, referees and commissioners play an important role in the court. However, many states are eliminating them in order to obtain permanent juvenile court judges.

THE DEFENSE ATTORNEY IN THE JUVENILE JUSTICE SYSTEM

Through a series of leading Supreme Court decisions—*Powell v. Alabama* in 1932, *Gideon v. Wainwright* in 1962, and *Argersinger v. Hamlin* in 1972—the right of a criminal defendant to have counsel at state trials has become a fundamental right in the criminal justice system.[14] Today, state courts must provide counsel to indigent defendants who face the possibility of incarceration.

Increasingly, the right to counsel has been extended to juveniles. A survey conducted by the Department of Justice in 1973 pointed out that before the *Gault* decision in 1968, only 4 percent of the major cities sampled indicated that more than half of the juveniles involved in delinquency cases were represented by counsel. Current results of the survey indicate that in 62 percent of the cities surveyed, more than 75 percent of the juveniles brought before the court are represented by counsel. Thus, the attorney plays an increasingly prominent role in the juvenile court system.

The American Bar Association has described the responsibility of the legal profession to the juvenile court in Standard 2.3 of *Standards Relating to Counsel for Private Parties*. The ABA states that legal representation should be provided in all proceedings arising from or related to a delinquency or in-need-of-supervision action—including mental competency, transfer, postdisposition, probation revocation and classification, institutional transfer, and disciplinary or other administrative proceedings related to the treatment process that may substantially affect the juvenile's custody, status, or course of treatment.[15]

Over the past two decades, the rules and procedures of criminal and juvenile justice administration have become extremely complex. Specialized knowledge is essential for the adversary process to operate effectively. Today, preparation of a case for juvenile court often involves detailed investigation of a crime, knowledge of court procedures, use of rules of evidence, and skills in trial advocacy. Prosecuting and defense attorneys must both have this expertise, particularly when a child's freedom is at stake. The right to counsel in the juvenile justice system is essential if children are to have a fair chance of presenting their cases in court.

In many respects, the role of defense attorneys in the juvenile process is similar to the role they play in the criminal and civil areas. Defense attorneys representing children in the juvenile court play an active and important role at virtually all stages of juvenile proceedings. For example, the lawyer helps to clarify jurisdictional problems and to decide whether there is sufficient evidence to warrant the filing of a formal petition at intake. The defense attorney also helps outline the child's position regarding detention hearings and bail and explores the opportunities for informal adjustment of the case. If no adjustment or diversion occurs, the attorney represents the child at adjudication, presenting evidence and cross-examining witnesses to see that the child's position is made clear to the court. Attorneys play a critically important role in the dispositional hearing. They present evidence bearing on the treatment decision and help the court formulate alternative plans for the child's care. Lastly, the defense attorney pursues any appeals from the trial, represents the child in probation revocation proceedings, and generally protects the child's right to treatment.

PUBLIC DEFENDER SERVICES FOR CHILDREN

To satisfy the requirement that indigent children and their families be provided with counsel at the various stages of the juvenile justice process, the federal government and the states have had to expand public defender services. Three primary alternatives exist for providing children with legal counsel in the juvenile court today: (1) an all-public defender program, (2) an appointed private counsel system, and (3) a combination of public defender and appointed private attorney.[16]

The public defender system is a statewide program organized by legislation and funded by the government to provide counsel to children at public expense. This approach brings to juvenile proceedings the expertise of lawyers who spend a considerable amount of time representing juvenile offenders every day. Defender programs generally provide separate office space for juvenile court personnel as well as support staff and training programs for new lawyers.

In many rural areas, individual public defender programs are not available, and defense services are offered through appointed private counsel. Private lawyers are assigned to individual juvenile court cases and receive compensation for the time and services they provide to the child and the family. When private attorneys are used in large urban areas, they are generally selected from a list established by the court, and they often operate in conjunction with a public defender program. A system of assigned counsel used by itself suffers from such problems as unequal case assignments, inadequate legal fees, and lack of supportive or supervisory services.

The mixed counsel system, which uses both public defenders and private attorneys, seems to be the preferred approach. First, it allows widespread coverage of defense needs. Second, it provides experienced attorneys. Third, it allows the child to have counsel at the preadjudication and postadjudication stages of the juvenile process.

There are also programs where advanced law school students provide representation.[17] Most jurisdictions have a student practice rule or procedure that allows such students to earn credit by providing supervised counsel to children who have not committed serious offenses. The National Advisory Commission on Criminal Justice Standards and Goals recommends using public defenders and private attorneys rather than relying solely on any one plan. Standard 16.9, "Organization of Defense Services," states: "Where possible, a coordinated plan to providing representation that combines public defender and assigned counsel systems should be adopted."[18]

Despite the fact that public defense services for children have grown in recent years, a major concern is the continued provision of quality representation to the child and the family at all stages of the juvenile process. In some jurisdictions today, counsel is available to children in only part of the juvenile proceedings. In other jurisdictions, children are not represented in PINS cases or neglect cases. Often, public defender agencies and the assigned counsel system are understaffed and lack adequate support services. Representation should be upgraded in all areas of the juvenile court system.

ADJUDICATION

At the adjudication stage of the juvenile process, a hearing is held to determine the merits of the petition claiming that a child is either a delinquent youth or in need of court supervision. The judge is required to make a finding on the evidence in the case and arrive at a judgment. Adjudication is comparable to an adult trial. The majority of juvenile cases do not reach the adjudicatory stage, but serious delinquency cases based on violations of the criminal law, situations where children deny any guilt, cases of repeat offenders, and cases where children are a threat to themselves or the community often reach the adjudication stage.

Much of the controversy over the adjudication process has centered on whether juveniles have been accorded fair procedures. State juvenile codes vary with regard to the basic requirements of due process and fairness. Basic to this stage, of course, is the right of a child to have a hearing. Most juvenile courts have bifurcated hearings—that is, separate hearings for adjudication and disposition.

Today, adjudication is conducted much more formally than it was in the past. Prior to *Gault* and the movement for children's rights, juvenile courts ignored rules of evidence or failed to establish fair procedures for fact-finding hearings. Today, the proceedings are more orderly, dignified, and formal.

Formal Rules of Procedure

Today, most state juvenile codes provide for specific rules of procedure and a finding at adjudication. These rules require that a written petition be submitted to the court. They assure the right of a child to have an attorney. They provide that the adjudication proceedings be recorded. They allow the petition to be amended and provide that a child's guilty plea be accepted. Where the child pleads guilty, the courts generally seek assurance that the plea is voluntary. Where plea bargaining is used, prosecutors, defense counsel, and trial judges take steps to assure the fairness of such negotiations.

When a juvenile denies guilt, this involves a contested adjudication before a judge or jury. The Supreme Court held in *McKeiver v. Pennsylvania* that a juvenile does not have a federal constitutional right to a trial by jury. Some states provide juveniles with a jury trial, but most adhere to the constitutional standard set by the Supreme Court.

Although the Sixth Amendment guarantees a public trial to a criminal defendant, almost all states limit public access to the juvenile court. Most juvenile hearings are closed hearings because the court seeks to protect children from the harmful effects of being stigmatized as criminals.

Other procedural rules used in juvenile trials today govern the exclusion of hearsay and immaterial evidence, the privilege against self-incrimination, and the right of juveniles to confront and cross-examine adverse witnesses. Also, as a result of the *In re Winship* case, the standard of proof beyond a reasonable doubt is the basis for judgments. This standard is universally used in delinquency adjudications, although some states may use lesser standards, such as "a preponderance of the evidence" in noncriminal behavior and neglect cases.

Finding by the Court

At the end of the adjudication hearing, most juvenile court statutes require the judge to make a factual finding on the legal issues and evidence reviewed in the child's hearing. In the criminal court, this finding is normally an entry of judgment involving a verdict. In the juvenile court, the juvenile court judge normally does the following: (1) makes a finding of fact that the child or juvenile is not delinquent or in need of supervision, (2) makes a finding of fact that the juvenile is delinquent or in need of supervision, or (3) dismisses the case due to insufficient or faulty evidence. In some jurisdictions, informal alternatives are used, such as filing the case with no further consequences or continuing the case without a finding. These alternatives involve no determination of delinquency or noncriminal behavior. Because of the philosophy of the juvenile court involving treatment and rehabilitation, a delinquency finding is not the same thing as a criminal conviction. The disabilities associated with conviction, such as disqualification regarding employment, entrance into the military service, or involvement in politics, do not affect an adjudication of delinquency.

CONSTITUTIONAL RIGHTS AT ADJUDICATION

This section discusses three of the most important constitutional issues at the trial stage of the juvenile justice system and reviews the cases in which decisions about these issues were made. These include *In re Gault, In re Winship*, and *McKeiver v. Pennsylvania*. Although reference has been made to these cases previously, Highlight 17-2 sets them out in detail because of their significance to the adjudication process.

Highlight 17-2. Three Landmark Decisions.

1. The Right to Counsel at Trial: In Re Gault 387 U.S. 1, 87 S.Ct 1248 (1967)

The Gault case guaranteed basic due process rights to children charged with juvenile delinquency in the juvenile court.

Facts Gerald Gault, fifteen years of age, was taken into custody by the sheriff of Gila County, Arizona, because a woman complained that he and another boy had made an obscene telephone call to her. At the time, Gerald was under a six-month probation as a result of being delinquent for stealing a wallet. Because of the verbal complaint, Gerald was taken to the children's home. His parents were not informed that he was being taken into custody. His mother appeared in the evening and was told by the superintendent of detention that a hearing would be held in the juvenile court the following day. On the day in question, the police officer who had taken Gerald into custody filed a petition alleging his delinquency. Gerald, his mother, and the police officer appeared before the judge in his chambers. Mrs. Cook, the complainant, was not at the hearing. Gerald was questioned about the telephone calls and was sent back to the detention home and then subsequently released a few days later.

On the day of Gerald's release, Mrs. Gault received a letter indicating that a hearing would be held on Gerald's delinquency a few days later. A hearing was held, and the complainant again was not present. There was no transcript or recording of the proceedings, and the juvenile officer stated that Gerald had admitted making the lewd telephone calls. Neither the boy nor his parents were advised of any right to remain silent, or the right to be represented by counsel, or of any other constitutional rights. At the conclusion of the hearing, the juvenile court committed Gerald as a juvenile delinquent to the state industrial school in Arizona for the period of his minority.

This meant that, at the age of fifteen, Gerald was sent to the state school until he reached the age of twenty-one unless discharged sooner. An adult charged with the same crime would have received a maximum punishment of no more than a $50 fine or two months in prison.

Decision in the Case Gerald's attorneys filed a writ of *habeas corpus*, which was denied by the Superior Court of the State of Arizona. That decision was subsequently affirmed by the Arizona Supreme Court. On appeal to the United States Supreme Court, Gerald's counsel argued that the juvenile code of Arizona under which Gerald was found delinquent was invalid because it was contrary to the due process clause of the Fourteenth Amendment. In addition, Gerald was denied the following basic due process rights: (1) notice of charges with regard to their timeliness and specificity, (2) right to counsel, (3) right to confrontation and cross-examination, (4) privilege against self-incrimination, (5) right to a transcript of the trial record, and (6) right to appellate review. In deciding the case, the Supreme Court had to determine whether or not procedural due process of law within the context of fundamental fairness under the Fourteenth Amendment applied to juvenile delinquency proceedings in which a child is committed to a state industrial school.

The Court, in a far-reaching opinion written by Justice Abe Fortas, agreed that Gerald's constitutional rights had been violated. Notice of charges was an essential ingredient of due process of law, as was right to counsel, right to cross-examine and to confront witnesses, and privilege against self-incrimination. The questions of appellate review and a right to a transcript were not answered by the Court in this case.

Significance of the Case The *Gault* case decided that a child had the procedural due process constitutional rights listed above in delinquency adjudication proceedings where the consequences were that the child could be committed to a state institution. It was confined to rulings at the adjudication stage of the juvenile process.

However, this decision was significant not only because of the procedural reforms it initiated but because of its far-reaching impact throughout the entire juvenile justice system. *Gault* instilled in juvenile proceedings the development of due process standards at the pretrial, trial, and posttrial stages of the juvenile process. While recognizing the history and the development of the juvenile court, it sought to accommodate the motives of rehabilitation and treatment with children's rights. It recognized the principle of fundamental fairness of the law for children as well as for adults. Judged in the context of today's juvenile justice system, *Gault* redefined the relationship between juveniles, their parents, and the state. It remains the single most significant constitutional case in the area of juvenile justice.

2. Standard of Proof: In Re Winship
397 U.S. 358, 90 S.Ct. 1068, (1970).

Following the *Gault* case came the decision of *In re Winship*. This case expressly held that a juvenile in a delinquency adjudication must be proven guilty beyond a reasonable doubt.

Facts Winship, a twelve-year-old boy in New York, stole $112 from a woman's pocketbook. The petition that charged Winship with delinquency alleged that this act, if done by an adult, would constitute larceny. Winship was adjudicated a delinquent on the basis of the preponderance of the evidence submitted at the court hearing. During a subsequent dispositional hearing, Winship was ordered placed in a training school in New York State for an initial period of eighteen months, subject to extensions of his commitment until his eighteenth birthday—six years in total. The New York State Supreme Court and the New York Court of Appeals affirmed the lower court decision, sustaining the conviction.

Decision The problem in the case was whether Section 744(b) of the New York State Family Court Act was constitutional. This section provided that any determination at the conclusion of an adjudicatory hearing must be based on a preponderance of the evidence. The judge decided Winship's guilt on the basis of this standard and not on the basis of proof beyond a reasonable doubt, which is the standard in the adult criminal justice system. The issue in the case was whether proof beyond a reasonable doubt was essential to due process and fair treatment for juveniles charged with an act that would constitute a crime if committed by an adult.

Significance of the Case Although the standard of proof beyond a reasonable doubt is not stated in the Constitution, the court said that *Gault* had established that due process required the essentials of fair treatment, although it did not require that the adjudication conform to all the requirements of the criminal trial. The Court went further to say that the due process clause recognized proof beyond a reasonable doubt as being among the essentials of fairness required when a child is charged with a delinquent act. The State of New York argued that juvenile delinquency proceedings were civil in nature, not criminal, and the preponderance of evidence standard was therefore valid. The United States Supreme Court indicated that the standard of proof beyond a reasonable doubt plays a vital role in the American criminal justice system and ensures a greater degree of safety for the presumption of innocence of those accused of a crime.

Thus, the *Winship* case required proof beyond a reasonable doubt as a standard for juvenile adjudication proceedings and eliminated the use of lesser standards such as a preponderance of the evidence, clear and convincing proof, and reasonable proof.

3. Right to a Jury Trial: McKeiver v. Pennsylvania. 403 U.S. 528, 91 S.Ct. 1976 (1971).

One of the most controversial issues in the areas of children's rights at adjudication involves the jury trial. Although the Sixth Amendment guarantees to the adult criminal defendant the right to a jury trial, the Supreme Court had not seen fit to grant this right to juvenile offenders. In fact, the Constitution is silent on whether all defendants, including those charged with misdemeanors, have a right to a trial by jury. In the case of *Duncan v. Louisiana*, the Supreme Court held that the Sixth Amendment right to a jury trial applied to state and federal cases and jury trial applied to state and federal cases and to all adult defendants accused of serious crimes. However, no mention was made of the juvenile offender.

The case of *McKeiver v. Pennsylvania* deals with the right of the juvenile defendant to a jury trial.

Facts Joseph McKeiver, age sixteen, was charged with robbery, larceny, and receiving stolen goods, all of which were felonies under the Pennsylvania law. McKeiver was subsequently declared delinquent at an adjudication hearing and placed on probation after his request for a jury trial was denied.

In another case, Edward Terry, age fifteen, was charged with assault and battery on a police officer, misdemeanors under Pennsylvania law. He was declared a juvenile delinquent after an adjudication following a denial of his request for trial by jury.

In an unrelated case in North Carolina, a group of juveniles were charged with willful, riotous, and disorderly conduct, declared delinquent, and placed on probation. Their request for a jury trial was denied.

The Supreme Court heard all three cases together on the single issue of whether a juvenile has a constitutional right to a jury trial in the juvenile court system.

Decision The Court was required to decide whether the due process clause of the Fourteenth Amendment guarantees the right to a jury trial in the adjudication of a juvenile court delinquency case. It answered in the negative, stating that the right to a jury trial guaranteed by the Sixth Amendment and incorporated in the Fourteenth Amendment, is not among the constitutional safeguards that the due process clause requires at delinquency adjudication hearings.

The Court's reasons were as follows:

1. A jury trial is not a necessary component of accurate fact-finding, as are the procedural requirements stated in the *Gault* case.

2. Not all the rights constitutionally assured to an adult are to be given to a juvenile.

3. Insisting on a jury trial for juvenile offenders could fully turn the adjudication into an adversary process.

4. Insisting on a jury trial would not remedy the problems associated with the lack of rehabilitation in the juvenile court.

5. The preferable approach would be to allow states to experiment and adopt for themselves a jury trial concept in their individual jurisdictions.

6. The jury trial, if imposed in the juvenile court, would certainly result in delay, formality, and the possibility of a public trial, which at this point is not provided in most jurisdictions.

Significance of the Case The *McKeiver* case temporarily stopped the march toward procedural constitutional due process for juvenile offenders in the juvenile justice system. The majority of the Court believed that juvenile proceedings were different from adult criminal prosecutions. The case also emphasized the fact that, as Justice Blackwell said, jurisdictions are free to adopt their own jury trial position in juvenile proceedings. The Court further noted that the majority of states denied a juvenile the right to a jury trial by statute. Thus, the Court believed that granting the juvenile offender the right to a jury trial would hinder rather than advance the system of juvenile justice in America.

DISPOSITIONS

The stage of the juvenile justice process after adjudication is called disposition. At this point, the juvenile court orders treatment for the juvenile to prevent further delinquency. Disposition is the most important phase of juvenile proceedings.[19] Paul Piersma, Jeanette Ganousis, and Prudence Kramer describe the disposition as the heart of the juvenile process.[20] The Hon. Lindsay G. Arthur, who has spent many years working on behalf of the National Council for Juvenile and Family Court Judges, speaks about the importance and the philosophy of disposition in the following way:

A disposition is not simply a sentencing. It is far broader in concept and in application. It should be in the best interest of the child, which in this context means effectively to provide the help necessary to resolve or meet the individual's definable needs, while, at the same time, meeting society's needs for protection.[21]

The dispositional process has not received much attention from the courts. None of the Supreme Court decisions dealing with juvenile justice refer to its significance. Consequently, according to most legal commentators, one of the most important issues in the disposition is the lack of proper procedure and due process for the child. Today, in most jurisdictions, the bifurcated hearing separates the adjudication and the disposition. In addition to a separate dispositional hearing, a child is generally accorded the right to counsel.

The Supreme Court has not ruled on the right to counsel at disposition, but counsel's participation is generally allowed by either a state statute or general practice. Defense counsel often represents the child, helps the parents understand the court's decision, and influences the direction of the disposition. Others involved at the dispositional stage include representatives of social service agencies, psychologists, social workers, and probation personnel. Their information about the child's background may often be disputed at the disposition, and many states now allow cross-examination at this stage of the juvenile process.

Another important issue at the dispositional hearing is the need to obtain information about the child to formulate the treatment plan. In determining the type of disposition to be imposed on the child, juvenile court statutes often require the completion of a predisposition report. Fox describes the needs and purposes of this report:

Individualized justice is often taken to be the most salient characteristic of juvenile court dispositions. In order to have the disposition conform to this ideal, the juvenile court judge requires information about each particular child. This is usually provided by an investigation, usually performed by a member of the probation staff, and report, known as the social study or disposition report.[22]

The predisposition report in the juvenile court is similar to the presentence report in the adult criminal justice system. Its use at the adjudication may result in prejudicial error against the child and often results in a mistrial. However, social service information is often used at the intake phase of the juvenile process as well as at the disposition. In some jurisdictions, statutes mandate the completion of a predisposition report, particularly before a child can be placed in a youth program.

A third issue, a very controversial one, is determining what disposition or action to take against the child. This continues to be a critically difficult task. The basic dispositions that are available in practically every jurisdiction include: (1) dismissal, (2) fine or restitution, (3) probation, and (4) commitment or institutionalization. Other dispositions include examination or placement in a hospital setting, transfer of custody from the parents to another individual or family member, release from jurisdiction, suspension of the commitment order, and the imposition of special counseling orders.

Often, the criteria for applying particular dispositions are not stated in the statutes. Statutes vaguely suggest that the disposition be in the best interest of the child and for the protection of the community. In reality, the type of disposition imposed and its duration ordinarily depend on what the child has done, the age of the child, the child's prior record, and the child's capacity to benefit from rehabilitation programs conducted under the auspices of the juvenile court system.

TRENDS IN JUVENILE SENTENCING

In order to achieve the traditional goal of rehabilitation, juvenile court dispositional orders have been based on totally indeterminate sentences for juvenile offenders. The indeterminate sentence used for adults is often defined as a term of incarceration with a stated minimum and maximum period. For instance, prison terms of from three to ten years or up to a period of ten years are indeterminate sentences. The idea behind indeterminate dispositional orders is that such sentencing provisions allow for individualized programs of treatment and provide for flexibility in sentencing. In some jurisdictions, juvenile court judges can sentence the juvenile for an indeterminate period to a particular type of program. In other jurisdictions, judges are required to send a child to a department such as a division of youth services within the given jurisdiction, and that agency is responsible for the child's placement and treatment.

Over the past few years, juvenile justice experts and the general public have become aroused about the constantly rising juvenile crime rate, particularly with children committing serious crimes. Reform groups, particularly law enforcement officials and legislators, have demanded that the juvenile justice system deal with dangerous juvenile offenders more severely. Some state legislatures have amended their juvenile codes and passed harsh laws that tighten up the juvenile justice system. For instance, in New York, children as young as thirteen who are accused of murder can be sent to the adult courts and sentenced to terms as long as life under the New York Juvenile Justice Reform Act of 1976.[23] Other jurisdictions have lowered the age for transferring juvenile offenders to the adult courts to sixteen.[24]

Trying juveniles who commit serious crimes as adults is not new. The transfer or waiver proceeding exists in almost all states. However, the juvenile judge is required to hold a hearing to transfer the child to the adult court. In some states, such as Colorado, Delaware, and Florida, legislators are passing mandatory prison sentences for juveniles convicted of serious felonies. This approach automatically requires the court to try thirteen-, fourteen-, fifteen-, and sixteen-year old children in the criminal rather than in the family court.[25]

A second reform movement involves status offenders. Reformers suggest that status offenders and other minor juvenile offenders be removed from the juvenile justice system and kept out of institutional programs that accept juvenile delinquents. Because of the development of numerous diversion programs, many children who are involved in truancy and incorrigible behavior and who have ordinarily been sent to closed institutions, are now placed in community programs. Thus, dispositional orders regarding institutionalization for such children have declined, and the number of children in juvenile institutions has dropped over the past few years. As a result of this movement, the kinds of young people now being committed are those generally convicted of very serious juvenile crimes.

The American Bar Association has developed standards that affect the dispositional process. Stanley Fisher points out that these standards point to a shift in juvenile court philosophy from traditional rehabilitation to the concept of "just desserts."[26] The standards recommend that juveniles receive determinate or flat sentences without the possibility of parole, rather than the indeterminate sentences that most of them now receive. The standards further recommend that punishment be classified into three major categories: nominal, conditional, and custodial. Nominal sanctions consist of reprimands, warnings, or other minor actions that do not affect the child's personal liberty. Conditional sanctions deal with such regulations as probation, restitution, and counseling programs.

Custodial sanctions, which are the most extreme, remove the juvenile from the community into a nonsecure or secure institution. The National Advisory Commission on Criminal Justice Standards and Goals also recommended in 1976 that the dispositions available to the court include nominal, conditional, and custodial categories.[27]

The state of Washington has adopted a determinate sentencing law for juvenile offenders. All juveniles convicted of delinquency are evaluated on the basis of a point system. Points are awarded to children on the basis of their age, prior juvenile record, and type of crime committed. Minor offenders with less than a certain number of points are ordinarily handled in the community. Those committing more serious offenses are generally placed on probation. Children who commit the most serious offenses are often subject to institutional penalties. Institutional officials, who had total discretion in the past for releasing children, now have limited discretion. As a result, juvenile offenders who commit very serious crimes, such as rape, armed robbery, or murder, are being incarcerated for two, three, and four years. Thus, the use of presumptive sentencing provisions or proportionality in sentencing has become a factor in juvenile justice dispositional procedures.[28]

Although traditional juvenile court sentencing is changing, most jurisdictions continue to be preoccupied with rehabilitation as a primary dispositional goal. Joseph Goldstein, Anna Freud, and Albert Solnit, in their classic work, *Beyond the Best Interest of the Child,* say that placements of children should be based on the least detrimental alternative philosophy available in order to foster the child's growth and development.[29] This should be the goal whether the children are delinquents or status offenders and for those who are neglected, abandoned, or abused. In reality, most states apply custodial restrictions or institutionalization only to children who commit the most serious offenses.

In sum, rehabilitation and treatment remain the most realistic goals in the dispositional process. Proportionality in juvenile sentencing is being recognized and implemented by some jurisdictions. Whether a policy of just desserts is the answer to juvenile criminality remains unclear. Some critics suggest that the ABA standards would "destroy the nation's juvenile court system and replace it with a junior criminal justice system."[30] There is no question that fitting the penalty to the child's behavior effects a radical change in current juvenile justice sentencing philosophy.

PREDISPOSITION REPORT

After the child has admitted to the allegations in the petition or after they have been proved in a juvenile trial, the judge normally orders the probation department to complete a predisposition report. Investigating and evaluating the child coming before the court for juvenile disposition is one of the most important tasks of juvenile probation officers. The predisposition report has a number of purposes:

1. It helps the judge decide which disposition is best for the child.
2. It aids the juvenile probation officer in developing treatment programs where the child is in need of counseling or community supervision.

3. It helps the court develop a body of knowledge about the child that can aid others in treating the child.

4. It serves as a source of basic information for systematic research in criminal justice.

The style and content of predisposition reports vary among jurisdictions and also among juvenile probation officers within the same jurisdiction. The requirements for the use of the report, the sources of dispositional information, the techniques for obtaining it, and the conditions of its distribution vary among jurisdictions and are based on rules of law and procedure.

Some juvenile court probation departments require voluminous reports covering every aspect of the child's life. Other jurisdictions require information about the basic facts of the case and only limited information about the child's background. Individual probation officers bring their personal styles and educational backgrounds to bear on the development of the report. The probation officer who is a trained social worker, for example, might stress the use of psychological data, while the probation officer who is a lawyer might concentrate on the child's prior record and how dangerous the child is to him- or herself and to the community.

Sources of dispositional data include questioning the juvenile, as well as collecting information about the child from family and school officials. In addition, the results of psychological testing, psychiatric evaluations, and intelligence testing may be considered relevant to the dispositional report. Furthermore, the probation officer might include information about the juvenile's feelings and attitudes regarding the present situation.

Some state statutes make the dispositional report mandatory. Other jurisdictions require the report only when there is a probability that the child will be institutionalized. In Massachusetts, for example, the law reads that "in every case of a delinquent child, a probation officer shall make a report regarding the character of such child, his school record, home surroundings, and previous complaint, if any."[31] Some appellate courts have reversed orders institutionalizing children where the juvenile court did not use a predisposition report in reaching its decision.

Access to predisposition reports is an important legal issue. The Supreme Court ruled in the case of *Kent v. United States* that the child and counsel must be given access to the social service report at transfer proceedings.[32] The National Advisory Commission on Criminal Justice Standards and Goals recommends that no dispositional decision be made on the basis of facts or
· information in a report if they have not previously been disclosed to the defense attorney for the child and to the prosecutor representing the state.[33]

A number of national organizations—among them the American Bar Association, the National Council on Crime and Delinquency, and the National Advisory Commission on Criminal Justice Standards and Goals—have attempted to identify the most important criteria needed for the predisposition investigation. Standard 3.3 of the American Bar Association standards on the juvenile probation function incorporates many of these criteria and is outlined below:

3.3   Scope of investigation; formulation of postdispositional plan; format, contents, length, and disclosure of report.

A. The scope of a predisposition investigation that the investigating officer conducts should be carefully tailored to the needs of the individual case and should vary depending upon the type of case and the issues involved. The officer should only collect evidence relevant to the court's dispositional decision.

B. When it is appropriate for the investigating officer to conduct a comprehensive investigation, the officer may secure information from existing records of the juvenile court, law enforcement agencies, schools, and other agencies with which the juvenile has come in contact and from interviews and conferences with the juvenile, the juvenile's family, school personnel, and individuals having knowledge of the juvenile.

C. An officer conducting a predisposition investigation may refer a juvenile for a physical or mental examination to a physician, psychiatrist, or psychologist only if a court order authorizing an examination is obtained. Such a court order should be issued only after a hearing on the need for such an examination.

D. The officer conducting the predisposition investigation should explore community resources as well as other resources that might be available to assist the juvenile. The officer should then formulate a postdisposition plan for the care and, where appropriate, for the treatment of the juvenile.

E. A written predisposition report summarizing the significant findings of the investigation should be prepared. The format, contents, and length of the report should be flexible. A comprehensive report should ordinarily include the following:

    1. a summary of the facts that led to the adjudication, with respect to the conduct of the juvenile;
    2. a summary of the juvenile's prior contacts with the juvenile court and law enforcement agencies;
    3. a summary of the juvenile's home environment, family relationships and background;
    4. a summary of the juvenile's school and employment status and background;
    5. a summary of the juvenile's interests and activities;
    6. a summary of any significant physical problems of the juvenile and description of any behavior problems of the juvenile that the officer learns of or observes in the course of the investigation, provided the officer is careful not to represent these observations as qualified professional evaluations;
    7. a summary of the results and recommendations of any significant physical and mental examinations; and
    8. an evaluation of the foregoing information, a recommendation as to disposition, and a suggested postdisposition plan of care and treatment.

F. The predisposition report should contain only information that is relevant to the court's dispositional decision, and all information should be presented in a concise, factual, and unbiased manner. The report should indicate how much time and effort was expended upon the investigation and the sources of information in the report.

G. The predisposition report should not be open to public inspection, but the juvenile's counsel and the attorney representing the state in connection with dispositional proceedings should be given access to the report.[34]

In the final section of the predisposition report, the probation department recommends a disposition to the presiding judge. This is a very critical aspect of the report, since it has been estimated that the court follows more than 90 percent of all probation department recommendations. Thus, it is essential that the purpose of the report, which is to determine the care or treatment plan the child needs and not to prove or disprove the child's innocence or guilt, be accomplished.

THE CHILD'S RIGHT TO APPEAL IN THE JUVENILE COURT

According to Sanford Fox, juvenile court statutes normally restrict appeals to cases where the juvenile seeks review of a "final order" or a final judgment.[35] Paul Piersma and associates define a final order as one that ends the litigation between two parties by determining all their rights and disposing of all the issues.[36]   The appellate process gives the juvenile the opportunity to have the case brought before a reviewing court after it has been heard in the juvenile or family court. Today, the law does not recognize a federal constitutional right of appeal in juvenile or adult criminal cases. In other words, the Constitution does not require any state to furnish an appeal to a juvenile charged and found to be delinquent in a juvenile or family court setting.

Appellate review of a juvenile case is a matter of statutory right to appeal in each jurisdiction. Today, the majority of states provide juveniles with some method of statutory appeal.

The appeal process was not always a part of the juvenile law system, however. J. Addison Bowman found, for example, that in 1965 few states extended the right of appeal to juveniles.[37] According to the President's Commission on Law Enforcement and Administration of Justice, appellate review was equally limited in 1967:

By and large the juvenile court system has operated without appellate surveillance. . . . Two factors contribute substantially to the lack of review. The absence of counsel in the great majority of cases is the first. . . . The other important factor is the general absence of transcripts of juvenile court proceedings.[38]

Even in the *Gault* case in 1967, the Supreme Court refused to review the Arizona juvenile code, which provided no appellate review in juvenile matters. It further rejected the right of a juvenile to a transcript.[39]

Today, however, most jurisdictions that provide a child with some form of appeal also provide for counsel and for the securing of a record and transcript, which are crucial to the success of any appeal. Since adult criminal defendants have both a right to counsel at their initial appeal and a right to a stenographic transcript of trial proceedings, it would violate equal protection if a juvenile were denied the same rights.

Since juvenile appellate review is a matter of statutory right, each jurisdiction determines for itself what method or scope of review will be used. There are two basic methods of appeal: the direct appeal and the collateral attack. The direct appeal normally involves an appellate court review to determine whether the rulings of law and the judgment of the court based on the evidence presented at the trial were correct. This approach is laid out in Section 59 of the Uniform Juvenile Court Act of the National Conference of Commissioners on Uniform State Laws: "The appeal should be heard upon the files, records, and minutes or transcripts of the evidence of the juvenile court, giving appreciable weight to the findings of the juvenile court."[40] A similar approach is suggested by the National Advisory Commission on Criminal Justice Standards and Goals: "The appeal should be heard upon the files, records, and transcript of the evidence of the family court."[41]

A broader review procedure, which is a form of direct review, is the *de novo* review. A trial *de novo* is a complete retrial of the original case based on the original petition. All evidence produced at the first trial can be resubmitted, as can additional evidence. The trial *de novo* appeal is limited to only a few jurisdictions in this country. It is usually encountered when a juvenile is originally tried in a court of very limited jurisdiction and in some administrative proceedings before masters or referees.

The second major area of review involves the collateral attack of a case. The term *collateral* refers to a secondary or indirect method of attacking a final judgment or order of the court. Instead of appealing the original juvenile trial because of errors, prejudice, or lack of evidence, collateral review uses extraordinary legal writs to challenge the lower court position. Two such procedural devices include the writ of *habeas corpus* and the writ of *certiorari*. The *habeas corpus* writ, known as the Great Writ, refers to a procedure for determining the validity of a person's custody. In the context of the juvenile court, it is used to challenge the custody of a child in detention or in an institution. The writ of *certiorari* is an order from a higher to a lower court commanding that the case be brought forward for review. This writ is often the method by which the Supreme Court exercises its discretionary authority to hear cases regarding constitutional issues. In spite of the facts that there is no constitutional right to appeal a juvenile case and that each jurisdiction provides for appeals differently, juveniles have a far greater opportunity for appellate review today than in years past.

CHAPTER SUMMARY

The purpose of this chapter has been to describe two major aspects of the juvenile justice system, adjudication and disposition. Most jurisdictions have a bifurcated juvenile code system that separates the adjudication hearing from the dispositional hearing. Juveniles alleged to be delinquent as well as children in need of supervision have virtually all the rights given to a criminal defendant at trial—except possibly the right to a trial by jury.

The types of dispositional orders that the juvenile court gives include dismissal, fine, probation, and institutionalization. The use of these dispositions has not curtailed the rising rate of juvenile crime, however. As a result, legislatures and national commissions have begun to take a harsher position with regard to the sentencing of some juvenile offenders. The traditional notion of rehabilitation and treatment as the proper goals for disposition is now being questioned, and some jurisdictions have replaced it with proportionality in sentencing procedures.

The presentence investigation report is the primary informational source for assisting the court in making a judgment about a child's care and treatment.

Although it is impossible to determine which aspect of the juvenile justice system is most critical, disposition probably holds the final solution to juvenile criminality. Once a juvenile is found delinquent or in need of supervision, the juvenile court is empowered through the dispositional process to make fundamental changes in the child's life. If there is any chance for juvenile crime to be reduced in the future, it may well depend upon the need for fair, just, and effective disposition.

DISCUSSION QUESTIONS

1. Discuss and identify the major participants in the conduct of a juvenile adjudication. What does each person do in the course of the juvenile trial?
2. The criminal justice system in America is based on the adversary process. Does the same adversary principle apply in the juvenile justice system?
3. Children have certain constitutional rights at adjudication, such as the right to an attorney and the right to confront and cross-examine witnesses. But they do not have the right to trial by jury. Should juvenile offenders have a constitutional right to a jury trial? Should each state make that determination?
4. What is the point of obtaining a predisposition report in the juvenile court? Is it of any value in cases where the child is often released to the community? Does it have a significant value in serious juvenile crime cases?
5. The standard of proof in a juvenile adjudication is to show that the child is guilty beyond a reasonable doubt. Explain the meaning of this standard of proof in the American judicial system.

SUGGESTED READINGS

Alschuler, Albert W. "The Defense Attorney's Role in Plea Bargaining." *Yale Law Journal* 84 (1975): 1179–1201.

American Bar Association. Project on Standards for Juvenile Justice. *Standards Relating to Adjudication.* Cambridge, Mass.: Ballinger Press, 1977.

____Project on Standards for Juvenile Justice. *Standards Relating to Dispositional Procedures.* Cambridge, Mass.: Ballinger Press, 1977.

____Project on Standards for Juvenile Justice. *Standards Relating to Dispositions.* Cambridge, Mass.: Ballinger Press, 1977.

____Project on Standards for Juvenile Justice. *Standards Relating to Appeal and Collateral Review.* Cambridge, Mass.: Ballinger Press, 1977.

Coffee, James. "The Future of Sentencing Reform: Emerging Local Issues in the Individualization of Justice." *Michigan Law Review* 73 (1975): 1361–1380.

Douglas v. California, 372 U.S. 353, 83 S.Ct. 814 (1963).

Fay v. Noia, 372 U.S. 391, 83 S.Ct. 822 (1963).

Fisher, Stanley. "The Dispositional Process under the Juvenile Justice Standards Project." *Boston University Law Review* 57 (1977): 732–753.

Gross, S. "The Prehearing Juvenile Report, Probation Officers' Conceptions." In *Probation and Parole,* edited by R. Carter and L. Wilkins. New York: Wiley, 1970.

Hufnagel, Lynne, and Davidson, John. "Children in Need: Observations of Practices of the Denver Juvenile Court." *Denver Law Journal* 51 (1974): 337–369.

In re Oliver, 333 U.S. 257, 68 S.Ct. 499 (1948).

Ketchum, Orman W. "McKeiver v. Penn: The Last Word on Juvenile Court Adjudications." *Cornell Law Review* 57 (1972): 56-575.

National Council on Crime and Delinquency. "Corrections in the United States." *Crime and Delinquency Journal* 13 (1967): 1-280.

Newman, Donald. *Conviction: The Determination of Guilt or Innocence without Trial*. American Bar Foundation. Boston: Little, Brown, 1966.

Note. "A Right to Jury Trial for Juveniles—The Implications of McKeiver." *Notre Dame Law Review* 49 (1973): 625-634.

Note. "Appellate Review of Juvenile Court Dispositions: Gault's Forgotten Footnote." *Connecticut Law Review* 5 (1972): 117-129.

Note. "Pre-Adjudicatory Confessions and Consent Searches: Placing the Juvenile on the Same Constitutional Footing as an Adult." *Boston University Law Review* 57 (1977): 778-789.

President's Commission on Law Enforcement and Administration of Justice. Task Force Report. *Juvenile Delinquency and Youth Crime*. Washington, D.C.: Government Printing Office, 1967.

Rosenheim, Margaret K., ed. *Justice for the Child—The Juvenile Court in Transition*. New York: Free Press, 1962.

Rubin, Ted. *The Courts: Fulcrum of the Justice System*. Sacramento, Calif.: Goodyear, 1976.

Sheridan, William. *Standards for Juvenile and Family Courts, Children's Bureau*. Washington, D.C.: Government Printing Office, 1966.

Skoler, Daniel, and Tenney, Charles. "Attorney Representation in Juvenile Court." *Journal of Family Law* 4 (1964): 83-94.

REFERENCES

1. U.S. Department of Justice, *Prosecution in the Juvenile Courts* (Washington, D.C.: Government Printing Office, 1973), p. 9.

2. 383 U.S. 541, 86 S.Ct. 1045, 16 L.Ed. 2d 84 (1966); 387 U.S. 1, 87 S.Ct. 1428, 18 L.Ed. 2d 527 (1967); and 397 U.S. 358, 90 S.Ct. 1068, 25 L.Ed. 2d 368 (1970).

3. U.S. Department of Justice, *Prosecution in the Juvenile Courts*, pp. 14-15.

4. National Conference of Commissioners on Uniform State Laws, Uniform Juvenile Court Act (1968).

5. See National Council on Crime and Delinquency, *Model Rules for Juvenile Courts* (Hackensack, N.J.: NCCD, 1969).

6. William Sheridan, *Legislative Guide for Drafting Family and Juvenile Court Acts*, Department of Health, Education and Welfare Children's Bureau Publication 472. (Washington, D.C.: Government Printing Office, 1969).

7. American Bar Association, *Standards Relating to Juvenile Prosecution* (Cambridge, Mass.: Ballinger, 1977), p. 13.

8. Daniel Skoler and Charles Tenney, "Attorney Representation in Juvenile Courts," *Journal of Family Law* 4 (1964): p. 83.

9. 191 Neb. 5231 (1974).

10. U.S. Department of Justice, *Prosecution in the Juvenile Courts*, p. 15.

11. National Advisory Commission on Criminal Justice Standards and Goals, *Report of the Task Force on Juvenile Justice and Delinquency Prevention* (Washington, D.C.: Law Enforcement Assistance Administration, 1976).

12. See Sari Escovitz with Fred Kurland and Nan Gold, *Judicial Selection and Tenure* (Chicago: American Judicature Society, 1974), pp. 3–16.

13. Advisory Council of Judges of National Council on Crime and Delinquency, *Procedure and Evidence in the Juvenile Court—A Guidebook for Judges* (New York: NCCD, 1962), p. 2.

14. 287, U.S. 45, 53 S.Ct. 55, 77 L.Ed. 158 (1932); 372 U.S. 335, 83 S.Ct. 792, 9 L.Ed. 2d 799 (1963); and 407 U.S. 25, 92 S.Ct. 2006, 32 L.Ed. 2d 530 (1972).

15. See H. Lou, *Juvenile Courts in the United States* (Chapel Hill, North Carolina: University of North Carolina Press, 1927), p. 1.

16. Joseph Senna and Larry Siegel, *Introduction to Criminal Law* (St. Paul, Minn.: West Publishing, 1978), pp. 235–239.

17. See Massachusetts Supreme Judicial Court Rule 11.

18. National Advisory Commission on Criminal Justice Standards and Goals, *Report of the Task Force on Juvenile Justice and Delinquency Prevention.*

19. National Advisory Commission on Criminal Justice Standards and Goals, *Report of the Task Force on Juvenile Justice and Delinquency Prevention*, p. 431.

20. Paul Piersma, Jeanette Ganousis and Prudence Kramer, "The Juvenile Court: Current Problems, Legislative Proposals, and a Model Act," *St. Louis University Law Review* 20 (1976): p. 43.

21. See Lindsay Arthur, "Status Offenders Need a Court of Last Resort," *Boston University Law Review* 57 (1977): pp. 63–644. See also Lindsay Arthur, ed., *National Bench Book for Juvenile Courts* (St. Paul, Minn.: American Case Law Corp., 1978), p. 43.

22. Sanford Fox, *Juvenile Courts in a Nutshell* (St. Paul, Minn.: West Publishing, 1977), p. 208.

23. Fred Cohen, "Juvenile Offenders: Proportionality vs. Treatment," *Children's Rights Report* (New York: American Civl Liberties Union, 1978), pp. 2–7. See also Juvenile Justice and Reform Act of 1976 and New York Family Court Act, Secs. 711–717 (Chap. 878, Laws of 1976).

24. See such jurisdictions as California, Hawaii, Idaho, Kansas, New Jersey, and Rhode Island.

25. See, generally, American Bar Association/Institute of Judicial Administration, Juvenile Justice Standards Project, *Standards Relating to Transfer between Courts* (Cambridge, Mass.: Ballinger Press, 1977).

26. Stanley Fisher, "The Dispositional Process under the Juvenile Justice Standards Project," *Boston University Law Review* 57 (1977): p. 732.

27. National Advisory Commission on Criminal Justice Standards and Goals, *Report of the Task Force on Juvenile Justice and Delinquency Prevention*, pp. 452–459.

28. See Michael Serrill, "Police Write a New Law on Juvenile Crime," *Police Magazine*, September 1979, p. 47. See also N. P. Leggi, "How Fifteen-Year-Olds Get Away with Murder," *New York Magazine*, June 13, 1977; p. 11 and Lucy Komisar, "Putting Johnny in Jail," *Juris Doctor*, June–July 1978, p. 29.

29. See Joseph Goldstein, Anna Freud, and Albert Solnit, *Beyond the Best Interests of the Child* (New York: Free Press, 1973).

30. Fisher, "The Dispositional Process under the Juvenile Justice Standards Project," p. 732.

31. Mass. Gen. Laws, Chap. 119, Sec. 57.

32. Kent v. United States, 383 U.S. 541, 86 S.Ct. 1045 (1966).

33. National Advisory Commission on Criminal Justice Standards and Goals, *Report of the Task Force on Juvenile Justice and Delinquency Prevention*, p. 445.

34. American Bar Association, *Standards Relating to Juvenile Probation Function* (Cambridge, Mass.: Ballinger Press, 1977), pp. 113–114.

35. Fox, *Juvenile Courts in a Nutshell*, pp. 254–255.

36. Paul Piersma et al., *Law and Tactics in Juvenile Cases* (Philadelphia: American Law Institute–American Bar Association, Committee on Continuing Education, 1977). p. 397.

37. See Addison Bowman, "Appeals from Juvenile Courts," *Crime and Delinquency Journal* 11 (1965): pp. 63–77.

38. President's Commission on Law Enforcement and Administration of Justice, Task Force Report, *Juvenile Delinquency and Youth Crime* (Washington, D.C.: Government Printing Office, 1967), p. 115.

39. 387 U.S. 1 (1967).

40. National Conference of Commissioners on Uniform State Laws, Uniform Juvenile Court Act (1968), Sec. 59.

41. National Advisory Commission on Criminal Justice Standards and Goals, *Report of the Task Force on Juvenile Justice and Delinquency Prevention*, p. 428.

PART VI

JUVENILE CORRECTIONS

Chapter 18

Chapter Outline	Key Terms, Names, and Cases
Introduction	juvenile probation
Juvenile Probation	community treatment
The Organization and Administration of Juvenile Probation Services	diagnostic study
	probation revocation
Restitution as a Form of Community Treatment	restitution
	therapeutic program
The Trend toward Deinstitutionalization	Provo Project
Residential Treatment Alternatives to Incarceration	Key Program
	CTP
Nonresidential Community Treatment	CDCP
Criticisms of the Community Treatment Approach	Earn-It Program
	deinstitutionalization
Chapter Summary	training schools
	recidivism
	Essexfields
	New Pride
	Juvenile Delinquency and Prevention Act of 1974
	residential treatment
	group homes
	foster homes
	Highfields Project
	Silverlakes Experiment

Community Treatment
of the Juvenile
Offender

INTRODUCTION

In the middle of the 1960s, America began to realize that the juvenile justice system was a failure. During this time, violent juvenile crime and property crimes such as burglary, larceny, and auto theft increased considerably. In addition, persons under twenty-five accounted for a larger percentage of the total crimes committed each year, and recidivism rates for juveniles were far higher than the rates for adult offenders.

Supreme Court Justice Harry Blackmun underlined this failure in the case of *McKeiver v. Pennsylvania*:

We must recognize as the court has recognized that the fond and idealistic hopes of the juvenile justice proponents and early reformers of three generations have not been realized. The devastating commentary of the system's failures as a whole contained in the task force report: Juvenile Delinquency and Youth Crime, reveals the depth of disappointment in what has been accomplished. The community's unwillingness to provide people and facilities and to be concerned, the insufficiency of time devoted, the scarcity of professional help, the inadequacy of dispositional alternatives, and our general lack of knowledge, all contribute to dissatisfaction with the experiment.[1]

Whether we agree with Justice Blackmun's assessment or not, it is necessary to realize that the juvenile justice system has not lived up to its promise; nor has it improved much since Justice Blackmun's statement of a decade ago. Many experts believed that in the *McKeiver* case, Justice Blackmun gave juvenile justice a reprieve. Instead of implementing the due process concept completely and creating a system totally akin to the criminal system, Justice Blackmun pointed out the following:

The juvenile concept held high promise. We are reluctant to say that, despite disappointments of grave dimensions, it still does not hold promise and we are particularly reluctant to say, as do the Pennsylvania appellants here that the system cannot accom-

417

plish its rehabilitative goals. So much depends on the availability of resources, on the interest and commitment of the public, on willingness to learn, and on understanding as to cause and effect and cure. In this field, as in so many others, one perhaps learns best by doing.[2]

Over the past ten years, juvenile justice experts have been acting on Justice Blackmun's statement. Community treatment programs have proliferated throughout the country. As the term is used here, community treatment refers to a wide variety of efforts at the dispositional stage to provide care, protection, and treatment for children defined as delinquent and in need of supervision. These efforts include probation, a variety of treatment services such as social casework, group work, and the use of volunteers in probation, as well as the concept of restitution. The term *community treatment* also refers generally to the use of nonsecure and noninstitutional residences such as foster homes, small group homes, boarding schools or semi-institutional cottage living programs, forestry camps or outdoor camps, and overnight schools and residences. Finally, *community treatment* refers to the use of nonresidential programs where youths remain in their own homes and receive counseling, education, family assistance, diagnostic service, casework service, or vocational training. Often, parole is considered an extension of community treatment, but parole will be discussed in the following chapter. Community treatment includes preventive programs such as street work with antisocial gangs or early identification and treatment of predelinquents. Such programs are discussed in Chapters 9 and 10.

This chapter will discuss the concept of community treatment as a dispositional alternative for juveniles who have violated the law and who have been found guilty by the juvenile court. Their hope for rehabilitation and the hope of society for resolving the problems of juvenile crime lie in the use of community treatment programs. First, the chapter will discuss probation in detail. Next it will review restitution, which is being used in many jurisdictions to supplement probation supervision. It will then trace the historical development of the alternatives to incarceration, with particular emphasis on programs in the 1950s and 1960s. Finally it will discuss contemporary, community-based, nonsecure treatment programs.

JUVENILE PROBATION

Probation is the primary form of community treatment in the juvenile justice system. *Probation* ordinarily refers to a disposition. The child is placed and maintained in the community under the supervision of a duly authorized officer of the court. The term also denotes a status or process whereby the child on probation is subject to rules that must be followed and conditions that must be met in order for the child to remain in the community. *Probation* often refers to an organizational structure—a probation department (either an independent agency or one attached to a court) that manages, supervises, and treats children and carries out investigations for the court. Although the term has many other meanings too, *probation* usually refers to a legal disposition of a nonpunitive type for delinquent youths and those in need of supervision, emphasizing maintenance in the community and treatment without incarceration.

Juvenile probation is based on the idea that the juvenile offender is not generally dangerous to the community and has a better chance of being rehabilitated within the community. Advocates of probation and community treatment suggest that the institutional experience can force juveniles to become further involved in antisocial behavior. Probation provides the child with the opportunity to be closely supervised by trained personnel who can help reestablish forms of acceptable behavior in a community setting.

In its *Adult Standards on Criminal Justice Relating to Probation*, the American Bar Association points out the desirability of probation for adults, and the advantages it cites apply equally to juveniles:

Standard 1.2. Probation is a desirable disposition in appropriate cases because (1) it maximizes the liberty of the individual while at the same time vindicating the authority of the law and effectively protecting the public from further violations of law; (2) it affirmatively promotes the rehabilitation of the offender by continuing normal community contacts; (3) it avoids negative and frequently stultifying effects of confinement which often severely and unnecessarily complicate the reintegration of the offender into the community; (4) it greatly reduces the financial cost to the public of an effective correctional system.[3]

In practice, probation is a legal disposition, and only a court system can place a juvenile under an order of probation. Two methods are generally used. One is a straight order of probation for such a time and under such conditions as the judge deems proper. The other method involves ordering a child to be committed to an institution or department of youth services and then suspending the order and placing the child on probation. In the majority of jurisdictions, probation is a direct order similar to a sentence and is exercised under wide statutory discretion. In particular, the conditions to be followed during the probationary period are subject to the court's discretion.

Where a suspended incarceration is used, the probation implies a contract between the court and the juvenile. The court promises to hold a period of institutionalization in abeyance; the juvenile promises to adhere to a set of rules or conditions mandated by the court. If the rules are violated, and especially if the child commits another juvenile offense, the probation may be revoked. The contract between the court and the child is over, and the original commitment order may be enforced.

In the juvenile court, probation is often ordered for an indefinite period of time. Depending on the statutes of the jurisdiction, the seriousness of the offense, and the juvenile's adjustment on probation, a child can remain under the court's supervision until the court no longer has jurisdiction over him or her. In most jurisdictions, the status of probation is reviewed regularly to assure that a child is not kept on probation needlessly. Generally, discretion lies with the probation officer to discharge the child if the child is adjusting to the supervision and treatment plan.

Since virtually all the states have adopted the Inter-State Compact for Juveniles, the supervision of a juvenile probationer can be transferred from one state to another when it is necessary for a child to move from the original jurisdiction.[4] The Compact adopted by virtually all the states, provides jurisdiction over all nonresident children by allowing for the return of runaway children to their home state and for supervision of out of state children.

The Historical Development of Juvenile Probation

Though juvenile probation has had its major development in the present century, its roots go back through history. In England, specialized procedures for dealing with youthful offenders emerged as early as 1820, when the magistrates of the Warwickshire quarter sessions adopted the practice of sentencing youthful criminals to prison terms of one day, then releasing them conditionally under the supervision of their parents or masters. This practice was developed further in Middlesex, Birmingham, and London, where probation supervision was first supplied by police officers, then by volunteer philanthropic organizations, and finally by public departments.[5]

In the United States, juvenile probation developed as part of the wave of social reform characterizing the latter half of the nineteenth century. Massachusetts took the first step toward the development of a juvenile probation service. Under an act passed in 1869, an agent of the state board of charities was authorized to appear in criminal trials involving juveniles, to find them suitable homes, and to visit them periodically. These services were soon broadened and strengthened so that by 1890 probation had become a mandatory part of the court structure throughout the state.[6]

Probation made a central contribution to the development of the concept of the juvenile court. In fact, in some states the early supporters of the juvenile court movement accepted probation legislation as the first step toward achieving the benefits that the new court was intended to provide. The rapid spread of the juvenile court during the first decades of the present century encouraged the development of probation. The two closely related and to a large degree interdependent institutions sprang from the same dedicated conviction that the young could be rehabilitated and that the public was responsible for protecting them.

By the mid-1960s, juvenile probation had become a major social institution, large and complex and touching the lives of an enormous number of children in America. In 1976, almost a half million children were placed under juvenile probation.[7] Today, probation departments have the main responsibility for processing and servicing the majority of cases referred to the juvenile court.

THE ORGANIZATION AND ADMINISTRATION OF JUVENILE PROBATION SERVICES

Juvenile probation systems are organized according to two main patterns.[8] In the most prevalent one, the court or a group of courts administer probation services. In the other, an administrative agency such as a probation department provides the services to the court. Today, juvenile probation is administered predominantly by courts in the majority of states. Other organizational structures include state correctional agencies, public welfare departments, or a combination of such agencies. The relationship between the court (especially the judge) and the probation staff, whether it is under the court or in a separate administrative agency, is an extremely close one.

In the typical juvenile probation department, the chief probation officer sets policy, supervises hiring, determines what training should be emphasized, and sometimes recommends dispositions to the juvenile court judge. The leader-

ship role of the chief probation officer is central to the operation of a good probation department. Where the probation service is under the responsibility of
the juvenile court, the judge is the chief administrative officer and exercises
leadership over probation with the chief probation officer.

Large probation departments include one or more assistant chiefs. Each of
these middle managers is responsible for one aspect of probation service. One
assistant chief will oversee training. Another will supervise and treat special
offender groups. Another might act as liaison with juvenile, police, or community service agencies. The probation officers are in direct and personal contact
with the supervisory staff. They investigate and supervise juvenile cases.

In major cities and states, juvenile probation services are quite complex.
They control detention facilities, juvenile court treatment programs, and research and evaluation staffs. For example, since there are no federal juvenile
courts, children under eighteen who break federal laws are handled in United
States district courts as juvenile delinquents. If they are placed on probation,
they are supervised by federal probation officers in geographic districts established throughout the country.

The states have their own jurisdiction and laws over juvenile offenders.
Their approach to juvenile probation organization varies. In some
states Massachusetts, for example—a state-wide probation service exists, but
actual control over departments is localized within each district court. New
York, on the other hand, has in each of its counties a family court with exclusive
original jurisdiction over children sixteen or under. There, county probation
departments provide services, and a single department handles probation for
the five boroughs of the city of New York. In Maryland, the State Department of
Juvenile Services provides probation services to the juvenile courts in each
county.[9] The organization of probation services depends on the size of the service and the number of children under its supervision and control.

Duties and Responsibilities of Juvenile Probation Officers

The juvenile probation officer is responsibile for the initial contact with the
child, for continuing to process the case, and for providing services for the child
while he or she is under court supervision.

According to the American Bar Association's standards for juvenile justice,
juvenile probation officers are involved at four stages of the court process. At
intake they screen complaints by deciding to adjust the matter, refer to an
agency for service, or refer to the court for judicial action. During the interim
status or predisposition stage they participate in release or detention decisions.
At the postadjudication stage, they assist the court in reaching its dispositional
decision. During postdisposition they supervise juveniles placed on probation.[10]

At intake, the probation staff engages in preliminary explorations with the
child and the family to determine if court intervention is necessary or if the matter can be better resolved by some other community service. If the child is
placed in a detention facility, the probation officer helps the court decide if the
child should continue in or be released from detention pending the adjudication and disposition of the case.

The juvenile probation officer exercises tremendous influence over the child and the family by developing a social investigation report and submitting it to the court. This report is a clinical diagnosis of the child's problems and his or her need for court assistance. It is based on the child's social functioning. The report evaluates the child's personality and relationship to family, peers, and community in order to provide a future treatment plan. The National Council on Crime and Delinquency summarizes the purpose of the report as follows:

If the diagnostic study is to accomplish its purpose, it must include skilled analysis of the child's perceptions of and feelings about his violations, his problems and his life situation. It must shed light on the value systems that influence behavior. It must consider the degree of his motivation to solve the problems productive of deviant behavior as well as his physical, intellectual, and emotional capacity to do so. It must examine the influence of members of his family and other significant persons in his life in producing and possibly solving his problems. Neighborhood and peer group determinants of his attitudes and behavior must be analyzed.

All of this information must be brought together into a meaningful picture of a complex whole composed of the personality, the problem, and the environmental situation which must be dealt with. This configuration must be considered in relation to the various possible alternative dispositions available to the court. Out of this, a constructive treatment plan must be developed.[11]

The most important function of the juvenile probation officer is to provide the child with supervision and treatment in the community. The treatment plan is a product of the intake, diagnostic, and investigative aspects of probation. Treatment plans vary. Some children simply report to the probation officer and follow the conditions of probation. In other cases the probation officer may need to counsel the child and family extensively or refer them to other services, such as group therapy, provided by various community agencies.

The following list summarizes the probation officer's role and reflects the diversity of skills the role requires:

1. Providing direct counseling and casework services.
2. Interviewing and collecting social service data.
3. Making diagnostic recommendations.
4. Maintaining working relationships with law enforcement agencies.
5. Using community resources and services.
6. Using volunteer case aides and probation officers.
7. Writing predisposition reports.
8. Working with families of children under supervision.
9. Providing specialized services such as group work, behavior modification counseling, or reality therapy counseling.
10. Supervising specialized caseloads involving children on drugs or with special psychological or emotional problems.
11. Making decisions about the revocation of probation and its termination.

Performing all these functions requires a high quality probation staff. Today, juvenile probation officers have legal backgrounds, social work backgrounds, or special counseling skills. Most jurisdictions require juvenile probation officers to have a background in the social sciences and a bachelors degree. Because referrals to juvenile courts usually involve large numbers of minority children, the American Bar Association recommends the following: "Agencies should recruit and employ as juvenile intake and investigative officers individuals including minority group members and women from a wide variety of backgrounds."[12]

Conditions of Juvenile Probation and Its Revocation

Conditions of probation are rules and regulations mandating that a juvenile on probation behave in a particular way. They are important ingredients in the accomplishment of the treatment plan that has been devised for the child. Conditions can include restitution or reparation, intensive probation counseling, participation in a therapeutic program, or participating in an educational or vocational training program. In addition to these specific conditions, state statutes generally allow courts to insist that probationers lead law-abiding lives during the period of probation, that they maintain a residence in a family setting, that they refrain from associating with certain types of people, and that they remain in a particular geographic area unless they have permission to leave.

Probation conditions vary, but they are never supposed to be capricious or cruel or beyond the capacity of the juvenile to accomplish. Furthermore, conditions of probation should relate to the crime that was committed and to the conduct of the child.

In recent years, appellate courts have invalidated probation conditions that were harmful and that violated the child's basic due process rights. Restricting a child's movement, insisting on a mandatory program of treatment, ordering indefinite terms of probation, and demanding financial reparation where this is impossible are all grounds for an appellate court review.[13]

If a child violates the conditions of probation or breaks the law again, the court can revoke probation. The juvenile court ordinarily handles a decision to revoke probation upon recommendations of the probation officer. Today, as a result of Supreme Court decisions dealing with the rights of adult probationers, a juvenile is normally entitled to legal representation and a hearing when a violation of probation occurs.[14]

Effectiveness of Juvenile Probation

Probation is the primary disposition used in the juvenile court in America today. In any given year, more than half a million children are placed on probation. In recent years, the predominant question asked by probation personnel and other juvenile justice practitioners has been, "Is juvenile probation effective, and under what conditions is it successful?"

Although the American Bar Association recognizes probation as one of the critical elements of the juvenile process, it also points out that probation is one of the greatest community treatment disappointments. It further indicates that the performance of juvenile probation has been erratic, unreliable, and ineffective.[15]

The ABA statements may generally be correct, but an occasional piece of documented evidence shows probation to be a successful rehabilitation method in the juvenile court system. Ralph England, in a summary of fifteen probation studies from various jurisdictions, reported success rates of about 75 percent.[16] A more recent study by Frank Scarpitti and Richard Stephenson in

1968 revealed that over 70 percent of male probationers between sixteen and eighteen years of age were discharged favorably from probation supervision.[17] As LaMar Empey points out, however, these studies do not necessarily prove that juvenile probation rehabilitates the juvenile offender.[18] Such research generally does not take into account the fact that most children under normal probation supervision reveal a high success rate anyway. In addition, many children are released from probation and generally receive only a minimal amount of treatment and supervision. England points out that many offenders are "self-correcting" and are not likely to become recidivists regardless of whether they receive a minimum, moderate, or maximun amount of supervision.[19]

Much research has dealt with reducing the caseloads of probation officers. Experts have believed that limiting the number of individuals under supervision would give probation supervision a higher probability of success. A 1959 parole research project in Oakland, California, tested whether reduced caseloads improved the overall performance of young parolees. No substantial difference was found.[20]

Most experts believe that small caseloads are no more effective than large ones without systematic matching of offender type, treatment, and probation officer. As a result, the emphasis in probation research has shifted over the past two decades from reducing caseloads to classifying juvenile offenders and finding appropriate treatment for different types of children.

One of the most widely acclaimed projects of this type is the Community Treatment Program (CTP) of the California Youth Authority. The purpose of the project was to determine whether intensive supervision of juveniles in the community would be more successful than the normal program of institutionalization.[21] The project was established in 1961 and has served as a research model in juvenile justice for two decades. The study took children committed from the juvenile courts of the cities of Sacramento, Stockton, San Francisco, and Modesto and classified them according to a measure of interpersonal maturity (I-level). The children were divided into an experimental group treated in an intensive community parole program and a control group treated in a traditional program. Individual treatment plans were developed for each child in the experimental group. Certain types of youths did especially well; others did not respond to community treatment.

Over the years, numerous researchers have examined the data from the California community treatment project.[22] On the whole, recidivism rates seem to be lower for those in community treatment than for those in traditional programs. Intensive probation and treatment programs are less costly and probably less harmful than traditional institutional commitment.

Another significant project was established in 1964, also in California—the Community Delinquency Control Project (CDCP) of the California Youth Authority, operating in Los Angeles and Oakland.[23] The purposes of this project were to reduce overcrowding in youth authority institutions and to determine the effectiveness of community treatment. Children receiving intensive treatment were placed in small caseloads. They were given more supervision as well as individual counseling and the opportunity to do remedial school work. They also received psychiatric services. Other children were placed in subsidized foster homes and group homes. The results were immediate and dramatic. Commitments to institutions dropped, and the youthful offenders in the community treatment program did better than those in institutions. Neither the CTP nor the CDCP program offers absolute proof that community treatment is an unqualified success, but their approach holds out more hope for treating young offenders than does incarceration.

Numerous jurisdictions have adopted intensive programs of community supervision. Massachusetts, for example, operates intensive probation programs that are more successful than limited probation supervision.[24] For many years, the juvenile court of Boulder County, Colorado, has provided an extensive volunteer program of delinquency prevention and treatment.[25] Local volunteers work with juvenile offenders, providing tutoring, group counseling, and job training. The variety of community treatment programs available today allows the court greater flexibility in disposing of children's cases.[26] Highlight 18–1 describes a probation program that uses volunteers.

Highlight 18–1. Project CREST—Counseling for Juveniles on Probation.

Project Crest

Kids get into trouble for many different reasons. For Tommy, it was more or less a matter of growing into trouble. Tommy's father disappeared years ago. Because his mother worked at two jobs, she wasn't around when Tommy needed supervision. Very early he began tagging along with older kids in the neighborhood—skipping school, hanging out, occasionally participating in some vandalism. Known to the police by the time he was 12, Tommy had never been caught at anything more serious than breaking street lights. Until now.

This time it was serious. Tommy and a couple of older boys had been caught breaking into a house. He was now officially a delinquent. The other two youths, who were repeat offenders, were committed to a state institution. Since Tommy was only 14 and this was his first serious offense, the court placed him on probation with the Florida Youth Services Program (YSP).

The probation officer assigned to the case felt that Tommy lacked structure and clear limits in his life. Equally important, he needed caring and a belief that someone would help him work through his problems.

In the probation officer's judgment, Tommy was a prime candidate for Project CREST.

Project CREST (Clinical Regional Support Teams) uses volunteer, graduate-level university students to counsel delinquent youth in north-central Florida. Complementing the more authoritative role of probation officers, CREST counselors give youngsters an opportunity to discuss their problems openly without fear of being judged or adversely affected. CREST tries to help clients develop more positive attitudes about themselves and society, and thus to reduce delinquent behavior. CREST began in 1972 when a professor at the University of Florida in Gainesville helped Columbia County obtain an LEAA grant for a counseling program involving graduate students in the University's Department of Counselor Education. With the support and encouragement of Youth Service Program probation officers, the project quickly became a respected partner in the area's juvenile justice system. Since 1976, all financing for Project CREST has been provided by the State. The founder has served as project director throughout the life of the program and has built a strong and active constituency, including juvenile authorities and advocates, the University and the public schools. His continuing ties to the University's Counselor Education Department, where he is an adjunct professor, help to ensure the quality and commitment of the students involved in the program.

How Is CREST Organized?

CREST brings together three organizations with mutual interest in helping juveniles—Project CREST itself, the University of Florida and the Florida Youth Services Program (YSP). Each benefits from the relationship: YSP has access to a valuable resource; the University counseling program is strengthened, and its students receive training, experience and academic credit; and CREST gets its volunteers. But the most important beneficiaries of this network are youth like Tommy who get the help they need.

Outreach is key to CREST's operations. Counselors do not wait for clients to come to them. Rather, CREST goes into the communities, into the homes, and into the schools to serve the youngsters referred to the program. Three counseling teams, one for each of the three counties served by CREST, work out of a small central office in Gainesville. Each team consists of 4 to 6 volunteer counselors and tutors supervised by a doctoral student who functions as the team leader.

CREST volunteers come from the University of Florida's Department of Counselor Education, which requires graduate students to complete three to five practica (10-week work experiences in their field of specialization). CREST is one of several programs students may choose to fulfill that requirement. During each practicum, students receive academic credit for working 20 hours a week in their chosen agency while continuing to take classes at the University. Students enrolled in the two-year graduate specialist program must also complete a one quarter internship during which they work full time in the agency of their choice. Doctoral students are required

to complete a full year of internship.

A smaller number of CREST workers, known as counselor aides, come from Santa Fe Community College, also in Gainesville. These are undergraduate students who, unlike the University's graduate students, are not required to complete courses in counseling before beginning their work experience. . . .

How Are Volunteers Supervised?

Structured supervision and ongoing training and support are vital to the success of CREST. All new volunteers receive an intensive 12-hour orientation and training workshop before they are paired with clients. Staff and volunteers meet together every week for a least an hour to review cases, discuss problems and exchange ideas for treatment. In addition to the full staff meeting, which is mandatory for all personnel, volunteers meet each week with their team leaders, all of whom began as CREST counselors. Team leaders know all of the clients assigned to their team members and are able to provide first-hand knowledge and much-needed encouragement for counselors. They are also able to smooth the transition for the longer term client from one volunteer counselor to another.

CREST counselors also meet weekly with each client's probation officer to discuss problems and progress. In addition, at the end of every month, counselors submit detailed reports of their work to the project director. . . .

Who Are CREST'S Clients?

Probation officers decide which youngsters to refer to CREST. Because they see CREST services as a valuable resource not to be wasted, they tend to refer neither the hardest nor the easiest cases to the program. They are more likely to send difficult youngsters who want help or who might be responsive to counseling—youngsters like Tommy who might be diverted from the legal system with some extra help. Youth who come to CREST often have psychological and family problems, and many have trouble dealing with authority.

What Kind of Treatment Does CREST Provide?

CREST counseling is designed to build trust and increase the client's sense of self worth and self awareness, so that youngsters not only understand better why they do the things they do, but can better plan and control their actions.

CREST counselors attempt to develop a helping relationship with clients using a variety of counseling techniques and therapy models taught in the University's Department of Counselor Education. Individual counselors are encouraged to choose the techniques that they feel are most appropriate for each client. They may use reality therapy to help some youngsters confront the problems of the present rather than living in the past or in a fantasy world. In other cases, it may be necessary to separate irrational associations in the client's mind ("I did something bad; therefore, I am bad."). Or perhaps a client centered approach which focuses on the youngster's needs and perspectives is the basis upon which counseling proceeds. But whatever method a counselor chooses to use with a particular youngster, the basic approach for CREST workers is non-authoritarian and oriented toward the feelings and attitudes of the clients.

In addition to individual and family counseling, CREST workers often organize small group sessions to help clients learn that their problems are not unique and to encourage them to help each other. Counselors spend extra time with their clients attending cultural or sports events or participating in recreational activities.

How Does CREST Work With Probation Officers?

CREST workers are taught to be part of a treatment *team* and to work closely with the responsible juvenile authorities. CREST's dual treatment concept underlies the relationship between CREST and the Youth Services Program. Probation officers provide structure and limits and can invoke sanctions. CREST counselors provide guidance and support in a non-threatening, helping environment.

In fact, YSP staff see CREST as an important supplement to probation. Before CREST came along, they had to be both probation officers and counselors, and many of them found those roles conflicting. CREST's assumption of some responsibility for counseling has reduced this tension. And CREST has also dramatically increased the amount of counseling time provided to clients. While CREST workers have no fixed schedule for counseling, they usually see their clients once or twice a week, the family once a week, and the school once every other week. Often probation officers, who may have more than fifty clients in their caseloads, are only able to see each client once a month for an hour or so. Sometimes clients tell counselors about offenses they have committed that the probation officer doesn't know about CREST's stated policy is to give priority to the trust between counselor and client, except where a danger to life is involved. Probation officers understand and respect this position. . . .

What Has Been the Impact of CREST on its Clients?

With few exceptions, CREST has met or exceeded its service delivery goals every year since it began. In 1977–78, for example, CREST:

● provided weekly individual counseling for 90 delinquent youth for an average of five months per child;
● counseled more than 50 families of delinquent youth;
● provided extended group counseling and therapy for 84 youngsters;
● counseled 40 delinquency-prone

youngsters referred by the high school and another 24 such youth referred jointly by YSP and the high school;
• gave consulting assistance to schools for 81 CREST clients.

Officials of the Florida Department of Health and Rehabilitative Services, YSP's parent agency, say they consider CREST's performance over the years to be excellent.

What does that record mean for the clients? Several studies have attempted to measure the project's impact upon its clients. In one study, evaluators looked at episodes of misconduct among two groups of youngsters, 30 CREST clients and 34 youth who had committed similar offenses but had not received treatment. While the groups differed somewhat in terms of age and sex, the CREST youngsters did show a dramatic reduction in official acts of misconduct during treatment as compared to the other group. The total number of such acts committed by the CREST clients declined from 39 to 8, while those of the comparison group remained essentially the same—26 and 25.

A follow-up study almost 2 years later found that youngsters who had received CREST counseling were charged with offenses less often than the comparison group. Thirty-one individuals in the comparison group were charged with 65 offenses, while in the same post-project period, 30 former CREST clients were charged with only 23 offenses. Felony charges dropped from 54 to 7 for the CREST group and from 56 to 30 for the comparison group.

Youngsters receiving CREST treatment have also shown significant improvement in school attendance when compared to similar youth who were not involved with CREST. The grades of CREST clients improved and they had fewer suspensions from the school than the comparison group.

Source: U.S. Department of Justice, National Institute of Justice, *Exemplary Project—CREST* (Washington, D.C.: U.S. Government Printing Office, 1978) pp. 1–11.

RESTITUTION AS A FORM OF COMMUNITY TREATMENT

An innovative and promising program in the area of community treatment is the concept of restitution. Restitution can take several forms. A child can reimburse the victim of the crime or pay money to a worthy charity or public cause. In other instances, a juvenile can be required to provide some service directly to the victim or to assist a worthwhile community organization.[27]

Requiring children to pay the victims of their crimes is the most widely used method of restitution in America. Less widely used but more common in Europe is restitution to a community charity. In the past few years, numerous programs have been set up to enable the juvenile offender to provide service to the victim or to participate in community programs—for example, working in schools for retarded children and cleaning and fixing up neighborhoods.

Restitution programs can be employed at stages of the juvenile justice process. They can be part of a diversion program prior to conviction, they can be a method of informal adjustment at intake, or they can be a condition of probation. In some cases, children are required to contribute both money and community service.

Restitution has a number of justifications.[28] It provides the courts with alternative sentencing options. It offers direct monetary compensation or service to the victims of a crime. It is rehabilitative (because it gives the juvenile the opportunity to compensate the victim and take a step toward becoming a productive member of society). It relieves overcrowded juvenile courts, probation caseloads, and detention facilities. It has the potential for allowing vast savings in the operation of the juvenile justice system. Probation costs approximately $500 to 1,000 per person, and institutional placement costs between $10,000 and $15,000 per child, but restitution programs cost far less. Monetary restitution programs in particular, may improve the public's attitude toward juvenile justice by affording equity to the victims of crime and ensuring that offenders assume the obligations of their actions.

Despite what seem to be its many advantages, however, some believe that restitution contributes to retribution rather than rehabilitation because it emphasizes justice for the victim and criminal responsibility for illegal acts. There is some concern that restitution creates penalties for juvenile offenders where none existed before.

The use of restitution is increasing around the country. Many states—among them Minnesota, Massachusetts, Arizona, and Oklahoma—have developed novel approaches to restitution. Legislation authorizing restitution programs either has been passed or is being considered in numerous jurisdictions throughout the country.[29]

Most restitution programs service nonviolent adult and juvenile offenders. One of the most well-known projects is the Win-Onus program in Winona County, Minnesota.[30] The program services about 10 percent of the adults in the county who commit misdemeanors or who break traffic laws. The judge decides whether a person is eligible for the program. Then, the offender and a court service officer agree to a plan. If the judge accepts the plan, the court service department monitors its execution. It can take the form of monetary payment or community service. A recent evaluation of the program revealed a 2.7 recidivism rate as compared to the county jail's 27 percent. In addition, offenders have contributed thousands of hours to charitable organizations and have returned large amounts of money to victims.[31]

Another novel approach to restitution has been developed in the Quincy, Massachusetts, district court. The Alternative Work Sentencing Program, or Earn-It, handles juveniles referred by the court, the county probation department, and the district attorney's office. The program brings the child together with the victim of the crime in order to develop an equitable work program. Program staff members determine the extent of the victim's loss and place the child in paying jobs to earn the required restitution. Some children are placed in nonpaying community service jobs to work off court orders. By all indications, Earn-It has been a success. During its first year of operation in 1975, the program returned $36,000 in restitution payments. In 1978, over $100,000 was returned to victims, the courts, and the community.

The success of Earn-It and similar programs has encouraged .the development of restitution programs in other communities.[32] However, certain problems remain. Offenders often find it difficult to make monetary restitution without securing new or additional employment. Since most of them have been convicted of a crime, many employers are reluctant to hire them. Problems also arise when offenders who need jobs suffer from drinking, drug, or emotional problems. Public and private agencies are likely sites for community service restitution, but their directors are sometimes reluctant to allow convicted children or adults access to their organizations. Thus, even voluntary charitable work is difficult to obtain.

Some juvenile probation officers view restitution programs as a threat to their authority and to the autonomy of their organizations. Interestingly, courts believe that police officers view restitution more positively than social workers because the police are quick to grasp the retributive nature of restitution.

Another problem restitution programs must deal with is the charge that they foster involuntary servitude. For the most part, the courts have upheld the legality of restitution even though it has a coercive element. Some people believe that restitution is inherently biased against indigent clients. A person who is unable to make restitution payments can have probation revoked and thus face incarceration. It is necessary to determine why payment has stopped and to suggest appropriate action for the court to take rather than simply to treat nonpayment as a matter of law enforcement. A final concern is that it is difficult to calculate loss to the victim accurately and therefore difficult to judge how much restitution is equitable.

It is possible that restitution programs are an important alternative to incarceration, benefiting the child, the victim, and the juvenile justice system. However, such programs should be evaluated carefully to answer questions like the following:

1. What types of offenders would be most likely to benefit from restitution?
2. When is monetary restitution more desirable than community service?
3. What is the best point in the juvenile justice process to impose restitution?
4. What is the effect of restitution on the juvenile justice system?
5. How successful are restitution programs?

THE TREND TOWARD DEINSTITUTIONALIZATION

The term *deinstitutionalization* refers to efforts of juvenile justice practitioners, law reform and citizen groups, and judges and legislators to divert children from public custodial institutions to community treatment programs. Probation and restitution programs are two examples of deinstitutionalization, as are residential and nonresidential placement in small, community-based facilities.

Past experiences with the training school, the reform school, and the industrial institution have been unsatisfactory. Because of the current emphasis on diverting children into community programs, the number of juvenile offenders in state institutions has been declining over the past fifteen years. In the early 1960s about 45,000 children were in state secure institutions. By 1970 the number had declined to about 35,000; by 1975 it had dropped to 28,000; and in 1978 the number was approximately 26,000 children.[33]

Massachusetts in particular has, since the early 1970s, led the movement to keep juvenile offenders in the community. In the mid-1960s, its Department of Youth Services housed over 1,000 youngsters in secure training schools. Under Dr. Jerome Miller, who became the commissioner of the department in 1969, Massachusetts began a massive deinstitutionalization of juvenile offenders. Today, only about seventy children are in secure facilities. All the other are in small, community-based private and public programs.[34] Table 18–1 surveys the number of juveniles who were in secure and semisecure institutions in the various states from 1965 to 1978, including children charged as persons in need of supervisions.

Two other factors have affected the decline in the number of juvenile offenders in secure institutions. The first was the Juvenile Justice and Delinquency Prevention Act of 1974, which tied the receipt of federal funds for juvenile justice programs to the removal of status offenders from institutions.[35] Consequently, many states have reformed their juvenile codes to support new community-based treatment programs and to remove status offenders from institutions. Massachusetts, New York, and California now prohibit the commitment of status offenders to juvenile correctional institutions and to places of closed detention.

The second factor to fuel the deinstitutionalization movement has been the recent effort to grant children the general right to services and, in particular, the legal right to treatment.[36] This concept recognizes the principle that where the juvenile justice system places the child in some custody, basic concepts of fairness and humanity suggest that the system be required to supply the child with rehabilitation. Consequently where states have failed to provide such treatment approaches, it has been necessary for the government to evaluate the continued operation of its institutional programs where the promise of treatment is not fulfilled. As such, judicial recognition of a right to treatment, on constitutional or statutory grounds, has given impetus to the deinstitutionalization movement and required states to provide treatment to children in institutions or close them.

RESIDENTIAL TREATMENT ALTERNATIVES TO INCARCERATION

Most adjudicated children are placed under probation supervision or in a residential nonsecure facility. Residential programs can be divided into three major categories: (1) group homes, including boarding schools and apartment-type settings; (2) foster homes, and (3) rural programs.

Group homes are nonsecure, structured residences that provide counseling, education, job training, and family living. They are staffed by a small number of qualified persons, and they generally hold a maximum of twelve to fifteen youngsters. The institutional quality of the environment is minimized, and children are given the opportunity for a close but controlled interaction and relationship with the staff. Children reside in the home, attend public schools, and participate in community activities in the area.[37]

In the foster care program, one or two juveniles live with a family—a husband and wife who serve as surrogate parents. The juveniles enter into a close relationship with the foster parents and receive the attention, guidance, and care that they did not receive before. The quality of the foster home experience depends on the foster parents and their emotional relationship with the child. Foster care for adjudicated juvenile offenders has not been extensive in this

Table 18-1. Corrections Magazine Survey of Juveniles under 18 in Secure and Semisecure Facilities

STATE JUVENILE SYSTEMS

	1/1/65	1/1/70	1/1/75	% change 70-75	1/1/78	% change 75-78
Alabama	773*	406*	369	– 9	315	–15
Alaska	NA	63*	97	+54	108	+11
Arizona	677*	468*	362*	–23	344*	– 5
Arkansas	516	490	476	– 3	335	–25
California	3,577	2,643	1,256	–52	1,389	+10
Colorado	586	360	297	–17	369	+24
Connecticut	300*	275*	160*	–42	170*	+ 6
Delaware	NA	NA	249 (1/31/75)	NA	176	–29
D.C.	868	935	606	–35	530	–12
Florida	NA	1,012	1,070	+ 6	1,087	+ 2
Georgia	713	1,534††	2,453††	+60	1,468	–40
Hawaii	143	68	112	+65	77	–31
Idaho	172	176	123	–30	109	–11
Illinois	2,100*	2,030	1,172	–42	1,121	– 4
Indiana	860	919	600	–35	674	+12
Iowa	288	343	295	–14	382	+29
Kansas	350	358	349	– 2	380	+ 9
Kentucky	772*	611	362	–41	470	+30
Louisiana	1,382	1,321	1,191	–10	880	–26
Maine	204	212	142	–33	208	+46
Maryland	NA	1,253	1,002	–20	1,052	+ 5
Massachusetts	1,118	895	49	–94	71	+45
Michigan	1,200*	1,199	562	–53	669	+19
Minnesota	670*	763	424	–44	248	–41
Mississippi	NA	500 (2/19/70)	631 (12/16/74)	+26	331	–47
Missouri	713	553	450	–19	361	–20
Montana	249	181	163	–10	179	+10
Nebraska	369	293	218	–25	212	– 3
Nevada	191	220	229	+ 4	169	–26
New Hampshire	NA	184	188	+ 2	165	–12
New Jersey	1,894	1,122	659	–41	784	+19
New Mexico	342	262	247	– 6	321	+30
New York	2,046**†	2,280 (31/12/69)**†	567**†	–75	471 (7/1/78)	–17
North Carolina	1,653 (6/30/65)	NA	939	NA	807	–14
North Dakota	130	101	92	– 9	118 (11/30/77)	+28
Ohio	NA	2,786	2,476	–11	1,709	–31
Oklahoma	607 (6.30/65)	350 (6/30/70)	377 (6/30/75)	+ 8	375 (6/30/77)	0
Oregon	569	507	414	–18	680	+64
Pennsylvania	959	927	1,082	+17	750	–31
Rhode Island	172*	120*	79*	–34	74	– 6
South Carolina	NA	NA	650	NA	469	–28
South Dakota	161	136	98	–28	110	+12
Tennessee	NA	1,160 (3/2/72)	1,063	– 8	1,134	+ 6
Texas	2,310*	2,215*	756	–66	1,274	+68
Utah	329	279	184	–34	156	–15
Vermont	185	183	95	–48	98	+ 3
Virginia	1,148	1,324	944	–29	820	–13
Washington	1,400*	1,015*	760	–25	703	– 8
West Virginia	444	264	286	+ 8	211	–26
Wisconsin	944	1,078	763	–29	749	– 2
Wyoming	158	133	110	–17	138	+25
Total States	34,242	36,507	28,298	–28	26,000	– 8
	(42 jurisdictions)	(48 jurisdictions)				

NA means not available.   *Estimate.   **Includes some volunteers.   †Excl. youth in camps (325 on 7/1/78).   ††Increase largely due to takeover of county systems.

Source: *Corrections Magazine*, September 1978, p. 11. Reprinted with permission.

country. It is most often used for orphans or for children whose parents cannot care for them. Welfare departments generally handle foster placements, and funding has been a problem for the juvenile justice system. However, foster home services for delinquent children and status offenders are a promising new approach in the area of community treatment.[38]

Rural programs include forestry camps, ranches, and farms that provide specific recreational activity or work in a rural setting. Individual programs handle from thirty to fifty children. Such programs have the general disadvantage of isolating children from the community. However, reintegration can be achieved if the child's stay is short and if family and friends can visit.

Over the past two decades, extensive work has been done on group home settings. Highlight 18–2 illustrates three comprehensive community-based residential treatment programs in the field of juvenile corrections.

Highlight 18–2. Residential Treatment Programs.

1. The Highfields Project. Highfields was a short-term residential nonsecure program for boys that began in 1950. Boys in the program were kept at Highfields, New Jersey, for periods of three or four months. They were permitted to leave the grounds under responsible adult supervision. They were also granted furloughs over weekends to visit their families and to continue to relate to the community. The youths lived in groups of no more than twenty boys in a large home on an estate. They also worked twenty to forty hours a week at a neuropsychiatric clinic. The most important treatment technique was peer pressure exerted through active participation in guided group interaction sessions.

The Highfields project was evaluated by using a controlled group of boys sent to Annandale, a juvenile reform school in the same state. One year after release, Highfields boys had a lower recidivism rate than Annandale boys. The Highfields project was considered to be as successful as any training school and was much less expensive to operate. However, the validity of the recidivism rates was questioned because of the difficulties associated with matching the control and treatment groups.

Source: H. Ashley Weeks, *Youthful Offenders at Highfields* (Ann Arbor, Mich.: University of Michigan Press, 1958).

2. The Silverlake Experiment. The Silverlake experiment occurred in Los Angeles County in the mid-1960s. Like Highfields, this program provided a group home experience seeking to create a nondelinquent culture for male youths between the ages of fifteen and eighteen. Seriously delinquent youths were placed in a large family residence in a middle-class neighborhood. Some of them attended local high schools, and many returned to their homes on weekends. Only twenty boys at a time lived in the residence. They were responsible for maintaining the residence and for participating in daily group interaction meetings. These sessions were the major formal treatment approach for implementing programs goals. The Silverlake program sought to structure a social system with positive norms by discussing the youths' problems and offering positive alternatives to delinquent behavior in the group sessions.

To evaluate the Silverlake experiment, experimental and control groups were selected at random from the youths participating in the program. There was no significant difference in the recidivism rates of the two groups tested, and it was unclear whether one program over the other reduced recidivism. Since both control group youths and treatment youths lived in the facility, the researchers concluded that the experimental group receiving guided group interaction and the control group were positively affected by the program. Recidivism rates twelve months after release indicated a general reduction in delinquent behavior on the part of participants.

Source: LaMar T. Empey and Stephen Lubeck, *The Silverlake Experiment: Testing Delinquency Theory and Community Intervention* (Chicago: Aldine Publishing, 1971).

3. The DARE Program. The DARE (Dynamic Action Residence Enterprise) Program was one of the first major attempts to establish community treatment alternatives to incarceration for children in Massachusetts. The organization began operation in 1964 and currently has ten specialized programs and thirteen community residences set up to provide children with structured living experiences. There are nine group homes, four foster home programs, two residential schools, shelter care programs, and an intensive care secure facility. Children are referred primarily from the Department of Youth

Services and the Department of Public Welfare.

What is unique about the DARE Program is that it provides a variety of different community services for children. The mentor program is one example. Children in need of immediate placement are put into the care of a concerned individual. rather than placed in a detention facility or an institution. The purpose is to help young people develop a trusting and secure relationship with an adult. Through the variety of its approaches, the DARE Program has been able to provide services for children charged with even the most severe juvenile offenses, as well as those in need of supervision under the Massachusetts CHINS Law.

Source: Information from Dynamic Action Residence Enterprise (DARE), Jamaica Plain, Mass.

Most residential programs use group counseling techniques as the major treatment tool. Although group facilities have been used less often than institutional placements in years past, there is definitely a trend toward developing community-based residential facilities.

NONRESIDENTIAL COMMUNITY TREATMENT

In nonresidential programs, youths remain in their homes or in foster homes and receive counseling, education, work study, diagnostic services, and casework services. A counselor or probation officer gives innovative and intensive support to help the child remain at home. In the mid-1960s, nonresidential programs or daycare facilities represented the major alternative to institutionalization.

Perhaps the most notable of such nonresidential programs were the California Community Treatment Project and the California Community Delinquency Control Project, both of which have been previously discussed. Others that are equally well known are discussed in Highlight 18-3.

Highlight 18-3. Nonresidential Treatment Programs.

The Provo Program. The Provo Program was established in 1959 in Provo, Utah, to provide an alternative to institutional placement for delinquent children. Boys sent to the Provo program were between the ages of fifteen and seventeen and had generally been involved in a series of juvenile offenses. The basic assumptions of the program were that continued delinquency is group influenced and that delinquents come from low-income families with limited opportunities for success. Treatment was based on intensive group participation and on the development of ongoing critical interaction with peers. The program handled a maximum of twenty boys at a given time. They participated in a daily schedule of work or school followed by guided group interaction sessions. After their sessions, the boys normally returned to their homes. Boys in the Provo Program had less recidivism than those in institutions.

Source: LaMar T. Empey and Maynard L. Erickson, *The Provo Experiment: Evaluating Community Control of Delinquency* (Lexington, Mass.: D.C. Heath, 1972).

The Essexfields Rehabilitation Project. Essexfields was developed in the early 1960s in Essex County, New Jersey. It was a short-term, group-oriented nonresidential rehabilitation effort. The local citizenry arranged for the twenty boys in the program, ages sixteen and seventeen, to work in a county mental hospital. The boys were referred by the juvenile court and remained in the program for four to five months as a condition of their probation.

Essexfields was evaluated by comparing its recidivism rates with the rates of children in residential group homes and in state institutions. Nonresidential group treatment fared as well as, and on occasion better than, residential treatment programs and programs in state institutions.

Source: Paul Pilnick, Albert Elias, and Neale Clapp, "The Essexfields Concept: A New

Approach to the Social Treatment of Juvenile Delinquents," *Journal of Applied Behavioral Sciences* 2 (1966): 109–121.

Project New Pride. Project New Pride was a successful effort to help juvenile offenders, many of whom had previous records, to break a pattern of antisocial behavior by developing their ego strength and self-pride. The project stressed education, employment counseling, and cultural assistance. Children between the ages of fourteen and seventeen in Denver County, Colorado, with arrest or conviction records for burglary, robbery, and other serious offenses were placed in the program. Many of the children also had learning disabilities.

During a twelve-month period, the rearrest rate of children in Project New Pride was less than that of a control group. In addition, over 75 percent of the children were placed in full-time or part-time jobs. The rearrest rate for employed children was one-third the rate for unemployed children.

Source: Carol Blew, Daniel McGillis, and Gerald Bryant, *Project New Pride: An Exemplary Project* (Washington, D.C.: Government Printing Office, 1977).

The Key Program. The Key Program in Massachusetts offers a wide range of counseling and advocacy services to delinquent and nondelinquent youth. Supervision and intensive counseling are used to intervene in the child's daily life and activity in the community in order to prevent delinquency. Counselors help children deal with educational and vocational planning, with the juvenile court, and with their personal lives. Advocacy programs exist in store fronts, and services also involve the use of foster-care facilities.

The program was recently evaluated to determine which Key Program services provided the most assistance to children. Recidivism studies found that about half of the children who had been in juvenile court before they became involved with the program reappeared in the court within six months. On the other hand, the Key Program was able to reduce children's contacts with the court while they were actually in the program. Key Program services were most helpful to children who had committed property offenses or who had lost interest in school. They were less successful with those who had a serious criminal history.

Source: Jonathan Katz, *An Evaluation of Community Based Services for Delinquent Youth: The Key Program* (Worcester, Mass.: Key Inc., 1979).

CRITICISMS OF THE COMMUNITY TREATMENT APPROACH

The community treatment approach has some limitations. Public opinion may be against community treatment, especially when it is offered to juvenile offenders who pose a real threat to society. Institutionalization may be the only answer for the violent young offender. As the juvenile crime problem worsens, society may be less and less willing to accept reforms that liberalize policies and practices in the field of juvenile corrections.

Evaluations of recidivism rates do not show conclusively that community treatment is more successful than institutionalization. Some experimental programs indicate that young people can be treated in the community as safely and as effectively as children placed in an institution. However, commitment to an institution guarantees that the community will be protected against further crime, at least during the time of the child's placement. More research is essential to evaluate the success of community treatment programs.

Much of the early criticism of community treatment was based on poor delivery of services, shabby operation, and haphazard management, follow-up, and planning. In the early 1970s, when Massachusetts deinstitutionalized its juvenile correction system, a torrent of reports flowed forth about the inadequate operation of community treatment programs. This was caused by the absence of uniform policies, different procedures in various programs, and the lack of accountability.[39] The development of needed programs was hampered, and available resources were misplaced.

It is possible that deinstitutionalization will result in the increasing use of pretrial detention for children. Also, it may cause more children to be transferred to adult courts and subsequently to be committed to adult prisons. Finding out if this is actually happening is a difficult task, but there is no question that law and order forces are seeking to turn more children over to the adult system.

To a great extent, fewer children are in institutions because status offenders are in community corrections programs. Thus, deinstitutionalization is widening the net of the juvenile justice system.[40] Instead of contracting to deal directly with law violations, the system has expanded to include all kinds of community programs. Consequently, the number of children in juvenile corrections and in residential care remains about the same as it was ten years ago.

Theoretical breakthroughs in the behavioral sciences, such as Freud's work on personality development in the 1930s and efforts in the 1950s and 1960s to explain the etiology of crime, have not occurred for many years. The place of treatment has changed from the institution to the community, but the juvenile justice practitioners are using the same basic approaches to treatment. What is different, of course, is that the damaging effects of institutionalization are not present when the child is handled in the community. In addition, rehabilitation is a more realistic goal when placed in a community treatment environment.

Major proponents of community treatment argue that the approach has not been as successful as it should because of the lack of resources available to develop community treatment programs. For more than a half century, numerous national commission reports have documented the need for more human and monetary resources. When caseloads in court systems are high, when children are placed in custodial institutions without treatment, and when there are too few judges in the juvenile court, we are forced to conclude that the funding of agencies to combat juvenile delinquency is a low-priority item in most jurisdictions.

Yet, since the establishment of Law Enforcement Assistance Administration in 1968 and the Juvenile Delinquency and Prevention Control Act of 1974, large amounts of federal funds have been given to the states for delinquency prevention programs. More money would help to improve the system, but it is unclear how much is needed and whether it would have a serious impact on today's juvenile delinquency problem.

In sum, deinstitutionalization and the community treatment approach are here to stay. Although most experts agree that community treatment is more successful than institutionalization, the most compelling argument for its continued use is an economic one. Community treatment is cheaper. It costs anywhere from $10,000 to $20,000 a year to keep a child in a secure institution and $5,000 to $7,000 a year to keep a child in a nonresidential program. Thus, the future of community treatment hinges on politics rather than new empirical information. Various organizations may have an important effect on the future shape of juvenile corrections because they can lobby for legislative change and financial resources. Of course, research documenting the success of community treatment programs is also important. Two research efforts are those of Robert Vinter, who is in charge of the National Assessment of Juvenile Corrections Project, and those of the Harvard Center for Criminal Justice, under Lloyd Ohlin, which has monitored the Massachusetts deinstitutionalization program for the past decade. This latter project found that overall recidivism rates dropped for those in community-based programs.[41]

CHAPTER SUMMARY

More often today than ever before, probation is the predominant disposition chosen in the juvenile court system. It is also recognized as the most promising alternative to incarceration for treating the child in the community. One novel approach to community treatment is restitution as a sentence and as a condition of probation.

Residential and nonresidential community treatment programs represent efforts to help children in settings that are free from the stifling, inhumane, and isolated characteristics of institutions. Some early programs have been the subject of in-depth evaluations and have had some success.

One question is whether America will proceed with the development of community treatment or emphasize institutionalization. Since the early 1970s the closing of most juvenile institutions has received growing support. The 1973 National Advisory Commission on Criminal Justice Standards and Goals recommended phasing out all major juvenile institutions within five years. That period of time has elapsed, but many jurisdictions still rely on traditional institutions. Whether the move toward community-based alternatives will continue is unclear. Since it is generally impossible to prove that a juvenile correctional institution or community treatment program will lead to a more successful postdispositional result, it is likely that the youth correctional systems in the future will contain a variety of residential programs and some secured settings for children who are a threat to the general community.

DISCUSSION QUESTIONS

1. What is juvenile probation? Why is it considered the most significant of all community treatment methods?
2. Discuss the traditional argument associated with the use of community treatment in juvenile correction. What is the significance and meaning of such terms as CTP, Essexfields, Silverlake, and Highfields.
3. With juvenile delinquency rates at an all-time high and violent juvenile crime soaring, why is the country moving toward a program of deinstitutionalization for juvenile offenders?
4. Over the past two decades, legal decisions have provided criminal and juvenile offenders with due process rights. Such decisions have not taken into account the injustices done to the victims of crime. Does the concept of juvenile restitution provide the defendant and the victim with a fair settlement?
5. Do you know of any community treatment programs in the juvenile justice system for juvenile offenders in your jurisdiction? If so, describe them.

SUGGESTED READINGS

American Bar Association. Project on Standards for Juvenile Justice. *Standards Relating to Juvenile Probation Function.* Cambridge, Mass.: Ballinger Press, 1977.

____Project on Standards for Juvenile Justice. *Standards Relating to Non-Criminal Behavior.* Cambridge, Mass.: Ballinger Press, 1977.

Brantley, J. R. *Alternatives to Institutionalization—A Definitive Bibliography.* U.S. Department of Justice, Law Enforcement Assistance Administration. Washington, D.C.: National Criminal Justice Reference Service, 1979.

Chudd, William, and Donnelly, Agnes. "Characteristics of Investigative Process in a Children's Court." *Social Casework* 40 (1959): 262–271.

Empey, LaMar T., and Erickson, Maynard. *The Provo Experiment: Evaluating Community Control of Delinquency.* Lexington, Mass.: D. C. Heath, 1972.

Empey, LaMar T., and Lubeck, Steven. *The Silverlake Experiment: Testing Delinquency Theory and Community Interventions.* Chicago: Aldine Publishing, 1971.

Geenstma, Robert. "Group Therapy with Juvenile Probationers." *Federal Probation* 24 (1960): 45:52.

Hardman, Dale. "The Function of the Probation Officer." *Federal Probation* 24 (1960): 3:12.

Jennings, W. K. *Project Pride—A Positive Approach to Vandalism.* San Francisco: Project Pride Association, 1976.

Kayden, Xandra. *Alternative Court Programs in Massachusetts.* A Report Sponsored by the Gardner Howland Snow Foundation. Boston 1978.

Klapmusts, Norma. "Community Alternatives to Prison." *Crime and Delinquency Journal* 5 (1973): 305.

Martin, John, and Fitzpatrick, Joseph. *Delinquent Behavior: A Redefinition of the Problem.* New York: Random House, 1965.

Nelson, E. K., and Harlow, N. *Promising Strategies in Probation and Parole.* Sacramento, Calif.: American Justice Institute, 1978.

Norman, Sherwood. *Delinquency Prevention: Three Basic Approaches.* New York: National Council on Crime and Delinquency, 1968.

Ohlin, L., Coates, R.; and Miller, A. "Radical Correctional Reform: A Case Study of the Massachusetts Youth Correctional System." *Harvard Educational Review* 37 (1973): 52.

Palmer, Ted. "California's Community Treatment Program for Delinquent Adolescents." *Journal of Research in Crime and Delinquency* 8 (1971): 74.

Stark, Herman. "Alternatives to Institutionalization." *Crime and Delinquency Journal* 13 (1967): 323.

Susmann, A. "Practitioner's Guide to Changes in Juvenile Law and Procedure." *Criminal Law Bulletin* 14 (1978): 311–321.

U.S. Department of Justice, Office of Juvenile Justice and Delinquency Prevention, Law Enforcement Assistance Administration. *Community Alternatives.* Washington D.C.: U.S. Government Printing Office, 1978.

____*Foster Parenting.* Washington, D.C.: U.S. Government Printing Office, 1978.

____*Juvenile Restitution—An Alternative to Incarceration.* Washington, D.C.: U.S. Government Printing Office, 1978.

Vinter, Robert; Downs, George; and Hall, John. *Juvenile Corrections in the United States: Residential Programs and Deinstitutionalization.* Ann Arbor, Mich.: National Assessment of Juvenile Corrections, 1967.

Warren, Marguerite Q. "The Community Treatment Project: History and Prospects." In *Law Enforcement Science and Technology*, edited by S. A. Yafsky. Proceedings of the First National Symposium on Law Enforcement Science and Technology. Washington, D.C.: Thompson Publishing, 1967.

Weber, Robert, and Mayer, Mary. *A Strategy for Action in Establishing Alternatives to Training Schools.* New York: National Council on Crime and Delinquency, 1968.

Weeks, Ashley H. *Youthful Offenders at Highfields: An Evaluation of the Effects of the Short-Term Treatment of Delinquent Boys.* Ann Arbor: University of Michigan Press, 1958.

Willman, H., and Chun, R. "Homeward Bound, an Alternative to the Institutionalization of Adjudicated Offenders." *Federal Probation* 37 (1973): 52.

REFERENCES

1. 403 U.S. 528, 91 S.Ct. 1976 (1971).

2. Ibid., p. 547.

3. American Bar Association, *Standards Relating to Probation* (New York: Institute of Judicial Administration, 1968), Sec. 1.2, p. 10.

4. Uniform Interstate Compact on Juveniles. See also Ralph Brendes, "Interstate Supervision of Parole and Probation," in *Probation and Parole,* ed. Robert Certer and Leslie Wilkins (New York: Wiley, 1970).

5. George Killiner, Hazel Kerper, and Paul F. Cromwell, Jr., *Probation and Parole in the Criminal Justice System* (St. Paul, Minn.: West Publishing, 1976), p. 45.

6. National Advisory Commission on Criminal Justice Standards and Goals, *Corrections* (Washington, D.C.: Government Printing Office, 1973), p. 312.

7. U.S. Department of Justice, *Sourcebook of Criminal Justice Statistics—1978,* National Criminal Justice Information and Statistics, Law Enforcement Assistance Administration, Washington, D.C.: U.S. Government Printing Office 1979), p. 598.

8. National Council on Crime and Delinquency, *Correction in the United States—A Survey for the President's Commission on Law Enforcement and Administration of Justice* (New York: NCCD, 1967), p. 52.

9. For a general review of the organization of probation services in the United States, see National Council on Crime and Delinquency, *Probation and Parole Directory* (Hackensack, N.J.: NCCD, 1976).

10. American Bar Association, *Standards Relating to Juvenile Probation Function* (Cambridge, Mass.: Ballinger Press, 1977), p. 124.

11. "Correction in the United States—A Survey for the President's Commission on Law Enforcement by the National Council on Crime and Delinquency," *Crime and Delinquency Journal* 13 (1967): p. 44.

12. American Bar Association, *Standards Relating to Juvenile Probation Function,* p. 137.

13. Paul Piersma et al., *Law and Tactics in Juvenile Cases* (Philadelphia: American Law Institute—American Bar Association Committee on Continuing Education, 1977), pp. 358–367.

14. See *Morrissey v. Brewer,* 408 U.S. 471, 92 S.Ct. 2593, 33 L.Ed. 2d 484 (1972); and *Gagnon v. Scarpelli,* 411 U.S. 778, 93 S.Ct. 1756, 36 L.Ed. 2d 655 (1973).

15. American Bar Association, *Standards Relating to Juvenile Probation Function.* See also *Standards Relating to Disposition* (Cambridge, Mass.: Ballinger Press, 1977).

16. See Ralph England, "A Study of Past Probation Recidivism among Five Hundred Federal Offenders," *Federal Probation* 19 (1955): pp. 10–17.

17. Frank Scarpitti and Richard Stephenson, "A Study of Probation Effectiveness," *Journal of Criminal Law, Criminology and Police Science* 59 (1968): p. 361.

18. LaMar T. Empey, *American Delinquency—Its Meaning and Construction* (Homewood, Ill.: Dorsey Press, 1978), p. 508.

19. Ralph England, "What Is Responsible for Satisfactory Probation and Post-Probation Outcome?" *Journal of Criminal Law, Criminology and Police Science* 47 (1957): pp. 667–679.

20. Bertram Johnson, "The Failure of a Parole Research Project," *California Youth Authority Quarterly* 18 (1965): pp. 35–42.

21. Marguerite Q. Warren, "The Community Treatment Project: History and Prospects," *Law Enforcement Science and Technology,* ed. S. A. Yafsky. Proceedings of the First National Symposium on Law Enforcement Science and Technology (Washington, D.C.: Thompson

Publishing, 1967), p. 191.

22. See Paul Lerman, "Evaluating the Outcome of Institutions for Delinquents," *Social Work Journal* 13 (1968):

23. Esther Pond, "A Comparative Study of the Community Delinquency Control Project," in *Status of Current Research in the California Youth Authority*, (Sacramento: Department of Youth Authority, May 1968). p. 20.

24. See Massachusetts Gen. Laws, Chap. 119, Sec. 52–83; M. Levin and R. Sarri, *Juvenile Delinquency: A Comparative Analysis of Legal Codes in the United States* (Ann Arbor, Mich.: National Assessment of Juvenile Corrections, 1974).

25. "Volunteers in Probation," *Newsletter of the National Information Center on Volunteerism*, ed. Ivan Scheier, Boulder, Colo.: Boulder County Juvenile Court, 1972.

26. See National Clearinghouse for Mental Health Information, *Community Based Correctional Programs—Models and Practices* (Rockville, Md.: National Institute of Mental Health, 1971).

27. Larry Siegel, "Court Ordered Victim Restitution: An Overview of Theory and Action," *New England Journal of Prison Law* 5 (1979): p. 135.

28. For an extensive analysis of the pros and cons of restitution, see Anne Newton, "Sentencing to Community Service and Restitution," in *Criminal Justice Abstracts* (Hackensack, N.J.: National Council on Crime and Delinquency, September 1979). pp. 435–468.

29. Ibid.

30. See Stephen Schafer, "The Proper Role of a Victim-Compensation System," *Crime and Delinquency Journal* 21 (1975): p. 48.

31. Siegel, "Court Ordered Victim Restitution," p. 142.

32. Descriptive materials can be obtained from the Earn-It Program, District Court of East Norfolk, Quincy, Mass., 02169.

33. See Louise Fraza, "National Survey of Juveniles under 18 in Secure and Semi-Secure Settings," *Corrections Magazine*, September 1978, p. 4.

34. Commonwealth of Massachusetts, *Department of Youth Services Annual Report of 1978* (Boston: State Purchasing Agent, 1978).

35. Public Law pp. 93–145 (1974).

36. Patricia Wald and Laurence Schwartz, "Trying a Juvenile Right to Treatment Suit: Pointers and Pitfalls for Plaintiffs," *American Criminal Law Review* 12 (1974): p. 125.

37. American Bar Association, *Standards Relating to Disposition*, p. 68.

38. See E. Lawder, R. Andrews, and J. Parsons, *Five Models of Foster Family Group Homes*, Report of Child Welfare League of America (New York: Child Welfare League, 1974); Yitzhak Bakal, *Closing Correctional Institutions* (Lexington, Mass.: D. C. Heath, 1973); and Andrew Rutherford and Osman Berger, *Community Based Alternatives to Juvenile Incarceration*, U.S. Department of Justice, National Institute of Law Enforcement and Criminal Justice (Washington, D.C.: Government Printing Office, 1976), pp. 10–35.

39. Rob Wilson, "The Legacy of Jerome Miller," *Corrections Magazine*, September 1978, p. 11.

40. Empey, *American Delinquency*, p. 542.

41. See, for example, Robert Vinter, ed., *Time Out: A National Study of Juvenile Correctional Programs* (Ann Arbor, Mich.: National Assessment of Juvenile Corrections, 1976); Robert Vinter, George Downs, and John Hall, *Juvenile Corrections in the States: Residential Programs and De-institutionalization* (Ann Arbor, Mich.: National Assessment of Juvenile Corrections, 1976); and Robert Coates, Alden Miller, and Lloyd Ohlin, *Diversity in a Youth Correctional System: Handling Delinquents in Massachusetts* (Cambridge, Mass.: Ballinger Press, 1978).

══════════════════════════Chapter 19═

Chapter Outline

Introduction
History of Juvenile Institutions
Institutionalized Youth — A Profile
Juvenile Institutions
Treatment of Juveniles Within the
    Institution
Female Juveniles in Institutions
Institutional Rules and Discipline
Juvenile Aftercare
Violent Young Offenders
Chapter Summary

Key Terms, Names, and Cases

Lyman School
secure institution
treatment
Robert Vinter
psychotherapy
cottage
group counseling
guided group interaction
right to treatment
Boys Training School v. Affleck
training school
O'Connor v. Donaldson
Nelson v. Heyne
aftercare
violent young offenders
Martarella v. Kelly

Institutionalization ―――――――――

INTRODUCTION

In the past, institutionalization almost always referred to incarceration in a reform or training school—a large, closed setting where children could remain under supervision up to their majority. Today, however, institutionalization includes incarceration in detention facilities prior to adjudication and to treatment in smaller, residential institutions that are generally less secure than training schools and located in the community.

Secure institutions for youths are operated on federal, state, and local levels. They range from somewhat less secure ranches, camps, and farms with small populations to large training schools that exercise tight security and hold up to three hundred hungsters. There has been a general movement in the past ten years toward the use of fewer and smaller secure facilities, on the theory that community-based programs that allow more freedom stand a greater chance of rehabilitating young offenders than do large bureaucratic institutions. As noted in the previous chapter, Massachusetts closed down all its training schools in the early 1970s and now relies heavily on community programs.

Studies show that institutionalizing young offenders generally does more harm than good. It exposes them to debilitating, prison-like conditions and to more experienced delinquents without giving them the benefit of any constructive treatment programs. Moreover, community-based programs often have recidivism rates at least as low as, if not lower than, those in institutions. These facts have led to a general decline in the numbers of juveniles confined in secure institutions.

The authors wish to express their appreciation to Elizabeth Mills for her assistance in the research and development of this chapter.

Unfortunately, few treatment programs of any kind are effective in reducing recidivism rates for juvenile offenders. In addition, violent juvenile crime is rising rapidly, a situation that is causing increasing concern to government and to private citizens. The public is clamoring for increased protection from violent youths while youth advocates continue to argue for the deinstitutionalization of almost all categories of juvenile offenders.

Several agencies, including the American Bar Association, the National Advisory Committee on Juvenile Justice and Delinquency Prevention, and the Committee on Accreditation for Corrections, have published standards and goals for juvenile justice, many of which focus on institutions for juvenile offenders. These standards have been a positive step toward improving the juvenile justice system; and although they have not been adopted on a nationwide basis, their serious consideration would undoubtedly create more humane and more effective methods of treating young offenders within institutions of all kinds.

HISTORY OF JUVENILE INSTITUTIONS

Early History

Until the early 1800s, juvenile offenders as well as neglected and dependent children were confined in adult prisons. Physical conditions in these institutions were horribly punitive and inhumane, a fact that led social reformers to create a separate juvenile court system in 1899 and eventually to open correctional facilities solely for juveniles.[1] These early juvenile institutions were industrial schools modeled after adult prisons but designed to protect children from the evil influences found in adult facilities. The first was the New York House of Refuge, established in 1825.

Not long after this, states began to establish reform schools for juveniles. Massachusetts was the first to open a state reform school—the Lyman School for Boys in Westborough—in 1846. New York opened the State Agricultural and Industrial School in 1849, and Maine opened the Maine Boy's Training School in 1853. By 1900, thirty-six states had reform schools.[2] Early reform schools were generally punitive in nature and based on the concept of rehabilitation or reform through hard work and discipline.

In the second half of the nineteenth century, emphasis shifted from the massive industrial schools to the cottage system. Juvenile offenders were housed in a series of small cottages in a compound, each one holding twenty to forty children. Each cottage was run by cottage parents, who attempted to create a homelike atmosphere. It was felt that this would be more conducive to rehabilitation than the rigid bureaucratic organization of massive institutions. The first cottage system was established in Massachusetts in 1855, the second in Ohio in 1858.[3] The system was generally applauded for being a great improvement over the earlier industrial training schools. The general feeling was a movement away from punitiveness and toward rehabilitation: "By attending to the needs of the individual and by implementing complex programs of diagnosis and treatment, known offenders could not only be rehabilitated, but crime among dependent and unruly children could be prevented."[4]

Twentieth Century Movements

The twentieth century has seen some interesting changes in the structure of institutionalization for juvenile offenders. Because of the influence of World War I, reform schools began to adopt military styles: "Living units became barracks; cottage groups, companies; housefathers, captains; and superintendants, majors or more often, colonels."[5] Military style uniforms became standard.

As the number of juvenile offenders increased, the forms of institutions varied to include forestry camps, ranches, and educational and vocational schools. Beginning in the 1930s, for example, juvenile camps became a part of the correctional system. Modeled after the camps run by the Civilian Conservation Corps (CCC), the juvenile camps centered on conservation activities and outdoor living and work as a means of rehabilitation.

Los Angeles County was the first to utilize camps during this period.[6] Southern California had problems with transient youths who came to California with no money and then got into trouble with the law. Rather than filling up the jails, the county placed these offenders in conservation camps, paid them small wages, and then released them when they had earned enough money to return home. When the camps proved more rehabilitative than training schools, California established forestry camps in 1935 especially for delinquent boys, and the idea soon spread to other states.[7]

Another innovation came in the 1940s with the American Law Institute's Model Youth Correction Authority Act. This act emphasized the use of reception-classification centers. California was the first to try out this new idea when it opened the Northern Reception Center and Clinic in Sacramento in 1947. Today, there are seventeen centers scattered around the country.[8]

The Juvenile Justice and Delinquency Prevention Act of 1974 created a new office located in the Law Enforcement Assistance Administration called the Office of Juvenile Justice and Delinquency Prevention. It stressed prevention, but its major purpose was to promote changes in juvenile justice administration. Federal funding through this act is available only to states meeting the following requirements:

1. Federal funds must be used to develop or to maintain programs designed to prevent delinquency, to divert juveniles from the juvenile justice system, and to provide community-based alternatives to juvenile detention and correctional facilities.

2. After two years, each state must guarantee that juvenile status offenders will not be confined in juvenile detention or correctional facilities. Deinstitutionalization for them must be complete. If such children have no place else to stay, communities must create new shelters for them.

3. No delinquent can be detained or confined in any institution where he or she will have contact with adult offenders.[9]

Today, although new programs continue to emerge, the majority of institutionalized youths remain confined in traditional training schools. Only about 16 percent are held in ranches, forestry camps, or farms.[10]

INSTITUTIONALIZED YOUTH—A PROFILE

On June 30, 1974, a total of nearly 45,000 juveniles were being held in custody in 829 separate facilities (see Tables 19–1 and 19–2). About two-thirds of them, nearly 30,000, were in state-operated facilities, mainly in training schools, and in rural-based ranches, forestry camps, and farms.

Table 19–1. *Number of Public Detention and Correctional Facilities for Juveniles and Number of Juveniles, by Type of Facility and Level of Government, June 30,1974.*

Type of Facility	Total		State		Local	
	Facilities	Juveniles	Facilities	Juveniles	Facilities	Juveniles
Total	829	44,922	396	29,920	5433	15,002
Detention centers	331	11,110	50	1,214	281	9,796
Shelters	21	180	—	—	21	180
Reception and diag-nostic centers	19	1,376	17	1,352	2	24
Training schools	185	25,397	151	23,373	34	2,024
Ranches, forestry camps, and farms	107	5,232	61	2,706	46	2,536
Halfway houses and group homes	166	1,727	117	1,275	49	452

Source: U.S. Department of Justice, Law Enforcement Assistance Administration, Preliminary Tabulation from the LEAA/Census Juvenile Detention and Correctional Facility Census of 1974. Title: Preliminary LEAA Census Report 1974 U.S. Government Printing Office, Washington, D.C.

Table 19–2. *Juveniles in Custody by Type of Facility, 1971 and 1974.*

Type of Facility	Numbers						Percent Change 1971 to 1974		
	Total		State		Local				
	1971	1974	1971	1974	1971	1974	Total	State	Local
Total	54,729	44,922	38,265	29,920	16,464	15,002	–18	– 22	– 9
Detention centers	11,767	11,010	689	1,214	11,708	9,796	– 6	+ 76	– 9
Shelters	360	180	110	—	250	180	–50	—	–28
Reception/diagnostic	2,153	1,376	2,153	1,352	—	24	–36	– 37	—
Training schools	34,005	25,397	31,606	23,373	2,399	2,024	–25	– 26	–16
Ranches, farms, camps	5,471	5,232	3,074	2,706	2,397	2,526	– 4	– 12	– 5
Halfway houses and group homes	973	1,727	633	1,275	340	452	+77	+101	+33

Source: Special tabulations of the 1971 and 1974 Censuses of Juvenile Detention and Correctional Facilities, U.S. Department of Justice, LEAA. Data for 1971 are revised from those previously published to exclude youthful and adult offenders housed in the same facilities. Data for 1974 are preliminary.

Earlier statistics suggest that the population in juvenile institutions remained fairly stable (42,000 to 43,000) between 1965 and 1970 and began to decline in 1971. Law Enforcement Assistance Administration/Census data indicate a particularly sharp reduction in the number of juveniles in custody in residential facilities between 1971 and 1974. The residential population of all juvenile facilities declined by 18 percent, from 54,700 to 44,900. Most of this reduction was in the state training schools, whose resident population fell by nearly 9,000, or 25 percent.

Juvenile institution populations have declined since 1971 because of two closely related developments. Court decisions and policies in a number of states have precluded assigning status offenders to state institutions, and a number of states have adopted general policies of deinstitutionalization. However, the nationwide survey by the National Assessment of Juvenile Corrections (NAJC) in 1973–74 found that 35 percent of the juvenile corrections population and 29 percent of juveniles in institutions were still status offenders.[11]

Who are the children in institutions today? What are their characteristics? Are there major differences among them?

To answer these and other questions, the National Assessment of Juvenile Corrections undertook a survey in 1976 of forty-two juvenile correctional programs, including institutions, group homes, and day-treatment programs.[12] There were sixteen institutions in the sample, averaging 117 youths per institution.

The majority of inmates in the institutions were males, who outnumbered females 71 percent to 29 percent. Whites constituted 46 percent of the sample. Blacks, who represent less than 12 percent of the national population, comprised 30 percent of the population in institutions. Native Americans constitute less than 1 percent of the national population, but they represented 8 percent of the institutional sample. Chicanos (3 percent), Puerto Ricans (1 percent), Orientals (less than 1 percent), and persons with mixed heritages (11 percent) represented the remainder of the population. The average age of the institutionalized male was 15.6 years; females averaged 15.9 years. Over 40 percent of the youths were below the age of 16.

On the basis of reported parental occupations, the study found that 40 percent of the youths were from working-class families, 24 percent were from middle-class families, and 17 percent were from upper-class families. A notably high percentage (19 percent) were from unemployed families. These figures are consistent with theories relating delinquent behavior to economic and environmental factors.

The majority of youths in the sample had committed property or person offenses (37 percent and 17 percent, respectively), although a distressingly large number (29 percent) had committed status offenses. Smaller percentages of youths were admitted for drug offenses (10 percent), probation and parole violations (3 percent), or miscellaneous misdemeanors (4 percent). This is in line with assumptions that institutionalization is the most severe disposition available to a judge and that most commitments are positively associated with severity of offense.

Most institutionalized youths were previously involved in delinquent activities. Large percentages admitted to drinking alcohol (73 percent) or using marijuana or hashish (59 percent), and many had run away from home in the past (38 percent) or were truants (78 percent). Almost three-quarters of the youths admitted to either previous breaking and entering (43 percent) or robbery (30 percent).

The youths in the sample averaged 8 prior arrests, 4.5 times in detention, 3.2 times in jail, 5.5 times in court, 2 times on probation and 1.7 times in an institution. These figures suggest that the youths who ultimately end up in institutions are those for whom previous rehabilitation programs have failed.

Only 30 percent of the sample youths reported that they had spent no time in a residential correctional program. Of those who had spent any time at all in such a program, 32 percent had spent more than a year.

In conclusion, the study described the typical sample youth in the following manner:

He was likely to be male, non-white, about 16 years old, and lower-class. He had probably been committed for a property crime (although if female she probably had been committed for a status offense), and was no stranger to the police or juvenile court. He had probably been on probation or even in an institution at least once previously. He is no angel—he readily admits to drinking, using drugs, and skipping school, but neither is he a hardened criminal—he had probably not frequently engaged in serious criminal behavior such as robbery or breaking and entering. The girls in the sample were far less frequently or seriously delinquent but still had had considerable prior contact with the juvenile justice system.[13]

JUVENILE INSTITUTIONS

Public institutions for juveniles can be administered by any number of state agencies: child and youth services, mental health, youth conservation, health and social services, corrections, and child welfare.[14]

The institutions in some states fall under a centralized correctional system that covers adults as well as juveniles. Other states operate separate adult and juvenile systems. Institutional administration is not an easy task. It must cover not only business management (budgeting) but also program planning. The quality of administration often determines the effectiveness of a particular facility (see Highlight 19–1).

Highlight 19–1. The Delinquent Institution.

Institutions for the delinquent child usually have vastly different characteristics than those holding adults. Often they are located on a campus spreading over many acres. The housing units provide quarters for smaller groups invariably less than 60 and frequently less than 20. Often they also provide apartments for cottage staff. Dining frequently is a function of cottage life, eliminating the need for the large central dining rooms. Grills seldom are found on the cottage doors and windows, although sometimes they are covered by detention screens. Security is not the staff's major preoccupation.

Play fields dot the usually ample acreage. Other resources for athletics, such as gynmasiums and swimming pools, are common. Additional recreational activity often is undertaken in nearby towns, parks, streams, and resorts. Teams from youth institutions usually play in public school leagues and in community competition. The principal program emphasis at these children's centers quite naturally has been education, and many have fine, diversified school buildings, both academic and vocational.

Exterior security varies, but most juvenile centers have no artificial barriers separating them from the community at large. Space frequently provides such a barrier, however, as many juvenile centers are in rural settings. Fences do exist, especially where the institution borders a populated area. Usually they do not have towers. Walkaways are quite frequent and cause considerable annoyance to neighbors, who sometimes hold public subscriptions to raise money for fences. . . .

This section describes two predominant but conflicting philosophies about the care of delinquent children. This is done because they suggest profoundly different directions and consequently different facility requirements for the future.

One has its roots in the earliest precepts of both the penitentiary and reformatory systems. It holds that the primary cause of delinquent behavior is the child's environment, and the secondary cause is his inability to cope with that environment. The response is to provide institutions in the most remote areas, where the child is protected from adverse environmental influences and exposed to a wholesome lifestyle predicated on traditional middle-class values. Compensatory education, often

better than that available in the community, equips the child with tools necessary to face the world again, some day. This kind of correctional treatment requires expensive plants capable of providing for the total needs of children over prolonged periods.

The second philosophy similarly assumes that the child's problems are related to the environment, but it differs from the first model by holding that the youngster must learn to deal with those problems where they are in the community. Institutions, if required at all, should be in or close to the city. They should not duplicate anything—school, recreation, entertainment, clinical services that is available in the community. The child's entire experience should be one of testing himself in the very setting where he will one day live. The process demands that each child constantly examine the reality of his adjustment with his peers.

The first model clings to the traditional solution. Yet institutions that serve society's misfits have never experienced notable success. One by one, institutions have been abandoned by most of the other human services and replaced by community programs. The second model, still largely untested, moves corrections toward more adventurous and hopeful days.

Source: National Advisory Commission on Criminal Justice Standards and Goals, *Corrections* (Washington, D.C.: Government Printing Office, 1973), p. 348.

At the present time, the physical plans of juvenile institutions across the country vary tremendously. Many of the older training schools were built to last, but they are tremendously outdated. Obviously no single architectural structure is best for every area, but the American Bar Association devotes an entire volume of its standards to the architecture of facilities. Commenting on standards for security in institutional plant structure, the ABA concludes:

Youths concentrated in a secure setting shall be youths considered high risks because of destructive behavior patterns. The difficulty in developing design standards for facilities for such youths lies in balancing the legitimate needs for security felt by staff, administrators, and society, with the need for settings that provide the young resident with a reasonable quality of life and a sense of safety and well being.[15]

Older facilities still tend to place juvenile offenders in a single building. More acceptable structures today include a reception unit together with an infirmary, security unit, and dormitory units or cottages. Planners have concluded that the most effective design for training schools is to have facilities located around a community square. The facilities are a dining hall and kitchen area, a storage warehouse, academic and vocational training rooms and a library, an auditorium and a gymnasium, a laundry, maintenance facilities, an administrative building, and other basic facilities such as a commissary, barbershop, and beauty shop.[16]

Although the physical plant is not the most critical aspect of an institution, its impact can be important:

The physical plant of the training school, particularly a good, well-maintained plant, has far-reaching effects upon the school program. Not only is the statement "despair breeds disrespect" true among the children, but a physically deteriorated plant lowers morale and results in an unreasonable amount of administrative attention and staff time being devoted to rebuilding, repair, and maintenance. On the other hand, a well-planned, modern plant in good repair frees administration and staff to devote their full attention to the real "target"—a sound treatment program. It also facilitates the development of activities and lessens the problems of supervision.[17]

Physical conditions of individual living areas vary widely, depending on the type of facility and the progressiveness of its administration. In the past, most training school conditions were appalling, with children living in unbelievable squalor. Today, most institutions provide children with toilet and bath facilities, beds, desks, lamps, and tables. Following the recommendations of various standards, new facilities usually provide single rooms for each individual.

Also recommended are indoor and outdoor leisure areas, libraries, academic and vocational education spaces, chapels, facilities for youths to meet with their visitors, a reception and process room, security fixtures (which, when necessary, are normal in appearance), windows in all sleeping accommodations, and fire safety equipment and procedures.

The physical conditions and architecture of secure facilities for juveniles have come a long way from the training schools at the turn of the century. Unfortunately, however, many administrators and state legislators have not yet realized that more modernization is necessary to meet even minimum compliance with national standards for juvenile institutions.

TREATMENT OF JUVENILES WITHIN THE INSTITUTION

Nearly all juvenile institutions utilize some form of treatment program for the children in custody—counseling on an individual or group basis, vocational and educational training, various types of therapy, recreational programs, and religious counseling. In addition, most institutions provide medical and dental health programs of some kind, as well as occasional legal service programs. Generally, the larger the institution, the greater the number of programs and services offered.

The purpose of these various programs is to rehabilitate the youths within the institutions—to reform them into well-adjusted individuals and send them back into the community to be productive citizens. Despite generally good intentions, however, the goal of rehabilitation has rarely been attained. National statistics show that 74 to 80 percent of all juvenile offenders commit more crimes after release from incarceration.[18]

One of the most common problems is a lack of well trained staff members to run programs. Budgetary limitations are a primary concern when it comes to planning for institutional programs. It costs from $15,000 to $25,000 per year to keep a child in an institution—a staggering amount that explains why institutions do not generally employ large staffs of professionals.[19]

It is not clear which programs provide the most effective treatment. Coupled to this is the fact that studies overwhelmingly indicate that few, if any, of the treatment programs presently being utilized in juvenile institutions are effective in preventing future delinquency:

Treatment programs for delinquents have been notoriously unsuccessful, as indicated by the high recidivism rates usually reported. Efforts to keep delinquents free of crime are hampered by a strong peer culture which maintains the delinquent behavior. Even those treatments which are successful on a short-term basis have usually failed to document any long-term differences over similar nontreated youth in such variables as number of offenses. As such, the treatment of delinquent youth represents one of the greatest challenges to the fields of psychology, psychiatry, and social work.[20]

Most importantly though, not every program will work for every individual, which necessitates some type of diagnostic evaluation at the beginning of confinement to develop an individual treatment plan for each youth. The plan must help youths understand why they misbehave; that is, attitudes must be changed if behavior patterns are to change.

Probably the most glaring problem with treatment programs is the fact that they are not effectively utilized within the institution. While the official goals of many institutions may be treatment and rehabilitation, the actual program may center around security, control, and punishment.[21]

Individual Treatment Techniques

Probably the most commonly used treatment approach is individual counseling. Robert Vinter points out that over 90 percent of institutions utilize this approach to some extent.[22] Individual counseling does not attempt to change a youth's personality. Rather, it attempts to help individuals understand and solve their present adjustment problems. The advantage to individual counseling is that institutions can utilize it on a superficial basis with counselors who may not be professionally qualified.

Highly structured counseling can be based on psychotherapy or psychoanalysis. Psychotherapy is an outgrowth of Freudian psychoanalytic techniques and requires extensive analysis of the individual's past childhood experiences. An effective therapist attempts to help the individual solve conflicts and make a more positive adjustment to society through altering negative behavior.

Although individual counseling and psychotherapy are used extensively in institutions and may work well for certain individuals, there is little indication that this type of treatment is even marginally effective. In a 1978 review of ten such programs, Dennis Romig reported that eight of the ten had completely negative results.[23]

Another highly utilized treatment approach for delinquents is reality therapy.[24] This approach, developed by Dr. William Glasser, emphasizes the present behavior of offenders by making them completely responsible for their actions. Glasser feels that a psychoanalytical emphasis on the past may lead children to excuse present and future misbehavior by encouraging them to think of themselves as sick and unable to change their actions.[25]

The success of reality therapy depends greatly on the warmth and concern of the individual counselor. Unfortunately, many institutions rely heavily on this type of therapy because they assume that highly trained professionals are unnecessary. Actually, a skilled therapist is a must. The individual must be knowledgeable about the complexity of personalities and be able to deal with any situation that may come up in the counseling.

The object of the therapy is to make individuals more responsible people. This end is accomplished by giving them confidence and strength through developing their ability to follow a set of expectations as closely as possible.

Another treatment, transactional analysis (TA), has been used in the past primarily for adult offenders. However, its developer, Eric Berne, feels that it may have special value for adolescents.[26] Transactional analysis is based on the following assumptions:

1. Human relationships consist of competitive acts of social maneuvering that serve a defensive function and yield important gratification. Berne calls these acts *games*.
2. All persons manifest three different ego states: the *child*, a relic of the individual's past; the *parent*, whom the person has incorporated through identification with parents; and the *adult*, who is the mature and responsible self.
3. Each of these ego states perceives reality differently; the child prelogically, the parent judgmentally, and the adult comprehensively on the basis of past experience.
4. The three states operate constantly in response to the person's need and the games in which the person indulges at a given time.[27]

Through transactional analysis, an attempt is made to show the child that his or her behavior falls into these categories and that childish and undesirable behavior can be altered into more mature behavior.

Behavior modification is another method of treatment. It is used in almost three-quarters of all institutions.[28] It is based on the theory that all behavior is learned and that, as such, present behavior can be shaped through a system of rewards and punishments.

This type of program is easily utilized in an institutional setting that offers points and privileges as rewards for behaviors such as work, study, or the development of skills. It is a reasonably effective technique, especially when utilized on a contractual basis.[29] When youths are aware of what is expected of them, they plan their actions to meet these expectations and then experience the anticipated consequences. In this way they can be motivated to change.[30] Behavior modification is effective in controlled settings where a counselor can manipulate the situation, but once the youth is back in the real world it becomes difficult to use.

Group Treatment Techniques

There are advantages to group therapy.[31] First, it is more economical than individual therapy because one therapist can handle more than one individual at a time. Second, the support of the group is often highly valuable to the individuals in the group. Third, individuals derive hope from other members of the group who have survived similar experiences. Last, a group can often solve a problem more effectively than an individual.

There are some disadvantages to group therapy too. It provides less individualized attention, for example. Some individuals may be different from the other group members and need more highly individualized treatment. Others may be shy, afraid to speak up in the group, and thus fail to receive the benefits of the group experience. Some individuals may dominate group interaction, and the leader may be ineffective in handling the situation. Finally, group condemnation may seriously hurt rather than help a child.

More than any other group treatment technique, group psychotherapy probes into the personality and attempts to restructure it. Relationships in these groups tend to be quite intense. The group is used to facilitate expression of feelings, to solve problems, and to teach members to emphathize with one another.

Unfortunately, as Irving Schulman suggests, "the components necessary for an effective group psychotherapy situation such as personal interaction, cooperation, and tolerance, are in direct conflict with the antisocial, antagonistic, and exploitive orientation of delinquents."[32] This type of technique is often effective when the members of the group are there voluntarily. Obviously, institutionalized delinquents are often forced to attend.

Guided group interaction is a fairly common method of group treatment. It is based on the theory that through group interactions a delinquent can begin to realize and solve personal problems. A group leader facilitates interaction among group members, and a group culture develops. Individual members can be mutually supportive and can help develop more acceptable behavior. Guided group interaction was an instrumental factor in the success of programs at Highfields, New Jersey, and Provo, Utah.[33]

Milieu therapy seeks to make all aspects of an inmate's environment a part of his treatment and minimize differences between the custodial staff and the treatment personnel. It also emphasizes peer influence in the formation of constructive values.[34] Milieu therapy attempts to create an environment that encourages meaningful change, increased growth, and satisfactory adjustment. This is often accomplished through peer pressure to conform to group norms.

One early type of milieu therapy based on psychoanalytic theory was developed in Chicago during the late 1940s and early 1950s by Bruno Bettelheim.[35] This therapy attempted to create a conscience or superego in delinquent youths by getting them to depend on their therapists to a great extent and then threatening them with loss of the loving and caring relationship if they failed to control their behavior.

Vocational and Educational Programs

In addition to individual and group treatment programs, most institutions utilize vocational and educational treatment programs designed to teach juveniles skills that will help them adjust more easily when they are released into the community. Educational programs for juveniles are required in long-term facilities because children must go to school until they are of a certain age. Other reasons for education programs can be summarized as follows:

Since the educational program is developmental and has therapeutic value in addition to its instructional values, it is an essential part of the treatment program. What takes place under the auspices of education is related to all other aspects of the institutional program—the work activities, cottage life, recreation, and clinical services. In the class-room, as in all other settings within the training school, emphasis must be upon the development of constructive and satisfying human relationships. Stress should be placed particularly upon social training, teaching the basic principles of healthy family relationships, and the development of acceptable attitudes and behavior.[36]

Educational programs are probably some of the best staffed programs in training schools, but even at their best, most are inadequate. Training programs must contend with a myriad of problems. Many of the youths coming into these institutions are mentally retarded, or they have low IQs or learning disabilities. As such, they are educationally handicapped and far behind their grade levels in basic academic areas. Most of these youths dislike school and become bored with any type of educational program that is offered. Their boredom often leads to acting out and subsequent disciplinary problems.

Ideally, institutions should allow the inmates to attend a school in the community, or they should offer programs that lead to a high school diploma or GED certificate. As one recent study notes, not all institutions offer these types of programs.[37] The same study also noted, however, that institutions were more likely than group homes or day-treatment centers to offer supplemental educational programs such as remedial reading, physical education, and tutoring.[38] Some more modern educational programs offer computer learning and programmed learning modules.[39]

Vocational training has long been utilized as a treatment technique for juveniles. Early institutions were even referred to as industrial schools. Today, vocational programs in institutions are varied. Programs offered to boys include auto repair, printing, wood working, mechanical drawing, food service, barbering, welding. For girls they include sewing, food service, beauty shop techniques, secretarial training, and data processing.[40] One obvious problem here is sex typing, and the recent trend has been to allow equal access to all programs offered in institutions that house girls and boys. This is more difficult in single-sex institutions because funds often cannot be found to offer all types of training.

A recent review of twelve studies of vocational programs for youths concluded that "job placement, vocational training, occupational orientation, field trips, and work programs do not positively affect juvenile delinquency."[41] As Romig points out:

Job advancement skills, support educational programs, a career-ladder frame of reference, or skills for starting new and competing businesses all work to involve youths or inmates positively in careers. It is not simply vocational training or a job that counts; it is giving the individual a job where he or she can have hope for advancement. Programs are needed for delinquent youths that give them skills to advance, thus fostering a more positive outlook for the future.[42]

Recreational Programs

In a recent major study by the National Assessment of Juvenile Corrections, youths in institutional programs were asked to respond to the statement "most of the time it is boring here." Seventy-seven percent responded that the statement was true.[43] It is an unfortunate reality that many of the training schools in the United States do not offer adequate recreational facilities for institutionalized youth. Many are stark and furnished only with televisions and a few chairs. Little organized activity is available. On the other hand, many newer facilities have recreational programs and equipment offering institutionalized youth a wide scope of leisure time activities.

Recreational activity is an important way to help relieve adolescent aggressions, as evidenced by the many diversionary and delinquency prevention programs that focus on these activities as the primary treatment technique. The National Advisory Commission, for example, states:

Recreation and leisure activities are vital parts of a residential facility program. There should be many kinds of activities available and juveniles should have freedom of choice. The recreation program should allow the delinquent to engage in activities that he can continue and benefit from when he returns to the community. Because there are such diverse groups of juveniles in residential facilities, considerable planning and development must take place to insure meaningful participation for each person.

A recreation program should include active and sedentary activities both indoor and outdoor, for teams and individuals. Adequate equipment and supplies should be provided for a comprehensive program. In case of nonsecure facilities, maximum use of recreational facilities—such as swimming pools, parks, bowling lanes, and gymnasiums—in the community should be made.[44]

Medical and Dental Programs

Most juvenile institutions today offer some type of medical and dental services to their inmates. These programs vary widely in their comprehensiveness, often depending on the type of facility, the funding availability, and the foresight of the administration.

Most institutions have at least a dispensary with a full-time nurse. More comprehensive programs offer the services of one or more physicians, dentists, or psychiatrists.

Children in institutions need medical and dental treatment even more than adults in prison because the children may never have been examined before. Health problems discovered during adolescence can often be corrected, and some of them can affect delinquent behavior:

Physical condition and physical disabilities often contribute toward the delinquent orientation of young persons. Many adjudicated delinquents, because they come from poor families and areas with insufficient health care services, have a backlog of medical and dental need. Basic health needs must be met if the delinquent is to improve his behavior.[45]

This is especially true for youths with psychological or mental health problems.

Most institutions maintain resident medical and dental staffs. However, one recent study reported that youths do not feel that these services are accessible enough. The study concludes that utilizing community medical, dental, and mental health services might provide better care at lower costs.[46]

In 1973 the Committee on Youth of the American Academy of Pediatrics developed a set of program needs for youth in institutions entitled "Health Standards for Juvenile Court Residential Facilities."[47] Briefly, these standards recommend the following:

Screening or inspection on admission, a health evaluation or assessment based on a thorough medical history and physical examination soon thereafter, a sound medical records system, access to all levels of care from ambulatory care in the institution to hospitalization, and so on. Emphasis is placed on a multidisciplinary health council empowered to set policy for the institution's health program—a council composed primarily of senior health staff members, advised by a technical advisory committee of outside professionals and experts. Emphasis is also placed on dental care and preventive dentistry, on mental health considerations, on environmental health, and on health education.[48]

Right to Treatment

The goal of placing children in institutions is basically to prepare them for a positive adjustment in the community. Therefore, lawyers in the field of juvenile justice claim that children in state-run institutions have a legal right to treatment.

The concept of a right to treatment was first introduced to the mental health field in 1960 by Dr. Morton Birnbaum.[49] He theorized that individuals who are deprived of their liberty because of a mental illness serious enough to require involuntary commitment are entitled to treatment to correct that condition. People for whom treatment is not provided are entitled to release from the institution.[50]

It was not until six years later that any court acknowledged any such right to treatment. That year, in *Rouse v. Cameron*, the District of Columbia Circuit Court of Appeals found that mentally ill individuals were entitled to treatment, an opinion based on interpretation of a District of Columbia statute.[51] Although the court did not expressly acknowledge a constitutional right to treatment, it implied that it could have reached the same decision on constitutional grounds:

Had appellant been found criminally responsible, he could have been confined a year, at most, however dangerous he might have been. He has been confined four years and the end is not in sight. Since this difference rests only on need for treatment, a failure to supply treatment may raise a question of due process of law. It has also been suggested that failure to supply treatment may violate the equal protection clause. . . . Indefinite confinement without treatment of one who has been found not criminally responsible may be so inhumane as to be "cruel and unusual punishment."[52]

The constitutional right to treatment that was suggested by the *Rouse* court was further recognized in 1971 in *Wyatt v. Stickney*.[53] This case was particularly important because it held that involuntary commitment without rehabilitation was a denial of due process of law. There is an "unquestionalbe . . . constitutional right" for those in noncriminal custody "to receive such individual treatment as will give each of them a realistic opportunity to be cured or to improve his or her mental condition."[5']

Of greater significance, however, is the Supreme Court's decision in the case of *O'Conner v. Donaldson* in 1975.[55] This case concerned the right to treatment of persons involuntarily committed to mental institutions. The court concluded that, except where treatment is provided, a state cannot confine persons against their will if they are not dangerous to themselves or to the community. In his concurring opinion, however, Chief Justice Warren Burger rejected the idea that a state has no authority to confine a mentally ill person unless it provides treatment. He also denied that commitment is the *quid pro quo* for treatment. It is not clear what significance this case will have for juveniles claiming a right to treatment.

THE RIGHT TO TREATMENT IN THE JUVENILE JUSTICE SYSTEM   The right to treatment argument has expanded to include the juvenile justice system. One of the first court cases to highlight this issue was the 1972 case of *Inmates of the Boy's Training School v. Affleck.*[56] This case analyzed conditions that allegedly violated juvenile constitutional rights to due process and equal protection and that constituted cruel and unusual punishment. *Affleck* was one of the first cases to describe some of the horrible conditions existing in many of the nation's training schools. The court argued that rehabilitation is the true purpose of the juvenile court, and without that goal due process guarantees are violated. It condemned such devices as solitary confinement, strip-cells, and the lack of educational opportunities and held that juveniles have a statutory right to treatment. The court also established the following minimum standards for all juveniles confined in the training school:

1. A room equipped with lighting sufficient for an inmate to read by until 10:00 P.M.
2. Sufficient clothing to meet seasonal needs.
3. Bedding, including blankets, sheets, pillows, pillow cases, and mattresses. Such bedding must be changed once a week.
4. Personal hygiene supplies, including soap, toothpaste, towels, toilet paper, and a toothbrush.
5. A change of undergarments and socks every day.
6. Minimum writing materials: pen, pencil, paper and envelopes.
7. Prescription eyeglasses, if needed.
8. Equal access to all books, periodicals, and other reading materials located in the training school.
9. Daily showers.
10. Daily access to medical facilities, including the provision of a twenty-four-hour nursing service.
11. General correspondence privileges.[57]

These minimum requirements were expanded in *Martarella v. Kelly,* which analyzed juvenile treatment facilities and the confinement of persons in need of supervision in New York. The court held that failure to provide these juveniles with adequate treatment violated their right to due process and to be free from cruel and unusual punishment.[58]

In 1974, the case of *Nelson v. Heyne* was heard on appeal in the Seventh Circuit Court in Indiana. Because of its significance to the right to treatment issue, the case is outlined in Highlight 19–2.

Highlight 19–2. Nelson v. Heyne.

Facts: In a class civil rights action on behalf of juvenile inmates of the Indiana Boys' School, a state institution, a complaint to the district court alleged that defendants' (Robert Heyne, the Commissioner of Corrections; Robert Hardin, Director of the Indiana Youth Authority; and Alfred Bennett, Superintendent of Indiana Boys' School) practices and policies at the school violated the Eighth and Fourteenth Amendment rights of the juveniles under their care. The alleged practices included the use of corporal punishment, solitary confinement for periods ranging from five to thirty days, intramuscular injections of tranquilizing drugs, and censorship of inmate mail.

The school itself was a medium security state correctional institution for boys twelve to eighteen years of age, where about one-third were noncriminal offenders. The average length of stay at the institution was about six and one-half months; and although the school's maximum capacity was under three hundred boys, the usual population was about four hundred. The counseling staff included twenty persons, three of whom were psychologists with undergraduate degrees, and one part-time psychiatrist who spent four hours per week at the institution. The medical staff included one part-time medical physician, one registered nurse, and one licensed practical nurse.

The district court in this case found that it had jurisdiction over the case and thereafter held that the use of corporal punishment and the method of administering tranquilizing drugs by defendants constituted cruel and unusual punishment in violation of plaintiffs' Eighth and Fourteenth Amendment rights. In a separate judgment, the court found that the juveniles had a right to affirmative treatment and that the school had not satisfied the minimal

constitutional and statutory standards required by its rehabilitative goals. The defendants appealed on January 31, 1974, before final relief was granted. The Seventh Circuit of the United States Court of Appeals granted review.

Decision: In *Nelson v. Heyne* the circuit court dealt with the issue of a juvenile's constitutional affirmative right to treatment within a closed institution. Specifically, the questions were (1) whether the practices alleged by defendants were violations of the cruel and unusual punishment clause of the Eighth Amendment, and (2) whether defendants had a constitutional right to rehabilitative treatment, and if so, whether the treatment as provided by the school was adequate. The court discussed the practices of corporal punishment in light of the cruel and unusual punishment standard suggested in *Furman v. Georgia,* 408 U.S. 238, 279 (1971). By that standard, punishment is excessive if it is unnecessary, and it is unnecessary if less severe punishment would serve the same purpose.

Although the court did not find corporal punishment to be cruel and unusual *per se,* it did find that on the basis of undisputed expert testimony the beatings as applied were unnecessary and therefore excessive, thus violating the Eighth Amendment proscription against cruel and unusual punishment. The court next looked at the school's practice of administering tranquilizing drugs "to control excited behavior" without individual medical authorization and without first trying oral medication. Based on expert testimony at trial that established the possible serious side-effects of these drugs, the court rejected the school's assertion that the use of drugs was not punishment. After stressing the need to balance the school's desire to maintain discipline with the child's right to be free from cruel and unusual punishment, the court held that the school's interest in reforming juveniles through the use of drugs in maintaining a rehabilitative atmosphere, did not justify the cruel and unusual dangers resulting from poorly supervised administration of tranquilizing drugs.

Turning to the crucial holding by the District Court that incarcerated juveniles have an affirmative right to rehabilitative treatment, the Seventh Circuit noted that the Supreme Court has assumed, although it has not explicitly stated, that the state must provide treatment for incarcerated juveniles. In light of this, the court looked at several recent cases concerning the impact of the *parens patriae* doctrine on this right, most notably the case of *Martarella v. Kelly*, 349 F.Supp. 575 (S.D.N.Y. 1972), in which the court found a clear constitutional right to treatment for juveniles based on the Eighth and Fourteenth Amendments. The Seventh Circuit agreed then with the lower court that the juveniles did indeed have a

constitutional as well as a statutory right to rehabilitative treatment. Lastly, the court held that the Quay system of behavior classification utilized by the school was not treatment. Subsequently the case was remanded to allow the lower court to determine the "minimal standards of care and treatment for juveniles" needed to provide them with their "right to 'individualized' care and treatment."

Significance: Nelson v. Heyne is significant in that it is the first federal appellate court decision affirming that juveniles have a constitutional as well as a statutory right to treatment. It is also the first to hold that federal judges can require standards by which to judge minimal adherence by institutions to individualized treatment.

Source: 491 F.2d 353 (7th Cir. 1974).

In *Morales v. Turman*, the court held that all juveniles confined in training schools in Texas have a constitutional right to treatment. The court established numerous criteria for assessing placement, education skills, delivery of vocational education, medical and psychiatric treatment programs, and daily living conditions.[59] The order was later vacated on procedural grounds on appeal; and on *certiorari* to the Supreme Court, the case was remanded. A more recent case in New York, *Pena v. New York State Division for Youth*, held that the use of isolation, hand restraints, and tranquilizing drugs at Goshen Annex Center was punitive and antitherapeutic and therefore violated the Fourteenth Amendment right to treatment and the Eighth Amendment right to protection against cruel and unusual punishment.[60]

CURRENT STATUS OF THE RIGHT TO TREATMENT Although the Supreme Court has not yet ruled that juveniles have a constitutional right to treatment, some recent case discussions serve as a basis for many substantive changes in the juvenile justice system, most notably in the improvement of physical conditions in juvenile institutions and in the judiciary's recognition that it must take a more active role in the juvenile justice system.

Some argue that right to treatment decisions are not based on accurate analysis; others argue that the courts have not gone far enough in establishing juvenile rights.[61] Still others argue for a right to punishment beyond the right to treatment in order to challenge the practice of indeterminate sentencing of juveniles.[62] Recognition of a right to punishment would force the juvenile system either to live up to the rehabilitative justification for the peculiar incarceration it imposes or to provide an alternative method of dealing with the juvenile offender.

The future of the right to treatment for juveniles is somewhat uncertain, although case law has established it, whether it is constitutionally or statutorily based. The courts have not gone so far as to order the creation of new programs; nor have they decided what constitutes minimal standards of specific individual treatment. They have, however, decided whether certain existing programs are capable of treating individual children.

The courts will continue to involve themselves with this issue of a right to treatment if the juvenile justice system is to fulfill its goal—to assure that a child does not receive the worst of both worlds, "that he gets neither the protections accorded to adults nor the solicitous care and regenerative treatment postulated for children."[63] For the time being, the broad constitutional question of the right to treatment for any particular group remains unclear. Certainly, it does not exist at all for criminal offenders, but it seems to exist partially on a state constitutional and statutory basis for juvenile offenders, the mentally ill, and possibly the retarded.

FEMALE JUVENILES IN INSTITUTIONS

Females have traditionally been less involved in criminal activities than males. As a consequence, the number of females in institutions has generally been lower than the number of males. However, female involvement in all aspects of crime, including violent crime, has risen tremendously in the past ten years:

Recent statistics indicate a dramatic increase in the rate of women's offenses. The F.B.I. Uniform Crime Reports, released in August 1974, reveal that arrests for females under 18 years of age for violent crimes increased 393 percent and 334 percent for property crimes during the 1960–1973 period, while arrests for young males under 18 rose by 236 and 82 percent, respectively. . . .

This increase in arrests for serious crimes is even more dramatic when notice is made of the arrest figures for murder committed by the young female, which show an increase of 477 percent [versus] 290 percent for males; an aggravated assault increase of 350 percent [versus] 190 percent for males; and a burglary increase of 239 percent [versus] 100 percent for males.[64]

The growing involvement of girls in criminal behavior and the recent feminist movement have resulted in more attention being focused on the female juvenile offender. This focus has revealed a double standard of justice. For example, girls are more likely to be incarcerated than boys for status offenses such as truancy, running away, and sexual misconduct. Institutions for girls are generally more restrictive than those for boys. They have fewer educational and vocational programs and fewer services. They also perform a less than adequate job of rehabilitation. It has been suggested that this double standard operates through a chivalrous male justice system that seeks to "protect" young girls from their own sexuality.[65]

Profile of the Institutionalized Girl

According to a recent source, 4,767 female juveniles were held in public long-term custodial facilities in 1977. This is approximately 15 percent of the total long-term public institutional population. The mean age of these girls was 15.6 years.[66]

Several studies in recent years have shown that the majority of girls in state institutions are there for juvenile status offenses. One such study, conducted in 1976, surveyed 107 state training schools in fifty states. It found that 77 percent of all status offenders in institutions holding males and females are female, and 46.5 percent of the population in female institutions are status offenders. Only 18 percent of the population in all-male institutions were status offenders.[67]

Of all the girls committed to the California Youth Authority, 37 percent were from welfare homes and 78 percent from broken homes. Half had at least one parent or sibling with a criminal record. Seven percent of the girls were married at the time of their commitment, and 13 percent had children.[68]

Institutionalized girls are often runaways seeking escape from intolerable home situations. They are often involved in abusive or incestuous relationships. Many are poor and have been involved in crime or prostitution just to be able to eat. Some are pregnant and have no means of support. Only a few are true delinquents. Many are the "throw-aways" of society—those whom nobody wants. Highlight 19–3 is a case history of Sally, one of the many girls who each day pass through the juvenile justice system.

Highlight 19–3.   Sally.

Sally is 17 years old, white, and has spent the last two and a half years in a state training school. She was sent to the institution because of a long history of running away and truancy. She also allegedly had been involved in prostitution since age 13, although this was never proven in court.

Sally lived in the suburbs of a major metropolitan area with her mother and natural grandmother. Her mother, divorced since Sally was 12, is unskilled and has been living on welfare for the past five years.

Sally's problems began soon after her father left home. She began to stay out of school and ran away from home frequently. Her mother turned to alcohol and soon became so unable to cope with Sally that she asked her mother to come and live in their home to help raise Sally. The school finally turned Sally's case over to the county probation department. After extensive

testing the department recommended that Sally be placed out of the home. Although an institutional setting was not recommended for Sally, other alternatives, including foster care, had a three month waiting list for girls. Because there were no appropriate community-based residential programs for young women in Sally's community, she was sent to a state institution.

After she was released, she immediately started her pattern of running away again. She was eventually transferred to a secure institution, but her behavior did not improve. After spending eight months in a secure setting, Sally was paroled to her own home. This decision was made solely because the facility in which she was confined was being converted to a program for difficult boys. Sally was seen once by an aftercare counselor after returning home. During that visit, the counselor explained

the rules of parole but made no effort to
help her enroll in school or in a vocational
or job training program. Sally stayed at
home for two weeks. She disappeared one
evening and has not been heard from since.

Source: Office of Juvenile Justice and
Delinquency Prevention, Law Enforcement
Assistance Administration, *Little Sisters and the
Law* (Washington, D.C.: Government Printing
Office, 1976), p. 16.

Characteristics of Institutions for Females

The same double standard and inequality that brings a girl into an institution
continues to exist once she is in custody. The remedy for not being a "good
girl" at many reform schools is often twofold—training in womanly arts and
incarceration for a longer term than most males receive. Institutional programs for girls tend to be strongly oriented toward the reinforcement of "traditional roles" for women. It is questionable how well these programs rehabilitate young girls and ready them for life in a quickly changing society.

Although there is a recent movement toward the use of coed institutions for
juveniles, most girls remain incarcerated in antiquated single-sex institutions.
They are usually isolated in rural areas and rarely offer adequate
rehabilitative services. Results of a recent survey of training schools across
the country reveal a definite pattern of inequality in services for boys and
girls.[69]

Institutions for girls generally offered fewer programs than those for boys.
The training schools surveyed averaged 3.3 different types of vocational
training programs for girls per institution compared to 5.5 per institution for
boys, and 15.8 percent of the female institutions offered no vocational programs at all.[70] The programs offered to girls most frequently were cosmetol-
ogy (56.2 percent), business education (56.2 percent), nurses aid programs (50
percent), and food services (37.5 percent). Programs for boys included such
things as auto shop, welding, and small engine repair.[71] Obviously these programs tend to reinforce the sex stereotyping so rampant throughout the system.

Educational programs, job programs, institutional services and staff ratios
for girls also fall below those for boys. Several factors account for the
different treatment of girls. One is the sexual stereotyping of administrators
who feel that "girls should be girls" and that teaching them appropriate sex
roles in prison will help them adjust on the outside. This is often true for the
staff as well. Many of them have only a high school education as well as rigid
and highly sexist ideas of what is appropriate adolescent behavior for girls.
Girls' institutions tend to be smaller and less filled than boys'. They simply do
not have the money to offer as many varied programs and services as do the
larger male institutions.

Make-Believe Families

A unique characteristic of incarcerated girls is their tendency to form surrogate or make-believe families. Since the girls have little or no contact with

their real families during their incarceration, these relationships often provide substitues for the affection and support they are lacking:

The make-believe or prison family is ... a form of structured peer group interaction that is characterized by role-taking among the participants. Prison family members normally adopt roles traditionally assigned to family members in the larger society, e.g. father, mother, sister, brother, cousin, etc., and interactions between role-players often resemble those which occur in an actual extended family. Strong in-group loyalties typify inmate family relationships and a functional diversion of responsibility and labour characteristically takes place among family members. Family members also are likely to lend each other mutual advice and assistance, look out for one another's interests, and participate in institutional activities together.[72]

These kinship groups sometimes involve homosexual relationships between the girls.[73] It is unclear as to what percentage of girls involved in kinship groups engage in lesbianism.[74] Each institution is different in its tolerance of such activities. Some matrons understand the needs their girls have for human companionship and love and permit such families to exist as long as they are not detrimental to any of the members. Others display an active fear of homosexuality by forbidding close contact of the girls and drumming into their minds the evils and dangers of lesbianism.

A major study by Rose Giallombardo compared three institutions for female delinquents and reached the following conclusions about the kinship structures:

Transplanted to the institutions the adolescent girls find themselves many miles from the communities where their families and friends live. In the impersonal world of the institution, they desire to be accepted and to interact in the context of primary social relationships.

The courtship, marriage, and kinship relationships established by the adolescent inmates represent an attempt to provide a solution to the personal and social deprivations by duplicating the external world. . . .

The family group in the female prison is singularly suited to meet the inmates' internalized cultural expectations of the female role; it serves the social, psychological, and physiological needs of the adolescent offenders. Together, the prison homosexual marriage alliance and the larger kinship network provide structures wherein the female inmates' needs may find fulfillment and expression during the period of incarceration.[75]

In general, society is more negative about girls who act out and less concerned with their rehabilitation because the crimes they commit are not serious. These attitudes get translated into fewer staff, less modern buildings, and poorer vocational, educational, and recreational programs than those found in boys' institutions.[76] This is best illustrated by a report on juvenile institutions in Massachusetts. When asked to rate their overall institutional experience, 86 percent of the girls responded by saying it was fair or poor. Only 21 to 41 percent of the boys responded in that way.[77]

INSTITUTIONAL RULES AND DISCIPLINE

All secure institutions for juveniles must maintain a relatively high level of security within the facility. Consequently, most maintain lengthy sets of rules governing the daily activities of the inmates. Failure to abide by them results in serious consequences such as loss of privileges, a longer sentence, isolation, or transfer to a court or another more secure facility.

The following lists are examples of hypothetical rules used at secure institutional programs for female juvenile offenders:

1. Do not be disrespectful to any staff member.
2. Do not fight in or out of the cottage.
3. Do not become involved in negative campus activities, in or out of the cottage.
4. Do not bring, take out, or deliver bed and clothing issues in or out of the cottage.
5. Keep your room, dresser drawers, closets, beds, personal belongings clean and neat at all times.
6. Never under any circumstances enter another girl's room.
7. Do not talk or yell out your window at any time to anyone.
8. Do not go upstairs, downstairs, to the basement, outdoors, or to another girl's room without *first* getting permission from the staff member on duty.
9. Do not swap, borrow, loan, exchange, or give away any personal clothing, yours or state issue.
10. Do not at any time create a disturbance in the dining room.
11. Do not cause any trouble going to and from chapel, movies, and school or on walks.
12. Never leave the group for any reason when assembled in the recreation room, dining room, and so forth without *first* getting permission from the staff member on duty.
13. *Never leave your room without first getting permission of the staff member on duty (knock on door).*
14. Do not use profanity at any time.
15. Do not talk to girls in room confinement at any time.[78]

The next is a list of rule infractions at the Indiana Girls School for which brief detention can be utilized:

1. Upon being returned to Indiana Girls School from A.W.O.L.
2. Escape or attempted escape.
3. Attacking a staff member.
4. Attacking, threatening, bullying other inmates.
5. Fighting.
6. Destruction of property.
7. Theft.
8. Possession of cigarettes and matches.
9. Refusal to report for work assignment or leaving work assignment without permission.
10. Very foul abusive language directed toward a staff member or an inmate.
11. Consistent refusal to obey any certain rule or regulation.

12. Consistent, violent outbursts of temper, sass, impudence.
13. Illicit sexual activity.[79]

Juvenile institutions have a history of punishment practices that often reads like a horror story. Cases have been reported of brutal beatings, extended solitary confinement, and other inhumane practices in juvenile institutions across the country.[80] As recently as the early 1970s, major newspapers have published reports on conditions in these institutions that shocked the public.

Several court cases and a large amount of publicity have led a number of federal and state groups across the nation to develop standards for the juvenile justice system, including its institutions.[81] One of the areas they have all highlighted concerns rules and disciplinary measures. The following are the objectives for standards on the disciplinary system of the American Bar Association's Standards on Juvenile Justice:

Standard 8.2 Objectives
The objectives of these standards are:
A. to allow those charged with the custody and control of juveniles to reasonably regulate the behavior of those in their charge and to impose disciplinary measures congruent with the willful violation of the applicable regulation;
B. to promote fairness and regularity in the disciplinary system;
C. to separate major infractions from minor infractions and to prohibit the imposition of disciplinary measures in certain cases;
D. to promote the use of written regulations and to ensure that the juvenile know as precisely as possible what conduct is expected of him or her and what sanctions may be imposed;
E. to provide a procedural format for the imposition of disciplinary measures; and
F. to prohibit cruel and unusual punishment within juvenile correctional facilities.[82]

Many groups have developed standards requiring that rules be in writing, that the inmates be oriented to the rules as soon as possible after admission, and that the rules be posted conspicuously throughout the facility.[83]

The standards are adamant that corporal punishment be outlawed and that solitary confinement be used only as a last resort and only according to strict procedural requirements. Too often in the past, solitary confinement has been used for days at a time, serving no true rehabilitative purpose. The National Advisory Commission Standards, for example, recommend that secure restriction be used only in extreme cases such as when children are a danger to themselves or others or they are likely to escape.[84]

The American Bar Association Standards go even further by specifying conduct that should not be subject to disciplinary action at all:

Standard 8.6
Juveniles should not be subject to disciplinary action for any of the following behavior:
A. sexual behavior that is not forbidden by law;
B. refusal to attend religious services;

C. refusal to conform in matters of personal appearance or dress to any institutional rule that is not related to health or safety;

D. refusal to permit a search of the person or of personal effects that is not authorized by these standards;

E. refusal to continue participation in any counseling, treatment, rehabilitation, or training program, with the exception of school or class attendance mandated by the compulsory school attendance law;

F. refusal to address staff in any particular manner or displaying what is viewed as a negative, hostile, or any other supposed attitude deemed undesirable;

G. possession of any printed or otherwise recorded material unless such possession is specifically forbidden by these standards;

H. refusal to eat a particular type of food;

I. refusal to behave in violation of the juvenile's religious beliefs;

J. refusal to participate in any study, research, or experiment;

K. refusal to take drugs designed to modify behavior or to submit to nonemergency, surgical interventions without consent.[85]

Most institutions maintain disciplinary boards of some sort that regulate and hear appeals by juvenile inmates on their disciplinary procedures. The case of *Wolff v. McDonnell* focused on due process requirements for disciplinary proceedings in adult institutions.[86] To provide the same rights for juveniles, several sets of standards have recommended similar rules and regulations governing juvenile institutional boards—including notice, representation by counsel, and the right to a written record of the proceedings and decision.[87]

Ideally, rules and discipline should have two purposes. First, they should maintain security and control within the institution only to the level that is necessary to provide a sense of well-being to staff and inmates. Second, they should be therapeutic by teaching inmates to "understand the wisdom and necessity of a postponement of or substitution for immediate pleasure and gratification of a wish or need."[88]

JUVENILE AFTERCARE

Aftercare in the juvenile justice system is the equivalent of parole in the adult criminal justice system. When juveniles are released from an institution through an early release program or after completion of their sentences, they may be placed in an aftercare program of some kind. The feeling is that children who have been institutionalized should not be abruptly returned to the community without proper help and supervision. Whether individuals who are on aftercare as part of an indeterminant sentence remain in the community or return to the institution for further rehabilitation depends on their actions during the aftercare period.

One of the purposes of aftercare is to give an individual some extra assistance during this readjustment period in the community. As one authority has stated:

The principal rationale for modern aftercare is that the institutionalized minor is likely to have a difficult time coping with life in the community after release. The experience of being in the institution generally has negative effects. First, the minor's activities have been tightly regimented for some time; once such restraints are removed, he may not find it easy to make his own decisions. Second, his peers in the institution may have provided a speedy but effective course in advanced criminality. Furthermore, the community itself may view the returned minor with a good deal of prejudice; school adjustment problems or a discouraging job hunt may reinforce his impulses to seek refuge in his bad habits of deviant behavior.[89]

Juveniles in aftercare programs are supervised by a parole caseworker or counselor whose job is to provide surveillance by maintaining contact with the juvenile, to make sure that a corrections plan is followed, and to show interest and caring in order to help prevent further mistakes by the juvenile. The counselor also keeps the youth informed of available services that may assist in reintegration and counsels the youth and his or her family on the possible reasons for the original problems.

Unfortunately, aftercare caseworkers, like probation officers, often carry such large caseloads that their jobs are next to impossible.[90] Although the exact number of juveniles on aftercare is difficult to estimate, a recent Department of Justice source placed the total number of juvenile "parolees" as of September 1, 1976, at 53,347. Of this total, 42,703, or 80 percent, were male; 10,644 were female. The total reflects a decline of almost 42,000 youths from the 1975 figure of 94,150.[91]

Several reasons account for the lower figure. First of all, with the trend towards deinstitutionalization, fewer children are placed in long-term institutions, and therefore they do not require aftercare programs for reintegration into the community. Second, due to a recent public outcry against releasing violent young offenders back into the community too soon, early release may not be as prevalent as it once was. Third and perhaps most important, many jurisdictions are moving toward the idea of determinant sentencing, which eliminates aftercare from the juvenile justice system.

Another explanation for the decline in the number of juvenile parolees is that these programs are being phased out because they are ineffective. How a youth does on parole is one of the few indicators of the success of the rehabilitation programs in institutions. As early as 1962 at the National Conference of Superintendents of Training Schools and Reformatories, it was noted that:

What happens to a child after he leaves the training school is probably the most important link in the entire program for dealing with boys and girls who get into trouble. When a child is released from the institution, how he is released, how he is received back into the community, what he does there, how he is helped through this whole critical period and how it is decided whether he has broken parole, or supervision can be terminated, are all points demanding wise planning and serious consideration.[92]

A more recent statement by the National Advisory Commission Task Force on Corrections reported on juvenile parole organization, noting that:

The National Survey of Corrections found tremendous shortcomings in juvenile aftercare programs. In some States young persons released from training schools were supervised by institutional staff. In others they were made the responsibility of local child welfare workers, who simply included these youngsters in their caseloads of dependent or neglected children. In some States no organized program of juvenile parole supervision existed. Whether distinct juvenile correctional agencies should exist or whether such services should be carried out as a regular part of welfare services has been a matter of controversy for years.

The events of the last years have virtually ended that argument. Distinct divisions and departments of juvenile correctional services are emerging. There is less agreement about whether such departments should be combined with agencies serving adult offenders. Yet it is widely agreed that separate program units should be maintained, even if adult and juvenile programs are combined in a single agency. Statewide juvenile correctional services embracing both institutions and field aftercare represent an established trend that should be supported.[93]

A recent survey of eight juvenile parole studies of over 2,300 youths indicated that these two organizations were generally correct in their evaluation of juvenile parole. The survey reported that traditional parole programs (those involving casework and individual or group counseling) have generally had negative results. The researcher's suggestions for improvement included teaching more intellectual and interpersonal skills to parolees in lieu of extensive counseling of other types.[94]

The California Youth Authority (CYA) recently tried out some innovative juvenile aftercare programs. One is the Social, Personal, and Community Experience (SPACE) project in Los Angeles. Twenty-five parolees live in a half-way house in a converted hospital, work at assigned jobs, and take part in role training exercises and reality therapy. After they go out into the community, find a "real" job, and convince their parole board that their plans are working, they are released from the CYA.[95]

A final issue in aftercare for juveniles concerns revocation procedures. Although adult parolees have been entitled to certain procedural rights in revocation proceedings since 1972, the Supreme Court has not yet extended these same rights to juveniles.[96] However, at least twenty-seven states have extended these rights to juveniles on their own initiative.[97] The following list spells out some of the conditions that a juvenile parolee has to meet to avoid revocation:

1. Adhering to a reasonable curfew set by youth worker or parent.
2. Refraining from association with persons whose influence would be detrimental, including but not limited to persons convicted of crimes or persons of a known criminal background.
3. Attending school in accordance with the law.
4. Abstaining from drugs.
5. Abstaining from alcohol.
6. Reporting to the youth worker when required.
7. Refraining from acts that would be crimes if committed by an adult.
8. Refraining from operating an automobile without permission of the youth worker or parent.
9. Refraining from being habitually disobedient and beyond the lawful control of parent or other legal authority.
10. Refraining from running away from the lawful custody of parent or other lawful authority.

The following procedural safeguards have been set up to ensure that revocation is handled fairly.

1. Notice of specific conditions of parole.

2. Agreement among parole workers and legal personnel about the need to revoke and sufficiency of the evidence before proceeding.
3. Notice of allegations.
4. Right to legal counsel to be provided at state expense if necessary.
5. Right to confrontation and cross-examination.
6. Right to introduce documentary evidence and witnesses.
7. Right to an independent hearing officer who shall be an attorney but not an employee of the revoking agency.
8. Right to a speedy hearing to be held within twenty days from mailing notice of hearing where the releasee is not taken into custody.
9. Right to a verbatim record of the hearing.
10. A decision based on substantial evidence.
11. Right to judicial review.

Successful completion of an aftercare program generally marks the end of a juvenile's involvement with the juvenile justice system.

VIOLENT YOUNG OFFENDERS

In 1978, the Vera Institute of Justice completed a year-long study on violent delinquency.[98] The study found that diversion away from the juvenile justice system has increasingly been the norm for all but serious offenders. These offenders tend to receive the harshest dispositions; and although they are the ones most in need of rehabilitation, they are the least likely to receive it. They are often subjected to long delays before their cases are finally disposed of. Because most community-based programs will not accept problem youths or ones with a history of violent behavior, they often receive ineffective and possibly damaging treatment in securely locked institutions, when they might be better served in small community-based programs.[99]

No single treatment program for violent delinquents seems entirely viable. Intervention techniques such as probation, restitution, or commitment aim to reduce antisocial behavior, but there is little evidence to indicate which of the techniques works best or whether any of them work. Effective treatment must combine a number of options to try to solve the many types of problems that tend to characterize violent juvenile offenders.

Although delinquent behavior is a fairly widespread phenomenon, violent acts by juveniles are less frequent than other types of delinquent behavior. In the Vera study, only 11 percent of all the offenses researched were of a serious violent nature, and an additional 12 percent were less serious assaults and robberies. These figures are comparable to nationwide statistics showing that 10 percent of all juvenile arrests in 1975 were for serious violent crimes. It should be noted, however, that in 1975, the arrest rate of juveniles fifteen to seventeen years old for violent crimes was higher than the rate for those eighteen years old and older. The most common violent crime was simple assault. The most common serious violent crime was robbery followed by serious assault.

Juvenile violence appears to be on the increase. Between 1960 and 1975, for example, arrests for juvenile violent crimes rose 293 percent. Robbery lead the list, followed by aggravated assault, homicide, and rape. The total rate of increase was twice the adult rate.[100]

Alternatives for dealing with this pressing issue present planners and policy makers with unpleasant and difficult decisions. Some jurisdictions have moved toward deinstitutionalization by following the Massachusetts example, but many are responding to public outcry with more severe and punitive responses to serious juvenile offenders. Such approaches include the use of flat sentences, transferring more children to adult courts, lowering the age of criminal responsibility for juvenile actions, and giving children longer sentences.

Only time will tell which direction juvenile justice policy will take over the next several years. It seems inevitable, however, that if serious and violent youth crime continues unabated, more secure facilities will be needed in the future.[101]

CHAPTER SUMMARY

Judicial intervention in juvenile justice over the last two decades has raised the issue of whether a child has a legal right to treatment when confined in an institution. Although the legal definition of treatment remains unclear, right to treatment suits have become a major technique to obtain services for children in the juvenile justice system.

Attention was then given to the concept of aftercare, which allows the institutionalized child to move into the community. Once released, the child is often supervised in the community by aftercare treatment specialists.

Finally, this chapter noted that juvenile violence has become a major concern of the public, and of professionals in the juvenile justice system. Available statistics indicate a dramatic increase in violent juvenile crime, and society will have to be responsive to this problem in the future.

DISCUSSION QUESTIONS

1. What are some of the major characteristics of juvenile institutions? Have treatment programs in institutions been effective in reducing recidivism rates for juvenile offenders?
2. What kinds of young people are generally placed under correctional control in juvenile institutions? Is the population of juveniles placed in institutional programs increasing or decreasing? Explain.
3. Juvenile probation and parole are important community treatment methods in juvenile correction. What are their similarities and their differences? Are juvenile aftercare programs needed if children serve a fair and just sentence in an institution?
4. Most adult and juvenile institutions have been unable to provide a safe, humane, and adequate treatment environment for adult inmates and adjudicated juvenile offenders. What improvements would have to be made in juvenile institutions to provide the juvenile with a normal growth and development experience?
5. Violent juvenile crime is increasing in America. Are institutional programs the answer to such criminality?

SUGGESTED READINGS

American Bar Association. Project on Standards for Juvenile Justice. *Standards Relating to Architecture of Facilities.* Cambridge, Mass.: Ballinger Press, 1977.

_____ Project on Standards for Juvenile Justice. *Standards Relating to Corrections Administration.* Cambridge, Mass.: Ballinger Press, 1977.

Amos, William, and Manella, Raymond. *Delinquent Children in Juvenile Correctional Institutions.* Springfield, Ill.: Charles C. Thomas, 1966.

Bartollas, Clemons; Miller, Stuart J.; and Dinitz, Simon. *Juvenile Victimization: The Institutional Paradox.* New York: Wiley, 1976.

Carter, Robert M., and Wilkins, Leslie, eds. *Probation and Parole: Selected Readings.* New York: Wiley, 1970.

Cole, Larry. *Our Children's Keepers.* Greenwich, Conn.: Fawcett, 1974.

Fogel, David. *We Are the Living Proof: The Justice Model for Corrections.* Cincinnati, Ohio: W H. Anderson, 1975.

Fox, Sanford. "The Reform of Juvenile Justice: The Child's Right to Punishment." *Juvenile Justice Journal* 25 (1974): 15:22.

Giallombardo, Rose. *The Social World of Imprisoned Girls.* New York: Wiley, 1974.

Gibbons, Don C. *Changing the Lawbreaker: The Treatment of Delinquents and Criminals.* Englewood Cliffs, N.J.: Prentice-Hall, 1965.

Goffman, Erving R. *Asylums.* New York: Doubleday, 1961.

James, Howard. *Children in Trouble.* New York: David McKay, 1970.

Lerman, Paul. "Evaluative Studies of Institutions for Delinquents." *Social Work Journal* 13 (1968): 55–62.

Morales v. Turman, 326 F.Supp. 677 (E.D. Tex. 1971).

Morris, Albert. *The Future of Imprisonment.* Chicago: Univeristy of Chicago Press, 1974.

National Advisory Commission on Criminal Justice Standards and Goals. *Corrections.* Washington, D.C.: Government Printing Office, 1973.

Ohlin, Lloyd; Coates, Robert; and Miller, Alden. "Radical Correctional Reform: A Case Study of the Massachusetts Youth Correctional System." *Harvard Educational Review* 44 (1974): 74–111.

Richett, Lisa. *The Throwaway Children.* Philadelphia: Lippincott, 1969.

Sheer, Edwin. *Radical Non-Intervention: Rethinking the Delinquency Problem.* Englewood Cliffs, N.J.: Prentice-Hall, 1973.

Strasburg, Paul A. *Violent Delinquents.* New York: Monarch, 1978.

Street, David; Vinter, Robert; and Periow, Charles. *Organization for Treatment: A Comparative Study of Institutions for Delinquents.* New York: Free Press, 1966.

Wald, Patricia, and Schwartz, Laurence. "Trying a Juvenile Right to Treatment Suit: Pointers and Pitfalls for Plaintiffs." *American Criminal Law Review* 12 (1974): 125–163.

Wooden, Kenneth. *Weeping in the Playtime of Others: America's Incarcerated Children.* New York: McGraw-Hill, 1976.

REFERENCES

1. For a detailed description of juvenile delinquency in the 1800s, see J. Hawes, *Children in Urban Society: Juvenile Delinquency in Nineteenth Century America* (New York: Oxford University Press, 1971).

2. D. Jarvis, *Institutional Treatment of the Offender* (New York: McGraw-Hill, 1978), p. 101.

3. Clemons Bartollas, Stuart J. Miller, and Simon Dinitz, *Juvenile Victimization: The Institutional Paradox* (New York: Wiley, 1976), p. 6.

4. LaMar T. Empey, *American Delinquency—Its Meaning and Construction* (Homewood, Ill.: Dorsey Press, 1978), p. 515.

5. National Conference of Superintendents of Training Schools and Reformatories, *Institutional Rehabilitation of Delinquent Youth: Manual for Training School Personnel* (Albany, N.Y.: Delmar, 1962), p. 4.

6. Edward Eldefonso and Walter Hartinger, *Control, Treatment and Rehabilitation of Juvenile Offenders* (Beverly Hills, Calif.: Glencoe Press, 1976), p. 151.

7. Ibid., p. 152.

8. National Criminal Justice Information and Statistics Service, *Children in Custody: Advance Report on the Juvenile Detention and Correctional Facility Census of 1975* (Washington, D.C.: Government Printing Office, October 1977), p. 17.

9. Ibid.

10. Law Enforcement Assistance Administration, *Indexed Legislative History of the "Juvenile Justice and Delinquency Prevention Act of 1974"* (Washington, D.C.: LEAA, 1974), pp. 395–396.

11. The following four paragraphs are taken from The National Manpower Survey of the Criminal Justice System, Vol. 3. *Corrections*, National Institute of Law Enforcement and Criminal Justice, LEAA (Washington, D.C.: Government Printing Office, 1978), pp. 22–23.

12. Robert D. Vinter, ed., *Time Out: A National Study of Juvenile Correctional Programs* (Ann Arbor, Mich.: National Assessment of Juvenile Corrections, 1976), pp. 20–53.

13. Ibid., p. 51.

14. Mark M. Levin and Rosemary C. Sarri, *Juvenile Delinquency: A Study of Juvenile Codes in the U.S.* (Ann Arbor, Mich.: National Assessment of Juvenile Corrections, 1974), p. 55.

15. American Bar Association, Project on Standards for Juvenile Justice, *Standards Relating to Architecture of Facilities* (Cambridge, Mass.: Ballinger Press, 1977), Standard 5.1 Commentary, p. 50.

16. Eldefonso and Hartinger, *Control, Treatment and Rehabilitation of Juvenile Offenders*, p. 162.

17. U.S. Department of Health, Education and Welfare, Children's Bureau, *Institutions Serving Delinquent Children* (Washington, D.C.: Government Printing Office, 1962), p. 73.

18. Kenneth Wooden, *Weeping in the Playtime of Others: America's Incarcerated Children* (New York: McGraw-Hill, 1976), p. 95.

19. Constance Holden, "Massachusetts Juvenile Justice: Deinstitutionalization on Trial," *Science* 192 (1976): p. 450.

20. K. Daniel O'Leary and O. Terence Wilson, *Behavior Therapy: Application and Outcome* (Englewood Cliffs, N.J.: Prentice-Hall, 1975), quoted in Robert C. Trojanowicz, *Juvenile Delinquency: Concepts and Control*, 2d ed. (Engelwood Cliffs, N.J.: Prentice-Hall, 1978), p. 303.

21. See, for example, Edward Rolde et al., "The Maximum Security Institution as a Treatment Facility for Juveniles," in *Juvenile Delinquency: A Reader*, ed. James E. Teele (Itasca, Ill.: F. E. Peacock, 1970), pp. 437–444.

22. See Vinter, *Time Out*, p. 141.

23. Dennis A. Romig, *Justice for Our Children: An Examination of Juvenile Delinquent Rehabilitation Programs* (Lexington, Mass.: Lexington Books, 1978), p. 81.

24. See Vinter, *Time Out*; Vinter reports that reality therapy is utilized in 80 percent of the institutions surveyed.

25. See, generally, William Glasser, "Reality Therapy: A Realistic Approach to the Young Offender," in *Readings in Delinquency and Treatment,* ed. Robert Schaste and Jo Wallach (Los Angeles: Delinquency Prevention Training Project, Youth Studies Center, University of Southern California, 1965). See also Richard Rachin, "Reality Therapy: Helping People Help Themselves," *Crime and Delinquency* 16 (1974): p. 143.

26. See Eric Berne, *Transactional Analysis in Psychotherapy* (New York: Grove Press, 1961).

27. Lewis R. Wolberg, *The Techniques of Psychotherapy* (New York: Grune and Stratton, 1967), p. 257.

28. See Helen A. Klein, "Towards More Effective Behavioral Programs for Juvenile Offenders," *Federal Probation* 41 (1977): pp. 45–50; Albert Bandura, *Principles of Behavior Modification* (New York: Holt, Rinehart and Winston, 1969); and H. A. Klein, "Behavior Modification as Therpeutic Paradox," *American Journal of Orthopsychiatry* 44 (1974): p. 353.

29. See Robert B. Rutherford, "Establishing Behavioral Contracts with Delinquent Adolescents," *Federal Probation* 39 (1975): p. 29. For examples of token economies within institutions, see E. L. Phillips, "Achievement Place: Token Reinforcement Procedures in a Home-Style Rehabilitation Setting for Predelinquent Boys," *Journal of Applied Behavior Analysis* 1 (1968): p. 213; and D. Wexler, "Token and Taboo: Behavior Modification, Token Economies and the Law," *California Law Review* 61 (1973): p. 81.

30. Romig, *Justice for Our Children,* pp. 20–24.

31. See J. N. Yong, "Advantages of Group Therapy in Relation to Individual Therapy for Juvenile Delinquents," *Corrective Psychiatry and Journal of Social Therapy* 17 (1971): p. 34.

32. Irving Schulman, "Modifications in Group Psychotherapy with Antisocial Adolescents," *International Journal of Group Psychotherapy* 7 (1974): p. 310, quoted in Trojanowicz, *Juvenile Delinquency,* p. 296.

33. See LaMar T. Empey and Steven Lubeck, *The Silverlake Experiment* (Chicago: Aldine Publishing, 1971); H. Ashley Weeks, *Youthful Offenders at Highfields* (Ann Arbor: University of Michigan Press, 1958); and L. T. Empey and J. Rabow, "The Prove Experiment in Delinquency Rehabilitation," *American Sociological Review* 26 (1961): p. 679.

34. Maxwell Jones, Social Psychiatry in Practice (Baltimore: Penguin Books, 1968); also Loren Crabtree and James Fox, "The Overthrow of a Therapeutic Community," International Journal of Group Psychotherapy 22 (1972): p. 31.

35. Bruno Bettelheim, *The Empty Fortress* (New York: Free Press, 1967).

36. U.S. Department of Health, Education and Welfare, Children's Bureau, *Institutions Serving Delinquent Children,* p. 73.

37. Vinter, *Time Out.* p. 15.

38. Ibid., p. 152.

39. Ibid.

40. Ibid.

41. Romig, *Justice for Our Children,* p. 51.

42. Ibid., pp. 51–52.

43. Vinter, *Time Out,* p. 181.

44. National Advisory Commission on Criminal Justice Standards and Goals, *Report of the Task Force on Juvenile Justice and Delinquency Prevention* (Washington, D.C.: Government Printing Office, 1976), Standard 24.12 (Recreation and Leisure Time Activities), Commentary, p. 721.

45. Ibid., Standard 24.10 (Medicine/Dental and Mental Health Services), Commentary, p. 717.

46. Vinter, *Time Out,* p. 165.

47. See Edward M. Brecher and Richard D. Dealle Penna, *Health Care in Correctional Institu-*

tions, National Institute of Law Enforcement and Criminal Justice (Washington, D.C.: Government Printing Office, 1975), Appendix B.

48. Ibid., p. 36.

49. Morton Birnbaum, "The Right to Treatment," *American Bar Association Journal* 46 (1960): p. 499.

50. Discussed in Adrienne Volenik, "Right to Treatment: Case Developments in Juvenile Law," *Justice System Journal* 3 (1978): pp. 292–307.

51. 373 F.2d 451 (D.C. Cir. 1966).

52. Ibid., p. 453.

53. 325 F.Supp. 781 (1971).

54. 325 F.Supp. 373, 784 (1972).

55. 422 U.S. 563 (1975).

56. 346 F.Supp. 1354 (D.R.I. 1972).

57. Ibid., p. 1343.

58. 349 F.Supp. 575 (S.D.N.Y. 1972).

59. 383 F.Supp. 53 (E.D. Texas 1974).

60. 419 F.Supp. 203 (S.D.N.Y. 1976).

61. See, for example, "Limits on Punishment and Entitlement to Rehabilitative Treatment of Institutionalized Juveniles: *Nelson v. Heyne,*" *Virginia Law Review* 60 (1974): p. 864; Kenneth R. Hamm, "*Nelson v. Heyne:* The Misuse of Tranquilizing Drugs in a Juvenile Correctional Institution Constitutes Cruel and Unusual Punishment," *New England Journal of Prison Law* 1 (1975): p. 244.

62. See, for example, Robert E. Shepherd, Jr., "Challenging the Rehabilitative Justification for Indeterminate Sentencing in the Juvenile Justice System: The Right to Punishment," *St. Louis University Law Journal* 21 (1977): p. 12.

63. *Kent v. United States,* 383 U.S. 541, 556 (1966).

64. Testimony by Mary K. Jolly before the National Congress for New Directions in Federal Correctional Programming, *Juvenile Justice Digest* 3 (1975): p. 1.

65. Several authors have written of this sexual double standard. See E. A. Anderson, "The Chivalrous Treatment of the Female Offender in the Arms of the Criminal Justice System: A Review of the Literature," *Social Problems* 23 (1976): pp. 350–357; G. Armstrong, "Females under the Law: Protected but Unequal," *Crime and Delinquency* 23 (1977): pp. 109–120; M. Chesney-Lind, "Judicial Enforcement of the Female Sex Role: The Family Court and the Female Delinquent," *Issues in Criminology* 8 (1973): pp. 51–59; M. Chesney-Lind, "Juvenile Delinquency: The Sexualization of Female Crime," *Psychology Today,* July 1974, pp. 43–46; Allan Conway and Carol Bogdan, "Sexual Delinquency: The Persistence of a Double Standard," *Crime and Delinquency* 23 (1977): pp. 13–135.

66. U.S. Department of Justice, Law Enforcement Assistance Administration, *Children in Custody: Advance Report of the 1977 Census of Public Juvenile Facilities* (Washington, D.C.: Government Printing Office, 1979), p. 3.

67. Office of Juvenile Justice and Delinquency Prevention, Law Enforcement Assistance Administration, *Little Sisters and the Law* (Washington, D.C.: Government Printing Office, 1976), p. 16.

68. Ibid.

69. Ibid., p. 23.

70. Ibid., p. 16.

71. Ibid.

72. Thomas W. Foster, "Make-Believe Families: A Response of Women and Girls to the Deprivations of Imprisonment," *International Journal of Criminology and Penology* 3 (1975): p. 71.

73. Ibid.

74. Ibid.

75. Rose Giallombardo, *The Social World of Imprisoned Girls: A Comparative Study of Institutions for Juvenile Delinquents* (New York: Wiley, 1974), pp. 15–16.

76. Y. Bakal, *Closing Correctional Institutions: New Strategies for Youth Services* (Lexington, Mass.: Lexington Books, 1973), p. 26.

77. Ibid.

78. See, for example, Giallombardo, *The Social World of Imprisoned Girls*, pp. 309–310.

79. Statement of Dorothy VanBrunt, Superintendent, Indiana Girls School, Indianapolis, Indiana, in "Juvenile Confinement Institutions and Correctional Systems," *Hearings before the Subcommittee to Investigate Juvenile Delinquency of the Committee of the Judiciary,* U.S. Senate, 92nd Congress, First Session, May 3, 4, 17, and 18, 1971.

80. See generally, Edward Wakin, Children without Justice—A Report by the National Council of Jewish Women (New York: National Council of Jewish Women, 1975) pp. 43–55; Howard James, Children in Trouble—A National Scandal (New York: Pocket Books, 1971), pp. 102–125; also Martarella v. Kelly, 349 F.Supp. 575 (1972).

81. Harry Swanger, "Juvenile Institutional Litigation," *Clearinghouse Review* 11 (1977): pp. 219–221, reports that the National Juvenile Law Center in St. Louis has been involved in litigation since 1972 that has sought and obtained reform of such practices as solitary confinement, disciplinary procedures, corporal punishment, forced drugging, and institutional rules. Examples of the litigation include the following cases: Nelson v. Heyne, 355 F.Supp. 451 (N.D. Ind. 1972); Inmates v. Affleck, 346 F.Supp. 1354 (D.R.I. 1972); Morales v. Turman, 383 F.Supp. 53 (E.D. Tex. 1974).

82. American Bar Association, Project on Standards for Juvenile Justice, *Standards Relating to Corrections Administration* (Cambridge, Mass.: Ballinger Press, 1977), Standard 8.2.

83. National Advisory Commission on Criminal Justice Standards and Goals, *Report of the Task Force on Juvenile Justice and Delinquency Prevention*, Standard 20.4.

84. Ibid.

85. American Bar Association, Project on Standards for Juvenile Justice, *Standards Relating to Corrections Administration*, Standard 8.6. See also Standard 8.9.

86. 418 U.S. 539 (1974).

87. American Bar Association, Project on Standards for Juvenile Justice, *Standards Relating to Corrections Administration*, Standard 8.9 (Criminal Justice).

88. Eldefonso and Hartinger, *Control, Treatment and Rehabilitation of Juvenile Offenders*, p. 195. See also Brother Christian Hynes, "Discipline in a Treatment-Oriented School for Delinquent Boys," *Federal Probation* 33 (1969): p. 29, for discussion of purposes of discipline and how to administer it.

89. See, generally, William R. Arnold, *Juveniles on Parole* (New York: Random House, 1970).

90. See, for example, Paul A. Strasburg, *Violent Delinquents: A Report to the Ford Foundation from Vera Institute of Justice* (New York: Monarch, 1978), pp. 120–121, in which it is stated that the New York State Division of Youth's aftercare service workers have caseloads of 52 to 53 juveniles; it is suggested that it would cost close to $900,000 to reform to meet minimum standards.

91. U.S. Department of Justice, Law Enforcement Assistance Administration, *State and Local Probation and Parole Systems*, No. SD-0-1 (Washington, D.C.: Government Printing Office, 1978), pp. 37–39.

92. National Conference of Superintendents of Training Schools and Reformatories, *Institutional*

Rehabilitation of Delinquent Youth, p. 178, quoted in Arnold, *Juveniles on Parole*, pp. 5–6.

93. National Advisory Commission on Criminal Justice Standards and Goals, *Corrections* (Washington, D.C.: Government Printing Office, 1973), p. 408.

94. See Romig, *Justice for Our Children*, pp. 185–194.

95. Project Benchmark, *Juvenile Justice* (Berkeley, Calif.: Office of Criminal Justice Planning, 1974). pp. 2-22.

96. See *Morissey v. Brewer*, 408 U.S. 471, 92 S.Ct. 2593, 33 L.Ed. 2d 484 (1972). Upon revocation of parole, a defendant is entitled to the due process rights of (1) a hearing, (2) written notice of charges, (3) knowledge of evidence against him or her, (4) opportunity to present and cross-examine witnesses, and (5) written statement of reasons for parole revocation.

97. See Malcolm S. Goddard, "Juvenile Parole Revocation Hearings: The New York State Experience," *Criminal Law Bulletin* 13 (1977): pp. 552–573. A survey taken by the author showed that the following states have implemented juvenile parole revocation hearing procedures: Arizona, California, Colorado, Connecticut, Georgia, Hawaii, Idaho, Indiana, Iowa, Kentucky, Maine, Michigan, Minnesota, Missouri, Montana, Nebraska, New Jersey, New York, North Dakota, Ohio, Rhode Island, South Carolina, Tennessee, Virginia, Washington, and Wisconsin.

98. Strasburg, *Violent Delinquents*.

99. Ibid., pp. 11–43.

100. Ibid., p. 165.

101. *The Issue of Security in a Community-Based Juvenile Corrections System: The Final Report of the Task Force on Secure Facilities*, Commonwealth of Massachusetts, Department of Youth Services, November, 1977. See also U.S. Department of Justice, Law Enforcement Assistance Administration, *Reports of the National Juvenile Justice Assessment Project—A National Assessment of Serious Juvenile Crime and the Juvenile Justice System*, vol. 1, *Summary* (Washington, D.C.: Government Printing Office, 1980).

PART VII

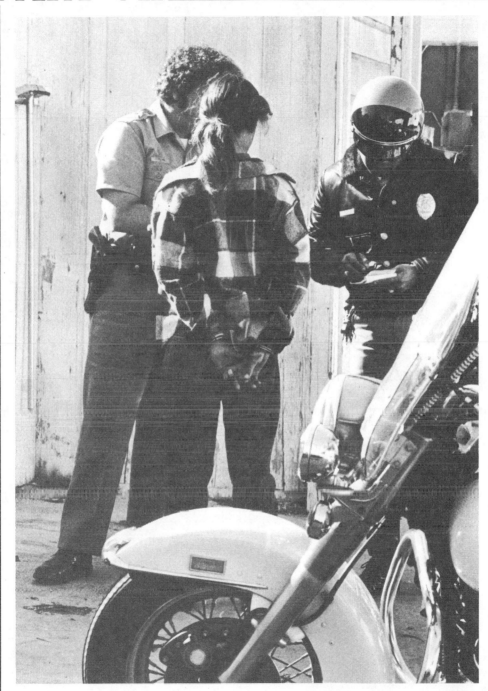

CHILDREN'S RIGHTS

Chapter 20

Chapter Outline

Children's Rights Within the Family
Children's Rights Outside the Family
Rights of Special Children
Bill of Rights for Children
Chapter Summary

Key Terms, Names, and Cases

in loco parentis
Wisconsin v. Yoder
passive speech
Tinker v. Des Moines School District
active speech
People v. Overton
emancipation
Peagle v. Scott
Ingraham v. Wright
Penn. Assn. for Retarded Children v. Penn.
Bill of Rights for Children
privacy
right to treatment
abortion
right to consent
Bellotti v. Baird
corporal punishment
People v. Bowers
In re Donaldson
special children

Rights of Minors

INTRODUCTION

In previous chapters, we discussed the legal rights of children who become involved with the juvenile justice system. This chapter moves beyond the problems of crime, delinquency, and antisocial behavior and considers the rights of minors in a broader sense, including child emancipation, medical care, support, education, employment, treatment, and First Amendment freedoms.

Although the Supreme Court hears thousands of cases each year, it seldom decides cases in childrens' rights. Even the landmark *Gault* decision was limited because it provided only due process rights under the Fourteenth Amendment to children charged with delinquency at the adjudicatory hearing. However, the *Gault* decision represented a critical departure in juvenile law since the turn of the century in its decision that generally children do have constitutional rights. Moreover, it gave impetus to the Supreme Courts further involvement in litigating childrens' rights.

Nevertheless, the rights of children in such areas as medical care, education, employment, and abuse remain unclear even today. In fact, the law has only begun to deal with the role of children in society. Few states have a completely unified jurisprudential code of laws for children. The major legislation is the juvenile court act in every jurisdiction, and its primary focus is children in trouble. Only recently have the courts begun to recognize the legal and constitutional issues affecting the lives of all children and to provide some legal guidance. As Sanford Katz states:

The future of the nuclear family is uncertain, and the centuries-old subservience of children in the family is being philosophically and practically protested. A growing

The authors wish to express their appreciation to Howard Lightman for his assistance in the research and development of this chapter.

awareness that children are people, with rights previously often ignored by the statutes and courts of the land, has led to increasing efforts to defend these rights. The result is a new concern for the child in American law.[1]

Although our society has established some case and statutory law dealing with the rights of children, the care and protection of children in the legal system remains a controversial issue. Many children continue to be institutionalized without proper legal safeguards. Thousands of children are physically and emotionally abused each year. Others are denied medical care because parents or guardians control the decision-making process. Still others are arbitrarily placed in schools where they receive inferior education. In addition, children who are emotionally disturbed, physically handicapped, and mentally limited are being deprived of opportunities because their legal rights are unclear and unenforceable.

It would be impossible in this chapter to deal with all the issues involved in the legal rights of minors. However, some areas relate directly to delinquency and deviant behavior. In our complex society, many agencies within government take action directly affecting the lives of children, often with negative results. Under obsolete laws, children suffer numerous discriminations and injustices. This chapter concentrates on a number of major areas with respect to the rights of children. They include: (1) children's rights within the family, with the right to medical care as the major example; (2) children's rights in society, with the legal problems that children face in the educational system as an example; and (3) the rights of special children. The chapter concludes with an analysis of a bill of rights for children. It spells out the basic rights that should be recognized by any modern society when dealing with children. In each of the areas discussed, the focus is on the intricate, three-part relationship of the child, the parents, and the state. Thus, when we ask whether a child should be treated as an adult with similar rights, we must explore the answer against a background of the interests of the different parties. We also recognize the general rule that the courts usually do not interfere with the care of the child unless the parents violate some statute that requires them to provide at least a minimum amount of care.

CHILDREN'S RIGHTS WITHIN THE FAMILY — MEDICAL CARE AND PRIVACY

In recent years, the Supreme Court has begun to recognize the child as an individual with some of the same constitutional rights enjoyed by adults. With this recognition has come respect for the child's right to privacy and the right to make decisions in his or her own best interest, as well as the subsequent erosion of the parents' absolute control over the child's development.

This process has been slow, however, because the government is reluctant to enter into traditional family matters. Even when the parents are suspected of neglect or abuse, the state is loath to interfere. This has been the dilemma—the sanctity of the family unit versus the constitutional rights of the child. As the Supreme Court stated in *Griswold v. Connecticut*, "various guarantees create what is known as a zone of privacy. . . . This right of privacy, which presses for recognition, is a legitimate one."[2] The critical issue in regard to children's rights in the family is whether the state can impose on the right of privacy enjoyed by the family in order to preserve certain rights for one of its own members—the child.

In its recent assertions of the child's right to privacy, the Supreme Court has had to overcome what it characterized as a family's liberty—the guaranteed freedom to marry, to establish a home, and to bring up children. The Court stated, for example, in the case of *Prince v. Massachusetts*, and reaffirmed later in the case of *Ginsberg v. New York*, that:

First of all, constitutional interpretation has consistently recognized that the parents' claim to authority in their own household to direct the rearing of their children is basic in the structure of our society. It is cardinal with us that the custody, care, and nurture of the child reside first in the parents, whose primary function and freedom include preparation for obligations the state can neither supply nor hinder.[3]

As a result of this hands-off policy, the state has in the past given parents a free hand in the area of medical care and privacy for their children, as well as in such areas as the discipline, limits on speech, searching of a child's belongings, and even choosing a child's religion. However, in recent years, the state has considered children's rights primarily in the realms of medical care and privacy.

Under common law, parents must consent to any medical treatment for the child. The assumption is that children do not have the capacity to choose wisely for themselves. Today, common law is still the norm. For example, the American Bar Association's Standards on the Rights of Minors suggests that a minor cannot obtain medical treatment or services without prior parental consent.[4] This policy of parental consent presumably strengthens the idea of family integrity, improves the child's ability to make decisions at a reasonable age, and provides the state with an interest in preventing physical harm to the child. Most states use the age of eighteen as the age of majority in medical treatment decisions.

Nonetheless, not all states and court decisions have recognized the assumption that prior parental consent is essential for children's medical treatment. In fact, parents often do not know what is best for their children, and some children can make decisions for themselves about their own lives. In addition, parents may have interests and preferences that do not coincide with those of the child. There are, for example, some well-recognized exceptions to the absolute necessity of parental consent in the area of medical care: (1) emergency treatment, (2) treatment of emancipated minors (minors living alone without financial support from their parents, and (3) treatment of mature minors, those minors above a given age with the capacity to understand the nature and consequences of a particular treatment program. Some states have passed statutes that allow various types of medical treatment without parental consent. Other jurisdictions have adopted comprehensive medical care statutes that in essence allow a minor to obtain any medical care without parental consent.

Some experts have called for more autonomy for minors in medical matters of a sensitive nature. For example, the American Bar Association suggests that minors not have to obtain parental consent for treatment involving venereal disease, contraception, and pregnancy.[5] Drug abuse and emotional disturbances are also sensitive areas where a rule requiring parental consent may be counterproductive to the child's interest. It remains for the various states to adopt such policies.

A good example of the Supreme Court's interjection into the area of parental consent and medical rights is the 1976 case of *Planned Parenthood of Central Missouri v. Danforth*. The Court ruled that a pregnant minor need not obtain prior consent from either her parents or her husband for an abortion during the first trimester of pregnancy.[6] Because of its significance to the children's rights movement, the Danforth case is summarized in Highlight 20–1.

Following the *Danforth* decision, the Supreme Court in the case of *Bellotti v. Baird* in July 1979 found unconstitutional a Massachusetts statute requiring a minor to seek parental consent before obtaining an abortion.[7] The Massachusetts statute also provided that, if parental consent were denied, a pregnant minor could seek a consent order from a superior court judge following a hearing. The Supreme Court voided the statute because it required the woman to go first to the parents for consent, a requirement that the *Danforth* decision had held unconstitutional.

Constitutional protections are as available to the newborn infant as to the most venerable adult in the nation.[8] Yet it is important to realize that in the area of intrafamily right to privacy and medical care the courts will balance the state's interest and need to protect the family and the individual child's best interests. Court decisions to date have not effectively given priority to either of these interests.

Highlight 20–1. The Danforth case.

Facts Two physicians brought suit to establish the constitutionality of a Missouri statute requiring women under eighteen to have the consent of parents, husband, or a person acting *in loco parentis* to the parents before being able to obtain an abortion. In addition, these women had to have their own informed consent.

Decision of the Case The Court decided that the state cannot constitutionally impose a blanket parental consent requirement as a condition for an unmarried minor's abortion during the first twelve weeks of her pregnancy. In its decision, the Court reasoned that there were no significant state interests to safeguard the family unit and parental authority in conditioning an

abortion on the consent of the parent with respect to a pregnant minor under eighteen.

Significance of the Case The Supreme Court recognizes that the choice to have an abortion is a decision of the pregnant adult and her physician during the first trimester of the pregnancy. It is a private decision, beyond state regulation. In *Danforth*, the Court extended that right to women under eighteen. As a result, such women can choose to have abortions without consent from parents, husband, guardian, or the child's father.

Source: 428 U.S. 52, 96 S.Ct. 2831 (1976).

CHILDREN'S RIGHTS OUTSIDE THE FAMILY

Two of the factors determining the scope and content of the rights of children in our society are the interrelationships of the child, the family, and the state and the doctrine of *in loco parentis*. Historically, the children's rights movement has recognized that the family has the paramount responsibility for the child's care and for decision-making about the child. In some instances the state exercises immediate control over a child and dictates the form and scope of parent-child relationships. In other cases the state maintains a hands-off policy and refuses to interfere in the relationship of the child with the parent and other social institutions. Schools, for example, have played a predominant role in making decisions about the care and education of the child for more than half a century. However, the rights of each of the parties—the parent, state, and child—are often ill-defined or confused. In recent years, the federal and state courts have taken an increasing interest in education and are attempting to define new legal rights for children.

The doctrine of *in loco parentis* comes into play when the child's parents are not accessible. For example, when a child is in school, the school authorities take the place of the parent in providing care, custody, and discipline. *In loco parentis* means that some adult or authority figure "takes the place of" the parent in caring for the child. This parental role in theory operates from the time students enter the school until the time they return home. While the school has custody of the children, it is to make decisions and take action as if it were their natural parents.

Many questions arise from this theory. What are the limitations under which the school can act? To what degree can the school control the students' rights in such areas as free speech, privacy, and property? Can the school impose curriculum matters on students and parents? What are the limits of school discipline?

Today, the school's right to control the child and the child's constitutional rights are often balanced by the courts. Thus, the almost absolute control that schools once had over children is slowly being tempered and redefined by the court system. When students challenge the right of the school to regulate certain conduct, it is the court's duty to balance the need for control against the students' individual constitutional interests. At issue is whether the necessity of maintaining order is more important in the child's education than the child's assertion of constitutional rights. In the past two decades court decisions have begun to emphasize individual student rights, particularly in the following areas: (1) the child's right to an education, (2) course content and curriculum development, (3) the right to free speech and assembly, (4) the student's right to make individual decisions about personal appearance and dress, (5) the child's right to protection from search and seizure in schools, and (6) the child's right to procedural due process of law within the school system.

The Right to Education

In America, compulsory school attendance statutes have been in effect for more than half a century.[9] Children are required by law to attend school until a given age, normally sixteen or seventeen.[10] Violations of compulsory attendance laws generally result in complaints that can lead to court action. Often, however, children are truant because of emotional problems or learning disabilities. They are then brought into the court system for problems beyond their control. Many of them might be better off leaving school at an earlier age than the compulsory education law allows. On the other hand, emotionally disturbed and nonconforming children are pushed out of many school systems and thus deprived of an education. Whether these children have a right to attend school is unclear. Many school systems ignore the difficult student, who may be classified as "bad" or "delinquent."

In 1925, the Supreme Court determined that compulsory education did not necessarily have to be provided by a public school system and that parochial schools could be a reasonable substitute.[11] From that time through the 1970's, the courts upheld the right of the state to make education compulsory. Then, in 1972, in the case of *Wisconsin v. Yoder*, the Supreme Court made an exception to the general compulsory education law by holding that traditional Amish culture was able to give its children the skills that would prepare them for adulthood within Amish society. Thus, their removal from school after the completion of the eighth grade was justified.[12] It is not clear, however, whether this decision speaks directly to the issue of compulsory education or whether it is simply another instance of freedom of religion. Thus, the state's role in requiring school attendance is still unsettled.

Curriculum Development

The right to determine what subjects a child studies does not rest solely with the state, or the parent, or even the child. Presumably the state has the superior expertise to determine what a school curriculum should contain. However, some courts have held that it is the fundamental right of the parent to raise the child.

In many instances, parental objection to school curriculums has led to court intervention. As early as 1923, the Supreme Court found a Nebraska statute unconstitutional because it forbade the teaching of a foreign language to a student who had not completed the eighth grade.[13] In 1943, the Court announced that reciting the Pledge of Allegiance to the flag should not be compulsory because it could violate a child's First Amendment right to freedom of speech.[14] Twenty years later, the Court held that mandatory participation in school prayers in public schools violated the child's First Amendment right to freedom of religion and therefore should not be part of the curriculum.[15]

These decisions do not give the parent a clear right to keep a child away from objectionable subjects and practices at school. Lower courts are mixed as to parents' rights in this matter. Where the subject is elective in nature—that is, beyond the basic three R's of reading, writing, and arithmetic—the parents have been able to have their children excused from school. However, where it involves the basic curriculum, the state can legitimately refuse the request to remove a child from the course.

These decisions reflect a position by the courts that provides every child with an education suitable to the child's physical, intellectual, and emotional needs.

As the American Bar Association's Juvenile Justice Standards Relating to School and Education state:

The right to an education . . . includes the right to an education that is appropriate for each individual student. . . . The particular educational needs of each student must be considered in that what happens to a student educationally must be a reflection of what will be appropriate to meet the student's educational needs. . . . The required effort should include an effort to obtain the funds necessary to provide an appropriate education and a careful judgment allocating available resources to achieve that end.[16]

This recognition of the child as an individual person with individual needs and interests moves counter to traditional notions of the child as a dependent person.

Freedom of Speech in Public Schools

Freedom of speech is granted and guaranteed in the First Amendment to the Constitution. The right has been divided into two major categories as it affects children in schools. The first category involves what is known as "passive speech," a form of expression not associated with the actual speaking of words. Examples include wearing armbands or political protest buttons. The most recent Supreme Court decision concerning a student's right to passive speech was in 1969 in the case of *Tinker v. Des Moines Independent Community School District*.[17] This case involved the right to wear black armbands to protest the war in Vietnam. High school students, aged sixteen and seventeen, were told they would be suspended if they demonstrated their objections to the Vietnam War by wearing black armbands. They went ahead and attended school wearing the armbands and were subsequently suspended. According to the Court, in order for the state, in the person of a school official, to justify the prohibition of an expression of opinion, it must be able to show that its action was caused by something more than a mere desire to avoid the discomfort and unpleasantness that accompany the expression of an unpopular view. Certainly, where it cannot be shown that the forbidden conduct will interfere with the discipline required to operate the school, the prohibition cannot be sustained. In the *Tinker* case, the Court indicated that there was no evidence that the school authorities had reason to believe that the wearing of the armbands would substantially interfere with the work of the school or infringe upon the rights of the students.[18]

The significance of this decision is that it recognizes the child's right to free speech in a public school system. As Justice Abe Fortas stated in his majority opinion, "Young people do not shed their constitutional rights at the schoolhouse door."[19] *Tinker* accomplished two things:

1. A child is entitled to free speech in school under the First Amendment of the United States Constitution.
2. The test used to determine whether the child has gone beyond proper speech is whether he or she materially and substantially interferes with the requirements of appropriate discipline in the operation of the school.

This was the first Supreme Court decision to define what was included in a student's right to free speech. More significantly, the decision asserted that students' rights were not to be ignored or overshadowed by the school's right to maintain order.

The second category of free speech is active speech, which involves the use of words, by one person or by a group, in the form of a demonstration. In this area, the courts have given much more support to the schools' efforts to maintain order and discipline. Because active speech often fails to pass the *Tinker* test of "material or substantial interference," schools have been permitted to discipline students involved in racial conflicts, sit-ins, walkouts, hall demonstrations, and refusals to attend class. The general justification for not allowing this form of speech is that the school is required to safeguard the best interests of all students, not just those participating in the demonstration. In other words, the right to freedom of speech must be balanced by the right to an orderly education. The courts have therefore allowed schools to prohibit and consequently punish interferences with the right of the general student population to an education.

The Right to Assembly and the Right to One's Own Appearance

Related to the issue of free speech are the right of students to assemble and the issue of their general appearance. For the most part, school systems have not been allowed to prohibit students from promoting and forming clubs or fraternities that meet on school grounds. Such groups can be prohibited only when the school can show that they do not pass the *Tinker* test of material or substantial interference with the school process. As far as student appearance is concerned, case law has established that students have the right to wear clothes and hair styles of their choice. Again, however, the decisions hinge on whether or not the student's appearance interferes significantly with the daily school process and the administration of the educational system.

Search and Seizure in Schools

One of the more significant issues in the area of student rights is the law of search and seizure as applied to students and their possessions on school grounds. Searches of students' persons or lockers become necessary when it is believed that a student is in the process of violating the criminal law. Drug abuse, theft, assault and battery, and racial conflicts in schools have increased the need for school authorities to protect the general welfare of their students. In some states, schools have a statutory right to conduct searches or report suspicious behavior to the police. Schools sometimes rely on students to inform the authorities about suspected violations of the law.

However, a considerable amount of confusion remains about students' constitutional rights under the Fourth Amendment with regard to search and seizure. How much authority does a school have acting *in loco parentis* to conduct a search, and how far can the school go in protecting other students' interests. Such questions as, "What are the due process rights of students who are to be searched?" "Who may conduct the search?" and "What is the extent of the search?" remain unanswered. Would a child's own parent, for example, who found the child smoking marijuana, be able to take the marijuana and turn it over to the police? Can a school that stands *in loco parentis* to the child turn the child over to the police if the drugs are found in the child's possession? Are the police required to give the child the *Miranda* warning prior to questioning the child at school? Does such a warning have to be given by a school administrator prior to such questioning? These are the kinds of issues that are constantly being litigated when children are accused of violating juvenile and criminal penal codes in school.

The most significant Court decision in recent years in the area of school searches is the case of *People v. Overton*.[20] In this case, detectives presented a Mt. Vernon high school vice-principal with a search warrant to search the persons and lockers of two students in the school. After unsuccessful body searches of the students, a detective went to the locker of the defendant's friends while another officer asked the defendant if his locker contained marijuana. Under persistent questioning, the defendant acknowledged that he did possess marijuana. Then the detective, the vice-principal, and the school custodian went to the child's locker. The locker was opened by the vice-principal and the detective. Marijuana was found in it. The trial court found that although the warrant was defective, the evidence taken from the locker was to be admitted at the trial because the school could and did consent to the legitimacy of the search on its premises.

This case is significant because it concludes that a student's locker is the school's property and that therefore only the school, not the student, needs to consent to the search. Although the police had a warrant that the court found improper and thus invalid, the search was legal because the owner of the property—the school—consented to it.

Other, lower-court, decisions have helped establish, limit, and define the scope of the school's authority in student searches and seizures. In the case of *In re Donaldson*, the court determined that a school official's warrantless search was permitted because the school official was not considered a public official and therefore not restricted by the necessity of a search warrant.[21] In the case of *People v. Bowers*, the court held that a school official can search a student's locker in the presence of police without a search warrant.[22] In the case of *In re W.*, a California court stated that the warrantless search of a student's locker was a right and a duty within the concept of *in loco parentis* provided that it was a reasonable search.[23] On the other hand, in an interesting twist, a Pennsylvania court held that a school official, as a private citizen and not as a state or public servant, could search without a warrant.[24] It further held that if the search was reasonable, it was not critical if the school official was a servant of the state or not. Finally, in the case of *People v. D.*, a New York court established specific criteria to be used in determining the validity of the search: (1) the student's age, (2) the student's history, (3) the student's record, (4) the student's previous history as to school disciplinary problems, (5) the seriousness of the current suspicion, and (6) the necessity for an immediate warrantless search.[25]

To determine whether or not a school official is justified in searching a student's body, most courts have required a standard of cause called "reasonable suspicion." In other words, the police officer or government official must have a reasonable suspicion that a child has violated the law in order to justify the search.

In summary, the critical issue with regard to the rights of the child and school searches is the extent of the student's Fourth Amendment protection against unreasonable searches and seizures as compared with the extent of the school's authority to conduct searches and the duty of the school under *in loco parentis* to protect other students. Basically, this means that the courts are faced with determining whether or not the student is entitled to due process before a search. That is, is a search warrant required prior to the search? Using Justice Fortas's comment as a basis, it would seem that a warrant is necessary. However, courts have generally excused the necessity of a warrant by concluding that the status of the individual conducting the search determines whether it is required. In other words, if a school official is considered a private citizen rather than an arm of the state, then the search is justified without a warrant. A private citizen is not held to the same standard of reasonable search as a state or public servant. Citizens are to be protected from government intrusion, but a private citizen need not get a warrant to search another's property. This does not excuse an unreasonable search, but it does excuse a reasonable warrantless search.

If the government or police are to search, or if the school official is considered a government official, a warrant is necessary even for a reasonable search. Yet it is important to recognize that courts have excused warrantless searches and made them legitimate by school officials who are considered public servants. The reason is that the school official acts as a public official consenting to a search of public property. What has emerged from these decisions is that regardless of how a teacher or school official is categorized, the search may be upheld. "Reasonableness" as the standard of the search is basically the major criterion for warrantless searches.

If school officials suspect that a certain student's locker contains drugs or stolen property, and if the subsequent warrantless search is based on the reasonable suspicion standard, the search is generally considered valid. In one of the latest school search cases, the Supreme Court in 1975 validated a Louisiana Supreme Court decision that held that a warrantless search of a student's possessions was *per se* unconstitutional, unless the search was for easily destructible evidence or evidence that could easily be removed from the place of the search. This case, *State v. Mora*, significantly increased students' rights to be free from unreasonable searches and seizures under the Fourth Amendment.[26]

School Discipline

Most states have statutes permitting teachers to use corporal punishment to discipline students in public school systems. Under *in loco parentis*, discipline is one of the assumed parental duties given to the school system. In two recent decisions, the Supreme Court upheld the schools' right to use corporal punishment. In the case of *Baker v. Owen*, the Court stated:

We hold that the Fourteenth Amendment embraces the right of parents generally to control the means and the discipline of their children, but that the state has a countervailing interest in the maintenance of order in the schools . . . sufficient to sustain the right of teachers and school officials to administer reasonable corporal punishment for disciplinary purposes. We also hold that teachers and school officials must accord to students minimal due process in the course of inflicting such punishment.[27]

In 1977, the Supreme Court again spoke on the issue of corporal punishment in school systems in the case of *Ingraham v. Wright,* which upheld the right of teachers to use corporal punishment.[28] The facts in this case were that James Ingraham and Roosevelt Andrews, two students, sustained injuries as a result of paddling in the Charles Drew Junior High School in Dade County, Florida. The legal problems raised in the case were (1) whether corporal punishment by teachers was a violation in this case of the Eighth Amendment against cruel and unusual punishment and (2) whether the due process clause of the Fourteenth Amendment required that the students receive proper notice and a hearing prior to receiving corporal punishment. The Court held that neither the Eighth Amendment nor the Fourteenth Amendment was violated in this case. Despite the fact that Ingraham suffered hematomas on his buttocks as a result of twenty blows with a wooden paddle and that Andrews was hurt in the arm, the Supreme Court ruled that such punishment was not a constitutional violation. The court established the standard that only reasonable discipline was allowed in school systems, but it excepted the degree of punishment administered in this case. The Court ruling seemed to indicate that the child's legal remedies in such cases should be handled administratively or on a case-by-case basis. The court agreed that the schools are open to public scrutiny and that statutory and other kinds of remedies should deter excesses such as those alleged in the Ingraham case. The key principle in *Ingraham* is that the reasonableness standard that the Court articulated represents the judicial attitude that the scope of the school's right to discipline a child is by no means more restrictive than the rights of the child's own parents to impose corporal punishment.

Other issues involving the legal rights of students include their due process rights when interrogated, if corporal punishment is to be imposed and when suspension and expulsion are threatened. When students are questioned by school personnel, no warning as to their legal rights to remain silent or right to counsel need be given. However, when school security guards, on-campus police officials and public police officers question students, such constitutional warnings are required. In the area of corporal punishment, procedural due process established with the case of *Baker v. Owen* requires that students at least be forewarned as to the possibilities of corporal punishment being used as a discipline. In addition, the *Baker* case requires a witness to the administration of corporal punishment and allows the student and the parent to elicit reasons for the punishment. The *Ingraham* case, however, did not reinforce the nature of these due process rights. With regard to suspension and expulsion, in 1976 the Supreme Court ruled in the case of *Goss v. Lopez* that any time a student is to be suspended up to a period of ten days, he or she is entitled to a hearing.[29] The hearing would not include a right to counsel or a right to confront or cross-examine witnesses. The Court went on to state in *Goss* that the extent of the procedural due process requirements would be established on a case-by-case basis. That is, each case would represent its own facts and have its own procedural due process elements.

In conclusion, the rights of students in primary, high school, and university settings are evolving. The schools are required to maintain order and administer an educational program, but the student has a right to constitutional and due process protection and treatment. The courts must balance the need for order and respect with the right of the individual student. The consequences for the juvenile justice system and society in general as to whether or not children receive their rights is considerable. When children are involved in obtaining illegal medical care (for example, abortion) or when they need medical care that is not available because their rights are not clear, these same children become troubled youths with a higher probability of entering the juvenile justice system. Youths whose problems in school result in truancy, or youths who have emotional problems because of the imposition of corporal punishment, tend to commit antisocial or delinquent behavior. These same children also may enter the juvenile justice system. Thus, when we do not recognize the rights of children generally, there is more of a possibility that children and adults will enter the juvenile and adult criminal justice systems.

THE RIGHTS OF SPECIAL CHILDREN

Special or exceptional children are those with physical or mental handicaps or learning disabilities. For many years this group of children received the lowest level of legal rights.

Among the many rights denied special children are the right to an education at public expense, the right to proper testing, evaluation, and classification, rights in the juvenile justice system, and the right to treatment when institutionalized at public expense.

The Right to Education at Public Expense

Major national organizations such as the National Advisory Committee on Criminal Justice Standards and Goals and the American Bar Association strongly advise that children with physical handicaps, emotional disturbance, and severe mental retardation have special educational opportunities developed for them.[30] Both groups recommend that schools develop special educational programs and that states review and recommend special educational statutes to permit more flexibility for providing resources and services for children in this category. An example of such an approach is the legislation passed in 1976 in Massachusetts establishing an extensive program in the public school system for children with special needs.[31]

The growth of special children's rights comes after many years of complete lack of interest and banishment from the public educational system. Children between the ages of seven and sixteen are subject to compulsory school attendance requirements. However, the laws did not necessarily apply to children who were physically or mentally incapacitated. Thus the implication was that school attendance of retarded or physically handicapped children was less important than the attendance of the overall school population. Handicapped children and special children were placed in special classes if they were available or excluded from school entirely. Even in the states that did make provision for educating special children, the teachers were often too few and too poorly trained. Long waiting lists made it difficult for children to gain access to programs.

However, in 1972, two federal district court decisions began to establish legal rights for special children. In the case of *Pennsylvania Association for Retarded Children v. State of Pennsylvania,* the district court of Pennsylvania held that special children are educable and therefore entitled to an education at public expense.[32] In addition, the case established due process requirements for children with special needs. The court held that any time an allegedly mentally retarded child between the ages of five years, six months and twenty-one years was recommended for change in educational status by a school department, due process must be afforded. The child must have an informal hearing, with the right to an attorney and the right to present evidence and cross-examine witnesses with regard to the change in educational status. This case was significant in that the court not only provided handicapped children with the right to an education but recognized that such children have individual problems and require individual programs and services. Therefore the school could not make decisions for the child without justification, purpose, and adequate information.

In the second case, that of *Mills v. Board of Education,* a federal district court took the Pennsylvania decision one step further and held that any child, regardless of classification, is entitled to a publicly funded education adequate for his or her needs and a constitutionally adequate hearing regarding the classification process.[33] The *Mills* case emphasized the difficulties associated with classifying children who have different levels of intellectual ability. Many moderately retarded persons have erroneously been classified as extremely retarded and institutionalized for life. Thus the *Mills* case emphasizes that a proper hearing regarding classification, reclassification, and educational program alternatives is needed when dealing with the treatment of the special child. Today, extensive rights in the area of procedural due process of law exist for students who may be in need of special treatment due to physical or mental handicaps or for any students in publicly supported educational systems.

Although the law seems reasonably clear with regard to the rights of special children in the area of education, an interesting dilemma occurred when the Supreme Court ruled in *San Antonio Independent School District v. Rodriguez* in 1973.[34] This case generally stated that there is no constitutional right to an education. However, the students involved in the *Rodriguez* case were not being denied access to an education, as were the children in the *Pennsylvania* and the *Mills* cases. They were contesting inconsistent allocation of state revenues between students from different school districts. Thus *Rodriguez* was not concerned with a complete denial of an education. Assuming this analysis is correct, the *Rodriguez* decision should not affect future litigation in the area of continuing the movement of providing rights for special or exceptional children. In fact, the American Bar Association points out that children have a right to an education that is appropriate for each individual student.[35]

Use of Testing Procedures for Special Children

A second major area of rights of special children deals with the adequacy and reliability of testing procedures. Retarded children and adults have most often been deprived of their rights because of major inaccuracies in the classification of mentally retarded persons. Many children who are inadequately classified may be placed in institutions. Others may be excluded from educational programs. Many retarded adults may be excluded from employment opportunities. The IQ level is the standard used to classify people. Mental retardation is a condition—a deficiency—not a disease. Retarded children can learn to their level of ability and performance. Many states today recognize these principles but have been unwilling to actively ensure proper testing for children. The unwillingness of courts to indicate the criteria for proper testing for children with special needs is reflected in the quality of existing educational programs.

Special Children and Juvenile Justice

Another problem related to the needs of special children involves their rights under the juvenile justice system when brought to court. It is difficult for law enforcement officials to distinguish between those who are mentally retarded in some instances and those who are not when they charge a person with a crime. Thus, the juvenile justice system and the adult system have failed to recognize the special problems of the retarded defendant or delinquent.

In many cases mentally retarded suspects cannot understand the charges brought against them. When the court does not recognize retardation, a child may be institutionalized for a long period of time. In some cases mentally retarded defendant may be innocent and unable to present an adequate defense because of the mental deficiency. Furthermore, some mentally retarded suspects may lack the criminal intent needed to commit an act of delinquency or crime, yet be unable to take advantage of legal opportunities given to normal children and adults. For example, those who are mentally ill or retarded may fail to claim a valid legal defense under laws involving insanity. Those in the juvenile justice system—police officers, probation personnel, juvenile court judges and institutional personnel—should be given training and should have some understanding and recognition of the factors involved in mental deficiency, mental retardation, and the problems of the special child.

The Right to Treatment When Institutionalized

In addition to the right to a public education and the rights associated with proper and accurate testing, the courts have become concerned about the child's right to institutionalized treatment. This entire issue is treated in Chapter 19. However, it is important to mention here that children who require special training outside a public school setting do have rights to proper treatment and care. In the case of *Wyatt v. Stickney,* the Court held that the purpose of institutionalizing people was to train them to cope with their environment. Once a person was institutionalized, he or she had a right to treatment.[36] Judge Frank Johnson in the *Wyatt* case sought to explain the need for a statutory as well as constitutional right of treatment for all classes of children. According to Johnson, rehabilitation in the *Wyatt* case includes but is not limited to programs of formally structured education and treatment. Thus, when one analyzes the *Wyatt* decision in light of the previously discussed *Pennsylvania* and *Mills* cases, it seems to be established that the state is responsible for the educational care of all special children, no matter what their degree of mental illness or retardation or physical disability and no matter where they are living—whether at home or in an institution.

A BILL OF RIGHTS FOR CHILDREN

A bill of rights for children is a statement of principles not formulated in law that are intended to guarantee the welfare of children. Such a statement is essential for the following reasons:

1. Children are persons and have basic rights.
2. The definition of who is a child legally is essential to operate our legal system.
3. The treatment of children in the various institutions of our society requires an understanding of the rights and laws of child care.
4. The concept of delinquency prevention in health care, education, recreation, and employment requires that children be treated properly, lest they develop a greater propensity for deviant behavior.

Probably one of the clearest statements involving a bill of rights for children has been written by Foster and Freed. Its principles are enunciated in Highlight 20-2.

Highlight 20-2. A Bill of Rights for Children

A child has a moral right and should have a legal right (1) to receive parental love and affection, discipline and guidance, and to grow to maturity in a home environment which enables him to develop into a mature and responsible adult; (2) to be supported, maintained, and educated to the best of parental ability in return for which he has a moral duty to honor his father and mother; (3) to be regarded as a person with the family, at school; and before the law; (4) to receive fair treatment from all in authority; (5) to be heard and listened to; (6) to earn and keep his own earnings; (7) to seek and obtain medical care and treatment, and counseling; (8) to emancipation from the parent-child relationship when that relationship has broken down and the child has left home due to abuse, neglect, serious family conflict, or other sufficient cause, and his best interests would be served by the termination of parental authority; (9) to be free of legal disabilities or incapacities save where such are convincingly shown to be necessary and protective of the actual best interest of the child; and (10) to receive special care, consideration, and protection in the administration of law and justice so that his best interests always are a paramount factor.

Source: Henry Foster, Jr., and Doris Freed, "A Bill of Rights for Children," *New York Law Journal,* 1972.

The substance of these principles recognizes the child as a person under the law, with legal rights. Furthermore, these principles address the need to balance the concept of *parens patriae* and establish the philosophical base of *In re Gault* in regard to the pragmatic need to safeguard rights instead of simply having good intentions when dealing with the child. A bill of rights for children recognizes the inherent danger of *parens patriae* power while acknowledging its desire for the best interests of the child. In addition, these principles take into account the idea of *in loco parentis*, whereby certain other people or institutions take on the parental role. When that occurs, it is important that children know their rights and are able to contribute to what is in their own best interests.

The first two rights stem from the basic need of the child. The child has a right to love, affection, and maintenance. As the child becomes increasingly recognized as a person, with rights and the ability to make decisions, the courts have become more aggressive in insisting that parents perform the necessary duties to provide for the child's needs. Despite the courts' historical reluctance to get involved in family matters, recent case decisions indicate a willingness to ensure that these rights are honored. Public policy and human decency dictate that the care and custody of the community's children be guaranteed. In the future, family autonomy will probably not be a barrier to the courts' involvement in ensuring that the child's interests are protected. This trend is visible today with efforts against arbitrariness in the juvenile court, the establishment of rights for children in areas of civil commitment, and the development of laws and controls with regard to child abuse.

Rights three, four, and five combine to give the child status equal with adults in the eyes of society. The essence of these principles is expressed in the care of *In re Gault*. This landmark decision placed checks and balances on the arbitrary exercise of parental and institutional authority over the welfare of children.

Principle six deals with the problem of youth employment in our society. Children are expected to keep their own earnings when employed and to be paid for work performed. This principle embodies the need to reconcile employment during school, problems of the minimum age of employment, and employment in hazardous activities. In addition it recognizes the right of children to earn and to keep their own earnings rather than to turn them over to the family. It further recognizes that when children make purchases, they have a right to keep them.

Principle seven, that of medical treatment, is one of the areas where children's rights have noticeably improved. Many highly personal and sensitive areas of medical care are now available to children without prior parental consent. The Supreme Court has already recognized such rights in the area of abortion and contraception. State statutes cover medical care for venereal disease, psychiatric problems, drug addiction, and emergencies. In addition, some states have created mature minor or emancipated minor laws that recognize certain children to be capable of consenting to their own medical treatment. Some states have gone so far as to adopt statutes permitting children to consent to any form of medical treatment. The ultimate goal inherent in this principle is not to eliminate the parent in medical decision making but to further recognize the child as a person who knows what is in his or her best interest.

Principle eight deals with the issue of emancipation. The traditional doctrine of emancipation involves the continued use of parental authority over the child. Many jurisdictions have different ages for emancipation in general and for the concept of majority with regard to voting, drinking, driving, employment, and so on. The American Bar Association recommends that the emancipation doctrine should be reviewed by various state legislatures in order to make uniform the laws and rules governing legal relationships between parents and children. In addition, the ABA standards recommend that parents not be able to recover from a child's employer wages due the child and that a child be permitted to sue parents for damages arising from intentionally damaging or negligent behavior.

The right to be considered emancipated from the control of a parent before reaching the age of majority permits children in various domestic situations to be considered independent of their parents and capable of asserting their own rights as individuals. When a child is neglected or abused or in a difficult domestic conflict, it is possible that the parent cannot determine what is in the child's best interests. The right to be considered emancipated before reaching majority allows children a voice in developing solutions to their problems. Today, literally thousands of minors have left home or are alienated from their families. They drift from city to city and from district to district within the cities. Runaways of both sexes abound throughout the country. In legal theory many of these children are still subject to parental control. An appropriate emancipation law would help clarify their legal interests. States have already adopted statutes giving minors the right to participate in various activities such as voting, drinking, and marriage. This practice could very well be extended to establish that the right to consent hinges not on parental control but on a doctrine of emancipation under which children are capable of making decisions for themselves.

Principle nine deals with freeing children from legal disabilities in such areas as employment and compulsory school education, as well as freeing them from limitations on ownership of property, on suing family members, and on entering into validly drawn contracts. This principle is consistent with the growing acceptance of children as people. The blanket assumption that children are in need of protection in all of these areas pervades most aspects of their lives. It is not necessarily in their best interests. Rather than assume that a minor is incapable of contracting, for example, it would be preferable to adopt a general rule that minors have the capacity to contract and are bound by agreements. This principle is in keeping with the statement of Commissioner Patricia Wald in her dissenting view in the American Bar Association Standards dealing with the Rights of Minors. Wald disagrees with the existing theories about emancipation, minors' contracts, and support obligations because they are premised on a doctrine of family autonomy. Instead, Wald suggests that children from birth forward should be assumed to have all legal rights of adults against anyone who intentionally or negligently harms them.

Principle ten emphasizes the fact that although children are entitled to rights similar to adults, they should be given every opportunity to develop and assert themselves as individuals. In addition, children are still a special concern in our society, and that factor should be taken into account to improve their chances for adequate care and development. Thus action should be taken to improve educational programs in schools, to ensure a fair system of justice in the courts, and to accept the fact that students as individuals have rights with regard to speech, privacy, and appearance, particularly in the educational system.

In summary, the most practical use of a bill of rights for children is to help establish these rights under the law. The Foster and Freed statement is philosophic in nature, but it includes pragmatic concerns. Both the pragmatic and philosophic statements recognize children as persons. Many inconsistencies between the treatment of children and adults continue to exist today. For example, children can be tried and sent to a correctional institution for being incorrigible. Adults are not tried and convicted for such a crime. Children can be sent to jail for refusing to attend school. Adults cannot. Children are often denied the opportunity to vote, to serve on juries, and, generally, to participate in the political process.

At the same time, the courts have continued to recognize the concept of family autonomy and control by parents, although in recent years some effort has been made to recognize the independence of children. What the future will bring in the area of minors' rights is unclear. Many legal and constitutional issues remain to be decided—the constitutional right to treatment for children in institutions, the rights of children involved in foster care programs, the continuing battle for the rights of children who are mentally retarded, the rights of children under support obligation, and the rights of children of separated and divorced parents. If these issues are neglected by the courts, such children could be cast aside and lose the opportunity for a decent and meaningful existence.

The issue of age is a significant factor in the juvenile court system. Jurisdiction over a child is determined by age, and the various jurisdictions in this country have different age determinations. Yet the Twenty-sixth Amendment to the Constitution provides "that the right of citizens of the United States who are 18 years of age or older to vote shall not be denied or abridged by the United States or by any state on account of age." This Amendment establishes a minimum age for voter qualification in America. However, it does not deny states the opportunity to use different ages for other legal actions, such as marriage, drinking, and employment.

Most states have reduced the age of majority to eighteen for virtually all legal purposes. Using eighteen as the age of majority in all areas is a valid approach to creating uniformity and improving the general framework of legal rights for children. It helps to place in perspective the role of the child-adult in our society and makes for a clearer definition and understanding of the usefulness of the juvenile justice system.

CHAPTER SUMMARY

Legal rights of minors concerns the rights of children vis-a-vis the parent and the state. Previous chapters discussed the rights of children charged with delinquency and status offenses in the juvenile justice system. This chapter concerns the other side of the coin, mainly areas where the parent or state controls the child who has not committed criminal acts.

In years past, civil libertarians were primarily concerned with the rights of parents. The courts litigated the rights of parents in the area of criminal justice, domestic relations, and medical care. Many condemned intrusions on the parents' privacy, individual liberty, and welfare.

On the other hand, today the focus is moving towards the juvenile's right to invoke the power of the court for his or her protection. Thus, this chapter deals with children's rights within the family, such as the right to medical care and privacy, and the children's rights outside the family, such as the rights to education, freedom of speech, and procedural due process in school discipline. The fundamental question has been to what extent a minor child should be given rights similar to those of an adult outside the juvenile justice system. In other words, should a child be subject to legal disabilities because of age? The courts, in years past, have almost always answered this question on the basis of such principles as the concept of family autonomy, the uniqueness of the parent-child relationship, and the concept of the child's best interests. But the courts have moved to eliminate the view that a child is without rights and is theoretically the parents' total possession.

The chapter concludes with an analysis of the rights of special children, such as those with physical and learning disabilities and those who are mentally retarded. Finally, from the standpoint of a just society, not just constitutional or statutory law, the concept of a bill of rights for children is discussed. Its emphasis is on showing the broad range of areas that need to be developed in approaching the issue of juvenile justice and children's rights today.

DISCUSSION QUESTIONS

1. Throughout the past two decades, the courts have expanded the legal rights of children. Define and discuss those areas where children's rights have been granted by the courts.

2. What is the meaning of the First Amendment to the Constitution? Does this Amendment mean that a child may speak out on any issue even if in conflict with a school system or parents' wishes?

3. A police officer arrests a child in school for possession of marijuana after a search of the child and the child's locker. Will the conduct of the search and whether or not the child voluntarily consented to the search be an issue when the case goes to the juvenile court?

4. Discuss how far you think the government or the court can go in providing children with due process rights. Is there need, for example, for a special bill of rights for children?

5. Numerous decisions are made daily about children by the courts in cases involving custody, juvenile delinquency, and neglect. Does the child have special rights to make his or her position known to the court? What is the relationship between the state, the parent, and the child in making such decisions? Who has the primary responsibility for the child's care in today's society?

SUGGESTED READINGS

Allen, Francis. *Legal Values and the Rehabilitative Ideal*. Chicago: University of Chicago Press, 1964.

Bartley v. Dremens, 402 F.Supp. 1039.

Brant, Irving. *The Bill of Rights: Its Origin and Meaning*. New York: Mentor Books, 1967.

Bykofsky v. Borough of Middletown, 401 F.Supp. 1242.

Cardozo, Benjamin. *The Nature of the Judicial Process*. New Haven, Conn.: Yale University Press, 1921.

Edwards, Leonard. "The Rights of Children." *Federal Probation* 37 (1973): 34–41.

Forer, Louis. "Rights of Children: The Legal Vacuum." *American Bar Association Journal* 55 (1969): 1151–1156.

Goldstein, Joseph; Freud, Anna; and Solnot, Albert. *Beyond the Best Interests of the Child*. New York: Free Press, 1973.

Katz, Sanford; Schroeder, William; and Sidman, Laurence. "Emancipating Our Children — Coming of Legal Age in America." *Family Law Quarterly* 7 (1973): 211–241.

Levine, Alan, with Eve Carey and Diane Divoky. *The Rights of Students*. New York: Avon Books, 1973.

Mack, Julian W. "The Juvenile Court." *Harvard Law Journal* 23 (1909): 104.

Note, "Parental Consent Requirements and Privacy Rights of Minors." *Harvard Law Review* 88 (1975): 1001.

Rawls, John. *A Theory of Justice*. Cambridge, Mass.: Harvard University Press, 1971.

Roe v. Wade, 410 U.S. 113, 93 S.Ct. 705 (1973).

Rodman, Hillary. "Children under the Law." *Harvard Educational Review* 43 (1973).

Rosenheim, Margaret K., ed. *Pursuing Justice for the Child*. Chicago: University of Chicago Press, 1976.

Rosen, Paul. *The Supreme Court and Social Science*. Urbana: University of Illinois Press, 1972.

Silverman, "Children's Rights and Social Work," *Social Service Review* 51 (1977): 171.

Wald, Patricia. "Making Sense out of the Rights of Youth." *Human Rights* 4 (1974): 13.

Wilkerson, *The Rights of Children: Emergent Concepts in Law and Society*. Philadelphia: Temple University Press, 1973.

Wilkins, Parental Consent Barrier to Medical Treatment of Minors." *Arizona State Law Journal* 31 (1975): Woodward, Bob, and Armstrong, Scott. *The Brethren—Inside the Supreme Court*. New York: Simon and Schuster, 1979.

REFERENCES

1. Sanford Katz, ed. *The Youngest Minority—Lawyers in Defense of Children* (American Bar Association, 1974), p. 1.

2. 381 U.S. 479, 85 S.Ct. 1678 (1965).

3. 390 U.S. 629, 88 S.Ct. 1274 (1968).

4. See American Bar Association, *Standards on Juvenile Justice: Standards Relating to Rights of Minors* (Cambridge, Mass.: Ballinger Publishing, 1977).

5. Ibid., p. 50.

6. 428 U.S. 52, 96 S.Ct. 2831, 49 L.Ed. 2d 788 (1976).

7. 443 U.S. 622, 99 S.Ct. 3035 (1979).

8. See *Miller v. Gillis,* 315 F.Supp. 94 (1969).

9. For an interesting article on compulsory education, see S. Arons, "Compulsory Education: The Plain People Resist," *Saturday Review* 15 (1972): pp. 63-69.

10. Ibid.

11. See *Pierce v. Society of Sisters,* 268 U.S. 510, 45 S.Ct. 571, 69 L.Ed. 1070 (1925).

12. 406 U.S. 205, 92 S.Ct. 1526, 32 L.Ed. 2d 15 (1972).

13. *Meyer v. Nebraska,* 262 U.S. 390, 43 S.Ct. 625 (1923).

14. See *West Virginia State Board of Education v. Barnette,* 319 U.S. 624, 63 S.Ct. 1178 (1943).

15. *School District of Abington v. Schemmp,* 374 U.S. 203, 83 S.Ct. 1560, 10 L.Ed. 2d 844 (1963).

16. American Bar Association, *Standards of Juvenile Justice: Standards Relating to Schools and Education* (Cambridge, Mass.: Ballinger Publishing, 1977), p. 37.

17. 393 U.S. 503, 89 S.Ct. 733 (1969).

18. Ibid.

19. Ibid., p. 741.

20. 24 N.Y.2d 522, 301 N.Y.S.2d 479, 249 N.E.2d 366 (1969).

21. 75 Cal. Rptr. 220 (1909).

22. 77 Misc.2d 697, 356 N.Y.S.2d 432 (1974).

23. 29 Cal.App.3d 777, 105 Cal. Rptr. 775 (1973).

24. See *Com. of Penn. v. Dingfelt,* 227 Pa. Super. 380, 323 A.2d 145 (1974).

25. 34 N.Y.2d 483, 358 N.Y.S.2d 403, 315 N.E.2d 466 (1974).

26. 307 So.2d 317 (La. App. 1975).

27. 423 U.S. 907, 96 S.Ct. 210, 46 L.Ed. 2d 137 (1975).

28. 430 U.S. 651, 97 S.Ct. 1401 (1977).

29. 419 U.S. 565, 95 S.Ct. 729 (1976).

30. See, generally, National Advisory Commission on Criminal Justice Standards and Goals, *Report of Task Force on Juvenile Justice and Delinquency Prevention* (Washington, D.C.: Law Enforcement Assistance Administration, 1976); American Bar Association, *Project on Standards for Juvenile Justice: Standards Relating to Schools and Education.*

31. See Chapter 766, M.G.L. 1972, Law and Procedure Aiding the Special Needs of Children.

32. 343 F.Supp. 279 (D.C. Pa. 1972).

33. 348 F.Supp. 866 (1972).

34. 411 U.S. 959, 93 S.Ct. 1919, 36 L.Ed. 2d 418 (1973).

35. American Bar Association, *Project on Standards for Juvenile Justice: Standards Relating to Schools and Education,* p. 11.

36. 344 F.Supp. 387 (M.D. Ala. 1972).

Appendix A
Glossary

acquittal   Release or discharge, especially by verdict of a jury.

action   Lawsuit; a proceeding taken in a court of law. Actions are either civil, to enforce a right, or criminal, to punish an offender.

adjudicated   Having been the subject of completed criminal or juvenile proceedings and having been convicted or declared a delinquentt, status offender, or dependent.

adjudication (juvenile)   Juvenile court decision, terminating a hearing, that the juvenile is a delinquent, a status offendor, or a dependent or that the allegations in the petition are not sustained.

adjudicatory hearing   In juvenile proceedings, the fact-finding process wherein the juvenile court determines whether there is sufficient evidence to sustain the allegations in a petition.

adjustment   Settlement or bringing to a satisfactory state so that parties are agreed without official intervention of the court.

adversary system   Procedure used to determine guilt or innocence that pits the defense (advocate for the accused) against the prosecution (advocate for the state), with the judge acting as arbiter of the legal rules. Under the adversary system, the burden is on the state to prove the charges beyond a reasonable doubt.

affidavit   Written statement of fact, signed and sworn to before a person having authority to administer an oath.

aftercare   Supervision given children for a limited period of time after they are released from a training school but still under the control of the school or of the juvenile court.

appeal   Review of lower court proceedings by a higher court. There is no constitutional right to appeal; however, the right has been established by statute in some states and by custom in others.

appellant   Party who initiates an appeal from one court to another.

appellee   Party in a lawsuit against whom an appeal has been taken.

arrest   Taking persons into custody to restrain them until they can be held accountable for an offense at court proceedings. The legal requirement for an arrest is probable cause.

arrest warrant   Written court order by a magistrate authorizing and directing that an individual be taken into custody to answer criminal charges.

bail   Amount of money that has to be paid as a condition of pretrial release, normally set by a judge at the initial appearance. The purpose of bail is to ensure that people accused of crimes will return for subsequent proceedings. If they are unable to make bail, they are detained in jail.

beyond a reasonable doubt   Degree of proof required for conviction of a defendant in criminal proceedings. It is less than absolute certainty but more than high probability. If there is doubt based on reason, the accused is entitled to the benefit of that doubt by acquittal.

booking   Administrative record of an arrest made in police stations. It involves listing offender's name, address, physical description, date of birth, employer, time of arrest, offense, and name of arresting officer. Photographing and fingerprinting of the offender are also part of booking. The *Miranda* warning is given again (the first time was at the scene of the arrest). In addition, the accused is allowed to make a telephone call.

burden of proof   Duty of proving disputed facts on the trial of a case. The duty commonly lies on the person who asserts the affirmative of an issue and is sometimes said to shift when sufficient evidence is furnished to raise a presumption that what is alleged is true.

case law   Law derived from previous court decisions; opposed to statutory law, which is passed by legislatures.

certiorari   Literally, to be informed of, to be made certain in regard to. The name of a writ of review or inquiry.

chancery court   Court proceeding to the forms and principles of equity.

child abuse   Willful action or actions by a person causing physical harm to a child.

child neglect   Willful failure by the person(s) responsible for a child's well-being to provide for adequate food, clothing, shelter, education, and supervision.

commitment   Action of a judicial officer ordering that an adjudicated and sentenced adult or adjudicated delinquent or status offender who has been the subject of a juvenile court disposition hearing be admitted to a correctional facility.

common law   The basic legal principles that developed in England and became uniform (common) throughout the country. Judges began following previous court decisions (precedent) when new, but similar, cases arose.

community facility (nonconfinement facility, adult or juvenile)   Correctional facility from which residents are regularly permitted to depart, unaccompanied by an official, to use community resources such as schools or treatment programs or to seek or hold employment.

concurrent sentences   Literally, running sentences together. The condition set for serving sentences of imprisonment for multiple charges. When people are convicted of two or more charges, they must be sentenced on each charge. If the sentences are concurrent, they begin the same day and are completed after the longest term has been served.
See also Consecutive Sentences.

conflict theory   Theory that conflict among interest groups, especially those of opposing socioeconomic classes, is the main determinant of human behavior.

consecutive sentences   Literally, sentences that follow one another. Upon completion of one sentence, the other term of incarceration begins. *See also* Concurrent Sentences.

consent decree   Decree entered by consent of the parties. Not properly a judicial sentence, but in the nature of a solemn contract or agreement of the parties that the decree is a just determination of their rights based on the real facts of the case, if such facts are proved.

constitutional law   Branch of the public law of a state that maintains the framework of political and government authorities and functions in accordance with the Constitution.

conviction   Judgment of guilt; verdict by a jury, plea by a defendant, or judgment by a court that the accused is guilty as charged.

correctional institution   Generic name for long-term adult confinement facilities that are often called prisons, federal or state correctional facilities, or penitentiaries, and for juvenile confinement facilities that are often called training schools, reformatories, boy's ranches, and the like.

correctional institution (juvenile)   Confinement facility having custodial authority over delinquents and status offenders committed to confinement after a juvenile disposition hearing.

corrections   Generic term that includes all government agencies, facilities, programs, procedures, personnel, and techniques concerned with the investigation, intake, custody, confinement, supervision, or treatment of alleged or adjudicated adult offenders, delinquents, or status offenders.

court   Agency of the judicial branch of government authorized or established by statute or constitution and consisting of one or more judicial officers that has the authority to decide upon controversies in law and disputed matters of fact brought before it.

crime   Offense against the state; behavior in violation of law for which there is prescribed punishment.

criminal justice process   Decision-making process from the initial investigation or arrest by police to the eventual release of offenders and their reentry into society; the various sequential criminal stages through which offenders pass.

criminal justice standards   Models, commentaries, or recommendations for the revision of criminal justice procedures and practices; for example, the American Law Institute's Model Penal Code, the American Bar Association's Standards for Criminal Justice, and the recommendations of the National Advisory Commission on Criminal Justice Standards and Goals.

criminal justice system   Group of agencies and organizations—police, courts, and corrections—as well as the legislation and appellate courts responsible for the administration of criminal justice and crime control.

criminal law   Body of law that defines criminal offenses and prescribes punishments (substantive law) and that delineates criminal procedure (procedural law).

criminology   Study of the causes and treatment of criminal behavior, criminal law, and the administration of criminal justice.

culpable   Implication of a wrongful act but one that does not involve malice. It connotes fault rather than guilt.

deinstitutionalization   Closing of institutions and moving inmates to community-based programs.

delinquency   Juvenile actions or conduct in violation of criminal law and, in some contexts, status offenders.

delinquent   Juvenile who has been adjudicated by a judicial officer of a juvenile court as having committed a delinquent act.

delinquent act   Act committed by a juvenile for which an adult could be prosecuted in a criminal court. A juvenile who commits such an act can be adjudicated in a juvenile court or prosecuted in a criminal court if the juvenile court transfers jurisdiction.

dependency   Legal status of juveniles over whom a juvenile court has assumed jurisdiction because the court has found their care by parents, guardians, or custodians to fall short of a legal standard of proper care.

dependents   Juveniles over whom a juvenile court has assumed jurisdiction because the court has found their care by parents, guardians, or custodians to fall short of a legal standard of proper care.

detention   Temporary care of a child alleged to be delinquent who requires secure custody in physically restricting facilities pending court disposition or execution of a court order.

detention center   Government facility that provides temporary care in a physically restricting environment for juveniles in custody pending court disposition.

detention facility (juvenile)   Confinement facility having custodial authority over juveniles confined pending and after adjudication.

detention hearing   In juvenile proceedings, a hearing by a judicial officer of a juvenile court to determine whether a juvenile is to be detained, to continue to be detained, or to be released while juvenile proceedings are pending in the case.

differential association   A theory positing that criminal behavior is learned when an individual encounters an excess of definitions favoring law violations over those that support conformity to law; also learned in primary groups characterized by intimacy.

discretion   Privilege conferred by law on officials or official agencies to act in certain situations according to the dictates of their own judgment and conscience; subject to review if abused. Ability to distinguish between good and evil.

disposition (juvenile court)   Decision of a juvenile court concluding a disposition hearing that a juvenile be committed to a correctional facility, be placed in a care or treatment program, be required to meet certain standards of conduct, or be released.

disposition hearing   A hearing in juvenile court conducted after an adjudicatory hearing and subsequent receipt of the report of any predisposition investigation to determine the most appropriate disposition of a juvenile who has been adjudicated a delinquent, a status offender, or a dependent.

diversion   The official halting or suspension of formal criminal or juvenile justice proceedings against an alleged offender at any legally prescribed processing point after a recorded justice system entry and the referral of that person to a treatment or care program administered by a nonjustice public agency or a private agency or the recommendation that the person be released.

due process   Constitutional principle based on the concepts of the primacy of the individual and the limitation of government power; a safeguard against arbitrary and unfair state procedures in judicial or administrative proceedings. Embodied in the concept are the basic rights of a defendant in criminal proceedings and children in juvenile proceedings and the requisites for a fair trial. These rights and requirements have been expanded by appellate court decisions and include (1) timely notice of a hearing or trial that informs the accused of the charges; (2) the opportunity to confront accusers and to present evidence on one's own behalf before an impartial jury or judge; (3) the presumption of innocence under which guilt must be proved by legally obtained evidence and the verdict must be supported by the evidence presented; (4) the right of accused persons to be warned of their constitutional rights at the earliest stage of the criminal process; (5) protection against self-incrimination; (6) assistance of counsel at every critical stage of the criminal process; and (7) the guarantee that an individual will not be tried more than once (double jeopardy) for the same offense.

emancipation   Relinquishment of the care, custody, and earnings of a minor child and the renunciation of parental duties.

family court   Court with broad jurisdiction over family matters, such as neglect, delinquency, paternity, support, and noncriminal behavior.

felony   Criminal offense punishable by death or by incarceration in a state or federal confinement facility for a period whose lower limit is prescribed by statute in a given jurisdiction, typically one year or more.

finding of fact   Court's determination of the facts presented as evidence in a case, affirmed by one party and denied by the other.

fine   The court-imposed penalty requiring that a convicted person pay a specified sum of money.

gang   Group of persons who act in concert, mainly for criminal purposes.

group home   Nonconfining residential facility for adjudicated adults or juveniles or those subject to criminal or juvenile proceedings, intended to reproduce as closely as possible the circumstances of family life and at minimum providing access to community activities and resources.

guardian   Person who has the legal responsibility for the care and custody of a minor child.

habeas corpus   Literally, you have the body. A variety of writs whose objective is to bring a party before a court or judge. The function of the writ is to release the person from unlawful imprisonment.

halfway house   Nonconfining residential facility for adjudicated adults or juveniles or for those subject to criminal or juvenile proceedings, intended to provide an alternative to confinement for persons not suitable for probation or in need of a period of readjustment to the community after confinement.

hearing   Presentation of evidence to the juvenile court judge, the judge's consideration of it, and the decision on disposition of the case.

hearing (probable cause)   Presentation of evidence to the juvenile court judge, the judge's consideration of it, and the decision on disposition of the case.

incarceration   Putting a person in prison. The basic purposes of such confinement have been punishment, deterrence, rehabilitation, and integration into the community.

index offenses   Crimes used by the FBI to indicate the incidence of crime in the United States and reported annually in the Uniform Crime Reports. They include murder and nonnegligent manslaughter, robbery, rape, aggravated assault, burglary, larceny $50 and over, and motor vehicle theft.

indictment   Written accusation returned by a grand jury that charges an individual with a specified crime after determination of probable cause. The prosecutor presents enough evidence to establish probable cause.

indigent   Person who is needy and poor or who lacks the means to provide a living.

inmate   Person in a confinement facility.

insanity Unsoundness of mind that prevents one from comprehending the consequences of one's acts or from distinguishing between right and wrong.

intake Process during which a juvenile referral is received and a decision is made to file a petition in juvenile court, to release the juvenile, to place the juvenile under supervision, or to refer the juvenile elsewhere.

intake unit Government agency or unit of an agency that receives juvenile referrals from police, other government agencies, private agencies, or individuals and screens them, resulting in closing of the case, referral to care or supervision, or filing of a petition in juvenile court.

jail Confinement facility, usually administered by a local law enforcement agency, that is intended for adults but sometimes also contains juveniles. It detains persons pending adjudication and persons committed after adjudication for sentences of a year or less.

judge Judicial officer who has been elected or appointed to preside over a court of law. The position is created by statute or by constitution, and the officer's decisions in criminal and juvenile cases can be reviewed only by a judge of a higher court and cannot be reviewed de novo.

judgment Statement of the decision of a court that the defendant is convicted or acquitted of the offense(s) charged.

judicial officer Any person exercising judicial powers in a court of law.

jurisdiction Every kind of judicial action; the authority of courts and judicial officers to decide cases.

just desserts Idea that the distribution of penalties among convicted offenders should be decided chiefly by reference to the seriousness of the offense and the number and seriousness of prior convictions.

juvenile court Court that has original jurisdiction over persons defined by statute as juveniles and alleged to be delinquents, status offenders, or dependents.

juvenile delinquent Youth, within the age established by statute, who has been adjudicated by a juvenile court to have committed a prohibited act or to be in need of supervision. Age limitations of "juveniles" vary among the states from sixteen to twenty-one years, with the most common being eighteen years.

juvenile justice agency Government agency or subunit thereof whose functions are the investigation, supervision, adjudication, care, or confinement of juveniles whose conduct or condition has brought or could bring them within the jurisdiction of a juvenile court.

Juvenile Justice and Delinquency Prevention Act of 1974 Federal law establishing an office of juvenile justice within the LEAA to provide funds for the control of juvenile crime.

juvenile justice process Court proceedings for youths within the juvenile age group that differ from the adult criminal process.

juvenile record   Official record containing, at a minimum, summary information pertaining to an identified juvenile concerning juvenile court proceedings and, if applicable, detention and correctional processes.

labeling theory   Theory that views society as creating deviance through a system of social control agencies that designate certain individuals as deviants. The stigmatized individual is made to feel unwanted in the normal social order. Eventually, the individual begins to believe that the label is accurate, assumes it as a personal identity, and enters into a deviant or criminal career.

law   Method for the resolution of disputes. A rule of action to which people obligate themselves to conform, via their elected representatives and other officials. The principles and procedure of the common law, as distinguished from those of equity.

law enforcement agency   Federal, state, or local criminal justice agency of which the principal functions are the prevention, detection, and investigation of crime and the apprehension of alleged offenders.

law enforcement officer   Employee of a law enforcement agency who is an officer sworn to carry out law enforcement duties or a sworn employee of a prosecutorial agency who performs primarily investigative duties. Also called police officer.

law guardian   Person with the legal authority and duty of taking care of someone and managing the property and rights of that person, if the person is considered incapable of administering the affairs personally.

Law Enforcement Assistance Administration   Unit in the United States Department of Justice established by the Omnibus Crime Control and Safe Streets Act of 1968 to administer grants and provide guidance for crime prevention policy and programs.

line-up   Pre-trial identification procedure in which a suspect is placed in a group for the purpose of being identified by a witness.

mandamus   Literally, we command. A legal, not an equitable, remedy. When issued, it is an inflexible peremptory command to do a particular thing.

manslaughter   Voluntary (nonnegligent) killing. Intentionally causing the death of another with reasonable provocation.

minor   Person who is under the age of legal consent.

Miranda warning   The result of two Supreme Court decisions (*Escobedo v. Illinois*, 378 U.S. 478, 1964 and *Miranda v. Arizona*, 384 U.S. 436, 1966) that require a police officer to inform individuals under arrest of their constitutional rights. Although aimed at protecting individuals during in-custody interrogation, the warning must also be given when the investigation shifts from the investigatory to the accusatory stage—that is, when suspicion begins to focus on an individual.

misdemeanor   Offense punishable by a fine or by incarceration for not more than one year in a county jail. There is no uniform rule; an offense can be a misdemeanor in one jurisdiction and a felony in another.

Model Penal Code   Generalized modern codification of that which is considered basic to criminal law, published by the American Law Institute in 1962.

murder   Intentionally causing the death of another without reasonable provocation or legal justification or causing the death of another while committing or attempting to commit another crime.

National Council on Crime and Delinquency   Private national agency promoting efforts at crime control through research, citizen involvement, and public information efforts.

neutralization theory   Theory that disputes the common belief that delinquents belong to subcultures adhering to separate norms. Neutralization theory holds instead that delinquents experience guilt when involved in illegal activities and that they respect leaders of the legitimate social order. Their delinquency is episodic rather than chronic. Delinquents adhere to conventional values while "drifting" into periods of illegal behavior. In order to drift, the delinquent must first neutralize legal and moral values.

nonjudicial disposition   Rendering of a decision in a juvenile case by an authority other than a judge or court of law. Often an informal method used to determine the most appropriate disposition of a juvenile.

nonresidential program   Program enabling youths to remain in their homes or foster homes while receiving services.

nonsecure setting   Setting in which the emphasis is on the care and treatment of youths without the need to place constraints on them and to worry about the protection of the public.

parens patriae   Power of the state to act in behalf of the child and provide care and protection equivalent to that of a parent.

parole agency   Correctional agency that may or may not include a parole authority and whose principal functions are the supervision of adults or juveniles placed on parole.

parole authority   Person or correctional agency having the authority to release on parole adults or juveniles committed to confinement facilities, to revoke parole, and to discharge from parole.

parolee   Person who has been conditionally released from a correctional institution prior to the expiration of his or her sentence and who has been placed under the supervision of a parole agency.

penalty   Punishment meted out by law or judicial decision on the commission of a particular offense. It may be death, imprisonment, fine, or loss of civil privileges.

petition   Document filed in juvenile court alleging that a juvenile is a delinquent, a status offender, or a dependent and asking that the court assume jurisdiction over the juvenile or that the juvenile be transferred to a criminal court for prosecution as an adult.

petition not sustained   Finding by a juvenile court in an adjudicatory hearing that there is insufficient evidence to sustain an allegation that a juvenile is a delinquent, status offender, or dependent.

person in need of supervision   Persons usually characterized as ungovernable, incorrigible, truant, and habitually disobedient.

plea bargaining   Discussion between the defense counsel and the prosecution by which the accused agrees to plead guilty for certain considerations. The advantage to the defendant may be in the form of a reduction of the charges, a lenient sentence, or, in the case of multiple charges, dropped charges. The advantage to the prosecution is that a conviction is obtained without the time and expense of lengthy trial proceedings.

predisposition report   Document resulting from an investigation undertaken by a probation agency or other designated authority, which has been requested by a juvenile court, into the past behavior, family background, and personality of a juvenile who has been adjudicated a delinquent, a status offender, or a dependent, in order to assist the court in determining the most appropriate disposition.

probable cause   Reasonable ground to believe the existence of facts that an offense was committed and the accused committed that offense.

probation   Sentence entailing the conditional release of a convicted offender into the community under the supervision of the court (in the form of a probation officer) subject to certain conditions for a specific time. The conditions are usually similar to those of parole. (Note: probation is a sentence, an alternative to incarceration; parole is administrative release from incarceration.) Violation of the conditions of probation may result in revocation of probation.

probation agency   Also called probation department. Correctional agency of which the principal functions are juvenile intake, the supervision of adults and juveniles placed on probation status, and the investigation of adults and juveniles for the purpose of preparing presentence or predisposition reports to assist the court in determining the proper sentence or juvenile court disposition.

probation officer   Employee of a probation agency whose primary duties include one or more of the probation agency functions.

probationer   Person required by a court or probation agency to meet certain conditions of behavior, who may or may not be placed under the supervision of a probation agency.

procedural law   Rules that define the operation of criminal proceedings. The methods that must be followed in obtaining warrants, investigating offenses, effecting lawful arrests, using force, conducting trials, introducing evidence, sentencing convicted offenders, and reviewing cases in appellate courts. Substantive law defines criminal offenses; procedural law delineates how the substantive offenses are to be enforced.

prosecutor   Representative of the state (executive branch) in criminal proceedings; advocate for the state's case—the charge—in the adversary trial, for example, the attorney general of the United States, United States attorneys, attorneys general of the states, district attorneys, and police prosecutors. The prosecutor participates in investigations both before and after arrest, prepares legal documents, participates in obtaining arrest or search warrants, decides whether or not to charge a suspect and, if so, with which offense to charge. The prosecutor argues the state's case at trial, advises the police, participates in plea negotiations, and makes sentencing recommendations.

prosecutorial agency   Federal, state, or local criminal justice agency whose principal function is the prosecution of alleged offenders.

public defender   Lawyer who works in a public agency or under private contractual agreement as defense counsel to indigent defendants.

recidivism   Repetition of criminal behavior; habitual criminality. The National Advisory Commission on Criminal Justice Standards and Goals recommends a standard definition of recidivism in its volume *Corrections* (1973): "Recidivism is measured by (1) criminal acts that resulted in conviction by a court, when committed by individuals who are under correctional supervision or who have been released from correctional supervision within the previous three years, and by (2) technical violations of probation or parole in which a sentencing or paroling authority took action that resulted in an adverse change in the offender's legal status."

referral to intake   In juvenile proceedings, a request by the police, parents, or other agency or person that a juvenile intake unit take appropriate action concerning a juvenile alleged to have committed a delinquent act or status offense or to be dependent.

reform school   Institution in which efforts are made to improve the conduct of those forcibly detained within. Educational and psychological services are employed to achieve this goal.

rehabilitation   Restoring to a condition of constructive activity.

release (pretrial)   Procedure whereby an accused person who has been taken into custody is allowed to be free before and during trial.

release from detention   Authorized exit from detention of a person subject to criminal or juvenile justice proceedings.

release on bail   Release by a judicial officer of an accused person who has been taken into custody, upon the accused's promise to pay a certain sum of money or property if he or she fails to appear in court as required. The promise may or may not be secured by the deposit of an actual sum of money or property.

release on own recognizance   Release, by a judicial officer, of an accused person who has been taken into custody, upon the accused's promise to appear in court as required for criminal proceedings.

residential child care facility   Dwelling other than a detention or shelter care facility that provides living accommodations, care, treatment, and maintenance for children and youths and is licensed to provide such care. Such facilities include foster family homes, group homes, and halfway houses.

residential treatment center   Government facility that serves juveniles whose behavior does not necessitate the strict confinement of a training school, often allowing them greater contact with the community.

responsible   Legally accountable for one's actions and obligations.

restitution   Restoring of property, or a right, to a person who has been unjustly deprived of it. A writ of restitution is the process by which a successful appellant may recover something of which he or she has been deprived under a prior judgment.

revocation   Administrative act performed by a parole authority that removes a person from parole or a judicial order by a court removing a person from parole or probation, in response to a violation on the part of the parolee or probationer.

right to counsel   Right of the accused to assistance of defense counsel in all criminal prosecutions.

right to treatment   Philosophy espoused by many courts that offenders have a statutory right to treatment. A federal constitutional right to treatment has not been established.

rights of defendant   Powers and privileges that are constitutionally guaranteed to every defendant.

runaway   Juvenile who has been adjudicated by a judicial officer of a juvenile court as having committed the status offense of leaving the custody and home of his or her parents, guardians, or custodians without permission and failing to return within a reasonable length of time.

search and seizure   The Constitution protects against any search or seizure engaged in without a lawfully obtained search warrant. A search warrant will be issued if there is probable cause to believe that an offense has been or is being committed.

secure setting   Setting that places constraints on youths for care and treatment and for the protection of the public.

security and privacy standards   Set of principles and procedures developed to ensure the security and confidentiality of criminal or juvenile record information in order to protect the privacy of the persons identified in such records.

sentence   Criminal sanction imposed by the court upon a convicted defendant, usually in the form of a fine, incarceration, or probation. Sentencing may be carried out by a judge, jury, or sentencing council (panel of judges), depending on the statutes of the jurisdiction.

sentence, indeterminate   Statutory provision for a type of sentence to imprisonment where, after the court has determined that the convicted person shall be imprisoned, the exact length of imprisonment and parole supervision is fixed within statutory limits by a parole authority.

sentence, suspended   Court decision postponing the pronouncing of sentence upon a convicted person or postponing the execution of a sentence that has been pronounced by the court.

standard of proof   Proof beyond a reasonable doubt—the standard used to convict a person charged with a crime. Many Supreme Court decisions have made the beyond-a-reasonable-doubt standard a due process and constitutional requirement.

status offender   Juvenile who has been adjudicated by a judicial officer of a juvenile court as having committed a status offense.

status offense   Act that is declared by statute to be an offense, but only when committed by a juvenile. It can be adjudicated only by a juvenile court.

statutory law   Law relating to a statute, created or defined by a statute, required by a statute, conforming to a statute.

take into custody   The act of the police in securing the physical custody of a child engaged in delinquency. Avoids the stigma of the word *arrest*.

training school   Correctional institution for juveniles adjudicated to be delinquents or status offenders and committed to confinement by a judicial officer.

transfer hearing   Preadjudicatory hearing in juvenile court for the purpose of determining whether juvenile court jurisdiction should be retained or waived over a juvenile alleged to have committed a delinquent act and whether he or she should be transferred to criminal court for prosecution as an adult.

transfer to adult court   Decision by a juvenile court resulting from a transfer hearing that jurisdiction over an alleged delinquent will be waived and that he or she should be prosecuted as an adult in a criminal court.

treatment   Rehabilitative method used to effect a change of behavior in an inmate, juvenile delinquent, or status offender. It may be in the form of therapy programs or educational or vocational training.

trial   Examination of issues of fact and law in a case or controversy, beginning when the jury has been selected in a jury trial or when the first witness is sworn or the first evidence is introduced in a court trial and concluding when a verdict is reached or the case is dismissed.

UCR   Abbreviation for the Federal Bureau of Investigation's uniform crime reporting program.

verdict   In criminal proceedings, the decision made by a jury in a jury trial or by a judicial officer in a court trial that a defendant is either guilty or not guilty of the offenses for which he or she has been tried.

victim   Person who has suffered death, physical or mental suffering, or loss of property as the result of an actual or attempted criminal offense committed by another person.

waiver   Voluntary relinquishment of a known right.

youth services bureau   Neighborhood youth service agency that coordinates all community services for young people and provides services lacking in the community or neighborhood, especially those designated for the predelinquent or the early delinquent.

youthful offender   Person adjudicated in criminal court who may be above the statutory age limit for juveniles but who is below a specified upper age limit, for whom special correctional commitments and special record sealing procedures are made available by statute.

Appendix B
Excerpts from
the U.S. Constitution

Amendment I (1791)

Congress shall make no law respecting an establishment of religion, or prohibiting the free exercise thereof; or abridging the freedom of speech, or of the press; or the right of the people peaceably to assemble, and to petition the government for a redress of grievances.

Amendment II (1791)

A well regulated Militia, being necessary to the security of a free State, the right of the people to keep and bear Arms, shall not be infringed.

Amendment III (1791)

No Soldier shall, in time of peace be quartered in any house, without the consent of the Owner, nor in time of war, but in a manner to be prescribed by law.

Amendment IV (1791)

The right of the people to be secure in their persons, houses, papers, and effects, against unreasonable searches and seizures, shall not be violated, and no Warrants shall issue, but upon probable cause, supported by Oath or affirmation, and particularly describing the place to be searched, and the persons or things to be seized.

Amendment V (1791)

No person shall be held to answer for a capital, or otherwise infamous crime, unless on a presentment or indictment of a Grand Jury, except in cases arising in the land or naval forces, or in the Militia, when in actual service in time of War or public danger; nor shall any person be subject for the same offence to be twice put in jeopardy of life or limb; nor shall be compelled in any criminal case to be a witness against himself, nor be deprived of life, liberty, or property, without due process of law; nor shall private property be taken for public use, without just compensation.

Amendment VI (1791)

In all criminal prosecutions, the accused shall enjoy the right to a speedy and public trial, by an impartial jury of the State and district wherein the crime shall have been committed, which district shall have been previously ascertained by law, and to be informed of the nature and cause of the accusation; to be confronted with the witnesses against him; to have compulsory process for obtaining witnesses in his favor, and to have the Assistance of Counsel for his defence.

Amendment VII (1791)

In suits at common law, where the value in controversy shall exceed twenty dollars, the right of trial by jury shall be preserved, and no fact tried by a jury, shall be otherwise reexamined in any Court of the United States, than according to the rules of common law.

Amendment VIII (1791)

Excessive bail shall not be required, nor excessive fines imposed, nor cruel and unusual punishment inflicted.

Amendment IX (1791)

The enumeration in the Constitution, of certain rights, shall not be construed to deny or disparage others retained by the people.

Amendment X (1791)

The powers not delegated to the United States by the Constitution, nor prohibited by it to the States, are reserved to the States respectively, or to the people.

Amendment XIV (1868)

Section I. All persons born or naturalized in the United States, and subject to the jurisdiction thereof, are citizens of the United States and of the State wherein they reside. No State shall make or enforce any law which shall abridge the privileges or immunities of citizens of the United States; nor shall any State deprive any person of life, liberty or property, without due process of law; nor deny to any person within its jurisdiction the equal protection of the laws.

Appendix C
Children's Rights

A historical survey of the rights of children from the Constitution to date. The authors wish to express their appreciation to Dr. Lynn Sametz of Kent State University for the use of this material:

1787 Signing of the Constitution of the United States.

1791 Passage of the Bill of Rights.

1824 New York House of Refuge founded.

1826 Boston House of Refuge founded.

1838 *Ex Parte Crouse—Parens patriae* concept relied upon. The right of the parent is not inalienable.

1841 John Augustus, first official probation officer in United States, began working in Boston.

1847 State institutions for juvenile delinquents opened in Boston and New York.

1850 The House of Refuge in Philadelphia closed.

1851 The first adoption act in the United States was passed in Massachusetts.

1853 New York Juvenile Asylum started by the Children's Aid Society.

1866 Massachusetts established that the state has power over children under sixteen whose parents are "unfit."

1868 Passage of the Fourteenth Amendment to the Constitution.

1870 Illinois Supreme Court reversed Dan O'Connell's vagrancy sentence to the Chicago Reform School due to lack of due process procedures in *People v. Turner*.

1881 Michigan began child protection with the Michigan Public Acts of 1881.

1875-1900 Case law began to deal with protective statutes.

1884 The state assumed the authority to take neglected children and place them in an institution. See *Reynolds v. Howe*, 51 Conn. 472, 478 (1884).

1886 First neglect case was heard in Massachusetts.

1889 Board of children's guardians established in Indiana and given jurisdiction over neglected and dependent children.

1890 Children's Aid Society of Pennsylvania, a foster home for the juvenile delinquent used as an alternative to reform schools, was established.

1891 Supreme Court of Minnesota established the doctrine of parental immunity.

1897 Ex Parte Becknell, a California decision that reversed the sentence of a juvenile who had not been given a jury trial.

1899 Illinois Juvenile Court Act.

1903-1905 Many other states passed juvenile court acts.

1905 *Commonwealth v. Fisher.* Pennsylvania Supreme Court upheld the constitutionality of the Juvenile Court Act.

1906 Massachusetts passed an act to provide for the treatment of children not as criminals but as children in need of guidance and aid.

1908 *Ex Parte Sharpe* defined more clearly the role of the juvenile court to include *parens patriae.*

1910 Compulsory school acts.

1924 Federal Probation Act.

1930 Children's Charter.

1954 *Brown v. Board of Education*, a major school desegregation decision.

1959 Standard Family Court Act of National Council on Crime and Delinquency established that juvenile hearings are to be informal.

1966 *Kent v. United States.*—initial decision to establish due process protections for juveniles at transfer proceedings.

1967 President's Commission on Law Enforcement — the Juvenile Justice System.

1967 *In Re Gault,* a Supreme Court decision establishing that juveniles have the right to counsel, notice, confrontation of witnesses, and the avoidance of self-incrimination. The decision also applied procedural due process to juveniles in the adjudicatory phase of a hearing and if loss of liberty is threatened. In general, the court held that Fourteenth Amendment due process applied to the juvenile justice system, specifically in adjudicatory hearings.

1968 *Ginsberg v. New York* established that it is unlawful to sell pornography to a minor.

1969 *Tinker v. Des Moines School District* established that the First Amendment applies to juveniles and protects their constitutional right to free speech.

1970 *In re Winship* established that proof beyond a reasonable doubt is necessary in the adjudicatory phase of a juvenile hearing. A juvenile can appeal on the ground of insufficiency of the evidence if the offense alleged is an act that would be a crime.

1970 White House Conference on Children.

1971 *McKeiver v. Pennsylvania* established that a jury trial is not constitutionally required in a juvenile hearing but states can permit one if they wish.

1971 The Twenty-sixth Amendment to the Constitution was passed, granting the right to vote to eighteen year olds.

1972 *Wisconsin v Yoder* gave parents the right to impose their religion on their children.

1973 *In re Snyder* gave minors the right to bring proceedings against their parents.

1973 *San Antonio Independent School District v. Rodriguez* established that differences in education based on wealth were not necessarily discriminatory.

1974 Federal Child Abuse Prevention Act.

1974 Buckley Amendment to the Education Act of 1974, the Family Education Rights and Privacy Act. Students have the right to see their own files with parental consent.

1974 Juvenile Justice and Delinquency Prevention Act.

1975 *Goss v. Lopez* established that student facing suspension has the right to due process, prior notice, and an open hearing.

1977 Report of the Committee of the Judiciary, especially concerning the rights of the unborn and the right of eighteen year olds to vote.

1977 Juvenile Justice Amendment of 1977.

1977 *Ingraham v. Wright* established that corporal punishment is permissible in public school and is not a violation of the Eighth Amendment.

1977 American Bar Association, Standards on Juvenile Justice.

1979 International Year of the Child.

1980 National concern over child abuse and neglect.

Subject Index

A

Academic achievement, and delinquency, 221-222

Academic tracking, 225

Active speech, students' right to, 486

Addict gangs (Cohen & Short), 212

Adjudication, 4, 399

Adjudicatory hearings, 259, 276, 278, 279, 399-403
due process rights at, 315, 322, 331, 400-403
finding of fact by the court at, 400
formal rules of procedure at, 399

Adolescent Girl in Conflict, The (Konopka), 182

Adult justice system,
versus juvenile justice system, 144-145, 280-284, 382, 466, 496
transferring children to, 331

Adult Standards on Criminal Justice Relating to Probation (American Bar Association), 419

Affleck decision (1972), 457

Aftercare, 332, 466-469. *See also* Parole

Age,
arrest trends by, 25, 26
and delinquency, 33
of gang members, 203-204
by type of victimization, 57, 58
as determinant of court jurisdiction, 335-336, 353, 383
drug abuse by, 51-52

Aggravated assault, 23

Agreeing to a finding, 330

Alcohol abuse. See Drug and alcohol abuse

Alienation, student, 225-226

Alternative Work Sentencing Program (Earn-It), 429

Anabolic females (Thomas), 179

Anal stage (Freud), 84

Anomie theory (Merton), 107-110

Anthropological view of delinquent gang formation (Block & Niederhoffer), 207-209

Appeals, 332
right to and types of, 409-410

Appearance, right to one's own, 486

Apprenticeship systems, 303, 305

Argersinger v. Hamlin (1972), 397

Army Alpha Examination, 78

Arrest stage of juvenile justice process, 324-325, 353, 354

Arrest trends, 24-29

Arrest warrants, 353

Assault, aggravated, 23

Assembly, right to, 486

Atavistic anomalies (Lombroso), 178

Attachment, as social bond element, 136, 137-138

Attorneys, *See individual entries, such as* Defense attorneys; Prosecuting attorneys

Autonomy, as lower-class focal concern (Miller), 104

B

Bail,
for children, 380-381
right to, 330, 381

Bail hearing, 381

Baker v. Owen (1975), 488, 489

Baldwin v. Lewis (1969), 330
Barfield decision (1975), 327
Barker v. Wingo (1972), 324
Battered child syndrome (Kempe), 252
Behaviorism, 83
Behavior modification, 452
Belief, as social bond element, 136, 138
Bellotti v. Baird (1979), 482
Belonging, as lower-class focal concern of
    gangs (Miller), 104-105
Bifurcated hearings, 399, 403
Bill of rights for children, 493-496
Binding out of children, 305
Bindover. *See* Transfer (waiver) proceedings
Biological determinism theories, 72-82
    defined, 69
Biometric method of studying criminals
    (Goring), 73
B.J.R. decision (1975), 336
Body-build theories, 76
Bopping gangs, 203
Boston Juvenile Court, 340, 393-394
Bowers decision (1974), 487
Brasher decision (1971), 336
Breed v. Jones (1975), 323, 384, 385-386
Burglary, defined, 23

C

California Youth Authority, 424-425, 468
Cambridge-Somerville Youth Study, 142
Capitalist society, viewed by conflict
    theorists, 165-167
Cecilia R. decision (1975), 332
Certiorari, writ of, 332, 410
Chancery court system, 303-305
Chicago Area Project, 101, 119-120
Chicago Reform School, 309
Child abuse and neglect, 13, 251-263
    causes of, 254-256
    definitions of and types of, 252-253
    in the nineteenth century, 305-306
    rates of, 253-254
    related to delinquency, 261-263
    by social class, 254-255
Child abuse and neglect cases,
    disposition of, 260-261
    police handling of, 349
    role of juvenile courts in, 256-257, 259, 312,
        313
    state intervention in, 257-260
Child Abuse Prevention and Treatment Act
    (1974), 256
Child dependency. *See* Dependency of
    children
Child protection systems, 256-260
Children. *See also* Juvenile *entries;* Minors
    care of,

in the Middle Ages, 299-302
    reforms in, 306-310
in colonial America, 304-305
in Great Britain in the nineteenth century,
    305-306
legal protections of, 7
legal status of, 6
noncriminal. *See* Noncriminal children
police work with. *See* Police work with
    children
special. *See* Special children
Children in Need of Supervision (CHINS),
    10, 159, 315, 336
Children's Aid Society, 309-310
Children's Bureau, 392
Children's court movement in Great Britain,
    306
Children's rights, 321-340, 392, 479-496. *See
    also* Due process of law
    *and individual rights entries,
    such as* Counsel, right to;
    Trial by jury, right to
    bill of, 493-496
    outside the family, 483-490
    within the family, 480-482
Children's rights movement, 483
Children without Justice (National Council
    of Jewish Women), 368
Childsavers, 307-308
    defined, 6
    influencing juvenile justice reform, 311
    influencing reform school movement, 309
Childsavers, The (Platt), 167
CHINS (Children in Need of Supervision),
    10, 159, 315, 336
Cuilla v. State (1968), 326
Civil law, defined, 6
Civil rights for children. *See* Children's
    rights; Due process of law
Classical theory, 69-72
Cocaine use, by age, 52
Cognitive operations stage (Piaget), 85
Coleman Report (Coleman), 221
Collateral attack, 409, 410
Collateral review, 410
College boys (Cohen), 112
Commissioners, 396
Commitment, as social bond element, 136,
    138
Common law, 257, 352-353
Commonwealth v. Brasher (1971), 336
Community Delinquency Control Project
    (CDCP) of California Youth Authority,
    424-425, 434
Community Treatment Program (CTP) of
    California Youth Authority, 424, 425, 434
Community treatment programs, 405, 417-437
    advantages of, 338

criticisms of, 436-437
defined, 418
diverting children into, 430
nonresidential, 434-436
parole as extension of. *See* Parole of
  juvenile offenders
and probation. *See* Probation
proliferation of, 418, 425
rehabilitation through, 418
scarcity of, 338
Compulsory education law, 484
Concrete operations stage (Piaget), 85
Conditional sanctions, 405-406
Conflict gangs, 212
Conflict subculture (Cloward & Ohlin), 115
Conflict theory, 163-169
Conformity to social goals, as social
  adaptation (Merton), 108
Consent, right to, 495
Containments, inner and outer, 140, 142
Containment theory, 139-142
Contemporary Woman and Crime, The
  (Simon), 185
Control theory, 135-139
Corner boys (Cohen), 112
Corporal punishment in schools, 489
Cottage system, 444
Counsel, right to, 315, 324, 329, 354, 397,
  400-401, 409
Counseling in institutions, individual, 451
Court decisions,
  affecting juvenile justice process, 324-333
  Argersinger v. Hamlin (1972), 397
  Baker v. Owen (1975), 488, 489
  Baldwin v. Lewis (1969), 330
  Barker v. Wingo (1972), 324
  Bellotti v. Baird (1979), 482
  Breed v. Jones (1975), 323, 384, 385-386
  Cecilia R. decision (1975), 332
  Cuilla v. State (1968), 326
  Commonwealth v. Brasher (1971), 336
  defined, 67
Criminology, new, 163-169
"Crimogenic" families, 75
Critical theory, 163-169
Crouse case (1838), 308-309
Cultural transmission,
  according to Shaw & McKay, 100
  defined, 98
Cultural transmission theory, 98-106
Curriculum development, right to determine.
  484-485
Custodial sanctions, 406
Custody, taking into,
  due process safeguards for, 353-354
  guidelines for, 353, 354
  interrogation after, 326-329
Cyclothyme body type (Kretschmer), 76

D

D. decision (1975), 487
Danforth decision (1976), 482
DARE (Dynamic Action Residence
  Enterprise) Program (Massachusetts),
  434
Defense attorneys, 397. *See also* Private
  attorneys; Public defenders
"Defensible space" concept (Newman), 78
Definition against delinquency, 127
Definition toward criminality, 130
Definition toward delinquency, 127, 128,
  129-130, 142
Dei delitti e delle pene (Beccaria), 70
Deinstitutionalization of juveniles. *See also*
  Community treatment programs;
  Institutionalization of juveniles;
  Institutions, juvenile
  criticisms of, 436-437
  defined, 430
  trend toward, 430-431
Delinquency. *See also* Status offenses
  affected by tracking, 225
  and age. *See* Age, and delinquency
  causes of, 4
    according to Cohen, 111
    according to Shaw and McKay, 99-100
  chronic, and disposition of case, 33
  and court jurisdiction, 336-337
  defined, 5
    by various states, 336
  definition against, 127
  definition toward, 127, 128, 129-130, 142
  drug and alcohol abuse as, 50-52, 229-230
  and ecology (Shaw & McKay), 100-102
  extent of, 55, 57, 58
  and the family, 248-251
  female. *See* Female delinquency
  gang. *See* Delinquent gangs
  and IQ, 32-34, 78-82
  and juvenile justice system, 168, 187-190,
    287
  and learning disabilities, 223-224
  as legal concept, 311-313
  lone, 50, 58
  and lower-class focal concerns (Miller),
    105
  measures of (Shaw & McKay), 99
  official. *See* Official delinquency *entries*
  and personality testing, 87-89
  and physique, 76
  psychology of (Erikson), 86-87
  punishment as solution to, 71, 87
  and race, 27-29, 33-34, 49-50
  related to child abuse and neglect, 261-263
  school-related. *See* Schools, and
    delinquency

self-report studies of. *See* Self-report
    surveys of delinquency
and sex, 48-49. *See also* Female
    delinquency, linked to sexuality
and social class, 45-48, 206, 222
and socioeconomic status (SES), 32-34
studied through official records, 30-34
in transitional neighborhoods, 98-106, 206
UCR as predictor of, 49-50
understanding and treating, 339
urban (Cloward & Ohlin), 115
utilitarianism applied to, 70-71
viewed by conflict theorists, 167-168
violent, study of, 469
Delinquency and Drift (Matza), 131
Delinquency and Opportunity (Cloward &
    Ohlin), 114
Delinquency concept, 7, 167-168
Delinquency Evaluation Project (New York
    City), 212
Delinquency in a Birth Cohort (Wolfgang,
    Figlio, & Sellin), 31-34
Delinquency label,
    effects of, 152
    history of, 6
    and juvenile justice process, 159-162
Delinquency prevention,
    and employment, 144-360
    and family services, 143-144
    as goal of juvenile justice system, 287
    and health system, 143
    and housing, 145
    and human services, 143-146
    and mass media, 146
    role of schools in, 236-239, 359-360
    through police work, 358-360
    and social process theories, 142-146
District of Columbia v. B.J.R. (1975), 336
Doe v. State (1971), 330
Ellery C. decision (1972), 332
Escobedo v. Illinois (1964), 324
Ex parte Crouse (1838), 308-309
Ex parte Sharp (1908), 282-283
Fare v. Michael C. (1979), 327-329
Gallegos v. Colorado (1962), 315
Gideon v. Wainwright (1963), 324, 397
Ginsberg v. New York (   ), 481
Goss v. Lopez (1976), 489
Griswold v. Connecticut (1965), 480-481
Haley v. Ohio (1948), 315, 327
Ingraham v. Wright (1977), 489
Inmates of the Boy's Training School v.
    Affleck (1972), 457
In re Donaldson (1969), 487
In re Gault (1967), 279, 310, 315, 322, 323,
    324, 326, 331, 353, 354, 392, 397, 399,
    400-401, 409, 479, 494
In re Holley (1970), 329

In re Joseph S. (1969), 325
In re Marsh (1968), 326
In re Moten (1973), 325
In re Nelson (1969), 326-327
In re Rich (1966), 332
In re Robert F. (1968), 332
In re Roberts (1971), 331-332
In re Stanley M. (1972), 332
In re W. (1973), 487
In re William M. (1970), 330
In re Winshop (1970), 322-323, 392, 399,
    400, 401-402
Kent v. United States (1966), 315, 322, 323,
    331, 354, 369, 384-385, 386, 392, 394,
    407
Kirby v. Illinois (1972), 329
Lamb v. Brown (1972), 335-336
McKeiver v. Pennsylvania (1971), 323, 331,
    382, 399, 400, 402-403, 417-418
Mapp v. Ohio (1961), 324
Martarella v. Kelly (1972), 374, 457, 459
Mills v. Board of Education (1972), 491,
    492-493
Miranda v. Arizona (1966), 324, 326
Morales v. Turman (1974), 459
Morrissey v. Brewer (1972), 332
Moss v. Weaver (1974), 326
Nelson v. Heyne (1974), 457-459
O'Connell v. Turner (1870), 309
O'Connor v. Donaldson (1975), 457
Pena v. New York State Division for
    Youth (1976), 459
Pennsylvania Association for Retarded
    Children v. State of Pennsylvania
    (1972), 491, 492-493
People v. Bowers (1974), 487
People v. D. (1975), 487
People v. Fields (1972), 331
People v. Lara (1967), 327
People v. Overton (1969), 487
Planned Parenthood of Central Missouri
    v. Danforth (1976), 482
Powell v. Alabama (1932), 397
Prince v. Massachusetts (1968), 481
Rivera v. Freeman (1972), 330
Rouse v. Cameron (1966), 456
San Antonio Independent School District
    v. Rodriguez (1973), 491
Santobello v. New York (1971), 382
State v. Grayer (1974), 393
State v. Mora (1975), 488
State v. Redeman (1971), 325
Tinker v. Des Moines Independent
    Community School District (1969), 485
U.S. v. Barfield (1975), 327
U.S. v. Wade (1967), 329
Wellesley v. Wellesley (1827), 304, 306
West v. U.S. (1968), 327

Wisconsin v. Yoder (1972), 484
Wolff v. McDonnell (1974), 466
Wyatt v. Stickney (1971), 456-457, 492-493
Courts. *See* Jurisdiction of courts; Juvenile
    courts
Court statistics, accuracy of, 101-102
Crime, Pauperism, Disease and Heredity
    (Dugdale), 75
Crime rates, women's, changes in, 185-187
Crime reporting practices, 34-36. *See also*
    Victimization
Crimes. *See individual entries, such as* Index
    crimes; Violent crimes
Crime statistics, official, 34-36, 55
Criminal atavism theory (Lombroso), 73
Criminal behavior,
    and court jurisdiction, 336-337
    learning, 126-128
Criminal gangs (Cloward & Ohlin), 212
Criminality, definition toward, 130
Criminality of Women, The (Pollak), 180, 181
Criminal justice systems, nineteenth century,
    306. *See also* Adult justice system;
    Juvenile justice system
Criminal law, 167, 306
    defined, 6
Criminal subculture (Cloward & Ohlin), 115
Criminological theories, 67-68
    and social reaction theories, 168-169
    and social structure theories, 119-120
Delinquency rates,
    explained by anomie theory (Merton), 109
    official, defined, 44
    of school dropouts, 235
    in suburban areas, 102
Delinquency statistics,
    official. *See* Official delinquency statistics
    unofficial sources of, 41-60
Delinquency theories,
    anomie (Merton), 107-110
    as basis for treatment and control, 348
    biological determinism, 72-82
        defined, 69
    body-build, 76
    classical, 69-72
    conflict, 163-169
    containment, 139-142
    control, 135-139
    criminal atavism (Lombroso), 73
    criminology, new, 163-169
    critical, 163-169
    cultural transmission, 98-106
    delinquent subculture, 110-114
    differential association (Sutherland),
        126-131, 142
    drift, 131-135
    female. *See* Female delinquency, theories
        of

hereditary insanity, 83
heredity, 75
individualistic, 68-90
inheritance, 75
IQ, 78-82
labeling, 151-163
learning (Bandura), 87
lower-class focal concern (Miller),
    105-106, 202
Marxist, 163-169
middle-class, 118-119
neutralization, 131-135
opportunity (Cloward & Ohlin), 114-117,
    202
physical anomalies, 72-75
positivist, 72-82
    defined, 72
psychobiological, 75
psychological, 69, 82-89, 249
social process, 125-146, 249
social reaction, 151-170
social structure, 97-120, 249
sociobiology, 76-82
    defined, 69
strain, 106-110
subcultural (strain), 110-117
Delinquent boys (Cohen), 112-113
Delinquent Boys (Cohen), 110, 114
Delinquent careers, as result of labeling, 152,
    160
Delinquent Child and the Home, The
    (Lathrop), 282
Delinquent gangs, 197-213
    age of members of, 203-204
    behavioral approach to typing
        (Yablonsky), 211-212
    behavior of, as similar to primitive
        puberty rites (Block & Niederhoffer),
        208
    causes of, 207-210
    characteristics of (Yablonsky), 198-199
    character traits of members of
        (Yablonsky), 210
    definitions of, 197-199
        by Yablonsky, 211-212
    ethnic and racial composition of, 205
    extent of problem with, 212-213
    formation of,
        anthropological view (Block &
            Niederhoffer), 207-209
        psychological views, 210
        social-cultural view, 209
    history of, 200-203
    joined by abused and neglected children,
        261
    leadership of, 206-207
    location (neighborhoods) of, 206
    versus lone delinquency, 50

by types of victimization, 57
as near groups (Yablonsky), 198-199
in schools, 232
sex of members of, 204
social class of, 206
structural approach to typing
(Klein), 210-211
structure of, 203-207
as subcultures (Cloward & Ohlin), 114-115
teenage, 98, 99-100, 101
focal concerns unique to
(Miller), 104-105
lower-class (Miller), 104-105
types of, 203, 210-212
Delinquent Girl, The (Vedder & Somerville),
182-183
Delinquents. *See also* Status offenders
versus adult criminals, 5-6
defined, 5
disposition of. *See* Disposition of cases
female. *See* Female Delinquents
in Great Britain, nineteenth century,
305-306
incorrigible, 159, 314, 315, 336, 349, 371, 405
multiple offenses committed by, 32-33
observation of and biographical data on, as
source of unofficial delinquency
information, 59-60
official, defined, 21
process of becoming, 8-9
rehabilitation of. *See* Rehabilitation of
juvenile delinquents
treatment of, evaluated, 4
violent, 469-470
Delinquent subcultures,
development of (Cohen), 111
general properties of (Cohen), 113
varieties of (Cohen & Short), 114
Delinquent subculture theory (Cohen),
110-114
Demystification of capitalist society, 166-167
De novo review, 410
Dental programs in institutions, 455-456
Denying the petition, 330
Dependency of children, 253
in colonial America, 305
under Illinois Juvenile Court Act of 1899,
312, 314
Detached street worker project, 203
Detention, 368-373
defined, 368
of neglected and abused children, 372
procedural safeguards during, 353
of status offenders, 13, 371
Detention facilities, 368
jails as, 370-371
for noncriminal children, as violating due
process of law, 374

placing runaways in, 369
secure, 368
standards for care in, 373-374
typical, 373-374
Detention hearings, 278, 329-330, 369-370
Determinate sentencing, 405, 406
Determinism theories of female
delinquency, 184-187
Developmental theories of female
delinquency, 181-184
Deviance,
four-fold model of (Becker), 157-159
primary, 154
primary-secondary model of (Lemert),
154-157, 158
secondary, 154, 157, 163
Deviant label, 153-154
Deviants,
pure, 159
secret, 158
Dialectic method (Hegel), 165
Differential association,
empirical research on, 128-129
principles of, 126-128
Differential association theory (Sutherland),
126-131, 142
"Different treatment" hypothesis, 224
Direct appeal, 409
Direct review, 410
Discretion,
at different stages of juvenile justice
system, 369
of police. *See* Police discretion
of probation officers, 419
of prosecutors, 393
Disintegrative gangs (New York City Youth
Board), 212
Dispositional hearings,
ABA standards affecting, 405
in child abuse and neglect cases, 259
in juvenile court, 279, 331-332, 403-404
Dispositional reform, 292-293
Disposition of cases,
of child abuse and neglect, 260-261, 312,
313
involving delinquents, 312-313
reassessment of purpose of, 292
rehabilitation and treatment as
goals of, 406
related to chronic delinquency, 33
related to race, 33-34
types of, 279, 293, 404
District of Columbia v. B.J.R. (1975), 336
Diversion, 291-292, 376-377
arguments for use of, 376
definitions of, 291, 376
distinguished from screening, 376
as goal of juvenile justice system, 287, 358,

377
    role of police in, 349
Diversionary programs, 291-292
    effectiveness of, 378-379
    illustrations of, 377-379
    position of National Advisory Commission
        on Criminal Justice Standards and
        Goals on, 379
    youth services bureaus as, 358
Doe v. State (1971), 330
Donaldson decision (1969), 487
Double jeopardy, 323
Dower system, 300-301
Drift, 131-132
Drift theory, 131-135
Dropouts, school, 235-236
Drug and alcohol abuse,
    in schools, 229-230
    self-report data on, 50-52
Due process of law. See also Juvenile justice
        entries
    in adjudicatory hearings, 331
    during arrest stage, 324-325, 353, 354
    children's rights under, 279, 283, 288,
        290-291, 310, 315, 321-322
    defined, 12, 290
    in pre- and postadjudication proceedings,
        324
    role of, in juvenile justice (five
        major decisions), 322-324
    vagueness of, in applying to juvenile
        justice process, 333
    in waiver proceedings, 331

E

Earn-It, 429
Economic and social determinism theories of
    female delinquency, 184-187
Ectomorphs (Sheldon), 76
Education. See also Schools
    children's right to, 483-484
    and delinquency, 144, 221-227, 239
        See also Schools entries on delinquency
    as key to success, 220-221
    special children's right to, 490-491
Ego (Freud), 83-84
Egocentrism stage (Piaget), 85
Electra complex (Freud), 84
Ellery C. decision (1972), 332
Emancipated minors, defined, 481
Emancipation doctrine, 495
Emotional abuse or neglect of children, 253
Employment,
    children's rights in, 494
    and delinquency prevention, 144, 360
Endangered children, 253
Endomorphs (Sheldon), 76

English Convict, The (Goring), 73
Escobedo v. Illinois (1964), 324
Essexfields Rehabilitation Project (New
    Jersey), 435
Ethnicity of delinquent gangs, 205
Evaluation as goal of juvenile justice system,
    288
Excitement as lower-class focal concern
    (Miller), 104
Exclusionary rule, in state court proceedings,
    324
Ex parte Crouse (1838), 308-309
Ex parte Sharp (1908), 282-283
External pressures, in containment theory,
    140
External pulls, in containment theory, 140,
    142
Extinction of a behavior, 87
Extroverts (Eysenck), 85

F

Factory Act (early nineteenth century), 305
Fairness, concept of, applied to juvenile
    delinquency proceedings, 331, 333, 353,
    354
Fair treatment, through juvenile justice
    process, 323
Falsely accused individuals, 158, 159
Families,
    children's rights outside, 483-490
    children's rights within, 480-482
    "criminogenic," 75
    and delinquency, 111, 248-251
    make-believe, formed by incarcerated
        females, 462-463
Families in Need of Supervision (FINS), 315
Family autonomy, doctrine of, 495
Family courts. See Juvenile courts
Family services and delinquency prevention,
    143-144
Family structure,
    early changes in, affecting juvenile justice
        system, 302-303
    as influencing delinquency (Cohen), 111
    in Middle Ages, 300-301
Fare v. Michael C. (1979), 327-329
Fate as lower-class focal concern (Miller),
    104
Federal Bureau of Investigation (FBI). See
    Uniform Crime Reports (UCR)
Female criminality,
    changing pattern of, 184-185, 460
    changing types of, 185-187
    stages of (Pollak), 181
Female delinquency, 177-190
    affected by changing patterns of female
        behavior (Adler), 184-185

barriers to understanding, 48-49
and deviousness (Pollak), 180-181
linked with sexuality, 180, 188-190, 460
    Freud's view of, 181-182
    Konopka's view of, 182
    Thomas's view of, 180
Lombroso's view of, 178-179
major influences on (Konopka), 182
nature of, 178-181
theories of,
    developmental, 181-184
    economic and social determinism,
        184-187
Female delinquent gangs, 204
Female delinquents,
  in institutions. *See* Institutions, juvenile
  and the juvenile justice system, 187-190
  self-report studies of, 186-187
  as troubled adolescents (Konopka), 182-183
  as unadjusted girls (Thomas), 179-180
Female Offender, The (Lombroso), 178, 179
Females, anabolic (Thomas), 179
Feminist movement. *See* Women's liberation
    movement
Fields decision (1972), 331
Fighting gangs (Miller), 212
Final order, 409
Finding of fact by the court, 400
FINS (Families in Need of Supervision), 315
Five Hundred Delinquent Women (Glueck &
    Glueck), 183
Focal concern theory (Miller), 105-106, 202
Forcible rape, defined, 23
Foster care, 279
  in child abuse and neglect cases, 260
Foster homes, 431-432
Freedoms. *See individual entries,* such as
    Speech, freedom of, in public schools

G

Gain-oriented gangs (Miller), 212
Gallegos v. Colorado (1962), 315
Gang, The (Thrasher), 202
Gangs, types of, 210-212
Gault decision. *See In re Gault* (1967)
Genital stage (Freud), 84
Gideon v. Wainwright (1963), 324, 397
Ginsberg v. New York (1968), 481
Goss v. Lopez (1976), 489
Gough Socialization Scale of the California
    Personality Inventory, 116
Grayer decision (1974), 393
Griswold v. Connecticut (1965), 480-481
Group homes, 431, 433-434
Group psychotherapy, as treatment in
    institutions, 453

Guardian *ad litem,* 259
  defined, 256
Guided group interaction, as treatment in
    institutions, 453

H

Habeas corpus, writ of, 332, 410
Haley v. Ohio (1948), 315, 327
Hallucinogen use by age, 52
Haryou-Act (Harlem Youth Opportunities
    Unlimited), 120
Health system and delinquency prevention,
    143
Hearing on the petition, 380
Hearings. *See individual entries, such as*
    Adjudicatory hearings; Bail
    hearings
Hereditary insanity theory, 83
Heredity theories, 75
Highfields Project (New Jersey), 433, 453
Holley decision (1970), 329
Horizontal gangs (New York City Youth
    Board), 212
Horizontal pattern of gangs (Klein), 211
House of Reformation (Boston), 308
Houses of Refuge,
  New York, 308, 444
  Philadelphia, 308
Housing and delinquency prevention, 145
Human services and delinquency
    prevention, 143-146

I

Id (Freud), 83-84
Identification from lineups, procedural
    safeguards during, 329, 353, 354
"Identity crisis" (Erikson), 86
Illinois Juvenile Court Act (1899), 9, 274,
    310-313, 339
Incarceration. *See* Institutionalization
Incorrigible delinquents, 159, 314, 315, 336,
    349, 371, 405
Indenturing of children in colonial America,
    305
Indeterminate sentencing, 292, 404-405
Index Crimes, definitions of, 23-24
Individual counseling as treatment in
    institutions, 451
Individualistic theories, 68-90
Industrial schools, 444
Ingraham v. Wright (1977), 489
Inheritance theory, 75
In loco parentis, doctrine of, 483, 486-488,
    494
Inmates of the Boy's Training School v.

Affleck (1972), 457
Inner containments, 140, 142
Innovation as social adaptation (Merton), 108, 109
In re Donaldson (1969), 487
In re Gault (1967), 279, 310, 315, 322, 323, 324, 326, 331, 353, 354, 392, 394, 397, 399, 409, 479, 494
In re Holley (1970), 329
In re Joseph S. (1969), 325
In re Marsh (1968), 326
In re Moten (1973), 325
In re Nelson (1969), 326-327
In re Rich (1966), 332
In re Robert F. (1968), 332
In re Roberts (1971), 331-332
In re Stanley M. (1972), 332
In re W. (1973), 487
In re William M. (1970), 330
In re Winship (1970), 322-323, 392, 399
Insanity, 83
Institutionalization of juveniles, 443-470.
    See also Deinstitutionalization of juveniles
    changes in structure of, 445
    residential treatment alternatives to, 431-434
Institutions, juvenile,
    female juveniles in, 460-463
        profile of, 460-462
    for females, 462-465
    history of, 444-448
    medical and dental programs in, 455-456
    physical facilities of, 448-450
    profile of juveniles in, 446-448
    recreational programs in, 455
    rules and discipline in, 464-466
    sex typing in, 454
    treatment programs in, 450-460
    vocational and educational programs in, 453-454
Intake, defined, 374-375
Intake process, 278, 374-376
Intelligence. *See* IQ *entries*
Internal pushes, in containment theory, 140, 142
Interrogation, limits on, 326-329, 353, 354
Inter-State Compact for Juveniles, 419
Interstitial areas (Thrasher), 202, 206
Intervention by the state in child abuse and neglect cases, 257-260
Introverts (Eysenck), 85
Involuntary apprenticeship, 303, 305
Involvement as social bond element, 136, 138
IQ,
    and delinquency, 32-34, 78-82
    used to classify people, 492
IQ research, 81-82

IQ tests, 78-79
IQ theories, 78-82

J

Jails used as detention facilities, 370-371
JINS (Juveniles in Need of Supervision), 10
Jointure, 300
Joseph S. decision (1969), 325
Judge Baker Foundation and Clinic, 340
Judges, juvenile court,
    qualifications of, 396
    role of, 394-395
    selection of, 395-396
Jukes family, 75
Jukes in 1915, The (Estabrook), 75
Jurisdiction of courts, 287, 331, 335-338, 352-353
    transfer of waiver of. *See* Transfer (waiver) proceedings
Justice systems. *See* Adult justice system; Juvenile justice system
Juvenile camps, 445
Juvenile Court Act (1899), 9, 274, 310-313, 339
Juvenile court records as research tool, 30
Juvenile court reform movement, 280, 282-284, 420
Juvenile courts,
    adjudicatory hearings in. *See* Adjudicatory hearings
    appeals in. *See* Appeals
    dealing with noncriminal behavior, 314-315. *See also* Status offenders; Status offenses
    detention in. *See* Detention
    dispositional hearings in. *See* Dispositional hearings
    diversion in. *See* Diversion
    establishment of, 273-274, 312, 314-315, 349
    findings of fact in, 400
    intake process in, 278, 374-376
    interests guiding, 257
    judges in. *See* Judges, juvenile court
    jurisdiction of, 287, 331, 335-338, 352-353
    major characteristics of, 333-334
    modern, 314-315
    organization of, 333-335
    postdisposition of cases from, 279-280, 332-333, 392
    pretrial procedures of, 278
    probation in. *See* Probation
    procedural guarantees in, 279, 283, 288, 290-291
    processing children through, 367-386
    prosecution in, 393-394. *See also* Prosecutors
    purpose of, 280

role of, in child abuse and neglect cases,
        256-257, 259, 312, 313
screening in, 376
trial of juveniles in. *See* Trial
Juvenile Courts in the United States (Lou),
        281
Juvenile court statutes, constitutionality of,
        274
Juvenile delinquency (JD). *See* Delinquency;
        Delinquents
Juvenile gangs. *See* Delinquent gangs;
        Gangs, types of
Juvenile institutions. *See* Institutions,
        juvenile
Juvenile justice,
        defined, 272
        development of, 273-274, 306-310
        fields of study in, 272-273
        goals of, 284-288
        history and philosophy of, 299-315
        major issues in administering, 288-293
Juvenile Justice and Delinquency Prevention
        Act (1974), 13, 271, 289, 339, 431, 437, 445
Juvenile justice process,
        adjudication stage of. *See* Adjudication;
                Adjudicatory hearings
        arrest stage of, 324-325, 353, 354
        court decisions affecting, 324-333
        and delinquency label, 159-162
        disposition stage of. *See* Dispositional
                hearings; Disposition of cases
        due process and fair treatment in. *See* Due
                process of law
        postdispositional stage of, 279-280, 332-333,
                392
Juvenile justice standards, 253, 257-259,
        286-287, 289-290
Juvenile justice system,
        children's rights in, 274, 490. *See also*
                Due process of law
        compared with adult justice system,
                144-145, 280-284, 382, 466, 496
        criticisms of, 338-340
        defense attorneys in, 337. *See also* Private
                attorneys; Public defenders
        and delinquency,
                creating and sustaining, 168
                female, 187-190
        and delinquency prevention, 287
        discretion in, 369
        diverting children from. *See* Diversion
        in England, 302-304
        major components of, 275-276
        major functions of, 314
        overview of, 271-293
        planning policy in, 288-289
        plea bargaining in, 330, 382-383, 399

position of status offenders in, 293,
        336-337, 405
proposed structure of, 359
reform movement in, 280, 282-284, 310-313
rehabilitation as goal of, 280, 314, 323, 347
significant 1960s events in, 314-315
and special children, 492
stages in, 276-280
standards for, concerning rules and
        discipline, 465-466
systems approach to, 275-276
treatment in,
        benign setting for, 339
        of girls, 187-190
        right to, 457-459
Juvenile police officers. *See* Police officers
Juvenile probation. *See* Probation
Juvenile prosecutors, 391-393
Juveniles in Need of Supervision (JINS), 10
Juveniles, legal rights of. *See* Children's
        rights; Due process of law

K

Kallikak family, 75
Katabolic males (Thomas), 179
Kent v. United States (1966), 315, 322, 323,
        331, 354, 369, 384-385, 386, 392,
        394, 407
Key Program (Massachusetts), 435-436
Kinship structures, female, in institutions,
        463
Kirby v. Illinois (1972), 329
Known group method of validating
        delinquency self-reports, 53-54

L

Label acceptance, 152, 157, 163
Labeling,
        of delinquents. *See* Delinquency label
        self, 152, 157, 163
        societal response to, 153-154
        of students in low tracks, 225
Labeling process, 154-157, 339
Labeling theory, 151-163
Lamb v. Brown (1972), 335-336
Lara decision (1967), 327
Larceny-theft, defined, 24
Latency stage (Freud), 84
Law Enforcement Assistance Administration
        (LEAA), 289, 339, 437, 445
Law-violating youth group (Miller), 199. *See
        also* Delinquent gangs; Gangs, types of
Laws. *See individual entries, such as*
        Civil law; Common law
LD/JD link, 223-224

Leadership of delinquent gangs, 206-207
Learning disabilities (LD), 223-224
Learning theory (Bandura), 87
Life stages,
    Freud's, 84
    Erikson's, 86
Lineups, procedural safeguards during,
    329, 353, 354
Lone delinquency, 50
    by types of victimization, 58
Lower-class culture (Miller), 102-103
Lower-class focal concerns (Miller), 103-105
Lower-class focal concern theory (Miller),
    105-106, 202
Low visibility decision making,
    defined, 355

M

McKeiver v. Pennsylvania (1971), 323, 331,
    382, 399, 417-418
Maltreatment syndrome, 253
Manny: A Criminal Addict's Story (Rettig et
    al.), 59-60
Mapp v. Ohio (1961), 324
Marijuana use by age, 51-52
Marsh decision (1968), 326
Martarella v. Kelly (1972), 374, 457, 459
Marxist theory, 163-169
Marxist thought, 164-165
Mass media and delinquency prevention,
    146
Mature minors, defined, 481
Measurement of Intelligence (Terman), 78
Medical care, children's right to, 481-482, 494
Medical programs in institutions, 455-456
Mens rea, defined, 7
Mental ability. *See* IQ
Mental retardation, 492. *See also* Special
    children
Mesomorphs (Sheldon), 76
Mid-City Program, 119
Middle-class delinquency, 117-119
    theories of, 118-119
Middle-class measuring rods (Cohen),
    111-112, 222
    lower-class reactions to, 112-113
Mills v. Board of Education (1972), 491,
    492-493
Minnesota Multiphasic Personality
    Inventory (MMPI), 88-89
Minors,
    emancipated, defined, 481
    legal protections of, 7. *See also* Due
        process of law
    legal status of, 6
    mature, defined, 481

rights of. *See* Children's rights
Minors in Need of Supervision (MINS), 10,
    315
Miranda rights, waiver of, 327
Miranda v. Arizona (1966), 324, 326
Miranda warnings, 326, 354, 487
MMPI, 88-89
Mobilization for Youth (MFY), 120
Modeling of behavior, 87
Model Rules for Juvenile Courts, 392
Model Youth Correction Authority Act
    (American Law Institute), 445
Mora decision (1975), 488
Moral development,
    stages of (Piaget), 85
    theory of (Kohlberg), 86
Moral entrepreneurs, 157
Morales v. Turman (1974), 459
Morrissey v. Brewer (1972), 332
Moss v. Weaver (1974), 326
Moten decision (1973), 325
Motor vehicle theft, defined, 23
Murder, defined, 23

N

National Advisory Commission on
    Criminal Justice Standards and Goals,
    14-15, 236, 237, 248, 253, 258, 285-286,
    370, 379, 410
National Assessment of Juvenile Corrections
    (NAJC) surveys, 447
National Center for State Courts, 224
National Council on Crime and Delinquency
    (NCCD), 289, 368, 370, 392
National Crime Survey (NCS), 35, 49, 55-59
National Education Association, 228
National Institute for Juvenile Justice and
    Delinquency Prevention, 224
National Institute of Education, 233, 238
National Institute on Drug Abuse, 50-52
National Juvenile Justice Standards Project,
    14
National Organization for Women (NOW),
    184
National Strategy to Reduce Crime, A
    (National Advisory Commission on
    Criminal Justice Standards and
    Goals), 237
*National History of a Delinquent Career,
    The* (Shaw), 59
Nature-nurture controversy, 79-82
Nature theory of intelligence, 79, 81-82
Near group (Yablonsky), 198-199
Negative reinforcement, 87
Neglected or dependent children. *See also*
    Child abuse and neglect

under Illinois Juvenile Court Act of 1899,
312, 313, 314
as legal category, 13
placed in detention facilities, 371-372
Neighborhoods,
of delinquent gangs, 206
transitional, delinquency in, 98-106, 206
Nelson decision (1969), 326-327
Nelson v. Heyne (1974), 457-459
Neurotics (Eysenck), 85
Neutralization inventory (Ball), 134
Neutralization techniques, 132-133
Neutralization theory, 131-135
New York City Youth Board, 204, 212
New York Juvenile Justice Reform Act
(1976), 405
New York State Assembly Select Committee
on Child Abuse study, 262
Nominal sanctions, 405-406
Noncriminal children. *See also* Status
offenders
and court jurisdiction, 336-337
placed in detention facilities, 374
Nonnegligent manslaughter, defined, 23
Nonproblem gangs (New York City's
Delinquency Evaluation Project), 212
Nonresidential (community) treatment
programs, 434-436
Nonsecure facilities, 431
Norton Street Gang, 202
Nurture theory of intelligence, 80-81

O

O'Connell v. Turner, (1870), 309
O'Connor v. Donaldson (1975), 457
Oedipus complex (Freud), 84
Official crime statistics, 34-36, 55
Official delinquency,
defined, 21
importance of, 21-22
measures of, 21-36
Official delinquency rate, defined, 44
Official delinquency records, 30-31. *See also
Uniform Crime Reports (UCR)*
Official delinquency reports, 50
Official delinquency statistics, 22, 41, 250.
See also Delinquency statistics,
unofficial sources of; Official crime
statistics
Official delinquents, defined, 21
Official police records, 30, 31, 53
Official police statistics, 45, 101-102
Ohio Unruly Child Statute, 12
Omnibus Crime Control and Safe Streets
Act, 289
On Crime and Punishment (Beccaria), 70

Opportunity theory (Cloward & Ohlin),
114-117, 202
Oral stage (Freud), 84
Order of probation, 419
Outer containments, 140, 142
Overton decision (1969), 487

P

Parens patriae, defined, 6
Parens patriae doctrine,
attacks on, 7
in child abuse and neglect cases, 257
versus children's rights, 494
in colonial America, 305
in English juvenile justice system, 303-304
juvenile courts acting under, 274, 314
legal challenges to, 308-309
and legal responsibility, 6-7
used in juvenile justice reform, 311
Parents Anonymous (PA), 260
Parole of juvenile offenders, 279, 332, 418,
468
revocation of, 468-469
Passive speech, students' right to, 485-486
Peer informants, defined, 53-54
Pena v. New York State Division for Youth
(1976), 459
Penis envy (Freud), 181-182
*Pennsylvania Association for Retarded
Children v. State of Pennsylvania*
(1972), 491, 492-493
People v. Bowers (1974), 487
People v. D. (1975), 487
People v. Fields (1972), 331
People v. Lara (1967), 327
People v. Overton (1969), 487
Personality, components of (Freud), 83-84
Personality inventories (tests), 88-89
Personality testing and delinquency, 87-89
Personality types (Eysenck), 85
Persons in Need of Supervision (PINS), 10,
159, 315, 332, 336, 374, 398
Petitions, 380
Phallic stage (Freud), 84
Physical anomalies theories, 72-75
Physical neglect of children, 253. *See also*
Child abuse and neglect
PINS (Persons in Need of Supervision), 10,
159, 315, 332, 336, 374, 398
*Planned Parenthood of Central Missouri v.
Danforth* (1976), 482
Plea bargaining, 330, 382-383, 399
Pleading guilty or not guilty, 330, 382-383, 399
Police department, metropolitan,
organization of, 351
Police discretion,

controlling, 357-358
defined, 354
with juveniles, 354-358, 360-361
Police investigation of juvenile crimes, 278
Police officers,
    primary responsibility of, 347
    recruitment and training of, 350-352
    roles of, in dealing with juveniles, 348-349
Police records, 30, 31, 53
Police services for children, 349-350, 351
Police work with children, 347-361
    directions in, 360-361
    legal aspects of, 352-354
    to prevent delinquency, 358-360
Poor Laws,
    in colonial America, 305
    in England, 303
Positive reinforcement, 87
Positivist theory, 72-82
    defined, 72
Postdisposition of juvenile cases, 279-280,
    332-333, 392
Powell v. Alabama (1932), 397
Predelinquent children, 314
    schools dealing with, 359-360
Predisposition reports, 276, 404, 406-409
    access to, as legal issue, 407
    purposes of, 406-407
Preliminary investigations, procedural
    safeguards during, 353, 354
Preponderance of the evidence, as judgment
    standard, 399
President's Commission on Law
    Enforcement and the Administration of
    Justice, 34-35, 285, 315, 359
Presumptive sentencing, 406
Pretrial conferences in child abuse and
    neglect cases, 259
Pretrial court procedures, 278
Pretrial detention of status offenders, 13
Pretrial release, 329-330, 353, 354
Primary deviance, 154
Primogeniture, 300
Prince v. Massachusetts (1968), 481
Principles of Criminology (Sutherland), 126
Privacy, right to, 480-481
Private attorneys, 398
Probation, 418-428. *See also* Community
    treatment programs
    ABA standards on, 407-408
    based on rehabilitation, 419
    conditions to be followed during, 419, 423
    counseling of juveniles on, 425-428
    definitions of, 418

as disposition of choice in juvenile justice
    system, 338, 418
effectiveness of, 423-428
historical development of, 420
introduction of concept of, 306
order of, 419
revocation of, 423
Probation officers,
    caseloads of, 424
    discretion of, 419
    duties and responsibilities of, 421-423
    establishing position of, 312
    helped by predisposition reports, 406-407
    lack of qualified, 338
Probation services, 420-428
Problem gangs (New York City's
    Delinquency Evaluation Project), 212
Procedural guarantees. *See* Children's
    rights; Due process of law
Professional Thief (Sutherland), 59
Project CREST (Clinical Regional Support
    Teams), 425-428
Projective techniques (tests) of personality,
    88
Project New Pride (Colorado), 435
Proof beyond reasonable doubt, as judgment
    standard, 399, 401-402
Property offenses, arrest trends for, 26, 27
Prosecuting attorneys, 391, 392
Prosecution, general principles for, 393-394
Prosecutors, 391-393
Prototypic marginals, 168
Provo Program (Utah), 435, 453
Psychic or moral anomaly concept
    (Garofalo), 74
Psychobiological theory, 75
Psychological theories, 69, 82-89, 249
Psychological views of delinquent gang
    formation, 210
Psychology of delinquency (Erikson), 86-87
Psychotherapy or psychoanalysis as
    treatment in institutions, 451, 453
Psychotics (Eysenck), 85
Public defenders, 398
Punishment as solution to delinquency, 71,
    87
Pure deviants, 159
Pygmalion in the Classroom (Rosenthal &
    Jacobsen), 80

R
Race,
    arrest trends by, 27-29
    of delinquent gangs, 205
    differences in delinquency by, 33-34, 49-50
    and disposition of case, 33

problems of, in schools, 360
Rape, forcible, defined, 23
Reaction formation (Cohen), 113
Reality therapy in institutions, 451-452
Rebellion as social adaptation (Merton),
   108-109
Recidivism,
   in community treatment programs, 436, 437
   decreased through diversion, 292
   defined, 4
   rate of, 339, 417
Recidivists, 32, 33
Recreational programs in institutions, 455
Recreation and delinquency prevention, 145,
   360
Redeman decision (1971), 325
Referees, 396
Reform school movement (late nineteenth
   century), 309-310
Reform schools, 308, 310, 444, 445
Rehabilitation, 4
   through community treatment programs,
      418
   concept of, attacked, 293, 294
   as goal of juvenile justice system, 280, 314,
      323, 347, 404, 406
   in institutions, 444, 450-460
   probation based on, 419
   through restitution, 429
Reinforcement, positive and negative, 87
Religion and delinquency prevention,
   145-146
Residential treatment programs, 431-434
Restitution, 169
   as form of community treatment, 428-430
Retreatism as social adaptation (Merton),
   108, 109
Retreatist gangs (Cloward & Ohlin), 212
Retreatist subculture (Cloward & Ohlin), 115
Review hearings in child abuse and neglect
   cases, 259
Rich decision (1966), 332
Rights. *See* Children's rights
*Rights of Juveniles: The Juvenile Justice
   System* (Davis), 335
Ritualism as social adaptation (Merton), 108
Rivera v. Freeman (1972), 330
Robbery, defined, 23
Robert F. decision (1968), 332
Roberts decision (1971), 331-332
Rorschach Inkblot Test, 88
Rouse v. Cameron (1966), 456
Runaways, 306, 315, 336, 349, 369, 371, 495
Rural programs, 431, 433

S

"Safe school," 238
Safe School Study (National Institute of

Education), 233
*San Antonio Independent School District v.
   Rodriguez* (1973), 491
Santobello v. New York (1971), 382
Schizothyme body type (Kretschmer), 76
School attendance statutes, 483-484
School curriculum development, right to
   determine, 484-485
School discipline, 488-490
School dropouts, 235-236
School intruders, 233-234
Schools. *See also* Education
   corporal punishment in, 489
   and delinquency, 31-32
      delinquency within, 227-236
      delinquency prevention role of, 236-239,
         359-360
      delinquent gangs within, 232
      responses to delinquency by, 234-235
      student alienation related to, 225-226
      students' failures as contributing to,
         222-223
      tracking related to, 225
   drug abuse, in, 229-230
   freedom of speech in, 485-486
   as increasing students' propensity to fail,
      223
   after Middle Ages, 302-303
   in modern America, 220-221
   racial and minority problems in, 360
   reform, 308, 310, 444, 445
   right of to control children, versus
      children's legal rights, 483-491
   "safe," 238
   search and seizure in, 486-488
   social class orientation of, 227
   suggested improvements in, 238-239
   violence and vandalism in, 228-234
Scientific method, 68
Screening, 376
Search and seizure, freedom from
   unreasonable, 325-326, 353, 354, 486-488
Secondary deviance, 154, 157, 163
Secret deviants, 158
Secure detention facilities, 368, 432
Self-concept, 152
Self-contained gangs, 212
Self-esteem, loss of, 222
Self-incrimination, privilege against, 315,
   322, 324, 326
Self-labeling, 152, 157, 163. *See also*
   Delinquency label
Self-report surveys of delinquency, 42-54
   data generated by, 44-52
      on drug and alcohol abuse, 50-52
      on gang versus lone activity, 50
      on race, 49-50
      on sex differences, 48-49
      on social class, 45-48

female, 186-187
functions of, 42
versus official delinquency reports, 50
sample of, 43
testing Eysenck's theoretical model, 85
ways of validating, 52-54
Semisecure detention facilities, 432
Sentencing,
determinate, 405, 406
indeterminate, 292, 404-405
presumptive, 406
proportionality in, 406
trends in, 404-406
Sex,
arrest trends by, 26
of delinquent gang members, 204
differences in delinquency by, 48-49
incarceration by, 460
Sex and Society (Thomas), 179
Sexual abuse of children, 253, 254
Sexual delinquency of females. *See* Female
delinquency, linked with sexuality
Sharp decision (1908), 282-283
Shelter care, 368
Silverlake experiment (Los Angeles), 433-434
Sisters in Crime (Adler), 184, 185
Slum, stable, 206
Smartness as lower-class focal concern
(Miller), 104
Social adaptations for coping with society
(Merton), 107-109
Social bond with society (Hirschi), 100-107
Social class. *See also* Socioeconomic status
(SES) and delinquency
and delinquency, 45-48, 206, 222
of families,
in eighteenth century, 302-303
in Middle Ages, 300, 301
related to child abuse and neglect, 254-255
school orientation toward, 227
Social control, 165
Social-cultural view of delinquent gang
formation, 209
Social determinism theories of female
delinquency, 184-187
Social gang (Yablonsky), 211
Social, Personal, and Community
Experience (SPACE) project (California
Youth Authority, Los Angeles), 468
Social process theories, 125-146, 249
Social reaction theories, 151-170
Social structure theories, 97-120, 249
Social theory, purposes of, 67
Social typing (Tannenbaum), 159
Society for Prevention of Cruelty to
Children, 252
Sociobiology theory, 76-82
defined, 69
Socioeconomic status (SES) and

delinquency, 32-34. *See also* Social class
Sociopathic youth (Yablonsky), 210
Somatotype school, 76
Special children,
defined, 490
and juvenile justice system, 492
rights of, 490-493
testing procedures for, 491-492
Special courts. *See* Juvenile courts
Speech, freedom of, in public schools,
485-486
Splinter clique (Klein), 211
Spontaneous gang (Klein), 210
Stable slum, 206
*Standards and Guides for the Detention of
Children and Youth* (National Council
on Crime and Delinquency), 368, 370
Standards for Juvenile Justice (IJA/ABA),
289, 290
*Standards Relating to Counsel for Private
Parties* (American Bar Association), 397
Standards Relating to Interim Status
(American Bar Association), 369-370
*Standards Relating to Police Handling of
Juveniles* (American Bar Association),
349, 352, 353
Stanley M. decision (1972), 332
State intervention,
in child abuse and neglect cases, 257-260
and childsaving movement, 307
State v. Grayer (1974), 393
State v. Mora (1975), 466
State v. Redeman (1971), 325
Status as lower-class focal concern of gangs
(Miller), 105
Status offender concept,
future of, 14-16
opposition to, 12-13
support for, 13-14
Status offenders, 9-16. *See also* Delinquents;
Incorrigible delinquents; Runaways
changing state policies toward, 18-19
dealt with by police, 349
defined, 5
diversion of, 292
eliminating from juvenile justice system,
293, 337, 405
juvenile court jurisdiction over, 336-337
pretrial detention of, 13
treatment of, 9-11, 14-15, 308
Status offense categories, 10, 13, 18
Status offense statutes, 9-10, 12
Status offenses,
defined, 9
of females, 460
Statutory law, 257
Strain theory, 106-110
Street corner gang (Whyte), 211
Street Corner Society (Whyte), 59, 202

Structural approach to typing delinquent gangs (Klein), 210-211
Student alienation, 225-226
Subcultural (strain) theory, 110-117
Subterranean values and behaviors, 132
Success, education as key to, 220-221
Summons, defined, 380
Superego (Freud), 83-84
Supreme Court decisions. *See* Court decisions
Suspects, as falsely accused, 159
Swaddling, 301
Symbolic interaction school of sociology, 152
System, defined, 275
System operations, studies of, 4
Systems approach to juvenile justice system, 275-276

T

Task Force on Juvenile Delinquency, 221
Teenage gangs. *See* Delinquent gangs; Gangs, types of
Teenage subculture (Matza), 132
Theft,
  larceny, defined, 24
  motor vehicle, defined, 23
Theft gangs (Cohen & Short), 212
Thematic Apperception Test (TAT), 88
Theories of delinquency. *See* Delinquency theories
Tinker v. Des Moines Independent Community School District (1969), 485-486
Totality of the circumstances doctrine, 327
Toughness as lower-class focal concern (Miller), 103-104
Toward a Marxian Theory of Deviance (Spitzer), 168
Tracking, 225
Traditional gangs, 211
Training schools, 457, 462
Transactional analysis (TA) as treatment in institutions, 452
Transcript, right to, 409
Transfer (waiver) proceedings, 7, 337-338, 383-386
  due process of law in, 331, 384-386, 407
  statutory criteria for, 383-384, 405
Transitional neighborhoods, delinquency in, 98-106, 206
Treatment,
  evaluated, 4
  as goal in dispositional process, 406
  right to, 332-333, 431
    current status of, 459-460
    defined, 279-280

in institutions, 456-460, 492-493
  in juvenile justice system, 457-459
  theories of delinquency as basis for, 348
Treatment programs,
  in child abuse and neglect cases, 260
  within institutions, 450-460
    group, 453
    individual, 451-452
Trial, 276, 278, 279, 314, 391-410. *See also* Juvenile courts
  in child abuse and neglect cases, 259
  by jury, right to, 323, 331, 399, 402-403
  right to counsel at, 400-401
  right to speedy, 324
Trial *de novo*, 410
Trouble as lower-class focal concern (Miller), 103
Truancy, 233-234
  dealt with by community program placement, 405
  dealt with by juvenile courts, 314, 315, 336, 371
  dealt with by police, 349
  as form of delinquency, 233
Turf gangs (Miller), 212

U

Unadjusted Girl, The (Thomas), 179
Under Lock and Key: Juveniles in Jail and Detention (Sarri), 370
Uniform Crime Reports (UCR),
  conclusions of, 29
  inaccuracy of, 55
  as predictors of delinquency, 49-50
  as source of official delinquency statistics, 22-30
Uniform Juvenile Court Act (1968), 353, 392, 409
Urban delinquency (Cloward & Ohlin), 115
U.S. v. Barfield (1975), 327
U.S. v. Wade (1967), 329
Utilitarianism, 70-71

V

Vandalism in schools, 228-234
Vertical gangs, 212
Victimization,
  estimates of, 35, 55, 56, 57, 58
  types of, 56, 57, 58
Victimization surveys, 49, 55-59
  analysis of, 57-59
Victimless crimes, 58
  drug and alcohol abuse as, 50
Violence in schools, 228-234
Violent crimes, trends in, 25, 27

Violent delinquency, study of, 469
Violent gangs (Yablonsky), 212
Vocational programs in institutions, 453-454
Voluntary apprenticeship, 303

W

W. decision (1973), 487
Wade decision (1967), 329
Waiver (transfer) of jurisdiction. *See*
    Transfer (waiver) proceedings
Wayward youth, catchall status of, 159
Wellesley v. Wellesley (1827), 304, 306
West v. U.S. (1968), 327
William M. decision (1970), 330
Win-Onus program of restitution, 429
Winship decision (1970), 322-323, 392, 399

Wisconsin v. Yoder (1972), 484
Wish fulfillment, categories of, 179-180
Wolff v. McDonald (1974), 466
Wolfgang-Sellin Delinquency Index, 31
Women's liberation movement, 184
    and female involvement in crime, 460
Writ of *certiorari*, 332, 410
Writ of *habeas corpus*, 332, 410
Wyatt v. Stickney (1972), 456-457, 492-493

Y

Yoder case (1972), 484
Young Lords (The): Warriors of the Streets
    (Keiser), 59
Youth service bureaus, 358
Youths in Need of Supervision (YINS), 10

Name Index ────────────────────

A

Adams, Reed, 129
Adams, William, 183
Adler, Freda, 184-185, 188, 189
Ageton, Suzanne, 47-48, 49-50, 161
Akers, Ronald, 47, 129, 162
Alfaro, Jose, 262
Arnold, William, 46-47
Arthur, Judge Lindsay G., 14, 337, 403
Austin, James, 168

B

Baker, Judge Harvey, 340
Ball, Robert, 134
Bandura, Albert, 87, 250
Barker, Gordon, 183
Baron, Roger, 378
Bayh, Senator Birch, 284
Beccaria, Cesare, 70
Becker, Howard, 127, 157-159
Bennett, William, 204
Bentham, Jeremy, 70
Berne, Eric, 452
Bernstein, Saul, 206
Besharov, Douglas J., 253, 301
Bettelheim, Bruno, 453
Binet, Alfred, 78
Birnbaum, Dr. Morton, 456
Black, Donald, 356
Black, Justice Hugo, 322
Blackmun, Justice Harry A., 323, 417
Blake, Gerald, 378
Blew, Carol, 435
Block, Herbert, 207-209
Bordua, David, 162, 163

Bowman, J. Addison, 409
Brace, Charles, 309-310
Briar, Scott, 356, 357
Bronner, Augusta, 79
Bryant, Gerald, 435
Burger, Chief Justice Warren, 457
Burgess, Robert, 129
Burks, Barbara, 80
Burt, Cyril, 79

C

Capwell, Dora, 88
Cartwright, Desmond, 198
Chappell, Duncan, 35
Chesney-Lind, Meda, 189
Cicourel, Aaron, 159, 357
Clapp, Neale, 435
Clark, John, 46, 54, 186
Clinard, Marshall, 116
Cloward, Richard, 114-117, 120, 202, 212, 339
Cohen, Albert, 109-114, 115, 117, 212, 222, 339
Cohn, Yona, 30, 189
Conway, J., 79
Cooper, Charles, 204
Cooper, Sara, 307
Cottrell, L., 339
Couzens, Michael, 35
Cressey, Donald, 89, 126, 129-130
Czikszentmihalyi, Mihaly, 227

D

Davis, Kenneth Culp, 355, 357-358
Davis, Samuel, 335, 336
Dentler, Robert, 46
Detrick, David, 113

Dinitz, Simon, 89, 141, 161-162
Dugdale, Richard, 75
Durkheim, Emile, 107

E

Eels, Kenneth, 80
Elias, Albert, 435
Elliott, Delbert, 47, 49-50, 161, 219, 235
Emerson, Robert, 9
Empey, Lamar, 47, 116-117, 292, 340, 376, 424,
    434, 435
England, Ralph, 118, 423, 424
Erickson, Kai, 153
Erickson, Maynard, 47, 50, 116-117, 435
Erikson, Erik, 86-87
Estabrook, Arthur, 75
Eve, Raymond, 48, 187
Eysenck, Hans, 85

F

Fakouri, Ebrahim, 221
Fannin, Leon, 116
Feeney, Floyd, 378
Ferdinand, Theodore, 30, 188
Ferri, Enrico, 74-75
Figlio, Robert, 31-34
Fisher, Stanley, 405
Fitzpatrick, Joseph, 340
Flexner, P., 281-282
Flowers, Lucy, 307
Fontana, Vincent J., 253
Fortas, Justice Abe, 310, 324, 485, 488
Foster, Henry, Jr., 493, 496
Foster, Jack, 161-162
Fox, Sanford, 309, 310, 311, 313, 333, 404, 409
Frease, Dean, 222
Freed, Doris, 493, 496
Freud, Anna, 406
Freud, Sigmund, 83-85, 181-182, 437, 451
Friedan, Betty, 184

G

Ganousis, Jeanette, 403
Garfinkel, Harold, 160
Garofalo, Raffaele, 74
Geis, Gilbert, 35
Gelles, Richard, 253-254, 261
Giallombardo, Rose, 463
Gibbons, Don, 183, 378
Gibbs, Jack, 162
Glaser, Daniel, 235
Glasser, Dr. William, 452
Glueck, Eleanor, 76, 183, 234, 340
Glueck, Sheldon, 76, 183, 234, 340
Goddard, Henry, 75, 79
Gold, Martin, 45, 47, 48, 186, 188, 222-223, 250
Goldman, Nathan, 355-356, 357
Goldstein, Joseph, 355, 406

Gordon, Robert, 134
Goring, Charles, 73-74
Gottfredson, Michael, 35
Gould, Leroy, 49
Green, Edward, 30
Griswold, Manzer, 183

H

Hackler, James, 53
Hartgen, Clayton, 70-71
Hathaway, R. Starke, 88
Haurek, Edward, 186
Healy, William, 79
Hegel, George, 165
Helfer, Ray, 261
Herrnstein, Richard, 81-82
Hindelang, Michael, 35, 48, 49, 50, 81, 88,
    134, 138-139, 186
Hirschi, Travis, 81, 129, 135-136, 137-139, 226,
    227, 250
Hood, Roger, 41, 42
Howard, M., 79

I

Inciardi, James, 200-202

J

Jacobsen, Lenore, 80
Jeffrey, C. Ray, 4, 77
Jenkins, Richard, 262
Jensen, Arthur, 81-82
Jensen, Gary, 48, 160-161, 187
Jerse, Frank, 221
Johnson, Richard, 47

K

Kamin, Leon, 79
Kantor, David, 204
Katz, Jonathan, 436
Katz, Sanford, 479-480
Keiser, R. Lincoln, 59
Kempe, Dr. C. Henry, 252, 261
Ketcham, Judge Orman, 337
Kitsuse, John, 113
Klein, Malcolm, 198, 204, 205, 207, 209, 210,
    211
Klineberg, Otto, 80
Kobrin, Solomon, 203-204
Kohlberg, Lawrence, 86
Konopka, Gisela, 182-183, 340
Kramer, Prudence, 403
Kretschmer, Ernst, 76
Krisberg, Barry, 168, 207
Kvaraceus, William, 222

L

Landis, Judson, 115-116
LaPook, Judith, 284, 340

Larson, Reed, 227
Lathrop, Julia, 282
Lautt, Melanie, 53
Lemert, Edwin, 154-157, 158
Liazos, Alexander, 236
Lightman, Howard, 479
Lipsett, Paul, 160
Locke, John, 302
Lombroso, Cesare, 72-73, 178-179
Lou, Herbert, 281
Lubeck, Stephen, 434
Luchterhand, Elmer, 30, 188
Lundman, Richard, 378

M
McCandless, B. R., 76
McCord, Joan, 250
McCord, William, 250
McGillis, Daniel, 435
McKay, Henry D., 30-31, 98-102, 109, 115, 250
McKinley, J. Charnley, 88
Manning, Peter, 162
Martin, John, 340
Martin, Lawrence, 13-14
Marx, Karl, 164-165
Matza, David, 131-133, 134, 135-136, 159
Maudsley, Henry, 83
Meier, Robert, 165
Mennel, Robert, 308
Merton, Robert, 107-110, 114, 117
Miller, Dr Jerome, 430-431
Miller, Walter, 50, 98, 102-106, 109, 115, 119, 199, 202, 203, 204, 205, 206, 209, 212-213, 339
Mills, Elizabeth, 443
Minton, Sophia, 307
Monachesi, Elio, 88
Monroe, Lawrence, 46
Murray, Ellen, 141
Myren, Richard, 348

N
Nejelski, Paul, 284, 340, 376-377, 378
Newman, Oscar, 78
Niederhoffer, Arthur, 207-209
Norman, Sherwood, 340, 358
Nye, F. Ivan, 42, 45-46, 48, 251

O
Ohlin, Lloyd, 114-117, 120, 202, 212, 339, 437
Olsen, Virgil, 46
Oppenheimer, N., 281-282
Otis, Arthur, 78

P
Packer, Herbert, 355
Perrow, Charles, 161
Piaget, Jean, 85

Piersma, Paul, 403, 409
Piliavin, Irving, 356, 357
Pilnick, Paul, 435
Platt, Anthony, 167, 311, 313
Polk, Kenneth, 220, 222, 223, 227, 235
Pollak, Otto, 180-181, 187-188
Poole, Eric, 134
Pound, Roscoe, 351

Q
Quinney, Richard, 165

R
Rathus, Spencer, 43, 44, 88, 89
Reckless, Walter, 140-141, 142, 161-162
Regoli, Robert, 134
Reiss, Albert A., Jr., 128-129, 356
Rendleman, Douglas, 304
Rhodes, A. Lewis, 128-129
Richmond, F. Lynn, 222
Rivera, Ramon, 116
Robey, Ames, 183
Romig, Dennis, 157, 451, 454
Rosenthal, Robert, 80
Rousseau, Jean Jacques, 302

S
Sarri, Rosemary, 13, 189-190, 370
Saunders, Frank, 183
Scarpitti, Frank, 116, 141, 423-424
Scarr, Sandra, 82
Schafer, Stephen, 35
Schafer, Walter, 220, 222, 223, 227, 235
Schrag, Clarence, 105, 111, 130-131, 142, 351
Schuessler, Karl, 89
Schulman, Irving, 453
Schur, Edwin, 153, 162
Schwendinger, Herman, 166, 167-168
Schwendinger, Julia, 166, 167-168
Seidman, David, 35
Sellin, Thorsten, 31-34
Shaw, Clifford R., 30-31, 59, 98-102, 109, 115, 119-120, 250
Sheldon, William H., 76
Short, James, 42, 45-46, 48, 114, 116, 128, 205, 212
Siegel, Larry, 35, 43, 44, 80, 88, 134
Silberman, Charles, 28-29
Simon, Rita James, 184, 185-186
Simon, Theodore, 78
Slawson, John, 80
Snyder, Eloise, 160
Snyder, Phyllis, 13-14
Solnit, Albert, 406
Somerville, Dora, 182-183
Sparks, Richard, 41, 42
Spergel, Irving, 205, 209
Spitzer, Stephen, 168

Spock, Dr. Benjamin, 117
Steffensmeier, Darrell, 187, 190
Steffensmeier, Renee Hoffman, 187, 190
Steinmetz, Dr. Suzanne, 261
Stephenson, Richard, 423-424
Stinchcombe, Arthur, 222, 226-227
Strasburg, Paul, 355
Straus, Murray, 253-254, 261
Street, David, 161
Streib, Victor, 355
Strodtbeck, Fred, 205
Strouse, Jean, 188
Sutherland, Edwin H., 59, 79, 117, 126-128,
    129, 130, 131, 339
Swanson, Lynn, 348
Sykes, Gresham, 131-133, 134, 135-136,
    165-166

T

Tannenbaum, Frank, 159
Tennyson, Ray, 116
Terman, L. M., 78
Terry, Robert, 30, 189
Thomas, Charles, 14
Thomas, W. I., 179-180
Thornton, Justice, 309
Thornton, Warren, 378
Thrasher, Frederick, 101, 198, 202, 203-204,
    205, 206
Thurber, Emily, 250
Tifft, Larry, 51
Toby, Jackson, 169, 222
Tuthill, Judge Richard, 307

V

Van den Haag, Ernest, 71-72, 293
Vaz, Thomas, 118
Vedeer, Clyde, 182-183
Vinter, Robert, 161, 437, 451
Voltaire, Francois Marie Arouet de, 302
Voss, Harwin, 27, 219, 235

W

Wald, Patricia, 495
Waldo, Gordon, 89
Warren, Marguerite, 340
Wattenberg, William 183
Weeks, H. Ashley, 433
Weeks, Herbert, 340
Weinberg, Richard, 82
Weis, Joseph, 81, 88
Wellford, Charles, 162-163
Wenninger, Eugene, 46, 54
Wheeler, S., 339
Whyte, William F., 59, 202, 203-204, 206, 211
Williams, Jay, 47, 48, 188
Wilson, James Q., 71, 72
Wines, Enoch, 307
Wise, Nancy, 186-187
Wolfgang, Marvin, 31-34, 81, 118, 119
Wooden, Kenneth, 190

Y

Yablonsky, Lewis, 198-199, 205, 210, 211
Young, Lawrence, 88

†